PHILIPPINES
BUSINESS

World Trade Press
Country Business Guides

ARGENTINA Business
AUSTRALIA Business
CHINA Business
HONG KONG Business
JAPAN Business
KOREA Business
MEXICO Business
PHILIPPINES Business
SINGAPORE Business
TAIWAN Business
USA Business

PHILIPPINES
BUSINESS

The Portable Encyclopedia For Doing Business With The Philippines

James L. Nolan, Ph.D.   Karla C. Shippey, J.D.
Molly E. Thurmond, J.D.   Alexandra Woznick
Edward G. Hinkelman

Dean Engel   John DeCaire, J.D.   David L. Gold
Daniel Edelstein   Cynthia G. Sewell   Robin E. Kobayashi, J.D.
Stan Draenos   Patrick Sullivan   Christopher Mahon

Philippine Board of Investments • International Monetary Fund
SyCip Salazar Hernandez & Gatmaitan • Villaraza & Cruz
Bengzon Narciso Cudala Pecson Bengson & Jimenez
Ernst & Young • International Chamber of Commerce
Colliers International • CIGNA Property and Casualty • The East West Group Inc.
Auerbach International • Reed Publishing (USA) Inc. • Magellan Geographix

Series Editor: Edward G. Hinkelman

WORLD
TRADE
PRESS®

Resources for International Trade

1505 Fifth Avenue
San Rafael, California 94901
USA

Published by World Trade Press
1505 Fifth Avenue
San Rafael, CA 94901, USA
Tel: (415) 454-9934
Fax: (415) 453-7980
USA Orderline: (800) 833-8586
E-mail: WorldPress@aol.com

Cover and book design: Brad Greene
Illustrations: Eli Africa
Maps: Magellan^{sm} Geographix
Desktop design and publishing: Peter G. Jones
Charts and graphs: Peter G. Jones
Copy Editor: Michael Levy

Library of Congress Cataloging-in-Publication Data

Philippines business : the portable encyclopedia for doing business
        with the Philippines / James L. Nolan . . . [et al.].
            p.   cm. – (World Trade Press country business guides)
        Includes bibliographical references and index.
        ISBN 1-885073-08-9
        1. Philippines–Economic conditions–1986–   2. Philippines-
-Economic policy. 3. Investments, Foreign–Government policy-
-Philippines. 4. International business enterprises–Philippines.
I. Nolan, James L., 1951–.   II. Series.
HC455.P5273   1996   95-37479
350.9599 ' 097–dc20   CIP

Printed in the United States of America

ACKNOWLEDGMENTS

We owe many leaders in the international business community a debt of gratitude. Hundreds of trade and reference experts have brought this book to life. We are indebted to numerous international business consultants; reference librarians; travel advisors; consulate, embassy, and trade mission officers; bank officers; attorneys; global shippers and insurers; and multinational investment brokers who answered our incessant inquiries and volunteered facts, figures, and expert opinions. To all these many individuals, named and unnamed, we extend our thanks.

We are particularly grateful to Durgha Edson of AMCORP, whose warm and generous support of our cause got us noticed all the way to the shores of the Philippines, and to Donna Cancio of the Goodwill Trading Company in the Philippines, who encouraged the publication of this book.

This publication would not have been possible without the professional talents of many researchers, authors, and editors. Special acknowledgment goes to Trade Representative Mike T. Haresco of the Los Angeles Office of the Trade Representative, Philippine Consulate General for supplying current statistical information and materials on Philippine business, industries, investment, and culture.

Multitalented author and attorney Molly Thurmond contributed a number of chapters and then joined our in-house staff. International trade specialist and corporate writer Stan Draenos searched source after source for hard-to-find data on Philippine labor issues and requirements. A thorough treatment of Philippine culture was provided by human resources consultant Dean Engel, senior partner in The East West Group Inc., a consulting firm that develops cross-cultural strategies for clients operating worldwide. The special research and analytical skills of Patrick Sullivan were essential to compiling the demographic and trade fair materials. We also recognize Merdona C. Bautista and Carmelita R. Bernado with appreciation for reviewing Tagalog materials.

Attorney John DeCaire spent long hours exploring the practical aspects of Philippine commercial law and entities, often by interviewing Philippine practitioners to learn the current status of legislation. For taking time from their busy days to brief us on the Philippine legal system, we are most obliged to Hector M. de Leon, Jr. (SyCip Salazar Hernandez & Gatmaitan, Makati), Jose V.E. Jimenez (Bengzon Narciso Cudala Pecson Bengson & Jimenez, Makati), and Cynthia D. Nuval-Ambrosio (Villaraza & Cruz, Makati).

Travel writer Daniel Edelstein took us on a Philippine business tour. International marketing analyst Cynthia Sewell sifted through the intricacies of developed and undeveloped Philippine markets. Legal author Robin Kobayashi analyzed Philippine import and export policies and sorted through often conflicting procedural data to get to the hard facts. Author Christopher Mahon delved into Philippine industries, opportunities, and trade zones, while investment manager David Gold (Transamerica Investment Services, Los Angeles) analyzed oceans of data on Philippine foreign investment requirements and financial institutions to come up with the practical basics.

For reprint permissions, we found helpful allies in Cassie Arnold (Ernst & Young, San Francisco office); Kenneth Young (Publications Services, International Monetary Fund); Steve Fahrbach, Doug Crawford, and Rick Wood (Magellan^sm Geographix); and Barry Tarneff (CIGNA Property and Casualty Co.). Thank you also to Denise Getty of Colliers International for coordinating the real estate market survey and to the researcher in Colliers Jardine, Philippines, who charted the information. We further acknowledge the valuable contributions of Philip B. Auerbach and Naomi Baer (Auerbach International, San Francisco) for translations.

We relied heavily on the reference librarians and resources available at the libraries of the University of California at Berkeley, San Francisco Public Library, San Rafael Public Library, Marin County Civic Center Library, and Marin County Law Library. Of particular note, reference librarian Gail Lockman at the San Rafael Public Library has always been a most willing accomplice in research.

DISCLAIMER

We have diligently tried to ensure the accuracy of all of the information in this publication and to present as comprehensive a reference work as space would permit. In determining the contents, we were guided by many experts in the field, extensive hours of research, and our own experience. We did have to make choices in coverage, however, because the inclusion of everything one could ever want to know about international trade would be impossible. The fluidity and fast pace of today's business world makes the task of keeping data current and accurate an extremely difficult one. This publication is intended to give you the information that you need in order to discover the information that is most useful for your particular business. As you contact the resources within this book, you will no doubt learn of new and exciting business opportunities and of additional international trading requirements that have arisen even within the short time since we published this edition. If errors are found, we will strive to correct them in preparing future editions. The publishers take no responsibility for inaccurate or incomplete information that may have been submitted to them in the course of research for this publication. The facts published are the result of those inquiries, and no warranty as to their accuracy is given.

Contents

Philippines at a Glance

INTRODUCTION

In a Nutshell The Philippines is in the process of recovering its previous luster as it builds for the next century. The country's leaders and business community are easing it away from a stagnant and closed economy toward a new, dynamic future. Although the Philippines is still developing and changing its systems, there is much reason to be optimistic that it will reach its goals. With more opportunities than ever before, the Philippines is a complex, challenging, and compelling place to do business.

This island nation offers abundant tropical agricultural production—long the mainstay of its economy. It is the world's top producer of coconut, exports substantial amounts of shrimp and prawns from aquaculture farms, and ranks among the top ten producers of chromium, gold, and copper. Deforestation has taken a toll on the timber industry, and most of the remaining timber is on the steeper slopes and upper elevations. The manufacturing sector's share of the nation's GDP has grown to more than 20 percent and has diversified into both heavy—cement, glass, chemical, steel, petroleum—and light—apparel, electronics, furniture—industries.

Opportunities

. . . for buyers—nontraditional intermediate products and more advanced goods. The Philippine industrial sector is growing and the country is fast becoming a competitive producer in world and regional markets.

. . . for sellers—the Philippines needs capital and intermediate components for its industries, household goods to meet increasing consumer demands, business and professional services, and technological expertise to support ambitious infrastructure projects nationwide.

. . . for manufacturers—the nation offers a large, generally well educated, cost-competitive, and skilled workforce.

. . . for investors—the country is in the midst of a campaign of investment liberalization. It seeks overseas involvement to deepen and sustain its development. Especially welcome are build-operate-transfer (BOT) arrangements, but greater foreign ownership is being accepted in many sectors and businesses, and there are relatively few restrictions in the opened areas.

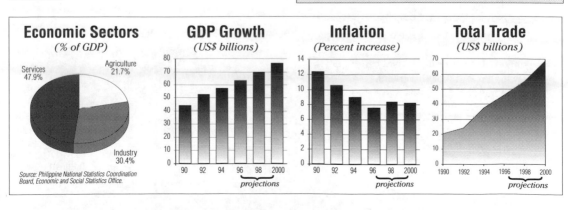

Economic Sectors
(% of GDP)

Services 47.9%
Agriculture 21.7%
Industry 30.4%

Source: Philippine National Statistics Coordination Board, Economic and Social Statistics Office.

GDP Growth
(US$ billions)

90 92 94 96 98 2000
projections

Inflation
(Percent increase)

90 92 94 96 98 2000
projections

Total Trade
(US$ billions)

1990 1992 1994 1996 1998 2000
projections

TEN REASONS FOR DOING BUSINESS IN THE PHILIPPINES

1. The Philippines is creating incentives to entice foreign investors, opening opportunities particularly in the areas of industrial and infrastructure development.
2. Earnings and capital can be freely converted and repatriated.
3. A wave of privatizations and deregulation has added substantially to the investment attractions.
4. Philippine financial markets, while still volatile, have been among the most rewarding emerging securities markets, posting remarkable performances in recent years.
5. The Philippines is one of Asia's most accessible countries for many Westerners because of its historic links with Spain and the US.
6. At the crossroads of international shipping and air routes, this island nation is strategically positioned as a perfect intermediary between Asia and the rest of the world. It is both a potential source for those seeking suppliers worldwide and a prime location from which to serve rapidly growing Asian markets.
7. The country offers a skilled, highly trainable, and inexpensive labor force of more than 26 million people, many of whom speak English.
8. The Philippines has a long-established reputation as a significant exporter of agricultural products, minerals, and other raw materials and commodity goods.
9. The Philippines' reawakening industrial sector has already begun to produce and export a range of competitive, higher-value-added industrial products, and its efforts at diversification are succeeding. The country is fast becoming a competitive producer in regional and world markets.
10. The nation's 69 million people constitute a huge domestic market for modern consumer goods. Policies encouraging exports mean a demand for imports of intermediate goods, high-tech machinery, and raw materials.

Climate

Eastern coastal areas

Dry season	December to May
Monsoon and typhoon season	June to November

Western coastal areas

Dry season	March to May
Monsoon and typhoon season	June to February

Interior, mountainous areas

Rainy season	All year

People

Languages:
Official—Pilipino (Tagalog-based with elements taken from other native languages)
Other major languages used—most urbanites are bilingual in English or at least speak some English; English is the standard business language.

Literacy rate:
90 percent

Ethnicity:
Primarily of Malayan descent; about 10 percent belong to one of the 60 recognized ethnic minorities. Two-thirds of the minorities are Muslim groups; others include peoples of Chinese, Spanish, and US extraction.

Population distribution:
40% of population is concentrated in urban centers.

1994 average density:	233 persons per sq km (604 per sq mi)
1994 urban density: (Metro Manila)	21,676 per sq km (56,141 per sq mi)

Religion:

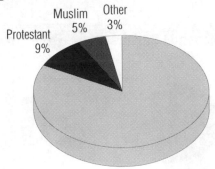

Muslim 5%
Other 3%
Protestant 9%
Roman Catholic 83%

Source: CIA World Factbook

REPUBLIKA NG PILIPINAS

The Luzon Region

The largest island in the chain and site of Metro Manila, the nation's capital and primary industrial center and port of entry. Home to nearly half of the Filipino population.

Metro Manila

The 11th largest city in the world, with a 1995 estimated population of 11.3 million. Encompasses 17 distinct cities. Business opportunities make this area a magnet, and it is fast becoming one of the densest population centers in the world.

The Visayas

The central Visayas include eight major islands and a number of smaller ones. Agriculture, mining, and tourism are mainstays of the economy here.

An Island Nation

The Philippines is a nation of islands located south of mainland Asia. To the west is the South China Sea; to the east, the Pacific Ocean; north is the Bashi Channel, and south, the Sulu and Celebes Seas. It has no contiguous land borders with any other nation. Its nearest neighbors are Malaysia, Indonesia, and Brunei to the southwest.

Cebu

The growing port city of Cebu is the nation's second largest international gateway. Located in the central Visayas, this city is well positioned for shipping and is the transit point for a growing Philippine tourist trade.

Mindanao

The southern island of Mindanao is the second largest in the chain. On its Pacific coast is the growing urban center of Davao. Historically the center of Islam in the islands, today it is also the focus of East ASEAN Growth Area development.

Land area distribution

Total islands	7,107
Total land area	299,404 sq km
	(115,600 sq mi)
11 islands account for 92% of total land area.	
Provinces	73
Regions	12

ISLAND FEATURES

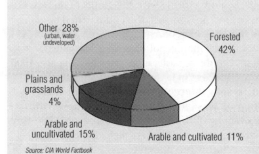

Other 28%
(urban, water undeveloped)

Forested 42%

Plains and grasslands 4%

Arable and uncultivated 15%

Arable and cultivated 11%

Source: CIA World Factbook

COMPARABLE IN SIZE TO ITALY

The Philippines' 229 thousand square miles encompasses an area similar to that of Italy.

National Leaders

FIDEL RAMOS (1928–)

Successor to President Aquino, Fidel Ramos was endorsed by her in consideration of his loyal support, first as leader of the military and then as her Minister of Defense. Immediately after his election in 1992, Ramos proceeded to institute ambitious social, economic, and political reforms. Under his leadership, the administation developed the Philippines 2000 program, designed to make this nation a major economic force in international markets by the century's end.

JOSE RIZAL (1861–1896)

The country's primary national hero in its fight for independence, José Rizal was an influential physician, artist, author, and Filipino patriot. He was educated in Europe, where he published several books and many essays advocating an end to Spanish control in the Philippines. On returning to the islands, he founded the Liga Filipina reform movement, was arrested shortly thereafter, and exiled to Mindanao. After a nationalist rebellion was quelled in 1896, the Spanish convicted him of treason and executed him at the Manila site known today as Rizal Park.

CORAZON AQUINO (1933–)

Widow of opposition politician Benigno Aquino, who was assassinated while returning from exile in 1983, Aquino became a central opposition leader against the Marcos regime. In the disputed 1986 election, she took presidental power and proceeded to reform the country's government and legal structure. During her six-year term, her administration withstood seven military coup attempts. For lack of funds from a nearly bankrupt government, she was unable to institute promised social and industrial reforms. Nor was she able to loosen monopolistic control held by prominent familes and the military. Her political legacy is the restoration of democracy to the Philippines.

FERDINAND MARCOS (1917–1989)

A distinguished guerrilla fighter during World War II, Ferdinand Marcos was elected to the presidency in 1965. He held executive power for another 20 years, through two terms as president and then under martial law into the early 1980s. Although he instituted social reforms, applied a heavy hand against rampant crime, and strengthened the country's international ties, he also outlawed opposition groups, suppressed freedom of expression, and allowed family influence ("cronyism") to reach extremes, often violently. In 1984 political opposition gained strength in Parliament, and following a disputed 1986 election, he was ousted by Corazon Aquino's supporters and went into exile in the US.

THE TIGER CUB OF SOUTHEAST ASIA

The Philippines has experienced a radical rebirth since the social and political "People Power" revolution during the mid-1980s. The country has made great strides in reordering its old system by opening its markets and linking them more closely with the global economy.

Once considered prosperous, the country had become known as the "sick man of Asia." However, as Filipinos say, lately the sick man is not only up but jogging. Although its economy came under pressure in early 1995 from the sudden loss of favor for emerging markets worldwide among international investors, the Philippines' situation was far less structurally problematic than that of many of the other nations affected. The May 1995 election of a new legislative majority favoring progressive reforms has added even more reasons for optimism concerning the future direction of this island nation.

The Philippines in Time

BC–1400AD   Asian immigrants settle islands.

900–1300   Trade ties with China and India.

1380–1500   Islamic influences spread.
First sultanate on Mindanao.

1521   Magellan claims islands for Spain.

1543   Villalobos claims islands for Spain and
names them Filipinas for Philip II.

A Center for Exploration
With a strategic position in southeast Asia, the
Philippines has long been an important maritime stop
in the Pacific Ocean.

1575   Spain takes control over non-Islamic
areas and monopolizes trade.

1872 Cavite revolt against Spain; some
trade restrictions are relaxed.

1896 Spain quells armed revolt and
executes nationalist José Rizal.

1898   US purchases Philippines at end of Spanish-American War.

1900   US quells nationalist resistance and institutes commonwealth government.
US enacts law to grant Philippines independence by 1944.

1935   New constitution is adopted; Manuel Luis Quezon y Molina is elected president.

1941   Japan invades the islands.

1945   US expels Japan. Philippines joins UN as charter member.

1946   Philippines gains full independence. Manuel A. Roxas y Acuna is elected president.

1950   Philippines rebuilds after war, becoming second most prosperous nation in Asia.

1965   President Ferdinand Marcos is elected.

1966   Asian Development Bank (ADB) is headquartered in Manila.

1967   Philippines joins Association of Southeast Asian Nations (ASEAN).

1969   Reelection of President Marcos.

1972   Marcos declares martial law.

1973   Philippines becomes provisional member of GATT.

1981   Martial law is lifted and new constitution is adopted to preserve strong executive.
President Marcos is reelected amid widespread charges of election fraud.

1983   Opposition leader Benigno Aquino is assassinated.

1984   Opposition candidates gain strength in congressional elections, coalescing
around Corazon Aquino. People Power revolt gains momentum.

1986   Corazon Aquino wins disputed election with support of the military.
Marcos is exiled. Aquino restructures government.

1987   New constitution is ratified. First free election in two decades is held.

1989   Limited autonomy granted to Muslim provinces. Dispute with China
over Spratly Islands escalates.

1990   7.7 earthquake kills more than 1,600. Super-typhoon hits Visayas.

1991   Mount Pinatubo erupts; more than 20,000 are evacuated.
Philippines refuses to renew leases on US military bases.
New Foreign Investment law is enacted

1992   Fidel Ramos is elected president. Philippines 2000 plan
is adopted. US withdraws from military bases.

1994   Cease-fire signed with Moro National Liberation Front.

1994   Philippines weathers emerging markets crisis.

1995   Midterm elections support Ramos reforms.

What's Inside

PHILIPPINES Business is designed by businesspeople experienced in international markets to give you a head start for doing business in the Philippines. It will tell you how the business, legal, and social systems work, what the conditions are, who to contact, and where to get more details. **PHILIPPINES Business** is your invitation to this fascinating society and market. Mabuhay!—Welcome!

Economy surveys the financial and social sectors of Philippine life. A must-read chapter to gain insight into the past, present, and future of the Filipino people.

Current Issues explores the significant events that affect the country's development, with a focus on what you can expect when doing business there.

Opportunities highlights hot prospects in industrial, service, agricultural, and public sectors that hold high potential for importers, exporters, and investors.

Foreign Investment details the ease and risk of the Philippines investment environment, including the policies, incentives, restrictions, and procedures.

Foreign Trade considers the Philippines' relative role in international trade, both in relation to domestic production and in comparison with other countries.

Trade Agreements presents the latest information on multilateral and bilateral trade arrangements, with special reference to ASEAN and GATT.

Trade Zones offers an alternative for doing business in the Philippines and explains the requirements and procedures for operating within a special zone.

Import Policy & Procedures surveys the regulatory environment for importing and gives a nuts-and-bolts guide, from preshipment through customs.

Export Policy & Procedures views transborder shipping from the opposite side: the practice and procedure of moving goods out of the Philippines.

Industry Reviews outlines the competitive positions of the most prominent industries and offers industry-specific resource contacts.

Trade Fairs is a comprehensive listing of Philippine trade fairs, complete with contact information and tips on how to maximize the benefits of these events.

Business Travel is a quick reference for the information that a businessperson on the go needs to know—visas to hotels to taxis to business centers.

Business Culture offers a primer on how to adapt to local business and negotiating styles, improve business effectiveness, and avoid inadvertent gaffes.

Demographics supplies the basic statistical data that you will need to begin assessing the nature and demands of local Philippine markets.

Marketing outlines consumer trends, urban and rural markets, and the channels for market entry and advertising that are specific to the Philippines.

Business Entities & Formation discusses the requirements for recognized business entities and the registration procedures for operating in the Philippines.

Labor assembles information on the availability, capabilities, and cost of labor, as well as terms of employment and labor-management relations.

Business Law gives practical guidelines on the legal system and an abridged digest of commercial law prepared by legal publishing authority Martindale-Hubbell.

Financial Institutions surveys the banking and financial markets and provides a useful guide to financing and related services available to foreign businesses.

Currency & Foreign Exchange explains the foreign exchange system and presents the Philippine annual report prepared by the International Monetary Fund.

International Payments is an illustrated, step-by-step guide to using documentary collections and letters of credit in trade with the Philippines.

Taxation incorporates the Ernst & Young international personal and corporate tax guides to explain the tax benefits and liabilities of doing business in the Philippines.

Transportation & Communications brings you current information on available ports, airports, roads, and communications throughout the islands.

Business Dictionary is a unique resource of more than 400 entries focused specifically on Philippine business slang and Tagalog usage.

Important Addresses compiles more than 750 listings for Philippine government agencies; business and trade associations; financial, professional, and service firms; transportation and shipping agencies; media outlets; electronic information services; publications; and other resources.

Economy

HISTORY OF THE ECONOMY

The Republika ng Pilipinas—the Philippines—is a nation of islands located south and east of the Asian mainland. Although strongly Asian in heritage and culture, the Philippines has a complex western overlay that includes Spanish and US colonial influences. The first waves of migrants from the Asian mainland built the agricultural systems that have sustained the country for thousands of years. Indian and, to an even greater degree, Chinese trade influences were strong from AD 800 to AD 1300, with Islamic inroads beginning around AD 1400.

Spanish influence began with the landfall of Magellan in 1521, and colonial control was established by around 1575. The Philippines was maintained as a distant Spanish colony until the late 19th century, when, as part of the treaty that ended the Spanish-American War, it was transferred to US control. By that time, Filipino nationals had gained strength in their quest for independence from all colonial powers, but by 1902 the US had quelled active resistance and taken over the administration.

The US installed a friendly local government—consisting primarily of prominent local families to whom administrators delegated broad authority to manage Philippine affairs—as well as infrastructure and an educational system that shifted the focus from Spanish to English. In 1935 the Philippines gained US Commonwealth status with limited self-rule, and full independence was slated for 1944.

The swift Japanese conquest of US and other European forces in Asia—including the Philippines—in 1941–1942 led to yet another period of foreign domination. Japanese rule was generally considered to be particularly harsh. Among other things, the Japanese attempted to extinguish Spanish and English, substituting Pilipino—codified in 1936—and Japanese as more appropriate Asian languages. US forces expelled the Japanese in 1944–1945.

Post–World War II As of the end of World War II, the Philippines had been maintained largely as a colony throughout much of its modern history. Except for the mostly low-value-added commodity goods produced for export, its economy remained largely subsistence-based well into the 20th century. Local industry was absent or underdeveloped, and it was not until after World War II that the Philippines began to industrialize; even then, development was spotty.

After the war, many Filipinos perceived the US as neither culturally nor politically invincible; many felt that they had been sacrificed by the US, which had promised but failed to defend their interests. In 1946 the US granted full independence to the Philippines; however, the Philippines and the US continued to maintain close (albeit ambivalent) political, commercial, and military ties. The US remained the country's main trading and investment partner, using the Philippines as its primary base of operations in Southeast Asia.

Despite—or, some would say, because of—this continued close association, the Filipino political and economic systems failed to develop in the direction and at the rate anticipated. Development was slow, and many observers, both inside and outside the Philippines, considered the system to be inefficient and corrupt. In the first decades after the war, most production was controlled by a small group of prominent families, who constantly feuded with each other over economic, political, and social dominance. These local conditions—as well as a lack of basic infrastructure, corruption, and a high crime rate—kept many foreigners from investing in the country. Nevertheless, during much of the 1950s, 1960s, and 1970s, the Philippines was one of the more prosperous nations in Asia, second only to Japan until the 1960s.

Ferdinand Marcos, the sixth president since independence, began serving in 1965. His foremost program was to stabilize the country's economic and social systems. The Marcos regime did reduce rampant crime, improve delivery of some public services, increase the role of the Philippines in regional and international affairs, and open the country to foreign investors. However, Marcos' rule created about as many problems as it solved. Reelected in 1969, Marcos declared martial law in 1972, ostensibly to clean up abuses and get the country moving again. However, domestic criticism was suppressed, corruption among those associated with the government soared, and violent insurgencies sprang up, particularly among the Communists and Islamic separatists. Investment and development continued to lag.

Marcos was reelected for an unprecedented third term in 1981 amid widespread charges of election fraud. Within three years, the opposition had gained sufficient strength to make a significant showing in the midterm congressional elections of 1984. Marcos' suppression of the opposition became less effective as more Filipinos took to the streets as part of the "People Power" movement. This movement united behind the presidential candidacy of Corazon Aquino, widow of a former senator who was assassinated while returning from exile to oppose Marcos. Both candidates claimed victory in the 1986 election. The turning point came when the military threw its support to Aquino, driving Marcos into exile.

Following an initial burst of euphoria on the heels of the People Power revolution, economic conditions actually worsened for many sectors of the population. Aquino abolished the constitution and the legislature and set out to restructure the government and to restore democracy, but she was unable to effectively rein in either the military or the prominent families. She spent most of her political capital in trying to do so and was unable to make needed investments and reforms for lack of funds. In 1991 Filipino legislators also moved the country away from the US by refusing to renew the leases on major US military facilities. Aquino, who

withstood seven military coup attempts during her tenure, largely because of the support of military chief General Fidel Ramos, endorsed Ramos as her replacement in the election of 1992.

Known as "Steady Eddie," Protestant outsider Ramos narrowly defeated multiple opponents and began to institute reform policies through a cabinet composed largely of technocrats rather than the anticipated cronies. Major policy goals have included job creation; deregulation of protected domestic industries; foreign debt reduction; foreign investment reform; political reform (decentralization of authority and decriminalization of opposition parties, including the Communist party); and improvement of infrastructure, especially the inadequate national electric power system. Ramos' main policy, the Philippines 2000 program, was designed to reform and modernize the economic system to make the Philippines more international and market oriented.

SIZE OF THE ECONOMY

In 1994 the gross domestic product (GDP) of the Philippines was approximately US$57.6 billion, calculated at the average exchange rate for the year. This represented a rise of more than 4 percent from the previous year's US$53.7 billion. Since 1965, when the GDP was US$6 billion, it has grown nearly tenfold, at a compound annual growth rate (CAGR) of 7.8 percent during these 19 years. Official sources are projecting continued GDP growth in the range of 5.4 to 6.1 percent in 1995.

The Philippine economy took off following World War II; however, the pace slowed in the 1950s and early 1960s. Although the economy has risen steadily over the past 30 years in peso terms, it dipped significantly from 1982 through 1986 when measured in US dollar terms. During this period, the GDP fell by nearly 19.4 percent (by 10.5 percent in 1983 alone) before trending upward again in 1987. This drop coincided with the turmoil leading up to the departure of Marcos and the establishment of the Aquino administration. Since 1986 the nation's GDP has shown strong growth at a CAGR of 8.5 percent, nearly doubling in current US dollar terms.

Standard of Living By a somewhat different measure, a significant rise in the Philippines per capita GDP during the past 20 years is visible: from P740 (US$28) in 1965 to P21,801 (US$825) in 1994, an increase of nearly 30-fold representing a CAGR of almost 12 percent. However, in current US dollar terms, the increase in per capita GDP during this same period has not been so large, growing at a CAGR of 5.2 percent (from US$178 to US$825).

During the last years of the Marcos regime and the transition years of the Aquino administration, per capita GDP in fact decreased slightly in terms of both constant pesos and current US dollars. From 1982 to 1986, per capita GDP fell by 26.9 percent when measured in current US dollars (from US$731 to US$534). During the last years of Aquino's term, per capita GDP showed the signs of recovery as the drop slowed, falling by only 4.7 percent in constant peso terms from P11,620 in 1989 to P11,078 in 1993. The goal of the Ramos administration is to boost per capita GDP to US$1,000 by 1998.

The reality is that perhaps as much as half of the population in the Philippines is involved in essentially subsistence or extremely low level market activities. The cash economy and purchasing power in nonurban areas is relatively undeveloped. Of course, this also means that effective purchasing power in the cities is in general significantly higher than the overall per capita level and is even more concentrated at higher income levels.

CONTEXT OF THE ECONOMY

The Philippine economy has historically been characterized by boom-and-bust cycles. Shortly after independence in 1946, the leadership chose a strategy based on import substitution rather than export promotion. This policy led to the building of narrowly focused, uncompetitive industries largely dependent on imported raw materials and capital equipment.

During the 1970s, the Philippines attempted to capitalize on local labor advantages for assembly functions—primarily of electronics and apparel—but these operations have often been low-value-added without much influence on or connection to the economy as a whole. Still, the Philippines was considered relatively prosperous from the 1950s

until the 1980s, when it was dubbed "the sick man of Asia." In 1991 the official poverty rate was about 50 percent, while the self-reported poverty rate was nearly 70 percent.

Nowadays, many Filipinos and outsiders alike argue that the picture of the 1980s is no longer accurate because the Philippines has begun to overcome some of the problems that have plagued its people and economy in modern times. While much of the Philippines remains rural, Manila—the nation's primary industrial and business center—is regaining its status as the "Pearl of the Orient."

The Philippine economy is played out against a backdrop of a number of limiting constraints. One of the most noticeable is the inadequate domestic power grid, which was neglected during much of the 1970s and 1980s. By the time Aquino took office in 1986, not only were the existing generating and distribution systems inadequate, but the deferral of maintenance had made the available capacity inefficient and unreliable. Until very recently, the Philippines was unable to sustain even its relatively low level of industrial development, much less develop new industry, and the problem grew worse with increasing dependence on imported petroleum to fire the generating plants. Government initiatives have begun to bring new capacity on line—including coal- and oil-fired, as well as hydroelectric and geothermal generators. Parts of the state-run power company are also being privatized in the interest of enticing new investment and achieving greater efficiency by the end of this century.

Another structural difficulty in the economy has been the Philippines' significant foreign debt. In 1994 total foreign debt—most of which was left over

The Philippines' Gross Domestic Product (GDP)

Note: (e) = estimate; US dollar value calculated using average exchange rate for the year.

Source: International Monetary Fund, International Financial Statistics Yearbook, 1994

from the Marcos era, when a substantial portion of borrowed funds went into consumption or graft instead of investment—was roughly US$42 billion, equal to two-thirds of GDP. However, only about one-quarter of the Philippine foreign debt is short-term (compared with more than three-quarters for Mexico, which experienced financial difficulties in early 1995). In the late 1980s, foreign debt service routinely ate up more than one-third of all Philippine export-derived foreign exchange earnings. Through rescheduling, buybacks of debt at a discount, increased exports, and general growth in GDP, this debt service was reduced to less than 20 percent of GDP in the mid-1990s.

For many past decades, the Philippines maintained a relatively closed economy in which local monopolies and cartels operated by insiders or by the government were largely protected from both domestic and foreign competition. During much of the post–World War II period, the "system" operated in an often anticompetitive manner, with bureaucratic roadblocks protecting the status quo and derailing most attempts by outsiders to penetrate Philippine markets. With the advent of Aquino, some of these foundations became a little shaky, but most stayed in place. Beginning with the Ramos administration in 1992, the executive strongly pushed for the further easing of foreign exchange, foreign investment, and banking restrictions; the lowering of tariff and nontariff barriers to trade and market entry; and the general deregulation of the system. While progress has been made, entrenched interests and some members of the legislature continue to resist many of the changes. Since 1986 the government has begun to privatize its holdings, and additional privatizations are anticipated. The government has also cut the solid protection once given to the national telephone monopoly, allowing outside competitors to provide service.

The government's attempts to deal with economic problems have met with the further difficulty of lack of funds for necessary investments or even for seeding the opportunities. Attempts to allow foreign investors to build industrial capability and imports to provide competition have often foundered because of local resistance. Moreover, attempts to upgrade domestic industry through imports of capital goods and necessary raw materials have resulted in a growing trade deficit that might destabilize the economy in the short term because of the outflow of foreign reserves needed to pay for them. The government must rely largely on private investment to fund development.

A final and significant aspect of the Philippine economy is that a lack of employment opportunities at home has caused substantial numbers of Filipinos to work abroad as contract labor or on some

other guest worker basis. In recent years the estimated US$2 billion remitted annually by overseas workers has represented one of the country's largest single sources of foreign exchange. However, the status of Filipino workers abroad is often problematic at best and marginal at worse, a fact brought into poignant light by the 1995 execution of a Philippine domestic worker in Singapore, an event that became a political cause célèbre. But despite the social disruptions caused by the absence of workers from home, a decrease in overseas employment could have a greater negative impact on the economy than its continuation because of the relatively few employment options at home and the importance of the hard currency earnings generated by these workers.

THE UNDERGROUND ECONOMY

Tracking informal transactions—those that occur outside what is commonly accepted in more developed countries as the formal economic system—is a formidable task. As a result the lines of demarcation between the formal and informal, or underground, economies are not always clear. The Philippine underground economy is difficult to quantify, although some observers argue that it is equal to one-third of the total official, regulated economy. Many underground transactions are based on traditional patron-client relationships; others exist primarily to evade regulation and taxation; yet others exist to engage in illegal activities. Competition for power among relatively few prominent families and a general lack of resources have added impetus to the conduct of business other than through arm's-length market interchanges. Although these deals may work reasonably well for local operators, they are unlikely to function well in most international exchanges.

The historically narrow, family power structure in the Philippines has led to a tradition in which payoffs represent a more or less accepted way of doing business, a situation that became highly developed during the Marcos regime. In the 1980s, it was estimated that an amount equal to one-quarter of the national budget was lost through payoffs. Although the Aquino and Ramos administrations have made some progress toward eliminating these practices, business operations are often less than transparent, and the payment of "financial incentives" remains relatively common. Foreigners may encounter unofficial requests for undisclosed payments and quid pro quo arrangements, and they may find themselves effectively prevented from carrying out their plans without at least some accommodation with those demanding such considerations.

The Philippine tax and tariff systems have also

been marked by considerable evasion. Smuggling and bribing customs officials to avoid the high tariffs has been commonplace; in recent years an estimated 60 percent of the goods entering the Philippines have passed the border without payment of the duties owed. In the early 1990s fewer than 40 percent of the nation's businesses and only about one-quarter of the individuals even bothered to file tax returns. Only a fraction of the 12 million individuals employed in the private sector were on the tax rolls at all, and tax agents were notorious for accepting bribes to reduce the amount of tax owed. Collection has improved, but the level of revenue is still far below that which should be generated under existing laws. President Ramos has had tax reform on his agenda, but he has had difficulty in forcing the reforms because of opposition from entrenched interests. However, the administration has made the reduction of corruption a major focus of its program and penalties have been increased— all the way to the death penalty for the most egregious acts of corruption.

For the most part, the criminal excesses of past decades have been checked, and between 1989 and 1993 the overall crime rates, including violent crimes, have dropped by more than half. As in any society, crime and violence are still factors primarily for the unwary. The Philippines is marked by drug enforcement agencies as a main transshipment point for heroin and related illegal drugs between Southeast Asia and the US, and there are segments of the population noted for running innovative scams on incautious travelers. Both organized and lower level street crime are visible, particularly in Manila. The Filipino belief in honor and sensitivity to loss of face can sometimes lead to rapid escalation of violence in circumstances that would not provoke similar responses in more passive cultures. Interpol notes that the murder rate in the Philippines is among the highest in the world. Although most crime is economically motivated, the Philippines has its share of ideologically motivated groups that resort to violence as a means of financing, publicizing, and achieving their political ends. Such groups seldom select foreigners as primary targets, but their actions are fairly indiscriminate.

Enforcement of Intellectual Property Rights
Philippine laws are designed to protect intellectual property rights, and the country is a party to international conventions that protect such rights. As a signatory of the General Agreement on Tariffs and Trade (GATT), the Philippines is obligated to upgrade its available protections to international standards. In the past, enforcement has often been ineffective. Problems cited by companies that have done business there include trademark counterfeiting; piracy of audio, video, and computer software materials; infringement of copyright; and failure to pay royalties. The Philippines follows a rather broad definition of fair use for copyrighted works. Bureaucratic regulations make protection difficult because of the costs and delays in registering licensing agreements and, for some arrangements, in gaining government approvals. Nevertheless, the government has declared its commitment to strengthen legal enforcement. Largely on that basis, in 1993 the US downgraded the Philippines from "priority" to "regular" status on the US Special 301 list of countries that fail to protect intellectual property rights.

Philippine Consumer Price Index

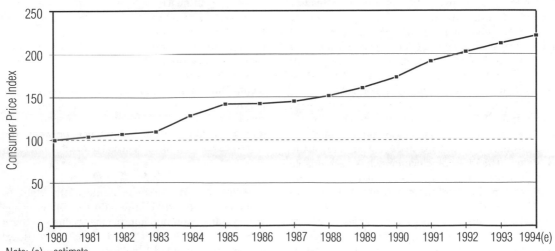

Note: (e) = estimate

Source: International Monetary Fund, International Financial Statistics Yearbook, 1994

INFLATION

Inflation has been highly variable in the Philippines; the most recent trend has been slightly downward. In 1994, inflation ran 9 percent, down from 9.6 percent the previous year. With only a 6 percent rise in the first quarter of 1995, officials have predicted an inflation rate of no more than 5 percent for the year.

During the 1970s, annual inflation averaged only 1.4 percent, while during the 1980s it averaged 6.5 percent. However, between 1990 and 1994, it averaged 12.1 percent, at a time when inflation rates were generally falling in much of the developed world. Between 1980 and 1994, inflation ranged as high as 18.7 percent (in 1984 and 1991) and as low as 0.5 percent (1986); the CAGR was 5.4 percent during this period.

Because the Philippines has had such low domestic productivity and depends so heavily on imports—of energy, consumer goods, capital goods, and basic and intermediate inputs—it has a significant structural problem with supply and demand for foreign goods that serve to drive up domestic prices. This situation tends to be exacerbated by local conditions, including such natural disasters as the eruption of Mount Pinatubo in 1991. At that time, the inflation rate surged to 18.7 percent, a level last seen during the turmoil surrounding the 1984 midterm elections when the opposition began to seriously challenge Marcos.

LABOR

The Philippines has a surplus of relatively inexpensive, capable, and generally well educated labor. Education is highly prized, and after the ten years of available public education the goal of many Filipinos is to attain as much additional education as possible. Job training and retraining is heavily promoted, and both public agencies and private firms offer continuing programs; roughly half of larger firms offer at least some training for their workers, although the training available varies widely by industry and size of firm. The nation claims a literacy rate of nearly 90 percent.

Most Philippine businesses are small, with fewer than 1 percent employing more than 200 workers, and the vast majority are undercapitalized and strongly affected by the cyclic nature of the economy. The Philippine economy has been unable to find places for many of its graduates, rendering significant numbers of them overqualified for available jobs. Many are unable to find work at any level. Conversely, employers in specialty areas may have difficulty in immediately locating qualified workers, but Filipino workers are considered to be fast at learning new skills. According to a survey taken in

the early 1990s, Filipino workers rated a 3 out of 10 (with 1 representing the best) for quality, a 1 for availability, and a 2 for cost in comparison with other Asian economies. The other Asian countries that ranked higher on quality also ranked much lower in terms of labor availability and cost.

Given its current high level of population growth, the Philippines needs to generate nearly one million new jobs annually during the rest of the 1990s to accommodate its burgeoning workforce. Many Filipinos—an estimated two million of them (or four million if permanent overseas residents are counted)—have emigrated abroad as temporary or long-term guest workers because of the lack of opportunity at home. Nearly 700,000—down in recent years because of reduced demand primarily in the Middle East—have signed formal, registered labor contracts; many others work informally. The lack of employment opportunities at home and financial need for the remittances of these overseas Filipinos makes this situation unlikely to change in the near future.

Unemployment

In early 1995 unemployment was estimated to be about 9 percent, although perhaps one-third of the workforce could be classified as underemployed. Unemployment was down slightly from 9.1 percent in 1994. Throughout the 1970s and into the early 1980s, unemployment averaged around 4.5 percent, and then it started to creep upward, reaching a high of 11.4 percent in 1989. During the late 1980s and early 1990s, unemployment has generally fluctuated between 8 and 10 percent, with underemployment ranging between 20 and 30 percent.

During the early 1990s, the job turnover rate began to rise, and the Philippine unemployment rate has shown a predictable annual pattern ever since. The annual swing in unemployment rates begins when many workers choose to quit during the first quarter of the year in search of better jobs or to live on year-end bonuses. In the fall, many of these workers again take jobs to pay for Christmas shopping, causing a drop in year-end unemployment. This phenomenon has resulted in an unemployment rate that peaks at the beginning of the second quarter and plummets at the end of the fourth quarter, with the difference between the extremes amounting to nearly 3 percent.

Role of Unions

Filipino workers are guaranteed the right to organize and to strike in an effort to obtain wage and working condition improvements. In 1993 there were 475 major unions, nearly 5,900 active local unions, and about 3.1 million union members—about 13 percent of the total workforce. Overall, unions have become less militant as the 1990s have proceeded, with the number of labor stoppages and the number of workers affected falling. In 1993 there were 122 strikes—affecting 35,000 workers—down by about 10 percent from the preceding year. However, both labor and management often threaten strikes or lockouts, engaging in brinksmanship before settling at the last minute.

Filipino unions are diverse and seldom cooperate because of differing ideologies and personalities. However, during the early 1990s, a broad spectrum of unions united to demand an increase in the minimum wage and a freeze in government-controlled commodities prices. The government has established a relatively effective mediation and conciliation program. It seldom intervenes directly in labor disputes, but can act strategically. During the early 1990s, the government has been lobbying unions to restrain demands for higher wages based on the claim that there is a close correlation between higher wages and greater unemployment.

Wages

In recent years, wages in the Philippines have generally been about one-quarter to one-third of what they are in more developed Asian countries. As of mid-1994, the daily minimum wage in the Philippines was P145 (US$5.35) for nonagricultural workers in the National Capital Region (Manila); agricultural minimum wages in Manila were between P124.5 (US$4.59) and P135 (US$4.98). Legal minimums also varied according to industry and—more importantly—by size of operation, with smaller firms being allowed to pay legal minimum wages that are as much as 17 percent lower.

Minimum wages outside the capital varied between P115 (US$4.24) and P129 (US$4.76). In mid-1994 local managers were earning about US$600 per month, intermediate level skilled employees US$225 per month, and low level workers about US$120 per month; domestics were paid between US$60 and US$120. In the early 1990s the minimum wage was estimated to be about 80 to 85 percent of average wages. However, in 1991, 44 percent of workers nationwide and 29 percent of those in Manila reported that they earned less than the minimum wage.

Philippine law requires employers to pay workers an extra month's salary as an annual bonus. Workers also receive many benefits, including paid vacation days, paid holidays, social security, and medical benefits. Larger employers often offer paid sick leave, private pension plans, additional private health and life insurance plans, profit sharing, subsidized meals, and rice and transportation allowances. Employers are not permitted to cancel unilaterally any previously granted benefits. Benefits generally cost a minimum of 15 percent of payroll, but can cost as much as 60 percent of payroll. Executive and management benefits are generally higher—often in line with those in more developed countries.

Workweek

The standard workweek in the Philippines is 48 hours, consisting of six 8-hour days, although more and more white-collar operations are limiting themselves to a 40-hour workweek. Laws mandate rest days, overtime and holiday pay, and night shift premiums. There are also prohibitions on child

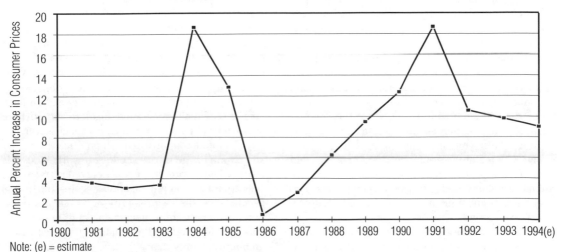

Philippine Inflation: 1980–1994

Note: (e) = estimate

Source: *International Monetary Fund, International Financial Statistics Yearbook, 1994*

labor and restrictions on the employment of women in hazardous jobs or at night. Refer to the "Labor" chapter, beginning on page 197, for discussion of the employment laws.

ELEMENTS OF THE ECONOMY

As noted, many Filipinos operate largely outside the formal market economy, making national statistics susceptible to a range of error. Nevertheless, the statistics are considered to present a relatively consistent, reasonable picture of the Philippine economy. Although in 1993 agriculture, fishing, and forestry pursuits employed about 45 percent of the workforce, the sector accounted for only 21.7 percent of GDP—down from 22.7 percent in 1989. Industry—employing about 15 percent of the workforce—represented 30.4 percent of GDP (down from 33.1 percent in 1989). The service sector accounted for 47.9 percent of GDP in 1993, up from 44.2 percent in 1989; in 1993 services employed slightly less than 40 percent of the workforce.

Agriculture

Agriculture was disrupted by political events during the 1980s and suffered even more during the series of natural disasters that hit the islands in the early 1990s. These events damaged not only production but also processing, storage, and transportation infrastructure, none of which were highly developed in the first place. Markets were established in 1986 to begin trading in major commodities—primarily rice, coconut, and sugar—following the breakup of the monopolies and cartel arrangements that had developed in these products over the years.

In 1994 agricultural production grew by 2.4 percent, up marginally from 1993. Most Philippine food crops—mainly palay (rice) and maize (corn)—are grown on a subsistence, sharecropping, or small market farming basis for domestic consumption. Productivity per worker in agriculture is the lowest of any major economic sector.

A number of industrial crops are cultivated on a large scale for export or as cash crops for domestic markets, the major ones being sugarcane and coconut. Sugarcane accounts for a bit more than 50 percent of all such production, while the coconut yield is nearly 30 percent of the total. Other crops include fruit (mainly pineapple, banana, and mango), specialty crops (tobacco, coffee, and cocoa), and industrial crops (abaca and rubber). Animal products include eggs, chicken, pork, and beef, although animal husbandry is relatively poorly developed.

The timber industry has declined in recent years because exploitation by clear-cutting has led to environmental concerns. Programs designed to counteract deforestation include the planting of fast-growing bamboo, which not only stabilizes the soil but also has economic value.

Filipinos are heavily reliant on seafood for subsistence. In recent years the Philippine catch has reached about 2.5 million metric tons, making it the 10th largest fishing nation worldwide. However, growth has begun to level off because of overfishing and a lack of investment. Some fisheries have turned to aquaculture, and a particularly successful export trade has developed in shrimp and prawns and in the breeding of ornamental fish.

Future Directions In general, the agricultural sector has a suffered from a lack of infrastructure and financing. Government intervention to break up monopolies is helping to invigorate the sector to some extent, but the level of investment needed to improve the situation substantially has not been available. The Department of Agriculture has targeted improvement of production and distribution of rice, maize, coconut, sugar, livestock and poultry, and fisheries. Agriculture and forestry are classified as "pioneer" industries and are thus entitled to various incentives under the terms of the Omnibus Investments Code established in 1987.

An agrarian reform program, in existence since 1988, is designed to redistribute land from large private and corporate holders to those who work it, making investment in productive land problematic. Landowners are to be compensated, and recipients are required to reimburse the government; this leads to disputes over land valuation, which have slowed the program. Although the government has been transferring land titles, the rate and extent of redistribution has been below expectations.

Manufacturing and Industry

In 1994 overall growth in the industrial sector was 6.1 percent, up sharply from an anemic showing of 1.6 percent in 1993. This performance was largely bolstered by the 10.9 percent increase in construction and was underwritten by a 5.1 percent rise in manufacturing; however, the rise was tempered by a 7 percent fall in mining activity.

Mining The Philippines has rich deposits of mineral wealth, but of an estimated 20 million hectares of potentially productive onshore and offshore areas, fewer than 75 percent have been surveyed. The Philippines is the top Asian producer of copper and is one of the top 10 producers worldwide. It is also the eighth largest producer of gold in the world. The combined output of copper, gold, and nickel accounts for the vast majority of its metal production. A variety of other metal and nonmetallic minerals are produced in smaller quantities, and a number of energy deposits have been found—coal, uranium, oil, and natural gas—but none of these

Structure of the Philippine Economy—1993

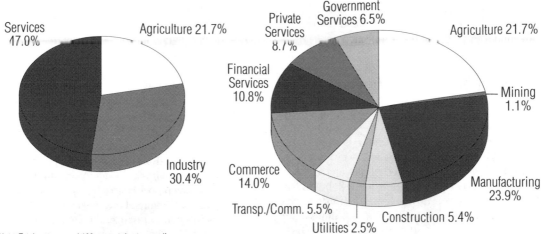

Note: Totals may exceed 100 percent due to rounding.
Source: Philippine National Statistics Coordination Board, Economic and Social Statistics Office

areas have been exploited to their full potential.

The relatively low-value-added nonmetallic sector provided the only growth in the mining subsector during the early 1990s, primarily because demand and prices for metals were hurt by the worldwide economic slowdown. In 1993 the mining sector accounted for only 1.1 percent of GDP (down from 1.7 percent in 1989) and employed only 0.5 percent of the workforce.

Construction Despite a housing shortage and building boom in recent years, the construction industry tends to operate in a boom-and-bust cycle, characterized in general by low investment and a lack of stability. In 1993 construction provided 5.4 percent of GDP—down from 6.2 percent in 1989— and employed 4.7 percent of the workforce, although property management (classified under financial services) has been a major growth area.

Manufacturing In 1993 only 9.8 percent of the workforce was employed in the manufacturing sector, which accounted for 23.9 percent of GDP, down from 25.2 percent in 1989. Nevertheless, the value-added per employee was the third highest of all major sectors, surpassed only by the utilities and financial services sectors. The value-added nearly doubled between 1989 and 1993, with production in transportation equipment, electrical machinery, nonmetallic minerals, and energy products rising in value by more than 75 percent.

In 1993 the main manufacturing areas were energy products (with a 9.7 percent share of value-added), followed by food and beverage processing (8.5 percent), chemicals (8.3 percent), and footwear and apparel manufacturing (7.2 percent), together accounting for about one-third of national output in

manufacturing by value. Heavy industry includes production of cement, glass, industrial chemicals and fertilizers, iron and steel, and petroleum products. Light manufacturing is centered around labor intensive assembly, primarily of imported components, including apparel, electronics, and electrical machinery, the main growth areas. Industry is concentrated in and around Manila and a few other urban areas—a result of the dominance of Manila as well as the lack of adequate power, transportation, and communications infrastructure in other areas of the country.

Future Directions Although the government wants to industrialize and upgrade Philippine manufacturing capabilities, it has not had the resources to further such development. Rather, programs—such as free trade and export processing zones—have been designed to encourage the creation of relatively low level assembly jobs producing exports that are financed by foreign investors. Another targeted area is the value-added processing of agricultural and mining products, again largely for export. Target areas designed to take advantage of the low cost of labor and available skill levels include the manufacture of textiles, garments, furniture and other wood products, gifts, and housewares; the assembly of electronic components and products; and the processing of food, beverage, and seafood products.

Petroleum exploration has been given priority in the mining subsector, and the government wants to attract foreign investment capital and expertise into this area. By executive order, foreign explorers were exempted from the value-added tax on imported materials used in the process. Part of the unexplored area includes the Spratly Islands, located in the

South China Sea, parts of which are also claimed by Indonesia, Malaysia, Brunei, Vietnam, Taiwan, and China. The value of potential deposits of petroleum and other resources in the area mean that resolution of ownership is likely to be difficult and prolonged, delaying development of the resources.

Services

Overall, the services sector grew by 3.8 percent in 1994, up from 2.5 percent in 1993. Although the Philippine services sector is contributing nearly half of the country's total GDP—it was 47.9 percent in 1993—it has remained relatively undeveloped. Overall, its workers have achieved low productivity, adding 1.2 times the value per employee (which is above the 0.5 rate for agriculture, but well below the 2.2 rate for industry). However, productivity varies widely by subsector, with utilities (6.2 times) and financial services (5.4 times) representing high productivity areas; trade, transportation, and communications (1.0 times) representing an essentially break-even level; and personal services (0.9 times) representing below par productivity.

Utilities The utilities subsector accounted for 2.5 percent of GDP and 0.4 percent of employment in 1993. This subsector has been a problem area for the Philippines, primarily because of a lack of investment. Although the country has the second highest rate of geothermal energy production in the world, as well as hydroelectric power and generation using alternative fuels (such as agricultural wastes), it remains heavily dependent on imported oil. Despite all the problems, utilities is the most productive subsector in the country in terms of output per worker, and the value of its output grew by 13.8 percent in 1994—the largest increase in any major subsector.

Commerce Retail and wholesale trade is important: with a 14 percent share of GDP, trade lags behind only agriculture and manufacturing in terms of its contribution to the economy. Trade also provides 14 percent of overall employment, second only to agriculture and the combined public and private personal services sectors. However, trade and distribution remain highly fragmented; foreign investors have not been allowed to operate retail stores, and entrenched local businesses have resisted changes that would arguably upgrade access and levels of service.

Transportation and Communications The contribution of transportation and communications to GDP has grown from 4.5 percent in 1989 to 5.5 percent in 1993, when these activities employed 5.4 percent of the workforce. Improvements in these areas are a necessary goal if the sprawling, and often poorly integrated, island chain is to improve its business climate.

Financial Services Financial services has been one of the high growth areas of the economy. In 1993 this subsector employed only 2 percent of the workforce but accounted for 10.8 percent of GDP, of which 60 percent represents the important real estate development and rental subsector. Financial services is slowly opening up to international practices and providers.

Government and Private Services Personal services—including private and government—together contributed 15.2 percent of GDP in 1993 (up from 13.8 in 1989) while employing 17.3 percent of the workforce.

Future Directions The Philippine services sector has grown almost by accident. Although the government has relaxed entry barriers to outsiders in such areas as financial and business services, it continues to maintain barriers in such prime areas as retail trade. The only services area actively targeted by the government for development has been tourism. Visitor numbers have been growing only slowly, but the contribution of tourism—especially of coveted foreign exchange—has been growing substantially, making this an area that ripe for more government incentives aimed at encouraging investment.

TRADE

The Philippines is heavily dependent on trade to acquire needed energy, capital goods, and inputs. During the past 30 years, foreign trade has grown at a CAGR of 11 percent to equal 65 percent of GDP (up from just 26 percent in 1965). In 1994 the Philippines merchandise trade reached an estimated total of US$37.4 billion—an all-time high—and up about 29 percent in nominal terms from the previous year. Although it has become more involved in international trade, the Philippines has yet to develop as a reexport center despite its strategic location; in 1993 reexports accounted for only about 1 percent of total exports.

The Philippines has a long-standing structural merchandise trade deficit that has been growing in recent years. Despite attempts to encourage exports, growth of imports continues to outstrip that of exports by a substantial and increasing margin. The merchandise trade deficit—which was equal to 2.5 percent of total trade in 1965—rose to a record US$7.84 billion in 1994, equal to 21 percent of total trade. Exports have grown at a CAGR of 10.3 percent during the past 30 years, while imports have increased at a CAGR of 11.8 percent. During 1994 exports grew at a faster rate than did imports (19.5 percent versus 17.9 percent), although exports still accounted for far less in actual value. Filipino officials have defended the country's import perfor-

Philippine Foreign Trade

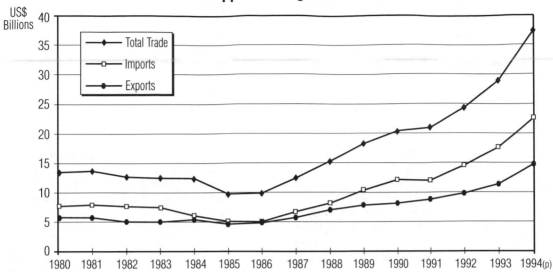

Note: (p) = preliminary.
Source: International Monetary Fund, International Financial Statistics Yearbook, 1994

mance, noting that only about 10 percent of imports consist of consumer goods, while the rest represent capital goods, raw materials, or intermediate components to be used in the production either of import substitution or export products. Refer to the "Foreign Trade" chapter, beginning on page 55, for discussion of exports, imports, and balance of trade.

The Philippines records a surplus in trade in services during most years based on remittances from overseas Filipino workers. From 1980 to 1993 total trade in services amounted to only about a third of what total merchandise trade posted, but it generated surpluses as high as US$2.5 billion in 1992. These surpluses have helped to offset chronic merchandise trade deficits.

The Philippine current account deficit has made growth in export receipts, remittances, and foreign investment increasingly important to the continued stability of the country. One generally positive sign has been the increase of foreign reserves, which ended 1994 at US$6 billion, growing to US$6.4 billion by the end of the first quarter of 1995. The Philippines began the decade of the 1980s with foreign reserves valued at US$2.8 billion; however, these fell to as low as US$602 million in 1984 before recovering in the 1990s. Since 1990 foreign reserves have nearly doubled. Nevertheless, even at US$6 billion, such reserves are only adequate to cover roughly one quarter's imports, not to mention debt service requirements.

Trading Partners

The Philippines' foreign trade is heavily concentrated, with the top two trading partners—the US

and Japan—accounting for 54.6 percent of all exports from and 42.6 percent of all imports to the Philippines. Although these two partners remain dominant, trade has been growing with other countries, especially the other members of the Association of Southeast Asian Nations (ASEAN). The Philippines has also been making a special effort to court members of the European Union (EU) in hopes of increasing trade with these potential large buyers and suppliers. Import trade is somewhat less concentrated than export trade: the top 10 sellers of Philippine imports represent 76.8 percent of all imports versus 82.3 percent taken by the top 10 buyers of Philippine exports. Refer to the "Foreign Trade" chapter, beginning on page 55, for a further breakdown of the contributions of various trading partners.

FOREIGN PARTICIPATION IN THE ECONOMY

The Philippine government recognizes that it needs foreign participation to acquire the technology, know-how, and capital required to improve its economy. Thus, after a prolonged period during which foreign investment policy was protectionist and generally exclusionary, the Philippines is becoming more welcoming to such investment. Under the Foreign Investments Act of 1991, foreigners are eligible to own 100 percent of export oriented ventures and certain companies serving the domestic market. However, a negative list is maintained of areas that are reserved for national ownership, some of which are completely restricted, while others allow up to 40 percent foreign ownership. Land ownership is generally restricted to Filipinos, although foreigners can obtain 75-year leases. Refer to the "Foreign Investment" chapter, beginning on page 43, for a thorough discussion of Philippine foreign investment laws.

The government offers significant incentives— including tax holidays, credits, and exemptions— especially for export oriented, nontraditional, or innovative activities, classified as "pioneer" enterprises. The Philippines also encourages build-operate-transfer (BOT) arrangements, by which the investor constructs and operates a facility for a specified period of time, after which it is turned over to a local entity. To encourage investment and dispersal of industry, the government offers incentives to foreign firms that locate in special free trade and export processing zones.

Registration of foreign investments is usually required, although formal approval is not always necessary. Investments cannot be completed—nor can capital or earnings be repatriated—without a registration certificate. The Philippines relaxed its exchange controls in 1992, and capital and earnings are eligible for immediate repatriation, provided the investment has been properly registered. Overseas borrowing by Philippine registered firms requires prior authorization, and remittances abroad may not be made using locally borrowed funds.

Size of Foreign Participation

Between 1970 and 1993, registered direct foreign investment in the Philippines was US$5.2 billion. In 1991 foreign investment accounted for almost half of total new investment in the Philippine economy, although the foreign share of such investment fell to one-quarter in 1992; the foreign share of new investment represented about 40 percent in 1993. In actual amounts invested, foreign investment fell by one-third from 1991 through 1993. Total net foreign investment—including both portfolio and direct foreign equity investment—in 1994 was roughly US$1.5 billion, up sharply from US$600 million in 1993.

Since 1987 after the Aquino government came into power and liberalization of foreign exchange restrictions began, the bulk of foreign investment has consisted of portfolio investment in securities. Although the influx of foreign exchange has been welcome, authorities continue to worry that conditions having little to do with the local situation will upset investors, who will then pull this international "hot money" out of the country on short notice. This is not an idle concern, as seen in the first quarter of 1995 when Philippine securities markets dropped sharply because investors suddenly began fleeing from all emerging markets in

the wake of the Mexican peso devaluation.

A greater long-term concern is that securities investment does little to create productive capacity or jobs. In 1994 some US$3 billion came into the Philippines as portfolio investment; however, US$2.1 billion flowed out during the same year, leaving net total foreign portfolio investment at roughly US$900 million—about the same level as in 1993.

The US$800 million that was registered as direct foreign investment in 1994 represented more than double the US$378 million in 1993. However, nearly two-thirds of this 1994 amount—about US$500 million—represented a single transaction: the acquisition of 40 percent of the government oil firm Petron by Saudi Aramco. Other new investment was thus about 20 percent below the 1993 level.

Origin of Foreign Investment

The US has been the main foreign investor in the Philippines, accounting for about 44 percent of total registered direct foreign investment. It is followed by Japan with 20 percent. The next largest foreign investors were Hong Kong (6.5 percent), the UK (6.5 percent), the Netherlands (4.0 percent), and Switzerland (2.0 percent). Together, these top five investors accounted for more than four-fifths of all direct foreign investment.

Between 1990 and 1994, Japan seized the lead in investment growth, investing more in the Philippines than the next four largest investors—the US, Hong Kong, Korea, and the UK—combined, and twice as much as the US alone during that period. The top investing countries in 1993 were Japan (US$112.3 million), the US (US$88.1 million), the Netherlands (US$79.6 million), Korea (US$40 million); and Singapore (US$40 million). Korean investment rose by almost 600 percent from the previous year, while that from Singapore soared by nearly 750 percent. Germany, Denmark, France, Hong Kong, and Malaysia rounded out the top ten foreign investors in 1993.

Areas of Foreign Investment

Some recent areas of investment that are gaining prominence include metalworking and engineering; the production and (mostly) the assembly of electrical components and consumer electronics; software development; construction materials; garment-making (including accessories, yarn, and related products); sporting goods; and tourism.

Of total direct foreign investment registered as of 1994, slightly more than half (53 percent) was invested in manufacturing. Mining, with a 20 percent share, was next, followed by financial services (11.1 percent). Remaining investments by sector were relatively minor: 5.0 percent in commerce (which was largely restricted to nationals); 4.6 percent in services (professional services also being restricted to Filipinos); 1.2 percent in public utilities (mostly state or private monopolies during this period); 1.5 percent in agriculture; and 0.6 percent in the construction industry. During the period 1990 through 1993, roughly two-thirds of all foreign investment went into manufacturing. Prominent targets included firms producing machinery, appliances, industrial and specialty chemicals, transportation equipment, and food products.

By contrast, in 1993 nearly one-third (32.7 percent) of foreign investment flowed into the energy sector, followed by the machine tools (22.3 percent), and construction (18.4 percent) industries. There were smaller investments in other sectors: electrical equipment and electronics (6.7 percent), processed foods (4.1 percent), textiles and apparel (3.6 percent), mining (2.1 percent), and the automotive industry (1.4 percent). Together these eight investment areas accounted for slightly more than 90 percent of all foreign investment in the Philippines in 1993.

However, foreign investment in new businesses (as distinguished from new investment in existing businesses) in 1993 gives a somewhat different picture. The largest share of capital invested by foreigners in newly opened (rather than acquired existing) businesses was in financial services and real estate (55.4 percent), followed by manufacturing (12.6 percent) and commerce (11.6 percent). The remaining 20 percent was invested in other personal services (6.4 percent), transportation and communications (5.2 percent), and construction (4.3 percent), with agriculture, mining, and utilities each accounting for less than 2 percent.

GOVERNMENT ECONOMIC DEVELOPMENT STRATEGY

A capitalist country, the Philippines has left economic development largely in the hands of private enterprise. Theoretically, the government has officially restricted its involvement to providing certain infrastructure and incentive programs, and to promoting its fiscal, monetary, and regulatory policies. However, much of the resulting economic structure has consisted of monopolies, cartels, and a state-run sector that kept growing well into the 1980s. On taking power in 1986, the Aquino government decreed the reorganization and privatization of state-run enterprises. In that year there were 296 state-run enterprises—which absorbed roughly one-quarter of the national budget in subsidies—and 399 additional entities transferred to the government as security for nonperforming development bank loans with a face value totaling US$4.6

billion. The government planned to keep about 30 percent of all state-run firms in one form or another, liquidate another 20 percent, and sell off the remaining 50 percent.

A National Economic and Development Authority, created in 1973, has produced a series of consecutive medium-term plans. Although performance has seldom reached the levels proposed in these plans, their existence has helped to set priorities. Since the 1950s, the Philippines has relied on incentives to attract domestic and foreign investment to meet its goals. These have become increasingly export oriented, although under the terms of GATT, actual or de facto export subsidies are to be eliminated.

The Philippines 2000 plan is the Ramos administration's development program for 1993–1998. It is designed to focus on five strategic areas: (1) getting the economy going, primarily through the creation of jobs; (2) ending the power shortage by expanding capacity and improving distribution; (3) strengthening environmental protections and mitigating existing environmental problems; (4) deregulating the system and streamlining the bureaucracy; and (5) fighting corruption. Each goal requires different implementing laws and regulations, most of which have been slow to get underway because of opposition from vested interests and a general lack of funds to pay for them. However, Ramos, who received additional backing in the midterm elections held in May 1995, is expecting to use his new majority to muscle more of his agenda through the legislature.

Specific goals call for an increase of the per capita GDP to US$1,000 by 1998 and Newly Industrialized Country (NIC) status by the year 2000; annual inflation of less than 10 percent; elevation of 70 percent of the population above the poverty line; sustainable growth of both domestic savings and foreign investment; and annual growth of export production by 15 percent. This program is to be accomplished through free market policies involving decentralization of control from Manila, deregulation, privatization, reduction in protections for domestic industries, and liberalization of foreign exchange regulations and foreign investment law.

POLITICAL OUTLOOK FOR THE ECONOMY

The Philippines is in the midst of a slowly developing change in its traditional political and economic system. Long controlled by a relative few regionally based family political and economic dynasties, the country is attempting to break out of this rule of the few to encompass a broader, more arm's-length and market oriented approach, in both

Philippine Leading Exports by Commodity—1993

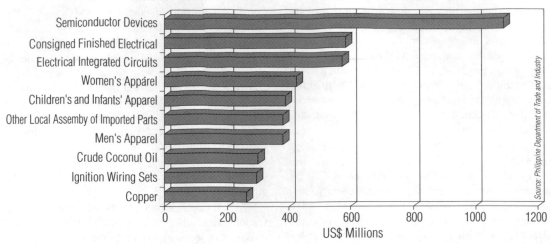

Source: Philippine Department of Trade and Industry

All other exports: US$6.586 billion or 58.4% of total.
Total 1993 exports: US$11.266 billion.

the economic and political spheres.

One of the forces that has limited the country's progress has been a historic focus on personalities and nepotism within the political sphere, which has consequently led to weakness of established political parties. During the first part of his term (1992–1995), Ramos was unable to accomplish much of his program because he lacked congressional support. Observers expect that more rapid progress will be made in the next three years, particularly because the results of the 1995 midterm elections—which were largely viewed as a referendum on Ramos' policies—gave him the support of the majority.

The gridlock experienced in the Philippine government during the post-Marcos regimes has led some—including Ramos—to float the idea of converting from a US-style, fixed-term political system (with a bicameral legislature and a balanced executive and judiciary) to a parliamentary form of government (with a unicameral legislature and an executive who serves an indefinite term). Such a switch is unlikely to happen anytime soon, especially given the fears that many present legislators have of losing their seats and influence in a smaller congress. These concerns are bolstered by opposition to what some view as an attempt by Ramos to circumvent the existing single six-year term limit on the chief executive (although Ramos has declared that he has no interest in extending his term).

The Philippines has been the location of ethnic and sectarian conflict since long before the 20th century. One long-simmering problem concerns the Islamic Moro National Liberation Front (MNLF), strongest in Mindanao in the south. The Spanish negotiated a settlement leaving these islands out of their direct colonial control. In the early 1900s, the US fought against a Moro insurgency, and the minority has periodically attempted to gain autonomy at various times ever since then. It has been split into factions, including the militant, fundamentalist Abu Sayyaf faction responsible for a massive raid at Ipil in March 1995. Another vocal minority, the National Democratic Front (NDF) of the Communist Party of the Philippines, has been sidelined by factional infighting among various doctrinal groups. Ramos legalized the previously outlawed Communist party, which served to dissipate its influence. This has seemed to work, at least for the present, although the government is likely to face continued difficulties from such breakaway groups in the future.

The Philippines has also faced problems on several international fronts. Its refusal to renew leases on US military bases at Clark Field and Subic Bay in 1991 led to cool relations between the two countries, although the special relationship between the US and the Philippines seems largely to have been restored. In 1994 the Philippines had a falling out with Indonesia after the Philippines hosted a conference on sovereignty in East Timor; Indonesia, which claims that island, broke off a variety of planned joint initiatives.

In early 1995 conflict heated up over the Spratly Islands, parts of which are claimed by the Philippines—among others—when Chinese naval vessels set out markers on several of these islands. The Philippines removed the markers and arrested some Chinese fishermen. There appears to be little danger that the conflict will escalate soon, although it could do so at any time. Finally, the execution of

Philippine Leading Imports by Commodity—1993

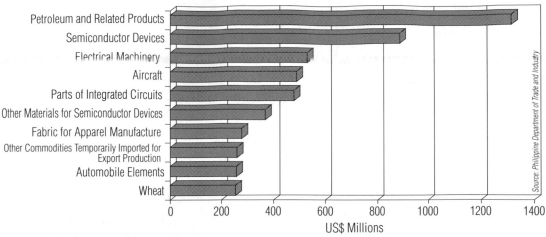

All other imports: US$12.506 billion or 71% of total.
Total 1993 imports: US$17.624 billion.

Flor Contemplación, a Filipino maid working in Singapore, by that country on a murder charge which many Filipinos believe was trumped up led to demonstrations, cancellation of diplomatic initiatives, and the firing of Ramos' foreign affairs secretary. The incident has also pointed up the plight of some Filipino guest workers overseas.

Back on the home front, the Ramos administration has faced slow going in its attempts to reform the election and tax systems, as well as on such other issues as privatization, deregulation, demonopolization, and agrarian reform. Although impressive advances have been made in some of these areas, many observers argue that the underlying patterns have yet to be altered. Economic reforms have been resisted by special interests as well as by populists arguing for economic nationalism. Privatizations have touched the power, petroleum, mining, paper, and shipbuilding industries, with additional opening slated for the hotel, steel, financial, petrochemical, and port service industries. The Ramos administration has been able to break the long distance telephone monopoly and to open banking to allow additional foreign participation, but the hold that the existing parties have on these industries remains strong. Local cartels have also resisted changes in the cement, shipping, and rice industries.

Government attempts to revise the tax codes to make them more effective have met resistance, as did an attempt to raise the value-added tax (VAT). Opposition politicians inserted so many exemptions into the proposed VAT law that it was considered to have been effectively gutted, and the administration tabled the issue until after the elec-

tions. The Ramos government also reaffirmed its support of agrarian reform, promising to double the rate of land distribution. However, most observers doubt that the government will be able meet its goals in this area, which have been stalled since its initiation during the Aquino administration.

Change is coming to the Philippines. However, to date, the rate of core change has made some observers skeptical. Nevertheless, the country is falling more in line with international standards and practices. Many analysts are anticipating enhanced progress from a reinforced Ramos administration.

THE PHILIPPINES' INTERNATIONAL ROLE

In recent years the Philippines has joined many international organizations and taken an active role regionally and internationally. The country is a member of most major international political and economic organizations and subscribes to most international conventions. It is a charter member of the United Nations and belongs to most of its subagencies. It also belongs to the General Agreement on Tariffs and Trade (GATT) and its successor body, the World Trade Organization (WTO); the International Monetary Fund (IMF); the International Bank for Reconstruction and Development (IBRD—the World Bank); and the Asian Development Bank (ADB). The country is also a member of such regional integration and trade oriented bodies as the Association of Southeast Asian Nations (ASEAN) and Asia Pacific Economic Cooperation (APEC). The Philippines has been attempting to enter into a new East ASEAN Growth Area (EAGA) alliance with neighboring Malaysia, Indonesia, and Brunei.

Current Issues

A NEW START FOR THE PHILIPPINES

The election of Fidel V. Ramos to the presidency in 1992 was a turning point for the Philippines; it marked the beginning of economic stability never before seen in the country. Under the direction of Ramos, who gained popularity as the military leader who helped oust Marcos, the economy has begun to rebound, and the Philippines has regained favor with the international investment community. Although its 1994 growth rate of 5 percent failed to match that of such fast-growth Asian economies as China, Singapore, and Malaysia, the Philippines is still widely regarded as a "tiger cub"—a viable contender among growing Pacific Rim economies. Subsequent parliamentary elections in May 1995 strengthened Ramos' hand in both houses of the Philippine legislature, giving him a convincing popular mandate to advance an ambitious modernization agenda that serves as the centerpiece of his political program.

However, the challenges are still enormous, due largely to the legacy of favoritism and corruption that reached extremes during the regime of dictator Ferdinand Marcos. But, if Ramos can overcome the fragmentation and corruption which continue to bedevil his country, the Philippines may yet become another Asian Tiger. Its prospects, say observers, are better now than they have been in decades.

CONTENTS

THE MODERNIZATION PROGRAM

Background In the 1960s, the Philippines was regarded as the second wealthiest country in Asia, surpassed only by Japan. Ferdinand Marcos, who came to power in 1965, continued the policies of his predecessors—attempting to achieve economic growth and independence through the protection of local producers, the creation of cartels and state-run monopolies in key economic sectors, and an effort to substitute domestic products for imported goods, regardless of comparative advantage—classic patterns of Third World development in the postwar era. He added a few policies of his own, including a system of "crony capitalism" that greatly rewarded and enriched a small group of large landowning families friendly with the ruling elite. After two decades of rule under Marcos, the Philippines' relative position had declined radically. While much of Asia enjoyed an era of explosive growth, it suffered massive unemployment and underemployment, losing many of its most skilled citizens through emigration. More than half of its population was living below international poverty standards, while the government survived by relying heavily upon foreign borrowing from international banks.

By the time Corazon Aquino came to power, the Marcos administration had run up US$25 billion in foreign debt.

Uncertainties of the Post-Marcos Era Though the election of Corazon Aquino to the presidency in 1986 brought great promise of reform, her government proved to be largely ineffective. Her administration was marked by political instability, civil unrest, and halting efforts to reform the economy. Natural disasters and a lingering hold on the economy by the landowning elite further dampened her efforts at reform and added to the Philippines' woes.

While the economy did recover somewhat between 1986 and 1989, it stalled again during the next three years as global recession created unfavorable conditions for Philippine exports. Labor uprisings, water and power shortages, and continued political unrest added to the country's economic woes. Political stability was tenuous and the economy was at an all-time low when Fidel Ramos came to power and initiated his reforms in 1992.

Philippines 2000 Modernization and industrialization lie at the core of the "Philippines 2000" program, unveiled by President Ramos in 1993. The Philippines has joined the ranks of emerging market countries that have adopted domestic free market reforms, trade liberalization, and the pursuit of foreign investment as the road to economic growth. The government's 1993–1998 development plan also stresses cultivating the country's human resources and improving its infrastructure. The government is mounting an effort to fulfill the country's infrastructure development needs by securing loans from international lending institutions and by attracting private foreign investment to infrastructure projects.

To achieve its development goals, the government has identified five "implementing mechanisms" that reflect conditions distinctive to the Philippines: (1) restoring political stability, (2) achieving economic recovery, (3) eliminating power shortages, (4) ensuring environmental protection, and (5) streamlining government bureaucracy. During its first few years in power, the Ramos government has scored a number of successes in advancing these goals.

Economic Reform and Recovery The most impressive achievements of the Ramos administration have been in the economic realm. Because President Ramos does not himself come directly from the country's powerful elite economic class, he has been far more willing than his predecessor to carry out reforms that challenge their dominance. Although his status as an "outsider" has made it difficult to achieve some of the goals he has set, he has made substantial progress. He should be able to achieve even more since the elections in May 1995 gave his regime a strong mandate to press forward with his reforms.

Import duties have already been slashed, and the government has ratified the country's participation in GATT as the administration presses toward substantial fulfillment of its obligations under that agreement. Foreign exchange controls have been eliminated, allowing the peso to float freely and find its own level. The banking, insurance, shipping, and telecommunications industries are now open to competition, both domestic and foreign. The newly consolidated Philippine Stock Exchange has become one of the best-performing equity markets in Asia—despite a plunge in the index during the first quarter of 1995. To encourage foreign investment, the Ramos

government enacted the "build-operate-transfer" (BOT) law, allowing full foreign ownership of domestic companies, which, after being operated privately for a specified period, are to be transferred to the government. Restrictions on foreign investment in particular economic sectors are also being reduced or phased out altogether.

The effects of these economic reforms are noticeable. Foreign equity investment more than tripled in 1994, while foreign direct investment reached record numbers, rising fivefold. By 1994 more than 12 foreign-domestic joint ventures were formed in the telecommunications industry in which the Philippine Long Distance Telephone Company (PLDT) once enjoyed a virtual monopoly.

While the reforms initially attracted the attention of Taiwanese and Japanese investors, investment from other countries is now rolling in as well; major investors include several large firms based in the US, Singapore, Malaysia, Switzerland, Korea, and Hong Kong. In 1994 Federal Express decided to make the Subic Freeport Zone its Asia-Pacific headquarters, bolstering prospects for the successful conversion of the former US bases at Clark and Subic Bay into international free trade zones.

Much of this foreign investment is direct, which means it is made in actual physical assets rather than in security holdings; thus international investors become active participants in the local economy instead of passive observers who could pull up stakes simply by selling their stock holdings. This shows international confidence in the long-term prospects of the economy and makes a crash of the equity markets or currency less likely.

Aided by general economic recovery worldwide, Philippine exports rose 20 percent in 1994 over the 1993 level. Gross domestic product (GDP) has been rising at a healthy pace and growth is expected to accelerate over the next few years. Inflation has moderated, and some order has been restored to public finances, with the ratio of national debt to national income declining from previous record levels. After a 10-year absence, the Philippines successfully reentered the international capital markets in 1993. In recent years, the government has also managed to obtain loans from major international lending institutions, such as the International Monetary Fund (IMF) and the Asian Development Bank (ADB). The loans are being used largely for infrastructure improvements and social services.

The Power Crisis Ends The earliest and most visible success of the Ramos regime was the resolution of the nation's electrical power crisis. Daily brownouts of up to 15 hours duration in the capital region between 1990 and 1993 were reduced to a total of 15 hours for all of 1994. This turnaround was a result of 21 projects, worth US$6 billion dollars, built by independent power producers under the government's BOT program.

The government has now shifted its attention from resolution of the immediate power crisis to ambitious efforts to reform and expand the country's energy industry. Following the British model, Ramos has decoupled power transmission and generation, leaving the nation's transmission system in the hands of Napocor, a state monopoly, while privatizing power generation and opening the industry to competition. The privatization of Napocor is also being explored.

In the meantime, recently discovered natural gas and oilfields on Camago-Malaypaya are being developed by a Shell-Occidental consortium, which is also building pipeline links to Manila. Plans for use of the gas include the possible conversion of the Bataan nuclear power plant into a gas-fired electrical power generating facility. Foreign investors are also considering the construction of plants to tap the country's rich, active seismic and volcanic sources of geothermal energy.

The Environment Enters the Public Agenda A 1994 opinion poll that was conducted to assess public priorities for the Philippines found that environmental issues were very important to nearly a third of respondents, a surprisingly high figure for a developing country that has never before focused on such issues. The high priority given to the environment may be related to the tremendous growth of industry and its impact on clean water and air, as well as to the spread of the population into previously undeveloped forest regions.

A World Resources Institute study found that economic losses due to logging—in terms of depletion of forest, soil, and fishery resources—equaled roughly 4 percent of the country's domestic product. Logging has reduced the usable forest acreage in the Philippines to less than 15 percent of what it was in 1950, when three-quarters of the country was covered by forests. Despite a 1989 ban on logging in regions with less than 40 percent tree cover, illegal logging continues to take its toll.

One key to environmental policy under Ramos has been the encouragement of ecotourism, an effort to tie the economic interests of the tourist industry to environmental protection. International lending institutions have provided funds for projects designed to protect the country's remaining forest resources and to encourage the development of sustainable forest management practices. Regulations have also been implemented to curtail air and water pollution, and penalties are being assessed against industrial offenders.

The Program Continues While its economic reform efforts have met with substantial success, the Ramos government has been less successful in addressing the thorny issue of political stability. The administration's program has had to deal with continuing civil unrest as well as corruption and other forms of lawlessness.

Communist rebels, right-wing military vigilantes, Muslim insurgents in the south, and both organized and street crime have long plagued the Philippines. The legalization of the Communist party and various peace offerings to other political groups, coupled with a crackdown on crime, have made headway in restoring civil peace, but have not yet achieved final resolution.

Corruption and more violent forms of lawlessness seem to be the more intractable problems. The violent reputation of the Philippine National Police—dominated as they are by the military—renders them largely ineffective in stemming criminal violence; many citizens fear the police force rather than admire its role in society.

The problem of corruption in government ranges from favoritism toward powerful private citizens to petty bribery as a means of securing government services and to the use of civil service appointments as a patronage tool. The tradition of patronage in the civil service has contributed to the creation of a bloated bureaucracy and makes it difficult to find ways to reduce the bureaucracy. Because the growth of the bureaucracy is due more to political constituency building than the need to provide services, civil servants are often called "15-30" workers: they show up for work only on paydays—the 15th and 30th of the month. A law of attrition passed during the Aquino administration has had some limited success in reducing the growth of the bureaucracy. But despite the apparent good intentions, it may be difficult for the current regime to address this perennial problem without jeopardizing its future political prospects.

Widespread income tax evasion is another problem the government must address if it is to implement its optimistic reforms. International lending institutions consider tax reform to be a prerequisite for the government to get its fiscal house in order and generate adequate funds to support its economic development programs. Yet, of the 26 million people who comprise the Filipino workforce, only two million pay taxes, and most of those are civil servants (whose pay cannot be hidden from the government). Corruption among tax collection agents is considered to be an important cause of underpayment and evasion by those whose salaries are not otherwise specifically known to the government. But the problem is systemic— so ingrained in the society that it is difficult to root it out without sustained, long-term efforts. Battling tax evasion entails taking on powerful, influential economic interests with ample means to fight back. The Ramos government is nonetheless pursuing several high-profile tax evasion cases against members of the economic elite. Broad-based reforms, including expanding the coverage of the value-added tax (VAT), modernizing the collection system, and creating a strong antifraud tax division, are among the government's current priorities.

STRONG SPECIAL INTERESTS

Background History and geography are at the roots of the powerful special interests which compete in Philippine society. An archipelago consisting of more than 7,000 islands, the country had no coherent precolonial identity and is largely a somewhat arbitrary European creation.

The population of the Philippines is comprised mainly of Malay, Chinese, Spanish, Negrito, and US stock, with members of 73 hill tribes and a large Muslim population as well. Many generations of intermarriage have somewhat lessened the cultural differences among these various groups, but language and religion remain points of contention. Overall, 11 major languages and 87 dialects are spoken in the Philippines, making the country's linguistic identity a political issue. At one time, Spanish was widely spoken and, later, English. Now, native Pilipino and English are the country's two official languages, although the use of English is declining somewhat in popularity as the educational system stresses Pilipino to a greater extent. However, English remains the primary language of international business.

Religion also lies at the root of many special interest conflicts. Muslim rule in the southern islands around Mindanao preceded Spanish colonization in the 16th century, and its continuing influence encourages ethnic rebellion and separatism in that region. Currently, the country's Muslim minority comprises about 10 percent of the country's total population. Other conflicts plague the majority religions. A high rate of population growth has contributed to poverty, and efforts by President Ramos—a Protestant—to encourage birth control have brought him into conflict with the hierarchy of the Roman Catholic church. Some 83 percent of Filipinos are Roman Catholic, making the Philippines the only predominantly Catholic nation in Asia.

Economic disparities and differences in rural and urban patterns provide additional fodder for special interests. Despite a growing middle class and a generally high level of education, Philippine society remains highly polarized. A world unto itself, the capital region—Metro Manila—is home to roughly 15 percent of the population, but produces half of the country's wealth and is the location of two-thirds of its cars and trucks. Statistics in 1988 found that the wealthiest 10 percent of the population earned more than one-third of the income, while the poorest third of the population generated less than 15 percent. While some changes have been made since 1988, there is little reason to believe that these figures have changed radically in the intervening years.

An Incomplete Democracy While a rough-and-tumble democratic tradition appears to be firmly entrenched in the Philippines, it also bears the marks of the country's hierarchical social structure. The socioeconomic structure that developed during the centuries of foreign rule was often somewhat feudal in nature, with large clans of Spanish-descent landowners creating vast disparities in political power and economic clout.

Although recent reforms have opened up the economy to a broader sector of the population, economic life is still dominated by an oligarchy consisting of the descendents of these families, along with a few wealthy ethnic Chinese business-people. As a consequence, the main factions competing in the country's democratic processes often represent conflicting interests within this oligarchy. In addition, Muslim and communist insurgencies on the left, and rebel military leaders on the right, are also disrupting factors which challenge the ability of the Philippines to develop into a fully democratic society.

President Ramos has pursued a policy of trying to co-opt the various renegade groups into the mainstream democratic political processes. In particular, he set up a National Unification Commission to deal with left-wing rebellion; this has met with some degree of success.

Although still an active political force, communist insurgency has waned in the post-Marcos years. The Communist party has fragmented over ideological issues, causing demoralization among the rank and file. The collapse of established communist regimes in Central Europe has contributed further to its decline. President Ramos legalized the party in 1992, releasing some jailed communist leaders from prison. Legalization has helped drive a wedge among party factions and defuse appeals for armed insurrection. The party's military wing, the New People's Army (NPA), is losing membership and support in the countryside.

Muslim insurrection in the south appears to be more intractable. Despite the government's efforts to negotiate a peace with the main Muslim independence organization—the Moro National Liberation Front (MNLF)—breakaway Muslim insurgents resumed violent actions in 1995. Known as Abu Sayyaf, this group is also suspected of international terrorist activities, including the 1993 bombing of the World Trade Center in New York.

Cliques of renegade military officers have been another destabilizing political force during the post-Marcos era. Because the army has traditionally been an active player in the country's political life, full civilian control over the army has been difficult to impose. Anti-Marcos army factions helped over-throw the dictator, but other factions loyal to Marcos, or with other political agendas, made several coup attempts against his successor, Corazon Aquino. Under Ramos, who formerly headed the Philippine Army, a number of renegade officers decided to campaign for political office. Unfortunately, a tradition of government collabora-tion with army cliques, as well as civilian anticom-munist vigilante groups in the countryside, has yet to become part of the Philippine past. In 1993 Amnesty International issued a report sharply crit-ical of factions of the army and of insurgent groups for human rights violations.

MOVING TOWARD INTERNATIONAL RESPECTABILITY

Like many countries that have experienced long periods of colonization, the Philippines is strug-gling to overcome the psychological scars of past dependence as it seeks to define its place in the world. Filipinos have long suffered from the feeling of being merely pawns of US foreign policy and therefore unable to gain the respect of their Asian neighbors. Recent international occurrences have contributed to their feeling that Filipinos are regarded internationally as second class citizens whose migrant sons and daughters are subject to unredressed discrimination and exploitation.

Such feelings have influenced Filipino attitudes towards the US. Although Filipinos are by no means hostile to people from the US as individuals, the country's former role as a subject territory and strategic base for the US has left Filipinos politically sensitive in their relations with that country. Tensions ran high during the post-Marcos era due to public resentments—even among the Filipino elite, who had benefited the most—at both former and supposed current US support for Marcos. Anti-US demonstrations and violence against US military personnel were frequent. However, the closure of US bases in 1992 has alleviated some Filipino resentments and allowed relations to normalize. Under President Ramos, relations have become more mutually friendly and respectful.

In the meantime, the Philippines is engaged in a potentially explosive sovereignty conflict with China over the Spratly Islands, located in the South China Sea north of Palawan. Although Vietnam, Brunei, Malaysia, Indonesia, and Taiwan also claim various parts of the island group, the Philippines and China are the parties in current active conflict. The Spratlys are potentially of great economic value because of recent oil and natural gas discoveries. Despite efforts to negotiate Spratly sovereignty issues in the context of the Association of Southeast Asian Nations (ASEAN), the dispute between the Philippines and China continued to simmer in 1995. Since the armed forces of the Philippines are ill equipped to enforce the country's claims militarily, the Philippine congress budgeted US$2 billion in 1995 for a modernization program directed at the islands.

The Philippines has emphasized regional coop-eration with its Asian neighbors and, despite various episodic tensions with Singapore and Indo-nesia, among others, it generally maintains good relations within the region. Relations with Japan, in particular, have been productive as the commercial intercourse between the two countries grows. Another positive factor has been the growing number of countries which have become important trade and investment partners, reducing its economic dependency on any single relationship.

The Middle East is an area where the interna-tional relations of the Philippines is more complex. The Philippines is heavily dependent on middle eastern oil, creating an economic stake in good rela-tions with the region. Also, many Filipino migrant workers live in the Middle East and send substantial remittances back home. Saudi Arabia alone has been host to more than 600,000 Filipino workers, making them the largest single group of overseas Filipinos. Complicating matters are the Muslim insurgencies in the Philippines, which create sensi-tivities about Philippine treatment of its Islamic minorities. Nur Misauri, leader of the MNLF, has lived and worked in both Libya and Saudi Arabia, but Middle Eastern leaders have generally main-tained their distance from the civil conflicts in the Philippines.

Opportunities

CONTENTS

OPPORTUNITIES FOR IMPORTING FROM THE PHILIPPINES

In 1993 export earnings in the Philippines increased 14.7 percent over the previous year, reaching a record US$11.3 billion. Leading exports by earnings were electronic products, garments, and fresh and processed foods. These and other exports should continue to grow as world markets improve and the Philippines remedies its infrastructure deficiencies. The country is building competitive production capabilities and is strongly pushing for increased export growth. Many new opportunities are being added to existing ones, providing traders with numerous opportunities for importing from the Philippines.

AGRICULTURAL PRODUCTS

In 1993 the Philippines exported fresh and processed foods worth about US$1.3 billion. Fish, fruit, and vegetables were the leading categories of exports. Fresh fish accounted for about 35 percent of these; fresh fruit and vegetables for 25 percent; processed fish for 11 percent; and processed fruit and vegetables accounted for 19 percent. Other exports that saw increased earnings were sugar preparations, cereals, and livestock.

The export potential of agricultural products for any given year depends primarily on weather conditions, politics, and world markets. Government promises of land reform (and the extent to which they are carried out), as well as government intervention in the form of market protection for the coconut industry, and its bolstering of the fishing industry, for example, have also had an impact on export potential.

The coconut and sugar industries in the Philippines have seen their ups and downs in recent years. Once a great source of wealth for the Philippine elite, production and earnings in these areas have suffered greatly in recent years. The capacity to produce sugar and coconuts is still great, and the Philippines remains one of the world's top exporters of coconut products, but falling world prices and inconsistent government policies have taken their toll on overall earnings.

Of the country's most important agricultural exports, the government has shown the greatest interest in developing the fishing industry. It has committed resources of its own as seed money to encourage increased investment from the private sector in both fisheries and in fish processing facilities. Thus, this sector should provide one of the best opportunities, especially if the Philippines can improve its fish processing sector and harvest its ample supply of off-shore seaweed. Policies are in place to do both.

Some hot items:

- bananas
- banana crackers
- chewing gum
- cocoa butter
- coconuts
- coffee
- copra cake
- corn (maize)
- mangos
- pineapples
- rice
- seaweed
- shrimp and prawns
- sugar
- tuna (canned, fresh, and frozen)

ARTS AND HANDICRAFTS

Combined export sales of basketry, Christmas decorations, and ceramics amounted to US$245.3 million in 1993. These products and others in the arts and handicrafts industries were manufactured by more than 2,000 exporters, indicating a diversity of supply. The industry is highly diversified, with the roughly 57 major manufacturers—led by H.S. Craft Manufacturing, Minami International, and Sosan Industries—accounting for only about 13 percent of total arts and handicrafts exports.

Some hot items:

- artificial flowers
- brassware
- basketware
- beach balls
- ceramics and porcelain
- Christmas decorations
- glassware
- lamps and lamp shades
- model ships in bottles
- novelty items
- papier-mâché figures (such as animals)
- sea shells
- silk flowers
- stoneware
- wallets and purses
- wall hangings
- wickerware
- wood carvings
- wooden frames for pictures and photographs

COMPUTER SOFTWARE AND SERVICES

Because it does not currently possess the technology to competitively manufacture computer hardware (although it does support some thriving hardware assembly operations), the Philippines has concentrated its efforts on software, and offers basic software at discount prices. The government wants to build this domestic industry. It encourages the growth of a large pool of high-tech professionals and offers generous grants for research and development. The government is also constructing a domestic information technology infrastructure. This is an area in which the Philippines hopes to become highly competitive, and it may now represent a bargain for consumers not wanting to pay the high research and development prices demanded by companies located in the US, Japan, and Europe. Philippine rates for such services are currently lower than those of its international competitors by as much as 40 to 50 percent. Many of the software companies are entrepreneurial spin-offs from larger companies and have set up joint operating agreements with foreign-based firms. Programmers are now concentrating on serving the banking, manufacturing, insurance, transportation, retail management, construction, pharmaceutical, and utilities industries.

Some hot items:

- applications software
- data entry
- network services
- systems integration
- systems software

ELECTRONIC AND ELECTRICAL PRODUCTS

Electronic products were the country's primary source of export earnings in 1993. Most of these earnings came from the sale of semiconductors, which accounted for roughly 60 percent of all electronics exports and almost 10 percent of total exports. Electronics manufacturing is conducted by several major multinational companies, including Texas Instruments, National Semiconductor, Philips, Intel, and Motorola (which together account for about 75 percent of electronic exports), supported by about 21 major independent subcontractors, most of which are Filipino-owned. The industry is characterized by cheap labor, modern management, technological expertise, on-time delivery, and a willingness to make special arrangements for expedited delivery.

Although electrical appliances and machinery do not have the earning power of electronic products, they too represent a fast-growing sector of the Philippine economy. In 1993 consigned electrical products accounted for about 5 percent of the country's exports—a value of US$585 million—growing by more than 20 percent from the previous year.

Some hot items:

- consumer electronics—color TVs, stereos, and video game players
- electric wire and cable
- incandescent lamps
- office machines
- semiconductors
- sound recording equipment

FASHION ACCESSORIES AND TRAVEL GOODS

A wide range of fashion accessories and travel goods accounted for Philippine exports worth more than US$250 million annually during the early 1990s. Leather and nonleather gloves accounted for a large portion of this. Other prominent items include precious gems and costume jewelry, duffel bags, handbags and totes, belts, and hats. The major export markets for these items are the US, Japan, Germany, Britain, and France.

Some hot items:

- beads
- brooches
- buttons
- bags of all kinds—duffel bags, handbags, tote bags
- costume jewelry
- earrings
- hair accessories
- hats and caps
- gems and jewelry
- gloves
- luggage
- scarves
- shawls
- sunglasses
- umbrellas

FURNITURE

The Philippines is home to about 15,000 furniture manufacturers and 1,100 furniture exporters. These range from large, established companies (the top three of which—Pacific Traders and Manufacturing, Mindanao Rattan, and Asian Rattan Manufacturing—in 1990 accounted for 10 percent of all exports) to small family-owned enterprises and individual craftsmen scattered throughout the country. The industry is dominated by medium-sized factories employing 100 to 300 workers, mostly located in Manila or Cebu.

In 1993 furniture exports were valued at US$202 million, which represented an increase of almost 12 percent from the previous year. Export sales of rattan furniture were the largest, accounting for roughly two-thirds of export earnings in the industry. The industry concentrates on rattan and wooden furniture, with little capacity to produce plastic and metal furniture.

In order to supply the furniture industry with raw materials, the Philippines has depleted much of its forestland during recent years, and campaigns by environmental activists are aimed at protecting the trees that remain. Although the large furniture manufacturers will undoubtedly continue to have significant political influence, the future of the industry will depend, in part, on how well the country can manage and restore the natural resources from which it draws its raw materials.

Some hot items:

- beds
- cabinets
- chairs
- chests of drawers
- dressers
- headboards
- kitchen storage units
- rattan and wicker furniture
- settees
- tables
- wardrobes

TELECOMMUNICATIONS

Domestic manufacturing of telecommunications equipment in the Philippines is limited to telephone sets, in which it is quite productive. About 80 percent of the sets assembled in the Philippines are intended for the export market, and the Philippines exported more than 1.8 million of these in 1992.

The Philippines is largely dependent on imports for almost all other telecommunications equipment, including network systems, fiber optic materials, fax machines, and teleprinters.

TEXTILES AND APPAREL

The Philippines produces all sorts of infants', children's, men's, and women's clothing. In 1993 earnings from exports of manufactured garments increased by more than 5 percent over the previous year to reach US$2.122 billion. The industry employs about 215,000 factory workers and about twice as many home workers. Many of the large manufacturers rely on subcontractors to produce much of their output. Such subcontractors accounted for about 30 percent of manufactured textile output in 1991. Despite the size of the workforce and the number of subcontractors, the industry is concentrated in a relatively few hands: about 9 percent of the manufacturers are responsible for roughly 56 percent of export sales.

The Philippine garment industry sells mainly to the US, Germany, Britain, and France. However, as these countries have increasingly tightened quotas on imported garments, the Philippines has also begun to develop markets in countries such as Japan and Hong Kong, and in nations in the Middle East. It currently sends its full quota limits to the US, Canada, and Europe.

The Philippines has also established itself as a manufacturer of footwear, especially athletic footwear. Rubberworld Philippines, the Asian manufacturer of Adidas shoes, is among world leaders in this sector. Other large companies have also contracted with local manufacturers, who are now beginning to produce goods in the country's Export Processing Zones (EPZs). Total revenue for exports of footwear amounted to US$141 million in 1991, representing an increase of 29 percent over the previous year.

Some hot items:

- blue denim
- boots
- brassieres
- children's wear
- cotton fabric
- embroidered garments
- lingerie
- men's wear
- sandals
- shoes of all kinds—athletic, casual, and dress
- slippers
- sportswear
- taffeta
- women's wear
- yarns of synthetic fibers

OPPORTUNITIES FOR EXPORTING TO THE PHILIPPINES

Imports into the Philippines have increased almost 20 percent per year over the past several years as the government has liberalized its trading policies and pursued infrastructure development programs. Increased development financing from international organizations has stimulated the demand for capital inputs and development materials and expertise. Opportunities to export to the Philippines abound across a wide range of sectors, and such opportunities should continue to grow over the medium term as the government continues its economic liberalization efforts, and infrastructure development stimulates economic growth.

AGRICULTURE

The Philippines is a fast-growing market for imports of bulk, intermediate, and consumer oriented agricultural products. Bulk commodities such as wheat, cotton, soybeans, and unmanufactured tobacco account for about one-half of total Philippine agricultural imports, with semi-processed intermediate commodities and consumer oriented foods quickly gaining in importance. In 1993 and 1994, significant growth was registered in several categories, most notably wheat, forest products, and such consumer items as fresh and processed produce, snack foods, and high-quality beef. Consumer oriented agricultural products are expected to continue to show high growth rates during at least the next three years. However, over the longer term imports of processed foods into the Philippines will probably reach limits as the country develops its own food processing industry.

Some hot items:

- beef
- corn (maize) and grain sorghum
- cotton
- fresh potatoes and other fresh vegetables
- fruit (fresh, dried, frozen, or processed)
- forest products
- poultry and poultry products
- pork and pork products
- snack foods
- soybean meal
- wheat

AUTOMOTIVE PARTS AND SERVICE EQUIPMENT

Sales of automotive parts and related service equipment have grown recently with increased sales of used cars and other motor vehicles. Total market demand is expected to grow by 18 percent annually between 1995 and 1998. Auto parts makers can capitalize on this growth through technology transfer or joint venture arrangements with local manufacturers, particularly under the government's Car Development Program. This program requires local assemblers to include 40 to 50 percent local content in its assembled units. The total market for automotive parts and service equipment in 1993 was US$120 million, 60 percent of which was supplied by imports.

Some hot items:

- engine blocks
- engines
- oil and fuel filters
- radiators
- tires
- transmissions
- wire harnesses

COMPUTERS

The computer and computer peripherals market offers many opportunities for exporters to the Philippines. Some observers expect this market to grow at an average annual rate of 45 percent between 1995 and 1997. This prediction is based on several factors, particularly the Philippine government's efforts to encourage greater use of information technology (IT) by both the government and the private sector, and an upturn in the country's economic activity, both of which are projected to lead to corresponding growth in IT usage and increased investment in computer equipment.

Since a variety of computer brands and models are sold in the Philippines, and because virtually every sector of the economy will increasingly rely on computers, a smaller supplier may find its niche in the overall market by concentrating on solving the IT problems of a particular market sector or industry. The current trend is for vendors to offer complete hardware/software packages—that is, total system packages—rather than to sell items individually. Foreign computer sellers who can provide competitive prices, conscientious customer service (including delivery, technical support, and after-sales service), reliable distributors and dealers, and a wide retail network should find the Philippines to be a receptive market. Product positioning and differentiation is important, and a foreign firm should work with a well-established importer/distributor who has a network of recognized dealers.

Some hot items:

- applications software

- combined input/output units
- computer aided design systems (CADs)
- computer storage devices
- financial software
- keyboards
- mainframe computers
- modems
- monitors
- multimedia systems
- network management software
- personal computers
- personal software
- portable computers (laptop, notebook, or handheld)
- printer units
- relational database management systems
- supercomputers
- telecommunications software

CONSTRUCTION EQUIPMENT

With its ambitious infrastructure development plans and limited domestic supply of technical and building equipment, the Philippines will have to import large amounts of building materials and construction machinery over the next several years. Some companies in the Philippines recondition used equipment and fabricate spare parts, but none are involved in actually producing major construction equipment. Virtually all market demand is filled by imports.

Total market demand for excavating, extracting, and earthmoving equipment amounted to US$60.1 million in 1992, representing a nearly 24 percent increase from the 1991 level. It is expected to increase further in the near future. Planned construction projects include roads and bridges, railways, airports, sea ports, rural electrification programs, and water supply and sewerage services.

Some hot items:

- backhoes
- bulldozers
- front-end loaders
- graders
- levelers
- off-highway trucks
- pile drivers
- pile extractors
- rollers
- scrapers
- shovels
- shovel loaders
- tamping/compacting machinery
- tracklaying-type tractors

ELECTRICAL POWER EQUIPMENT

In recent years, the Philippines has had difficulty meeting its electrical power needs (for more background on the electrical power sector in the Philippines *see* "Electrical Power Systems" on page 38 in the "Opportunities for Growth" section). But what was once a crisis is now close to being solved, and the country is dedicating itself to establishing and expanding a modern, reliable electrical power system. Numerous new power plants are either coming online or are under construction, and there are real and immediate opportunities for foreign suppliers of power equipment and related services.

The 1992 electrification level was figured at 60 percent, and the government aims to increase the country's electrification level to between 69 and 96 percent—depending on the geographic area—by the year 2000. The Philippine National Power Plan for the period 1993–2005 calls for expenditures that could reach a total of US$35 billion to correct current electricity shortfalls and meet expected growth in demand. This means that between one and five million additional customers need to be hooked into the power grid. These planned programs should boost demand for electric distribution equipment by an average annual rate of as much as 30 to 40 percent during the life of the plan. To achieve this target, distribution lines must be rehabilitated or expanded and substations installed. Much of the plan's successful implementation will depend on foreign investment in electrical power equipment. The government has proposed several build-operate-transfer (BOT) projects to draw the necessary investment.

The total market size for electrical power systems, which was estimated at US$887 million in 1993, is expected to grow at an annual rate of 50 percent in 1994 and 1995. Imports account for more than 92 percent of the market.

Some hot items:

- circuit breakers
- connectors
- electrical generation, distribution, and transmission equipment
- electrical wire and cable
- fuses
- meters
- protection devices
- relays
- steel and wood poles
- switches
- transformers
- voltage regulators

ENVIRONMENTAL TECHNOLOGIES

Pollution control is becoming an important issue in the Philippines. The Housing and Land Use Regulatory Board (HLURB) sets guidelines and requirements for the development of urban population centers and industrial estates. It is increasingly requiring that waste and water-treatment facilities and air pollutant control mechanisms be installed in growth centers. The demand for pollution control equipment grew from US$51.5 million in 1992 to US$58.5 million in 1993. It is expected to continue to grow at a rate of about 15 to 17 percent annually for the next few years.

Local producers are not yet equipped to handle either the quantity or quality demanded, so nearly 90 percent of the total market for pollution control equipment is imported.

Some hot items:

- centrifugal water pumps
- cleaning solutions
- filtering machines
- wastewater treatment chemicals—aluminum sulfate, caustic soda, sodium carbonate, ferric salts, other alkalies and polymers
- water aerating machines

INDUSTRIAL CHEMICALS, MINERALS, AND MATERIALS

The total market for industrial chemicals, which was estimated at US$846 million in 1993, is growing at an annual rate of about 13 percent. Imports account for approximately 70 percent of the market and demand for these products should continue to expand over the medium term. The improving economy and expanding local market for consumer and industrial products will benefit traders looking to export industrial chemicals into the Philippines.

Demand for industrial chemicals comes chiefly from companies manufacturing detergent, shampoo, and body care products, but many other industries also rely on imported chemicals, including: rubber, paint, ceramics, feeds, and pharmaceutical manufacturers (all utilize zinc oxide); paint, automotive battery, lead chemical, compounded resin manufacturers, and gold assayers (lead oxide); paint and glass manufacturers (selenium); manufacturers of vulcanizing chemicals (tellurium); textile, paper, cosmetics, and chemical manufacturers (hydrogen peroxide); dry cell or primary battery manufacturers (manganese oxide); rubber, tire, paint, soap, and detergent manufacturers (titanium oxide).

Due to government regulations, the detergent industry uses mostly locally produced surfactant (surface-active) chemicals. However, imports are a major source of detergent fillers and other ancillary ingredients. Also, the cosmetics, shampoo, body care, paint, textile, and leather industries rely mainly on imported surfactants.

Some hot items:

- detergent and surfactant chemicals, such as alkyl benzene, aluminum sulfate, detergent sulfur, fatty acids, phosphoric acid, and sulfuric acid
- hydrogen peroxide
- lead oxide
- manganese oxide
- selenium
- tellurium
- titanium oxide
- zinc oxide

INDUSTRIAL MACHINERY

Food Processing The market for food processing and packaging equipment is growing rapidly, representing a great opportunity for exporters of such products. New and expanding investments in fish, seafood, fruit and vegetable processing, and a growing demand for processed food from both the domestic and export markets, should ensure solid and growing demand for industrial equipment such as food processing machinery. Demand should remain high for the next several years, as the industry needs to retool, refurbish, and upgrade its equipment to improve its competitiveness in the world market.

The total market size for such equipment was about US$55 million in 1993, and is expected to grow at an average annual rate of 14 percent over the next few years. About 90 percent of the demand for food processing and packaging equipment is supplied by imports. An especially lucrative area is in machinery and equipment for processing fish and seafood and fruit and vegetables. Projections call for 50 percent average annual growth during the next two years, with imports also increasing by 50 percent annually.

Pumps, Valves and Compressors Most manufacturing industries—including chemical plants, electrical power plants, food processors, petroleum refineries, pulp and paper manufacturers, and textile manufacturers—need basic machine equipment such as pumps, valves, and compressors. The total market for these products in 1993 was valued at US$95.64 million; of that amount, 60 percent was supplied by imports. Imports accounted for 95 percent of the pumps used in the country, valued at nearly US$40 million. The market for these three products should expand through 1997 at an annual rate of about 10 percent.

Some hot items:

- boilers
- cookers/coolers
- depalletizers
- equipment for dehydration
- filtration equipment
- juice extractors
- refrigeration equipment
- seamers/closing machines
- tuna filling machines

MEDICAL AND DENTAL EQUIPMENT

The Philippine health care system is administered by two systems: public and private. The bulk of the market for the most sophisticated medical equipment and instruments exists in the private medical system, where demand is mostly supplied by imports.

Some hot items:

dental equipment
- amalgams, cements, and plaster
- dental chairs
- dental hand instruments
- drills
- sterilizers

surgical and medical instruments and supplies
- bandages
- blood pressure measuring devices
- catheters
- clamps
- hypodermic needles
- laparascopic devices
- prosthetics
- stethoscopes
- suture needles
- syringes
- wheelchairs

other
- magnetic resonance imaging (MRI) equipment
- mammography machines
- ophthalmic goods
- pacemakers
- patient monitoring systems
- rehabilitation and therapeutic equipment
- X-ray apparatus and tubes

SPORTING GOODS AND RECREATIONAL EQUIPMENT

The Philippine market for sporting goods and recreational equipment is increasing rapidly due to the promotion of sports and the population's relatively young age, as well as its growing overall health consciousness. Basketball and golf are especially popular in the Philippines.

The local market is dependent on imports since local production is limited and locally-made products are not price-competitive. Also, Filipinos perceive that the quality and durability of imported products are better than that of local products. Taiwan, Japan, and the US are the major sources of imported sporting goods and recreational equipment. These items offer attractive opportunities for exporters because manufactured sporting goods and recreational equipment carry significantly lower tariff rates than do the raw materials and machinery necessary to fabricate this equipment locally.

Some hot items:

- basketballs
- bicycles
- bowling equipment
- game tables
- golf equipment
- pool tables
- sporting shotguns

TELECOMMUNICATIONS

The Philippine government is embarking on a major campaign to improve its telecommunications network, and it estimates a total investment of US$28 billion will be required to achieve the targets (much of this expense to be borne by the private firms which must expand their service in return for licenses to operate). Its goals are ambitious and broad ranging, with substantial expenditures in virtually every field. The cost of increasing the country's telephone density is the largest single capital requirement for the project, accounting for more than half of the total.

Foreign telephone equipment manufacturers and service providers are expected to contribute significantly to the growth. The demand is high and growing for state-of-the-art equipment and services in both standard telephone usage and cellular services.

Some hot items:

- cellular telephones
- fax machines
- fiber-optic equipment
- fixed and mobile radio systems
- high-capacity switching systems
- radio transmitters, transceivers, and receivers
- signal switches
- telephones
- telecommunications networking systems
- television sets
- transmission equipment

OPPORTUNITIES FOR GROWTH

Substantial new investments in the Philippine economy are needed to reach the country's ambitious development targets. The government offers several fiscal and nonfiscal incentives to foreign investors, and it encourages foreign participation in many industries. It is pursuing the development of several Export Processing Zones (EPZs) to stimulate domestic production, and has liberalized its tariff rates to encourage imports. It has also opened many of its infrastructure development projects to foreign participation. In short, the country offers foreign traders and investors a broad range of opportunities across many sectors.

AGRICULTURAL PRODUCTS

The Philippine government has historically pursued a policy of protecting its domestic agricultural industry as much as possible from international competition. However, in recognition of its vast potential, the government has recently begun to encourage foreign investment in order to develop the industry into a world leader. It has the resources to supply much of its own food and to export large quantities of fresh and processed foods to the rest of the world. It is a large grower of vegetables and cereals—especially rice and corn (maize)—and many varieties of fruit. It also supplies a large quantity of fish. The country has the natural resources to establish a strong agricultural industry; what it needs to develop is the technological power to increase its processed foods sector.

The growth in manufacturing capacity for these purposes has already begun. Industry leaders of the processed shrimp, prawn, tuna, fruit, and vegetable industries project dramatic increases in exports during the near future, and government officials are bent on attracting local and foreign investors to the food processing industry.

COMPUTERS

One of the current goals of the Philippine government is to spread the application of information technology throughout the economy. Within the framework of the government's Philippines 2000 plan is a model for information technology development, called the National Information Technology Plan 2000 (NITP 2000). The opportunities for both domestic and foreign investors and suppliers are almost limitless since all areas of the Philippine economy can benefit from the introduction of the latest computer technology or the replacement of old equipment with state of the art technology.

NITP 2000 concentrates on five areas:

- **Education** The plan calls for the training of 30,000 to 50,000 IT workers and for the expansion of IT literacy to cover 60 percent of the population.
- **Government** The plan calls for computerization of government agencies and automation of the electoral process by 1998. The government plans to install a management information system for use in every local government office.
- **Industry** The plan encourages the use of information technology by all domestic industries.
- **Research and Development** The plan aims to identify key research and development areas. It offers government support for research and development on IT products that will increase the productivity and efficiency of the agricultural, governmental, and industrial sectors.
- **Telecommunications** The plan calls for a national telecommunications and data communications network to be established by 1998.

The Philippine government offers tax and other incentives to attract foreign investors and manufacturers to participate in these projects.

CONSTRUCTION

The Construction Industry Authority of the Philippines forecasts that the industry will grow at an average rate of 10 percent annually until 1998. The projected growth is expected to increase demand for engineering and construction services substantially. The bulk of the increase will be met by local engineering and construction firms which generally offer the same degree of expertise as foreigners, and whose cost is only about one-eighth of their foreign counterparts. Services of foreign consultants are usually engaged in projects funded by multilateral and bilateral lending institutions, and the governments of other countries.

Current projects include:

- The rehabilitation and construction of power plants, transmission lines, and substations in the Luzon, Visayas, and Mindanao grids.
- A full-scale rural electrification program.
- Improvement of many roads and bridges. About 16 percent of the country's roads, including the main Pan-Philippine Highway that runs through 21 provinces from north to south, are designated as national roads. They are paved and in fairly good condition, but about 80 percent of the country's roads, including most local road networks, are surfaced with gravel and need to be paved with asphalt or concrete.
- The construction and improvement of airports and sea ports.

- The expansion and development of urban rail transit and national railway.
- Construction of postal office buildings.
- The construction, rehabilitation, and maintenance of national irrigation facilities.
- The construction and upgrading of water supply and sewerage/sanitation facilities.
- The implementation of desirable flood control projects in the 12 major river systems in the country, including Metro Manila.
- The construction of housing for the significant numbers of people in Manila and other key cities who currently live in buildings that fail to meet minimum housing standards.

ELECTRICAL POWER SYSTEMS

The Philippines has substantial electrical and energy potential, but it has so far been unable to deliver anything near enough electrical capacity to meet existing demand, much less provide for future growth. The shortage of power-generating capacity is estimated to cost the economy about US$1.3 billion per year in lost output alone. It also has secondary effects on employment and consumer spending as many firms reduce work hours during brownouts, and unemployment soars. The government estimates it loses a total of about US$3 billion each year due to brownouts.

The power situation has recently improved, and studies indicate that from the present to the year 2005 power availability should generally be adequate. The utility sector grew at a rate of 2.9 percent in 1993 and 13.8 percent in 1994, and reserve capacity has been raised significantly. Having solved its immediate crisis, the country is now engaged in rehabilitating and privatizing its power systems, with a view toward expanding capacity in the future under private auspices. Thus, the sector offers many opportunities for domestic and foreign investors, as well as suppliers of electrical power equipment. Total market size in the sector was estimated at US$887 million in 1993, with imports supplying more than 92 percent of the market.

Hydroelectric power is expected to play a key role in the continuing development of electrical power. Construction contracts for anywhere from 18 to 52 hydroelectric power plants are expected to be assigned between 1993 and 2000. Some projects will be developed with the aid of international lending institutions, while others will be built under BOT arrangements between the government and the private sector. All of these will offer especially attractive opportunities for foreigners.

The country is also developing its geothermal power facilities. The Philippines has a vast potential for geothermal energy and the Department of Energy projects that geothermal developments will be the country's largest domestic source of energy by the year 2000.

Overall, the country offers many exciting opportunities in this area, but there are still some difficult issues to address. Privatizations will need to be expanded, and several major projects—including the conversion of the Bataan nuclear power plant to conventional use, the production of natural gas at the Malampaya field, and the interconnection of Luzon and Visayas grid—will need to move forward or be supplanted by other major projects to ensure sufficient and reliable power into the next century. There are problems connected with all of these projects, resulting in delays and investor concern. However, there is no doubt that the need exists, and that the country will require the investment of billions of dollars in equipment and expertise during the next decade. Much of this will have to come from abroad.

ENVIRONMENTAL TECHNOLOGIES

Although the market for environmental technologies in the Philippines is still small and developing, substantial long-term growth can be expected in this area. Both the public and the government are beginning to insist on pollution control for air, water, and land as the population grows and industry develops. Industries have so far not been quick to comply with pollution prevention requirements, but as the level of pollution becomes greater, the pressures on them will become more intense. Already, regulations—and the penalties for their violation—have been implemented and will affect the operations of many industries—including coal-fired power plants, geothermal power plants, sugar refining industry, metal works industry, pulp and paper manufacturing, and the textile industry. New operations are now required to present a certificate of environmental compliance from the Department of Environment and Natural Resources (DENR) to the Board of Investments before they will be allowed to register. More similar checks are sure to follow.

The government is also intent on reducing pollutant vehicle emissions, and intends do so by (1) replacing high-emitting vehicles with new ones designed to meet more stringent standards (the worst offenders are commercial vehicles such as trucks, buses, and jeepneys); (2) inspecting vehicles for excessive emissions and requiring repairs when necessary; and (3) converting existing vehicles to alternate fuels or purchasing new vehicles powered by alternate fuels.

Solid waste management projects are also increasingly becoming privatized to make waste collection and disposal more efficient and financially responsible.

INDUSTRIAL CHEMICALS, MINERALS, AND MATERIALS

Foreign investment in the petrochemical industry is being strongly encouraged by the government of the Philippines. The market for petroleum products in the Philippines is more than US$2 billion and 85 percent of this is supplied by domestic resources.

Projected growth in this industry is high, and opportunities for foreign suppliers of equipment, technological services, and engineering services abound. Exploration for oil and gas will continue to increase, especially in the large Malampaya field, located northwest of the island of Palawan, especially once international boundary disputes in the area have been settled. It is now widely accepted that the Palawan shelf offers opportunities to develop oil and gas fields that can produce several hundred million barrels of crude oil and several trillion cubic feet of gas. If estimates are accurate, this would be the largest oil find ever in the Philippines. Several oil companies are also undertaking other projects that will increase capacity and efficiency in order to meet growing demand for petroleum products.

The Philippines Department of Energy recently unveiled proposals to deregulate the domestic oil industry in order to encourage private investment with a view toward meeting unfilled energy needs. The initial stage, which requires congressional approval, provides for transitional measures to stabilize pricing for petroleum products. Full deregulation, including liberalized oil imports, could start as early as the end of 1996.

MINING

Mining has vast potential and is among the pioneer areas the government is promoting to both foreign and domestic investors. The Philippines has huge mineral resource, including reserves of metallic minerals such as copper, gold, nickel, chromite, silver, iron, lead, zinc and mercury.

The government is offering a variety of incentives and financial assistance to investors interested in developing mining properties, and it strongly recognizes that foreign capital is essential if it is to reach its goals.

TELECOMMUNICATIONS

The Philippine telecommunications industry, which has a vast and untapped potential, is gearing up for greater growth. Directing the growth—building and integrating new technologies with the existing telecommunications infrastructure in the country—is a high government priority. New government deregulation policies have already resulted in increased competition in the area of telecommunications services. Several financially powerful Filipino families have formed partnerships with technologically advanced foreign firms to create new players in the telecommunications market. The Philippine Long Distance Telephone Company (PLDT), which has long held a near-monopoly in both long distance and local service, still controls about 90 percent of the market. Observers anticipate a vigorous battle among competitors to determine who will be the second major provider, and overall growth is expected to provide enough opportunity to sustain several new competitors as the country's potential develops.

PLDT, once so lax about improving the Philippines telecommunications sector, has in fact responded to deregulation with a burst of energy and the addition of several hundred thousand new telephone lines throughout the country (but mostly in Metro Manila). It recognizes the threat from its newly powerful competitors, and a vigorous race is on between it and the several other telecommunications companies to install the most advanced and capable systems in the country. Although it clearly maintains the advantage in local telecom service, the competitors may have an edge in the more profitable long distance and cellular services. The government has required PLDT to allow its competitors to connect to its existing systems, and they often have the advantage of foreign expertise, state-of-the-art technology, and access to investment capital.

Universal access to basic telephone service is the major thrust of the government's telecommunications plans and programs. The ultimate objective is to interconnect all the islands in the archipelago using state-of-the-art technology. This means there will be new services, new facilities, and new lines, all of which calls for a tremendous variety of technology, equipment, and services. The introduction of more advanced technologies, such as fiber optic cables and digital-based networks, should further spur the development of the sector. Foreigners are expected to provide a majority of the equipment and services required.

The current developments in the Philippine telecommunications market should provide major benefits to the domestic consumer, who should receive much better service, and will demand yet more up-to-date services and options.

PUBLIC PROCUREMENT

OPPORTUNITIES

Major government procurement opportunities exist in the following six areas:

1. Airport development projects Current plans include the addition of a new international and a new domestic terminal at the Ninoy Aquino International Airport, as well as additional cargo facilities and new parking structures. There are also plans underway to transform Clark Air Force Base into either an auxiliary or primary international airport. Both of these projects should yield significant opportunities for supply and investment, although both have been delayed because of conflicting proposals and the government's indecision as to which project will take priority. For both, the work involves upgrading and extending runways, improving air navigation and safety facilities, expanding cargo capacity, constructing new passenger terminals, supplying and installing equipment for airfield maintenance, communications, navigation, meteorology, and accident response.

Six major projects on Mactan Island in Cebu Province are scheduled to be completed within the next couple of years, at a total cost of about US$359 million. These projects include upgrading existing facilities and building new terminals, hangars, and an administration building; building a training school; and constructing auxiliary airport terminal facilities—such as convention centers, hotels, and a commercial complex. Also, land now possessed by the Philippine Air Force is scheduled to be turned over to the project so it can be developed for industrial use. The six projects should result in 43,000 jobs and result in economic benefits of nearly US$962 million.

2. Energy The government plans large-scale rehabilitation and construction of power plants, transmission lines, and substations in the Luzon, Visayas, and Mindanao grids; exploration and development of indigenous energy resources; and comprehensive rural electrification through the construction, rehabilitation, and maintenance of distribution facilities.

3. Information technology The government will award contracts for supplying and installing computer equipment and services for the computerization of government agencies.

4. Municipal water supply projects The government aims to upgrade living conditions in urban areas through the rehabilitation and expansion of their water supply systems, and it wants to institutionalize and financially strengthen the agencies concerned. Planned projects involve the implementation of water supply expansion and improvement programs in existing urban water districts. It includes construction and rehabilitation of water source intakes, pumping stations, treatment facilities, storage reservoirs, transmission and distribution pipelines, service connections, and other facilities. Water works and sewerage systems contracts will also include the construction of water mains and water main extensions; interconnection works; surface restoration; installation of water service connections, gate valves, valve manholes, and fire hydrants.

5. Social infrastructure Plans call for the government to award contracts over the next several years to build, upgrade, and expand education facilities and equipment throughout the country. There are also plans to upgrade the capacities and capabilities of 13 regional hospitals and nine medical centers nationwide, including 14 National Capital Region (NCR) special hospitals; and the addition of 1.3 million new housing units in several areas of the country.

6. Transportation The Philippine government has recently been working on a program to ensure that 100 percent of its national roads are all-weather and 95 percent of them are paved. The condition of most local roads has historically been poor because of low design standards, substandard construction, inadequate maintenance, and damage from overloaded vehicles. They are also notoriously overcrowded. Government plans also include the expansion and development of urban rail transit in Metro Manila and the rehabilitation of the Philippine National Railways (PNR) commuter line south. About 50 km of the urban light rail and about 550 km of the inter-urban rail system are to be upgraded.

PROCEDURES

General Procedures

The general bidding procedures prescribed for the procurement of goods, supplies, and equipment, and services for major development projects are as follows:

1. Preparation of the invitation to bid and the bidding documents
2. Advertisement of the invitation to bid
3. Issuance of qualification statements and forms
4. Processing of prequalification statements and forms
5. Issuance of the bidding documents to prequalified bidders
6. Interpretation of the bid/tender documents and other supplemental notices
7. Preparation of bid, bid bond, and post-qualification statement

8. Submission, opening and abstracting of bids/tenders
9. Evaluation of bids and postqualification statements
10. Awarding of contract
11. Preparation of contract
12. Execution and approval of contract

Eligible Bidders

Contractors for government projects may include: (1) a Filipino citizen (including a single proprietorship) or a partnership or corporation duly organized under the laws of the Philippines, of which ownership is at least 75 percent held by Philippine nationals; (2) a joint venture between two or more contractors who are properly licensed by the Philippine Contractors Accreditation Board; and (3) a foreign contractor for an international bid, foreign-assisted contract as may be required by a foreign financial institution. The law favors the use of Filipino labor, domestic materials, and locally produced goods where possible.

Foreign contractors must submit certifications from their embassy or consulate stating that they are bona fide contractors. They must also maintain a registered branch office or a registered agent in the Philippines.

Advertisement of Contracts

For locally funded projects of more than one million pesos (about US$38,800), contracts must be advertised at least three times within a reasonable period, but in no case less than two weeks, in at least two general circulation newspapers. For projects costing one million pesos or less, the contract must be advertised at least once in a newspaper of general circulation within a reasonable time of announcing the project. For projects requiring special technology, the government contact contractors known for their expertise in the necessary field directly to request bids. Potential contractors may also be placed on the mailing list of bidders maintained by the agency with which the contractor hopes to do business.

Bid Security

The original copy of the bid must be accompanied by a bid security amounting to not less than 2.5 percent of the total bid price. The security must be in the form of cash, check, bank draft confirmed by a local bank, letter of credit, or security bond. This instrument serves to guarantee that the successful bidder will enter into a contract with the Philippines government within 30 calendar days (or less, at the discretion of the corporation or agency that awards the contract) from the receipt of notice of award. The successful bidder must also furnish the required performance security for the faithful and complete execution of the work specified in the contract at the time the contract is executed.

Submission of Bids

A bid is submitted in two sealed envelopes, one containing the technical proposal; the other containing the financial proposal. The former envelope is opened first, to determine the bidder's compliance with requirements. The second envelope is opened immediately afterwards. Bids which are not accompanied by the required bid security will be rejected outright.

After all bids have been received, a list will be prepared showing the names of the bidders and their corresponding bids, arranged from the lowest to the highest, and also showing their respective percentage variances from the approved agency estimate.

Awarding of Contract

A contract will not be awarded to a bidder whose bid price is higher than the Allowable Government Estimate (AGE) or the Approved Agency Estimate (AAE), whichever is higher, or lower than 70 percent of the AGE. The AGE is equal to one-half the sum of the AAE and the average of all responsive bids. For purposes of determining the average of all responsive bids, bids higher than 120 percent of the AAE or lower than 60 percent of the AAE are excluded from consideration.

The bidding will be declared a failure if no bids are received or if every bid received is higher than 120 percent of the AAE or lower than 60 percent of the AAE. In such a case the responsible agency or corporation will undertake a review of the AAE and the bidding specifications.

Normally a decision on a bid will be made within 30 calendar days from the date the evaluation of bids is completed. If the government decides to award a contract, the notice of the award will normally be issued within seven calendar days from the date of the decision. For foreign-assisted projects, the decision to award the contract should be transmitted to the relevant foreign financial institution for concurrence, as may be required, ordinarily within seven calendar days from the date the decision of award is made. Likewise, the notice of award should normally be issued by the implementing agency within seven calendar days from the date the concurrence of the foreign financial institution is secured. The successful bidder or the bidder's duly authorized representative should execute the contract with the responsible agency or corporation within 15 calendar days from receipt of award of the contract.

Performance Security

Once the contract is awarded and accepted, the contractor must post, upon the signing of the contract, a performance security in the form of cash, check, bank draft confirmed by a local bank, letter of credit, bank guarantee, or surety bond. If by surety bond, the security should be 30 percent of the total contract price; if by bank guarantee it should be 10 percent of the total contract price; and if by cash, check, letter of credit or bank draft, it should be 5 percent of the total contract price. The contractor shall post an additional performance security to cover any cumulative increase of more than 10 percent over the original value of the contract as a result of adjustments in unit prices and/or change orders, extra work orders, and supplement agreements.

Domestic and International Bidding

International competitive bidding is used for the procurement of imported materials and the selection of foreign contractors, while local competitive bidding is used for the procurement of locally available materials and the selection of local civil works contractors. The bidding procedures to be followed in the selection and award of contracts funded by international funding institutions—such as the International Bank for Reconstruction and development (IBRD—the World Bank), the Asian Development Bank (ADB), the US Agency for International Development (USAID), and the Overseas Economic Cooperation Fund of Japan (OECF)—will be based on the provisions of the loan agreement. For major projects funded by a multilateral institution, all eligible suppliers and contractors must be from its member-countries. For projects funded by bilateral aid agencies, the eligible suppliers and contractors will generally be from the lender country. However, such eligibility requirements may not exclude Filipino suppliers or contractors from participating in bidding for local civil works projects when the funding of the project component comes from funds of the Philippine government.

The borrower country, through its implementing agency, will be responsible for the selection of contractors and suppliers, and the award of contracts, as well as for the execution and implementation of the project. This allocation of responsibility does not preclude a funding institution from monitoring and, in some instances, directly participating in the selection and award process.

Exceptions to the Bidding Process

Projects may be negotiated rather than tendered publicly only in the following situations: (1) times of emergencies; (2) failure for valid cause to award a contract after bidding; or (3) when the subject project is adjacent to an ongoing project, thus making it more economical to hire the same contractor for the subject project.

Major Procuring Agencies

The major government purchasers are the National Power Corporation, the National Electrification Administration, the National Housing Authority, the National Irrigation Administration, the Local Water Utilities Administration, the Metropolitan Waterworks and Sewerage System, the Department of Transportation and Communication, the Department of Public Works and Highways, and the Department of Defense.

BUILD-OPERATE-TRANSFER LEGISLATION FOR PUBLIC PROJECTS

In 1990 the Philippines adopted legislation intended to allow the government to tap private capital to finance much-needed infrastructure improvements. The intent of this act is to attract private investors who will build facilities, operate them for a fixed term (not to exceed 50 years), and then relinquish ownership to the government. To recover its investment, the investor is allowed to charge user fees in accordance with a previously agreed upon schedule. The intended range of projects includes roads, railroads, airports, power generation and telecommunication facilities, water treatment plants, city markets, and slaughterhouses.

In May 1994 the government revised and expanded the original BOT law to make it more attractive to foreign investors. The amended BOT law permits a wider variety of financing, operating, and ownership arrangements; limits political intervention in the process; clarifies the procedural maze; and improves opportunities for better returns to investors. It also allows foreign firms to make unsolicited proposals for ventures that involve new technological concepts worth more than US$400 million. These will receive the same treatment as the government's 38 priority projects that are up for bidding over the next three years. The government's current short list of priority BOT projects (the top ten) on offer to private investors has a total value in excess of US$3.7 billion.

Foreign Investment

INVESTMENT CLIMATE AND TRENDS

Historically, the Philippines has shifted back and forth in its attitudes toward and regulation of foreign investment, swinging from periods of varying degrees of openness to periods of closed isolation. Political, crime, and labor considerations have all had their impact on the Philippine investment climate over the years. In the 1960s, the Philippines was one of the more economically advanced countries in Asia. But during much of the 1970s and 1980s, the Philippines lost ground, even as many of its Asian neighbors experienced rapid growth. During this period, the Philippines generally excluded foreigners from meaningful participation in its economy, which had become progressively more dominated by state-run businesses and privately-operated cartels. Foreign ownership was restricted, especially in some of the most critical and neediest industries. Cumbersome bureaucratic approval procedures also helped to keep foreigners away even

when legal restrictions did not. In many cases, foreigners were prohibited from managing the entities they owned because of regulations requiring that Filipinos occupy most of the senior management positions.

Unstable and fluctuating GDP growth and erratic inflation rates, coupled with an ever growing trade deficit and foreign debt position worked to divert government funds and energies away from vitally needed investment in infrastructure during recent years. The distorted economy led to a variety of inefficiencies, including lack of access to imported capital goods and necessary inputs; a deteriorating domestic industrial base starved for investment; a crumbling and inadequate infrastructure; and a growing inability to compete in world markets. Long-range planning was almost impossible; investors' confidence in the Philippines—so high shortly after Marcos was deposed—was shattered. The Philippines' abundant resources—not the least of which are its strategic location; its wealth of natural resources; and its educated, hardworking, and affordable labor force—have remained largely undeveloped.

The government has finally taken note, recently initiating bold steps to reverse its former, relatively unfriendly stance and to welcome foreign investment in order to underwrite the growth of the country's economy. While some Philippine statutes, regulations, and the constitution itself continue to limit or exclude foreign ownership in a number of industrial sectors and economic activities, the passage of the Foreign Investments Act of 1991 (FIA) has been a boon to the investment scene. The measure, coupled with the government's other reforms—such as import liberalization, tariff reform, and foreign exchange liberalization—has sent positive signals to outside investors, underscoring the country's commitment to encourage and protect foreign investment. The Philippines is taking advantage of the general trend toward internationalization in the

KEY CONTACTS AND REGULATORS

Bangko Sentral ng Pilipinas (BSP) The reorganized central bank of the Philippines. This agency is responsible for registering all foreign investment in the country. However, in many cases, if investors are required to register with either the SEC or the BTRCP, they are considered to have fulfilled their obligation to the BSP.

Board of Investments (BOI) The BOI is the agency that administers the incentives available to foreign and domestic investors under the Omnibus Investments Code of 1987.

Bureau of Trade Regulation and Consumer Protection (BTRCP) Foreign investors must register with this unit of the Department of Trade and Industry. Single proprietorships need only register with the BTRCP and not the SEC. Registration with the BTRCP is considered to satisfy the requirement that investors register with the BSP.

National Economic and Development Authority (NEDA) Mandated by the Philippine Constitution, this agency sets national developmental priorities and manages their implementation.

One-Stop Action Center (OSAC) Maintained by the BOI, this center houses representatives from the various agencies that have jurisdiction over foreign investment, including the BOI, BSP, and the SEC. Designed to provide a central source of information, it is also able to facilitate required approvals, licenses, permits, and registrations.

Philippine Securities and Exchange Commission (SEC) The SEC not only governs the offering of securities to the public, but also approves incorporations and partnerships. Foreign investments that fall into these categories must register with the SEC—such registration is considered to fulfill the requirement for registration with the BSP.

Addresses for these organizations can be found at the end of the chapter, under "Useful Addresses."

world economy and toward a free market orientation on the part of governments around the globe. The current crop of leaders is trying to institutionalize economic and political stability, while also encouraging foreigners to help it grow. The government seems to be making a genuine effort to correct the earlier distortions, take advantage of the country's capabilities, and move to actively promote economic growth and opportunity for Filipinos and foreign investors alike.

The current administration recognizes the need to attract new investment—especially direct fixed investment—if it is to reach its development goals. (The majority of the expansion in Philippine foreign investment inflows in past years has come in the form of portfolio investment in more liquid securities rather than from longer-term direct equity investments.) The administration continues to seek further liberalization of the investment regime and in particular welcomes foreign investment in infrastructure project—particularly in transportation and power generation—through its build-operate-transfer (BOT) program, which invites foreigners to construct facilities, operate them on a fee basis to recoup their investment and turn a profit, and then turn them over to the government at the end of their concession period.

Many Philippine regions—such as Cebu and Cavite—are now actively promoting themselves independently from the central government, and several enjoy a reputation for being actively pro-business. These have garnered levels of new investments and double digit growth far above those of the national economy as a whole. The former Subic Bay US Naval Base in Olongapo—the site of a free port zone development—and the city of Davao on Mindanao are examples of areas that are gearing up to attract foreign investment and export trade through local as well as national initiatives.

A myriad of other economic and structural factors have combined to boost investor confidence and encourage long-term foreign investment. The popularity of emerging markets worldwide and the improved prospects for the Philippine economy in particular have served to redirect investor attention toward the Philippines. Other specific measures—such as the restructuring of the central bank and the resultant stabilization of the financial system, a stock market boom, deregulation of the telecommunications sector, successful privatization of several state-owned firms, and elimination of power brownouts (periodic shutdowns of service because of insufficient capacity to serve demand) have all served to fuel the foreign investment boom.

The Philippine economy has responded encouragingly. It posted a 5.2 percent growth rate for the first quarter of 1995, rendering the official target of

6 percent feasible, although still optimistic. However, future long-term growth will depend heavily on continued economic and political reform, the institutionalization of stability, and the ability of the Philippine economy to get away from the boom-and-bust growth pattern that has characterized it in the past. Still, things look more favorable than at any time in the recent past as foreign investors begin to take advantage of the many opportunities available in the Philippines.

LEADING FOREIGN INVESTORS

Size of Foreign Investment

During the 1970s and most of the 1980s, direct foreign investment slowly trickled into the largely closed Philippine economy at a rate averaging less than US$50 million per year. But by 1990, with positive political and economic trends sweeping the nation, and the government easing its foreign investment posture by relaxing currency controls and discriminatory ownership regulations, annual foreign investment more than quadrupled, to more than US$200 million. As of year-end 1994, cumulative recorded direct foreign investment (other than portfolio investment in equity and debt securities) in the Philippines, amounted to approximately US$6 billion.

According to central bank registration statistics, net direct foreign investment in 1990 was US$195.9 million. Aided by the passage of the FIA and an economy that was bucking the trend toward global recession, the Philippines saw a huge surge of foreign investment activity in 1991. Net foreign investment doubled in 1991 to US$415 million, setting a record for annual foreign investment up to that time. The pace slowed slightly during 1992 and 1993, but remained relatively high because of declining inflation, a return to real growth, and a climate of improving political stability with the election of the Ramos administration. Total registered investment was US$328 million in 1992, and US$377.7 million in 1993. Investment for all of 1994 grew to around US$800 million, although observers note that nearly two-thirds of this amount represented a single transaction—the acquisition of a 40 percent holding in the state oil company—rather than new investment per se. Nevertheless, given continued stability and further liberalization, the Philippines should continue to register net positive foreign investment accumulation for the rest of the 1990s and possibly beyond.

Origin of Foreign Investment

As of the beginning of 1994, the US was the largest foreign investor in the Philippines, accounting for more than 44 percent of cumulative foreign direct investment. As of early 1995, a large percentage of US Fortune 500 firms maintained operations in the Philippines. At the beginning of 1994, cumulative direct investment by US entities was approximately US$2 billion (valued at cost). However, Japan has accounted for the largest share of annual net direct foreign investment in the Philippines thus far during the 1990s. Cumulatively, Japan accounts for more than 20 percent of total foreign investment, making it the second largest foreign investor in the country. Running a distant third and fourth are Hong Kong (US$286 million, with a 6.5 percent share) and the UK (US$285 million, 6.5 percent). Together, these top four investors account for slightly more than three-quarters of all direct foreign investment in the Philippines. The Netherlands and Switzerland also have significant investment positions in the Philippines, and investment from Korea and Singapore has also increased substantially in recent years.

Sectors of Foreign Investment

As of 1994, foreign investment in industry—US$2.33 billion—accounted for more than 53 percent of total cumulative direct foreign investment. The mining sector (particularly coal production) followed with a 20.5 percent share (US$898 million). Services (5.5 percent, US$242 million) and commerce (5 percent, US$224 million) round out the picture of the major sectors of foreign investments, accounting for about 84 percent of all such investment.

The sector trend has been rather stable, with investment by foreigners concentrated in manufacturing industries such as chemicals, machinery (especially appliances), and food processing. These three subsectors accounted for nearly 40 percent of the total foreign investment position in early 1994. On an annual basis, investment in the manufacturing sector accounted for more than 70 percent of net new investment. Other significant areas of investment for the period 1990 to 1994 include the petroleum and coal industries (US$142 million) and the service sector (more than US$110 million).

INVESTMENT POLICY AND CHANGES

Although the Philippine government has taken important steps in recent years to welcome foreign investment, its Constitution, statutes, and administrative regulations continue to limit or exclude foreign ownership in a number of industries. The FIA —which repealed Book II of the Omnibus Investments Code of 1987—has significantly simplified both the legal and procedural requirements for some foreign investments in the Philippines. However, the FIA repealed only Book II; the other five books of the Omnibus Investments Code, and existing laws in specific sectors, continue to govern in all other instances. The result is somewhat confusing. For example, banking and environmental laws, among others, continue to restrict the ability of foreigners to invest freely in many Philippine enterprises. Other sectors allow varying degrees of foreign ownership. Financing companies, public utilities, domestic air transport, educational institutions, and private domestic construction enterprises can be up to 40 percent foreign-owned. Advertising, savings and loan associations, and pawnshops can be 30 percent foreign-owned, while the maximum allowable ownership is 25 percent for private overseas construction and employment recruitment agencies. Filipinos must own a majority of the voting stock of an investment house. There are no longer any restrictions on foreign equity in insurance companies. However, in some industries existing laws continue to reserve executive and management positions for Philippine citizens even when majority foreign equity is allowed.

Several regulatory agencies oversee the various—and sometimes overlapping—aspects of investment, and the result is a tangle of restrictions, regulations, and opportunities that the foreign investor must navigate. The government has sought to alleviate this problem to some extent by creating a single One-Stop Action Center where representatives from each agency are on hand to answer questions, provide specific information, and help with applications and approvals. The entire process is expected to become simpler and proceed more smoothly in the future as reforms take hold, the economy strengthens, and participants become more used to the new ways and standards of doing things.

The current administration has gone on record as supporting further liberalization of the investment regime, including the easing of restrictions on foreign entry into retail trade, banking, and insurance. However, little legislative action has taken place recently, although now that the administration has gained additional support in the legislature following the May 1995 elections, new initiatives may be forthcoming. However, observers note that the removal of caps on foreign ownership in a variety of sectors—such as public utilities, exploitation of natural resources, and land ownership—which would require the amendment of the constitution are considered unlikely.

Foreign Investments Act of 1991 (FIA) The FIA covers all new foreign-owned enterprises or foreign nationals applying to do business in the Philippines who are not seeking incentives; existing Filipino-owned enterprises which would like to accept foreign equity participation of greater that 40 percent; and existing foreign-invested enterprises that would like to increase the percentage of their equity participation. It does not apply to investors who seek incentives or those locating in export processing zones; those seeking incentives will continue to be covered by the provisions of the more restrictive 1987 law, while those investing in special export processing zones are subject to the separate provisions governing those developments. The FIA states generally that the domestic market is open to foreign investors as long as the activity is not restricted in the negative list. The FIA defines a foreign-owned enterprise as one in which non-Philippine nationals own more than 60 percent of the equity.

The FIA's Negative List Areas of economic activity in which foreign ownership is limited are specified in the Negative List. Areas not included in the list—which is wide ranging and specific—are considered to be open to foreign investors without limits. The Negative List is made up of three sections: List A enumerates the areas of economic activity in which foreign ownership is limited by mandate of the Constitution and specific laws; List B includes sectors and enterprises limited for reasons of security or defense, or the protection of local small and medium-scale enterprises; List C is compiled upon request and application of a Philippine national, and includes industries or enterprises which, for various reasons, need to be specially protected from foreign intrusion. Once included, an area of investment remains on List C of the Regular Negative List for two years, after which it may be amended upon petition and following due process. To date, no applications have been submitted and the government has suspended List C.

The Negative List is designed to cover future investment activity: existing enterprises are not affected and are effectively grandfathered—that is, protected against retroactive prohibitions of existing operations should subsequent changes restrict new entrants from undertaking similar activities.

Registration Foreign investments must be registered with the Securities and Exchange Commission (SEC) for a corporation, or with the Bureau of Trade Regulation and Consumer Protection (BTRCP) for a sole proprietorship. Outside Manila, registration can be accomplished at any one of the many BTRCP local offices located throughout the country.

Foreign investments include all equity investments made by non-Philippine nationals in the form of foreign exchange or other assets actually transferred to the Philippines and registered with the Bankgo Sentral ng Pilipinas (BSP—the central bank). The profits derived from any assets not properly registered may not be repatriated.

Foreign export enterprises (those that export more than 60 percent of their production) must

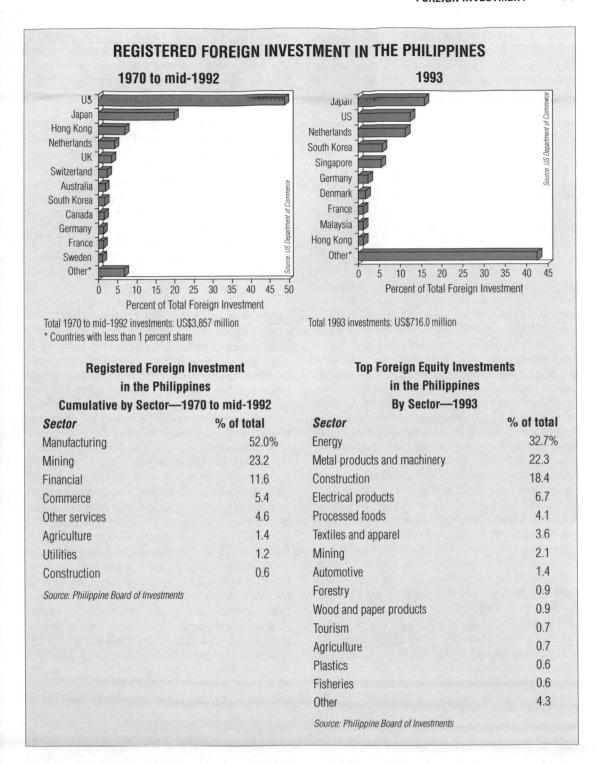

REGISTERED FOREIGN INVESTMENT IN THE PHILIPPINES

1970 to mid-1992

Total 1970 to mid-1992 investments: US$3,857 million
* Countries with less than 1 percent share

1993

Total 1993 investments: US$716.0 million

Registered Foreign Investment in the Philippines
Cumulative by Sector—1970 to mid-1992

Sector	% of total
Manufacturing	52.0%
Mining	23.2
Financial	11.6
Commerce	5.4
Other services	4.6
Agriculture	1.4
Utilities	1.2
Construction	0.6

Source: Philippine Board of Investments

Top Foreign Equity Investments in the Philippines
By Sector—1993

Sector	% of total
Energy	32.7%
Metal products and machinery	22.3
Construction	18.4
Electrical products	6.7
Processed foods	4.1
Textiles and apparel	3.6
Mining	2.1
Automotive	1.4
Forestry	0.9
Wood and paper products	0.9
Tourism	0.7
Agriculture	0.7
Plastics	0.6
Fisheries	0.6
Other	4.3

Source: Philippine Board of Investments

register with the Board of Investments (BOI) and agree to submit whatever reports may be required to ensure continuing compliance with the export requirements. Separately, the BOI now requires certification of compliance from the Department of Environment and Natural Resources (DENR) to obtain its approval to register new operations.

Rights and Guarantees All investors and enterprises are entitled to the basic rights and guarantees provided in the Philippine constitution. These include, among others: the right to full repatriation of investment, the right to remittance of earnings, the right to engage in and pursue foreign loans and contracts, freedom from expropriation (except under certain limited conditions), and the right of investment holdings to be free from requisition. The repatriation of investment capital and remittance of earnings are permitted in the currency in which the investment was originally made and at the exchange rate prevailing at the time of repatriation or remittance, providing that the investment was properly registered. The BSP is charged with valuing all non-cash foreign investments, and its valuation becomes the one officially used for determining eligible capital repatriation. The Philippines is a party to the World Bank Multilateral Investment Guarantee Agreement designed to protect foreign investment.

INVESTMENT INCENTIVES

The Philippine government, acting through the BOI, grants various incentives to foreign and domestic firms to encourage investment in designated priority activities. Most incentives are financially driven and come either in the form of exemptions from taxes and tariffs or through the granting of priority status in the allocation of below-market rate credits. The Omnibus Investments Code of 1987 governs the majority of the rules and regulations governing investment incentives; additional incentives are available to projects locating in less developed areas, to enterprises registered with the Philippine Economic Zone Authority (PEZA), and to multinational companies establishing regional headquarters in the Philippines. Under the terms of the Special Economic Zone Act of 1995 (R.A. 7916), the former Export Processing Zone Authority (EPZA) was transformed into the Philippine PEZA; this new organization is to have greater authority and broader functions, offering more potential opportunities to investors. However, because the new system only went into effect in June 1995, the details of its operations are as yet unclear.

Export enterprises, both foreign and domestic, seeking to take advantage of incentives under the Omnibus Investment Code must apply to the BOI. Properly registered investors are eligible for incentives for the investment in certain preferred areas, as specified annually by the government in the Investment Priorities Plan (IPP). The current IPP may be obtained from the One-Stop Action Center in Manila.

The IPP includes primarily "pioneer" activities. Pioneer enterprises may be up to 100 percent foreign-owned, but typically will require a commitment to transfer the operation to Filipino majority ownership within 30 years of the initial registration. Sectors qualifying for pioneer status are classified into four broad categories: (1) those involved in the manufacture, processing, or production of goods or raw materials not previously available in the Philippines on a commercial scale; (2) those using systems, designs, or methods to produce raw materials or products new to the Philippines; (3) agricultural, forestry, and mining activities and/or services predetermined by the BOI to support a specific declared national food and agricultural program designed to achieve self-sufficiency or some other social benefit; and (4) production of nonconventional fuels, manufacture of nonconventional fuel using equipment or vehicles, or use of or conversion to coal or other nonconventional fuels in production, manufacturing, or processing operations.

A foreign enterprise (one with more than 40 percent foreign equity) may still be entitled to incentives, even if the activity is not listed in the IPP, so long as 70 percent of its production is exported; a domestically-owned enterprise need only export 50 percent to be entitled to available incentives.

The incentives offered include a variety of fiscal and nonfiscal benefits. Newly registered pioneer projects are fully exempt from income taxes for six years from the start of commercial operations and nonpioneer firms for four years. The exemption period may be extended for an additional year under certain conditions. New and expanding registered enterprises may import machinery, equipment, and accompanying spare parts tax and duty free within five years of the date of registration, subject to certain terms and conditions.

Other incentives include additional tax deductions for labor expenses; tax credits equivalent to up to 100 percent for the use of domestic instead of imported capital equipment; exemption from contractor's tax; and tax credits on domestic breeding stocks and genetic material. In addition, tax credits are available for taxes and duties paid on raw materials used in the production of export products and forming parts thereof; access to bonded manufacturing or trading warehouse systems; exemption from taxes and duties on imported supplies and spare parts for consigned equipment; exemption from wharfage dues; and exemption from any export tax, duty impost, or fee.

Nonfiscal incentives include simplification of customs procedures and unrestricted use of consigned equipment. In addition, foreign nationals may be employed in supervisory, technical, or advisory positions within five years of project registration; this exemption may be extended for limited periods. Certain senior management positions of foreign-owned registered firms may be retained by foreign nationals for a longer than usual period.

Under Book V of the Code, foreigners who invest a minimum of US$75,000 in a Philippine company—

US$50,000 for certain approved tourism-related ventures—are entitled to a special investor's resident visa. This visa allows residence in the country as long as the investment remains in effect.

In addition to the items already noted, other incentives are available to enterprises locating in less developed areas. These incentives include: automatic entitlement to the pioneer incentives, regardless of nationality; income tax deductibility of up to 100 percent of the cost of construction of necessary, major infrastructure and public facilities; and a doubling of the tax deduction for labor expenses.

Firms registered with the PEZA are entitled to all the incentives available to firms registered with the BOI. Certain additional incentives available to PEZA-registered firms include: special tax treatment of merchandise within the zone; exemption from local taxes, licenses, and fees; exemption, during the first three years of operation, from real estate taxes due on the value of production equipment and machinery not secured to the real estate; and exemption from the 15 percent branch profits tax on earnings remitted by a branch to its head office.

Incentives also exist for multinational firms establishing regional headquarters or regional warehouses in the Philippines. These include certain tax and visa advantages for expatriates employed locally by the multinational. The operations of the regional headquarters are exempted from income and contractor's taxes, as well as from a host of local licenses, fees, and duties.

Offshore banking units (OBUs)—established by Presidential Decree No. 1,034—are eligible for tax exempt status on certain transactions. These include foreign currency transactions with nonresidents of the Philippines and on transactions with recognized Foreign Currency Deposit Units (FCDUs), local commercial banks, and local branches of foreign banks.

The Philippine government has sought to encourage the establishment of small-scale businesses outside the metropolitan Manila and other urbanized areas. The Magna Carta for Countryside and Barangay Business Enterprises—or Kalakalan 20—was approved in late 1989 to promote such activity. Kalakalan 20 exempts applicable entities from all taxes, including income and value-added taxes, license and building permit fees, and certain other business taxes.

INVESTMENT ASSISTANCE

The BOI maintains a One-Stop Action Center (OSAC), which can provide information on and accept and process applications regarding foreign investment in the Philippines. This office includes representatives of the BOI, the BSP, the SEC, and various other important agencies. Personnel of the BOI-OSAC answer business questions, arrange business meetings and visits to factory sites, promote joint ventures that match foreign investors with local Filipino firms, network with other government agencies, and facilitate action on various business permits, licenses, and registration. The BOI-OSAC maintains overseas representative offices in several locations worldwide.

To further enhance its operations, BOI-OSAC maintains a network of small staff units called Investment Promotion Units (IPUs) that operate in key government offices. The IPUs provide investors with answers to technical and legal inquiries as well as fast action on the approval of investment-related permits and licenses. Most Philippine government agencies have IPUs.

The similarly organized One-Stop Interagency Tax Credit and Duty Drawback Center—maintained by Customs and the Revenue Department—operates to aid in processing documents for those seeking tax credits and duty drawbacks.

ECONOMIC DEVELOPMENT PROGRAMS

The National Economic and Development Authority (NEDA) is the independent government agency mandated by the constitution to plan for national development and to coordinate program implementation. It reports directly to the president, who also acts as the agency's official chairman. A series of four and five year development plans are the cornerstone of the NEDA's efforts. The current plan (1993–1998) calls for rural industrialization to spread activity outside the metropolitan Manila area; agrarian reform; further development of the nation's natural resource base; and an increase in the contribution of the tourist industry to economic growth and regional development. The government generally looks to private sector investment, including foreign direct investment, and overseas development assistance to supplement the rather limited federal government contributions. Core investments are focused on agriculture and agro-industry, power, transportation, telecommunications, and the environment.

More specifically, NEDA-promoted projects are detailed in the Core Public Investment Program (CPIP) of the Philippines' medium-term development plan. More than 400 general projects, as well as 60 "flagship" projects, have been identified by the government's interagency Investment Coordination Committee (ICC), with the highest priority being given to a short list of 21 projects valued collectively at about US$4 billion. Some of

NEGATIVE OR APPROVED INVESTMENTS

This Negative List of the FIA governs areas of economic activity in which the degree of foreign ownership is limited to a specified maximum percentage of the equity capital of the enterprises engaged therein. The Regular Negative List supplanted the Transitory Negative List in October 1994 and remains in effect today. The Regular Negative is comprised of two parts, List A and List B. Transitory List C was repealed by presidential order and the Regular List C was suspended. If List C is ever put into effect it will include areas of investment in which existing enterprises already adequately serve the needs of the Philippine economy and do not require further foreign investment; hence no new foreign investment will be allowed in such areas. Note that these lists do not include banking and other financial institutions, because these activities are governed and regulated by the General Banking Act and other laws under the supervision of the BSP.

Regular Negative List Pursuant to Philippine Republic Act. 7042

List A

Foreign ownership is limited by the mandate of the constitution and specific laws.

No foreign equity allowed:

(1) mass media

(2) services involving the practice of licensed professions (such as engineering, medicine, accounting, and law)

(3) retail trade

(4) cooperatives

(5) private security agencies

(6) small-scale mining

(7) engaging in the rice and corn industry except as authorized

Up to 25 percent foreign equity allowed:

(1) private recruitment (for local or overseas employment)

Up to 30 percent foreign equity allowed:

(1) advertising

Up to 40 percent foreign equity allowed:

(1) exploration, development, and utilization of natural resources (subject to certain terms and conditions)

(2) ownership of private lands

(3) operation and management of public utilities

(4) ownership or establishment of educational institutions requiring Department of Education authorization

(5) financing companies

Varying foreign equity limitations:

(1) construction—locally funded public works (25 percent limit); contracts for supply of goods and materials to government-owned entities (40 percent limit); private domestic and overseas construction contracts (40 percent limit); contracts for defense-related buildings and facilities (40 percent limit); public utilities (40 percent limit)

List B

Foreign ownership is limited for reasons of security, defense, risk to health and morals, and protection of local small and medium-scale businesses.

Up to 40 percent foreign equity allowed:

(1) all activities related to firearms, ammunition, lethal weapons, military ordnance, explosives, pyrotechnics and parts, and peripherals and ingredients used in the manufacture thereof

(2) manufacture and distribution of dangerous drugs

(3) sauna and steam bathhouses, massage clinics, and other similar activities regulated by law

4) other forms of gambling, such as racetrack operation; racehorse ownership or importation

(5) domestic market enterprises with paid-in equity capital of less than equivalent of US$500,000, unless they involve advanced technology

(6) export enterprises which utilize raw materials from depleting natural resources and with paid-in equity capital of less than the equivalent of US$500,000

these projects are open to full private sector participation under the BOT program or through similar arrangements, while others are to be funded completely by the government or with the assistance of international agencies such as the World Bank (the International Bank for Reconstruction and Development, the IBRD), the Asian Development Bank (ADB), the US Overseas Private Investment Corporation (OPIC), or the US Agency for International Development (USAID). For foreign investors, the BOT programs are the most promising vehicle for many direct investment projects within this high priority strategic list. In return for this program, participating firms are given incentives—such as access to a wide array of business prospects and projects nationwide—and subsidiary funding through Official Development Assistance programs such as the Private Sector Infrastructure Development Fund.

Beginning under the Aquino administration, the Philippines launched a vast privatization program designed to divest the government of many of the businesses it had come to own either by design or by default during recent decades. This was begun with the idea of paring down government control of the economy while at the same time promoting economic development through the attraction of fresh infusions of capital to major industrial sectors needing rejuvenation. Divestiture has been conducted through the sale of shares, balance sheet assets, and physical assets through a public bidding process. Nearly a dozen government agencies are responsible for disposing of these assets, although the Asset Privatization Trust has taken the lead role. Some 400 separate assets of varying types have been sold or put up for sale since the late 1980s. A wide range of companies and their assets were and are available in sectors such as banking, mining, shipping, petroleum, and agro-industry. Foreign investment in these areas, as in other development programs, are generally subject to ownership limitations, with certain exceptions. Interested parties are encouraged to contact the appropriate agencies for further detail.

Geographically focused development—primarily involving dispersion of new development to previously undeveloped areas of the country—has become a growing priority of the federal government. Foreign investors have been encouraged to assist in the development of various regions of the country, and the central government has taken steps to decentralize certain areas of authority, allowing local governments to manage more of this development. Several regions have opened industrial centers which provide foreign investors with the infrastructure and facilities needed to do business. The facilities include Export

Processing Zones (EPZs), Industrial Estates (IEs), and Special Development Programs (SDPs). At present, four EPZs operate as self-contained enclaves, equipped to house various industries using imported raw materials and components to process, assemble, and manufacture goods for export. To date the Philippines has set up 11 IEs; these are large, fully integrated industrial facilities with a mix of infrastructure, including such elements as road networks, waste disposal systems, and independent power substations, designed to attract clusters of industrial operations. Five SDPs currently operate to facilitate rural development and redevelopment in areas including Calabarzon, Samar Island, Panay-Negros, South Cotabo-Santos City, and Iligan-Cagayan de Oro. (Refer to the "Trade Zones" chapter, beginning on page 71, for more information on these opportunities.)

Numerous specialty projects catering to the development or redevelopment of specifically identified economic zones or sectors exist. These include the Subic Bay Economic Freeport Zone and the Clark Economic Zone—both of which involve the conversion of former US military bases—and the Southern Mindanao and Regional Telephone Development Programs.

AVAILABILITY OF LOANS AND CREDIT

Foreign investor financing for general, nondevelopment project investment is available from the network of large, domestic commercial banks, finance companies, insurance companies, and branch offices of foreign banks. While the market for corporate debt and equity securities remains somewhat limited, these financial institutions provide a likely source of investment financing. However, the majority of available financing consists of short-term loans, with longer-term funding being considerably more difficult to obtain. Also, the BSP must approve any repayments to external lenders that require foreign exchange, which emphasizes reliance on domestic financing (although payments made from self-generated foreign exchange earnings may be used directly to make necessary payments).

Private sources of medium- and long-term funding are available, although on a limited scale and then only to the most creditworthy of borrowers. Public funds access is necessarily limited to those registered foreign entities involved in specific government sponsored or approved projects. Overseas development agencies regularly make funds available to foreign nationals for specific local development projects, subject to terms and conditions of the specific program.

REAL ESTATE—COMMERCIAL AND INDUSTRIAL SPACE

Land ownership in the Philippines is restricted by the Constitution to Philippine citizens and corporations or other similar business entities with a minimum 60 percent domestic ownership. In addition, public lands are available on a lease-only basis to both locals and foreigners. However, despite these restrictions, long-term land, residential, and commercial leases may be obtained by foreign operators in many instances. Land leases may be for a maximum term of 75 years. (This represents an extension from the previous 50-year limit in effect prior to mid-1993.)

Prime commercial office leases are generally readily available in metropolitan Manila. More limited opportunities for this property type are available outside of the country's main business region, and diligence is required to get good sites at good terms and rates. Commercial retail property is somewhat more difficult to come by, especially as one increases site quality and location (however, remember that foreigners are barred from participating in most retail activity). Industrial sites are in reasonably good supply. This is due primarily to recent government-sponsored development efforts coupled with the freeing up of existing space at former US military installations. Infrastructural support, such as rail access, power facilities, waste disposal, and shipping docks are relatively common, but availability varies widely according to location. Industrial parks are in generally good condition and can accommodate various processing, assembly, and manufacturing operations.

Site selection is substantially similar to the process elsewhere. However, certain critical differences exist: foreign firms wishing to locate or expand in the Philippines should retain the services of an industrial specialist with in-depth knowledge of the relevant markets and with access to general contractors, architects, engineers, and soil and environmental consultants. There are good Filipino professionals in all these areas (licensed foreign professionals may not operate in their professional capacities in the Philippines, although investors are free to use foreign practitioners informally as advisors), and the industrial specialist can play a vital role in coordinating the work of the various disciplines to assure that the client's requirements are met. In addition, because the local real estate market has been typically financed with the developer's own cash, no large, developed market exists to either deal in or finance real estate purchases. Foreign investors will generally need to rely on internally generated or other nondomestic sources of funding to finance any real estate-related activity.

The "Average Short and Long-term Lease Prices..." chart presents a snapshot of property rental costs one might expect to encounter based on conditions pertaining in mid-1994. Be aware that changes in market conditions and terms dictate that foreign operators must perform their own extensive property research.

USEFUL ADDRESSES

Board of Investments One-Stop Action Centers

Board of Investments One-Stop Action Center (BOI-OSAC)
Industry and Investments Bldg.
385 Sen. Gil J. Puyat Ave.
1200 Makati, Metro Manila, Philippines
Tel: [63] (2) 815-0702, 858-8322, 815-3731, 867-884
Fax: [63] (2) 810-9728, 761-2165

German Office, BOI-OSAC
Ground Fl., Industry and Investments Bldg.
Argelandstrasse 1
5300 Bonn 1, Germany

Japanese Office, BOI-OSAC
c/o Embassy of the Philippines
11-24 Nampeidai-machi, Shibuya-ku
Tokyo, Japan
Tel: [81] (3) 3462-1216, 3464-4177
Fax: [81] (3) 3462-2678

US Office, BOI-OSAC
c/o Consulate General of the Philippines
Philippine Center Bldg., Suite 516
447 Sutter St.
San Francisco, CA 94108, USA
Tel: [1] (415) 433-6666

United Kingdom Office, BOI-OSAC
c/o Embassy of the Philippines
1A Cumberland House
Kengsington Court
London W8 5NX, UK
Tel: [44] (171) 937-1898, 937-7998
Fax: [44] (171) 937-2747

Other Government Agencies

Bangko Sentral ng Pilipinas (BSP)
(Central Bank of the Philippines)
A. Mabini Street, cor. Vito Cruz Street
1004 Malate, Metro Manila, Philippines
Tel: [63] (2) 507-051, 593-380/1, 582-263, 582-372
Fax: [63] (2) 522-3987, 597-363

Bureau of Trade Regulation and Consumer Protection (BTRCP)
Department of Trade and Industry
2nd Fl., Trade & Industry Bldg.
361 Sen. Gil J. Puyat Ave.
Makati, Metro Manila, Philippines
Tel: [63] (2) 817-5280, 817-5340, 863-431, 818-5701
Fax: [63] (2) 810-9363

Department of Environment and Natural Resources (DENR)
DENR Bldg.
Visayas Ave.
Diliman
Quezon City, Metro Manila, Philippines
Tel: [63] (2) 976-626/9, 976-671/5, 990-691
Fax: [63] (2) 963-487, 922-6991

National Economic and Development Authority (NEDA)
NEDA Bldg.
Amber Avenue
1600 Pasig, Metro Manila, Philippines
Tel: [63] (2) 673-5031, 631-3716, 631-0945 to 64
Fax: [63] (2) 631-3747

One-Stop Interagency Tax Credit and Drawback Center
3rd Fl., Dept. of Finance Bldg.
Agripina Circle
Rizal Park, Metro Manila, Philippines
Tel: [63] (2) 482-455, 507-051
Fax: [63] (2) 530-0935, 461-015

Philippine Economic Zone Authority (PEZA)
4th Fl., Legaspi Towers 300
Roxas Boulevard
Metro Manila, Philippines
Tel: [63] (2) 521-9725, 521-04-19, 521-0546/7
Fax: [63] (2) 521-8659

Securities and Exchange Commission (SEC)
SEC Building
Epifanio de los Santos
Greenhills
Mandaluyong, Metro Manila, Philippines
Tel: [63] (2) 810-1145, 780-931/9
Fax: [63] (2) 722-0990

AVERAGE LEASE AND LONG-TERM LEASE PRICES FOR REAL ESTATE IN THE MANILA AREA (as of June 1994)

Type	Price	
	Manila	**Suburban Manila**
Annual quoted downtown office rent	US$327/sq m	US$316/sq m
Asking rent in class A building in prime downtown location for 1,000 sq m (10,000 sq ft). Includes all operating expenses plus taxes paid by tenant.		
Annual quoted suburban office rent		US$208/sq m
Asking rent in class A building in prime suburban location for 1,000 sq m (10,000 sq ft). Includes all operating expenses and taxes paid by tenant.		
Annual warehouse rent	US$97/sq m	US$92/sq m
Industrial space suitable for warehousing or light manufacturing for 2,000 to 4,000 sq m (20,000 to 40,000 sq ft) with 10 to 15 percent office space and 5 to 7 m (16 to 22 ft) ceilings. Does not include taxes, operating expenses, and insurance.		
Undeveloped industrial land long-term lease cost	US$60–120/sq m	US$26–31/sq m
Annual retail rent	US$420/sq m	US$300/sq m
Asking rent for retail space less than 1,000 sq m (10,000 sq ft) in a prime shopping area. Includes all expenses such as taxes and operating costs.		
	Asking Price	
Residential monthly rent	US$1,454–2,860	US$1,400–1,500
Two-bedroom apartment in a prestigious location.		
Purchase price		US$171,000–198,900
Two-bedroom Makati City apartment in a prestigious location.		

Source: Information provided by Colliers Jardine, Philippines.

Foreign Trade

THE ROOTS OF PHILIPPINE FOREIGN TRADE

During much of its modern history, the Philippines has focused on the export of primary low-value-added commodity (usually agricultural) products and the import of manufactured, high-value-added goods. As a result, its industries are generally heavily dependent on trade for energy and capital goods, as well as for many raw materials and intermediate components; the demands of its consumers for a wide range of items are also met largely by imports, with many Filipinos expressing a strong preference for foreign goods. The country has had a long-standing trade deficit that has not yet improved—despite recent increases in the quantity, quality, and diversity of Philippine exports—because of its continuing need to import expensive modern technologies to enhance the competitiveness of its exports in world markets.

Overall, Philippine foreign trade has been on the rise for many decades—albeit the rise has been moderate rather than explosive up until very recently in the 1990s. During the past 30 years, its foreign trade has grown at a compound annual growth rate (CAGR) of 11 percent. In 1965 total

foreign merchandise trade was equal to 26 percent of the country's gross domestic product (GDP), a figure which had more than doubled by 1994 to an amount equal to 65 percent of GDP. The trend toward increased involvement in international trade may now be considered to have become well established.

Growth in foreign trade, particularly in export receipts, is essential to the growth and stability of the Philippine economy. This fact is widely recognized by the country's political and business leaders, who are striving to develop export promotion and investment incentive programs. Transformation of the industrial sector is well underway, and numerous diverse and nontraditional products are being developed; observers expect that substantial progress will be seen over time.

Another promising area now being promoted is that of reexports. Given its strategic location between Asia and the Americas, as well as its intermediate geographic relationship to Europe, India, Australia, and the Middle East, the Philippines has the potential to develop as a major transshipment point for traffic moving between Asia and other ports throughout the world. Reexports still account for only about 1 percent of total exports, but are expected to grow substantially with the development of special trade zones and the conversion of the former US military bases at Subic Bay and Clark to allow increased local processing and transshipment through the Philippines. (Refer to the "Trade Zones" chapter, beginning on page 71, for a more detailed discussion of these zones.)

SIZE OF PHILIPPINE FOREIGN TRADE

During the past 25 years, Philippine foreign trade has been rising more rapidly than its GDP; this trend has been especially noticeable in the 1990s and is expected to continue. In 1994 the Philippines posted a GDP of US$57.6 billion and total

PHILIPPINE EXPORTS BY CATEGORY

Product Category	1993 US$ Billion	% of total	± from 1992 (%)
Semiconductor devices	1.090	9.7	24.7
Consigned finished electrical & electronic machinery, equipment & parts	.585	5.2	20.6
Electric integrated circuits	.574	5.1	53.5
Consigned women's wear	.426	3.8	5.4
Consigned children's & infants' wear	.389	3.5	8.0
Consigned menswear	.380	3.4	16.9
Consigned other products manufactured from imported materials	.380	3.4	136.0
Coconut oil	.300	2.7	−28.7
Ignition wiring sets	.295	2.6	13.0
Copper	.261	2.3	20.8
Top ten	4.680	41.5	20.6
Other	6.586	58.5	61.3
Total	11.269	100.0	14.7

Source: Philippine Department of Trade and Industry

merchandise trade of US$37.4 billion. The 1995 GDP projections are for growth of between 5 and 6 percent, or in dollar terms of roughly US$60.5 billion to US$61 billion. In 1995 total foreign trade—growing at a rate at least twice that of GDP—is expected to be the equivalent of nearly 70 percent of GDP, and it is anticipated that it will rise to about 70 to 75 percent of GDP by 1996. The faster growth rate of foreign trade in relation to GDP points up the country's relatively newfound orientation toward increasing its participation in world markets, following a period in which policy was generally protectionist and import substitution oriented.

The percentage equivalent of Philippine GDP represented by the country's foreign trade lies in the middle range of statistics measuring the economies of other nations. In 1992 Philippine foreign trade was roughly 46 percent of GDP, about the same percentage as that of the UK (43.8 percent). However, it was lower than that of such overtly foreign trade oriented countries as South Korea (53.8 percent of GDP) Germany (60 percent), and Taiwan (76.9 percent of GDP), but substantially higher than that of larger, more domestically diversified economies such as Japan (15.2 percent) and the US (17.5 percent) or some other developing countries such as Brazil (15 percent) and Mexico (23.4 percent).

The Philippines shows promising strength and potential in the trade area when compared with a sample of both developing and developed countries. At the moment, its rising foreign trade level is a function of the need to buy high-value imports to produce high-value-added exports. The investments it is now making in imports of capital goods for the modernization of its industries should begin to allow it to produce higher-value-added products that are competitive both at home and abroad. Its promotion of reexport centers should also hasten the country's progress.

EXPORTS

Labor intensive industrial manufactures continue to dominate the Philippine export scene, at least in terms of value. However, in terms of volume, Philippine exports are still largely lower-end commodity industrial and consumer products, that is, raw or semiprocessed extractive products—agricultural, forestry, and mineral goods. As a result, the Philippines continues to have difficulty generating sufficient export sales to pay for its imports of often more expensive raw and intermediate materials, industrial goods, and manufactured products.

The country has made considerable progress toward diversifying its exports in a short period of time. In 1950 the top ten exports together represented 85 percent of the value of the country's total trade. All but one of these were either agricultural or mineral products in a raw or minimally processed form, and the export picture stayed basically the same for the next 25 years, well into the 1970s, when the Philippines began to encourage diversification.

Although this shift has been largely incremental in nature, it has begun to register some success in turning the country away from its traditional roster of commodity goods, subject to the whims of the international commodity markets that work to remove a great deal of pricing power from the producers. In 1993 Philippine exports were categorized as manufactured goods (45.5 percent of total merchandise exports), consumer manufactures (29.5 percent), food and food preparations (11.7 percent), resource-based products (8.6 percent), and special transactions (4.6 percent). It should be noted that the dominance of industrial manufactures is more an indication of the relative value-added in such products than an indication of the overall volume produced. In 1993 the largest single export category was semiconductors, representing 9.7 percent of the value of total merchandise exports. This product category registered at nearly twice the value of the next largest export category—consigned, finished electrical and electronic machinery, equipment, and parts—with a 5.2 percent share of export value. Women's, children's and infants', and men's clothing—which reported separately are all in the top ten exports—collectively account for 10.6 percent of exports. Together the top ten export categories accounted for 41.6 percent of total merchandise exports.

During 1993 all the top ten export categories grew in value compared with 1992 except for coconut oil, which fell by 28.7 percent. Consigned other products manufactured from imported materials—the seventh largest export category, with a 3.4 percent share—grew by 136 percent from 1992, followed by electric integrated circuits—the third largest category, with a 5.1 percent share—up by 53 percent. In 1993 the top five export products in terms of foreign exchange earnings included electronics (US$3.5 billion), apparel (US$2.1 billion), frozen shrimp (US$222 million), furniture (US$202 million), and basketry (US$122 million). The next leading merchandise export earners included subcontracted metal parts, processed tropical fruit, Christmas decorations, fine and costume jewelry, decorative ceramics, seaweed, and marble.

IMPORTS

Following a post–World War II policy involving import substitution and protection of national industrial development during the 1950s through much of the 1970s, plus a period of political and economic crisis during the 1980s that resulted in reduced trade, the Philippines has embarked on a policy of economic renewal in the 1990s. This involves the recognition that capital goods, materials, and know-how are necessary to advance the economy and that these must be acquired primarily from outside sources. Thus, the government is allowing imports of a range of items broader than ever before, and it is allowing them to be purchased at the cost of having trade deficits, on the grounds that these imports constitute productive investments.

In 1993 petroleum and related products continued to be the largest import of the energy-poor Philippines, although owing to somewhat weaker international pricing and marginally reduced demand, the bill fell by 19 percent from the previous year to US$1.3 billion. (The Philippines has reduced its dependence on imported oil from 95 percent to around 65 percent.) Nevertheless, energy imports

PHILIPPINE IMPORTS BY CATEGORY

Product Category	1993 US$ Billions	% of Total	+ from 1992 (%)
Petroleum oils & oils from bituminous minerals	1.316	7.5	−19.3
Semiconductor devices	.890	5.0	39.5
Electrical & electronic machinery, equipment & parts	.530	3.0	54.5
Aircraft	.488	2.8	154.2
Parts of electronic integrated circuits	.478	2.7	32.4
Other materials & accessories for semiconductor devices	.368	2.1	17.9
Fabrics for embroidery or manufacture of garments	.278	1.6	−8.5
Other commodities temporarily imported	.260	1.5	50.3
Passenger cars & components	.257	1.5	57.7
Wheat	.253	1.4	7.7
Top ten	5.118	29.0	17.6
Other	12.506	71.0	23.0
Total	17.624	100.0	21.4

Source: Philippine Department of Trade and Industry

still exceeded the next largest import—semiconductors, which as reexports are also the major export product in terms of value—at US$890 million by 50 percent. Among the top ten imports, four represent electronic capital goods or components, together accounting for 12.9 percent of total imports. Other major imports involve transportation—aircraft and vehicles and their respective components—representing 4.2 percent of imports. The seventh and eighth largest import categories—fabric and other materials admitted temporarily for production—also represent goods imported primarily to fuel export production; together they represent only 1.5 percent of total imports. Fabrics represent the only top ten category besides petroleum to decline from 1992, largely an indication of the competitiveness of the

PHILIPPINE IMPORTS BY COUNTRY			
Country	1993 US$ Billions	% of total	± from 1992 (%)
Japan	4.002	22.7	29.6
US	.890	5.0	39.5
Taiwan	1.027	5.8	7.1
Singapore	.975	5.5	76.9
South Korea	.898	5.1	28.8
Hong Kong	.880	5.0	22.0
Saudi Arabia	.734	4.2	−15.9
Germany	.699	4.0	4.2
Australia	.472	2.7	16.0
UK	.379	2.2	26.3
Top ten	13.572	77.0	24.7
Other	4.052	23.0	11.5
Total	17.624	100.0	21.4

Source: Philippine Department of Trade and Industry

international garment industry. The final top ten category is wheat, which rose the least compared with 1992 among categories that increased in value from the previous year. Philippine imports are generally far more diversified than are its exports: the top ten imports account for only 29 percent of total imports, while the top 10 exports represent 41.5 percent of exports.

TRADE PARTNERS

Before the nation's independence in 1946, Philippine trade was heavily tied to the US, and as of 1950 approximately 80 percent of total Philippine trade was still conducted with the US. However, by 1970 the US share of Philippine export trade had declined to about 40 percent, although its share of Philippine imports had fallen less, to about 60 percent. At the same time, trade with Japan began to rise sharply, leveling off at a level somewhat lower than the US figures.

During the last three decades, Philippine traders have diversified into new markets, with the result that the share of trade held by its two largest trading partners has declined even further. Trade is increasing with the other members of the Association of Southeast Asian Nations (ASEAN) and with various members of the European Union (EU). Export trade remains slightly more concentrated than import trade, with the top ten buyers of exports taking 82.3 percent of the total exports versus the top ten sellers of imports, supplying 76.8 percent of the imports.

Today, the US and Japan remain the top two Philippine trading partners, together accounting for nearly half of all trade with the Philippines (54.6 percent of all export and 42.6 percent of all import trade). The US share of total merchandise trade in 1993 was US$7.9 billion (nearly 27 percent); Japan's share was somewhat lower at US$5.9 billion (about 20 percent), with the two together accounting for a total of 47 percent. Other major trading partners—as ranked from the next highest to the lowest—in 1993 were Hong Kong, Singapore, Taiwan, Germany, Korea, the UK, Saudi Arabia, and Australia. Trade with these second tier partners is still relatively low. Taken together, Hong Kong, Singapore, and Taiwan account for only about 15 percent of total trade. The next five top trading countries also combine to account for another 15 percent of total trade.

During 1993 trade increased with nine of the top ten partners, the exception being Saudi Arabia, with a decline of nearly 9 percent because of reduced oil prices. Singapore posted the highest growth rate in trade (75.6 percent) and Germany the lowest (2.8 percent). Trade with Japan and the US grew at about the same pace, around 20 percent.

PHILIPPINE EXPORTS BY COUNTRY			
Country	1993 US$ Billions	% of total	± from 1992 (%)
US	4.327	37.6	12.9
Japan	1.811	16.1	3.8
Germany	.579	5.1	10.9
Hong Kong	.546	4.8	17.7
UK	.534	4.7	14.3
Singapore	.378	3.4	50.0
Netherlands	.358	3.2	−11.8
Taiwan	.345	3.1	20.2
India	.226	2.0	2,712.5
South Korea	.220	2.0	22.9
Top ten	9.234	81.9	13.1
Other	2.035	18.1	22.6
Total	11.269	100.0	14.7

Source: Philippine Department of Trade and Industry

BALANCE OF TRADE

The Philippines has moved through several trade regimes during the 20th century, all of which have had difficulty in balancing the nation's foreign trade. In the immediate post–World War II era, the Philippines attempted to balance imports and exports by various means, including exchange and import controls and later tariffs; however, from the beginning, imports outpaced exports, and foreign exchange to pay for them became an issue. The last time the Philippine economy recorded a merchandise trade surplus was in 1973, and by the late 1970s imports had accelerated well beyond exports on a regular and growing basis. Many imports had to be financed by external debt, and the trade imbalance grew.

This structural merchandise trade deficit continues to grow despite attempts to encourage exports. The 1965 merchandise trade deficit equaled 2.5 percent of total trade, a share that in 1994 has risen to 21 percent of total trade—a record US$7.84 billion. During the past 30 years, exports have grown at a CAGR of 10.3 percent, compared with imports at a CAGR of 11.8 percent, a figure that has accelerated during the 1990s.

The imbalance in trade continued in 1994 although some change has become apparent since the implementation of export promotion programs. In 1994 the growth rate of exports (19.5 percent) actually topped the growth rate of imports (17.9 percent). However, the value of exports remains far below that of imports.

The imbalance in trade is likely to continue for at least the extended period required to modernize Philippine industry and infrastructure. This prediction is supported by the relative sizes of the categories of goods being imported. Only about 10 percent of the imports are consumer goods. The rest are intended for the production of import substitution products or exports, and thus consist of capital goods, raw materials, and intermediate components.

The trade deficit is eased somewhat by the trade in services, which in most years posts a surplus based on remittances from overseas Filipino workers; some argue that these workers represent one of the Philippines' most successful exports. In 1992 total trade in services generated surpluses as high as US$2.5 billion. From 1980 to 1993, the amount of total trade in services equaled on average nearly one-quarter of the average total merchandise trade during the same period.

PHILIPPINE TRADE POLICY

Beginning in 1946 the Philippine government agreed to accommodate the US through trade and fiscal policy. However, before decade's end the value of imports had so surpassed that of exports plus the inflow of US dollar aid that the Philippines initiated import and foreign exchange controls that remained in force throughout the 1950s. These controls also reflected the goals of national producers, who sought control over broad areas of the national economy and supported the development and protection of national industry. Despite these pressures, the relative share of exports and imports with respect to GDP remained stable until the 1960s, when structural trade imbalances and

The Philippine's Leading Trade Partners

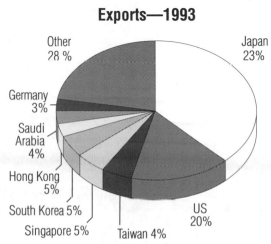

Exports—1993

Other 28 %
Japan 23%
Germany 3%
Saudi Arabia 4%
Hong Kong 5%
South Korea 5%
Singapore 5%
Taiwan 4%
US 20%

Total 1993 merchandise exports: US$11.3 billion

Imports—1993

Others 28%
Japan 23%
Germany 4%
Saudi Arabia 4%
Hong Kong 5%
South Korea 5%
Singapore 5%
Taiwan 6%
US 20%

Total 1993 merchandise imports: US$17.6 billion

Note: Figures rounded to nearest whole percent.
Source: Philippine Department of Trade and Industry

increasingly protectionist trade policies began to distort trade and the economy in general.

The basic political and economic structure continued into the 1970s, becoming generally more extreme as the economy grew more concentrated and centralized. By the 1980s the situation had reached crisis proportions, and the general lack of funds and impaired functioning of the economy during the ensuing political crisis served to reduce the level of trade even without added policy restrictions. The exile of Marcos in 1986 led to a different policy orientation, involving the easing of limits on trade, but it was not until the 1990s that the Philippines' more open policy was effectively codified and implemented. Broader government initiatives, including economic decentralization, demonopolization, privatization, and deregulation; promotion of foreign investment; infrastructure development; and export promotion have also led toward more liberal trade. The Philippines has, furthermore, become more attractive internationally following its abolition of exchange controls and the implementation of a policy allowing full and immediate repatriation of earnings.

As noted, Philippine policy has acknowledged the need to invest and has allowed the expansion of imports, even at the cost of rising deficits, while at the same time focusing attention and resources on offsetting export production. Moreover, Philippine membership in such bodies as the General Agreement on Tariffs and Trade (GATT), the Association of Southeast Asian Nations (ASEAN), and Asia Pacific Economic Cooperation (APEC) commit the country to standardizing and liberalizing its foreign trade regime to an even greater degree.

MEMBERSHIP IN INTERNATIONAL ORGANIZATIONS

For a country with a reputation for protectionism, the Philippines has been remarkably active in international organizations designed to promote international exchange and cooperation. It holds membership in most major international organizations, including charter membership in the United Nations and most of its agencies. The Philippines is a member of the International Monetary Fund (IMF), the International Bank for Reconstruction and Development (IBRD, or the World Bank), the Asian Development Bank (ADB, which set up its international headquarters in Manila on its founding in 1966), the G-24 and G-77 international economic policy cooperative groups, and GATT and its successor body, the World Trade Organization (WTO). The Philippines became a provisional member of GATT as early as 1973 and has ratified the WTO, which obligates it to reduce its tariffs over a period of no more than 10 years.

The Philippines is also one of the organizers of ASEAN, which includes neighboring Indonesia, Malaysia, Thailand, Singapore, Vietnam, and Brunei. Although disputes and some lingering mistrust among the members of ASEAN have prevented it from achieving the level of cooperation and mutual support envisioned by its founders, ASEAN is nevertheless becoming increasingly important as a regional entity, and plans for greater economic cooperation are beginning to make headway. Philippine endorsement of the APEC goal to create a pan-Pacific free trade area is in line with its more activist stance towards international exchange and issues.

Trade Agreements

INTRODUCTION

The Philippines has historically pursued a trade policy that favored closed, highly protected markets. However, the current administration, like that of its predecessor, is committed to improving the overall trade and investment climate in order to open the Philippine economy to greater foreign participation and thereby secure the resources necessary to improve the national economy. Trade liberalization measures have thus begun to reverse roughly 40 years of protectionist policy that kept the Philippines near the bottom among developing Asian economies. Under a World Bank Structural Adjustment Program initiated in 1981 and scheduled for completion by July 1, 1995, the Philippine tariff structure has been compressed so that it now has four tariff levels instead of seven; the duty rates are 3, 10, 20, and 30 percent, with an average nominal tariff of 20 percent. Notable exceptions to tariff liberalization remain, particularly with respect to imports of competing agricultural products. Quantitative restrictions also exist on more than 100 agricultural and industrial commodities for health, safety, or national security reasons, and until full and final implementation of the new market access rules established under the General Agreement on Tariffs and Trade (GATT) agreement

concluded in 1993, several agricultural commodities will continue to be prohibited for import. Many additional items are unconditionally prohibited from import into the Philippines, including: dynamite, explosives, and firearms; pornography and written material inciting treason or rebellion; gambling paraphernalia; articles manufactured of precious metal that do not clearly indicate the actual fineness of quality of said metal; misbranded food or drug articles; and habit-forming drugs or related paraphernalia. (Refer to the "Import Policy & Procedures" chapter, beginning on page 79, for a more detailed discussion of import restrictions.)

International trade in the Philippines is regulated by many government agencies, often having overlapping or conflicting mandates. Each of the following, for example, controls some portion of trade in agricultural products: the Fiber Industry Development Authority; the Bureau of Plant Industry; the Department of Environment and Natural Resources; the National Food Authority; the Philippine Coconut Authority; the Sugar Regulatory Administration; and the Department of Trade. The textiles and garment industry is governed by both the Garments and Textile Export Board and the Fiber Industry Development Authority, as well as the Department of Trade and Industry. The Philippine International Trading Corporation, the Board of Investments, and the Bureau of Fisheries and Aquatic Resources also have some authority over many of the Philippines' major imports and exports. There are, moreover, many other agencies and regulations. It is best to check with the Department of Trade and Industry to verify compliance with all requirements and procedures prior to attempting to import or export any specific products to or from the Philippines.

The Philippines participates in several important global and regional trade agreements. Trade agreements are usually based on the reciprocal extension of trade privileges between the nationals of the sovereign parties to the specific agreement. They generally serve to lower tariffs, eliminate quota restrictions, or otherwise remove protectionist barriers to cross-border trade. These agreements coupled with the Philippines' unilateral trade liberalization programs have freed its markets and reduced its tariffs significantly. Although the Philippines remains moderately restrictive in terms of its trade policies, it nevertheless offers a promising environment for traders who are willing to become familiar with its trade practices and current areas of opportunity; who establish good contacts in the market; and who have a solid understanding of Philippine trade regulations and treaties.

MOST FAVORED NATION STATUS (MFN)

Rather than the special preferential status that the name implies, most favored nation (MFN) status represents what has come to be seen as the norm in bilateral trade relationships between countries. In fact, the Philippines grants MFN status to every country with which it trades. Under MFN status both parties agree not to extend to any third-party nation any trade preferences which are more favorable than those available under the agreement concluded between them, unless they simultaneously make the same provisions available to each other. MFN status is reciprocal: each party agrees to grant the status to the other. Nonetheless, MFN must be negotiated on a separate basis with each and every country, and each such agreement will include additional and specific provisions relating to national security, dispute settlement procedures, trade promotion, and various other matters.

Although in theory MFN status requires equivalent treatment of all trading partners, international law and practice does recognize that specific countries may make additional arrangements granting special preferences to other nations without violating MFN precepts. Such arrangements include free trade areas between two or more countries and commodity-specific and/or country-specific preferences. International canons approve such arrangements provided the agreement contains explicit rules of origin specifying limits to the benefits and the special rate preferences are achieved by lowering internal rates among the participants rather than by raising external tariffs.

THE GENERALIZED SYSTEM OF PREFERENCES (GSP)

Under the terms of GATT, Generalized System of Preferences (GSP) programs have been set up by many industrialized nations to assist developing nations by granting selective waivers or reductions of tariffs on imports of products from these developing nations. Basically, GSP programs are designed to help products from underdeveloped countries become competitive in developed country markets. GSP programs in the US, Japan, Canada, and the European Union (EU) promote growth in and exports from developing countries while also reducing the cost to national consumers of many imported products.

The Philippines is a beneficiary of GSP programs of the US, Japan, the EU, and Canada, among others. Certain Philippine products can be imported either free of duty or subject to reduced duties into these countries if they meet the GSP requirements.

Basic Requirements Philippine goods must meet seven basic requirements to be imported into these countries duty-free under the GSP:

- The product must be imported from the Philippines;
- The product must be on the GSP eligible products list;
- The product must be entirely grown, produced, or manufactured in the Philippines, or it must be primarily the product of the Philippines with a minimum of 35 percent of its value coming from the cost of materials and/or direct costs of processing in the Philippines;
- Proper documentation, including a certified United Nations Conference on Trade and Development (UNCTAD) Certificate of Origin Form A, must be submitted in addition to normal customs entry documentation;
- The product must be exported directly from the Philippines to the grantee country;
- The exporter must formally request GSP status; and
- The product must meet the competitive needs limitations of the importing country, which can be used to limit preferential treatment of specific products from particular countries.

GSP rules exist in addition to regular customs regulations and procedures, and GSP imports remain subject to all regular customs requirements such as those governing packing, marking and labeling, and restrictions and prohibitions on products imported.

Eligible Products Raw materials are excluded from GSP programs, which generally cover processed and manufactured products. For importation into the US, for example, products eligible for special GSP status are identified in the Harmonized Tariff Schedule of the United States (HTSUS) by an "A" in column 1, next to the appropriate HTSUS product classification. If the product is marked by an "A*" it is GSP eligible, but may lose eligibility due to competitive needs limitations; that is, if GSP imports of specified products from particular countries exceed an established level—generally if they account for more than 50 percent of all such imports—the product loses its preferential treatment for as long as the situation persists. If GSP eligible products account for a disproportionate amount of total imports of the product, they are considered to be competitive without the advantage of preferential treatment. If products are not GSP eligible, the general MFN tariff rate applies.

GATT AND THE WTO

Known generally as GATT, the General Agreement on Tariffs and Trade is designed to provide a standard framework for global trade. Founded in 1947 with 23 members, GATT has passed through eight series of negotiations, known as rounds and named after the location where the opening sessions of each round were held. The most recent is the Uruguay Round, begun in 1986. Initially this round was to have been completed by 1990, but was extended as the agreement became more ambitious and more difficult to conclude. The Uruguay Round finally came to include an overall tariff reduction of 38 percent—higher than the less ambitious reduction originally targeted—the reduction of nontariff barriers, and the integration of a series of bilateral Multi-Fiber Arrangements (MFA) into a single multilateral agreement that has the effect of phasing out quotas on textiles. The final agreement also included provisions on services, intellectual property rights (IPR), and subsidies. The final document proposed the adoption of the provisions and an agreement to submit to the authority of a newly created body, the World Trade Organization (WTO), which will have the authority to hand down binding decisions in trade disputes.

Signed in December 1993 by 124 member countries, GATT was ratified by the Philippines on December 19, 1994. Since the agreement was signed, several other countries—including China, Russia, and Taiwan—have applied for membership.

Effects The agreement is expected to facilitate international trade through increased outsourcing of intermediate products and parts, allowing various producers to achieve greater economies of scale by removing artificial barriers to sources and markets.

GATT is also on record as promoting international free trade and opposing regional trade blocs that may lead to preferential treatment among members at the expense of nonmembers. This would theoretically include such bodies as, the Association of Southeast Asian Nations (ASEAN), of which the Philippines is a member.

Provisions The Uruguay Round final agreement consists of more than 20,000 pages of text, so the actual extent of its provisions is expected to remain unclear for some time. In general, GATT calls for the replacement of absolute quotas, which bar imports of quota items above a threshold level, with tariff rate quotas, which allow in essentially unlimited quantities but at higher duties. Eventually the levels on such tariff rate quotas are supposed to be reduced as well. Other notable provisions involve strengthened IPR protections; the elimination of local content requirements; an agreement to remove national health and safety regulations as barriers to international trade; and conventions regarding the opening of service industries.

Of major importance to the Philippines are the provisions involving trade in textiles and apparel. Under GATT, fiber, cloth, and garment imports and exports are to be deregulated over a period of 10 years. As a major exporter of these items, the Philippines anticipates a positive economic impact from the opening of these markets, although the lengthy phaseout period may serve to reduce the amount of the benefit actually received.

The Uruguay Round agreement also calls for limitations on voluntary restraint agreements; changes in how anti-dumping charges are calculated, assessed, and resolved; limits on government subsidies to various industries and activities; and an agreement to revisit the area of free trade in services.

Industrialized signatory countries are to eliminate tariffs on a variety of products, including beer, distilled spirits, construction equipment, farm machinery, medical devices, furniture, paper products, pharmaceuticals, steel, and toys. Tariffs on chemicals are to be phased out over a 15-year period, with some strategic exceptions allowed. Tariffs are to be lowered on electronic products such as semiconductors and pharmaceuticals, with both expected to receive added protection under IPR provisions. Under these new IPR rules, trademarks will be protected for 7 years, patents for 20 years, and copyrights for 50 years. Official research and development (R&D) subsidies will also be limited to no more than 75 percent for basic research and 50 percent for applied research.

Areas of Disagreement The Philippines' initial concern over the liberalization of agricultural imports was alleviated by the inclusion of what were felt to be appropriate safety provisions for affected farming sectors. However, the Philippines continues to maintain that as a developing country with a low per capita Gross Domestic Product (GDP) it cannot and should not be expected to assume all of its obligations under the GATT and WTO at the same pace as more developed countries.

Specific areas excluded from GATT due to a failure of the major parties to reach agreement include aircraft, entertainment, financial services, shipping, steel, and telecommunications. The main antagonists over most of these issues have been the US and the EU.

The WTO Designed along the lines of such independent international bodies as the International Bank for Reconstruction and Development (IBRD, or the World Bank) and the International Monetary Fund (IMF), the WTO will conduct future trade policy negotiations among GATT signatories and be responsible for adjudicating disputes. The WTO will operate through a bureaucracy and three judge panels which will arbitrate specific disputes in closed sessions. Unlike GATT, which required open procedures and a consensus verdict and in which the loser could simply veto an unfavorable ruling, WTO decisions may be appealed, but the final results will be binding. Nations failing to conform their practices and laws to WTO rulings may have compensatory sanctions levied against them. Any signatory may withdraw from the WTO, but this is expected to have major repercussions as the body becomes more established.

GATT and the WTO will become separate organizations, with GATT being phased out as new business is shifted over to the WTO. In reality the two will overlap for some time because the WTO is not ready to begin functioning. There was not even a chief executive appointed until spring of 1995 because of bickering among the major parties over whom to appoint.

ASSOCIATION OF SOUTHEAST ASIAN NATIONS (ASEAN)

Founded in 1967 with the signing of the Bangkok Declaration by the Foreign Ministers of Indonesia, Malaysia, the Philippines, Singapore, and Thailand (Brunei was added as a member in 1984, and Vietnam in 1995), ASEAN seeks to strengthen regional cohesion and self-reliance through economic, social, and cultural cooperation. The objectives of ASEAN are to accelerate economic growth, social progress, and cultural development in the region through joint endeavors in order to strengthen the foundation for a prosperous and peaceful community of Southeast Asian nations; to promote regional peace and stability; to promote active collaboration and mutual assistance in matters of common interest; and to collaborate more effectively for the greater utilization of agricultural and industrial resources, the expansion of trade, and improvement of transportation and communications throughout the region. ASEAN developed slowly during the first decade of its existence, partly because of the diverse economic interests, varied historical experience, and fragile

political ties among the original member states. ASEAN now presents itself as a powerful, more unified bargaining interest group within international organizations such as GATT and UNCTAD.

Economic ministers of the member countries usually meet twice a year to discuss common approaches to economic questions and to review cooperative programs. Decisions on economic questions are then referred to the foreign ministers or heads of government for final approval. Various sectoral committees and working groups have been established to deal with specific economic and social issues. Regular ministerial consultations also are held in such sectors as labor, social welfare, education, energy, and information.

The ASEAN region is one of the world's economic success stories in agriculture, industry, and trade. The economies range from resource-rich but still largely agricultural Indonesia, with a 1992 per capita GDP of US$661 (the per capita GDP of newly admitted Vietnam is even less, about US$230), to the highly industrialized city-state of Singapore, with a per capita GDP of US$17,215; in 1992 the Philippines had a per capita GDP of US$772. The ASEAN nations are mainly committed to market and export oriented economic growth strategies. Since the late 1980s, growth rates in these dynamic economies have increased steadily and in 1992 ranged from less than 2 percent for the Philippines to more than 10 percent for Thailand; the combined ASEAN economies (excluding Vietnam) grew by nearly 8 percent.

Pre-Vietnam ASEAN members account for 72 percent of the world's exports of rubber and compromise the world's largest source of tropical timber. Mineral resources include 26 percent of the world's tin exports and significant amounts of copper, coal, nickel, and tungsten. Although manufacturing sectors are gaining in importance, most ASEAN economies—except for those of Singapore and Brunei—are still largely agricultural, producing such commodities as rubber, palm oil, rice, copra, and coffee. The Philippines relies especially heavily on commercial cultivation and processing of primary agricultural products.

Although some achievements have occurred in all areas contemplated under ASEAN, the agreement has been unable to stimulate economic growth to the extent envisioned by the founders. As of 1994, Intra-ASEAN trade, although significant and growing, still accounts for less than 20 percent of total ASEAN trade. ASEAN is currently trying to increase this intra-organization activity, relying heavily on private sector initiatives. Indeed, the private sectors of all the member nations are playing an increasingly active role in ASEAN cooperation. The ASEAN Chambers of Commerce and Industry provide for closer cooperation among the private sector participants in the member countries and complement the efforts of the governments in building a stronger foundation for regional cooperation.

The primary trade aspects of the ASEAN compact have experienced some setbacks, as various member nations—particularly the Philippines, Indonesia, Malaysia, Brunei, and Vietnam—have advanced conflicting claims over portions of the Spratly Islands (although the most serious dispute over these islands has been between China and the Philippines). Alleged support by the Philippines for rebels on East Timor in their battle against Indonesia has also led to bad feelings between the two member nations.

ASEAN Supplemental Agreements

Preferential Trade Agreement (PTA) Under the 1977 PTA, members extend each other discounts on existing tariffs on a list of products traded. Initially these were products with little or no intra-ASEAN trade potential, and until 1987 the system covered only about 5 percent of trade between member states, including such regionally useless items as snowplows. Individual countries were also permitted to exclude any "sensitive" products from the list of preferential import tariffs. In December 1987 the meeting of ASEAN heads of government resolved to reduce such exclusions to a maximum of 10 percent of the number of items traded and to a maximum of 50 percent of the value of trade over the next five years (seven years for the less developed Philippines and Indonesia; Vietnam is to be incorporated into existing agreements as a less developed member). The items eligible for preferences have gradually risen in number, include items with market potential, and now number almost 20,000. Among these are such sensitive and important products as rice, sugar, crude oil, cement, and chemicals. In addition, discounts have risen to 50 percent. The Philippines is on schedule to enact its initial reductions by the deadline of July 1, 1995, and the liberalization of tariffs has clearly promoted the expansion of its trade with the rest of the region.

ASEAN Free Trade Area (AFTA) In January 1992, the Philippines and the other ASEAN countries agreed to create the ASEAN Free Trade Area (AFTA). AFTA covers several areas of cooperation, including the harmonization of standards, the reciprocal recognition of testing and certification, the removal of barriers to foreign investments, macroeconomic consultations, rules for fair competition, and the promotion of venture capital formation. When fully implemented, it will encompass a market of 425 million people that can draw foreign investment and compete more effectively with other Asian economies.

Common Effective Preferential Tariff (CEPT) At the heart of AFTA is the CEPT scheme, under which member countries agreed to reduce tariffs on products traded among themselves to a maximum of 20 percent within a period of 5 to 8 years and then further to range from 0 to 5 percent by the year 2008. CEPT originally covered all manufactured products, including capital goods and processed agricultural products (which together account for two-thirds of current intra-ASEAN trade), but excluded unprocessed agricultural products. However, because only Singapore and Malaysia adhered to the original tariff reduction schedule, it was modified in 1994 and now includes unprocessed agricultural products and other previously excluded items. There are still many details to be worked out, and AFTA trade has yet to show any significant growth. But the member nations appear to be committed to it and are expected to continue efforts toward full implementation. Unlike other ASEAN countries which began implementing CEPT on January 1, 1994, the Philippines will not begin implementation until its current tariff reforms are completed on July 1, 1995.

Included within CEPT are 15 products identified for "fast-track" tariff reduction to between 0 and 5 percent within seven years: vegetables, cement, chemicals, pharmaceuticals, fertilizers, plastics, rubber products, leather products, textiles, ceramic and glass products, gems and jewelry, copper cathodes, electronics, and wooden and rattan furniture. Other products that are not on the exclusion list or subject to fast-track treatment will undergo tariff reduction under normal time requirements.

CEPT allows member countries to exclude certain products from tariff reductions, including some unprocessed agricultural products, "general" products related to health or security, and "sensitive" products that go on a temporary exclusion list originally subject to review by the year 2001. The Philippine exclusion list consists of more than 350 unprocessed agricultural products, about 30 general exceptions, and roughly 650 temporary exclusions (mostly garments, processed food, paper, and motor vehicles). The total 1991 import value of these products was US$1.1 billion, of which less than 10 percent was imported from ASEAN. The Philippines claims its exclusion list is only "moderately restrictive," because only 12.8 percent of all tariff lines are excluded on a temporary basis. Negotiations continue regarding the gradual removal of products from the exclusion list.

ASEAN ministers agreed in late 1994 to shorten AFTA's implementation to 10 years. Tariffs now above 20 percent must be reduced to from 0 to 5 percent by 2003, and tariffs currently below 20 percent must fall to between 0 and 5 percent by

2000. Some additional goods will be subject to a new fast-track schedule under which tariffs are to be reduced to between 0 and 5 percent by 1998. The temporary list of excluded goods—originally subject to review in 2001—will be formally phased out over five years beginning in 1996. In all, AFTA should eventually cover virtually 100 percent of intra-ASEAN trade, up from the 85 percent of such trade originally envisioned.

ASEAN Industrial Complementation Agreement Begun in 1981, this program encourages member countries to produce complementary products in specific industrial sectors for preferential exchange among themselves to achieve specialization and economies of scale. Products include components to be used in the automobile industry. Another program defined projects—one to be undertaken by each member nation—which would serve to benefit the whole region. So far the Philippines has benefited little from this agreement. It selected phosphatic fertilizer for one of its projects, switched to pulp and paper, and later to copper fabrication, but has yet to implement this development in any significant way. Philippine participation has to date been limited to a couple of small-scale ventures.

ASEAN Industrial Joint Ventures (AIJV) The ASEAN program of greatest potential interest to foreign firms, an AIJV requires companies from only two of the six member countries to participate, and non-ASEAN firms can hold as much as a 49 percent equity share of the enterprise. Resultant products receive preferential treatment in the form of tariff reductions of up to 90 percent. The Philippines is currently cooperating with Malaysia in two AIJV projects involving mechanical engineering and with Thailand in one involving meat. Other projects include the manufacture of frit—an intermediate component in the ceramics industry—motorcycle electrical parts, constant-velocity joints, and steering mechanisms. Japanese investors have shown extreme interest in AIJVs, and there remains considerable room for growth in the program.

ASEAN Fund In 1988 the ASEAN Fund was established with capital of US$150 million to provide finance for portfolio investments in ASEAN countries, in particular for small and medium-sized companies.

ASEAN Reinsurance Corporation In 1988 this corporation was established after ASEAN members agreed to accelerate regional cooperation in the field of finance and banking in order to facilitate intra-ASEAN trade and investment; to increase the role of ASEAN currencies in regional trade; to assist in the avoidance of double taxation; and to improve the efficiency of tax and customs administrators.

ASEAN Agricultural Development Planning Centre This was set up to conduct research and

training and to draw up regional agricultural production plans.

ASEAN Emergency Grain Reserve Agreement An emergency reserve of grain is established each year; supplies are available to any member country on three days' notice.

ASEAN Fisheries Cooperation This agreement provides for the joint management of fish resources, the sharing of technology, and cooperation in marketing, as well as for the coordination and development of aquaculture in the region.

Other Agricultural Agreements Agreements for cooperation include: a Plant Quarantine Training Institute; an Agricultural Development Planning Center; a Forest Tree Seed Center; a post-harvest program for conserving grain; and an ASEAN center for training and research in poultry diseases.

ASEAN External Relations

The European Union A cooperation agreement exists between ASEAN and the EU providing for the strengthening of existing trade links and increased cooperation in the scientific and agricultural spheres. An ASEAN-EU Business Council provides a forum for businesspersons from the two regions and identifies joint projects. The EU adopted guidelines on development cooperation which increased assistance to ASEAN countries and changed the type of aid to be given to emphasize training, science and technology, and venture capital, rather than assistance for rural development. Two-way Euro-ASEAN trade is rising steadily; it approached US$57 billion in 1992.

Japan The ASEAN-Japan Forum was established to discuss matters of mutual concern in trade, investment, technology transfer, and development assistance. Tariff cuts on certain ASEAN exports were made by Japan in 1985, but ASEAN members continued to criticize Japan's attitude and called for Japan to import more manufactured products rather than raw materials. In 1987 Japan established an ASEAN-Japan Development Fund of about US$2 billion to assist ASEAN members over a three-year period, particularly in private sector industrial development projects. In May 1991 the Japanese Government declared its intention to continue to encourage economic growth in ASEAN members, while also trying to establish a framework for discussions on security and political matters. The first-ever meeting between ASEAN economic ministers and the Japanese Minister of International Trade and Industry was held in October 1992; ASEAN requested that Japan increase its investment in member countries and make Japanese markets more accessible to ASEAN products. At that time, Japan agreed to extend ASEAN's privileges under its generalized system of preferences until 2001. Japan also agreed to reduce its trade surplus with ASEAN members.

US The US gives assistance for the development of small and medium-sized businesses and other projects, and it supports a Center for Technology Exchange. In 1990 ASEAN and the US established an ASEAN-US Joint Working Group, the purpose of which is to review ASEAN's economic relations with the US and to identify measures by which economic links can be strengthened.

Indochina ASEAN has taken active steps to encourage trade with the countries of the former Indochina, although no formal agreements are yet in place. In 1992 Vietnam and Laos signed ASEAN's Treaty, the first stage toward becoming full members of the Association. In July 1993 ASEAN agreed to allow Vietnam to participate in regional cooperation programs in areas outside the economic and political sectors, including science and technology, the environment, health care, culture, and tourism. In mid-1995 Vietnam was extended full membership in ASEAN. ASEAN-Indochina trade links continue to grow, and greater cooperation is expected to develop between the nations involved.

Other Countries ASEAN holds regular dialogues on trade and other matters with the EU, US, Japan (as noted earlier), Australia, Canada, Korea, and New Zealand. It also receives assistance from these countries for various development projects. Under the ASEAN-Australia Economic Cooperation Programme, Australia provides financial support for ASEAN activities, and a joint Business Council was set up in 1980. New Zealand has given technical and financial assistance in forestry development, dairy technology, veterinary management, and legal aid training. ASEAN-Canada cooperation projects include fisheries technology, a joint program to reduce post-harvest crop losses, and a forest seed center. In July 1991 Korea was accepted as a dialogue partner; and a joint ASEAN-Korea Chamber of Commerce was established. There is discussion of establishing a center in Korea to promote trade and cooperation between ASEAN and that country. In July 1993 both India and Pakistan were accepted as sectoral partners, that is, nations that can participate in ASEAN meetings on sectors such as trade, transport and communications, and tourism.

OTHER AGREEMENTS

Special Trade Agreements

Cairns Group Established in 1986 by major agricultural exporting countries that do not provide subsidies for such exports, the goal of this agreement is to bring about reforms in international agricultural trade, including reductions in export subsidies, in barriers to access, and in internal support measures. It also represents its members' interests in GATT negotiations. Members include Argentina, Australia, Brazil, Canada, Chile, Colombia, Fiji, Hungary, Indonesia, New Zealand, Philippines, Thailand, and Uruguay. See page 69 for contact information

Pacific Economic Cooperation Conference (PECC) The PECC exists to bring senior government, business, and private institutional leaders together to examine key problems and issues influencing regional economic growth. It identifies regional interests in global issues as well, and it generally acts to facilitate regional cooperation in specific economic sectors. The PECC is increasingly viewed as the nucleus of a Pacific economic organization. With the establishment of a central fund to support greater participation by developing countries, the organization appears poised for further institutionalization. It was especially active in formulating common positions among Pacific region nations that helped produce substantive progress in the Uruguay Round of GATT trade negotiations. Members include: the ASEAN countries, plus Australia, Canada, China, Japan, Korea, New Zealand, Taiwan, and the US.

For further information contact the Philippine PECC Committee. See page 70 for contact information.

Asian Productivity Organization (APO) The APO was established 1961 under a convention signed by India, Japan, Korea, Pakistan, the Philippines, Taiwan, and Thailand in order to increase, by mutual cooperation, productivity in the countries of Asia.

Questions regarding current programs and other information may be addressed to the Secretary General of the APO in Tokyo. See page 69 for contact information.

Colombo Plan The Colombo Plan was established in 1950 to encourage economic and social development in Asia and the Pacific. It is primarily a funding program, and aid is provided bilaterally, with no central programming. Programs consist of grants and concessional loans for national projects; a technical cooperation program which provides experts and volunteers and awards training fellowships; a drug advisory program; and the Staff College for Technician Education in the Philippines. Members include Australia, Japan, New Zealand, the US (one of the program's primary donors), and nearly all of the Asian and Pacific countries. Canada and the UK left the organization in 1991–1992.

Customs Cooperation Council (CCC) The Philippines belongs to and adheres to the policies and procedures of the CCC, a multilateral body located in Brussels through which participating countries seek to simplify and rationalize customs procedures. The CCC also examines technical aspects and related economic factors of customs systems in order to obtain harmony and uniformity, while simplifying customs formalities.

United Nations Economic and Social Commission for Asia and the Pacific (ESCAP) The predecessor of ESCAP was originally set up in 1947 to initiate and participate in measures designed to facilitate economic and social development in Asia and the Pacific. It was further designed to strengthen relations among member nations, and between them and the rest of the world. ESCAP has been criticized for its failure to coordinate with other regional organizations, although it is currently revising its approach in an attempt to do so.

Related Agreements

The Asian Development Bank (ADB) The ADB's functions are to further investment in development projects within the region that contribute to the harmonious economic growth of the whole area; to assist Asian member countries in preparing and coordinating their development plans; and to provide technical aid for the preparation, financing, and execution of specific development projects.

The bank has expanded its assistance to the private sector, granting financial assistance in the form of equity and loans, without government guarantee, to small and medium-sized private enterprises. Interest rates are flexible and are set separately for each loan.

For questions regarding eligibility and procedures under current bank rules, contact the Information Director at ADB. See page 69 for contact information.

Intellectual Property Rights (IPR) The Philippines was removed from the US Trade Representative's special 301 "priority watch list" and placed on the "watch list" following a bilateral IPR agreement signed between the Philippines and the US in April 1993. The agreement commits the Philippine government to significantly strengthen the protection of intellectual property rights. The Philippine government is also a party to the Paris Convention for the Protection of Industrial Property, the Patent Cooperation Treaty, and the Berne Convention for the Protection of Literary and Artistic Works, and it is a member of the World Intellectual Property Organization. However, the lack of adequate and effective protection for IPR in the Philippines remains a trade concern.

Globalized Comprehensive Import Supervision Scheme (CISS) The Philippine government has engaged the services of the Société Generale de Surveillance S.A. (SGS) to implement the CISS.

Under this scheme, all importations into the Philippines valued at US$500 or more from whatever source are to be subject to preshipment inspection by the SGS in the country of origin. Guidance on this system and compliance procedures are available from SGS' main US office in New York City.

Commodities Agreements

Committee for Coordination of Joint Prospecting for Mineral Resources in Asian Offshore Areas (CCOP/East Asia) The CCOP/East Asia was formed in 1966 to reduce the cost of advance mineral surveying and prospecting and to work in partnership with technical advisers provided by developed nations.

Asian and Pacific Coconut Community Established to promote, coordinate, and harmonize all activities of the coconut industry, the community is designed to promote better production, processing, marketing, and research of coconut products.

Group of Latin American and Caribbean Sugar Exporting Countries This group was established to serve as a forum for consultation on the production and sale of sugar; to contribute to the adoption of joint positions at international meetings on sugar; to provide training and the transfer of technology; to exchange scientific and technical knowledge on agriculture and the sugar industry; to coordinate the various branches of sugar processing; and to coordinate policies of action in order to achieve fair and remunerative prices. Membership includes 22 Latin American and Caribbean countries and the Philippines. Together, the members account for about 45 percent of world sugar exports and 66 percent of world sugarcane production.

Others The Philippines is a signatory to several other international commodities agreements, including the International Sugar Agreement (with 33 members, headquartered in London); the International Wheat Agreement (36 members, headquartered in London); and the Agricultural Commodities Agreement with the US, under Title I of the US Agricultural Trade Development and Assistance Act.

Bilateral Agreements

Business Cooperation Network Known as BCNet, this newly signed agreement with the EU is expected to further strengthen Philippine trade relations with European countries. It provides for a package of investment programs that will enhance trade and investment opportunities between the Philippines and the EU.

Others The Philippines has recently concluded bilateral trade agreements with Saudi Arabia, Kuwait, the United Arab Emirates, Bulgaria, Cambodia, Romania, and some members of the Newly Independent States (NIS, the former USSR), all of which provide for more liberalized trade regulations and tariffs among the individual parties.

EMERGING TRADE AGREEMENTS

Asia Pacific Economic Cooperation (APEC) Founded in 1989, APEC is an informal working group composed of 18 Pacific Rim nations. Although no formal and legally binding agreement exists as yet, the members seem committed to forging a regional alliance of free and open trade. At their annual conference in Indonesia in November 1994, the members endorsed the "Bogor Declaration," which calls for "free and open trade and investment" throughout the region. The accord calls for the elimination of internal trade barriers by developed country members by 2010 and by developing country members by 2020. The group opposes protectionism and the creation of exclusionary regional trading blocs while promoting the expansion of trade. The accord also goes on record as supporting rapid implementation of the provisions of GATT; harmonization of international product testing and safety standards; simplification of customs procedures; and development of an international dispute resolution system.

Observers note that although the accord is long on generalities and short on specifics and definitions (participants could not even agree on the meaning of the term "free and open trade"), it is remarkable that the diverse nations were able to reach a consensus on any agreement. Many of the lesser developed countries lobbied for an even longer phase-in period and more gradual introduction for any significant provisions, and others disagreed on the implications of definitions to be used, questioning the intentions of some of the other members. In particular, some members questioned the good faith of the US, fearing that the country could try to turn the organization into a forum for advancing its own agenda at the expense of the interests of some of the other, less powerful, members.

Together the APEC member countries account for 42 percent of total world trade, 52 percent of world GDP, and 38 percent of world population. Members include the ASEAN countries, Australia, Canada, Chile, Taiwan, Hong Kong, Japan, Korea, Mexico, New Zealand, Papua New Guinea, China, and the US.

TRADE ZONES

Four areas in the Philippines and ten privately owned industrial sites have been designated as Export Processing Zones (EPZs) for purposes of encouraging investment, industrial expansion, employment generation, promotion of export production, foreign exchange generation, and

transfer of technology. They are open to foreigners as well as Philippine nationals and enjoy liberalized tax, customs, and labor procedures and regulations. (Refer to the "Export Policy & Procedures" beginning on page 93, and "Trade Zones" beginning on page 71, for a more detailed discussion of EPZs.)

USEFUL ADDRESSES

Philippine Government Organizations

Bureau of International Trade Relations
Department of Trade and Industry
361 Sen. Gil J. Puyat Avenue
Makati, Metro Manila, Philippines
Tel: [63](2) 817-8087
Fax: [63] (2) 818-7846

Philippine Economic Zone Authority (PEZA)
4th Fl., Legaspi Towers 300
Roxas Boulevard
Metro Manila, Philippines
Tel: [63] (2) 521-9725, 521-0546/7, 521-0585
Fax: [63] (2) 521-8659

International Trade Organizations

Asian Development Bank (ADB)
6 ADB Avenue
1501 Mandaluyong, Metro Manila, Philippines
Tel: [63] (2) 632-4444
Fax: [63] (2) 741-7961
WWW server: http://www.asiandevbank.org

Asian Productivity Organization (APO)
8-4-14 Akasata
Minato-ku
Tokyo 107, Japan
Tel: [81] (3) 3408-7221
Fax: [81] (3) 3408-7220.

Asia Pacific Economic Cooperation (APEC)
c/o Ministry of Trade and Industry
Public Relations
Treasury Bldg.
8 Treasury Way, No. 48-01
Singapore 0106
Tel: [65] 225-9911
Fax: [65] 320-9260

Cairns Group
c/o Department of Foreign Affairs and Trade
Bag 8
Queen Victoria Terrace
Canberra, ACT 2600, Australia
Tel: [61] (6) 261-9111
Fax: [61] (6) 273-3577

Colombo Plan
12 Melbourne Ave.
PO Box 596
Colombo 4, Sri Lanka
Tel: [94] (1) 581-813
Fax: [94] (1) 508-4240

Customs Cooperation Council (CCC)
26-38 rue de l'Industrie
1040 Brussels, Belgium
Tel: [32] (2) 508-4211
Fax: [32] (2) 308-4240

Pacific Economic Cooperation Council (PECC)
Philippine Committee
PO Box 10196
Makati, Metro Manila, Philippines
Tel: [63] (2) 816-2664

United Nations Economic and Social Commission
for Asia and the Pacific (ESCAP)
United Nations Bldg.
Rajadamnern Ave.
Bangkok 10200, Thailand
Tel: [66] (2) 282-9161
Fax: [66] (2) 282-9602

World Trade Organization (WTO)
Centre William Rappard
154, rue de Lausanne
CH-1211 Geneva, Switzerland
Tel: [41] (22) 739-5019
Fax: [41] (22) 731-4606

Trade Zones

INTRODUCTION

The Philippines has three main types of economic trade zones that can benefit international traders and investors: Export Processing Zones (EPZs), Special Export Processing Zones (SEPZs), and other Special Economic and Freeport Zones. These special zones are administered by the Philippine Economic Zone Authority (PEZA), the successor body to the Export Processing Zone Authority (EPZA). This new organization is the result of the Special Economic Zone Act of 1995 (R.A. 7916) , which took effect in June 1995. Under this act, the PEZA is to be granted additional authority and broader functions, although the details the new system have yet to be worked out.

All types of zones are basically similar in terms of their purposes and the benefits they offer to international traders. Their main purposes are to attract foreign investors to the Philippines, boost the Philippine economy, and offer incentives to companies manufacturing goods for export. The primary benefits include reduced taxes, exemption from certain fees, a streamlining of documentary procedures, a high-quality labor supply, and a high-quality business infrastructure.

The major difference between EPZs and SEPZs is that the former are owned by the government and the latter are owned by private investors. The

CONTENTS

government first sponsored EPZs in the late 1970s and early 1980s. Four EPZs were established at that time and continue to exist and expand today. However, the government has made no plans to open any more EPZs. Instead it has encouraged private investment in industrial estates, designating them as SEPZs and offering benefits identical to those offered by EPZs.

To receive economic benefits, EPZ and SEPZ companies are required to export 100 percent of the goods they manufacture. However, with prior approval from the Philippine Economic Zone Authority (PEZA) and upon payment of necessary taxes and duties, 30 percent may be sold locally. Goods may also be traded with other companies operating in the zone. The PEZA governs production within the individual EPZs and SEPZs. For the address of the PEZA, *see* "Useful Addresses" on page 77.

The Subic Bay Special Economic and Freeport Zone—the main one of this type to date—is identified separately primarily because of its unique infrastructure (when the US Navy left the Subic Bay Navy Base in November of 1992, it left behind facilities valued at US$8 billion) and because of the additional special benefits that are being offered to potential investors in the zone. Other similar operations are planned at the Clark Economic Zone on Luzon and Southern Mindanao Zone. All three types of zones—EPZs, SEPZs, and Special Economic and Freeport Zones—are regarded by the Philippine government as existing outside of the national customs territory.

Because there are differences in terms of origin, geography, and internal structure, EPZs and SEPZs will be discussed separately later. However, the advantages of using EPZs and SEPZs are essentially identical in all particulars, and the similar advantages will be described jointly. Following the discussion of EPZs and SEPZs, there is a separate discussion of the

Special Economic and Freeport Zones.

EXPORT PROCESSING ZONES

Overview

More than 200 companies are registered to operate in the four original EPZs. Production in the zones accounts for a significant proportion of the Philippines' export earnings. Total export earnings from EPZ operations in 1991 amounted to US$819 million—roughly 10 percent of total Philippine exports—and up from US$579.6 million in 1990 and US$444.1 million in 1989. The leading foreign investors in the EPZs consist of companies from Japan, the US, the Netherlands, South Korea, Bermuda, Taiwan, the UK, and Hong Kong.

All types of goods may be manufactured and traded in EPZs. These include food products, garments, wood products, metal products and machinery, chemicals, rubber and plastics products, minerals, electronics, and components—such as semiconductors—and computer equipment. However, the greatest emphasis has been on the manufacture of electronic products and apparel.

Practically all of the existing buildings in the four EPZs are now occupied, and any newcomers to the EPZs will need to build their own facilities.

Individual EPZs

Three of the four EPZs exist on the island of Luzon in the northern Philippines. They are the Bataan EPZ, the Baguio City EPZ, and the Cavite EPZ. The other EPZ—the Mactan EPZ—is located on the island of Mactan in the central Philippines, in the province of Cebu, near the city of the same name.

The Bataan EPZ is the largest and oldest of the four zones, but its development has been the slowest. Some 45 firms operate in the zone, with most being involved in the manufacture of garments. Other manufacturing activities include processing of food, beverages, wood products, metal products, chemicals, and other nonmetallic products.

The Baguio City EPZ houses two semiconductor firms: Texas Instruments—a US firm—and a German firm, Golf Electronics. Although only 12 firms in total operate in this zone, the Baguio City EPZ has the highest earnings of the four zones in the country. Located on the western end of the Central Cordillera mountain range in northern Luzon at 1,540 m (5,000 ft) above sea level, it enjoys cool weather all year round and is particularly suitable for operations requiring cool temperatures and humidity control.

The Cavite EPZ hosted 106 firms as of March 1993. It is the newest of the four EPZs, houses the largest number of firms, and is the closest of the EPZs to Manila. Garments and electronics account for 60 percent of the products exported. As the zone matures, investment is moving away from the traditional base of low-tech textile and light manufacturing toward more high-tech operations such as computer and consumer electronics assembly. The zone's future will depend on its ability to maintain its infrastructure as it expands, as well as on the results of competition from the newer and relatively nearby Subic Bay Special Economic and Freeport Zone.

The Mactan EPZ had 56 firms operating in April of 1994 and, next to the Baguio City EPZ, is the zone earning the highest income. It is located near the Port of Cebu, the second busiest port in the Philippines; it is also near Mactan International Airport. Profitable tenants in this zone include National Semiconductor, Timex, Asahi Optical Philippines Corporation, and United Technologies. Firms here produce electronics and electrical goods, car stereos, auto wire harnesses, garments, fashion accessories, gift items, and housewares. Cebu City has recently announced plans to expand the export zone in Mactan. The zone is known for its reliable labor supply. A current challenge is to ensure that the zone's infrastructure can be improved to support expansion. The development and maintenance of an adequate water supply is especially important as several water-intensive industries, such as semiconductor and electronic component manufacturers are located there.

Special Export Processing Zones

There are three industrial estates in the Philippines at which the entire area has been designated as a Special Export Processing Zone:

1. The Tabangao Special EPZ. Located in Batangas City, Southern Luzon, this SEPZ is operated by the Shell Gas Philippines Company, a 100 percent Dutch-owned company. Shell operates a liquefied petroleum gas production plant in this zone.

2. The Leyte Industrial Development Estate. Located in Isabel, Leyte in the Visayas, this SEPZ is occupied by four industrial firms that process and market copper slag, ammonium sulfate, and phosphate fertilizer.

3. The Philippine Shipyard and Engineering Corporation. Located near the Subic Bay Special Economic and Freeport Zone, this is the site of one of the largest shipbuilding and repair companies in Southeast Asia.

In addition to these three industrial estates, seven other private industrial estates registered with the Board of Investments (BOI) have cooperated to form the Philippine Industrial Estates Association. Certain areas within these private estates have been classified as SEPZs Six of the industrial estates are located within 30 km (19 mi) of Manila—in the fast-

ADVANTAGES OF USING EPZS AND SEPZS

1. Tax benefits. EPZs and SEPZs offer a number of tax benefits, including: (1) an exemption from local taxes, contractor's taxes, franchise taxes, amusement taxes, and occupation taxes; (2) a fixed tax on manufacturing, producing, and wholesaling; (3) a six-year exemption from all income tax for "pioneer" firms (firms that produce goods currently not produced, use materials or employ technologies not previously exploited, develop new applications for the agricultural sector, or develop new fuel sources for use in the Philippines) and a four-year exemption for nonpioneer (that is, all other preferred investment) firms; and (4) an exemption from the 15 percent branch profits remittance tax on profits remitted abroad.

2. No customs duties. No customs duties are levied on materials brought into the zone. This includes raw materials, foreign and domestic equipment, and machinery and spare parts.

3. Exemption from fees. Exemption from wharfage, storage, and water rental fees.

4. Simplified documentation procedures. Exporting firms are exempt from filing the Report of Foreign Sales (BSP), Export Entry (Customs), and Export Clearance (Bureau of Internal Revenue) documents. Imports do not need an import clearance from the Board of Investments (BOI) or release documents from the BSP. EPZs and SEPZs handle various bureaucratic requirements directly on behalf of the user, from immigration to drafting articles of incorporation and registering with the Securities and Exchange Commission and the Board of Investment.

5. Exemption from government inspection. Goods bound for zone enterprises are exempt from government inspection because zones are not officially part of Philippine customs territory.

6. Management support. Zone management works to meet the needs of individual and collective investor demands.

7. Superior infrastructure. EPZs and SEPZs usually offer better infrastructure and facilities than are to be found in most other areas of the country. The industrial sites have already been prepared. Because civil works have been completed and utilities installed, investors can concentrate on installing their production lines and operating their businesses. Utilities—such as power, telecommunications, sewage, industrial waste disposal, and water—are usually more dependable than in the rest of the country.

8. High-quality labor. The Philippine workforce is efficient, trainable, and cost competitive, and it compares favorably to the workforces in other countries in the region.

9. Expatriate employment is welcome. Zone enterprises may employ non-Philippine citizens in supervisory, technical, or advisory positions during the five-year period after registration. Immigration requirements are simplified for these employees and their families.

10. No limits on foreign ownership or equity. Companies may be wholly owned and controlled by non-Filipinos.

growing CALABARZON region south of Manila—while the seventh is located within 100 km (62 mi) of Manila. Like the firms located in the EPZs, the operations found in these SEPZs produce all kinds of goods, with a growing emphasis on electronic and other higher-value-added technology items. For a list of these seven industrial estates, *see* "Useful Addresses" on page 77.

Other industrial estates in the Philippines continue to be designated as SEPZs. Potential investors should contact local officials to learn of opportunities and new developments.

Considerations for Potential Investors

The best investment opportunities appear to be for financially strong, high-technology companies that have experience doing business overseas. Potential investors should negotiate strongly for their minimum requirements, make independent arrangements if necessary, and ensure that they have a guaranteed stake in future resource allocations. Smaller investors—such as electronic component makers able to supply computer companies using the zones—who align themselves with established companies can probably also successfully operate within the framework of the export

PHILIPPINE
TRADE ZONES

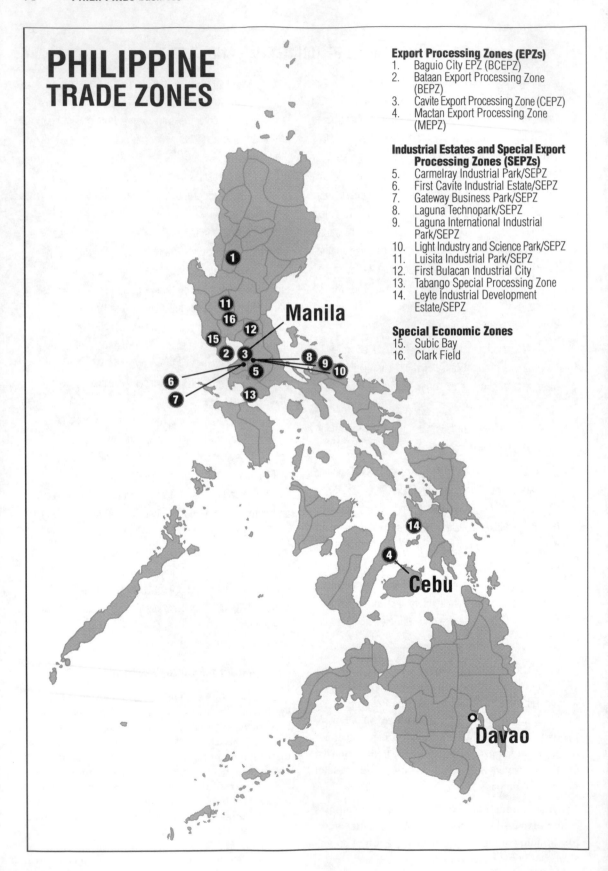

Export Processing Zones (EPZs)
1. Baguio City EPZ (BCEPZ)
2. Bataan Export Processing Zone (BEPZ)
3. Cavite Export Processing Zone (CEPZ)
4. Mactan Export Processing Zone (MEPZ)

Industrial Estates and Special Export Processing Zones (SEPZs)
5. Carmelray Industrial Park/SEPZ
6. First Cavite Industrial Estate/SEPZ
7. Gateway Business Park/SEPZ
8. Laguna Technopark/SEPZ
9. Laguna International Industrial Park/SEPZ
10. Light Industry and Science Park/SEPZ
11. Luisita Industrial Park/SEPZ
12. First Bulacan Industrial City
13. Tabango Special Processing Zone
14. Leyte Industrial Development Estate/SEPZ

Special Economic Zones
15. Subic Bay
16. Clark Field

Manila

Cebu

Davao

processing zones. But investors who have not yet clearly identified their market and with little or no previous overseas experience are likely to find doing business in the Philippines a difficult, if not daunting, prospect.

ADVANTAGES OF EPZS AND SEPZS

The main advantages of EPZs and SEPZs are a reduction of customs duties and taxes and a simplification of documentation procedures. Also, because sites are dedicated solely to manufacturing, industry, and trade, conducting business with a zone is more efficient and easier than maintaining business outside a zone.

All sites have the basic infrastructure necessary for manufacturing, including water supply, electric power, telecommunications facilities, housing and commercial complexes, banks, post offices, transportation services, roads, sewage and garbage disposal facilities, and security services. Local officials in the areas of the EPZs and SEPZs have been especially supportive of the operations.

The Philippines is a good source of relatively cheap and highly trainable labor. The productivity of the Philippine worker is ranked high compared with that of workers in many neighboring countries. And because EPZs and SEPZs often offer the choicest jobs in a region, labor relations are generally smooth. (However, some observers note that a rivalry may be developing between those who work in the more prestigious high-tech industries and those working in low-tech industries.) Each export zone is expected to publish a labor productivity record, and potential investors should ask to see these reports before deciding to invest.

PROCEDURES FOR USING EPZS

Application

Any person, firm, or corporation, regardless of nationality or ownership of controlling capital, may apply for registration as a zone export enterprise. A company applying for space in an EPZ must submit a report to the Philippine Economic Zone Authority (PEZA) in which the technical, financial, and market viability of the enterprise is detailed. It must contain a five-year projection of the company's revenues, expenses, and cash flow. The company must also supply copies of its articles of incorporation, a list of major officers and stockholders, and income tax returns for the previous three years or covering the full period of the company's existence, if less than three years.

The proposal will be evaluated by the PEZA's Project Evaluation and Review Department, which submits a recommendation to the PEZA Board, which makes its decision within two weeks after receiving the recommendation. If the project is approved, the applicant is given 20 days in which to accept and sign the registration agreement with the PEZA.

Production, Manipulation, and Transportation of Goods

As a general rule, the production of all types of permitted goods is allowed in an EPZ. However, the manufacture of guns, explosives, firearms, ammunitions, and similar items requires clearance from the Department of National Defense.

Most of the EPZs are located conveniently near an airport or seaport, allowing firms to import raw materials and other goods easily into the EPZ. Goods need not be inspected to enter the zone. While in a zone, goods can be manipulated in any standard business fashion.

All zone cargo in transit between a seaport or airport and an EPZ is escorted and guarded by PEZA police; a nominal fee is charged for this service. Eighty service companies registered with the PEZA offer customs brokerage, trucking, and freight handling services in the zones.

In 1988 the PEZA and the Philippine Bureau of customs cooperated to form the EEZA-Customs Documentation Unit (ECDU). The ECDU expedites imports, exports, and the movement of cargo for all PEZA enterprises. The ECDU has offices in the South Harbor, at the Manila International Container Port, the Ninoy Aquino International Airport, and the Port of Cebu.

Although procedures for using SEPZs are basically the same as those for EPZs, potential investors should contact individual SEPZs for specific application requirements and procedural information. For more information in general, contact the PEZA. (See "Useful Addresses" on page 77 for address and contact information.)

SUBIC BAY SPECIAL ECONOMIC AND FREEPORT ZONE

The Subic Bay Metropolitan Authority (SBMA) administers the Subic Bay Freeport, formerly a US naval base. Because of the extensive infrastructure left by the US Navy when it vacated the Subic Bay Naval Base in November1992, plus the potential it holds for international traders, the Subic Bay Special Economic and Freeport Zone has several special characteristics apart from the EPZs and SEPZs. Everything at Subic Bay is available on a 25-year lease, renewable for a second 25-year period. The freeport zone guarantees—for the life of the lease—a 5 percent flat tax on profits, no controls on foreign exchange, free repatriation of profits and dividends, and exemption from all other national and local taxes.

History and Infrastructure

On November 24, 1992, the US Navy turned over the Subic Bay Naval Base (the largest US naval base outside of the US) to the Philippine Government. The 6,000 hectare (15,000 acre) site contains infrastructure and facilities, including:

- Public utilities such as power plants, electricity, water, and sewer systems.
- More than 1,000 buildings of various sizes that can be converted to manufacturing and commercial use.
- More than 1,800 fully air conditioned housing units with supporting community facilities such as schools, shopping, and commercial centers.
- Sports and medical facilities.
- One large airport.
- Dry-dock and harbor facilities which can safely anchor and harbor 600 ships.
- A nature reservation that could possibly be developed for tourism. The jungle around Subic offers numerous species of native wildlife, including iguanas, pythons, wild boar, exotic birds, and many species of monkeys.

Purpose

The new Subic Bay Freeport encourages enterprises from any country in any area of economic activity—other than those restricted by Philippine law—to do business in the freeport zone. Subic Bay's master plan calls for the establishment of a convention center to attract business from neighboring Asian countries; a trade and exposition center; and a commercial business complex. Opportunities in tourism-related activities are also available.

Advantages and Disadvantages at Subic Bay

Incentives for doing business in Subic Bay include:

1. Duty-free import and export of all goods and materials;
2. Unrestricted foreign ownership of business;
3. No foreign exchange controls;
4. Free markets in gold, futures, and securities;
5. No limit on the sale of goods into the Philippine domestic economy (although to qualify for tax incentives, registered firms must export at least 70 percent of production);
6. No taxes except for a 5 percent tax on gross income (compared to a 35 percent corporate income tax in the rest of the country);
7. Permanent resident visas issued to investors of at least US$250,000 valid for the duration of the investment; and
8. An efficient, motivated, trainable, and relatively inexpensive labor force; some 20,000 skilled and semiskilled Philippine workers who had been employed by the US Navy are available to readily transfer to private sector firms who establish operations in Subic Bay.

Concerns for the potential investor include the fact that although a great deal of money has been raised for the Subic Bay Freeport, the extent of its financial foundation is still uncertain. Unlike the EPZs, the Subic Bay Freeport hopes to pay for itself. In addition, traffic connections between the Subic Bay Freeport and Manila will need to be improved substantially. There is also a natural risk from nearby Mount Pinatubo, which erupted in June of 1991 and covered Subic with volcanic ash. Fortunately, intermediary mountain ranges protected the Subic Bay Navy base from mudflows, but the risk remains. Finally, political rivalries among officials who want to influence the future of Subic Bay may make doing business there a bit less inviting, but in light of the economic potential of this site, the future of Subic as a freeport is likely to be the decisive factor in any disagreements among local political factions.

Investors

One year after the US Navy left Subic Bay, more than 300 investment proposals had been received and processed, and more than 100 other proposals were under evaluation. A variety of international investors from the US, Hong Kong, Switzerland, Australia, Malaysia, Taiwan, and other areas of the Philippines have been interested in Subic. Since 1992, the number of actual investors has grown dramatically, from two companies in 1992 to 36 by the end of 1993 and 75 by the middle of 1994. By the end of the first quarter of 1994, there were seven banks and eight duty-free shops operating in the freeport. Investments are expected to accelerate in 1995, averaging US$1.2 billion per year thereafter.

Manufacturing Opportunities

Specific manufacturing opportunities include electronics manufacturing and assembly; vehicle assembly; pharmaceutical manufacturing; computer hardware manufacturing; software development, and data processing; jewelry, garment, and footwear manufacture and assembly; industrial and electrical equipment manufacturing, and the production of toys. Sites for heavy industries such as shipbuilding are available in the immediate off-base vicinity.

The Future of Subic Bay and Its Effect on EPZs

There has been a great deal of activity at Subic Bay, but it is still too early to call the zone an unqualified success. Nevertheless, the development of the Subic Bay Freeport is considered to be a top priority of the Philippine government and, for the potential investor, this means maximum support and a minimum of bureaucratic delays.

It is not yet known what effect the Subic Bay Freeport will have on the preexisting EPZs. The zone most likely to be hurt is the Bataan EPZ, which is closest to Subic geographically and which has none of its infrastructure advantages. The Baguio EPZ, dominated by its Texas Instruments facility, is least likely to be affected, and may even benefit from high-tech suppliers that could establish operations at Subic Bay.

The Cavite EPZ, which is still developing, should be able to compete with the Subic Bay Freeport. An advantage of the Cavite EPZ is that it is very close to Manila. However, if the Subic Bay Freeport begins to prosper greatly, the Cavite EPZ may have a difficult time attracting the additional investors it needs to secure its own future. Other Cavite Industrial Estates that have just recently begun to do business may also have reason for concern.

The Mactan EPZ should be protected from any adverse impact; it is already operating at near-capacity, and it is geographically far enough away from Subic Bay to avoid direct competition.

OTHER ECONOMIC ZONES

Clark Air Force Base This former US Air Force base, located to the north of Subic Bay, will also be turned into a freeport and special economic zone. Clark's industrial estate is to be dedicated to light manufacturing, tourist resorts, and golf courses. There are plans to expand the base to serve as an alternative international airport.

Southern Mindanao Abundant natural and agricultural resources in this area, together with its location (which makes it East Indonesia's gateway to the world), are combining to make this an area where major international agricultural companies such as Dole, Del Monte, Cargill, General Milling, and Coca-Cola are beginning to invest. Southern Mindanao is emerging as a major trading corridor for the ASEAN (Association of Southeast Asian Nations) region. Mindanao also represents a market opportunity for many corporations because of the region's large population.

There are also ongoing special development programs designed to revitalize communities so that the social, industrial, and public infrastructure networks can all work together for the economic well-being of the community. The five major projects are the CALABARZON project, the Samar Island Special Development Project, the Panay-Negros Agro-Industrial Development Project, the South Cotabato–General Santos City Area Development Project, and the Iligan–Cagayan de Oro Industrial Corridor.

USEFUL ADDRESSES

Export Processing Zones

Philippines Export Zone Authority (PEZA)
4th Fl., Legaspi Towers
300 Roxas Boulevard
Metro Manila, Philippines
Tel: [63] (2) 521-9725, 521-04-19, 521-0546/7
Fax: [63] (2) 521-8659, 521-0419

Baguio City Export Processing Zone (BCEPZ)
Loakan Road
Baguio City, Philippines
Tel: [63] (74) 442-6589

Bataan Export Processing Zone (BEPZ)
Mariveles
Bataan, Philippines
Tel: [63] (47) 935-4004
Fax: [63] (47) 731372

Cavite Export Processing Zone (CEPZ)
Rosario
Cavite, Philippines
Tel: [63] (96) 437-6090
Fax: [63] (96) 742-1022

Mactan Export Processing Zone (MEPZ)
Lapu-Lapu City
Cebu, Philippines
Tel: [63] (32) 400-590
Fax: [63] (32) 400-591

Industrial Estates

Philippines Industrial Estates Association (PHILEA)
PHILEA Desk (OSAC)
Ground Fl., Industry & Investment Bldg.
385 Sen. Gil J. Puyat Ave.
Makati, Metro Manila, Philippines
Tel: [63] (2) 818-1831/9
Fax: [63] (2) 810-9728

Carmelray Industrial Park
Carmelray Development Corporation
7th Fl., Rufino Plaza
Ayala Avenue
Makati, Metro Manila, Philippines
Tel: [63] (2) 810-6306
Fax: [63] (2) 817-5051
Located in Canlubang, Calamba, Laguna

First Cavite Industrial Estate
3rd Floor, First Bank Bldg.
Sen. Gil Puyat Ave.
Makati, Metro Manila, Philippines
Tel: [63] (2) 817-1308
Fax: [63] (2) 817-0939
Located in Langkaan, Dasmariñas, Cavite

Gateway Business Park
Gateway Business Holdings
Ground Fl., Jaycem Bldg.
104 Rada St.
Legaspi Village
Makati, Metro Manila, Philippines
Tel: [63] (2) 892-2916, 819-1146
Fax: [63] (2) 817-9576
Located in Amadeo Road, Bgy. Jalavera, Gen. Trias, Cavite

Laguna International Industrial Park
Laguna International Industrial Park, Inc.
3rd Fl., Solid House Bldg.
P. Tamo Ext., cor. Lumbang St.
Makati, Metro Manila, Philippines
Tel: [63] (2) 859-041 to 52
Fax: [63] (2) 819-5123
Located in Ganado and Mamplasan, Biñan, Laguna

Laguna Technopark
Laguna Technopark, Inc.
Ground Fl., MSE Bldg.
Ayala Avenue
Makati, Metro Manila, Philippines
Tel: [63] (2) 814-7676
Fax: [63] (2) 812-1386
Located in Sta. Rosa and Biñan, Laguna

Light Industry and Science Park of the Philippines
Science Park of the Philippines, Inc.
15th Fl., Solidbank Bldg.
Paseo de Roxas
Makati, Metro Manila, Philippines
Tel: [63] (2) 810-2931
Fax: [63] (2) 819-0941
Located in Diezmo, Cabuyao, Laguna

Luisita Industrial Park
Luisita Reality Corporation
119 De la Rosa St., cor. C. Palanca St.
Legaspi Village
Makati, Manila, Philippines
Tel: [63] (2) 818-3911, 818-1516
Fax: [63] (2) 817-9309
Located in Hacienda Luisita, San Miguel, Tarlac

Special Economic Zones

Bases Conversion Development Authority (BCDA)
2nd Fl., Rufino Center
Ayala Avenue, cor. Herrera St.
1226 Makati, Metro Manila, Philippines
Tel: [63] (2) 813-5383, 864-006/9
Fax: [63] (2) 813-5424/7

Contact the BCDA for information on the conversions of the former Clark Air and Subic Naval Bases.

Subic Bay Metropolitan Authority (SBMA)
Bldg. 229, Waterfront Ave.
Subic Bay Freeport Zone
2200 Olongapo City, Philippines
Tel: [63] (47) 222-5454/6, 222-2731, 384-5849
Fax: [63] (47) 222-5278
The SBMA also has a telephone number in Metro Manila, which is [63] (2) 817-3994.

Import Policy & Procedures

INTRODUCTION

The Philippine economy is largely import oriented in terms of the value of merchandise trade. A sizable trade deficit continues primarily because of merchandise imported to meet the strong demand for raw materials, intermediate goods, industrial upgrades, and infrastructure-related capital goods. An emerging market, the Philippine economy continues to recover from the political instability of the 1980s, a series of natural disasters in the 1990s, and additional disruption caused by the closing of important US military bases in the early 1990s.

Many of the products being imported are for improvement of the country's production capabilities. The development of industry has been hindered by such factors as electric power shortages and a still-developing infrastructure. Thus, the importation of modern technology, power generating equipment, specialized industrial machinery, and telecommunications and transport equipment is of prime importance to the nation. The largest import item is fuel, which accounts for 10 percent of total imports into the country.

Since 1992 the government has enacted various measures designed to spur the nation's economy and stimulate foreign trade. These measures include the reduction of import duties, the opening of the telecommunications market, the liberalization of the foreign exchange regime, an increase in the supply and reliability of electric power, and

CONTENTS

measures to encourage a more hospitable investment climate. In 1993 Philippine imports reached US$17.1 billion in value. The Philippines' major trading partners are the US, Japan, the European Union (EU), and fellow member states of the Association of Southeast Asian Nations (ASEAN).

This section discusses Philippine policies toward and procedures for importing into the country. Such information is useful to persons seeking to sell goods and services to the Philippines, firms that decide to establish a manufacturing facility or other operation in the Philippines, foreign investors who are considering acquiring an interest in an entity located in the Philippines, and persons in the Philippines who are seeking to import from sources outside the country. (Refer to the "Marketing" chapter, beginning on page 169, for a discussion of sales channels in the Philippines and to the "Business Entities & Formation" chapter, beginning on page 185, for information on establishing a local business presence.)

IMPORT POLICIES

Government Regulation

The Philippine government has taken several significant steps to reduce bureaucratic regulations and to foster competition. In recent years, it has revised and enacted tax, labor, health, safety, environmental, and other laws and policies with the aim of regulating industry and investment more efficiently. Nevertheless, doing business in the Philippines is like doing business in any other country: one must deal patiently with bureaucratic red tape. In addition, the government cannot always supply the most effective or uniform means of law enforcement, and therefore one must seek various means—contractual and otherwise—to protect business rights and interests.

The primary authority controlling imports is the Bureau of Customs (BOC). It enforces the country's Tariff and Customs Code. Other important regula-

IMPORTING GLOSSARY

ad valorem tariff A tariff assessed as a percentage of the value of the imported merchandise.

Association of Southeast Asian Nations (ASEAN) ASEAN, established in 1967, is comprised of Thailand, Singapore, Malaysia, Indonesia, Brunei, Vietnam, and the Philippines. The purpose of the organization is to strengthen regional cohesion and self-reliance through economic, social, and cultural cooperation. In 1992 the ASEAN leaders agreed to reduce intra-ASEAN tariffs (the Common Effective Preferential Tariff scheme) to levels of between 0 and 5 percent within a 15-year period and to create an ASEAN Free Trade Area—Common Effective Preferential Tariffs (AFTA–CEPT) in hopes of overcoming barriers to greater integration among the economies of the ASEAN states.

cost, insurance, and freight (CIF) value The CIF value of goods includes the value of the goods, the freight costs required to bring the goods to the named port of destination, plus the costs of obtaining insurance and the premiums paid to insure the goods during the carriage.

General Agreement on Tariffs and Trade (GATT) A multilateral trade agreement aimed at expanding international trade. GATT's main goals are to liberalize world trade and place it on a secure and stable regulatory basis. GATT is the only multilateral instrument that lays down agreed-upon rules for international trade. The organization that oversees the agreement—to be succeeded by the World Trade Organization (WTO)—is the principal international body concerned with negotiating the reduction of trade barriers and improvement of international trade relations.

Generalized System of Preferences (GSP) An international program under which the members allow imports of merchandise from developing countries to enter duty-free or at reduced tariff rates in order to make exports from those countries competitive in more developed country markets.

Harmonized System (HS) A multipurpose international goods classification system designed to be used by manufacturers, transporters, exporters, importers, customs officials, statisticians, and others in classifying goods that move in international trade to standardize.

Home Consumption Value (HCV) The HCV is the domestic wholesale price at the first line of distribution in the home country, plus packing and other related export costs. The Philippines is the only country in the world that uses this particular system to assess import duties.

Import Liberalization Program (ILP) This governmental program was started in 1981, suspended in 1984 during a balance of payments crisis, and resumed in 1986 to shrink the list of regulated import items. In addition to lifting quantitative restrictions, the Philippine government is implementing a tariff reform program to rationalize and simplify its tariff structure.

Magna Carta of Small Farmers Though restrictions have been lifted on many farm commodities, the Magna Carta of Small Farmers prevents importation of agricultural products that are produced locally in sufficient quantity, such as corn, corn substitutes (including feed wheat), meat, and meat products (except beef and beef products). However, the Philippine government has made commitments under the Uruguay Round of GATT to convert most of these restrictions to tariffs, which will be gradually reduced.

most favored nation (MFN) A nondiscriminatory trade policy commitment on the part of one country to extend to another country the lowest tariff rates it applies to any other country, thus effectively establishing a standard common tariff. All contracting parties to GATT undertake to apply such treatment to one another.

transaction value The price actually paid or payable for merchandise.

value-added tax (VAT) An indirect tax on consumption that is assessed on the increased value of goods at each discrete point in the chain of production and distribution, from the raw materials stage to final consumption. The tax on processors or merchants is levied on the amount by which they increase the value of the items they purchase and resell.

tory agencies include: the National Economic and Development Authority (NEDA); the Bangko Sentral ng Pilipinas (BSP, or the Central Bank); the Industry Section of the Department of Trade and Industry (DTI); the Board of Investments (BOI) of DTI; the Environmental Management Bureau (EMB); the Department of Health (DOH); the Technology Transfer Board (TTB); the Bureau of Food and Drugs (BFAD); the Dangerous Drugs Board (DDB); the Bureau of Fisheries and Aquatic Resources (BFAR); the National Meat Inspection Commission (NMIC); the Bureau of Animal Industry (BAI); the Bureau of Plant Industry (BPI); and the Energy Regulatory Board (ERB).

Tariffs

Classification and Rate of Tariffs Customs uses the Harmonized System (HS) to classify all products for purposes of assessing import duties. In August 1991, Executive Order 470 cut the number of tariff categories and established the following four-tiered structure:

- 3 percent for agricultural commodities, such as purebred breeding animals and vegetable alkaloids
- 10 percent for raw materials and selected equipment
- 20 percent for intermediate, semi-processed materials
- 30 percent for finished goods

This new system, which was scheduled to take full effect as of July 1, 1995, affects approximately 94 percent of the roughly 5,560 tariff line item classifications. The adoption of this system of tariffs will mean a substantial drop in the tariffs assessed against agricultural products, including high-value-added processed agricultural products such as canned fruit, processed foods, and poultry, most of which have been subject to tariffs of 50 to 60 percent. Restrictions against the importation of some agricultural products—for example, feed corn and meat other than beef—are also being lifted.

Executive Order 470 also identified about 200 strategic items that will continue to enjoy 50 percent tariff protection after July 1995. These items include cut flowers, locally available fresh and dried fruits, rice, coconut oil, sugar, fruit juices, wines and spirits, tobacco, cosmetics, bags and suitcases, leather clothing accessories, fur skins, plywood and veneer, tableware and ornamental ceramics, molasses, and candies (including chocolate bars). Some commodities presently subject to quantitative restrictions (QRs) may be subject to a higher tariff rate once the QRs are lifted.

Value Assessed Customs assesses import duties based on Home Consumption Value (HCV) rather than on the specific transaction value of the goods. The HCV is the domestic wholesale price at the first line of distribution in the home country plus export packing and other export costs. Foreign exporters unfamiliar with the HCV system can obtain guidance from the Foreign Commercial Service (FCS) in Manila.

The HCV has greatly increased the landed cost of many imported products, significantly raising dutiable values in many cases. Critics of the system say it has led to inconsistent valuation of products that have passed through a country after leaving the country of manufacture. The private sector has been pressuring the government to eliminate the HCV scheme, despite strong opposition from the Finance Department, which has made ominous projections of the revenue losses that would result. In the Uruguay Round of the General Agreement on Tariffs and Trade (GATT), the Philippine government has committed itself to replace the HCV with transaction or invoice value, a change that traders should look for in the not too distant future.

Preferential Tariff Treatment The Philippines is a signatory to the following treaties that affect the tariff rates assessed against imports from member countries:

- General Agreement on Tariffs and Trade (GATT) The Philippines is entitled to most favored nation (MFN) status and is eligible for duty-free treatment for designated articles under the Generalized System of Preferences (GSP). (Refer to the "Trade Agreements" chapter, beginning on page 61, for further information on GATT, MFN status, and GSP.)
- Association of Southeast Asian Nations (ASEAN) The ASEAN Free Trade Area—Common Effective Preferential Tariffs (AFTA-CEPT) serves as the mechanism for the conversion of ASEAN into a free trade regional market. In addition to the Philippines, member countries include Indonesia, Malaysia, Singapore, Thailand, Brunei, and Vietnam. (See the "Importing Glossary" sidebar on page 80 for further information on ASEAN and AFTA-CEPT.)

Subsidies Companies investing in preferred areas and registered with the BOI have traditionally received incentives such as income tax holidays, tax deductions for labor expenses, and duty-free importation of capital equipment. Foreign equity in BOI-registered entities is generally limited to 40 percent, although foreigners can own up to 100 percent of companies that export at least 60 percent of their production. As a member of GATT, the Philippine government has committed itself to eliminating various privileges that have been accorded to exporters who registered with BOI on or after March 15, 1985.

Antidumping and Countervailing Duties The

Philippine Tariff and Customs Code provides for both antidumping and countervailing duties to counteract unfair trade practices or laws. If a specific kind or class of foreign goods is imported into or sold in the Philippines at less than its fair value, this code imposes an antidumping duty equal to the difference between the actual purchase price and the fair market value of the article. It also imposes a countervailing duty equal to the estimated amount of the subsidy granted to a foreign article on its production in its country of origin.

Other Fees and Taxes

Excise Taxes Certain products are subject to one of two types of excise taxes: specific or ad valorem. A specific excise tax is calculated based on weight, volume, capacity, or another physical unit of measurement. An ad valorem tax is based on the selling price or other specified value of the article. Customs levies excise taxes on such items as alcohol products, petroleum, minerals, jewelry, perfume, automobiles, films, cigarettes and other tobacco products, fireworks, saccharine, and yachts and other vessels for pleasure or sport.

The categories and specific items subject to excise tax can change fairly frequently, and therefore information on excise taxes must be sought from customs at the time of importation. For example, excise taxes on compounding liquors, matches, and videotapes have been eliminated recently. Excise taxes are levied in addition to the VAT.

Value-Added Tax (VAT) The uniform VAT system has replaced the advance sales tax and compensating tax, miller's tax, contractor's tax, broker's tax, and fixed tax. A uniform VAT rate of 10 percent applies to all sales of goods and services, including capital goods regardless of acquisition date; raw materials used in production (such as petroleum); real estate sales; and hotel and restaurant operations. The 10 percent VAT applies to imported goods, regardless of their intended use. However, agricultural items, such as cotton, are exempted from the VAT.

The rate on imported goods is based on the duty-paid value of the goods, plus any other charges—such as postage and commissions—levied prior to release from customs. If customs computes the value of the products on the basis of volume or quantity, the landed cost is used to compute the VAT. Landed cost consists of the invoice amount plus customs duties, freight, insurance, and other charges. If the imported goods are subject to an excise tax, the excise tax is included in calculating the VAT base.

Persons who may be subject to the VAT must register with customs. Any person required to register for VAT purposes but failing to do so remains liable for VAT taxes owed on sale of taxable goods or services.

Import Processing Fee A fixed import processing fee of P250 (about US$9.60) must be paid by importers or consignees to an authorized agent bank on all imports covered by a formal entry and having an invoice value of P5,000 (about US$190) or more.

Restrictions and Prohibitions on Imports

Before certain goods may be imported, the Philippine importer or foreign exporter must obtain prior approval from the government agencies in the Philippines responsible for regulating the product. Some items deemed to adversely affect public security, health, or morality cannot be imported at all. In addition, the importer or exporter may be required to obtain advance government permission to use certain shipping methods for the delivery of particular goods. These various restrictions and prohibitions are covered in this section.

Quotas Recent trade reforms have eliminated most quantitative restrictions (QRs) on imports, although roughly 137 items remain subject to QRs. About 60 commodities remain protected indefinitely by QRs for reasons of health, safety, or national security. These include chemicals for manufacturing explosives, dangerous drugs, and vehicle parts for the light commercial vehicle development program. The government is expected gradually to reduce and eliminate remaining quantitative restrictions on imports.

Import Permits and Licenses Generally, most merchandise may be imported without a license. Licensing rules have been lifted on about 2,770 items, representing nearly 96 percent of the 2,900 products identified for liberalization over a 12-year period. The government classifies imports into three categories:

- Freely importable, which may be processed by authorized bank agents without prior approval from CBP.
- Regulated, which require clearance and permits from various governmental agencies and which may need prior approval from CBP (see "Import Procedures" on page 85).
- Prohibited, which affect public health and safety, national security, international commitments, or development or rationalization of local industry (see "Import Procedures" on page 85).

Items that are generally prohibited from importation may nevertheless be imported if they are intended for use in the production of exports. For example, raw materials or intermediate components that would otherwise be banned may be imported for use in export production. To import such items, import authority must be obtained from the Commodity Classification Office of the BSP.

Prohibited Imports The following products are prohibited from importation into the Philippines:
- explosives, firearms, and weapons of war
- pornographic materials
- narcotics, drugs, and items for inducing unlawful abortions
- printed materials that advocate the overthrow of the government, urge forcible resistance to any law, or threaten to take the life of or inflict bodily harm on any person in the Philippines
- gambling paraphernalia
- toy guns
- misbranded or adulterated food or drugs items
- lottery and sweepstakes tickets, including advertisements and lists of such drawings
- precious metals and alloys of precious metals with no indication of fineness or quality

In addition, the following agricultural products are prohibited from importation:
- corn (maize)
- feedgrains
- poultry and poultry products
- pork and pork products
- prepared or preserved meat and meat products
- fresh garlic
- fresh cabbage
- fresh onions
- fresh potatoes
- sugar
- coffee
- live swine, chicken, and horses, except for those certified for breeding purposes
- all agricultural products covered by the Magna Carta of Small Farmers (see the "Importing Glossary" on page 80)

Carnets

The Philippines has not joined the Admission Temporair/Temporary Admission (ATA) Convention, which establishes the use of an international customs document known as the ATA Carnet. An ATA Carnet would allow a person to bring merchandise temporarily into a member country for demonstration, show, and similar purposes without paying duties on it.

Admission of Sample Merchandise

Commercial samples valued at no more than US$1,500 are eligible for import without payment of duties, subject to certain conditions. One of these conditions is the filing of a bond for an amount equal to twice the ascertained duties and taxes, guaranteeing that the samples will be reexported within six months of entry. Failure to export within this period will lead to collection of the corresponding duties.

Customs may also assess duties if it deems that the quantity of the imported samples is excessive. For single shipments valued at more than US$1,500, the importer may select any portion of the shipment not exceeding US$1,500 in value for entry as a duty-free commercial sample. The remainder must be entered in bond or for consumption with payment of the applicable import duties and tax.

Individual commercial samples that have been defaced or have no commercial value (such as swatches of material or shoes with cut soles) are usually admitted duty-free, and so are samples of medicine that are marked "Physician's Sample, Not for Sale." Items with inherent value, such as jewelry, cannot be entered as a commercial sample.

Admission of Advertising Materials

Printed material, including pictures and photographs containing printed material—such as lithographs, posters, signs, catalogs, price lists, pamphlets, booklets, and folders for advertising foreign products and foreign businesses—should be marked "Advertising Materials, No Commercial Value" to avoid payment of duties. Accompanying documents should indicate that the articles are advertising materials and are not for sale. No special rate for postage exists on leaflets and pamphlets in quantity.

Advertisements of Philippine products, businesses, firms, offices, associations, corporations, trades, or professions intended for use within the country are subject to payment of duties, as are calendars of all kinds.

Mandatory Technical Standards

Product Requirements and Standards With respect to product standards, a manufacturer or other person exporting goods to the Philippines should follow the instructions of the Philippine importer. The standards for imported products may also be included in contract specifications.

For industrial goods, local inspection for standards compliance is required for imports of 28 specific products. These include lighting fixtures, electrical wires and cables, sanitary wares, household appliances, pneumatic tires, and portland cement. For electrical products, the Philippine standards are 220 or 110 volts, AC, 60 cycles. Flat and round 2- and 3-pin plugs are used, and electrical lamp fittings are of the screw type. For other products, customs will generally accept a manufacturer's certification of conformance to the product requirements or standards of the country of origin. A Product Standard (PS) quality mark is affixed on products manufactured by companies that comply with national or internationally accepted standards.

The DTI requires a product standard license and certification from the Bureau of Product Standards

(BPS) for products that affect life, health, safety, and property. These products include medical oxygen, consumer goods, electrical and firefighting equipment, and construction materials. The BPS must also grant prior clearance to imports of nonmetric measuring devices, instrumentation, and apparatus.

The Philippines adheres to the Standards Code accepted during the Tokyo Round of GATT. Under this code, a standard is a technical specification contained in a document that specifies characteristics of a product such as levels of quantity, performance, safety, or dimensions. Standards may include, or deal exclusively with, terminology, symbols, testing and test methods, packaging, marking, or labeling requirements as they apply to a product.

Environmental Protection and Pollution Control The Department of Environment and Natural Resources (DENR) has primary responsibility for implementing the government's environmental strategies and policies. The Environmental Management Bureau (EMB) of DENR spearheads the government's efforts to protect the Philippine people and resources from environmental pollution. Historically, compliance with environmental regulations has been relatively low, although local nongovernmental organizations have increased the pressure on plants and factories to comply with these regulations. Polluting industries must secure an Environmental Compliance Certificate from the EMB in order to operate in the Philippines.

Food, Health, and Safety Regulations The Bureau of Food and Drugs (BFAD) enforces special regulatory standards on the importation of food products. Phytosanitary restrictions and strict licensing requirements apply to the importation of fresh fruit, frozen meats, and meat products. If low-growing vegetables and fruit are imported from areas infected with certain pests, quarantine restrictions are enforced, a fumigation certificate may be required, and a quarantine officer must place an official stamp of authorization in the vessel's cargo manifest before the cargo can be unloaded. Special regulations also apply to imported tobacco.

Used personal apparel can be imported only with a disinfection certificate from the port of embarkation.

The Department of Health (DOH) promulgates and enforces safety regulations for the import of hazardous materials. These materials must be labeled, sold, and distributed in accordance with strict DOH standards. Hazardous substances covered by these regulations include irritants and substances that are corrosive, flammable, combustible, or radioactive.

Labeling and Marking

Adherence to all required marking and labeling requirements is extremely important because failure to comply with such requirements can cause the entire shipment to be seized and disposed of.

General Requirements Imported products must be labeled with at least the following information:

- registered trade or brand name
- registered trademark
- registered business name
- address of manufacturer or importer
- general make or active ingredients
- net quantity of contents—stated in a metric measurement—for weight, volume, size, numerical count, or other appropriate measure, rounded to at least the nearest tenth

Specific Agency Requirements If the import or sale of a product is subject to regulation by a particular government agency—such as the DOH or BFAD—that agency may require additional information on the product's label. For example, the product label may require information such as flammability risk; directions for use; toxicity warnings; usage of wattage, voltage, amperes; or the process of manufacture. Specific formats may also be required.

Retail Products Most imported merchandise intended for retail markets should be labeled clearly with the country of origin in Pilipino, English, or Spanish. Packages that contain such merchandise must also be marked with the country of origin. In the absence of country-of-origin labeling or marking, a duty of 5 percent ad valorem is assessed. The label or marking must be sufficiently permanent to remain on the package or product when it reaches the ultimate purchaser.

Articles containing precious metals that are intended for sale in the Philippines must be labeled to indicate the true character, amount, value, contents, properties, and conditions of the articles or of the materials of which they are composed.

If the product is certified to be in compliance with a consumer product standard prescribed by the BPS, the label must contain the PS quality mark.

Except for the country-of-origin labels or markings, no labeling or marking requirements apply with respect to any retail product that cannot be labeled or marked at all; cannot be labeled or marked before shipment without injury or prohibitive expense; consists of a crude substance; is entered for the importer's use and is not intended for resale in the imported form; or was produced at least 20 years prior to the date of importation.

Drugs Pharmaceuticals are subject to special labeling regulations of the DOH. The DOH adopts and implements labeling standards and approves all new labels. Under the Generic Act of 1988, the DOH requires that the generic name of most drugs appear above the brand name in a slightly larger typeface and enclosed in a box that has a contrasting background.

Textiles and Apparel Mandatory labels are required for most textiles and garments. The labels must be reasonably legible, with letters not less than 1.5 mm in size. The label information can be stamped, printed, woven, or shown on tags. Textile products that are subject to these labeling requirements include finished textile fabrics in rolls or folded, textile piece goods, ready-made garments, household and institutional linens, handkerchiefs, umbrellas, socks, hosiery, neckties, and scarves. Labels are not necessary for narrow fabrics, artificial flowers, purses, doilies, bags, hats, belts, and gloves.

Shipping Cases All cases of imported merchandise in a single shipment must be numbered consecutively and must be declared and entered by the consecutive numbers in addition to all other required markings. However, this requirement does not apply to goods shipped in bulk—such as petroleum, gasoline, benzine, coal, flour, rice, fresh vegetables, fresh eggs, and frozen goods. Shipments of 500 or more barrels or cases of beer, wine, liquor, iron nails, bolts, or uniform canned goods are also considered shipments in bulk. Consignments consisting of fewer than 500 barrels or cases must be numbered.

Articles or cargos must have clear, legible markings that state the name and address of the consignee, package number, and other necessary shipping information. Any article or cargo that cannot be marked must have an attached registry tag that contains this data.

Credit and Payment Conditions

Import payments in the Philippines are made through a relatively straightforward process subject to minimal controls. Commodities may be imported against letters of credit (L/Cs), based on documents against acceptance (D/A) or documents against payment (D/P), under open account (O/A) arrangements, or by direct remittances. Any one of these payment methods may be used regardless of the type and amount of importation.

Under the government's import liberalization program, prior clearance is no longer needed to open L/Cs for most imports. However, clearance requirements for certain restricted or controlled items still apply. Self-funded (no dollar) imports and imports on a consignment basis are permitted without prior approval by the BSP. However, importers of capital goods financed through foreign credits must obtain prior approval from the BSP if payments in foreign exchange are to be made through the banking system.

In the past, only export producers could use the D/A and O/A procedures. The liberalization of exchange controls in 1992 opened D/A and O/A procedures to oil firms, export producers or manufacturers, franchised public utility concerns, and domestic producers or manufacturers approved by the BSP. Importations under D/A and O/A are covered by a BSP Release Certificate (RC), which is issued by commercial banks on receipt of complete shipping documents, the duly accomplished Record of Goods Imported (RGI), and any pertinent import permit.

Import payments valued at more than US$1,000 are almost always made using commercial bank L/Cs. Payment through O/A is used for prequalified importers, but L/Cs remain the dominant payment mechanism. Use of an irrevocable L/C is strongly advised. Payment terms tend to average three months, while exchange delays may last 60 to 90 days, and in some cases four months if CBP finances are tight. Arrangements requiring more than one year to close require BSP approval.

Countertrade

The Philippines has very limited exposure to barter and countertrade activities. Executive Order No. 427 restricted barter trading to the Sulu archipelago, a province in Western Mindanao where the economy has traditionally depended on barter trade. However, countertrade proposals by private sector firms are considered on a case-by-case basis by the BSP or the DTI. Imports of essential raw materials and finished goods are allowed under countertrade transactions, but only "nontraditional" exports, such as electrical equipment, textiles, minerals and ores, farm products, coconut products, chemicals, fish, and forest products, are encouraged. The DTI's trading arm, the Philippine International Trading Corporation (PITC), has completed a number of countertrade deals; it prefers that at least 50 percent of the total contract represent countertrade.

IMPORT PROCEDURES

In an international transaction, the seller and buyer must comply with two sets of requirements: the export regulations of the country from which the goods are shipped and the import regulations of the country to which the goods are delivered. This discussion focuses on the second step: bringing goods into the Philippines. Also, shippers must abide by the export regulations of their own countries; these may include export documentation, declarations, and licenses.

Importers usually appoint a customs broker or freight forwarding agent to deal with the required documentation. In the past, the most frequent complaints about the Bureau of Customs were related to the complexity of its bureaucracy, inefficiency of the import process, and frequent changes in procedures. Customs has substantially improved the importation process by creating a One-Stop Import Documentation Center (OSIDC) that houses, in a single location, all the offices involved in documentation. Customs has also reduced the number of approval signatures required for importation. Nevertheless, snags still exist in the system, particularly in the release of imported cargo.

The average time required for customs to release imported cargo is one to two weeks, despite the fact that on paper it appears that it should take about four days to release cargo categorized for consumption entry or immediate use. If an importer has an outstanding balance in its account with customs or has committed import violations in the past, the processing delay is likely to increase. If customs has reason to believe that a shipment is in violation of import requirements, the shipment will probably be delayed pending investigation.

Import Registration and Permits

Registration Importers must register with the Customs Intelligence Investigation Service (CIIS). The importer will be issued a control number, which must be received before Customs will classify the goods for importation.

Goods Requiring Import Permits Although most licensing requirements have been eliminated, the importation of some commodities is still restricted or regulated. The following products require a permit or clearance from the government agency listed:

- dangerous drugs, such as acetic anhydride—DDB
- sodium cyanide, chlorofluorocarbon, and penicillin—BFAD
- refined petroleum products and coal—ERB
- fish and fish preparations—BFAR
- animals, animal products, meat, and meat products—NMIC, BAI
- onions, garlic, potatoes, and cabbage for seeding purposes—BPI
- specific consumer durable goods such as motor vehicles and parts—DTI or BOI
- pesticides including agricultural chemicals—Fertilizer and Pesticide Authority (FPA)
- raw sugar—Sugar Regulatory Administration (SRA)
- trucks, tires, and tubes—DTI
- rice, corn, and other feedgrains—National Food Authority (NFA)
- imports originating from socialist countries or nations with centrally planned economies—PITC

Application for Permit For beef, poultry, pork, and other meat products, the import permit is a Veterinary Quarantine Clearance (VQC) issued by NMIC. For fresh produce and planting seeds and plants, the BPI issues the import permit. For both commodity groups, the respective agencies take into account not only domestic sanitary and phytosanitary regulations, but also domestic production and supply levels. For other commodities, the importer should contact the appropriate governmental agency to determine the procedures for obtaining a permit.

Preshipment Stage

Advance Classification for Tariffs If an importer is unable to identify the classification of a product in the Tariff and Customs Code, advance classification may be sought from the Philippine Tariff Commission in Manila. A sample should be sent with a request for information. If that is impractical, a complete description of the article along with photographs may be submitted to assist the customs appraiser. Duties will be assessed against the article under the heading indicated by the Tariff Commission at the rate in effect at the time of importation.

Preshipment Inspection With a few narrow exceptions, all imports to the Philippines are subject to preshipment inspection pursuant to the Comprehensive Import Supervision Scheme (CISS). Under this scheme, the independent Swiss concern Société Generale de Surveillance (SGS) must inspect shipments on behalf of Customs prior to shipment in order to prevent misdeclaration of goods and tariff evasion. The BSP will refuse to negotiate a letter of credit for imports without a Clean Report of Findings (CRF) from the SGS. Exceptions to the preshipment inspection include shipments valued at US$5,000 or less, semiconductors, and some textile inputs.

The SGS has offices throughout the world, including nine in Japan, four in Taiwan, and one in Hong Kong. The seller should carefully read SGS instructions concerning the Philippine Tariff and Customs Code HCV definition. To avoid providing incorrect or misleading price information to the SGS, the seller requires a thorough understanding of HCV. Once the SGS has reached a determination of the HCV of the seller's product or shipment based on information supplied by the seller and other market sources, the seller will have difficulty persuading the SGS to change its findings. A seller should establish a cooperative, direct working relationship with the SGS inspector who handles the seller's industry.

As soon as the importer opens an L/C to cover the shipment, the seller should provide complete address and contact information to facilitate SGS contact for preshipment inspection. Better yet, as

TEN TIPS FOR EXPORTING TO THE PHILIPPINES

1. Advice and assistance for exporters selling goods to the Philippines can be obtained through Philippine commercial offices, as well as most government agencies and banks, but the assistance they offer may be limited because of the expense of staffing all such offices with such personnel.

2. Exporters should obtain or carry out market surveys to determine the most rational five-year horizon strategy to follow in penetrating the Philippine market.

3. To secure any necessary approvals from government agencies:
   — regular communication is needed between the buyer and manufacturer;
   — all documents should be in order, and the metric system should be used;
   — the manufacturer should follow up with documents submitted to the specific agency because there is no guarantee that the agency will notify the manufacturer of any discrepancy that is holding up the approval process;
   — if the agency still refuses to grant approval, the manufacturer should seek assistance from the appropriate industry association to which it belongs and request, if possible, that its officials intercede on behalf of the manufacturer.

4. Exporters should establish a network of resources; government agencies, freight forwarders, bankers, international marketing consultants, accountants, marine insurance companies, local world trade associations, and port authorities can serve as important sources for information on the Philippines.

5. Because the key to making a successful transaction is getting paid, exporters should carefully manage the terms of sale and payment; exporters should understand all Incoterms.

6. Exporters should understand the geography, physical profile, and infrastructure system in the Philippines because this can affect the manner in which products should be shipped, warehoused, or distributed.

7. Exporters should understand document requirements in the Philippines; the importer's customs broker, as well as the freight forwarder or shipping agent, can be used as a source of information

8. Exporters should be conscious of insurance issues and know whether appropriate coverage has been obtained; advice can be obtained from local insurance brokers and marine underwriters.

9. Exporters should know the legal definition of HCV and work directly with SGS inspectors at the exporter's port of departure; SGS will not work with third parties, such as freight forwarders or other agents.

10. To avoid delays at the port of entry and to be accredited to use customs' express lane to import cargo, clean documentation is needed, and both exporter and importer should have clean track records with customs.

soon as the shipment date is known, the seller should contact the local SGS office to arrange a physical inspection in the seller's factory, warehouse, or port of loading.

The SGS does not charge any inspection fee. It checks whether the quantity and quality conform to the specifications of the Philippine importer and whether the declared value is correct according to the market price information. However, the price comparison made by the SGS does not affect the seller's final invoice price. If the SGS finds problems with the goods, it will notify the importer and wait for written instructions from the importer as to whether the goods will still be accepted.

When a seller provides the SGS with the final documents, the seller should request a "plain paper draft" of the CRF that the SGS transmits electronically to Manila. The seller should further make sure that the SGS inspector affixes a security label to the products after completing the preshipment inspection. These two steps will enable the seller to negotiate changes with the SGS before the shipment arrives in Manila. For reasons of confidentiality, the SGS will not provide a plain paper draft to freight forwarders or agents.

To appeal a valuation decision, the seller should contact the general manager of the local SGS office. If the seller disagrees with the general manager's decision, the seller can appeal to the SGS head office in Geneva, Switzerland. In the event that the seller and the SGS cannot reach a satisfactory agreement on the proper HCV for the product or shipment, the seller can appeal the valuation to Customs' SGS Import Valuation and Classification Committee in Manila. Standard forms for filing valuation appeals can be obtained from either the Manila office of the SGS or the Philippine Office of the Deputy Customs Commissioner.

Once an appeal has been filed, the seller can proceed to clear the contested shipment through customs on payment of import duty based on the disputed invoice value, and deposit of a 60-day postdated check in the amount of the additional import duty claimed on the basis of the SGS HCV valuation. The seller may also wish to consider transshipping the product through another Asian port, such as Singapore, where the local HCV for the product may be lower. This stratagem is "legal" under the HCV system, which bases valuation on the HCV of the country of immediate export, not the country of manufacture or origin.

Insurance Arrangements Most importers prefer to arrange locally for insurance of incoming goods. Importers should be familiar with shipping terms or Incoterms because they determine which party is responsible for the insurance costs and at which point such responsibility begins and ends.

Documentation at Packing

The following documents are required when packing articles for shipment to the Philippines. However, none of these documents are required for shipments valued at less than US$100, but a copy of the invoice should be included in the package showing the value to be less than US$100.

- certificate of origin, if requested; follow importer's instructions (further discussion follows)
- commercial invoice, usually three copies required; follow importer's instructions (further discussion follows)
- bill of lading (air waybill for air shipments), usually three negotiable and five nonnegotiable copies, although number requested may vary; freight and other charges must be annotated by the carrier or its agent, not by the forwarder; "to order" bills of lading are permitted
- packing list, one copy usually required to be duly certified by the exporter, shipper, manufacturer, or authorized representative and issued to cover each shipment; attach to the invoice
- pro forma invoice, if requested by the importer to support an import letter of credit application when a firm offer or contract is not available; invoice should include a complete description and specifications of the goods and quantity to be imported

- insurance certificate, following importer's and insurance company's instructions
- Shipper's Export Declaration, required for US exporters if value of exported goods is more than US$2,500 or when a validated license is needed
- Certificate of Non-Availability of Philippine Flag Vessel or Air Carrier if shipped by another vessel or carrier (see "Documentation at Shipping" on page 89)
- SGS Clean Report of Findings (CRF) on shipments valued at less than US$500,000 FOB or the equivalent in other foreign currencies
- Special certificates, if required due to the nature of the goods being shipped or if requested by the importer, bank, letter, or credit clause.

Certificates for Agricultural Goods, Food, and Drugs Special certificates are often required for particular products or for goods that contain particular substances. Thus, food and drug products must be shipped with a Declaration of Food and Drug Products, which must be furnished in three copies, attached to the invoice, and visaed for US$20 by a Philippine Consul (or for a shipment of small value coming from a place with no consular office, notarized and sent attached to the commercial invoice). Imported meat and meat-food products from cattle, sheep, swine, and goats must be accompanied by a Certificate of Ante-Mortem and Post-Mortem Inspection from an officially recognized veterinarian of the exporting country, district, or city where the animal was slaughtered or the meat was processed. This certificate must also be visaed for US$20 by a Philippine Consul. A notarial grower's certificate must be included for specified agricultural products from some countries, including the US. If importing wheat flour, the shipment must include a Certificate of Classification and Analysis of Wheat Flour, showing the protein, ash, and moisture content and extraction for the particular brand indicated in the invoice or the importer must present a certificate of analysis from the DOH before Customs will release the goods.

Certificates for Hazardous Materials Every shipment of insecticides, Paris greens, lead arsenates, or fungicides must be covered by a Declaration of Shipper or Manufacturer, which must state that the merchandise is not falsely labeled and is not dangerous to health and must be visaed for US$20 by a Philippine Consul. The importer must also be registered with the Pesticides and Insecticide Authority and must obtain prior clearance to import.

Other Special Certificates For aluminum products, the importer must present a notarial manufacturer's certificates to Customs. If importing any product containing ethyl alcohol, a Certificate of Products Containing Ethyl Alcohol (Distilled

Spirits) must be submitted, stating the source of the alcohol used in the manufacture of such products and visaed for US$20 by a Philippine Consul.

Commercial Invoice All commercial shipments, regardless of shipment value and mode of transport, must be accompanied by a commercial invoice. If goods are being returned to the Philippines, the invoice must so indicate. Special care should be taken with regard to the following information:

- brand and name of articles being shipped
- name and address of manufacturer
- date of departure of carrying vessel from country of export
- port of exportation
- port of entry in the Philippines
- cost of packaging
- inland freight costs
- other charges, excluding authentication fees

Generally the following information must be included in the commercial invoice:

- place where the articles were sold or agreed to be sold
- date when the articles were sold or agreed to be sold
- names of the seller and buyer
- port of entry in the Philippines
- BSP code classification number of each item
- detailed description of the articles, either according to the terms of the headings or subheadings as mentioned in the Tariff and Customs Code or in sufficient detail to allow the articles to be classified; this material must indicate the correct commodity description, in customary terms or commercial designation, including grade or quality numbers, marks or symbols under which they are sold by the seller or manufacturer, together with marks and numbers of the packages in which the articles are packed, the quantities in both the weights and measures of the country from which the articles are being shipped and those prescribed by the Philippine Tariff and Customs Code
- if the articles are shipped according to the conditions of a purchase or an agreement to purchase, the purchase price of each article in the currency of the purchase and in the unit of quantity in which the articles were bought and sold in the place or country of exportation
- if the articles are shipped other than as part of a purchase or an agreement to purchase, the value of each article in the unit of quantity in which the articles are usually bought and sold, and in the currency in which the transactions are usually made; in the absence of such value, the price in the currency in which the manufacturer, seller, shipper, or owner would have received or was willing to receive for such articles if sold in the

ordinary course of trade and in the usual wholesale quantities in the country of exportation; FOB value of the shipment should be shown separately from the cost and freight (C&F) or cost, insurance, and freight (CIF) value

- if the articles are intended for exhibition, display, or demonstration, a statement of such purpose and the phrase "No Commercial Value;" the value of the shipment must be indicated on the invoice for customs purposes as well as the venue of the exhibit
- all charges on the articles itemized by name and amount when known to the seller or shipper; if such amounts are unknown to the shipper or seller, all charges by name that are included in the invoice prices, such as commission, insurance, freight, cases, containers, coverings, and costs of packing
- all discounts, rebates, drawbacks, and bounties, itemized separately
- all internal and excise taxes applicable to the home market
- fair market value or price at which the same, like, or similar articles are sold freely in the usual wholesale quantities in the ordinary course of trade in the principal markets of the country of exportation on the date of exportation, or date nearest to the date of exportation
- any other fact deemed necessary for customs to properly classify and appraise the articles
- any statements or declarations regarding the truthfulness and correctness of the information given on the invoice, if required, and signed by the appropriate party, be it the manufacturer, seller, exporter, or authorized agent of the exporter

Certificate of Origin A certificate of origin attests to the country of origin of the goods. When the importer's bank requires such a certificate, the importer should have the certificate certified by a chamber of commerce (if one exists) before it is sent to the Consulate General of the Philippines for certification. Even if the importer's bank does not require such a certificate, certification by a chamber of commerce—but not by Philippine consulate—should be obtained.

Documentation at Shipping

The documentation requirements for shipping goods to the Philippines vary depending on the mode of transport: land (truck or rail), sea, air, or mail. In addition to the bill of lading documents described below, a shipper may request to see insurance, health, and other certificates.

Shipments by Sea Government Decree No. 769 of January 1982 reserves 40 percent of all liner trade to Philippine vessels and an additional 40 percent to a bilateral partner. Applications for waiver from the use of Philippine vessels must be made at the nearest Philippine Consulate. The application must include certified true copies of the purchase order, letter of credit or the sales contract, proposed charter party (if the vessel is to be chartered), and other pertinent documents. For liner service, the application must be filed not later than 20 regular working days prior to the estimated date of loading. When a foreign vessel is chartered, the application must be made not later than 45 working days before the estimated date of loading. Before a vessel is chartered, inquiry must be made about the availability of suitable Philippine vessels with the Freight Booking and Cargo Consolidation Center (FBCCC). Applications for waivers that are filed late, are incomplete, or are grossly inaccurate will not be approved without a valid reason.

Interisland shipping in the Philippines is dominated by the Conference of Interisland Shipowners and Operators (CISO).

Air Freight To ship goods in packages via air express an air waybill is needed—instead of a bill of lading—as are an original and three copies of the commercial invoice. To ship documents via air express, only an air waybill is needed. To ship goods via air freight, an air waybill and an original plus three copies of a commercial invoice are required. Generally, the freight company handling the air freight will fill out the air waybill, as long as a completed shipper's letter of instruction (SLI) has been provided. The commercial invoice should be on company letterhead, and all copies should be hand-signed. A certificate of origin and an import license are not required for air shipments.

Exporters should follow any applicable International Civil Aviation Organization (ICAO) rules governing labeling and packing of dangerous and restricted goods as well as any requirements for a shipper's certificate. Exporters should also take care to follow the importer's instructions with regard to textile shipments because special declarations or documentation may be needed.

Mail Service Parcel post packages weighing not more than 10 kg (22 lb) may be accepted for delivery to a number of the main cities of the Philippines. Parcels cannot be sent C.O.D. A customs declaration must be attached to each package. Before a package can be handed over to the recipient, the recipient normally arranges for clearance through customs by personally paying customs duty and all other charges involved. Both mail and parcel post shipments require postal documentation instead of bills of lading.

Philippine Customs

Ports of Entry Most goods imported into the Philippines enter through Manila. Other ports of entry include Ninoy Aquino International Airport, Cebu, Mactan International Airport, Iloilo, Davao, Tacloban, Zamboanga, Cagayan de Oro, Surigao, Legaspi, Batangas and San Fernando, and La Union.

Entry Customs has set up an express import lane for the speedy release of import cargo. However, only accredited importers can use the express lane. To qualify, the importers must show that they have a clean compliance record with customs rules and regulations. Express processing means quicker processing of entry documents, direct and immediate transfer of cargo from the vessel to the importer's premises, and temporary release of shipments pending the presentation of certain required documents. However, if the shipments have incomplete SGS documents or a dispute exists regarding the valuation, customs will allow tentative release of the goods only on deposit of a 60-day postdated check covering the redemption value of the shipment in the case of incomplete documentation, or the value of the difference between SGS's valuation and the importer's lower estimate in the case of a disputed valuation.

Entry of imported articles must take place within seven days from the date of discharge of the last package from the vessel by the importer (as the holder of the bill of lading), by a duly licensed customs broker acting under authority from the holder of the bill, or by a person duly empowered to act as agent or attorney-in-fact for the holder.

Bonded Warehouses and Reexports There are two bonded warehouse schemes in the Philippines. The Bonded Manufacturing Warehouse (BMW) scheme authorizes a firm to store and manufacture imported products without going through the normal customs import procedures or paying taxes. Under this arrangement, the firm is required to post a bond covering the amount of duties, taxes, and charges that would be due on standard importation of the items; if the finished products are exported within the designated period, the bond is canceled. A letter of request or application to establish a BMW must be filed with the Commissioner of Customs or with the Executive Director of the Garment and Textile Export Board (GTEB) for apparel products. Firms are required to pay a performance bond, a general warehousing bond, and annual warehouse supervision fees. Duty drawbacks are available on reexports. The goods may be kept in the bonded warehouse for a period of six months, which period may be extended for not more than three additional months. Goods not withdrawn or reexported at the end of the prescribed period are sold by auction.

The Customs Common Bonded Warehouse (CCBW) scheme caters to small and medium-sized exporters who cannot afford to operate individual

BMWs. Companies operating the CCBWs serve as import agents and carry out all the necessary import procedures for a service fee—a minimum of 3.5 percent of the importation's value. The service fee covers any expenses incurred through the use of CCBW. Operations and terms are similar to BMWs.

Abandoned Goods Customs will deem an implied abandonment if the interested party fails to file an import entry within seven days (or within the allotted time if an extension has been granted), or, having already filed an entry, fails to claim the imported goods within seven days after entry (or within such time granted by an extension). The implied abandonment becomes effective when the Collector gives notice to the interested party of the declaration of implied abandonment. A person who abandons an article or fails to claim the importation is deemed to have renounced all interest and property rights in the importation.

Within 10 days after filing of the import entry, the owner or importer of any article may abandon to the government all or a part of the articles included in an invoice and will be relieved from the payment of duties, taxes, and all other charges and expenses due on the importation. However, the portion abandoned must not represent less than 10 percent of the total invoice and not less than one package, except in cases of articles imported for personal or family use. The abandoned article must be delivered by the owner or importer at the place within the port of arrival designated by the collector. Failure to comply with the Collector's instructions may make the owner or importer liable for all expenses incurred in connection with the disposition of the articles.

The rules governing abandonment do not relieve the owner or importer from any criminal liability that may arise from a violation of law committed in connection with the importation of the abandoned article.

TRADE ZONES

The Philippine government refers to free trade zones (FTZs) as Export Processing Zones (EPZs). The government has designated four EPZs: Bataan, Cavite, Baguio City, and Mactan in the Visayas (near Cebu). These zones were established to promote industrial expansion, jobs, and exports, as well as to generate foreign exchange and technology transfers by offering incentives and benefits such as exemption from both customs duties and internal revenue taxes on supplies, raw materials, and spare parts, whether foreign or domestic, that are used for production and later exported. Foreign companies may locate facilities in any EPZ, but must register first with the Philippine Economic Zone

Authority (PEZA). There are about 250 registered companies in the EPZs, most of which are involved in the manufacture and export of electronics, garments, rubber products, fabricated metals, plastics, electrical machinery, transport equipment, and industrial chemicals.

The PEZA has also designed 10 sites as "Special Export Processing Zones." These sites include Cavite, Batangas, Laguna, Zambales, and Tarlac on Luzon Island, and Leyte in the Visayas. ASEAN has also agreed to create an FTZ by the year 2003, five years ahead of schedule, and to make substantial cuts in tariffs.

USEFUL ADDRESSES

Bangko Sentral ng Pilipinas (BSP)
(Central Bank of the Philippines)
A. Mabini St., cor. Vito Cruz St.
Malate, Metro Manila, Philippines
Tel: [63] (2) 507-051, 593-380/1, 595-263, 582-372
Fax: [63] (2) 522-3987, 597-363

Bureau of Customs
Port Area
Manila, Philippines
Tel: [63] (2) 530-0966, 484-161/9
Fax: [63] (2) 474-421/4, 530-0966, 818-2971

Bureau of Food and Drugs
DOH Compound
Alabang
Muntinlupa, Metro Manila, Philippines
Tel: [63] (2) 842-4583, 807-0751
Fax: [63] (2) 842-4603

Bureau of Plant Industry
Department of Agriculture
692 San Andres
Malate, Metro Manila, Philippines
Tel: [63] (2) 571-726, 571-776, 586-201
Fax: [63] (2) 521-7650

Bureau of Product Standards
3rd Fl., Trade and Industry Bldg.
361 Sen. Gil J. Puyat Ave.
Makati, Metro Manila, Philippines
Tel: [63] (2) 817-5527
Fax: [63] (2) 817-9870

Department of Agriculture (DOA)
DOA Bldg.
Elliptical Road
Diliman
Quezon City, Metro Manila, Philippines
Tel: [63] (2) 99-8741 to 65, 997-011
Fax: [63] (2) 978-183

Department of Energy (DOE)
One-Stop Action Center
3rd Fl., DOE Building, PNPC Complex
Merritt Road
Fort Bonifacio
Makati, Metro Manila, Philippines
Tel: [63] (2) 851-021, x238, 815-2098
Fax: [63] (2) 877-633

Department of Health (DOH)
San Lazaro Compound
Rizal Avenue
Santa Cruz, Manila, Philippines
Tel: [63] (2) 711-6080, 711-9502/3
Fax: [63] (2) 711-9509, 711-6055

Department of Trade and Industry (DTI)
Trade and Industry Bldg.
361 Sen. Gil J. Puyat Ave. Ext.
Makati, Metro Manila, Philippines
Tel: [63] (2) 818-5705 to 25, 818-1831, 818-5701
Fax: [63] (2) 856-487

Environmental Management Bureau
6th Floor, Philippine Heart Center
East Avenue
Quezon City, Metro Manila, Philippines
Tel: [63] (2) 980-421 x3627, 975-609
Fax: [63] (2) 973-254

Freight Booking and Cargo Consolidation Center (FBCCC)
Philippine Shipper's Council
6th Floor, Filcapital Building
Ayala Ave.
Makati, Metro Manila, Philippines

National Agriculture and Fishery Council (NAFC)
Department of Agriculture
Elliptical Road
Diliman
Quezon City, Metro Manila, Philippines
Tel: [63] (2) 962-2706, 978-234, 988-608
Fax: [63] (2) 922-8622

National Economic and Development Authority (NEDA)
NEDA Bldg.
Amber Avenue
Pasig, Metro Manila, Philippines
Tel: [63] (2) 631-3716, 631-0945 to 64, 673-5031
Fax: [63] (2) 631-3747

National Meat Inspection Commission (NMIC)
Bureau of Animal Industry
Visayas Avenue
Diliman
Quezon City, Metro Manila, Philippines
Tel: [63] (2) 924-3119
Fax: [63] (2) 924-3118

One Stop Import Documentation Center (OSIDC)
International Trade Center
Roxas Blvd.
Manila, Philippines

Philippine Economic Zone Authority (PEZA)
4th Fl., Legaspi Towers 300
Roxas Boulevard
Metro Manila, Philippines
Tel: [63] (2) 521-9725, 521-04-19, 521-0546/7
Fax: [63] (2) 521-8659, 521-0419

Société Generale de Surveillance (SGS)
8th Floor Mondragon House
324 Sen. Gil Puyat Ave.
Makati, Metro Manila, Philippines
Tel: [63] (2) 816-3786
Fax: [63] (2) 818-1560

Tariff Commission
5th Fl., Philippine Heart Center
East Avenue
Quezon City, Metro Manila, Philippines
Tel: [63] (2) 998-106
Fax: [63] (2) 921-7960

Export Policy & Procedures

INTRODUCTION

The Philippine economy, while not yet export oriented, is experiencing an upward trend in the total value of products exported. The nation continues to post trade deficits with all of its major trading partners, except with the US—its largest trading partner. As is the case in many other nations that are just beginning to develop high-value-added industries, Philippine export trade has been beset by outmoded and low-capacity production and a lack of capital resources. Additional factors—mainly political unrest, natural disasters, and labor difficulties—have slowed the nation's advance toward becoming an internationally competitive exporter. With the introduction of government incentives targeted at exporters and the recent liberalization of investment laws, the economic trajectory is becoming more positive.

Although Philippine exports have grown from US$5.8 billion FOB (free on board) in 1980 to US$11.1 billion FOB in 1993, the country's export volume pales in comparison with that of many of its Asian neighbors. The Philippine's major exports include electronics and garments (more than 40 percent of total receipts), although these goods depend heavily on imported raw materials. Other significant foreign exchange earners are coconut, minerals, and aquatic products. Service exports, particularly the remittances of overseas contract workers, are also important sources of foreign

exchange. With the aid of heavy foreign investment, the Philippines has developed a major computer software export industry. For many years, the country has been recognized by its largest trading partners as an important strategic offshore site with a substantial pool of skilled professionals and comparatively low labor and development costs.

The following section discusses Philippine export policy and the procedures for exporting from the country. This information is useful for those interested in purchasing goods and services from the Philippines, expanding their current operations in the Philippines to export markets, establishing an enterprise in the Philippines that will supply foreign markets, or investing in an export business located in the Philippines.

EXPORT POLICY

Government Regulation

The Bureau of Customs (BOC) and the Bureau of Export Trade Promotion (BETP) of the Department of Trade and Industry (DTI) are the governmental agencies that primarily oversee exporting procedures in the country. In addition, the Export and Investment Development Council (EIDC), chaired by the president, coordinates and enhances export promotion efforts. The Bangko Sentral ng Pilipinas (BSP, the Central Bank) technically monitors all export transactions in the country, although in practice it has transferred its authority to issue the Export Declaration (ED) (for manufactured items), and the Report of Foreign Sales (for commodities) to authorized agent banks (AABs).

Other government agencies of particular importance to the exporting process include the Garments and Textile Export Board (GTEB), Board of Investments (BOI), Bureau of Fisheries and Aquatic Resources (BFAR), Bureau of Plant Industry (BPI), Bureau of Animal Industry (BAI), the Depart-

EXPORTING GLOSSARY

Association of Southeast Asian Nations (ASEAN) ASEAN, established in 1967, is comprised of Thailand, Singapore, Malaysia, Indonesia, Brunei, Vietnam, and the Philippines. The purpose of the organization is to strengthen regional cohesion and self-reliance through economic, social, and cultural cooperation. In 1992 the ASEAN leaders agreed to cut intra-ASEAN tariffs (the Common Effective Preferential Tariff scheme) to levels of 0 to 5 percent within a 15-year period and to create an ASEAN Free Trade Area—Common Effective Preferential Tariffs (AFTA-CEPT) in hopes of overcoming barriers to greater integration among the economies of the ASEAN states.

Bangko Sentral ng Pilipinas (BSP) The BSP—the renamed Central Bank—monitors all export transactions in the country, although in practice it has transferred its authority in several respects (such as issuing the Export Declaration form for manufactured items) to Authorized Agent Banks (AABs).

Bureau of Product Standards (BPS) The BPS is a governmental body under the Department of Trade and Industry (DTI) that undertakes rigid testing and assessment of products manufactured locally based on standards set by itself. It affixes a Philippine Standard (PS) quality mark on products manufactured by companies that comply with national or internationally accepted standards. It also issues the Export Commodity Clearance Certificate of Exemption when exporters have goods that are exempt from inspection and export clearance requirements.

Export Assistance Network (EXPONET) EXPONET, which is part of the Department of Trade and Industry, was formed to assist exporters set up their business transactions.

Export Declaration (ED) Once goods are ready to be shipped for exportation, the exporter must file an ED with the Authorized Agent Bank (AAB). This document is the equivalent of the export permit in other countries.

General Agreement on Tariffs and Trade (GATT) A multilateral trade agreement aimed at expanding international trade. Its main goals are to liberalize world trade and place it on a secure basis, thus contributing to economic growth and development. GATT is the only multilateral instrument that lays down rules agreed to by the members for regulating international trade. The organization that oversees the agreement—formerly also known as GATT, but now called the World Trade Organization (WTO)—is the principal international body concerned with negotiating the reduction of trade barriers and improving international trade relations.

Generalized System of Preferences (GSP) An international program under which the members allow, as a means of encouraging economic growth, imports of merchandise from developing countries to enter duty-free or at reduced tariff rates.

Harmonized System (HS) A multipurpose international goods classification system designed to be used by manufacturers, transporters, exporters, importers, customs, statisticians, and others in classifying goods that are moving in international trade under a single commodity code.

ISO 9000 Series of Standards The International Standards Organization (ISO), a worldwide federation of national bodies, has established ISO 9000, a new series of voluntary international quality standards. Adoption of ISO standards has become a virtual prerequisite for doing business internationally.

most favored nation (MFN) A nondiscriminatory trade policy commitment on the part of one country to extend to another country the lowest tariff rates it applies to any other country. All contracting parties to GATT are obligated to apply this treatment with respect to one another.

One-Stop Export Documentation Center (OSEDC) The Philippine government established several branches of the OSEDC, which houses under one roof all the offices involved in export documentation, thus reducing the legwork for exporters and their staffs.

ment of Environment and Natural Resources (DENR), and the Protected Areas and Wildlife Bureau (PAWB).

Export Incentives to Foreign Investors

Foreign investors doing business in the Philippines generally receive the same treatment as nationals in the application of import restrictions and trade-related incentives. An exception is that a foreign-owned enterprise is required to export a higher level of production (70 percent versus the usual 50 percent) to qualify for investment incentives. Export-oriented BOI-registered firms are entitled to a tax credit for taxes and duties on imported raw materials. They may also be exempt from taxes and duties on imported spare parts (for firms exporting at least 70 percent of production), wharfage dues, and any export tax, duty, impost, or fee for exports of nontraditional products. These firms are also allowed access to bonded manufacturing warehouses.

Export Financing

Export financing is available to all Philippine exporters. No preferential rate exists for domestic companies. Exporters may avail themselves of Foreign Currency Deposit Unit (FCDU) loans from local commercial banks up to 100 percent of the letter of credit (L/C), purchase order, or sales contract without prior approval from the BSP. The BSP will lend to exporters at less than treasury bill rates using commercial paper as collateral. In 1993 an Export-Import Banking Program was launched to address the needs of the export community, especially those export-oriented activities that are labor intensive and will use local raw materials.

Export Payments Payments may be made using the following mechanisms:

- letter of credit (L/C)
- documents against payment (D/P)/cash against documents
- documents against acceptance (D/A)
- open account (O/A)
- intercompany open account offset arrangement (which can be used only by firms with parents located abroad)
- consignment
- export advance (which refers to the remittance of payments received more than 30 days before shipment)
- prepayment (which refers to the remittance of payments received within 30 days before shipment)

Because these methods require the use of foreign exchange obtained through the Philippine banking system, D/A and O/A arrangements require prior registration with the BSP if used by other than

exporters of manufactured (which generally may use them without special approval). Since 1992 D/A and O/A have been available—upon approval—to firms operating in the oil and franchised public utility industries and to some approved domestic manufacturers, as well as to those involved in the export of manufactured goods.

Registration of Exporters

Only duly registered businesses are allowed to engage in export activity. A first-time Philippine exporter expecting to be paid in foreign exchange must register with the BSP to receive an export permit. A sole proprietorship must register with the Bureau of Trade Regulation and Consumer Protection (BTRCP). A merchandise broker must register with the Broker's Division at BTRCP for a Certificate of Authority. Partnerships and corporations must register with the Securities and Exchange Commission (SEC). A mayor's permit and municipal license are also required for businesses and must be obtained in the municipality in which the business is located. To export to a socialist country, the exporter must obtain approval from the Philippine International Trading Corporation (PITC).

Regulated Products

The following products require export approval from the relevant governmental agency:

- aircraft (Department of Transportation and Communications—DTC)
- all plants, planting materials, and plant products capable of harboring pests, as well as live and dead insect specimens (BPI)
- animals and animal products (BAI)
- antiques, cultural artifacts, and historical relics (National Museum)
- cement and clinker (BOI)
- coffee (DTI)
- copper concentrates (BOI)
- exports destined to the Republic of South Africa (PITC)
- exports to socialist and centrally planned economy countries (PITC)
- firearms and ammunition (Firearms and Explosives Office, Philippine National Police, Department of Interior & Local Government)
- garments, textiles, carpets, polyester stable fiber, filament yarns, fabrics, upholstered furniture, and other natural and synthetic fibers, plus all products made in whole or in part of these fibers for export to all countries, with or without quota restrictions (GTEB)
- gold from small-scale mining or panned gold (BSP)
- grains and grain by-products (National Food Authority—NFA)

- legal tender, Philippine notes and coins, checks, money orders, and other bills of exchange greater than P5,000 (about US$190) (BSP) drawn in pesos against banks operating in the Philippines
- lumber, logs, poles, and piles, including log core, flitches, and railroad ties (DENR)
- motion pictures, television films, and related publicity materials (Movie and Television Review and Classification Board—MTRCB)
- natural fibers (Fiber Industry Development Authority—FIDA)
- oil and petroleum products (Energy Regulatory Board–ERB)
- radioactive materials (Philippine Nuclear Research)
- undersized raw shells of Trocas, Gold lip, Black lip, *Turbo narmoratus* and *Kapis tridacna crocea* (BFAR)
- sugar and molasses (Sugar Regulatory Administration—SRA)
- wild marine species, such as water snakes, seasnakes, frogs, and products from their skin or meat (BFAR)
- wild terrestrial species, such as certain mammals (Philippine monkeys and cloud-rats), certain birds, reptiles, flora, and all species of butterflies (PAWB)

Prohibited Exports

The BETP has identified the following as "prohibited" exports, which are controlled by the designated government agency. Included are:
- abaca and ramie seeds, seedlings, suckers, root stocks, and other planting materials (FIDA)
- bakawan (mangrove) (DENR)
- bangus fry and Mother bangus (BFAR)
- buri seeds and seedlings (BPI)
- matured coconuts and coconut seedlings (Philippine Coconut Authority—PCA)
- prawn spawn and fry (BFAR)
- raw materials for cottage industries (DTI)
- trumpet shells, helmet shells, raw shells, and their by-products including meat of giant clams (BFAR)
- stalactites and stalagmites (DENR)
- wild marine species and their by-products, including precious, semiprecious, and all ordinary corals (BFAR)
- certain wild terrestrial species and their by-products (PAWB)

Tariffs

Philippine foreign trade policy provides encouragement for commodity exports that generate foreign exchange earnings for the country. All such export commodities are classified as freely export-able, regulated, or prohibited. Most commodities are freely exportable unless a determination of national interest requires regulation of a commodity.

Quality Standards

Product Standards Quality Marking Scheme The Bureau of Product Standards (BPS), a governmental body under the DTI, undertakes rigid testing and assessment of products locally manufactured according to established standards. The BPS affixes a Philippine Standard (PS) quality mark on products manufactured by companies that comply with national or internationally accepted standards.

Metric System The BPS requires the use of the metric system (SI units) in the measurement of all products, commodities, materials, services, and utilities, as well as in commercial transactions, contracts, and other legal instruments, official records, and documents.

ISO 9000 Certification In 1992 the Philippine government launched ISO 9000 Certification to spur business growth and provide greater assistance to Philippine manufacturers and exporters in becoming more competitive globally. The requirements set by the International Standards Organization under the ISO 9000 Series of Standards have been adopted as the Philippine National Standards (PNS) 1000 Series. The standards can be applied in the services sector (including banking, insurance, tourism, and health and medical services), as well as in manufacturing.

The BPS has concluded a Memorandum of Understanding with foreign certification bodies for joint quality system assessment work in specific fields. These organizations are TUV Product Service GmbH (Germany) and BVQI (United Kingdom).

A certification from BPS shows that a company is structured to produce quality products and services. As of April 1994, BPS had certified 34 local companies as being in compliance with ISO 9000.

Trade Preferences

The Philippines is a signatory to the following treaties:
- *General Agreement on Tariffs and Trade (GATT)* The Philippines is entitled to most favored nation (MFN) status and is eligible for duty free treatment for designated articles under the Generalized System of Preferences (GSP). For further information on GATT, MFN status, and GSP, *see* the "Exporting Glossary" on page 94.
- *ASEAN* The Philippines is a member of ASEAN, the other members of which include Indonesia, Malaysia, Singapore, Thailand, Vietnam, and Brunei. The ASEAN Free Trade Area–Common Effective Preferential Tariffs (AFTA-CEPT) serves as the mechanism for the conversion of

ASEAN into a free trade regional market. (For further information on ASEAN and AFTA-CEPT, *see* the "Exporting Glossary" on page 94.)

Incentives for Exporters

Exporters enjoy a variety of incentives, including simplified import and export procedures and exemption from the payment of excise taxes on exports. With the liberalized policies on foreign exchange, exporters of commodities may retain 100 percent of the foreign exchange proceeds from exports; they may now freely use these for any purpose.

Exporters also receive refunds of value-added tax (VAT) paid on imports for reexport, foreign exchange assistance, and the use of low-cost facilities in the country's Export Processing Zones (EPZs).

Imports of Raw Materials for Export Purposes To assist Philippine manufacturers in obtaining the raw materials—many of which must be imported—necessary to produce high-quality exports, manufacturers of export products are permitted to import such raw materials duty-free on consignment or through a drawback program.

Imports on consignment are raw materials supplied to the manufacturer by the foreign buyer of the finished product. Only registered exporters having total capital (assets net of financing) not more than P5 million (about US$190,000) and able to present a certified copy of an existing contract may qualify for consignment arrangements. Consignment requires the exporter to obtain an Import Authority from the BSP's Current Import and Commodity Classification Department; this must be done before shipment of the imported materials. Exporters not registered with the appropriate authority should apply for a Certificate of Qualification with Customs.

On a duty-drawback basis, the Philippine supplier pays the appropriate duties for the import, claiming an offsetting refund or tax credit at a later date. Exporters using this method must export their finished product within one year of the import of the raw materials and then must apply for a rebate within a year of exporting that product. A refund of 99 percent is allowed for taxes and duties paid on the imported materials, including packing, covering, labeling, and other costs associated with obtaining imported materials.

Bonded Warehouses There are two bonded warehouse schemes in the Philippines.

Bonded Manufacturing Warehouse (BMW) Scheme This scheme authorizes a firm to store and manufacture imported products without going through the usual customs import procedures and payment of taxes. Under this arrangement, the importing firm must post a bond to cover the duties, taxes, and other charges due on importation and to ensure the exportation of the finished products within the designated period.

Customs Common Bonded Warehouse (CCBW) Scheme This scheme caters to small and medium-sized exporters who cannot afford individually to operate individual BMWs. Companies operating CCBWs serve as import agents and take care of all the necessary import procedures for a minimum service fee of 3.5 percent of the value of the import. The service fee covers any expenses incurred through the use of CCBW. Operations and terms are similar to those for BMWs.

Free Trade Zones The Philippine government refers to free trade zones (FTZs) as Export Processing Zones (EPZs). The government has designated four EPZs: Bataan, Cavite, Baguio City, and Mactan (near Cebu) in the Visayas. These zones were established to promote industrial expansion, jobs, and exports, as well as to generate foreign exchange and technology transfers by offering incentives and benefits such as exemption from both customs duties and internal revenue taxes on supplies, raw materials, and spare parts—whether foreign or domestic—that are used for production slated to be exported. Foreign companies may locate facilities in any EPZ, but must register first with the Philippine Economic Zone Authority (PEZA). There are about 250 registered companies in the EPZs, most of which are involved in the manufacture and export of electronics, garments, rubber products, fabricated metals, plastics, electrical machinery, transport equipment, and industrial chemicals.

PEZA has also designed 10 sites as Special Export Processing Zones (SEPZs). These sites include Cavite, Batangas, Laguna, Zambales and Tarlac on Luzon Island, and Leyte in the Visayas. ASEAN has also agreed to create an FTZ by the year 2003, five years ahead of schedule, and to make substantial cuts in tariffs.

Restrictions and Prohibitions on Exports

Unfair Competition Restrictions An importing country may assess anti-dumping and countervailing tariffs against Philippine exports that are found to have unfairly flooded the market in the importing country with goods priced below market. These tariffs vary depending on the anti-dumping charges brought at any one time against Philippine exports.

Quotas and Other Restrictions Quota restrictions exist on exports of textiles and garments. In addition, Generalized System of Preferences (GSP) status may be revoked by an importing country if the volume of a specific category of Philippine exports to that country becomes disproportionate. The standard often used is 50 percent of total imports of the specific product.

EXPORT PROCEDURES

Parties to an export-import transaction must basically comply with two sets of requirements: the export regulations of the Philippines and the import regulations of the country to which the goods will be delivered. This discussion focuses on the first step: sending the goods out of the Philippines. Once this is done, it is generally the responsibility of the foreign buyer to satisfy the import regulations of the buyer's country. However, it should be noted that these may include import documentation, declarations, or licenses, which may require documentation available only from the exporter.

Export transactions are handled primarily through customs brokers and freight forwarders. Philippine export procedures can be quite complex. In response to concerns raised by exporters, the government has taken several steps to simplify export procedures. For example, the Export Assistance Network (EXPONET) has been formed by the DTI to assist exporters in structuring their business transactions. In addition, the government has established several branches of the One-Stop Export Documentation Center (OSEDC), which brings together in a single location all the offices involved in documentation, lessening the legwork necessary for exporters and their staff members.

Exporting Registrations and Licenses

Registration First-time exporters must fill out an Information Sheet for Exporters and submit it to the Export Department of BSP through an AAB. This information sheet must be renewed every three years. BOI-registered and EPZA-registered firms must file their export permits with the AAB once export goods are ready to be shipped.

Export Licenses If an export license or certificate is required, the exporter must apply to the appropriate governmental agency. A customs broker should be consulted on this matter.

Preshipment Stage

Preshipment Customs Clearance If the exported goods are garments or textiles, the exporter must obtain clearance from the GTEB. It usually takes one day for the GTEB to process applications for a Textile Export Clearance (TEC). If the item is subject to a quota restriction, the exporter must obtain an Export Quota (EQ) or an Export Authorization (EA) from the GTEB in addition to export clearance. These documents must be obtained before the exporter files the ED with the AAB. The GTEB furnishes information on quota categories and quota situations of other countries to both the Confederation of Garment Exporters of the Philippines (CONGEP) and the Foreign Buyers Association of the Philippines (FOBAP); it also issues special documents (such as the export license and the certificate of origin, or the Special Customs Invoice required by US Customs) required by quota countries.

If traditional products are being exported, the exporter must file a Report on Foreign Sales with the BSP through an AAB.

Insurance Arrangements An exporter should consider insuring the goods until the risk of damage or loss passes to the importer. European buyers, however, often favor shipment on a cost plus insurance plus freight (CIF) basis, whereby the seller pays for the insurance and handles all the necessary arrangements. US buyers, on the other hand, tend to favor free-on-board (FOB) in which the buyer bears the cost of the insurance from the point at which the seller has loaded the merchandise. Oftentimes, the L/C spells out all the insurance details. In the absence of such a provision, the standard practice is to insure the goods for CIF value plus 10 percent.

Documentation at Packing

Commercial Invoice The commercial invoice is the document containing the seller's charges for the goods being sent to the foreign buyer. The BOC requires it before the cargo can be loaded, and the negotiating bank needs to see it before the exporter will receive payment for selling the goods. The commercial invoice includes the following information:

- date
- name and address of buyer and seller
- order or contract number
- quantity and description of goods
- unit price including other charges and the total price
- weight of the goods
- number of packages being sent in the shipment
- shipping marks and numbers
- terms of delivery and payments
- shipment details

Certificate of Origin To obtain preferential tariff treatment by the country of destination under GSP, the exporter must obtain a Certificate of Origin Form A, approved and signed by customs. Customs will determine the tariff classification of the product under the Harmonized System (HS), check and double-check the product's eligibility for preferential treatment, and determine the ceiling or quota, if any, set by the country of destination. The exporter should also verify specific rules applicable for the country of destination. In addition, the exporter should be wary of export sales contracts in which the importer has added a clause that the price of the exported goods relates to the preferential tariff treatment of those goods under GSP, as this exposes the exporter to liability for the difference if the goods are found ineligible for preferential tariff treatment.

Export Declaration Once goods are ready to be shipped for exportation, the exporter must file an ED with the AAB. This document serves as the equivalent of the export permit in other countries. ED1 and ED4 must be sent to Customs; ED2 and ED5 must be sent to the Export Department of BSP; ED3 must be sent to Customs to obtain the Authority to Load; ED6 remains with the BSP; ED7 remains with the exporter; ED8 must be sent to the Arrastre Office; ED9 must be sent to the Philippine Ports Authority for wharfage fees; and ED10 must be sent to the carrier.

Authority to Load To authorize loading at the Port of Manila, the exporter must present the following documents:

- ED1 and ED4 (both of which were previously submitted to customs by the AAB)
- ED3
- ED8
- original copy of the commodity clearance or license to use the PS certification mark
- Bureau of Internal Revenue tax clearance
- commercial invoice
- photocopy of sales contract for commodities subject to export tariff
- packing list (if merchandise is packed in multiple containers or cases, or if the quantities, weight, or contents of individual units in a shipment vary)

Documentation at Shipping

The documentation requirements for shipping goods from the Philippines vary, depending on the mode of transport: overland (truck or rail), sea, or air. The most vital document in sea transportation is the bill of lading (the analogous air waybill serves the same function for shipments made by air) because it is the document that gives title to the merchandise. Therefore, the bill of lading must conform to the conditions and terms of the L/C in every particular. In addition to the usual bill of lading documents, a shipper may request to see insurance, health, and other required certificates. The foreign importer or the bank that is handling payment for the goods may have additional documentary requirements that must be met before the shipper will accept the shipment. For a fee, exporters can have freight forwarders deal with shipping documentation, cargo consolidation, and loading. Most freight forwarders in the Philippines do not handle insurance; rather, the shipper or consignee is usually responsible for insuring the consignment.

Air Freight Due to the high costs associated with air freight, exporters rarely choose to ship goods by air unless the goods have a high value relative to their weight, are perishable, or must reach the buyer as soon as possible. Sometimes the high costs incurred in shipping by air can be offset by savings in packing, handling, inventory documentation, and delivery. Semiconductor exports, for example, are always sent by air because of their transit requirements, whereas garments are usually shipped by sea unless the shipment is late. If air shipment is chosen, four copies of the standard International Air Transport Association (IATA) form air waybill are required and must be signed by the carrier or its agent and stamped "For Consular Purposes Only."

Shipments by Sea The most common transport method used by exporters is ocean freight. Three negotiable bills of lading specifying freight and other charges are required. The bills of lading must be signed by the carrier or its agent and stamped "For Consular Purposes Only." "To order" bills of lading are allowed.

With the increase in containerized shipping, the combined transport bill of lading (CBL) has become common. The CBL is used when the merchandise is transshipped using more than one method of transport. Banks no longer require that special authorization for CBLs be granted in the L/C. The CBL lists both the place of acceptance of the merchandise (where the goods are taken in charge rather than loaded on board) and the place of delivery (rather than the port of discharge).

Exporters can choose from four types of sea vessels: conference, nonconference, charter, and tramp. The choice often depends on the shipper's requirements. Conference vessels provide regular service, but their rates are generally 15 to 20 percent higher than nonconference vessels. To obtain better rates, regular shippers can sign a shipper's contract with a conference vessel. Some carriers will waive standard rates and give a discount to a regular shipper on a case-by-case basis. Some regular shippers find the nonconference vessels more flexible.

Overland Transport One type of bill of lading that involves overland transport is the through bill of lading. It covers receipt of the cargo at the point of origin for delivery to the ultimate consignee, using two or more modes of transportation, such as sea and rail. It is noteworthy that the improvement of roads and bridges is Metro Manila and other key parts of the country is a priority under the Philippine Government's Medium-Term Development Plan.

TIPS FOR AVOIDING AND REMEDYING DOCUMENTARY DISCREPANCIES

In dealing with banks and L/Cs, the exporter must submit clean documents. The banks will scrutinize the terms of the L/Cs and compare them with the documentation submitted by the exporter. The bank's responsibility begins and ends with the documentation itself, and not with the actual condition of the merchandise. The banks will make payment on the L/Cs if the proper documents with the correct number of copies are submitted in an orderly and timely manner. However, even minor irregularities in the documents, such as spelling errors and small technicalities, can prevent payment from being made.

Exporters should keep in mind the following matters when completing and submitting documents to the banks:

- Documents must be of the exact type and number requested by the foreign buyer; substitutions are not acceptable.
- Items may not be included in one document when they are normally included in another document.
- Documents can be read together to form one fully complying description of the merchandise; however, other documents tendered, if not required under the terms of the L/C, will not be acknowledged by the banks even if they give a complete and full description of the merchandise.

Some common documentary discrepancies between the L/Cs and the documentation include the following:

Missing information

- Some documents are missing..
- Clean "on board" bill of lading is not tendered.

Inconsistencies

- Some documents are inconsistent with each other with respect to dates, signatures, or merchandise description.
- Shipping marks and numbers do not coincide with all the documents.
- Amounts on the invoice and the draft differ or exceed the credit amount without authorization.
- Draft is drawn on a third party and not the beneficiary of the credit.
- Draft is payable at an indeterminable date.
- Late submissions.
- Insurance certificate does not comply with the conditions stated in the L/C.
- Insurance certificate is in a currency other than that

of the L/C.

- Insurance certificate provides insufficient coverage.
- Insurance policy does not begin as of the shipping date.
- Documents are tendered after the L/C date expires.
- Documents are presented late, after the bill of lading has issued, thus preventing the negotiating bank from negotiating the L/C before arrival of the goods at the port of destination; these documents are often termed "stale."

The following guidelines should help foreign importers reduce the chance of documentary discrepancies and, thus, reduce delays in filling orders from foreign buyers:

- Keep documentary requirements clear and simple.
- Eliminate all unnecessary or extraneous documents.
- Provide adequate time for the exporter to receive documentation from the shipper, then assemble and transmit all further required documents to the importer or importer's agent.
- Provide the exporter with correct details of order, including the correct spellings and translations of pertinent information.
- Make sure that the terms and conditions of the purchase are thoroughly understood.
- Select a bank that has experience in international trade and can give advice on opening and negotiating L/Cs, dealing with discrepancies, and methods of financing the purchase under the L/C terms.
- Promptly notify the exporter if it becomes necessary to change any of the conditions and terms of the purchase after the order has been placed.

The exporter can attempt to correct any irregularities in the documentation and retender the documents for negotiation before they become stale or before the L/C expires. The exporter should keep in mind the following tips for remedying documentary discrepancies:

- Resubmit documents if sufficient time exists: retrieve the documents from the bank, rectify any errors in the documents, or ask foreign buyer to amend the L/C.
- Request authority to pay: request the negotiating bank on the Philippine end to cable or telex the issuing bank regarding the documentary discrepancy and requesting an authority to pay;

issuing bank will then notify the foreign buyer of the discrepancy and the request, and then wait for the foreign buyer's decision.

- Request collection basis at exporter's own risk: request the negotiating bank to send the documents at the exporter's own risk to the issuing bank on a collection basis; when issuing bank receives the documents, the foreign buyer has a chance to review them along with the discrepancies before making a decision whether to authorize payment; if foreign buyer accepts the documents as they are, foreign buyer then instructs issuing bank to telex or cable the negotiating bank to pay the exporter.

- Request payment under reserve: request that negotiating bank accept the documents containing the discrepancies and pay exporter under reserve, or set aside funds for the exporter in a suspense account until reimbursement is received from the issuing bank. This remedy works best when the exporter has a good relationship with the negotiating bank; negotiating bank retains the right of recourse against the exporter if the foreign buyer does not accept the documents and refuses to pay.

- Issue letter of indemnity: issue a letter of indemnity to the negotiating bank, stating that exporter will be fully responsible for the consequences of any discrepancy; exporter is liable to refund the proceeds, plus any interest or other charges, to the bank if the foreign buyer refuses to accept the documents as tendered; it should be noted that, oftentimes, foreign buyers will request that their L/Cs contain a stipulation that "letters of indemnity are prohibited."

Customs Clearance

If the goods to be exported fall under Executive Order No. 1016, which withdrew the inspection, commodity clearance, and export clearance requirements on a number of exports, the exporter must apply for an Export Commodity Clearance Certificate of Exemption from the BPS. The BPS issues the clearance under the following conditions:

- when voluntarily requested by a Philippine exporter
- when required of a Philippine exporter by a foreign buyer, which requires that the exporter satisfy a specific quality standard

- when a prior export shipment is reported to the BPS as having been rejected in another country, which means that the succeeding shipment involving essentially the same specifications should be given an all-clear by the BPS before it can clear customs

If the goods do not fall under Executive Order No. 1016, the AAB must file the ED and Export Permit, if required, with Customs. Customs will then issue an Authority to Load if everything is in order. Next, the exporter must pay arrastre (hauling) charges unless the exporter is the BOI or is PEZA-registered.

When cargo is accepted for shipping, the exporter will receive a bill of lading (if the goods are being shipped by sea) or an airway bill (if the goods are being shipped by air freight).

Within a week after loading is completed, the exporter should present the following documents to the AAB:

- covering draft for negotiation or collection
- bill of lading or air waybill
- signed commercial invoice
- insurance certificate
- standard packing list, if required
- certificate of inspection or commodity clearance
- certificate of origin
- consular invoice
- certificate of shipment by BOC

USEFUL ADDRESSES

Bangko Sentral ng Pilipinas (BSP)
(Central Bank of the Philippines)
A. Mabini St., cor. Vito Cruz St.
Malate, Metro Manila, Philippines
Tel: [63] (2) 507-051, 593-380/1, 595-263, 582-372
Fax: [63] (2) 522-3987, 597-363

Bureau of Customs (BOC)
Port Area
Manila, Philippines
Tel: [63] (2) 530-0966, 484-161/9
Fax: [63] (2) 474-421/4, 530-0966, 818-2971

Bureau of Export Trade Promotion
Department of Trade and Industry
5th Fl., New Solid Bldg.
357 Sen. Gil J. Puyat Avenue
Makati, Metro Manila, Philippines
Tel: [63] (2) 817-5298, 817-5203, 818-5701
Fax: [63] (2) 817-4923, 819-1816

Bureau of Product Standards (BPS)
3rd Fl., Trade and Industry Bldg.
361 Sen. Gil J. Puyat Ave.
Makati, Metro Manila, Philippines
Tel: [63] (2) 817-5527, 817-5339, 817-9602
Fax: [63] (2) 817-9870

Bureau of Trade Regulation and Consumer Protection
Department of Trade and Industry
2nd Fl., Trade and Industry Bldg.
361 Sen. Gil Puyat Ave.
Makati, Metro Manila, Philippines
Tel: [63] (2) 817-5280, 817-5340, 863-431, 818-5701 to 35
Fax: [63] (2) 810-9363

Confederation of Garment Exporters of the Philippines, Inc.
Suite 103, Marlis Bldg.
121 Tordesillas St.
Makati, Metro Manila, Philippines
Tel: [63] (2) 818-0224, 861-059

Department of Trade and Industry
Trade and Industry Bldg.
361 Sen. Gil J. Puyat Ave. Ext.
3117 Makati, Metro Manila, Philippines
Tel: [63] (2) 818-5705 to 25, 818-1831, 818-5701
Fax: [63] (2) 856-487

Foreign Buyers Association of the Philippines
Suite 607, Philbanking Bldg.
Ayala Avenue
Makati, Metro Manila, Philippines
Tel: [63] (2) 818-9472
Fax: [63] (2) 817-9160

Garment and Textiles Export Board
4th Fl., New Solid Building
357 Sen. Gil J. Puyat Avenue
Makati, Metro Manila, Philippines
Tel: [63] (2) 817-4321, 817-4323
Fax: [63] (2) 817-4339

International Standards Organization (ISO)
1 rue de Varembé
P.O. Box 56
CH-1211 Geneva 20, Switzerland
Tel: [41] (22) 749-0111
Fax: [41] (22) 733-3430

One-Stop Export Documentation Center (OSEDC)
International Trade Center
Roxas Boulevard
Manila, Philippines

Philippine Economic Zone Authority
4th Fl., Legaspi Towers 300
Roxas Boulevard
Metro Manila, Philippines
Tel: [63] (2) 521-9725, 521-04-19, 521-0546/7
Fax: [63] (2) 521-8659, 521-0419

Industry Reviews

INTRODUCTION

This chapter describes the status of and trends in major Philippine industries. It also lists key contacts useful for finding sources of supply, developing sales leads, and conducting economic research. Industries are grouped into 10 categories. Some smaller sectors of commerce are not detailed here, while others may overlap into more than one area. If your business even remotely fits into a category, don't hesitate to contact several of the organizations listed; they should be able to assist you further in gathering the information you need. We have included industry-specific contacts only. For general trade organizations, which may also be very helpful (particularly if your business is in an industry not specifically covered), refer to the "Important Addresses" chapter, beginning on page 297.

Each section has two segments: an industry summary and a list of useful contacts. The summary discusses the nature of the industry and gives an overview of the range of products available and that industry's ability to compete in worldwide markets. Key contacts include government departments, trade associations, publications, and trade fairs, all of which can provide information specific to the industry. Addresses, telephone numbers, and fax numbers are in the Philippines unless otherwise noted. The country code for calling the Philippines is [63]. An entire volume could probably be devoted to each area, but such in-depth coverage is beyond the scope of this book; instead the intention is to give you a basis for your own research.

It is strongly recommended that readers also peruse the "Trade Fairs" chapter, beginning on page 121, and "Important Addresses", beginning on page 297, where there are additional resources, including a variety of trade promotion organizations, chambers of commerce, business services, and media.

AGRICULTURAL PRODUCTS AND PROCESSED FOODS

In 1993 the agricultural sector accounted for about 22 percent of the country's gross domestic production and employed about 45 percent of the labor force (crops and livestock-raising account for 75 percent of this production and forestry and fishing together account for the remaining 25 percent). For many decades, agricultural production has grown steadily, meeting most of domestic demand except for specialty products. However, production generally fell during the 1980s with the exception of corn (maize), which was subject to growing demand as an animal feed. Rates have been increasing since the beginning of the 1990s. The agricultural sector grew at a rate of 2.4 percent in 1994, up from a rate of 2.1 percent in 1993.

The percentage of the population living in rural areas declined from 68 percent in 1970 to about 60 percent in 1990, and the share of the workforce engaged in agricultural production declined to less than 40 percent. Roughly two-thirds of agricultural workers farm their own lands, while the rest of the workers are landless tenants.

Land Crops

In 1988 palay (unhusked rice) and corn accounted for about half of the total crop area in the Philippines. In 1992 nearly 9.1 million metric tons of palay were produced. In the same year, the Philippines produced 4.5 million tons of corn, 11.4 million tons of coconuts, 21.5 million tons of sugarcane, and 3 million tons of bananas to round out the inventory of its major cash crops. The country also produced 1.1 million tons of pineapples and 3.1 million tons of vegetables.

Coconut products—including coconut oil, copra (dried coconut), and desiccated coconut—accounted for approximately 5.9 percent of Philippine exports by dollar value in 1992. About 25 percent of cultivated land is planted with coconut trees, and it is estimated that between 25 percent and 33 percent of the country's residents are at least partly dependent on coconuts for their livelihoods. The Southern Tagalog and Bicol regions of Luzon and the Eastern Visayas are the centers of coconut production. In the 1980s, western and southern Mindanao also became important coconut growing regions. The average coconut farm is a medium-sized unit of less than four hectares (10 acres). Many owners employ local peasants to collect coconuts rather than engage in active farming through tenancy relationships. The Philippines is the world's leading exporter of coconut products, but their relative importance has been declining.

Historically, from the mid-1800s to the 1970s, sugar has also been an important crop, grown on larger farms and accounting for much of the wealth of the Filipino elite. In the 1950s and 1960s, sugar accounted for more than 20 percent of Filipino exports, but by 1992 it had fallen to less than about 1 percent of exports by value. Although its special trading relationship with the US has provided a constant market for its exports, the Philippine sugar industry has severely declined since its prosperous days of previous decades.

Pineapples and Cavendish bananas (a dwarf variety) are additional important earners of foreign exchange, although they accounted for a relatively small portion of cultivated areas.

Products Chief crops are sugar, rice, corn, pineapple, bananas, and coconut. Lesser cash crops include coffee, mangos, tobacco, abaca (hemp), rubber, and cacao.

Competitive Situation The government has had only limited success in stabilizing agricultural prices because it has limited funds with which to subsidize farmers and buy imported crops for subsidized sale. However, official agencies have distributed irrigation water below-cost. The government encourages producers to diversify crop production in a way that meets market demand yet concentrates on maintaining the most important crops, such as rice and corn, despite low market returns. Whether the country can continue to meet its own demand and sell crops profitably in international markets depends on many nonagricultural forces: tropical storms, economic crises, and rising debt and declining income for farmers. Climatic conditions are a major determinant of crop production. Soil type, topography, government policy, and regional conflict between Christians and Muslims have also played a role in agricultural activity.

Since the 1970s, the government has had an active role in the coconut industry, merging coconut-related governmental operations, acquiring banks to serve the coconut industry, levying taxes on the industry, and making plans to reforest coconut plantations with newer hybrid strains. In principle, farmers were to benefit from much of the government taxes and programs (for example, such benefits were to include life insurance, educational scholarships, and farm subsidies), but to date the actual benefits received have been marginal. When coconut prices began to fall in the early 1980s, pressure mounted to alter the structure of the industry and the government dismantled the government operated United Coconut Oil Mills.

Land reforms—in which those working the land would acquire ownership—have been promised but seldom delivered. Although some land has been distributed, it is only a small percentage of the acreage promised. Because the government is required to compensate the owners and recipients have to reimburse the government, the programs continue to operate at a very low level without adequate funds.

Being a tropical country, the Philippines grows a large variety of fruit, a good number of which are still rare in the importing developed countries. So far, the majority of the country's exported fruit has consisted of canned pineapple. However, consumers in developed markets are becoming more sophisticated and adventurous. Because of their exotic appeal, demand for some Philippine fruits may grow. Thus the industry must expand trade contacts and undertake more promotional activities.

Livestock and Dairy

In 1990 the livestock industry, consisting primarily of cattle, carabao (water buffalo), hogs, and chickens, accounted for almost 20 percent of value added in the agricultural sector, up from 12 percent in 1980. Much of the growth came from an increase in chicken raising. In the late 1980s, hogs provided 60 percent of total domestic meat production, chickens 15 percent, and cattle and carabao about 20 percent. The dairy industry in the Philippines is quite small. Liquid milk is generally not available in the market, and virtually all canned and dry milk is imported.

Products Carabao, cattle, chickens, hogs.

Competitive Situation The Philippines is relatively self-sufficient in hog and chicken production, but imports approximately 4,500 tons of beef annually. The economic difficulties of the 1980s made the lower-priced chicken and carabao attractive substitutes for higher-priced pork and beef, but carabao raising remained oriented primarily toward providing work animals.

Forestry

There is presently concern in the Philippines about diminishing forests. Although as much as 42 percent of the Philippine territory is classified as forested, much of it lies at higher elevations and on steep slopes and is relatively inaccessible and of poor quality. And because tropical logs and lumber have been a major export product in recent decades, some observers argue that actual exploitable forest area has fallen almost by half, and the dangers of deforestation are becoming far more apparent. The contribution of logs and lumber to total Philippine exports declined from 25 percent in 1969 to less than 1 percent in 1992. Reforestation programs have met with only limited success, and some officials believe a timber shortage could occur within the next decade.

Fishing

Fishing accounts for between 3.5 and 4.5 percent of GDP annually. Among seafood exports, tuna is the biggest earner, and about 95 percent of the catch of this type of fish is sold abroad as canned tuna. Roundscad is caught in greater volume, but is consumed domestically. Prawn production, mostly through aquaculture, developed rapidly in the 1980s, averaging more than 30,000 tons per year during the period. Shrimp and prawns are exported mainly to Japan and the US.

Of total fish production, about half has been caught by the roughly 574,000 municipal and subsistence fishermen who operate small boats in shallow water, usually less than three km (2 mi) offshore. About one-quarter comes from the approximately 45,000 commercial fisherman who can work beyond 15 km (9 mi) from shore, while the remaining quarter was harvested by the aquaculture industry.

Aquaculture production has been rising steadily while capture production fluctuates. Commercial catches (such as tuna) and aquaculture products (such as prawns) have a higher value than most municipal varieties, so despite the sluggish growth in catch volume, catch value grew by 9 percent in 1994. The commercial fishing and aquaculture sectors have recently grown in both volume and value, while the municipal (near-shore) sector has declined in production. Near-shore waters have been overfished and poorly managed for years. Future declines in municipal production are to be expected, as long as no effective corrective measures are taken.

The Philippines is also one of the world's leading suppliers of *Eucheuma* seaweed and carrageenan. It is one of the few countries in the world that has successfully grown marine algae (seaweed) in commercial quantities. Seaweed grows abundantly throughout coastal and reef areas, and the island regions of the central and southern Philippines provide ideal conditions for sea algae plantations.

Products Mollusks, prawns, roundscad, shrimp, seaweed, tuna.

Competitive Situation Although the Philippines has great natural resources for fishing and continues to tap the potential, there is growing concern over environmental pollution and destruction. The fishing industry has been hurt recently by industrial pollution, destruction of coral reefs, and silting from excessive erosion resulting from deforestation. There is also some concern for quality control problems in its fishing industry. Japanese importers have reported high levels of bacteria in the Philippines prawns. The government is working to correct the problems and the fishing industry should remain strong. World demand for tuna and other marine species is likely to remain strong, and the Philippines has a competitive pricing edge in the world market because labor can be had at costs below those in most other countries.

Processed Foods

The processed foods industry accounted for about 40 percent of food exports in 1991 (compared with 60 percent for fresh or semiprocessed foods), and the industry is growing at a fast rate. Exports of processed fruit and vegetables in 1991 were worth US$193 million—an increase of 186 percent over their value in 1990—although nearly half of this total represented exports of canned pineapple. Exports of processed fish, crustaceans and mollusks were worth US$114.7 million. Other areas of major growth were sugar preparations, cereals, and livestock. In 1993 processing of food products accounted for nearly 40 percent of manufacturing value added, four times the contribution of the next largest energy industry, energy products.

Although about 450 companies in the Philippines export processed foods, seven companies dominate the market: Del Monte Philippines, Dole

Philippines, Mar Fishing, Permex Producers, Pure Foods, Sancanco Canning, and Century Canning. Other major companies include specialty producers, such as San Miguel Corporation (beverages), and chocolate and confectionery firms Philippine Cocoa, Wrigley Philippines, Nestlé Philippines, and Cocoa Specialties.

Products Bananas, banana crackers, beans, canned and frozen tuna, centrifugal sugar, chewing gum, cocoa butter, coconut (desiccated), copra cake and meal, cucumber, eggs, eggplant, fresh pineapple, guava, mangos, meat products (chicken, pork, and beef), papaya, pepper, pineapples in syrup, raw Robusta coffee, shrimps and prawns, tomato.

Competitive Situation The Philippine government is eager to attract both local and foreign investors to its food processing industry. The industry needs to retool, refurbish, and upgrade equipment to improve its competitiveness. Some medium- and large-scale enterprises have started to upgrade their equipment. However, cottage and small-scale companies which would like to modernize have been hampered by lack of funds and high interest rates. Industry leaders predict dramatic increases in exports in the processed seafood—shrimp, prawn, and tuna—and fruit and vegetables industries.

Government Agencies and Corporations

Bureau of the Animal Industry (BAI)
Visayas Ave.
Diliman
Quezon City, Metro Manila
Tel: (2) 966-883

Bureau of Fisheries and Aquatic Resources
Arcadia Bldg.
Quezon Ave.
Quezon City, Metro Manila
Tel: (2) 965-498

Bureau of Food and Drugs
DOH Compound
Alabang
Muntinlupa, Metro Manila
Tel: (2) 842-4583, 807-0751
Fax: (2) 842-4603

Bureau of Forest Development
Visayas Ave.
Diliman
Quezon City, Metro Manila
Tel: (2) 964-826

Bureau of Plant Industry
Department of Agriculture
692 San Andres
Malate, Manila
Tel: (2) 571-726, 571-776, 586-201
Fax: (2) 521-7650

Department of Agrarian Reform
Elliptical Rd.
Diliman
Quezon City, Metro Manila
Tel: (2) 997-031   Fax: (2) 973-968

Department of Agriculture
DOA Bldg.
Elliptical Rd.
Diliman
Quezon City, Metro Manila
Tel: (2) 998-741 to 65, 997-011
Fax: (2) 978-183, 995-140

Fertilizer and Pesticide Authority
6th Fl., Raha Sulayman Bldg.
Benavidez St.
Legaspi Village
Makati, Metro Manila
Tel: (2) 818-5115

National Agriculture and Fishery Council
Department of Agriculture
Elliptical Rd.
Diliman
Quezon City, Metro Manila
Tel: (2) 962-2706, 978-234, 988-608
Fax: (2) 922-8622

National Food Authority
Matimyas Bldg.
E. Rodriguez Blvd.
Quezon City, Metro Manila
Tel: (2) 712-1719

National Meat Inspection Commission (NMIC)
Bureau of Animal Industry
Visayas Ave.
Diliman
Quezon City, Metro Manila
Tel: (2) 924-3119   Fax: (2) 924-3118

National Sugar Trading Corporation
Traders Royal Bank Bldg.
Aduana St.
Intramuros, Metro Manila
Tel: (2) 408-667

Philippine Coconut Administration
Elliptical Rd.
Diliman
Quezon City, Metro Manila
Tel: (2) 994-501   Fax: (2) 921-6173

Philippine Cotton Corporation
4th Fl., JJACIS Bldg.
31 Shaw Blvd.
Pasig, Metro Manila
Tel: (2) 673-1476

Philippine Dairy Corporation
Philsucom Bldg.
North Ave.
Quezon City, Metro Manila
Tel: (2) 998-741

Trade Associations

Chamber of Agriculture and Natural Resources
of the Philippines
5th Fl., Rico House
Amorsolo St.
Legaspi Village
Makati, Metro Manila
Tel: (2) 856-296

Coffee Exporters Association of the Philippines
708 National Life Insurance Bldg.
Ayala Ave.
Makati, Metro Manila
Tel: (2) 816-2942, 810-0543, 819-0533

Federation of Fishing Associations of the
Philippines
4th Fl., Domestic Insurance Bldg.
Bonifacio Drive
Port Area, Manila
Tel: (2) 403-724, 481-929

Philippine Association of Prawn Growers
c/o NPPMCI
Ground Fl., JTL Bldg.
North Drive
Bacolod City
Tel: (34) 24-426, 81-404

Philippine Banana Growers and Exporters
Association
c/o Davao Fruits Corp.
State Condominium 1, Salcedo St.
Legaspi Village
Makati, Metro Manila
Tel (2) 817-0158

Philippine Chamber of Food Manufacturers, Inc.
8th Fl., Liberty Bldg.
Pasay Rd.
Makati, Metro Manila
Tel: (2) 865-011

Philippine Coconut Producers' Federation, Inc.
2nd and 3rd Fls., Lorenzo Bldg.
Cor. Taft and Vito Cruz Streets
Metro Manila

Philippine Fish Canners Association, Inc.
Room 106, Cabrera Bldg. I
130 Timog Ave.
Quezon City, Metro Manila

Philippine Food Exporters and Processors
Organization (PHILFOODEX)
Rm. 712, L 7 S Bldg.
1414 Roxas Blvd.
Manila
Tel: (2) 521-4466, 521-2299

Philippine Sugar Millers' Association
14th Fl., Pacific Bank Bldg.
6776 Ayata Ave.
Makati, Metro Manila
Tel: (2) 815-1279, 810-1286
Fax: (2) 810-1291

Philippine Wood Processors and Exporters
Organization, Inc.
c/o Marigold Commodities, Inc.
131 F. Manalo St.
San Juan, Metro Manila
Tel: (2) 772-763

Seaweed Industry Association of the Philippines
Room 307–308, Casa Mendoza
Ariston Cortes Ave.
Mandaue, Cebu City
Tel: (2) 84-012, 83-456

Tuna Canners Association of the Philippines
Room 106, Cabrera Bldg. I
130 Timog Ave.
Quezon City, Metro Manila

United Coconut Association of the Philippines
(UCAP)
4th Fl., G and A Bldg.
2303 Pasong Tamo
Makati, Metro Manila
Tel: (2) 816-7495

Publications

Asia Pacific Food Industry Business Report
(Monthly)
Asia Pacific Food Industry Publications
24 Peck Sea St. #03-00, Nehsons Bldg.
Singapore 0207
Tel: [65] 222-3422   Fax: [65] 222-5587

Directory of Philippine Processed Foods Exporters
Department of Trade and Industry
Trade and Industry Information Center
4th Fl., Industry and Investments Bldg.
385 Sen. Gil J. Puyat Ave.
3117 Makati, Metro Manila
Tel: (2) 818-5705   Fax: (2) 856-487

Farming Today
(Monthly)
Room 201, Catalina Bldg.
New York St.
Cubao
Quezon City, Metro Manila

Selected Statistics in Agriculture
(Annual)
Department of Agriculture
Bureau of Agricultural Statistics
BEN-LOR Bldg.
1184 Quezon City, Metro Manila
Tel: (2) 992-641
Also publish Development Indicators in Philippine
Agriculture *(Annual),* Livestock, Poultry, and
Fishery Statistics Bulletin *(Annual),* Rice and Corn
Situation Outlook *(Quarterly),* Retail Market Price
Bulletin *(Weekly)*

Sugarland Magazine
(Monthly)
Sugarland Publications
Room 207–209, Sugar Center Bldg.
San Juan St.
Bacolod City, Negros
Tel: (34) 22-643
About the sugar industry

Trade Fairs

Refer to the "Trade Fairs" chapter, beginning on page 121, for complete listings, including contact information, dates, and venues. Trade fairs with particular relevance to this industry include the following, which are listed under the headings given below:

Trade Fairs outside the Philippines

- Germany: Anuga
- Hong Kong: Philippine Food Festival & Mission
- Singapore: Philippine Food Festival & Mission
- USA: Food Festival & Mission to the US

Agriculture, Livestock & Horticulture

- National Garden & Pets Exhibition
- Philippine Agri-Aqua Fair '95
- Plants and Flower Fair

Food, Beverages & Hospitality

- Asiafood Expo '95
- International Trade Fair on Food and Beverage
- National Food Festival

COMPUTERS AND OTHER INFORMATION PRODUCTS

Although the Philippines information technology industry does not have the materials or expertise to compete in the computer hardware market, it has been able to concentrate its efforts and become a credible player in the computer software and computer services sectors. There are at least 150 software houses in the country, 30 of which are registered with the Board of Investments (BOI). At least nine of the major ones are majority-owned or wholly owned by foreign companies. Many of the software companies are entrepreneurial spinoffs from larger companies and would like to execute joint operating agreements with foreign-based firms to increase capital, facilitate technology transfer, and build or gain access to national and international marketing networks. Contract programming dominates Philippine sector exports. Philippine applications software programmers serve international clients engaged in the banking, manufacturing, insurance, transportation, retail management, construction, pharmaceuticals, and utilities industries.

During the late 1980s, earnings from this sector topped US$300 million, and were growing at a fast rate in the early 1990s. By 1990, computer software foreign exchange earnings were beginning to represent about 15 percent of this amount.

Products Applications software, data entry, network services, systems integration, systems software.

Competitive Situation The Philippine software industry has set high goals. It aims to generate export revenues of US$300 million by 1998, becoming the biggest supplier in Southeast Asia. Its specific priority target markets are the US, Germany, the UK, France, and Japan. The industry has lobbied for support, including: (1) an exemption from tariffs on imported hardware, peripherals, and software; (2) special financing; (3) grants for research and development; (4) an increasing use of information technology by government and industry; and (5) strengthening of the authority of government technology organizations and policies such as the Information Technology Coordinating Council (ITCC), the National Information Technology Plan (NITP), and the National Computer Center (NCC). Another project being proposed is the establishment of a Software Development Institute.

The Philippines software industry offers two important competitive advantages: (1) it has a large available pool of trained professionals in a labor intensive industry, and (2) it can offer competitive pricing based on the relatively low salaries for such quality professional labor. The industry's rates are lower than those of most of its overseas competitors by as much as 40 to 50 percent.

Government Agencies

Bureau of Patents, Trademarks and Technology Transfer
Department of Trade and Industry
361 Sen. Gil J. Puyat Ave.
Makati, Metro Manila
Tel: (2) 815-4919, 818-3109, 818-3944, 882-350
Fax: (2) 818-4145

Department of Science and Technology (DOST)
Gen. Santos Ave., Bicutan
Taguig, Metro Manila
Tel: (2) 837-2071, 837-3171, 822-0960/7, 823-8939
Fax: (2) 822-0564, 823-8937

National Computer Center
Camp Gen. Emilio Aguinaldo
Cubao
Quezon City, Metro Manila
Tel: (2) 797-631   Fax: (2) 781-172

Trade Associations

Computer Distributors and Dealers Association of the Philippines (COMDDAP)
7th Fl., SEDCCO I Bldg.
Legaspi St., cor. Rada St.
Legaspi Village
Makati, Metro Manila
Tel: (2) 810-3814   Fax: (2) 815-6-31

Philippine Computer Society
6th Fl., Emmanuel House
115 Aguirre St., Legaspi Village
Makati, Metro Manila
Tel: (2) 818-4227, 817-1820
Fax: (2) 818-0381

Philippine Software Association, Inc. (PSA)
Mezzanine, Republic Glass Bldg.
115 Aguirre St.
Legaspi Village
Makati, Metro Manila
Fax: (2) 818-5368

Semiconductor Electronics Industry Foundation,
Inc. (SEIFI)
5th Fl., Kings Court II
Pasong Tamo, cor. de la Rosa St.
Makati, Metro Manila
Tel: (2) 877-938, 866-995

Publications

Asia Computer Weekly
(Bimonthly)
Asian Business Press Pte., Ltd.
100 Beach Rd. #26-00, Shaw Towers
Singapore 0718
Tel: [65] 294-3366   Fax: [65] 298-5534

Asian Computer Directory
(Monthly)
Asian Computer Monthly
(Monthly)
Computer Publications Ltd.
Washington Plaza, 1st Fl.
230 Wanchai Rd.
Wanchai, Hong Kong
Tel: [852] 2932-7123   Fax: [852] 2832-9208

Asian Sources: Computer Products
(Monthly)
Asian Sources Media Group
22nd Fl., Vita Tower
29 Wong Chuk Hang Rd.
Wong Chuk Hang, Hong Kong
Tel: [852] 2555-4777   Fax: [852] 2873-0488

Asiatechnology
(Monthly)
Review Publishing Company Ltd.
6-7th Fl., 181-185 Gloucester Rd.
GPO Box 160
Hong Kong
Tel: [852] 2832-8381   Fax: [852] 2834-5571

Directory of Philippine Electronics Exporters
Department of Trade and Industry
Trade and Industry Information Center
4th Fl., Industry and Investments Bldg.
385 Sen. Gil J. Puyat Ave.
3117 Makati, Metro Manila
Tel: (2) 818-5705   Fax: (2) 856-487

Trade Fairs

Refer to the "Trade Fairs" chapter, beginning on page 121, for complete listings, including contact information, dates, and venues. Trade fairs with particular relevance to this industry include the following, which are listed under the headings given below:

Computers, Communications & Electronics
• Electronics and Electrical Asia '96
• Mediasia

ELECTRICAL AND ELECTRONIC PRODUCTS

The Philippines has a strong and growing electronics industry. It has become the country's leading exporting industry. In 1993 electronic products accounted for more than half of the value of the Philippines' top 10 earning exports, and about 22 percent of the country's total export earnings. Export sales of major electronic products in that year reached US$2.5 billion; this followed an annual growth rate in the sector exceeding 20 percent during the late 1980s and early 1990s. The major electronic export products in 1992 were semiconductors (with export sales valued at US$2 billion), telecommunications equipment (with export sales valued at US$400 million), and electrical machinery (with export sales valued at US$350 million). The US, Japan, Europe, and other ASEAN countries (Singapore, Thailand, Indonesia, Malaysia, Vietnam, and Brunei) buy most of the Filipino electronic products. Some 43 percent of the goods are sold to the US, 18 percent to Japan, 18 percent to Europe, and 7 percent to ASEAN countries.

Three-quarters of Philippine semiconductor production is manufactured by major multinational corporations. Among those now established in the Philippines are US-based multinational firms Texas Instruments, National Semiconductor, Intel, and Motorola, and the Anglo-Dutch firm, Philips. The remainder of these products are manufactured by 20 independent subcontractors, most of which are Filipino-owned. Altogether there about 200 electronic companies BOI-registered in the Philippines. Electronic products are assembled, tested, and packaged at companies in the Philippines; most raw materials and many components are imported for manufacture and assembly for shipment overseas. Factories are concentrated in the areas immediately south of Manila.

Although electrical appliances and machinery do not command as much earning power as electronic products, they, too, represent a growing aspect of the Philippine economy. In 1991 electrical products accounted for 7 percent of the country's exports—up by 204 percent from the previous year—and earned US$646 million. Export sales of telecommunications and sound recording equipment also increased by 35 percent from the previous year.

Products Electronic products include semiconductors, integrated circuits, and consumer electronics such as color TVs, stereos, and video game players. Electronic components are manufactured for telephone sets, citizens' band (CB) radios, and radio scanners. Electrical products include home appliances such as washing machines and incandescent lamps, as well as industrial and office products such as electric wire, cable, bars, microphone parts, and office machines.

Competitive Situation The Philippine electronics industry is marked by a highly trainable workforce, competitive wages, the availability of competent management teams, adherence to modern manufacturing practices such as just-in-time and other smooth-flow production techniques, and flexibility. However, the industry is facing stiff competition from other countries in the region, particularly as such low cost economies as China, Indonesia, and Vietnam develop the capabilities to offer competent, even lower cost assembly. The industry is responding to this challenge by focusing on productivity and higher-value-added products. Other areas of concern are the Philippines' underdeveloped infrastructure and support industries, as well as the relatively high cost—and sometimes problematic availability—of power, communications, and working capital. These areas are being addressed by both government and industry and hopefully will be mitigated in the near future.

Government Agencies

Department of Energy
PNPC Complex
Merritt Rd.
Fort Bonifacio
Makati, Metro Manila
Tel: (2) 850-251, 852-850, 857-051/9, 851-021/9
Fax: (2) 817-8603, 851-021

Department of Energy
One-Stop Action Center
3rd Fl., DOE Bldg., PNPC Complex
Merritt Rd.
Fort Bonifacio
Makati, Metro Manila
Tel: (2) 851-021, x238, 815-2098
Fax: (2) 877-633

National Electrification Administration
3rd Fl., D&E Bldg.
1050 Quezon Ave.
Quezon City, Metro Manila
Tel: (2) 922-9009, 922-5688
Fax: (2) 922-9058

Trade Associations

Consumer Electronic Products Manufacturing Association (CEPMA)
c/o Philippine Electrical and Allied Industries Federation
3rd Fl., Ajinomoto Bldg.
Sen. Gil J. Puyat Ave.
Makati, Metro Manila
Tel: (2) 818-5487

Philippine Electronics and Telecommunications Federation (PETEF)
6th Fl., Telecoms Plaza Bldg.
316 Sen. Gil J. Puyat Ave.
Salcedo Village
Makati, Metro Manila
Tel: (2) 813-6398, 815-8921
Fax: (2) 813-6397

Publications

Asian Electricity
(11 per year)
Reed Business Publishing Ltd.
5001 Beach Rd. #06-12, Golden Mile Complex
Singapore 0719
Tel: [65] 291-3188   Fax: [65] 291-3180

Asian Electronics Engineer
(Monthly)
Trade Media Ltd.
29 Wong Chuck Hang Rd.
Hong Kong
Tel: [852] 2555-4777   Fax: [852] 2870-0816

Asian Sources: Electronic Components
(All publications are monthly)
Asian Sources Media Group
22nd Fl., Vita Tower
29 Wong Chuk Hang Rd.
Wong Chuk Hang, Hong Kong
Tel: [852] 2555-4777   Fax: [852] 2873-0488

Directory of Philippine Electronics Exporters
Department of Trade and Industry
Trade and Industry Information Center
4th Fl., Industry and Investments Bldg.
385 Sen. Gil J. Puyat Ave.
3117 Makati, Metro Manila
Tel: (2) 818-5705   Fax: (2) 856-487

Electronic Business Asia
(Monthly)
Cahners Publishing Company
275 Washington St.
Newton, MA 02158, USA
Tel: [1] (617) 964-3030   Fax: [1] (617) 558-4506

Trade Fairs

Refer to the "Trade Fairs" chapter, beginning on page 121, for complete listings, including contact information, dates, and venues. Trade fairs with particular relevance to this industry include the following, which are listed under the headings given below:

Computers, Communications & Electronics
• Electronics and Electrical Asia '96
Machinery & Tools
• AIMS '95: Asian Industrial Machinery Show
• Industrial Seconds/Machinetech
• Industry Philippines
• PIM '95

FURNITURE

In 1993 total export earnings from the furniture industry reached US$202 million. This came as a result of efforts by more than 1,100 furniture exporters, although the top three—Pacific Traders and Manufacturing, Mindanao Rattan, and Asia Rattan Manufacturing—accounted for 9 percent of these export earnings. Other major export manufacturers include Mehitabel Furniture, Calfurn Manufacturing, and Maitland-Smith. About 400 exporters belong to the Chamber of Furniture Industries, which accounted for 70 percent of exports.

Most of the industry is not involved in exports. The Philippines supports a total of about 15,000 furniture enterprises, from the wood furniture centers in Manila to the rattan factories in Cebu, or the expert handcarving workers at Angeles in Pampanga Province. Between 90,000 and 100,000 Filipinos are employed as cabinetworkers and wood carvers. Most of the work involves the manufacture of rattan furniture in medium-sized factories employing 100 to 300 workers. Rattan furniture has been the top seller, accounting for about 60 percent of export sales. Wood furniture was next in export earnings, accounting for about 15 percent of category earnings. Although other sectors of the furniture industry—such as metal and plastic furniture—do not generate revenues approaching those in rattan and wood, they are growing.

Products Beds, cabinets, chairs, chests of drawers, dressers, headboards, kitchen storage units, rattan furniture, settees, tables, wardrobes, wicker furniture, wood furniture, wooden juvenile furniture.

Competitive Situation The Philippine furniture industry must now contend with an intermittently precarious environmental situation: forests are becoming depleted, which makes it more difficult to provide the high volume of wood from domestic sources needed to support sustained growth in production. Environmental activists have been campaigning to place much of the country's remaining natural resources off limits to manufacturers. In addition, some production suffers from low quality of materials. As a response to this and other new difficulties, the industry has turned to nontraditional materials, such as buri, which was once used exclusively for hats and bags but is now being used for barrel chairs, stools, bookcases, display stands, and headboards. Although workers have the ability to produce goods made of metals and plastics, little of either material is available locally. The Philippines offers able craftsmen, laborers, and manufacturers who have the ability to produce competitively. However, in large part the future of the industry will depend on how well the industry and the government can work together to manage the natural resources needed by the industry. Some furniture manufacturers, certainly, at least for the immediate future, may fall on harder times.

Trade Associations

Chamber of Furniture Industries of the Philippines
Unit H, 9th Fl., Strata 100 Bldg.
Emerald Ave.
Pasig, Metro Manila
Tel: (2) 673-7940, 673-8874

Wooden Gifts and Accessories Manufacturers Association, Inc.
6 South Bayview Drive
Sunset Village
Parañaque, Metro Manila
Tel: (2) 831-1316, 832-1633

Trade Fairs

Refer to the "Trade Fairs" chapter, beginning on page 121, for complete listings, including contact information, dates, and venues. Trade fairs with particular relevance to this industry include the following, which are listed under the headings given below:

Trade Fairs outside the Philippines
- Israel: Modern Living Fair
- Italy: Carrara
- United Arab Emirates: Index
- USA: International Home Furnishings Market

Furniture & Hardware
- Homemakers Furniture Show
- Manila F.A.M.E

GIFTS, HANDICRAFTS, HOUSEWARES, AND JEWELRY

Gifts and Housewares

Small enterprises account for the bulk of this industry. There are more than 2,000 small and 57 major manufacturers. Most of the firms in the gifts and housewares sector are wholly Filipino-owned, with the majority representing family enterprises with "mom-and-pop" production and management. The export oriented Philippine giftwares and houseware industries have become established in the US, Japan, the UK, Germany, Italy, Spain, and the Netherlands. A majority of the new and smaller handicraft producers use manual production, but a number of the more progressive, higher-volume firms are mechanized. Technology is being more frequently used in the ceramic subsector and in state-of-the-art embroidery and sewing machines found among producers of textile items. Major products include wickerwork, woodcraft, Christmas decorations, and ceramics and stoneware. Together, they earned more than US$250 million in exports in 1993.

In the early 1990s Philippine exports accounted for just 0.1 percent of the world demand for giftwares and housewares, with growth following roughly the same level as world demand.

Products Artificial flowers, brassware and metal, basketware, beach balls, ceramics and stoneware, Christmas decorations, decorative accessories, fabric articles, glassware, handicrafts, housewares, lamps, shades, novelty items, paper, papier mâché figurines, porcelain and ceramic pots, promotional gift items, shellcraft, model ships in bottles, silk flowers, tropical giftware, wallets and purses made of exotic skins, wall hangings, wood carvings, and wood frames for decorated plates or pictures.

Competitive Situation The main strengths of the industry are the abundance of a wide range of indigenous materials (such as rattan, bamboo, buri, twigs, rice stalks, and other nonthreatened forest products, fabrics and laces, lead, brass, wire, glass, and copper sheets); minimal need for imported components; Filipino talent for creating unique goods; and an industrywide understanding of Western tastes.

Jewelry

The supply of raw materials for the jewelry industry in the Philippines is stable and sufficient. The main raw materials used for jewelry are gold, white gold, sterling silver, precious or semiprecious stones, and diamonds. There are about 10,000 privately owned establishments engaged in manufacturing, gem cutting, and trading. Only about 30 of these firms are large corporations with foreign connections and established foreign markets. Gold, silver, and semiprecious stones are mined locally. Gold can be bought not only from the Central Monetary Authority (the former Central Bank), but also from local miners, panners, and refiners. Silver is common in Baguio, while pearls are abundant in the Southern Philippines. There are also cultured pearl farms in Davao, and semiprecious stones (such as jade) are mainly from Mindoro and Mindanao. The more valuable raw materials—such as diamonds, emeralds, and other precious stones—are imported from abroad, including Hong Kong, Thailand, Japan, Italy, and Israel.

Philippine exports of jewelry rose from US$2.9 million in 1987 to US$56.5 million in 1993. A reduction of tariff and taxes applicable to the fine jewelry industry is expected to boost export of this product significantly.

Products Fine jewelry produced in the Philippines consists mainly of precious metal jewelry made of gold or silver, which may be adorned with precious or semiprecious stones. There are also loose pearls and precious and semiprecious cut stones such as diamonds, rubies, and emeralds, and specific products include rings, earrings, bracelets, necklaces, and costume jewelry sets.

Competitive Situation There is an abundance of raw materials for the industry, especially gold. The workforce in this skilled, labor-intensive industry consists mainly of primary or secondary school graduates who are willing and able to be highly trained. The sector's existing technology is still below international standards. Production is still largely by hand, using tools such as mallets and tweezers. Few local jewelers have casting machines

and wax injectors. Upgrading of technology is being undertaken to make the industry more competitive in the world market. Fine jewelry producers are also seeking extension of the distribution network by authorizing gold and silver outlets to sell gold and silver sheets, wires, grains, and solder in various karats and purities.

Fashion Accessories and Travel Goods

In 1991 the top seller in this sector was gloves of both leather and nonleather material. In that year sales totaled US$136.2 million, down from the previous year by 5.6 percent. Other big sellers in the sector included travel goods (with sales of US$31.9 million), handbags and belts (with sales of US$14.5 million), and hats (with sales of US$5.4 million). The main markets for these products are the US, Japan, German, Britain, and France.

Products Beads, brooches, buttons, casual bags, duffel bags, handbags, tote bags, hair accessories, hats and caps, gloves, luggage, scarves, sunglasses, and umbrellas.

Trade Associations

Association of Philippine Leathergoods
Manufacturers (APLEM)
51 Xavier St.
Greenhills, Metro Manila
Tel: (2) 706-894

Cebu Gifts, Toys, and Housewares Manufacturers and Exporters Association
Room 207, Jessever Bldg.
Fuente Osmeña, Cebu City
Tel: (32) 216-216   Fax: (32) 310-132

Ceramic Exporters and Manufacturers Association
c/o Cardinal Ceramics Mfg. Inc.
SAKAP Bldg.
121 Dao St.
San Antonio Village
Makati, Metro Manila
Tel: (2) 816-19-83, 816-1213
Fax: (2) 810-8707

Christmas Decoration Producers and Exporters
Association of the Philippines
Rm. 304, MCR Bldg.
495 Boni Ave.
Mandaluyong, Metro Manila
Tel: (2) 788-956, 788-957

Guild of Philippine Jewelers
32 Greenhills St.
New Manila
Quezon City, Metro Manila
Tel: (2) 721-2451   Fax: (2) 721-5073

Fashion Jewelry and Accessories Association
51 Xavierville St.
Greenhills West
San Juan, Metro Manila
Tel: (2) 785-243, 706-842
Fax: (2) 721-6897

Philippine Chamber of Handicraft Industries, Inc.
Rm. T-2, 3rd Fl., Sunvar Plaza
Pasay Rd., cor. Amorsolo St.
Makati, Metro Manila
Tel: (2) 887-734, 887-818

Wooden Gifts and Accessories Manufacturers
Association, Inc.
6 South Bayview Drive
Sunset Village
Parañaque, Metro Manila
Tel: (2) 831-1316, 832-1633

Publications

Asian Sources: Gifts & Home Products
Asian Sources: Timepieces
Fashion Accessories
(Monthly)
Asian Sources Media Group
22nd Fl., Vita Tower
29 Wong Chuk Hang Rd.
Wong Chuk Hang, Hong Kong
Tel: [852] 2555-4777   Fax: [852] 2873-0488

Asia Pacific Leather Directory
(Annual)
Asia Pacific Leather Yearbook
(Annual)
Asia Pacific Directories, Ltd.
6th Fl., Wah Hen Commercial Centre
381 Hennessy Rd.
Hong Kong
Tel: [852] 2893-6377   Fax: [852] 2893-5752

Directory of Philippine Gifts and Housewares
Directory of Philippine Leather Goods and Footwear
Department of Trade and Industry
Trade and Industry Information Center
4th Fl., Industry and Investments Bldg.
385 Sen. Gil J. Puyat Ave.
3117 Makati, Metro Manila
Tel: (2) 818-5705   Fax: (2) 856-487

World Jewelogue
(Annual)
Headway International Publications Co.
907 Great Eagle Center
23 Harbour Rd.
Hong Kong
Tel: [852] 2827-5121   Fax: [852] 2827-7064

Trade Fairs

Refer to the "Trade Fairs" chapter, beginning on page 121, for complete listings, including contact information, dates, and venues. Trade fairs with particular relevance to this industry include the following, which are listed under the headings given below:

Trade Fairs outside the Philippines
- Australia: Sydney International Gift Trade
- Germany: Frankfurt Int'l Fair–Ambiente
- Germany: Frankfurt Int'l Autumn Fair
- Hong Kong: Hong Kong Jewelry
- Hong Kong: Asia Pacific Leather Fair
- Italy: Chibicar International Fair
- Italy: Macef Autunno

- Japan: Tokyo International Gift Show
- USA: New York Visual Marketing & Store Design Show

Comprehensive
- Export Overruns Fair
- Philippine Boat Show

Apparel & Textiles
- Stylefest Asia '95

Footwear & Leather Goods
- Phil Shoetech/Phil Leather '95

INDUSTRIAL MINERALS, CHEMICALS, AND MATERIALS

Much of the industrial manufacturing of materials from minerals and chemicals is rooted in the postwar recovery period, when the Philippines attempted to manufacture goods that would otherwise be imported. During the mid-1980s, an ambitious US$6 billion industrial development program begun under Marcos in 1979 resulted in functional copper smelter-refinery operations, coco-chemical manufacturing, and phosphatic fertilizer projects. A cement industry rehabilitation and expansion program and an integrated iron and steel mill project had still to be completed. A proposed petrochemical complex has remained bogged down in disputes over location and financing. The political crisis of the mid-1980s severely hurt production—some plants were operating at as little as 40 percent capacity at the height of the turmoil—but by 1988, most plants were again working at full capacity. In 1990 the Board of Investments approved investment projects valued at US$3.75 billion, including nearly US$1.5 billion earmarked for the manufacturing sector.

Minerals

The country has large deposits of coal, copper, chromium, gold, and nickel, plus smaller deposits of cadmium, iron, lead, manganese, mercury, molybdenum, and silver. Industrial minerals include asbestos, gypsum, limestone, marble, phosphate, salt, and sulfur. The use of coal and hydroelectricity development have reduced the nation's dependence on imported oil from 95 percent of the energy supply in 1973 to 60 percent in 1990. In 1988 the Philippines was the sixth largest producer of chromium in the world, ninth in gold, and tenth in copper. But the overall industry has not always performed so well. Mineral exports accounted for 17.8 percent of trade in 1980 and only 5.4 percent in 1988. The country's nickel mining company, Nonoc Mining and Industrial Corporation, closed its doors in 1986 because of labor and financial difficulties. It has since been taken over and sold by the government and the new owners may help to restore the Philippines as a major exporter of nickel. The mining sector grew marginally at a rate of 0.7 percent in 1993, but fell by 7.0 percent in 1994.

Products Asbestos, cadmium, coal, cobalt, copper, chromium, gold, gypsum, iron, lead, limestone, manganese, marble, mercury, molybdenum, nickel, phosphate, salt, silver, and sulfur.

Competitive Situation The Philippine mining sector has had its ups and downs. In the early 1990s, rising operational costs, a depressed market, labor disputes, higher mandated wages and unfavorable interest rates, typhoons, an earthquake, and power shortages combined to hurt the industry. By 1990 both production and value in exports had decreased substantially from the levels of 10 years before. Nevertheless, the country has large deposits of a wide variety of mineral resources, and the government is working to strengthen the infrastructure that supports the mining industry, while making it more attractive to investors.

Petrochemicals

In 1991 market demand for fuel and petroleum products increased by 24 percent, rising from US$1.7 billion to US$2.1 billion. The bulk of the market was supplied by locally produced petroleum products; less than 15 percent was supplied through imports. The Philippines has three oil refineries: Petron Corporation's Bataan Refinery, Pilipinas Shell Petroleum Corporation's Tabangao Refinery, and Caltex Incorporated's Batangas Refinery. Petron accounts for 52 percent of the industry's refining capacity, while the balance is shared almost equally by Caltex and Shell. Petron, the state-owned oil company (the petroleum subsidiary of the Philippine National Oil Company) has been partially privatized, with Saudi Aramco taking a major 40 percent share. However, this has provoked controversy, because Petron was one of the few relatively up-to-date and profitable government-run enterprises.

Products Asphalt, automobile and aviation gasoline, diesel fuel, fuel oil, kerosene, lubricants and greases, and solvents.

Competitive Situation Recent developments in the oil and gas sector in the Philippines have created significant opportunities for petroleum exploration and development. After nearly seven years in the doldrums, a resurgence of interest in oil and gas prospecting has occurred following major discoveries of oil in West Linapacan and gas condensate at Camago in 1990, as well as oil and gas in the Camago-Malampaya field—reputed to be the largest oil find ever in the Philippines—in 1992. All of these finds are in the Spratly Islands located northwest of the island of Palawan, and it is now widely accepted that the Palawan shelf offers

opportunities to develop oil and gas fields that can produce several hundred million barrels of crude oil and several trillion cubic feet of gas. However, the sovereignty over this area remains in dispute among the Philippines and China, Vietnam, Indonesia, Malaysia, and Taiwan, with the most active conflict being between the Philippines and China, which has begun fortifying some of the islets in the Spratlys. Active development of these resources awaits resolution of these disputes.

To meet projected growth in demand for petroleum products and to correct the existing gap between demand and production, oil companies are undertaking projects to increase capacity and efficiency. In addition to these developments, the Philippine Department of Energy recently unveiled proposals to deregulate the domestic oil industry. Deregulation is intended to encourage private investment to meet unfilled energy needs. The initial stage, which will require congressional approval, provides transitional measures for stable pricing of petroleum products. Full deregulation, including liberalized oil imports, could start as early as the end of 1996.

Detergents and Other Chemicals

Given that the Philippines is the world's largest producer of coconuts, domestic production of detergent and surfactant (that is, surface active) chemicals, especially coconut-based chemicals, is sizable. Local producers have been protected by government limits on the use of imported surfactants in the soap and detergent industry to no more than 40 percent of active agents in products. The government also promotes the utilization of local raw materials (such as coconut oil) as well as of other raw materials that do not endanger the environment. Local detergent manufacturers have invested heavily to retool their factories and comply with government policy; and they are spending more in the production of coconut fatty alcohol (CFA) based detergents. The cosmetics industry is one of the largest manufacturing sectors in the country. Output in the cosmetics, shampoo, and body care industry contributed nearly US$300 million in 1993.

The Philippines imports active ingredients or technical materials that can be used to make pesticides for the agricultural industry. Most pesticides are produced in the domestic market. Imported insecticides capture about 61 percent of the Philippine market, herbicides about 24 percent, and fungicides about 7 percent. Pesticides are used mainly in rice, banana, and vegetable cultivation, while insecticides are used mainly in rice fields. Fungicides are used mostly for treating bananas.

Packaging Materials

Packaging materials manufacturers enjoy a large, steadily growing market. The industry also benefits from the local availability of some of its most important raw materials. For example, the bulk of the raw materials of glassmakers come from local sources. About 50 percent of the kraft paper for corrugated carton boxes and 85 percent of tin plates required by the industry are also from local sources. Some plastic resins are also available locally, but the industry has a high dependence on imports in some subsectors. Because of the absence of a plastic-based petrochemical industry, the plastic-based subsector has to import most of what it needs. The paper-based and metal-based subsectors also must rely on imports to serve goods destined for export markets which demand higher quality packaging.

Manufacturers of packaging materials are located mostly in Metro Manila and the surrounding areas. Packaging materials come mostly from Luzon, although glass plants are located primarily in Cebu and corrugated box makers in Mindanao. Some 60 percent of the output of the industry goes into packaging processed food products, but the packaging industry has the potential to expand in all areas.

Products Packaging products are grouped into four categories: (1) glass based: bottles, jars, and vials of glass, used mainly for food products, beverages, cosmetics, and pharmaceuticals; (2) plastic based: plastic sheets, bags, bottles, jars, tubes, crates, insulation, and shockproofing materials such as foam, laminated sheets, and packaging tapes; (3) paper-based: corrugated carton boxes, folded boxes, multilayered kraft and paper adhesive tapes; and (4) metal-based: tin cans, metal closures, tubes, and aluminum foil.

Competitive Situation Despite the relative availability of many necessary raw materials and the growing domestic demand for packaging products, the industry faces a number of important challenges. It needs to invest in new equipment if it is to meet growing demand (not always an easy choice for manufacturers). Some companies may hesitate to buy new, state-of-the-art, electronically advanced equipment because it is expensive and may soon be outdated by rapid changes in technology. Many investors now buy secondhand machines from Taiwan. Other packaging manufacturers may lack high quality raw materials in the case of paper and metal packaging materials. Such manufacturers have to import kraft paper and tin plates to meet the requirements of the export market. The industry has also been heavily affected by power outages, but recent improvements should correct that situation.

Government Agencies and Corporations

Department of Environment and Natural Resources
DENR Bldg.
Visayas Ave.
Diliman
Quezon City, Metro Manila
Tel: (2) 976-626/9, 976-671/5, 990-691
Fax: (2) 963-487, 922-6991

Philippine National Oil Company (PNOC)
PNOC Bldg.
7901 Makati Ave.
Makati, Metro Manila
Tel: (2) 817-5395, 859-961, 859-061
Fax: (2) 815-2721, 812-1070
Responsible for geothermal energy development, power plants, oil exploration

Trade Associations

Chemical Industries Association of the Philippines
c/o Exxon Chemical Philippines
15th Fl., BA-Lepanto Bldg.
Paseo de Roxas
Makati, Metro Manila
Tel: (2) 816-2795   Fax: (2) 815-1686

Packaging Institute of the Philippines
Rm. 216, Comfoods Bldg.
Sen. Gil J. Puyat Ave.
Makati, Metro Manila
Tel: (2) 817-2936, 827-8509
Fax: (2) 817-2936

Philippine Plastics Industrial Association, Inc.
317 Rizal Ave. Ext., Grace Park, rear Block
Solidbank Bldg.
Caloocan City, Metro Manila
Tel: (2) 361-1160   Fax: (2) 361-1168

Publications

Asia Mining
(Monthly)
Asiaworld Publishing House, Inc.
7514 Bagtikan, cor. Pasong Tamo
3117 Makati, Metro Manila
Tel: (2) 874-348

Asian Oil & Gas
(Monthly)
Intercontinental Marketing Corp.
PO Box 5056
Tokyo 100-31, Japan
Fax: [81] (3) 3667-9646

Asian Plastic News
(Quarterly)
Reed Asian Publishing Pte., Ltd.
5001 Beach Rd. #06-12, Golden Mile Complex
Singapore 0719
Tel: [65] 291-3188   Fax: [65] 291-3180

Philippine Mining and Engineering Journal
(Monthly)
*Philippine Mining and Engineering Journal
Annual & Directory*
(Annual)
Business Masters International
55 U.E. Tech Ave.
University Hills
Malabon
Rizal, Luzon

Polymers & Rubber Asia
(Bimonthly)
Upper West St.
Reigate Surrey RH2 9HX, UK
Tel: [44] (1737) 242-599   Fax: [44] (1737) 223-235

Trade Fairs

Refer to the "Trade Fairs" chapter, beginning on page 121, for complete listings, including contact information, dates, and venues. Trade fairs with particular relevance to this industry include the following, which are listed under the headings given below:

Environmental & Energy
• Energy & Environment Expo Manila '95
• Oil & Gas Asia '95
Machinery & Tools
• Philplas '95
Packing & Packaging
• Phil Propack '96

SERVICE INDUSTRIES

Financial Services

The Philippine financial services sector is composed of banking institutions and nonbank financial intermediaries, including commercial banks, specialized government banks, thrift and rural banks, offshore banking units, building and loan associations, investment and brokerage houses, and finance companies. The central bank and the Securities and Exchange Commission maintain regulatory and supervisory control. The Philippines has a sophisticated banking system, although the level of financial activity has been low relative to the size of the economy because wealth is heavily concentrated and many Filipinos operate outside the formal system. Foreign investment in domestic banks is limited to 40 percent of domestic bank equity.

Political and financial crises, compounded by soaring foreign debt, resulted in a virtual collapse of the Philippine banking system in the mid to late 1980s. Two important government-owned banks—the Philippine National Bank (the PNB—at the time the largest commercial bank in the country, holding between 25 and 30 percent of total commercial bank assets) and the Development Bank of the Philippines (the DBP—which allocated 70 percent of its loans to support industrial development) became insolvent. A number of financial institutions failed, including the three largest investment houses, three commercial banks, the majority of the more than 1,000 rural banks, and the largest savings bank.

Since the crisis, the private commercial banking sector has become more concentrated. By 1988 the five largest private domestic commercial banks accounted for about 55 percent of total private domestic commercial bank assets. The combined assets of the five private domestic commercial banks, the restructured PNB, and the two largest foreign branch banks accounted for two-thirds of total commercial bank assets. A 1991 memorandum from the World Bank noted that the extent of bank profits indicated a "lack of competition" and a "market structure for financial services characterized by oligopoly." Philippine banks had the widest interest rate spread (loan rate minus deposit rate) in Southeast Asia. As more recent reform efforts have led to a relaxation of the stranglehold of established institutions, observers are anticipating a greater role for competition from foreign providers.

Tourism

Tourism developed rapidly in the 1970s, with visitors numbering one million in 1980. Thereafter, the industry went into a slump, reaching the one million visitor mark again only in 1988. In that year, the average length of stay was 12.6 days, up from 8.9 days in 1987. However, many of these visitors were emigrant Filipinos returning for periodic visits with families and friends. In 1988 an average of 73 percent of Manila's 8,500 hotel rooms were occupied.

Estimates of tourism-generated revenues vary widely. In 1988 the central bank estimated it at US$405 million, or 11 percent of the country's nonmerchandise exports. Using a different formula, the Department of Tourism estimated tourism earnings at US$1.45 billion. Most tourists enter the country through Manila, but the city has developed relatively few tourist amenities and has suffered from congestion, pollution, and crime. Intramuros, the colonial Spanish walled city, has yet to be fully restored since its destruction at the end of World War II. Political instability in the country during the 1980s was also a deterrent to tourism. The government's Medium-Term Development Plan called for promotion of both domestic and international tourism, and greater attempts have been made to boost this activity.

Government Agencies and Corporations

Bangko Sentral ng Pilipinas
(Central Bank of the Philippines)
A. Mabini St.
Malate, Metro Manila
Tel: (2) 507-051, 593-380/1, 595-263, 582-372
Fax: (2) 522-3987, 597-363

Department of Tourism
DOT Bldg.
T.M. Kalaw St.
Rizal Park, Manila
Tel: (2) 599-031 to 48, 585-528
Fax: (2) 521-7373/4, 522-2194

Insurance Commission
1071 United Nations Ave.
Manila
Tel: (2) 583-534, 574-886, 599-221/5
Fax: (2) 522-1434

Philippine Convention and Visitors Corporation
4th Fl., Legaspi Towers 300
Roxas Blvd.
Manila
Tel: (2) 575-031   Fax: (2) 521-6165

Securities and Exchange Commission
SEC Bldg.
Epifanio de los Santos Ave.
Greenhills
Mandaluyong, Metro Manila
Tel: (2) 810-1145, 780-931/9
Fax: (2) 722-0990

Trade Associations

Bankers Association of the Philippines
11th Fl., Sagittarius Bldg.
De la Costa St.
Salcedo Village
Makati, Metro Manila
Tel: (2) 851-711, 810-3858, 810-3859
Fax: (2) 812-2870, 810-3860

Philippine Association of Finance Companies, Inc.
2nd Fl., PCCI Bldg.
118 Alfaro St.
Makati, Metro Manila
Tel: (2) 813-1541   Fax: (2) 819-3356

Publications

Annual Report, Central Bank of the Philippines
(Annual)
Bangko Sentral ng Pilipinas
A. Mabini St.
Malate, Metro Manila
Tel: (2) 507-051, 593-380/1, 595-263, 582-372
Fax: (2) 522-3987, 597-363

Asia Travel Guide
(Monthly)
Interasia Publications, Ltd.
190 Middle Rd. #11-01, Fortune Center
Singapore 0718
Tel: [65] 339-7622   Fax: [65] 339-8521

Bankers Handbook for Asia
(Annual)
Dataline Asia Pacific Inc.
3rd Fl., Hollywood Center
233 Hollywood Rd.
Hong Kong
Tel: [852] 2815-5221   Fax: [852] 2854-2794

Philippine National Bank Economic Brief
PNB International
Philippine National Bank Public Information Office
PNB Bldg.
257 Escolta St.
1099 Escolta, Manila
Tel: (2) 402-051   Fax: (2) 496-091

Travel News Asia
(Bimonthly)
Far East Trade Press, Ltd.
2nd Fl., Kai Tak Commercial Bldg.
317 Des Voeux Rd.
Central, Hong Kong
Tel: [852] 2545-3028   Fax: [852] 2544-6979

Travel Trade Gazette Asia
(Weekly)
Asian Business Press Pte., Ltd.
100 Beach Rd. #26-00 Shaw Towers
Singapore 0718
Tel: [65] 2943366   Fax: [65] 2985534

Trade Fairs

Refer to the "Trade Fairs" chapter, beginning on page 121, for complete listings, including contact information, dates, and venues. Trade fairs with particular relevance to this industry include the following, which are listed under the headings given below:
Business & Education Services
• Annual PACAP Finance Conference
• International Investments Forum
• Mediasia
Food, Beverages & Hospitality
• Hotelexpo '95
Sporting Goods, Toys, Entertainment & Travel
• Phildive
• Traveltour Expo '95

TELECOMMUNICATIONS

The telecommunications industry consists of the providers of telecommunications services and the manufacturers of telecommunications equipment. Although the telecommunications service sector is expanding rapidly, the manufacturing side of the business is still fairly limited. Much of the actual equipment needed to expand telecommunications service in the Philippines is currently imported.

Providers of telecommunications services are expanding at a rapid rate in the Philippines and expect to increase their business dramatically in the coming years. Deregulation of the telecommunications service industry is creating competition in the field. Although, eventually, there may be room for only a fraction of the companies now competing for a share of the lucrative business, the current competition is prodding the established providers—most notably the Philippine Long Distance Telephone Company—to upgrade their services, and this should create better service at more competitive rates. The government has developed an ambitious program to link the country with telecommunication lines. The program includes (1) connecting all major cities and municipalities through a digital telephone system; (2) installing subscriber lines and new exchanges; (3) establishing satellite service in 39 municipalities; (4) establishing a nationwide maritime mobile communications network, and providing adequate, effective, and stable maritime services such as public correspondence, port operation, ship movement and emergency and safety communications.

The manufacturing of telecommunications equipment in the Philippines is limited mostly to telephone sets. More sophisticated items—such as fax machines, teleprinters, fiber-optic cables, telecommunications network software systems, and hardware—are, for the most part, imported.

Demand for telephone sets has been increasing as new telephone lines are being installed throughout the country. For example, in 1992 demand for telephone sets nearly doubled. Total market sales of telephones, teleprinters, and fax machines amounted to US$19.9 million in 1992, an 80 percent increase from the 1991 level. In 1992 telephone sets constituted 89 percent of total market demand, fax machines about 10 percent, and teleprinters less than 1 percent. In 1992, 19 percent of the Philippine market for telephones, teleprinters, and fax machines was supplied by imports. More than 75 percent of domestic production was exported—largely due to the Philippines' advantage in producing competitive basic to intermediate telephone sets.

Products Philippine industries assemble and produce such telecommunications products as telephone sets, CB radios, and radio scanners.

Competitive Situation The Philippines will continue to be an important producer of less sophisticated telecommunications equipment, such as basic telephone sets. Although the telecommunications service providers sector will certainly expand during the coming years, the extent of the expansion will depend on how well the public will be able to afford the services. There is also some question as to whether the public will be able to subscribe to as many lines as the government would like to install. In this sense, the telecommunications industry will serve as a barometer of the economy as a whole, but it is also likely that there will be a shake-out in the industry in the intermediate term, following rapid gains in the near term.

Government Agencies and Corporations

Bureau of Telecommunications
A. Roces Ave.
Quezon City, Metro Manila
Tel: (2) 964-391

Department of Transportation and Communications
3rd Fl., Philcomcen Bldg.
Ortigas Ave.
Pasig, Metro Manila
Tel: (2) 631-8761/3, 631-8666, 721-3781
Fax: (2) 632-9985

National Telecommunications Commission
VIBAL Bldg.
Epifanio de los Santos Ave., cor. Times St.
Quezon City, Metro Manila
Tel: (2) 924-4042, 924-4008, 981-160
Fax: (2) 921-7128
Regulates telecommunications industry and formulates policies

Philippine Telegraph and Telephone Corp. (PT&T)
PT&T Spirit of Communication Center
106 Alvarado St.
Legaspi Village
Makati, Metro Manila

Telecommunications Office (TELOF)
2nd Fl., Multipurpose Bldg.
A. Roces Ave.
Quezon City, Metro Manila
Tel: (2) 951-961, 974-747
Fax: (2) 921-8977

Trade Associations

Consumer Electronic Products Manufacturing Association (CEPMA)
c/o Philippine Electrical and Allied Industries Federation
3rd Fl., Ajinomoto Bldg.
Sen. Gil J. Puyat Ave.
Makati, Metro Manila
Tel: (2) 818-5487

Philippine Electronics and Telecommunications Federation (PETEF)
6th Fl., Telecoms Plaza Bldg.
316 Sen. Gil J. Puyat Ave.
Salcedo Village
Makati, Metro Manila
Tel: (2) 813-6398, 815-8921
Fax: (2) 813-6397

Publications

Asia Pacific Broadcasting & Telecommunications
(Monthly)
Asian Business Press Pte., Ltd.
100 Beach Rd. #26-00, Shaw Towers
Singapore 0718
Tel: [65] 29423366   Fax: [65] 29825534

Asiatechnology
(Monthly)
Review Publishing Company Ltd.
6-7th Fl., 181-185 Gloucester Rd.
GPO Box 160
Hong Kong
Tel: [852] 2832-8381   Fax: [852] 2834-5571

Trade Fairs

Refer to the "Trade Fairs" chapter, beginning on page 121, for complete listings, including contact information, dates, and venues. Trade fairs with particular relevance to this industry include the following, which are listed under the headings given below:

Computers, Communications & Electronics

*   Phil Telecom '95
*   Telecomex Asia

TEXTILES AND CLOTHING

The Philippines is a producer of textiles, finished garments, and footwear. In 1993 exports of garments earned US$2.1 billion—up by 5.4 percent from the previous year—ranking as one of the top export earners in the Philippine economy. Seventy percent of garment manufacturers are located in Metro Manila, with most of the rest being located in the provinces surrounding the capital city. About US$1.4 billion represented exports of finished apparel. One of the more rapidly growing areas within this sector has been the footwear industry, dominated by Rubberworld Philippines, maker of Adidas. Total export earnings for footwear in 1991 was US$141 million, an increase of 29 percent from the previous year.

Products Textile products include blue denim, carsheet cover (tafetta), cordages, cables, ropes and twines of Manila hemp, woven cotton fabric, and yarns of synthetic fibers. Manufactured garments include children's and infants' wear; embroidered garments; jogging suits; brassieres and other lingerie; men's shirts, suits, and trousers; women's blouses, dresses, pants, and skirts. Footwear includes boots, sandals, and shoes of all kinds (athletic, casual, and dress, made of leather and rubber).

Competitive Situation The Philippine garment industry is internationally competitive because it is able to supply manufacturers with its many of its own textile products and can produce at low wages in a labor intensive industry. The footwear industry is expected to retreat from its earlier rapid growth because of a lack of growth in the domestic leather industry and a high 30 percent tariff on high-quality imported leather.

Trade Associations

Association of Philippine Leathergoods Manufacturers (APLEM)
51 Xavier St.
Greenhills, Metro Manila
Tel: (2) 706-894

Confederation of Garment Exporters of the Philippines
Suite 103, Marlis Bldg.
121 Tordesillas St.
Makati, Metro Manila
Tel: (2) 818-0224, 861-059

Garment Business Association of the Philippines
Room 608, Doña Narcisa Bldg.
8751 Paseo de Roxas
Makati, Metro Manila
Tel: (2) 813-7418, 883-943, 883-946, 883-939

Textile Mills Association of the Philippines (TMAP)
Alexander House
132 Amorsolo St.
Legaspi Village
Makati, Metro Manila
Tel: (2) 816-6605, 818-6601
Fax: (2) 818-3107

Textile Producers' Association of the Philippines
Rm 513, Downtown Center Bldg.
516 Quintin Paredes St.
Binondo, Metro Manila
Tel: (2) 499-069, 461-435, 530-1043

Publications

Asia Pacific Leather Directory
(Annual)
Asia Pacific Leather Yearbook
(Annual)
Asia Pacific Directories, Ltd.
6th Fl., Wah Hen Commercial Centre
381 Hennessy Rd.
Hong Kong
Tel: [852] 2893-6377   Fax: [852] 2893-5752

ATA Journal: Journal for Asia on Textile & Apparel
(Bimonthly)
Adsale Publishing Company
Tung Wai Commercial Bldg., 21st Fl.
109-111 Gloucester Rd.
Wanchai, Hong Kong
Tel: [852] 2892-0511   Fax: [852] 2838-4119

Directory of Philippine Leather Goods and Footwear
Department of Trade and Industry
Trade and Industry Information Center
4th Fl., Industry and Investments Bldg.
385 Sen. Gil J. Puyat Ave.
3117 Makati, Metro Manila
Tel: (2) 818-5705   Fax: (2) 856-487

Trade Fairs

Refer to the "Trade Fairs" chapter, beginning on page 121, for complete listings, including contact information, dates, and venues. Trade fairs with particular relevance to this industry include the following, which are listed under the headings given below:

Trade Fairs outside the Philippines

*   Germany: Igedo-Dessous
*   Germany: Kind & Jugend Fair
*   Hong Kong: Asia Pacific Leather Fair
*   Hong Kong: Hong Kong Fashion Weeks
*   Hong Kong: Hong Kong Int'l Footwear Fair
*   Italy: Oggi Pelleteria
*   Japan: Japantex
*   USA: New York Home Textile Show

Apparel & Textiles

*   HINABI Fabric Presentation
*   Phil Garmentech '95

- Phil Textile '95
- Stylefest Asia '95

Footwear & Leather Goods

- Phil Shoetech/Phil Leather '95

Sporting Goods, Toys, Entertainment & Travel

- Sports & Leisure Show

TOYS AND SPORTS EQUIPMENT

Toys

About 50 major companies produce a wide variety of toys in the Philippines. The industry has been sufficiently attractive to induce manufacturers from other countries to set up joint ventures with Philippine firms. Recently, a consortium of five Taiwan companies established a US$10 million toy manufacturing plant in suburban Manila to produce toy automobiles, trucks, airplanes, musical instruments, and other products. The plant employs 3,000 workers, and its sales reached US$12 million in 1990. Stuffed toys are the top seller within the overall industry, but a lack of high-quality plush fabric prevents manufacturers from producing as many stuffed toys as they could.

Products Battery operated toys, electronic and mechanical toys, dolls, doll parts and accessories, musical instruments, stuffed toys, toy models (planes, ships, cars, trucks, and others, including miniature motors) in wood and other materials, and wheeled toys.

Sporting Goods

Most of the sporting goods manufactured in the Philippines are those that can be produced at low cost and do not require specialized manufacturing equipment or materials. The industry is defined mostly by small enterprises, which account for nearly two-thirds of activity in the sector. Twenty percent of the manufacturers are capitalized at between US$200,000 and US$1 million, while 17.5 percent of all manufacturers are capitalized at more than US$1 million, with the remainder representing capitalizations of less than US$200,000.

One of the most significant areas in the sector is tennis equipment, dominated by Dunlop Slazenger, an international leader in the manufacturing of tennis equipment. Tennis balls represented 28 percent of all sporting goods exports in 1991, largely due to the contribution of this firm. Other sporting goods manufacturers continue to enter the market, many of them representing joint ventures with manufacturers in other Asian countries known for sporting goods, most notably Korea and Taiwan.

Products Baseball and other sports caps; baseball gloves; basketballs; fish nets and fishing tackle; golf and tennis bags and other sports bags; gym equipment; canvas and nylon tents; plastic sports nets; volleyballs; safety helmets; sporting arms; sports shoes; table tennis, badminton, and wooden tennis rackets; wooden bats; and wooden game tables.

Trade Associations

Cebu Gifts, Toys, and Housewares Manufacturers and Exporters Association
Room 207, Jessever Bldg.
Fuente Osmeña, Cebu City
Tel: (32) 216-216   Fax: (32) 310-132

Philippine Toy and Novelty Manufacturers Association (Philtoy)
25 Quezon Ave.
Quezon Ave.
Quezon City, Metro Manila
Tel: (2) 711-7415, 732-5141
Fax: (2) 731-8477

Wooden Gifts and Accessories Manufacturers Association, Inc.
6 South Bayview Drive
Sunset Village
Parañaque, Metro Manila
Tel: (2) 831-1316, 832-1633

Trade Fairs

Refer to the "Trade Fairs" chapter, beginning on page 121, for complete listings, including contact information, dates, and venues. Trade fairs with particular relevance to this industry include the following, which are listed under the headings given below:

Trade Fairs outside the Philippines

- Australia: Sydney International Gift Trade
- Germany: Frankfurt Int'l Fair–Ambiente
- Germany: Frankfurt Int'l Autumn Fair
- Hong Kong: Hong Kong Toys & Games Fair
- Italy: Macef Autunno

Sporting Goods, Toys, Entertainment & Travel

- Hobby and Leisure Fair
- Phildive '95
- Sports & Leisure Show

Trade Fairs

INTRODUCTION

Led by one of the first convention and visitors organizations in Southeast Asia, the Philippines has built state-of-the-art meeting facilities and all the requisite support systems to support a wide variety of trade shows. The convention centers are well established, and shows are well attended, although there are relatively few Philippine events compared with Singapore or Hong Kong, the other main trade show centers in the region. This chapter focuses primarily on shows taking place in the Philippines, but it also contains information related to shows in other Pacific Rim convention centers which draw a significant number of Philippine exhibitors or attendees.

CONTENTS

Most areas of commerce, from agricultural shows to the latest in high technology, are represented at Philippine trade events. The listings on the following pages contain information gathered from a number of different sources, including the Philippine government, convention bureaus, and trade show organizers themselves. While we have made every effort to verify that the entries are correct and current, before making plans to attend or exhibit, be sure to check with a trade show's organizer to ensure that the dates and location are firm. Dates for some 1995 fairs may have passed, but have been included to give you an idea of the range of fairs available, the contacts for various shows, and a basis for estimating timing and location for potential trade fairs in the future.

The vast majority of trade fairs taking place in the Philippines occur in Metro Manila, either in the city itself or in nearby business districts such as Makati or Mandaluyong. Expansion of convention business is a central goal of both the government and the business community. Other Philippine cities, particularly Cebu—the Philippines' second city and a major international shipping center—and Davao—center of the fast-growing Mindanao economy—are likely to begin to host more trade fairs in coming years; a growing number of major international fairs are expected to be held in Manila. The central location of Manila in Southeast Asia (less than two hours by air from Hong Kong or Taiwan, and a three-hour flight from Singapore) makes the city an increasingly attractive option for event organizers.

The trade fair listings are organized first by product category, then alphabetically by name within a given product category. The product categories are listed in the table of contents, along with cross-references to other categories. Shows falling into the "Comprehensive" category exhibit goods that bridge several categories. When reviewing these listings, be sure not to overlook any related categories. For other potential sources of trade show information—such as organizations, associations, and directories—*see* "Useful Addresses" on page 123.

- Each listing ideally provides the name of a trade show, recent or upcoming dates, city, specific site, frequency, and contact information; however, available data varies in its completeness.
- If you find a date given for a show has already passed, don't despair. Although some shows are single events, most occur regularly, either annually or every two (biennially) or three years (triennially). Some events, particularly fashion shows, occur more than once a year.
- Certain events are regularly held in the same location, while some change location from year to year.
- Remember that if the organizer of a particular show has changed since these listings were compiled, try contacting a trade association in your area of interest to confirm an upcoming show.
- You will probably discover some variations in the names of the fairs. These differences exist at several levels and for a number of possible reasons: larger fairs may include smaller events, associated congresses, or conferences; other fairs use acronyms to identify themselves; other variations arise as titles are translated from one language to another.

EXHIBITING IN THE PHILIPPINES

The facilities and procedures for exhibiting in the Philippines are similar to those elsewhere in the Pacific Rim region. Pay close attention to any information you receive from show organizers. If possible, get the names of some exhibitors from previous shows so that you can interview them concerning any special circumstances they encountered in the past; find out how best to avoid or cope with potential problems. Past exhibitors can also give you an opportunity to get the general flavor of a show and perhaps to discover some key contacts.

The type of displays used and the size, shape, and location of the available space should be confirmed early in the process. This information will assist you in making decisions about what to bring from your headquarters and what to rent at the fair location. Some exhibitors have greater success renting displays locally than shipping them. Not only will you avoid difficulties in clearing customs, but you may also be better accommodated; locally rented displays are more likely to be designed specifically for the size and layout of that particular exhibition space. If you do decide to bring your own display materials, make sure that you allow adequate time for everything to arrive and clear customs, especially if the materials are shipped in several separate packages. If you will require assistance to set up your display, be sure to communicate that clearly to the show organizers well in advance so that the necessary arrangements can be made. Fax may be the most effective method of communicating with show organizers because it circumvents any oral language differences and gives you a record of exchanges suitable for review with the organizers should any confusion arise.

Trade Fair Venues in the Philippines

The number of trade fairs in the Philippines has been rising steadily in recent years. There has been a strong push on the part of the Philippine government to expand the infrastructure within the country and at the same time expand the number of facilities available for trade fairs. Most major trade shows in the Philippines occur in Metro Manila, but there are a few convention facilities in other cities. The Bacolod City Crown Plaza Hotel and Convention Center in Negros Occidental opened in 1991 with a capacity of 2,000 in its main ballroom, plus several conference rooms for smaller groups, but it has yet to attract shows of an international caliber. The Cebu Plaza Hotel and Cebu Midtown Hotel are the main trade show and convention venues in Cebu City, while the Davao Insular Hotel in Davao has limited convention facilities.

You may also wish to explore some of the other Pacific Rim exhibition centers, particularly those in Singapore, Hong Kong, and Taiwan. You will note a number of abbreviated entries for shows in which the Philippine Center for International Trade Expositions & Missions (CITEM) will be participating, but which take place outside the Philippines.

In Metro Manila the principal venue is the Philippine International Convention Center (PICC), situated on more than 30 acres overlooking Manila Bay. Boasting a 15,250 sq m (164,000 sq ft) exhibition center, this site also features an auditorium capable of holding more than 4,000 attendees and an additional 18 meeting rooms. Other venues include the Philippine Trade Training Center, the 2,000-seat Cultural Center of the Philippines, the 8,400-seat Folk Arts Theater, the 1,300-seat Manila Metropolitan Auditorium, and some of the major hotels.

FOR FURTHER INFORMATION

The Philippine consulate in your home country is often the best source of information for trade fairs in this region. (Refer to the "Important Addresses" chapter, beginning on page 297, for listings of Philippine embassies, consulates, and trade offices.) In the Philippines, the Center for International Trade Expositions & Missions (CITEM) is an excellent source for listings on fairs—ask for the center's current events calendar, which lists both trade fairs within the Philippines and those in neighboring countries in which the Philippine business community participates.

There are several other strategies for researching information on trade shows that can help you successfully market your product or service or help you find suppliers in the Philippines. If you are interested in exporting to the Philippines, your country's embassy in Manila may be able to advise you about trade missions or trade fairs in that city. Foreign chambers of commerce in Manila, such as the American Chamber of Commerce or the European Chamber of Commerce of the Philippines, are other good sources; they often provide information on trade shows in their publications. Philippine professional organizations in your area of interest are often excellent sources of information on trade fairs (refer to the "Important Addresses" chapter, beginning on page 297, for relevant listings). Basic reference materials include *Exhibit Review* magazine, the *International Encyclopedia of Associations,* and *Trade Shows Worldwide* (the latter two are Gale Publications).

FURTHER READING

Books and Periodicals

The Complete Handbook of Profitable Trade Show Exhibiting, by Christine Christman. New York: Prentice-Hall, 1991. ISBN 0-13-155722-X. 448 p., US$59.95. Available from: Paramount Publishing, 200 Old Tappan Rd., Old Tappan, NJ 07657, USA; Tel: [1] (201) 767-5937.

The Exhibit Review, Phoenix Communications, Inc., PO Box 5808, Beaverton, OR 97006, USA; Tel: [1] (503) 818-8211.

How to Get the Most Out of Trade Shows, by Steve Miller. Lincolnwood, IL, USA: NTC Business Books, 1991. ISBN 0-8442-3193-2. 177 p., $29.95. Available from: NTC Publishing, 4255 W. Touhy Ave., Lincolnwood, IL 60646-1975, USA; Tel: [1] 708-5500.

Marketing by Exhibiting in the Global Market: A Complete Handbook to International Exhibiting, by Michael S. Muribi and Carol A. Fojtik. Available from: Expressions International, Inc., 330 N. Garfield, Suite 110, Lombard, IL 60148, USA; Tel [1] (708) 495-8740.

The Successful Exhibitor's Handbook: Trade Show Techniques for Beginners and Pros, 2nd ed., by Barry Siskind. Bellingham, Wash.: Self-Counsel Press, 1993. ISBN 0-88908-528-5. 200 p., US$10.95. Available from: Self-Counsel Press, 1704 N. State St., Bellingham, WA 98225, USA; Tel: [1] (206) 676-4350.

Trade Show Exhibiting: The Insider's Guide for Entrepreneurs, by Diane K. Weintraub, New York: McGraw-Hill, 1991. ISBN 0-07-157616-9. US$14.95.

Available from: McGraw-Hill, Princeton Rd., Highstown, NJ 08520, USA; Tel: [1] (212) 512-2000, (800) 722-4726 (toll-free in the US only).

Trade Shows Worldwide '95 and *International Encyclopedia of Associations,* available from Gale Research Inc., 835 Penobscot Bldg., Detroit, MI 48226, USA; Tel: (800) 877-GALE (toll-free in the US only); Fax: [1] (313) 961-6815.

USEFUL ADDRESSES

Center for International Trade Expositions & Missions Inc. (CITEM)
International Trade Center Complex
Roxas Blvd., cor. Sen. Gil J. Puyat Ave.
Pasay City, Metro Manila, Philippines
Tel: [63] (2) 831-2201/9, 832-5001, 832-3982
Fax: [63] (2) 832-3965

Center for Exhibition Industry Research
4350 East-West Highway, Suite 401
Bethesda, MD 20814, USA
Tel: [1] (301) 907-7626
Fax: [1] (301) 907-0277

Department of Trade and Industry
Trade and Industry Bldg.
361 Sen. Gil J. Puyat Ave. Ext.
Makati, Metro Manila, Philippines
Tel: [63] (2) 817-5280, 817-5340, 863-431, 818-5701
Fax: [63] (2) 810-9363

Philippine Center for International Trade and Exhibitions (Philcite)
CCP Complex
Roxas Blvd.
Manila, Philippines
Tel: [63] (2) 832-0304
Fax: [63] (2) 832-3414

Philippine Convention and Visitors Corporation (PCVC)
4th Fl., Legaspi Towers 300
Roxas Blvd.
Manila, Philippines
Tel: [63] (2) 575-031
Fax: [63] (2) 521-6165

World Trade Center Metro Manila (WTCMM)
15th Fl., Solidbank Bldg.
Paseo de Roxas
Makati, Metro Manila, Philippines
Tel: [63] (2) 819-7232, 819-7297
Fax: [63] (2) 819-7209
The WTC in Manila offers various member services, but does not yet have its own exhibition facilities

TIPS FOR ATTENDING A TRADE FAIR

Trade fairs can be extremely effective for making face-to-face contacts and sales or purchases, identifying suppliers, checking out competitors, and finding out how business really works in the host country. However, the cost of attending or exhibiting at such fairs can be high. To maximize the return on your investment of time, money, and energy, be very clear about your goals for the trip and give yourself plenty of time for advance research and preparation.

You should also be aware of the limitations of trade fairs. The products on display probably do not represent the full range of goods available on the market. In fact, some of the latest product designs may still be under wraps. While trade fairs give you an opportunity to make face-to-face contacts with many people, both exhibitors and buyers are rushed, which makes meaningful discussions and negotiations difficult.

These drawbacks can easily be minimized if you have sufficient preparation and background information. Allow several months for preparation—more if you first need to identify which fair you should attend. Even under ideal circumstances, you should begin laying the groundwork a year in advance. Don't forget that exhibiting at or attending a fair in a foreign country means more complex logistics: numerous faxes and phone calls involving you, the show operator, and local support people, plus customs and transportation delays.

Participating in international trade fairs, particularly at the outset, should be considered a means of fulfilling long-term goals. At domestic fairs, you may exhibit on a regular basis with short-term sales and marketing goals. But at a foreign fair, it is often best to participate as a way to establish your company, make contacts for the future, and learn more about a market, its consumers, and products. New exporters may not generate high sales, but they often come away with information that assists them with future marketing and product development.

Selecting an appropriate trade fair

Consult the trade fair listings in this book to find some that interest you. Note the suggestions in this chapter for finding the most current calendars of upcoming fairs. Once you have identified some fairs, ask the organizers for literature, including a show prospectus, attendee list, and exhibitor list. Ask plenty of questions! Be sure not to neglect trade organizations in the host country, independent show-auditing firms, and recent attendees or exhibitors. Find out whether there are "must attend" fairs for your particular product group. Fairs that concentrate on other, but related, commodities might also be a good match. Be aware that there may be preferred seasons for trade in certain products.

Your research needs to cover a number of points

• *Audience* Who is the intended audience? Is the fair open to the public or only to trade professionals? Are the exhibitors primarily foreigners looking for local buyers or locals looking for foreign buyers? (Many trade fairs are heavily weighted towards one or the other; others may be so oriented to local activity that they are not equipped to cater to international businesspeople.) Decide whether you are looking for an exposition of general merchandise produced in one region, a commodity-specific trade show, or both. Are you looking for a "horizontal"—one that covers a wide range of products—or a "vertical" show—one that covers those involved in the production and marketing of a narrow range of products through all stages of the process?

• *Statistics* How many people attended the fair the last time it was held? What were the demographics? What volume of business was done? How many exhibitors were there? How big is the exhibition space? What was the ratio of foreign to domestic attendees and exhibitors?

• *Specifics* Who are the major exhibitors? Are any particular publications or organizations associated with the fair? On what categories of products does the fair focus? Does the fair have a general theme or a changing theme? How long has the fair been in existence? How often is it held? Is it always in the same location, or does it move each time? How much does it cost to attend? Are there any separate or special programs connected with the event, and do they require additional entrance fees? What does it cost to rent space?

Before you go

• If you have not already spoken with someone who attended the fair in the past, be sure to find someone who will give you advice, tips, and general information.

• Make your reservations and travel arrangements well in advance, and figure out how you are going to get around once you get there. Even if the fair takes place in a large city, do not assume that getting around will be easy. If the site is in a small city or a less developed area, the transportation and accommodation systems are likely to become overburdened sooner than in metropolitan areas.

• Will you need an interpreter for face-to-face business negotiations? A translation service to handle documents? Try to line up providers well in advance of your need for their services.

• For printed materials, pay attention to language barriers and make preparations that will help you overcome them. Assess your literature and decide what should be available in translated or bilingual editions. Have the translation work done by a seasoned professional, particularly if technical terms are used. Consider having a bilingual business card, and add the country and international dialing code information to the address and telephone number. Find out from the show organizers which countries will be represented, and prepare information in the languages of those countries as well, if necessary.

• Do you need hospitality suites and/or conference rooms? Reserve them as soon as you can.

• Contact people you would like to meet before you go. Organize your appointments around the fair.

• Familiarize yourself with the show's hours, locations (if at multiple venues), and the schedule of events. Then prioritize.

While you are there

• Wear businesslike clothes that are comfortable. Find out what the norm is for the area and the season.

• Immediately after each contact, write down as much information as you can. Do not depend on remembering it. Several companies now make inexpensive portable business card scanners with optical character recognition (OCR) software to read the information into a contact management program.

• Qualify your prospects before launching into a full presentation. Are you dealing with the right person? Ask open-ended questions to find out his or her true interests.

• Consider arriving a day early to get fully oriented, confirm appointments, and rest up.

• It is common sense: make sure you take breaks, even if you have to schedule them. You'll end up having far more energy and being more effective.

After the fair

• Within a week after the fair, write letters to new contacts and follow up on requests for literature. If you have press releases and questionnaires, send them out quickly as well. Even better, send these leads back to your office while you are still at the fair so that your new contacts receive literature on their return home.

• Write a report evaluating your experiences while they are still fresh in your mind. Even if you don't have to prepare a formal report, spend some time organizing your thoughts on paper for future reference. Aim to quantify the results. Did you meet your goals? Why or why not? What would you do differently? What unforeseen costs or problems arose?

• With your new contacts and your experiences in mind, start preparing for your next trade fair.

If you are selling

• Familiarize yourself with import regulations for products that you wish to exhibit at the fair.

• Set specific goals for sales leads, developing product awareness, selling and positioning current customers, and gathering industry information. For example, target the numbers of contacts made, orders written, leads converted into sales, visitors at presentations, brochures or samples distributed, customers entertained, and seminars attended. You can also set goals for total revenue from sales, cost-to-return benefit ratio, amount of media coverage, and amount of competitor information obtained.

• Review your exhibitor kit. Is there a show theme that you can tie into? Pay particular attention to the show's hours and regulations, payment policies, shipping instructions and dates, telephone installation policies, security, fire regulations, and extra-cost services.

• Find out about the labor situation at the fair site. Is it unionized, and what are the regulations? Will you have to hire your own workers to set up and break down the booth, or can the organizer or showcase facility provide them for you?

• Gear your advertising and product demonstrations to the expected target audience. Should you stress certain aspects of your product line? Will you need brochures and banners in different languages? Even if you do not need to translate your current materials into another language, will you need to rewrite them for a different culture? Consider advertising in publications that will be distributed at the fair.

• Plan the display in your booth carefully; you will have only a few seconds to grab the viewer's attention. Secure a location in a high-traffic area—for example, near a door, a restroom, a refreshment area, or a major exhibitor. For banners use copy that is brief and effective. Focus on the product and its benefits. Place promotional materials and giveaways near the back wall so that people have to enter your area, but make sure that they do not feel trapped. If you plan to use videotapes or other multimedia, make sure that you have enough space. Remember to ascertain whether you will need special equipment or equipment designed for different electrical current. Such presentations may be better suited to hospitality suites, because in exhibition halls lights are bright and noise levels high .

• Attend to the details. Order office supplies and printed materials that you will need for the booth. Have all your paperwork—order forms, business cards, exhibitor kit and contract, copies of advance orders and checks, travel documents, and so on—in order and at hand. If you ordered a telephone line, obtain your own host-country-compatible telephone or arrange to rent one. Draw up a schedule for staffing the booth.

• Plan and rehearse your sales pitch in advance, preferably in a space similar to the size of your booth.

• *Don't:* sit, read, smoke, eat, or drink in the booth; badmouth your competitors or complain about the show; ignore prospects while chatting with colleagues; stand with your back to the aisle or lean on booth furniture.

• If you plan to return to the next show, reserve space while you are still on-site.

If you are buying

• Familiarize yourself with customs regulations on the products that you seek to purchase and import into your own country or elsewhere. Be sure to get such information on any and all products in which you might be interested.

• Set specific goals for supplier leads and for gathering industry information. For example, target the numbers of contacts made, leads converted to purchases, seminars and presentations attended, and booths visited. Other goals might be a cost-to-return benefit ratio, an amount of competitor information gathered, or a percentage of projected purchases actually made.

• List all the products that you seek to purchase, their specifications, and the quantities you plan to purchase.

• Know the retail and wholesale market prices for the goods in your home country and in the country where you will be buying. List the highest price you can afford to pay for each item and still get a worthwhile return.

• List the established and probable suppliers for each product or product line that you plan to import. Include addresses and telephone numbers and note your source for the information. Before you go, contact suppliers to confirm who will attend and to make appointments.

TRADE FAIRS OUTSIDE THE PHILIPPINES

Many Philippine exporters will exhibit at trade fairs outside their country—the following is a list of 1995 fairs with a significant Philippine presence. For more information on Philippine exhibitors at these fairs or on Philippine international trade missions, contact CITEM (*see* "Useful Addresses" on page 123).

Location	Trade Fair	Description	Dates
Australia	Industry Philippines–Australia	Industrial goods & services	Aug. 21–25, 1995
Australia (Sydney)	Sydney International Gift Trade	Gifts, toys & housewares	Feb. 18–22, 1995
Chile	Philippine Promo in Falabella	General merchandise	Oct., 1995
Germany	Anuga	Food	Sept. 21–30, 1995
Germany (Frankfurt)	Frankfurt Int'l Fair–Ambiente	Gifts, toys & housewares	Feb. 18–22, 1995
Germany (Frankfurt)	Frankfurt Int'l Autumn Fair	Gifts, toys & houseware	Aug. 26–30, 1995
Germany	Igedo-Dessous	Garments & textiles	Aug. 6–8, 1995
Germany (Hannover)	Industry Philippines at Hannover Fair	Industrial goods & services	April 3–8, 1995
Germany	Kind & Jugend Fair	Garments & textiles	Aug. 25–27, 1995
Hong Kong	Asia Pacific Leather Fair	Footwear & leathergoods	April 3–5, 1995
Hong Kong	Hong Kong Fashion Weeks	Garments & textiles	Jan. 18–21, 1995 and July 13–16, 1995
Hong Kong	Hong Kong Int'l Footwear Fair	Footwear	Sept., 1995
Hong Kong	Hong Kong Jewelry Fair	Fine jewelry	Sept. 18–22, 1995
Hong Kong	Hong Kong Toys & Games Fair	Gifts & toys	Jan. 11–14, 1995
Hong Kong	Phil. Food Festival & Mission	Food	June 6–18, 1995
Israel (Tel Aviv)	Modern Living Fair	Furniture	July 4–15, 1995
Italy (Carrara)	Carrara	Marble	May 17–21, 1995
Italy	Chibicar International Fair	Fashion accessories	Jan. 20–23, 1995
Italy	Macef Autunno	Gifts, toys & houseware	Sept. 1–4, 1995
Italy	Oggi Pelleteria	Leathergoods	Sept., 1995
Japan	Industry Philippines at the ASEAN Trade Fair	Industrial goods & services	Sept. 21–25, 1995
Japan	Japantex	Garmets & textiles	Jan. 25–28, 1995
Japan (Tokyo)	Tokyo International Gift Show	Gifts, toys & houseware	Sept. 7–9, 1995
Singapore	Baucon Asia	Construction materials	Sept. 27–30, 1995
Singapore	Phil. Food Festival & Mission	Food	June 6–18, 1995
Singapore	Philippine Promotion in Isetan	General merchandise	June, 1995
Taiwan	Philippine Promo in FEDS	General	July, 1995
Taiwan	Plant Mission to Taiwan	Plants	Mar. 31–Apr. 4, 1995
United Arab Emirates	Index	Furniture & furnishings	Sept. 27–Oct. 1, 1995
USA	BIG I/APAA	Car parts	Oct. 24–27, 1995
USA	Food Festival & Mission to the US	Food	June 12–25, 1995
USA	Int'l Home Furnishings Market	Furniture	April 27– May 5, 1995
USA (New York)	New York Home Textile Show	Garments & textiles	April 8–11, 1995
USA (New York)	New York Visual Marketing & Store Design Show	Gifts, toys & houseware	May 20–23, 1995
USA	Philippine ElectrSolo Expo & Business Opps. Conference	Industrial goods & services	July 17–20, 1995
Vietnam	Philippine Int'l Goods & Services Trade to ASEAN & Vietnam	Industrial goods & services	August 7–18, 1995

TRADE FAIRS IN THE PHILIPPINES

Trade Fair	Location & Date	Contact

COMPREHENSIVE

Trade Fair	Location & Date	Contact
Export Overruns Fair Export surpluses of consumer items	Mandaluyong, Metro Manila SM Megamall Hall Annual May 25–30, 1995	BHC & Co., Professional Project Managers 1138 A. Antipolo St. Rizal Village 1200 Makati, Metro Manila, Philippines Tel: [63] (2) 812-6764 Fax: [63] (2) 812-9426 Contact: Ms. Agnes H. Escalnate
Korean Trade Festival Korean-made products from food to gifts and manufacturing equipment.	Mandaluyong, Metro Manila SM Mega Trade Hall Annual March 8–12, 1995	BHC & Co., Professional Project Managers 1138 A. Antipolo St. Rizal Village 1200 Makati, Metro Manila, Philippines Tel: [63] (2) 812 6764 Fax: [63] (2) 812-9426 Contact: Ms. Agnes H. Escalnate
Philippine Best Show Products and services of the Philippines	Pasay City, Metro Manila Trade Training Center Annual May 3–7, 1995	BHC & Co., Professional Project Managers 1138 A. Antipolo St. Rizal Village, Makati 1200 Makati, Metro Manila, Philippines Tel: [63] (2) 812-6784 Fax: [63] (2) 812-9426 Contact: Ms. Agnes H. Escalnate

AGRICULTURE, LIVESTOCK & HORTICULTURE

Trade Fair	Location & Date	Contact
National Garden & Pets Exhibition Agriculture	Manila November 15–19, 1995	CITEM International Trade Center Roxas Blvd. Pasay City, Metro Manila, Philippines Tel: [63] (2) 831-2201, 832-5001, 832-3982 Fax: [63] (2) 832-3965
Philippine Agri-Aqua Fair '95 Agriculture trade show	Pasay City, Metro Manila Folk Arts Theatre Annual May 17–20, 1995	BHC & Co., Professional Project Managers 1138 A. Antipolo St. Rizal Village 1200 Makati, Metro Manila Philippines Tel: [63] (2) 812-6784 Fax: [63] (2) 812-9426 Contact: Ms. Agnes H. Escalnate
6th Plants and Flower Fair Plants, flowers, tropical birds, and fish	Manila Annual November	CITEM International Trade Center Roxas Blvd. Pasay City, Metro Manila, Philippines Tel: [63] (2) 831-2201, 832-5001, 832-3982 Fax: [63] (2) 832-3965

APPAREL & TEXTILES

Trade Fair	Location & Date	Contact
HINABI Fabric Presentation Fabric	Manila September–October	CITEM International Trade Center Roxas Blvd. Pasay City, Metro Manila, Philippines Tel: [63] (2) 831-2201, 832-5001, 832-3982 Fax: [63] (2) 832-3965
Phil Garmentech '95 Garment manufacturing machinery	Pasay City, Metro Manila Trade Training Center Annual September 19–21, 1995	Oriental Western Promotions Ltd. 6/F, China Harbour Bldg. 370-374 King's Rd. North Point, Hong Kong Tel: [852] 807-7633 Fax: [852] 2570-5917 Contact: Choy So Yuk

Trade Fair	Location & Date	Contact
Phil Textile '95 Fabrics and textiles	Pasay City, Metro Manila Trade Training Center Annual September 21–24, 1995	Oriental Western Promotions Ltd. 6/F, China Harbour Bldg. 370–374 King's Rd. North Point, Hong Kong Tel: [852] 2807-7633 Fax: [852] 2570-5917 Contact: Choy So Yuk
Stylefest Asia '95 Showcase for latest fashion trends	Ortigas, Metro Manila Robinson's Galleria Annual November 10–17, 1995	BHC & Co., Professional Project Managers 1138 A. Antipolo St. Rizal Village 1200 Makati, Metro Manila, Philippines Tel: [63] (2) 812-6784 Fax: [63] (2) 812-9426 Contact: Ms. Agnes H. Escalnate

AUTOMOTIVE & TRANSPORTATION

Trade Fair	Location & Date	Contact
Trans Sport Show Exhibitors are automotive manufacturers, dealers and distributors	Mandaluyong, Metro Manila SM Megatrade Hall Annual September	Trade & Show Management, Inc. Unit 514, Valle Verde Terraces Meralco Ave. 1600 Pasig, Metro Manila Philippines Tel: [63] (2) 634-2539 Fax: [63] (2) 634-2539 Contact: Sophia S. Delos Santos
Aviation, Maritime & Defense (AMD) '95 Exhibit Aviation trade show	Pasay City, Metro Manila Trade Training Center Annual March 7–10, 1995	Philippine Exhibition Services Organization (PESO) Unit 1205, Centerpoint Office Condo Julia Vargas Ave., cor. Garnet St. Ortigas Complex 1600 Pasig, Metro Manila, Philippines Tel: [63] (2) 633-6557/9 Contact: Miroan Sy, Project Manager
Transhow International Transportation trade show	Manila Annual since 1982 1995 dates not available	Philcite–Philippine Center for International Trade and Exhibitions CCP Complex Roxas Blvd. Manila, Philippines Tel: [63] (2) 832-0304 Fax: [63] (2) 832-3414 Contact: Transhow Secretariat

BUSINESS & EDUCATION SERVICES

Trade Fair	Location & Date	Contact
AIM Management Conference on Asia: How Business Can Compete More Effectively in Southeast Asia	Makati, Metro Manila Shangri-La Hotel Manila March 8–9, 1995	Asian Institute of Management Manila, Philippines Tel: [63] (2) 892-0014, 892-0435
Annual PACAP Finance Conference Emerging capital markets	Mandaluyong, Metro Manila Shangri-La EDSA Plaza Hotel Annual July 6–8, 1995	Philippine Stock Exchange, Inc. Exchange Rd. Ortigas Center Pasig, Metro Manila Philippines Tel: [63] (2) 636-0122 Fax: [63] (2) 634-5920 Contact: Mr. Rafael Llave, COO
International Investments Forum Investment trade show	Makati, Metro Manila Shangri-La Hotel Manila March 2–3, 1995	Space Marketing Philippines Inc. Manila, Philippines Tel: [63] (2) 818-8979, 818-2707 Fax: [63] (2) 818-2707

Trade Fair	Location & Date	Contact
Mediasia Advertising services, suppliers, publications, electronics and audio visual equipment	Mandaluyong, Metro Manila The Manila Hotel Annual September 6–9, 1995	BHC & Co., Professional Project Managers 1138 A. Antipolo St. Rizal Village 1200 Makati, Metro Manila, Philippines Tel: [63] (2) 812 6764 Fax: [63] (2) 812-9426 Contact: Ms. Agnes H. Escalnate
Phil-Ed '95: Philippines International Education Exhibit Educational training systems, tools, equipment and technology	Manila Manila Midtown Hotel Annual August 23–26, 1995	BHC & Co., Professional Project Managers 1138 A. Antipolo St. Rizal Village 1200 Makati, Metro Manila, Philippines Tel: [63] (2) 812-6784 Fax: [63] (2) 812-9426 Contact: Ms. Agnes H. Escalnate

COMPUTERS, COMMUNICATIONS & ELECTRONICS

Electronics and Electrical Asia '96 Electronics trade show	Manila Philippine International Convention Center (PICC) Biennial August 1996	HQ Link Philippines, Inc. Unit B, 8/F, Cacho-Gonzales Bldg. 101 Aguirre St. Legaspi Village Makati, Metro Manila, Philippines Tel: [63] (2) 810-3694, 810-5685, 819-2738 Fax: [63] (2) 815-3152 Contact: Ms. Carol Odvina
Mediasia Advertising services, suppliers, publications, electronics and audio visual equipment	Mandaluyong, Metro Manila The Manila Hotel Annual September 6–9, 1995	BHC & Co., Professional Project Managers 1138 A. Antipolo St. Rizal Village 1200 Makati, Metro Manila, Philippines Tel: [63] (2) 812 6764 Fax: [63] (2) 812-9426 Contact: Ms. Agnes H. Escalnate
Telecomex Asia Telecommunications	Manila Philippine International Convention Center (PICC) Annual August	HQ Link Pty. Ltd. 150 S. Bridge Rd. #13-01 Fook Hai Bldg. Singapore 0105 Tel: [65] 534-3588 Fax: [65] 534-2330
Phil Telecom '95 International telecommunications, broadcast, and transport communications exhibit	Pasay City, Metro Manila Trade Training Center Biennial February 9–12, 1995	Oriental Western Promotions Ltd. 6/F, China Harbour Bldg. 370–374 King's Rd. North Point, Hong Kong Tel: [852] 2807-7633 Fax: [852] 2570-5917 Contact: Choy So Yuk

CONSTRUCTION & HOUSING
See also Machinery and Tools

Philconstruct '95 Construction materials and equipment conference	Manila CCP Complex Annual November 8–11, 1995	BHC & Co., Professional Project Managers 1138 A. Antipolo St. Rizal Village 1200 Makati, Metro Manila, Philippines Tel: [63] (2) 812-6784 Fax: [63] (2) 812-9426 Contact: Ms. Agnes H. Escalnate

Trade Fair	Location & Date	Contact

ENVIRONMENTAL & ENERGY

Energy & Environment Expo Manila '95 Energy and environment trade show	Manila Philippine International Convention Center (PICC) January 17–20, 1995	Exposition Communication Group S-342/S-369, Secretariat Bldg. PICC, CCP Complex Roxas Blvd. Pasay City, Metro Manila, Philippines Tel: [63] (2) 833-7119. 833-5889 Fax: [63] (2) 831 3827 Contact: Mr. Jerry G. Gonzales
19th Annual National Convention of Institute of Integrated Electrical Engineers	Manila Annual November	Institute of Integrated Electrical Engineers 41 Monte de Piedad St. Cubao Quezon City, Metro Manila, Philippines Tel: [63] (2) 722-7383; 721-6442 Fax: [63] (2) 721-6442 Contact: Mr. Ernie Gabion
Electronics and Electrical Asia '96 Electronics trade show	Manila Philippine International Convention Center (PICC) Biennial August 1996	HQ Link Philippines, Inc Unit B, 8th Fl., Cacho-Gonzales Bldg. 101 Aguirre St. Legaspi Village Makati, Metro Manila, Philippines Tel: [63] (2) 810-3694, 810-5685, 819-2738 Fax: [63] (2) 815-3152 Contact: Ms. Carol Odvina
Oil & Gas Asia '95 Energy trade show	Mandaluyong, Metro Manila Shangri-La EDSA Plaza Hotel February 14–15, 1995	Geological Society of the Philippines c/o HQ Link Philippines, Inc. Unit B, 8/F, Cacho-Gonzales Bldg. 101 Aguirre St. Legaspi Village Makati, Metro Manila, Philippines Tel: [63] (2) 810-3694, 810-5685, 819-2738 Fax: [63] (2) 815-3152 Contact: Alberto P. Morillo
Powertrends 2000 Electrical power trade show	Manila Philippine International Convention Center (PICC) November 14–16, 1995	Philippine Convention and Visitors Corporation (PCVC) 4th Fl., Legaspi Towers 300 Roxas Blvd. Manila, Philippines Tel: [63] (2) 575-031 Fax: [63] (2) 521-6165

FOOD, BEVERAGES & HOSPITALITY
See also Agriculture, Livestock & Horticulture

Asiafood Expo '95 Food processing, packing and handling expo	Pasay City, Metro Manila Trade Training Center Annual October 25, 1995 October 23, 1996	Trade Information Marketing & Exhibitions Manila, Philippines Tel: [63] (2) 832-0309 Fax: [63] (2) 632-7081
First International Supermarket Show Supermarket trade show	Manila Philippine International Convention Center (PICC) September 27–30, 1995	Philippine Convention and Visitors Corporation (PCVC) 4th Fl., Legaspi Towers 300 Roxas Blvd. Manila, Philippines Tel: [63] (2) 575-031 Fax: [63] (2) 521-6165

Trade Fair	Location & Date	Contact
Hotelexpo '95 Hotel and restaurant trade show	Manila Philippine International Convention Center (PICC) September 21–23, 1995	Philippine Convention and Visitors Corporation (PCVC) 4th Fl., Legaspi Towers 300 Roxas Blvd. Manila, Philippines Tel: [63] (2) 575-031 Fax: [63] (2) 521-6165
International Trade Fair on Food and Beverage Latest food and beverage products, machinery, and tools	Mandaluyong, Metro Manila SM Mega Trade Hall Annual October 17–19, 1995	BHC & Co., Professional Project Managers 1138 A. Antipolo St. Rizal Village 1200 Makati, Metro Manila, Philippines Tel: [63] (2) 812 6764 Fax: [63] (2) 812-9426 Contact: Ms. Agnes H. Escalnate
Great American Food Show Consumer ready food show	Mandaluyong, Manila Shangri-La EDSA Plaza Hotel Annual March 20–22, 1995	US Foreign Agriculture Service c/o Embassy of the USA 1201 Roxas Blvd. Ermita, Metro Manila Tel: (2) 521-7116 Fax: (2) 522-4361 *In the US: Tel: [1] (202) 720-9423; Fax: [1]* *(202) 690-4374; Contact: Sarah Hanson*
National Food Festival	Manila November 15–19, 1995	CITEM International Trade Center Roxas Blvd. Pasay City, Metro Manila, Philippines Tel: [63] (2) 831-2201, 832-5001, 832-3982 Fax: [63] (2) 832-3965

FOOTWEAR & LEATHER GOODS
See also Apparel, Textiles & Jewelry

Trade Fair	Location & Date	Contact
Phil Shoetech/Phil Leather '95 Leather and shoemaking machinery and supplies	Manila Philippine International Convention (PICC) Annual September 19–21, 1995	Oriental Western Promotions Ltd. 6/F, China Harbour Bldg. 370–374 King's Rd. North Point, Hong Kong Tel: [852] 2807-7633 Fax: [852] 2570-5917 Contact: Choy So Yuk

FURNITURE & HARDWARE
See also Machines & Tools, Construction & Housing

Trade Fair	Location & Date	Contact
Homemakers Furniture Show Household furniture, appliances and homecare products	Ortigas, Metro Manila Robinson's Galleria Annual October 1–15, 1995	BHC & Co., Professional Project Managers 1138 A. Antipolo St. Rizal Village 1200 Makati, Metro Manila, Philippines Tel: [63] (2) 812-6784 Fax: [63] (2) 812-9426 Contact: Ms. Agnes H. Escalnate
Manila F.A.M.E. Home furnishings market week	Manila March 2–5, 1995	CITEM International Trade Center Roxas Blvd. Pasay City, Metro Manila, Philippines Tel: [63] (2) 831-2201, 832-5001, 832-3982 Fax: [63] (2) 832-3965
Manila F.A.M.E. Gifts and housewares market week	Manila April 24–27, 1995 October 14–17, 1995	CITEM International Trade Center Roxas Blvd. Pasay City, Metro Manila, Philippines Tel: [63] (2) 831-2201, 832-5001, 832-3982 Fax: [63] (2) 832-3965

Trade Fair	Location & Date	Contact

MACHINERY & TOOLS
See also other categories which may include exhibitions with machines specific to those industries

Trade Fair	Location & Date	Contact
AIMS '95: Asian Industrial Machinery Show Machine building, metalworking and construction machinery	Pasay City, Metro Manila Trade Training Center Annual September/October 1995	Oriental Western Promotions Ltd. 6/F, China Harbour Bldg. 370–374 King's Rd. North Point, Hong Kong Tel: [852] 2807-7633 Fax: [852] 2570-5917 Contact: Choy So Yuk
Industrial Seconds/ Machinetech Secondhand and class "B" machinery and tools	Pasay City, Metro Manila Trade Training Center Annual May 30–June 3, 1995	BHC & Co., Professional Project Managers 1138 A. Antipolo St. Rizal Village 1200 Makati, Metro Manila, Philippines Tel: [63] (2) 812-6784 Fax: [63] (2) 812-9426 Contact: Ms. Agnes H. Escalnate
Industry Philippines Industrial goods show	Manila August 24–27, 1995	CITEM International Trade Center Roxas Blvd. Pasay City, Metro Manila, Philippines Tel: [63] (2) 831-2201, 832-5001, 832-3982 Fax: [63] (2) 832-3965
Philplas '95 International plastic machinery and materials exhibit	Pasay City, Metro Manila Trade Training Center Annual November 9–12, 1995	Oriental Western Promotions Ltd. 6/F, China Harbour Bldg. 370–374 King's Rd. North Point, Hong Kong Tel: [852] 2807-7633 Fax: [852] 2570-5917 Contact: Choy So Yuk
PIM '95 Industrial machinery exhibit	Pasay City, Metro Manila Philippine International Convention Center (PICC) Annual Sept. 12, 1995	Enterprise Associates International London, UK Tel: [44] (171) 289 6982 Fax: [44] (171) 289 6982
Welding Show '95 Welding materials, supplies, tools, services, and technology	Manila CCP Complex Annual October/November, 1995	PHC & Co., Professional Project Managers 1138 A. Antipolo St. Rizal Village 1200 Makati, Metro Manila, Philippines Tel: [63] (2) 812-6784 Fax: [63] (2) 812-9426 Contact: Ms. Agnes H. Escalnate

MEDICAL & DENTAL

Trade Fair	Location & Date	Contact
Asia Medica '95 Medical equipment exhibit	Manila Annual May 22, 1995 May 20, 1996	Trade Information Marketing & Exhibitions Manila, Philippines Tel: [63] (2) 832 0309 Fax: [63] (2) 632 7081
Asian Pacific Dental Fed Dental trade show	Manila February 3, 1994	Dr. Oliver Hennedige 841 Mountbatten Rd. Singapore 1543 Tel: [65] 345-3125

Trade Fair	Location & Date	Contact
Intermed-Pediasia Exhibit Latest machinery, tools, equipment for pediatric medicine	Manila The Manila Hotel Annual May 16–19, 1995	BHC & Co., Professional Project Managers 1138 A. Antipolo St. Rizal Village 1200 Makati, Metro Manila, Philippines Tel: [63] (2) 812-6784 Fax: [63] (2) 812-9426 Contact: Ms. Agnes H. Escalnate

PACKING & PACKAGING

Packprint Plas Philippines '95 International packaging and graphic arts technology	Pasay City, Metro Manila Trade Training Center Annual November 9–12, 1995	Oriental Western Promotions Ltd. 6/F, China Harbour Bldg. 370–374 King's Rd. North Point, Hong Kong Tel: [852] 2807-7633 Fax: [852] 2570-5917 Contact: Choy So Yuk
Phil Propack '96 International processing and packaging machinery and materials	Pasay City, Metro Manila Trade Training Center Biennial November 1996	Oriental Western Promotions Ltd. 6/F, China Harbour Bldg. 370–374 King's Rd. North Point, Hong Kong Tel: [852] 2807-7633 Fax: [852] 2570-5917 Contact: Choy So Yuk

SPORTING GOODS, TOYS, ENTERTAINMENT & TRAVEL

Hobby and Leisure Fair Toys, model kits, novelties, sporting goods	Mandaluyong, Metro Manila SM Mega Trade Hall Annual March 11–19, 1995	BHC & Co., Professional Project Managers 1138 A. Antipolo St. Rizal Village 1200 Makati, Metro Manila, Philippines Tel: [63] (2) 812 6764 Fax: [63] (2) 812-9426 Contact: Ms. Agnes H. Escalnate
Phildive '95 Tourism and sporting show	Makati, Metro Manila Hotel Nikko Manila Garden March 30–April 1, 1995	Philippine Convention and Visitors Corporation (PCVC) 4th Fl., Legaspi Towers 300 Roxas Blvd. Manila, Philippines Tel: [63] (2) 575-031 Fax: [63] (2) 521-6165
Sports & Leisure Show Sports equipment and accessories	Ortigas, Metro Manila Robinson's Galleria Annual September 14–17, 1995	BHC & Co., Professional Project Managers 1138 A. Antipolo St. Rizal Village 1200 Makati, Metro Manila, Philippines Tel: [63] (2) 812-6784 Fax: [63] (2) 812-9426 Contact: Ms. Agnes H. Escalnate
Traveltour Expo '95 Travel industry trade show	Mandaluyong, Metro Manila SM Mega Trade Hall February 24–26, 1995	Philippine Convention and Visitors Corporation (PCVC) 4th Fl., Legaspi Towers 300 Roxas Blvd. Manila, Philippines Tel: [63] (2) 575-031 Fax: [63] (2) 521-6165

Business Travel

INTRODUCTION

Business travelers to the Philippines will find it to be a land of contrasting experiences, both frustrating and exhilarating. First comes the grim: the sinking feeling you will have—upon arriving after a long, tiring flight—confronting the nonstop chaos of wall-to-wall humanity at the airport. The challenge to your patience continues as massive traffic tie-ups conspire to block your progress into Manila, the capital. Once in Manila, expect a scenario similar to those encountered in other Southeast Asian capitals: an eclectic mélange of cultures—Asian, Western, and unidentifiable indigenous—complete with modern shopping malls that include internationally recognizable fast-food restaurant chains; a frenetic buzz of anarchic traffic; and omnipresent air, water, and noise pollution that constantly assail the already overloaded senses at almost every turn.

At the opposite extreme are the pleasures of visiting the fabled, ancient rice terraces of Banaue in the north and letting go of your business-driven sense of time as you linger in this tropical land where rainbow sunsets are commonplace. An escape from the big cities brings travelers face-to-face with the grandeur and simplicity of long, deserted beaches that encircle many of the Philippines' more than 7,000 islands. They beckon with verdant tropical forests that host myriad flora and fauna. Intrepid travelers with wanderlust tendencies and the means, time, and inclination to follow them may be intrigued to know that more than 2,000 of these wayward islands have not even been named.

Equally pleasing is the hospitality offered by most Filipinos to foreign visitors. Kindness and consideration seem to be national traits, and whether the occasion is business or leisure, Filipinos seem eager to please. Although some 90 native languages and dialects are spoken, English is the most important nonnative and business language. Like Pilipino (based on the Tagalog language), English is an official national language and is spoken by almost half of the population, including nearly all professionals, academics, government officials, and many lower level personnel as well. The Philippines has one of the highest literacy rates in the East Asian and Pacific area: about 90 percent of the population ten years of age and older are literate. A surprisingly high percentage hold college degrees.

Lying just north of the equator, the Philippine islands constitute a total land area of nearly 300,000 sq km (116,000 sq mi)—about the same size as Italy

PHILIPPINE ADDRESSES AND TELEPHONE NUMBERS

Addresses and telephone numbers listed in this chapter are in the Philippines unless otherwise noted. Country codes for international dialing appear in square brackets, such as [34] for Spain or [1] for the US and Canada. City codes appear in parentheses—(171) for London or (2) for Manila.

If you are calling the Philippines from outside the country you will first need to dial the local international access code, such as 011 from the US or 001 from Japan, then [63] (the Philippines' country code), followed by the city code and the local telephone number. Some of the codes for major cities in the Philippines are: (2) for Metro Manila, (32) for Cebu, and (82) for Davao.

Philippine street addresses often give the name of the building, followed on the next line by the building number and the street name. There is often a neighborhood given, particularly within Manila. Postal codes are in place, but still rarely used.

For more telephone dialing codes and information on Philippine address formats, refer to the "Important Addresses" chapter, on page 297.

United Kingdom Department of Tourism, 17 Albermarle St., London, W1X 7HA, UK; Tel: [44] (171) 499-5443, 499-5652, Fax: [44] (171) 499-5772.

Pacific Asia

Hong Kong Philippine Consulate General, 21st Fl., Wah Kwong Regent Centre, 88 Queen's Road Central, Hong Kong; Tel: [852] 2810-0770, 2810-0963.

Japan Philippine House, 11-24 Nampeidai-machi, Shibuya-ku, Tokyo, Japan; Tel: [81] (3) 3464-3630, 3464-3635, Fax: [81] (3) 3464-3690.

Philippine Tourism Center, 2nd floor, Dainan Building, 2-19-23 Sinmachi, Nishi-ku, Osaka 550, Japan; Tel: [81] (6) 535-5071/2, Fax: [81] (6) 535-1235.

Australia Highmount House, Level 6, 122 Castlereagh St., Sydney, NSW 2000, Australia; Tel: [61] (2) 267-2695, 267-2756, Fax: [61] (2) 283-1862.

United States

Los Angeles Philippine Consulate General, 3660 Wilshire Blvd., Suite 216, Los Angeles, CA 90010, USA; Tel: [1] (213) 487-4527, Fax: [1] (213) 386-4063.

New York Philippine Center, 556 Fifth Ave., New York, NY 10036, USA; Tel: [1] (212) 575-7915, Fax: [1] (212) 302-6759.

San Francisco Philippine Consulate General, 447 Sutter St., 6th Fl., San Francisco, CA 94108, USA; Tel: [1] (415) 956-4060, Fax: [1] (415) 421-2641.

VISA AND PASSPORT REQUIREMENTS

A valid passport and an onward or return ticket are required for travelers entering the Philippines at the international airports in Manila and Cebu, the main ports of entry. Foreign visitors, whether on business or pleasure, do not need visas if they are staying for no more than three weeks. (A person who is specifically restricted, stateless, or from a country with which the Philippines does not have diplomatic relations—which would include Albania, Austria, Belgium, Cambodia, China, Cuba, Denmark, Finland, France, Germany, India, Italy, Iran, Laos, Libya, Luxembourg, Macao, Netherlands, North Korea, Norway, Russia, South Africa, Spain, Sweden, Syria, Taiwan, and Vietnam—do require a visa issued in advance by a Philippine overseas mission.)

Regular travelers are exempt from payment of immigration fees and charges. A visa waiver may be extended for another 38 days by applying to the Commission of Immigration and Deportation on arrival. The fee is P500 (about US$20), plus P10 (about US$0.40) for a legal research fee. Thereafter, visitors must apply for extensions and pay immigrations fees at the Commission on Immigration and Deportation, Magallanes Drive, Intramuros, Metro Manila (Tel: (2) 407-651). If you are entering the Philippines with a visa obtained in advance, be sure to

or the US state of Arizona. Airline service into Manila and among the major regions and islands is ongoing and meets good standards. Direct flights arrive daily from major carriers throughout North America, Europe, and Asia. But the road system, though well developed, is often overcrowded and poorly maintained; many surfaces consist only of gravel or crushed stone, and many others are unpaved.

TOURISM DEPARTMENT OFFICES WORLDWIDE

Head Office

Philippines Department of Tourism, DOT Bldg., T.M. Kalaw Street, Rizal Park, Manila; Tel: (2) 599-031 to 048, 585-528, Fax: (2) 521-7274, 521-7373, 583-317, 522-2194, 501-751.

Europe

Germany Philippines Department of Tourism, Kaiserstrasse 15, 6000 Frankfurt am Main 1, Germany; Tel: [49] (69) 20494/5, Fax: [49] (69) 285127.

call this to the attention of the immigration officer at the time of entry; otherwise, your passport may be stamped with the customary 21-day visitor's visa, which could cause you problems later.

Fees due from travelers staying up to six months include an application and visa fee (P450; about US$18), an Alien Head Tax (P200; about US$8), an Alien Certificate of Registration (P400—about US$16—for the first application or P250—about US$10—for a second application within the same calendar year), an Extension Fee of P200 (about US$8) for each month of the extension period already in effect, and an Emigration Clearance Certificate (P500; about US$20) that can be paid when departing at the airport. Travelers remaining for more than six months must pay an additional P700 (about US$28) for a Certificate of Temporary Residence. On departing after a stay of one year or more, a travel tax of P1,620 (about US$63) is due.

Business travelers must bring a letter from their employers. In addition to guaranteeing the trip financially, a traveler's business letter must describe the nature of business to be conducted and the anticipated length of stay.

Whether entering with a visa or a tourist card, it is important to carry a passport at all times (some observers suggest that travelers carry a photocopy of the document and safeguard the original elsewhere). A driver will need an International License as well as a home country national, state, or provincial license.

IMMUNIZATIONS

The World Health Organization (WHO) does not recommend vaccinations or preventive medication against any endemic diseases, but business travelers planning visits to remote areas may want to take more precautions. Malaria is endemic in some remote parts of the Philippines, although precautions are considered unneccesary for those traveling to Manila and other urban areas. Vaccinations travelers should consider getting include those against typhoid, tetanus, diphtheria, and yellow fever. Proof of vaccination against yellow fever, plague, and typhus or other diseases is not required unless travelers arrive from an infected area. The most common requirement is yellow fever vaccination for travelers arriving from tropical South America and Africa.

CLIMATE

The Philippine archipelago stretches from north to south for 1,850 km (1,221 mi) and from east to west for 1,100 km (726 mi). The Philippines can be divided into four main island groups: Luzon in the north, the largest island and the site of the capital, Manila; a central group of islands called the Visayas; the southernmost island, Mindanao; and the southwestern province of Palawan, consisting of more than 1,700 islands.

Typically hot and humid year-round throughout the region, the Philippines does have a dry and a wet season. In the northern part of the country that includes Manila, the wet season is from June to October. Heavy rains may fall during these times and usually occur daily from July through September. You shouldn't be affected by these downpours unless they coincide with the arrival of typhoons, which may occur from June through October. During these times, flooding may occur in Manila, causing traffic tie-ups throughout the capital, including Makati, the main business district.

The best months to visit and to conduct business are from December to May. These months offer cooler and drier conditions, with high temperatures ranging in Manila from 21° to 31°C (70° to 88°F). Temperatures begin to rise again in March, the hottest occurring in April and May, when daytime temperatures may rise as high as 35°C (95°F) and nighttime lows remain as hot as 27°C (81°F).

The southern regions have similar ranges of temperatures, but rainfall is distributed more evenly throughout the year. In the highlands, temperatures are often 5° to 10°C (9° to 18°F) cooler than in Manila. Such areas—particularly Baguio in the north on Luzon island (a four- to five-hour drive from Manila)—are popular destinations for lowland Filipinos seeking relief during the hot summer months.

BUSINESS ATTIRE

Quick to notice the attire of newly arriving foreign visitors, Filipinos are fashion conscious and use their clothes to make a statement and a good impression. But, perhaps due to the ongoing, often oppressive, presence of heat and humidity, Filipinos accept comfort and neatness as the overriding rules in dress. Although sometimes expecting travelers to dress formally for initial business meetings, Filipinos also want their guests to be comfortable, which means dress is more relaxed. And the Filipino business style is usually relatively leisurely and informal.

For example, businessmen seldom wear suits unless they have scheduled an appointment that requires greater than usual formality; instead they usually wear a business shirt, usually with a tie, sometimes without. Some men wear a *barong tagalog*, a lightweight, long-sleeved, embroidered shirt worn outside the trousers. A foreign businessman traveling in the Philippines may adopt this local style; although some Filipinos will be pleased

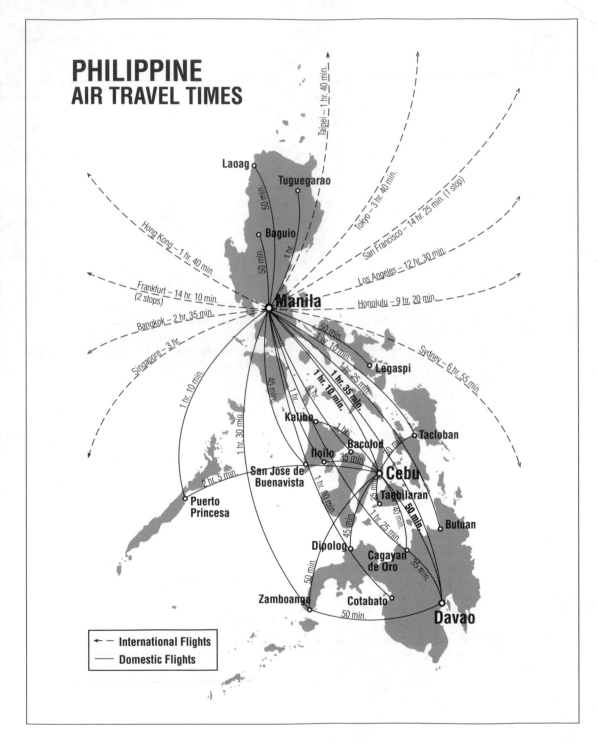

at this nod to local culture, others may expect somewhat more formality from visitors, at least initially. Two kinds of *barongs* are popular: an informal one made from cotton or polyester with short sleeves and minimal embroidery and a formal variety with long sleeves and elaborate embroidery. The formal garment is traditionally fashioned from

a sheer fabric composed of pineapple fiber; it is worn—always with a plain white undershirt—at social occasions and semiformal events.

Women in business wear conservative attire. Suits with skirts and elegant dresses are appropriate, while trousers and pantsuits are not. Ethnic fashions among women travelers—whether their own or the

Philippines'—are usually not well received.

When dining in someone's home, men should wear a coat and tie and women should wear dressy pants with a top, or a dress, or a skirt and blouse. (Because most upper class homes are air conditioned, you will most likely be comfortable even in this layered attire.)

Formal occasions, such as banquets, require men to wear a suit and women a short cocktail dress. Gowns are appropriate and necessary only for formal diplomatic receptions.

Casual wear for men is a sweater, shirt, and pants, with the sweater being optional, depending on the weather. For women, either pants or a skirt with a blouse is appropriate.

Neither men nor women should wear shorts in public, although they are fine for joggers. Sandals are acceptable as casual wear, but should not be worn when first entering the country or when going to a home, to a restaurant, out for the evening, or to any appointment involving anything official.

TIME CHANGES

The Philippines is 8 hours ahead of Greenwich Mean Time (GMT), or 13 hours ahead of US Eastern Standard Time (EST).

When in the Philippines, you can determine what time it is in any of the cities listed here by adding (+) or subtracting (–) the number of hours shown to or from Manila. The country does not observe daylight savings time.

City	Time Change (hours)
Auckland	+ 4
Beijing	0
Bangkok	–1
Frankfurt	–7
Hong Kong	0
Jakarta	–1
Kuala Lumpur	0
London	–8
Los Angeles	–16
New York	–13
Singapore	0
Sydney	+ 2
Taipei	0
Tokyo	+ 1

AIR TRAVEL TIME TO MANILA

- from Bangkok: 2 hours, 35 minutes
- from Hong Kong: 1 hour, 40 minutes
- from Honolulu: 9 hours, 20 minutes
- from Los Angeles: 12 hours, 30 minutes
- from Frankfurt: 14 hours, 10 minutes*
- from San Francisco: 14 hours, 25 minutes**
- from Singapore: 3 hours
- from Sydney: 6 hours, 55 minutes
- from Taipei: 1 hour, 40 minutes
- from Tokyo: 3 hours, 40 minutes

* with two stops   ** with one stop

AIRLINES

Air traffic in the Philippines is dominated by Philippine Airlines (PAL), the official state airline, although quality domestic service is also provided by two smaller companies, Aerolift and Pacific Airways.

PAL operates direct flights between Manila and the US, Australia, Taiwan, Japan, Brunei, Malaysia, Thailand, the United Arab Emirates, Saudi Arabia, Thailand, Germany, France, and the UK. Other international airlines serving Manila include Air France, British Airways, CAAC, Cathay Pacific, China Airlines, Japan Air Lines, KLM, Korean Air, Lufthansa, Malaysian Airlines, Northwest, PIA, Quantas, Saudia, Singapore Airlines, Swissair, Thai Airways International, and United.

Departure tax is P250 (about US$10) per passenger.

CUSTOMS ENTRY

Philippine customs officials usually ignore foreign visitors, but expensive cameras, laptop computers, and similar electronic items may arouse interest. It is a good idea to have a prepared list of such equipment, including serial numbers, ready for authorities to inspect and stamp. Inspectors at Ninoy Aquino International Airport in Manila are particularly vigilant.

Travelers are also subject to police inspection at internal checkpoints, usually at provincial borders and major highway junctions. Officials at international borders are generally efficient and helpful, but personnel at internal checkpoints tend to be more bureaucratic and formal in their approach.

Customs inspection follows the usual red and

green lane approach: green for nothing to declare, red for dutiable items. Personal items—including clothing, toiletries, and jewelry for normal use and in reasonable quantities—may be brought into the country duty-free. Each adult traveler is allowed to enter with two liters of alcoholic beverages and 400 cigarettes, 100 cigars, or two tins of smoking tobacco. Visitors may not bring in: firearms, ammunition, or explosives; narcotics and other internationally prohibited drugs—unless they are accompanied by a prescription; pornographic, seditious, or subversive literature; or gambling equipment. (Note that the Philippines may consider as pornographic some materials that are considered relatively innocuous in other cultures.)

FOREIGN EXCHANGE (PERSONAL)

The unit of currency is the peso (P), divided into 100 centavos. Paper currency is issued in 2, 5, 10, 20, 50, 100, 500, and 1,000 peso denominations. Coins in circulation are 1, 5, 10, 25, and 50 centavos and 1, 2, and 5 pesos. The exchange rate in June 1995 was 25.745 pesos per US dollar.

Traveler's checks and currency can be exchanged at banks, hotels, department stores, and the banking counter in the departure hall of Ninoy Aquino International Airport (NAIA) in Manila. Banks in Manila offer the best rate of exchange. Licensed money changers in Manila also offer competitive exchange rates. In the provinces, the exchange rate is lower, sometimes by as much as 20 percent, than at a bank in the capital. The business traveler should be aware that many provincial banks will only exchange traveler's checks up to a total value of US$100 or less. Transactions involving larger amounts may need special advance approval. Transactions require a passport and—if traveler's checks are being exchanged—the purchase receipt to authenticate the serial numbers of the checks. Receipts of exchange transactions are also needed for reconverting unused pesos at the time of departure.

A black market exists, but business travelers would be wise to avoid it. Schemes abound, and some travelers can recite horror stories about how they were swindled by suave, smooth-talking dealers. What is more, even straightforward transactions on the black market are rarely worthwhile; even if the black marketeer delivers as promised, most of these transactions result in a savings of only a few centavos per US$100. In some cases, the black market even pays substantially less than the going official rate.

US dollars are widely accepted, and—unlike the situation in many other places—cash is often easier to change than traveler's checks and commands a better rate. However, only clean, new bills in larger denominations (US$50–US$100) will be accepted; smaller denominations or worn bills are virtually impossible to negotiate. Cash is also widely available from automated teller machines (ATMs), particularly in Manila, for those with a Philippine bank account. Visitors expecting to remain in the Philippines for a while or anticipating the need for frequent transactions may wish to consider opening an account with a local bank, this can usually be done quite easily.

Credit cards (American Express, Diner's Club, MasterCard, Visa, and JBC) are widely accepted by hotels, restaurants, and businesses in the Philippines, especially in urban areas (acceptance is low to nonexistent in nontourist rural areas). A traveler can obtain cash or traveler's checks using a credit card at selected banks. American Express cardholders may obtain a cash advance or purchase traveler's checks from the company office in Manila using a personal check. Travelers should be aware that some businesses displaying signs for Visa accept only the credit card issued under that name by a Philippine bank, not the international card.

TIPPING

Tips are offered for most services in the Philippines, but recipients generally do not expect extravagant amounts. In restaurants, good service should be rewarded with a tip of 10 percent, although sometimes a service charge may already have been included in the bill. It is sometimes difficult to determine if a service charge is included, so if the bill is unclear you may wish to inquire. Hotel staff, such as doormen and porters, are accustomed to receiving tips of P10 to P20 (about US$0.40 to US$0.80). Taxi drivers are usually satisfied with a 10 percent tip—the fare is also usually rounded up to the nearest whole peso. If the driver assists with luggage, an additional tip of at least 10 percent is commonly given. Hired drivers of rental cars don't always expect a tip, but instead may be honored with a small gift.

ACCESS TO MANILA FROM AIRPORTS

Travelers arriving at Ninoy Aquino International will find themselves 7 km (4.5 mi) from downtown. Many hotels provide free limousine or minibus service for their guests, provided a room has been booked in advance and shuttle arrangements have been made. Some of the larger hotels provide shuttles for about US$3. For travelers taking a taxi, expect the taxi ride to cost from P60 to P100 (about US$2.50 to US$4), plus tip. This ride will take 15 minutes outside of rush hour, but up to one hour during bumper-to-bumper peak commuting times. Be aware that taxi drivers have been known to ask absurdly inflated fixed prices for their services, so before boarding be sure to demand that the driver use the (distance-based) meter. Note that air conditioned taxis are about 50 percent more expensive.

Reaching downtown by taxi from the Manila Domestic Airport terminal, (located across from the international airport) is an adventure in vigilance for the business traveler. A normal fare to downtown should be P50 (about US$2), but taxi drivers often attempt to charge a much higher, prearranged set fee; don't fall for this scheme. Again, it is a good idea to demand that the driver use the meter (and if the driver says that the meter is broken, insist on seeing that it is in fact not working). As an alternative to inflated taxi prices at the domestic airport, you can walk from the terminal to the road adjacent to the airport and flag down a passing taxi.

Car rentals are available at the airports and major hotels. Weekly rates start at US$390 for a small vehicle, not including fuel. (Rates at US car rental franchises tend to be higher than those of local firms.) However, because of the incessant heavy traffic in Manila, you may wish to avoid driving at all. Instead hire a driver to transport you between appointments. Drivers are available at relatively low cost through car rental companies (or ask at your hotel).

ACCOMMODATIONS

An unwritten Philippine rule dictates that a guest be treated like one of the family. For this reason, warm, effusive hospitality is a common feature wherever the business traveler lands. Beyond the kind, friendly people, the Philippines' solid selection of international class business hotels have all the expected amenities: heating (should you want it), air conditioning, satellite and local television, minibars, telephones, nightclubs, fitness centers, swimming pools, bars, and fine restaurants.

Business center staples—such as fax service and the use of computers—are available at many major hotels and are becoming increasingly common at smaller ones. Urban and industrial areas generally have quite good telephone service, unlike many outlying areas, where service is unreliable.

High-quality hotels are located in Makati—the business district—and in the Roxas Boulevard and nearby Manila Bay areas. Bayside hotels are often more tourist oriented and plush, offering impressive views, but business travelers may wish to stay elsewhere to prevent traffic delays: the 15-minute taxi rides between the beach and business appointments can take twice as long (or longer) during rush hour.

Most hotels offer corporate rates, but it is a good idea to inquire when making reservations. In the listings that follow, rates are quoted in US dollars but payable in pesos and do not include a 10 percent service charge and 13 percent value-added tax.

Note that the high rate season begins in March and lasts through May. Expect to pay US$200 per night—and up—for a top-end hotel in Manila. Hotels classified here as "expensive" generally have rack rates starting between US$125–US$150, while "moderate" hotels usually have rooms available for US$100 or less. In Cebu and Davao, the "expensive" hotels will run you US$75 to US$100, while the moderate hotels are about US$50. Prices may be about one-third less from December through February. Expect to pay no more than half the high season price during June through November.

Advance hotel reservations are a good idea, especially for travelers who want a limousine or shuttle bus pickup at the airport.

Because nine-tenths of business activity occurs in Manila, business infrastructure has been slow to develop outside the capital area. Virtually all international arrivals continue to be through Manila, as well. Travelers with other Philippine destinations in mind would do well to check locally regarding current developments in the provinces.

MANILA

The majority of Manila's business hotels are in or very near the Makati downtown business area or in the Manila Bay area or nearby.

Top-End

Hotel Inter-Continental Manila One Ayala Ave., Makati. Centrally located in the main financial and shopping district, with golf courses and tennis courts located nearby. More than 400 rooms, business center, 7 function rooms with capacities ranging from 500 to 1,000. A longtime favorite with businesspeople. Swimming pools, health club and fitness center. Tel: (2) 815-9711, Fax: (2) 817-1330.

Manila Hotel One Rizal Park, Ermita. This government-owned hotel is a Manila landmark, built in 1908 and fully renovated 20 years ago. Additional renovations made in 1995. Beautiful architecture, ornate decor throughout, several restaurants, including the noted Champagne Room and Maynila. Business Services Center, 8 meeting rooms; fitness facilities include squash and tennis courts. Tel: (2) 832-0701, 470-011, Fax: (2) 530-0325, 247-1124.

The Peninsula Manila Corner Ayala and Makati Aves., Makati. Located in the center of the Makati business and shopping district. Renovated in 1995, each room features bedside control panels and remodeled bathrooms; 13 meeting rooms for groups of up to 1000, A/V and secretarial services available, health club, outdoor pool, 24-hour business center. Rates: Tel: (2) 819-3456, 812-3456; Fax: (2) 815-4825.

Westin Philippine Plaza Hotel CCP Complex, Roxas Blvd. Part of the Cultural Center complex and near the Philippine Center for International Trade and Exhibitions. Show lounge features top names and a top-notch restaurant. Business center, convention facilities, health club, swimming pool, floodlit tennis courts, short nine-hole golf course. Tel: (2) 832-0701; Fax: (2) 832-3485.

Expensive

Century Park Sheraton Corner Pablo Ocampo Sr. and M. Adriatico Streets, Malate. Features well-lit rooms with bay views and large desks; located next to the Harrizon Plaza shopping mall, which includes stores, boutiques, restaurants, movie theaters, and the Reed Fitness Center. Meeting facilities to 800, business center. Tel: (2) 522-1011, Fax: (2) 521-3413.

Hyatt Regency 2702 Roxas Blvd., Pasay City. Located near the Makati business district; also overlooks Manila Bay. Home of the highly acclaimed Japanese restaurant Tempura-Misono. Relatively more quiet than some large Manila hotels; popular among business travelers. Business center, conference facilities, outdoor pool, shopping arcade with boutiques. Rates: Tel: (2) 833-1234, Fax (2) 833-5913.

Nikko Manila Garden Ayala Center, Makati. Located in the Makati business district; within walking distance to nightspots and entertainment. Plain, efficient decor is popular with business travelers. Restaurant is noted for Japanese cuisine; Japanese garden offers tranquil surroundings for the urban weary. Business center, meeting rooms, outdoor pool, health club, shops. Rates: Tel: (2) 810-4101, Fax: (2) 817-1862.

Traders Hotel 3001 Roxas Blvd., Pasay City. Formerly the Holiday Inn Manila; US$10 million renovation project was completed January, 1995. Located opposite Cultural Center and Philippine Convention Complex. Rooms are well equipped for business travelers wishing to work. Business center, meeting rooms, health club, coffee shop. Rates: Tel: (2) 597-961, Fax: (2) 522-3985.

Moderate

Admiral 2138 Roxas Blvd., Malate. Many rooms overlook Manila Bay. Renovated in 1988. Bargain rates for business travelers; friendly staff. Meeting rooms, restaurants, meeting facilities, A/V rentals available, business center, fitness center, outdoor pool. Tel: (2) 572-081, Fax: (2) 522-2018.

La Corona Located in the heart of the tourist and nightlife district. The majority of guests are tourists. The business center offers the basic necessities; all suites have jacuzzis. Tel: (2) 502-631, Fax: (2) 505-513 (US tollfree (800) 528-1234.)

Philippine Village Nayong Pilipino Park, Ninoy Aquino Ave., Pasay City. Located next to the airport, this hotel is a 10- to15-minute taxi ride to bayside or Makati locations. Business center services are matched by well developed convention facilities. Outdoor pool, tennis courts, restaurant, coffee shop. Tel: (2) 833-8081, Fax: (2) 831-7788.

Sulo Hotel Mataline St., Diliman, Quezon City. Located in the business district of Quezon City. Meeting rooms, shops, restaurant, outdoor pool, coffee shop. Rates: US$100 and up. Tel: (2) 924-5051.

CEBU

Business facilities in Cebu are minimal in comparison with Manila. The airport, which is 14 km (8.7 mi) from Cebu is served by Philippine Airlines. Avis, Hertz, and Budget have rental car offices here.

Expensive

Cebu Plaza Hotel Nivel Hills, Lahug. On a hilltop overlooking city and Mactan Island. Conference facilities, meeting rooms, business center, two swimming pools, tennis courts, coffee shop, seafood restaurant. Tel: (32) 311-231, (32) 312-069, 24-861.

Moderate

Magellan International Hotel Gorordo Ave., Lahug. Full-service hotel, attractive grounds, conveniently located, meeting facilities, restaurants (Puerto Galera and Camarin Filipino), lounges, swimming pool, golf course. Tel: (32) 74-611/9, Fax: (32) 216-417.

Montebello Villa Hotel Banilad. In the residential area. Renovations made in 1992, ask for rooms in the new wing. Business center, meeting rooms, outdoor pools, tennis courts, restaurant. Tel: (32) 313-681, Fax: (32) 314-455.

DAVAO

The airport, which is 10 km (6.2 mi) north of the city, is served by Philippine Airlines.

Expensive

Insular Hotel Davao Lanang. Located near the beach. Meeting rooms, business center, outdoor pool, tennis courts. Tel: (82) 76-051, 234-3050, Fax: (82) 62-959.

Moderate

Apo View Hotel 150 J. Camus Street. Located in the business district. Meeting rooms, restaurant. Tel: (82) 74-861/5, Fax (82) 63-802.

EATING

Satisfying the appetites of business travelers with diverse food preferences is no problem in the Philippines. In Manila in particular, but in any larger Philippine city as well, visitors can partake of cuisines from a variety of cultures. Aromas intermingle amid busy streets where, packed side-by-side with each other, Chinese, Malay, Japanese, Middle Eastern, Latin American, Indian, Southeast Asian, and other specialty eateries abound. Within this mixture are establishments not to be missed—both well-worn, tiny cafés and elaborate, elegant palaces serving Filipino specialties.

A general definition of Filipino cuisine is that it is a mixture of East and West. Centuries of Spanish rule, half a century of US occupation, and longterm Malayan, Chinese, and Islamic cultural influences have resulted in an eclectic smorgasbord of Filipino dishes. Common ingredients include pork (goat in Muslim areas), shrimp, fish, beef, and chicken mixed with vegetables using such flavorings as soy sauce, coconut milk, tomato sauce, peanut sauce, *patis* (the Philippine variant of Southeast Asia's ubiquitous fish sauce), and vinegar or lime juice.

Filipino dishes are often made with quite fresh ingredients easily accessible from the nearby sea and agricultural lands. *Kinilaw* or *kilawin,* one of the oldest dishes that is still popular, is fish or shrimp cooked lightly in vinegar until it is no longer raw. Other traditional dishes are made without heavy sauces, relying instead only on light seasonings to bring out their fresh, natural flavors. These dishes include *pinakbet* (mixed vegetables stewed in anchovy sauce), *kare-kare* (oxtail- or tripe-and-vegetable stew with a peanut flavor) and *adobo* (meat, poultry, or seafood stew with pepper, garlic, and vinegar).

Rice, the national staple, is as permanent a fixture in Philippine cuisine as it is in China or Japan. So dominant is its influence that the Filipino word for rice can—depending on declension—mean "to eat" or, generically, "food". Therefore, it should come as no surprise that many Filipinos eat rice at every daily meal. The many varieties of rice available form the basis of a great number of recipes with distinctive flavors. Perhaps the most common way to prepare rice is simply to boil it and serve it steaming hot on anything from bone china to banana leaves.

At best, wariness may be your reaction to another popular local dish. But your reward for eating *balut,* an incubated duck egg consumed about 10 days before it would have hatched, is the goodwill you will gain from the locals. However, be prepared before you offer to participate; legend claims that *balut* is a potent aphrodisiac.

For hints on ordering meals and general eating etiquette, watch the Filipinos. They often begin their meal with *sinigang,* a clear broth made with *bangus* (milkfish) or shrimp and made tart and slightly sour with the addition of fruit. And when the dishes are brought in, Filipinos usually reach automatically for a variety of condiments, such as vinegar mixed with hot chili or soy sauce enlivened with *kalamansi* (a small green citrus fruit) juice.

Although shunned by some as peasant behavior, eating with one's hands is not only acceptable, but in fact is considered an enjoyable and authentic way of eating. Plenty of washbasins are available for cleanup before and after a meal. However, if you are feeling inhibited, do not hesitate to use utensils.

Drinking water in Manila is generally considered safe, and towns and cities outside Manila usually have clean, drinkable water as well. However, in rural areas it is probably a good idea to drink bottled or boiled water. In these outlying areas, you are generally safe ordering beer, wine, other alcohol drinks, and sodas, as long as they are not served with ice (the alcohol option is—and certainly should be—restricted in predominately Muslim areas).

Filipinos are not surprised if breakfast includes a meeting to discuss business. They are used to an early start, usually eating between 7 am and 8 am. US-style bacon-and-egg breakfasts are common, but menus frequently offer the "Filipino Breakfast," consisting of fried rice, fried egg, beef *tapa* (preserved beef slices), *tocino* (Spanish-style bacon), or *longaniza* (a spicy, garlic sausage). Others make do with fruit, *ensaimada* (sugary bakery buns), and coffee. Still others skip breakfast entirely or drink only tea. More traditional Filipinos eat fish and rice.

Lunch is typically eaten from noon to 1 pm. Like breakfast and dinner, lunch is usually a large meal, often including *sinigang* (a sour soup), *adobo* (a marinated meat stew), rice, fruit, and cakes. Water and soda are the usual drinks with lunch.

Expect a snack, the *merienda,* during mid-afternoon. Filipinos, especially those who continue to follow Spanish traditions, like snacks featuring sweet fritters, cakes, and tarts. Coconut milk is a main ingredient in most desserts, such as *suman* (rice, palm sugar, and coconut milk steamed in banana leaves), *tsampurado* (rice and chocolate), and *halo-halo* (shaved ice and coconut milk mixed with grains of fried rice, corn, or mung bean).

Dinner is generally eaten around 7 pm, although traditional Hispanic Filipinos may eat as late as 9 pm or 10 pm. Entrees generally consist of fish or seafood dishes. Side dishes include vegetables, rice, and fruit. Desserts are sure to please visitors with a sweet tooth, although some may find them overly rich. Some of the most popular are *sans rival* (made of egg whites, cream, coconut, and a meringue base); steamed or baked rice cakes made with coconut milk and sugar; and *queso puti,* a white cheese made from water buffalo milk.

Business travelers should be aware that only men are offered alcohol drinks, usually beer and wine. Manila-brewed San Miguel beer is highly regarded. However, outside Manila it is brewed under different licenses and may vary in quality. Mixed drinks are often made with local rum, which is also popular in cocktails and punches. Rum may be palmed off in some establishments as some other liquor; imported alcohols are quite expensive. Other readily available drinks include orange juice, various sodas, and *calamansi,* a native drink made with a citrus fruit similar to the lemon.

MANILA

Eating native Filipino fare at reasonable prices is not a problem. A meal for two usually ranges from P250 to P350 (about US$10 to US$14). However, business travelers opting for meals at first-rate restaurants and top hotels will pay considerably more: usually about P440 (about US$17) and up. Because wine is imported, a good bottle will run you P500 (US$20) and up. Remember that most restaurants automatically add a service charge and sales tax to the bill. Also keep in mind that most first class restaurants also have a dress code that requires a jacket and tie for men—or a *barong tagalog* (if you are unsure, inquire when making the reservations that most restaurants also require).

Abelardo's French-Continental. First class, appropriate for quiet business conversation; a private dining room adjoins the main restaurant; reservations advised. Native-inspired dishes such as steamed fillet of *lapu-lapu* (grouper) with fresh chervil blossoms and full-blown continental fare such as breast of duck with orange sauce are well prepared. Westin Philippine Plaza Hotel, Cultural Center of the Philippines Complex, Roxas Blvd. Tel: (2) 832-0701.

Aristocrat International and native cuisine. Casual. Open 24 hours. A Manila legend, featuring two large eating areas. There are six locations in Metro Manila, but this is the most popular one. Moderately priced; reservations not required. Casual dress. 432 San Andres St., corner Roxas Blvd., Malate. Tel: (2) 507-671.

Champagne Room French. First class; the place to see and to be seen, especially if you want to impress clients. Popular specialties include pan-fried veal steak dressed with ham, tomato, and Gruyere, and king prawns flamed in Pernod; reservations required for dinner. The lunch buffet is a bargain. In the Manila Hotel, Rizal Park, Ermita. Tel: (2) 470-011.

Lolita's Steakhouse. Worth the half-hour taxi ride from most hotels, this restaurant extends Philippine tradition to the steakhouse: patrons can choose their own steak and specify the preparation (or you can order from the menu). P90 to P220 (about US$3.50 to US$8.50). No reservations; casual dress. 7 Scout Borromeo Street, Quezon City. Tel: (02) 961-564.

Maynila Filipino cuisine. First class. Primarily visited by businessmen and politicos, this restaurant is quintessential elegance adorned in Spanish-Filipino decor; reservations required. Dinner only. Manila Hotel, Rizal Park. Tel: (2) 470-011.

Old Manila Filipino cuisine. First class. Located in the business district; a good last-minute choice that will impress clients. Native dishes are succulent, especially home-smoked *tanguingue* (local version of salmon); reservations advised. Peninsula Manila Hotel, corner of Ayala and Makati Avenues. Tel: (2) 819-3456.

CEBU

Alavar's Seafood House Seafood. Music and dancing complement highly acclaimed dishes; specialties include dishes from Zamboanga on Mindanao. 46 Gorordo Ave., Cebu City; Tel: (32) 781-126.

Tung Yan Restaurant Chinese cuisine. Considered to be one of the best Chinese restaurants in Cebu. Gorordo Ave., Cebu City.

Camarin Filipino Filipino cuisine. Highly recommended local dishes. On the grounds of the Magellan International Hotel. Gorordo Ave., Cebu City; Tel: (32) 74-613.

DAVAO

La Parilla Filipino-Continental Located in the Davao Insular Hotel. Live music at night. Tel: (82) 76-051.

LOCAL CUSTOM OVERVIEW

Life in the Philippines has a reputation for being laid-back, so slow that even hard-charging foreign business people would find themselves drifting into acceptance of the supposed local habit of putting off until tomorrow decisions that are necessary today. This notion may have some validity, especially in rural areas and at island resorts catering to tourists.

However, in the cities, the pulse of life—and commerce—quickens considerably. While the Filipino businessperson appears languid and at times behaves with an almost baroque civility that seems to belong to some other, slower and simpler age, this facade often masks a strict underlying awareness of the time of day, schedules, deadlines, and hard business requirements and realities. Nevertheless, this level of concentration will likely not be apparent during an initial business meeting. Instead, it may strike the foreign traveler that the conversation is lightweight, mere small talk. However, this is how Filipinos will begin to size you up, and the wise businessperson will slip easily and enthusiastically into talk about Filipino life, and food, the visitor's trip, family, hometown, and even the weather without concern that undue time is being spent on trivialities. To your host, they are not trivial, nor should they be to you.

The purpose of such digression is anything but trivial. It is standard operating procedure for Filipinos to first get to know their counterparts in order to become comfortable with them before beginning to negotiate serious business arrangements. For this reason, it is a good idea to leave plenty of time to negotiate a business deal. This may mean expecting a morning meeting to extend into lunch and beyond or realizing that two overseas business trips will be necessary to conclude a business deal.

Casual, informal banter may creep into discussions during subsequent meetings and return visits, even entering at crucial points during the final negotiations. Of course this may be a tactic, but is usually designed to slow down a process that is in danger of moving too fast or to defuse a potential confrontation. Your counterpart also may just feel like a break. If and when this occurs, the best approach is to follow the lead of your Philippine counterpart. Staying jovial and avoiding comments designed to force things "back on track" is a good strategy until the Filipino returns to the business at hand.

The work ethic is alive and well in the Philippines, but Filipino businesspersons can be relaxed in their general attitude while being focused on specifics; for instance, they may prefer to consummate a deal around a swimming pool, on the golf course, or over lunch in an outdoor restaurant.

Business is bound up in bureaucracy and red tape, although not usually to the same degree as government. Businesspeople need to obtain the consent of many others before proceeding with a project—an arduous and time-consuming process. Travelers accustomed to moving quickly and finalizing details with a phone call will have to adjust their expectations. There is no way to push the pace of approvals, and impatience will only make a bad impression and delay, if not derail, the deal.

One of the most important business precepts is

PHILIPPINE HOLIDAYS

The entire country celebrates the following holidays:

New Year	January 1
Maundy Thursday	Thursday before Easter Sunday
Good Friday	Friday before Easter Sunday
Easter	Late March or April
Bataan, Corregidor Day	April 9
Labor Day	May 1
Independence Day	June 12
Philippine-American Friendship Day	July 4
National Heroes Day	Last Sunday of August
Thanksgiving Day	September 21
All Saint's Day	November 1
Bonifacio Day	November 30
Christmas Day	December 25
Rizal Day	December 30
New Year's Eve	December 31

USEFUL TELEPHONE NUMBERS

EMERGENCY
24-hour police assistance in Manila: 166

AIRLINES
Philippine Airlines
    Ticket office: ....(2) 816-6691, 819-1771
    24-hour Info Service: .... (2) 816-6691
Aerolift Philippines: ....(2) 812-6711
Pacific Airways: ....(2) 832-2731

TOURISM INFORMATION
24-hour tourist assistance: ....(2) 501-660, 501-728
Tourist Information Centers
    Manila: .... (2) 599-031
    Ninoy Aquino Airport: .(2) 828-4791, 828-1511
    Cebu City: ....(32) 91-503, 96-518
    Davao: ....(82) 64-688, 71-534
Philippine Convention & Visitors Corporation:
    .... (2) 575-031

TELEPHONE INFORMATION
Directory assistance: 114
Direct dialing assistance: 112
Operator-assisted domestic calls: 109
Operator-assisted international calls: 108

POSTAL SERVICE
Manila Central Post Office: .... (2) 484-761
Makati Central Post Office: .... (2) 850-150

AMERICAN EXPRESS
Manila office: .... (2) 815-9311
24-hour assistance: ....(2) 815-4159, 856-911

CAR RENTAL
Avis, Manila: .... (2) 844-8498
    Ninoy Aquino Airport: .... (2) 832-2088
Budget, Manila: ....(2) 832-0931, 816-2211
Hertz, Manila: .... (2) 832-5325
    Reservations: .... (2) 832-0520
    Ninoy Aquino Airport: 831-9827

honored, so make sure written agreements set forth the terms of any business deals and transactions in adequate detail. This will also serve to flag the most likely points of controversy sooner rather than later.

In addition, decisions are usually made by the most important executives. But decisions are reached slowly, and even chief executives may be reluctant to commit to a definite agreement. Executives are also known to say that a proposal should be presented to a board or committee when they really are trying to avoid saying no. In this case, note that executives would rather have a group of people be responsible for negative actions.

Ultimately, Filipinos are team players, meaning that they value cooperation and consensus when decisions must be made. Introducing ideas that a majority of a group might oppose should be done with great care; diplomacy, tact, and indirection during negotiation are all-important if you are to avoid implying criticism. Filipino counterparts should always be allowed to retain an escape route in any discussion; to force an issue may be considered an act of rudeness and even aggression that can spoil future relations. Maintaining the allegiance and loyalty of Filipino businesspersons can be difficult if they feel criticized, and public criticism is a cardinal sin in both business and personal relations.

Contacts and introductions are indispensable, especially when doing business with government at any level. Bringing letters of introduction from mutual friends or business associates is a good idea for first-time business travelers or for those who represent companies not known locally; a direct personal introduction or reference is even better. Participants in prior business dealings, professional organizations, chambers of commerce, mutual friends or acquaintances, even embassy referrals, no matter how tangential, are more likely to be successful than a cold call. Expect to make several visits to establish a personal relationship before concluding any negotiations. Personal impressions and relationships remain a critical part of every business deal.

Manners and politeness are extremely important. It is a good idea to address a businessperson by putting that person's title in front of the last name; thus: "Doctor Ramos" or "Architect Cruz." Confrontation and threats, either real or implied, are frowned upon. Anyone who is seen as abrasive or uncooperative is unlikely to succeed, as group consensus is always more valued than individual approaches, although Filipinos do tend to be somewhat more individualistic than some other Asians.

Foreign women should experience few problems conducting business as long as they remain profes-

to remember that Filipinos go out of their way to save face. They avoid confrontation or the appearance of being out of control; they may agree to something they disagree with or have no intention of undertaking simply to be polite. In business, you need to get Filipinos to confirm what they say in writing. Verbal commitments will not necessarily be

sional in manner and dress and otherwise behave with sensitivity to local norms. Filipino women often serve in important business and political positions.

Promptness is important, particularly for foreign businesspeople. Although Filipinos are accustomed to being late for social occasions, they are not as forgiving about business meeting times. Punctuality is a good idea, and appointments are even more important. Do not expect to see anyone without an appointment. But remember that although foreign business travelers are expected to show up on time, they should not always expect Filipinos to be quite as punctual. Local visitors are typically five to ten minutes late, and anyone receiving visitors is expected to keep them waiting for at least a few minutes. The higher people are in the organization, the longer they tend to keep visitors waiting.

Gift-giving can be an important gesture that will help business travelers promote goodwill; however, gifts are usually not of high value, and are best bestowed after the relationship has had a chance to develop rather than at the first meeting. Filipinos are impressed by tasteful gifts that represent an aspect of a traveler's firm, culture, or hometown, such as a craft or other item. Other good gifts include T-shirts, high-quality chocolate (a favorite with all age groups), and books with photographs of your home country. Avoid giving tacky souvenir gifts.

Finally, here are a few points on business customs and etiquette:

- Business cards are important as a clue to professional rank and standing. It is a good idea to carry a supply, but it is not important to have them translated into a language other than English— the main business language—before arrival.
- The party that invites another to lunch or dinner pays. The "guests" should therefore avoid ordering the most expensive items on the menu. Confirmation of dates is usually made through personal secretaries. One exception regarding who pays is that foreign businesswomen should never offer to pay the tab for entertaining Filipino businesspeople. It is considered an insult for the visiting traveler to attempt to pay with a credit card beforehand.
- Upon closing a business deal, it is a good idea to celebrate by inviting Filipino businesspersons (and their spouses) to a restaurant. In general, it is appropriate to invite wives of Filipino counterparts to social occasions, but only to dinner or a similar event, and never to a lunch or other event at which discussion can be expected to deal primarily with business.
- Western businessmen living in the Philippines will often invite foreign travelers home for dinner or suggest an early evening meal in a restaurant. Filipinos are more likely to ask foreign travelers out for dinner. Be prepared for the festivities to last until late in the evening.
- Avoid planning business trips during the holiday period of June through September, at Christmas (late December), or during Easter week (March or April).
- Firms run by ethnic Chinese are generally closed for extended periods during Chinese New Year, often including the week before and after the actual observed date.
- It is a good idea to schedule business appointments from abroad at least a month in advance. Remember to arrange meetings for morning or mid-afternoon because many Philippine operations close for lunch (a remnant of the Spanish *siesta*).

DOMESTIC TRANSPORTATION

Manila With more than 11 million people, Manila has world class traffic jams morning, evening, and often in between. City driving is best left to Manila residents and other brave competitors who are accustomed to aggressively forging their own path, regardless of lane markings, traffic lights, or other niceties.

Taxis Taxis are by far the best way to get around Manila. With a plentiful supply of taxis at the international airport, a ride to the business district and nearby hotels generally takes little more than 15 minutes during nonrush hours. (Travelers may want to get a taxi through their hotels, which often screen drivers.) In addition, most of the major hotels operate shuttles from the international airport.

In Manila, taxis wait outside hotels or can be flagged down from the street. Most have a meter, but make sure it is working before boarding. Meters measure distance rather than time. Air conditioned taxis, which cost more than those not so equipped, have an initial minimum charge of P16 (about US$0.65). Thereafter, a charge of P1 occurs for every 250 meters. For example, the fare from the business district to the international airport is around P60 (about US$2.50).

Drivers generally do not carry change, so it is a good idea for travelers to carry some. Reputable taxi companies include Golden Cabs (black and gold lettering), EMP cabs (white with yellow stripes), Fil-Nipon taxis, and City taxis.

Business travelers might be tempted to use the colorful "jeepneys" to get around Manila, but the experience is not likely to be enjoyable. These converted buses, jeeps, and carts are often crowded and have limited views, preventing travelers from seeing where they are going.

Trains Rail travel may be an option for travelers not in a hurry. The Metro Rail, also called Light Rail Transit (LRT), maintains a 5.5 km (9 mi) route that generally parallels Roxas Boulevard. Transfer stations are located throughout the route at major intersections and shopping malls. The fare is a flat rate of P6 (about US$0.25), with unlimited transfers allowed. The Metro Rail operates from 5:30 am until 10:30 pm every day except Good Friday. Be aware that during rush hours Metro Rail is jammed, and no large carried objects will be allowed on board at those times.

Trains traveling outside Manila are not an option for business travel. Only the railway line from Manila to Naga in South Luzon remains in operation, and it is a long, slow ride of 12 hours.

Buses Manila buses, though efficiently operated and air conditioned, are a poor travel option unless the business traveler has plenty of time and knows local routes. Locals appreciate the Love Buses: blue vehicles emblazoned with red hearts that travel along several routes and charge a flat rate of P10 (about US$0.40). Travelers riding local buses should bring plenty of small change, because drivers usually cannot change bills.

Private Car For some travel outside Manila, renting a car may be the best option. Rentals can be had by the day, week, or month through the franchisees of companies such as Avis, Budget, and Hertz, as well as from local outfits. Rates for a basic economy car with air conditioning and radio are US$65 a day or US$390 a week with unlimited mileage. Gasoline costs P10 (about US$0.40) per liter. For travel in Manila, it is a good idea to hire a driver. Rental companies will provide one at a relatively low cost—a worthwhile investment to avoid having to brave the omnipresent and anarchic traffic on one's own.

The Philippines has a fair system of roads, the best maintained ones being those located in and around Manila and near the provincial capitals elsewhere.

Air For travelers on a schedule, those who need to get to outlying islands, and those desiring a modicum of comfort, air travel is the best option for getting around this huge island nation. Businesspersons can choose from among three airlines for domestic travel. Philippine Airlines (PAL) is the official state airline, but quality domestic service is also provided by Aerolift and Pacific Airways. PAL operates the greatest number of flights throughout the islands, serving more than 40 locations. However, travelers should note that flight schedules vary considerably. For example, there are several daily flights from Manila to Cebu, but other destinations are served only a few times a week. Sample prices of one-way fares beginning in Manila

are: to Cebu P1400 (about US$55); to Davao P2515 (about US$100); to Baguio P560 (about US$22); to Puerto Princesa P1425 (about US$55).

Aerolift flies to El Nido, Catician, Daet, Cebu, Boracay, Bohol, Dipolog, Lubang, and Busuanga. Destinations serviced by Pacific Airways include Lubang, Boracay, Busuanga, Daet, Catician, and Cuyo.

Advance reservations are important. Domestic flight schedules are available from various tourist operators, although one of the best places to obtain one is from the PAL office on Roxas Boulevard. Flight schedules are also listed in the magazine *What's On in Manila*, which is available at newsstands and hotels.

PAL and Aerolift have better reputations for on-time operations, while Pacific Airway is known for being less punctual. Airport taxes on domestic flights are included in the price of the ticket. Smoking is not permitted on flights.

HOLIDAYS

Banks, offices, and most shops are closed on the national holidays listed in the chart "Philippine Holidays" on page 145. Towns and regions also celebrate local holidays when everything closes (check with local tourist offices for the dates). In addition, the president occasionally designates special public holidays.

Travelers should also be aware that Filipinos are particularly observant around Easter. During Holy Week (the week before Easter), Filipinos are generally quiet and somber, gathering at home and attending church daily. The period around Christmas is more festive, but also a less than opportune time to try to conduct business. Vacations are generally scheduled during the period from June through September, which is considered to be a less effective time to try to do business.

BUSINESS HOURS

Business hours at private offices usually begin between 8 am and 9 am and run until 5 pm or 6 pm. Private offices are usually open Monday through Friday, and many establishments are open for either a half-day or all day on Saturday. A one-hour lunch break is customary, and some offices and establishments close during this period, although most stores now remain open during lunch. Many establishments operate more flexibly, so it is a good idea to make appointments or to call first to confirm hours. Offices are closed on Sunday, although many commercial establishments remain open, usually from 10 am to 6 pm.

Banking hours are generally 10 am to 4 pm, Monday through Friday. Government offices are open Monday to Friday from 8 am to 5 pm, with a one-hour lunch break.

COMMUNICATIONS

Most of the information that appears in this section applies to Manila. Outside Manila, communications services are not as well developed. Business travelers will usually need to bring any crucial equipment with them. For example, carry a laptop with you if you rely on computers, because finding one to rent or borrow is likely to be difficult, if not impossible, in most places in the Philippines. Fax machines are also relatively uncommon except in Manila.

Telephones

Strangely enough, it is often easier to complete an international call in the Philippines than to make a local call. The litany of problems with local service begins with the fact that there are too few public telephones, and many of these are often inoperable. Fortunately, telephones are generally more common in business districts, although you cannot expect to find telephones on streets or along highways.

Connecting local calls sometimes takes an exhausting amount of time, even though the parties may be relatively near each other. (For this reason, businesses sometimes use messengers to deliver important communications instead of attempting to call.) Why telephone numbers change so frequently is also a mystery. (Having a local telephone directory handy is a good idea, although even this may not help a great deal.) Local calls have no time limit and cost 25 centavos. To complete a call, deposit the coins, then dial the number.

Domestic calls are relatively cheap: a one-minute call from Manila to Cebu City costs P25 (about US$1) for the first minute and P20 (about US$0.80) for each additional minute.

Good hotels have more dependable telephone service, and many of the better ones provide rooms with direct international calling service. However, travelers should be aware that hotels may add a substantial surcharge onto long distance calls; it is usually less expensive to use a credit card number or call collect. The regular rate to North America is about US$10 for a station-to-station call lasting three minutes. To save money, call outside the business hours of the country to which the call is being placed. In addition, calls made on Sunday are 25 percent cheaper.

Telecommunications are superior in the first class hotels in Manila, with many offering guests business center services complete with computers, typewriters, telephones, faxes, and modems. Sending faxes can be expensive for travelers working from their hotel rooms. For example, the rate for faxing one page to Europe can be P350 (about US$14). However, to avoid other undue costs and hotel surcharges, the best solution for business travelers is often to plan on receiving calls from foreign callers at appointed times.

Telex and microwave relay stations are also in operation. Telex service is reliable, with most hotel business centers offering this service. The telex rate to North America is approximately US$1.90 per minute.

To cut costs and increase efficiency, more Philippine businesses are beginning to use cellular phones. Communications companies have set up cellular telephone facilities, so users can now reach most parts of the country.

Access to the operator is obtained by dialing 04, while dialing 09 provides long distance service.

To dial international calls, dial 00 for international access, then the country code, area or city code, and telephone number. For example, to direct dial World Trade Press, call 00-1-415-454-9934.

Fax and Online Services

Fax machines and computer modem connections are slowly gaining popularity in the Philippines, but are still somewhat hampered by poor telephone service. Hotels and most active businesses have fax machines, as do most telephone company centers. A number of photocopying and business service centers can provide this service, and offices that send telegrams may also be able to transmit faxes and telexes. Fax charges vary widely. Connection to the Internet and other telephone-linked computer services is problematic.

Post Office

The Philippine postal system is usually considered to provide reliable service. Most post offices are open Monday through Friday from 8 am to noon and from 1 to 5 pm. However, many close early (for no apparent reason), often by noon, while others are open on Saturday. With few exceptions, post offices are always closed on Sundays. Home and business delivery of mail occurs Monday through Saturday.

Postal rates within the Philippines are P2 (about US$0.08) per 20 grams for regular three-week delivery. One-week delivery will cost P3 (about US$0.12), while overnight service is P16 (about US$0.62).

Airmail rates per 10 grams cost P6 (about US$0.24) to Southeast Asia, P7 (about US$0.27) to Australia and the Middle East, P8 (about US$0.31) to Europe and North America, and P9 (about US$0.35) to Africa and South America.

Outgoing airmail letters take about five days to reach the US or about a week to reach Western

Europe. Letters are likely to be processed faster if they are dropped off at the mail distribution center near the domestic airport in Manila.

Media

The Philippines is dominated by English-language publications. In contrast with the past, when biased reporting was the norm, current media offer more fresh, objective—and sometimes archly critical—views of contemporary life and politics in the Philippines. Of the 20 daily newspapers, 11 are published in English. The main English-language daily is the *Manila Bulletin*. The majority of employment ads appear in this newspaper on Sunday.

Business travelers may want to consult business and trade newspapers such as *Business Day*, *Economic Monitor*, and *Business World*. Visitors seeking international news should not expect to find much coverage in Philippine publications. Such international publications as *Newsweek*, *Time*, *Asiaweek*, *Far Eastern Economic Review*, and the *International Herald Tribune*—all of which are readily available at bookstores and newsstands—offer better international coverage. A good source for business news in the region is *The Asian Wall Street Journal*.

English-language radio stations are widespread throughout the country, although travelers may soon tire of listening to the frequent advertisements that interrupt programming. The 196 radio stations throughout the country offer diverse formats that feature news and various genres of music. Business travelers may appreciate DWBR Business Radio (104.3 FM) and DWCT Citylites FM (88.3), both of which provide regular business news updates every hour.

English-language news on television appears regularly on cable channels (from the US networks ABC, CBS, and NBC) courtesy of the Far East Network of the US Armed Forces Radio and Television Service (FEN) and at 10 pm on ABS/CBN-Channel 2, GMA-Channel 7, and RPN-Channel 9. Seven of the country's 22 television channels broadcast from Manila, offering programs in both English and Tagalog.

Messenger Service

A number of messenger companies operate in the Philippines, many of them offering 24-hour service.

Executive Centerpoint Prince Plaza, ground floor, 106 Legaspi Street, Legaspi Village, Makati, Manila. Tel: 815-9872 or 818-8825.

Courier Services

You must allow two to three business days for most courier shipments between the Philippines and international destinations. The transit time for

FedEx packages may improve once the company has set up its transit center at the former Subic Bay Naval Base. International couriers that serve the Philippines include:

DHL Manila; Tel: (2) 834-0418, Fax: (2) 831-1986, 813-5260.

FedEx c/o U-Freight Warehouse, Manila; Tel:(2) 833-7586, Fax: (2) 833-3288

TNT Skypak Manila; Tel: (2) 817-2871.

UPS c/o Delbros Cargo Center, Manila; Tel: (2) 832-1565/9, Fax: (2) 834-0431

LOCAL SERVICES

All of the familiar business services are available in the Philippines, both through hotel business centers and locations in Metro Manila's Makati business district. If it is feasible, you may want to bring necessary copies of documents, proposals, and other paperwork with you in order to save on expense and wear and tear in chasing down copy centers. Several photocopying services are available in business district locations, many providing high-quality copies, ring binding, and quick turnaround. Some providers of specialty business services available in Manila are mentioned here.

One particularly good resource for the foreign businessperson traveling in the Philippines is the Philippine Convention and Visitors Corporation (PCVC) on the 4th floor of Legaspi Towers, 300 Roxas Boulevard, just across the street from the Cultural Center of the Philippines. The telephone number is (2) 575-031, and it is open during business hours Monday through Friday.

Secretarial Services

Hotel business centers are often your best bet for short-term secretarial assistance, but if your hotel does not offer the services you require, there are alternative services, including:

EuroComm 81-I Masikap Extension Teachers' Village, Quezon City; specializes in providing consultancy regarding government procedures; writing, editing, and designing manuals, project proposals, and brochures; Tel: (2) 922-3961, Fax: (2) 922-3861

Executive Centerpoint 106 Legaspi Street, Legaspi Village, Makati; Tel: (2) 815-9872, 818-8825.

Mandarin Oriental Business Center Makati Avenue at Paseo de Roxas, Makati; services include fax, telex, photocopy, typing, computer rental, meeting room facilities; Tel: (2) 816-3601, x2327/9.

Computer Rentals

Executive Centerpoint Prince Plaza, 106 Legaspi Street, Legaspi Village, Makati; Tel: (2) 815-9872, 818-8825.

Mandarin Oriental Business Center Makati Avenue at Paseo de Roxas, Makati; Tel: 816-3601, x2327/9.

Conference Centers

Most of the major hotels and business service centers offer conference rooms for rent and will provide services related to business meetings and informal gatherings. Rooms vary in size, style, and luxury, and rental rates are dependent on these factors.

Translation Services

Written translations and simultaneous and technical interpreters are available from a number of companies, many located in the Makati business district. Hotel business centers may be able to provide reliable English-Tagalog (that is, English-Filipino) or Tagalog-English translations. Translations involving other languages may be somewhat more difficult to locate.

Executive Centerpoint 106 Legaspi Street, Legaspi Village, Makati business district; translations are made by appointment; Tel: (2) 815-9872, 818-8825.

Westin Philippine Plaza Cultural Center Complex; translation and interpretation service is available with advance notice; Tel: (2) 832-0701.

EuroComm 81-I Masikap Extension. Teachers' Village; translation services from Filipino to English, German, and French; Tel: (2) 922-3961, Fax: (2) 922-3861.

STAYING SAFE AND HEALTHY

The Philippines is generally a safe country for travel, but crime can be a problem, especially in Manila. Petty crimes, such as pickpocketing and purse or briefcase snatchings, are not uncommon, so travelers are advised to be wary and vigilant. (To protect valuables, travelers should remember that many business hotels have small safes and safe deposit boxes.) Credit card fraud is also common, and travelers are advised to carry (separately from money and credit cards) protection plans and telephone numbers of credit card customer service departments to cancel stolen cards and arrange for replacements in the event a mishap occurs.

Streets and sidewalks are well lit at night and crowded with car and pedestrian traffic until after midnight. It is not necessary to remove jewelry before leaving the hotel, although excessive displays are neither safe nor considered to be in good taste. It is a good idea to avoid dark or deserted streets unless walking in a group. Car travel away from national highways at night is not recommended.

Women do not need a male escort to go to restaurants, cafés, films, or the theater, although it is customary for women to go out in groups rather than alone. Reports of Filipinos sexually harassing foreign women are rare.

In recent years, political unrest has become more common. This is often due to religious tensions in more remote areas. One potentially volatile location is northern Luzon, where the New People's Army (NPA) guerrillas and armed bandits in the provinces of Abra, Aurora, Cagayan, Isabela, Kalinga-apayao, and Mountain (including Sagada and Bontoc) are situated. NPA units have also been active in southern Luzon, where travel may be dangerous in Quezon province and in the Bicol region (except Catanduanes). In the Visayas regions, small numbers of NPA rebels are occasionally active in the interior areas of Panay, Negros, and Samar Islands. Travel in the Mindanao region is usually considered perilous only in the autonomous regions of Muslim Mindanao (Armm—specifically the provinces of Tawi-tawi, Sulum Maguindanao, and Lanao Del Sur), Basilan Island, Zamboanga City, Cotobato City, and in the border areas of the provinces of Davao Del Norte and Davao Del Sur. Persons interested in traveling to these or nearby areas should check with their embassies in the Philippines to obtain current information on conditions.

Victims of the religious tensions have primarily been local Christians and Muslims, but foreign government employees, missionaries, military personnel, and resident foreign citizens associated with foreign or international organizations are often at risk, as they may be singled out as targets by insurgents.

Sanitary conditions in urban areas in the Philippines are generally good. Sewage disposal and water treatment facilities are modern and effective, especially in urban areas. Tap water is generally safe in the developed areas of the country, although in rural locations it is a good idea to buy bottled water. Tea and coffee should be safe to drink because the water has been boiled.

As noted earlier, no immunizations are necessary for the Philippines unless travelers are arriving from an area infected with yellow fever. However, travelers may want to make sure that their immunizations are current before coming to the Philippines. Malaria treatment may be indicated for those traveling to some more remote areas of the country.

EMERGENCY INFORMATION

Manila:
- Police, fire, or ambulance (free call from any telephone):........................166
- For non-emergency police calls:...........................(2) 599-011, 594-344

Makati:
- For non-emergency police calls:.......................(2) 816-0495, 816-1322

Mandaluyong:
- For non-emergency
  police calls: ....(2) 798-209, 701-871

Pasay City:
- For non-emergency
  police calls: ....(2) 831-8070, 831-5054

Quezon City:
- For non-emergency
  police calls: ....(2) 996-194

Doctors, Hospitals, and Medicine

Good medical care is available in major cities, but is more limited in rural and remote areas. Doctors and hospital personnel often expect immediate cash payment for health care services. Travelers should note that home-based medical insurance may not be valid in the Philippines—they may wish to check the provisions of policies with insurance carriers before leaving. In some cases, supplemental overseas medical insurance and coverage for medical evacuation is available for purchase.

Hospitals and Clinics

Makati Medical Center 2 Amorsolo Street (corner de la Rosa Street), Makati; Tel: (2) 815-9911.

Manila Medical Center 1122 Gen. Luna Street, Ermita; Tel: (02) 591-661.

Manila Doctor's Hospital 667 United Nations Ave., Ermita; Tel: (2) 502-011.

Pharmacy (late-night)

Mercury Drug 777 J.P. Rizal St., Makati; Tel: (2) 871-444; and 483 Padre Faura St., Ermita; Tel: (2) 585-495.

DEPARTURE FORMALITIES

Leaving the Philippines is relatively easy, but it is nevertheless a good idea to check airline schedules and reconfirm for outbound flights. These can sometimes change, leaving travelers little time to adjust. Flights are often overbooked, so it is also suggested that travelers arrive early for check-in.

Departure tax from Ninoy Aquino International Airport (NAIA) is P500 (about US$20). To convert pesos at the airport, you must present receipts from official money changers or banks to show that you have legally converted at least as much currency as you wish to reconvert. The NAIA bank counter is located in the exit hall. If it is short of the currency you need, consider changing pesos into US dollars or another common currency, such as Japanese yen or deutsche marks, which are easier to exchange for worthwhile rates at an overseas location than are Philippine pesos.

BEST TRAVEL BOOKS

No travel book can keep up with changing prices, addresses, and telephone numbers, especially when the local and national telephone systems are poorly developed. Most of the following books are oriented toward leisure travelers, but are as practical as any on the market in any language. Be sure to contact the nearest Philippine Department of Tourism (DOT) office to request *The Official Philippines Guide*, which is issued quarterly by the DOT and the Philippine Convention and Visitors Corporation.

Philippines, by Jens Peters, Hawthorn, Victoria, Australia: Lonely Planet Publications, 1994. ISBN 0-86442-224-5. 522 pages, US$15.95. Written for budget travel (although coverage of other hotels and restaurants has improved in recent years), but offers detailed, voluminous, and practical advice and lists important information for all travelers. Detailed maps are a definite plus. One of the only entire volumes available on the Philippines.

All-Asia Travel Guide, 17th ed. Hong Kong: Review Publishing Co., 1995. 512 pages, US$25.95 (also available in a three-volume boxed set for US$34.95). Newly revised, this *Far Eastern Economic Review* publication covers 32 countries. Only about 30 pages are devoted to the Philippines, but the information is oriented toward the business traveler. Note that *Review* subscribers receive a 20 percent discount. For more information, contact *Far Eastern Economic Review*, GPO Box 160, Hong Kong; Tel: [852] 2508-4300, Fax: [852] 2503-1553.

Far East 94/95, Antoinette DeLand, Wink Dulles, Robert Young Pelton. New York: Fielding Worldwide, 1994. ISBN 1-569-52-018-6. US$16.95. Handy, up-to-date guide for those traveling to several countries, but because it covers so many (16) countries, coverage of each is rather skimpy. Lively, useful descriptions of hotels, restaurants, and sites.

Insight Guides: Southeast Asia, ed. by Joseph R. Yogerst. Singapore: APA Publications, 1993. US$21.95, 349 pages. Covers six countries in Southeast Asia, including about 50 pages on the Philippines. Light on the practical information, but the historical and cultural information is good.

Do's and Taboos Around the World, edited by Roger Axtell. New York: John Wylie & Sons, 1993. ISBN 0 -7159-584. 196 pages, US$12.95. A comprehensive and humorous rendition of cultural "do's and don'ts" for the business traveler.

Philippines

Legend:
- National capital
- Region capital
- Province capital
- City
- International border
- Province boundary
- Primary road
- Railroad

50 100 150 200 km
50 100 150 mi

Philippines is divided into 12
[regions], and further into 73 provinces
[list at right] plus the National Capital
[Region] of Metro Manila.

✪ Manila (Capital Region)

Ilocos Region
1. Ilocos Norte
2. Abra
3. Ilocos Sur
4. Mountain
5. La Union
6. Benguet
7. Pangasinan

Cagayan Valley
8. Batanes
9. Kalinga-Apayao
10. Cagayan
11. Isabela
12. Ifugao
13. Nueva Vizcaya
14. Quirino

Central Luzon
15. Zambales
16. Tarlac
17. Nueva Ecija
18. Pampanga
19. Bataan
20. Bulacan

Southern Luzon
21. Aurora
22. Rizal
23. Cavite
24. Laguna
25. Batangas
26. Quezon
27. Mindoro Occidental
28. Mindoro Oriental
29. Marinduque
30. Romblon
31. Palawan

Bicol
32. Camarines Norte
33. Catanduanes
34. Camarines Sur
35. Albay
36. Sorsogon
37. Masbate

Western Visayas
38. Antique
39. Aklan
40. Capiz
41. Iloilo
42. Negros Occidental

Central Visayas
43. Negros Oriental
44. Cebu
45. Bohol
46. Siquijor

Southern Leyte
47. Northern Samar
48. Samar
49. Eastern Samar
50. Leyte
51. Southern Leyte

Western Mindanao
52. Zamboanga del Norte
53. Zamboanga del Sur
54. Basilan
55. Sulu
56. Tawi-Tawi

Northern Mindanao
57. Camiguin
58. Surigao del Norte
59. Misamis Occidental
60. Misamis Oriental
61. Agusan del Norte
62. Bukidnon
63. Agusan del Sur

Southern Mindanao
64. Surigao del Sur
65. Davao Oriental
66. Davao
67. Davao del Sur
68. South Cotabato

Central Mindanao
69. Lanao del Norte
70. Lanao del Sur
71. Maguindanao
72. North Cotabato
73. Sultan Kudarat

120°   124°

20°

16°

12°

8°

Batan Islands
Basco
Luzon Strait
Babuyan Islands
Claveria   Babuyan Channel
Aparri   Santa Ana
Laoag
Bangued   Tabuk
Vigan
La Trinidad
Bontoc
San Fernando   Lagawe
Bayombong   Ilagan
Baguio   Cabarroguis
Bolinao
Lingayen   Dagupan
San José
Tarlac   Palayan   Baler
Iba   Cabanatuan
Angeles
San Fernando   Malolos
Olongapo
Balanga   Manila   Pasig
Mariveles   Santa Cruz
Trece Martires   Daet   Pandan
Nasugbu
Batangas   Lucena   Naga   Catanduanes Island
Boac   Pili   Virac
Calapan   Marinduque   Legaspi   Sorsogon
Mamburao   Mindoro   Bulan
Romblon   Masbate   Catarman   Palapag
Mansalay   Mandaon   Allen
Busuanga Island   Placer   Catbalogan   Samar
Calamian Group   Coron   Kalibo   Borongan
Roxas   Tacloban
Daanbantayan   Ormoc   Guiuan
Panay   Leyte Gulf
San Jose de Buenavista   Iloilo   Bacolod
Cuyo Island   La Carlota   Cebu
Tagbilaran   Bohol   Maasin   Siargao Island
Dumaguete   Siquijor   Surigao
Negros   Siaton   Mambajao   Tandag
Puerto Princesa   Butuan   Prosperidad
Quezon   Palawan   Dapitan   Oroquieta   Cagayan de Oro
Dipolog   Ozamis   Iligan   Malaybalay
Brookes Point   Pagadian   Marawi   Tagum
Balabac   Ipil   Cotabato   Davao   Mati
Zamboanga   Kidapawan   Digos
Isabella   Basilan   Maganoy   Isulan
Jolo   Koronadal
Sandakan   General Santos
Tawi-Tawi Island   Balimbing

South China Sea
Scarborough Shoal
Sea
Palawan Passage
Sulu Sea
Cagayan Sulu Island
Balabac
Malaysia
Jolo Island
Sulu Archipelago
Celebes Sea
Philippine Sea
Visayan Sea
Samar Sea
Panay Gulf
Bohol Sea
Moro Gulf
Davao Gulf
Mindanao
Karakelong (Indonesia)
Polillo Islands
Manila Bay
Sibuyan Sea

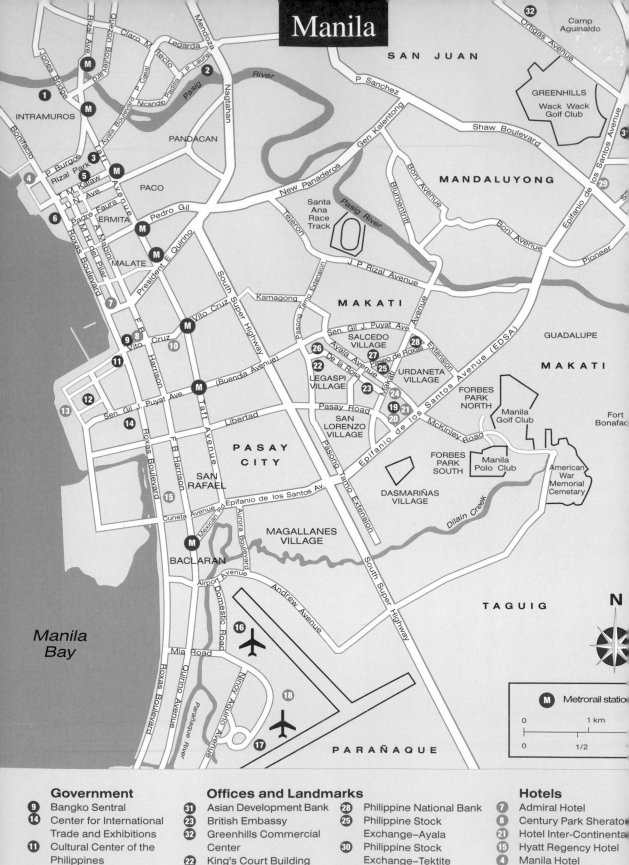

Manila

INTRAMUROS

SAN JUAN

GREENHILLS
Wack Wack
Golf Club

PANDACAN

PACO

MANDALUYONG

Santa Ana
Race
Track

ERMITA

MALATE

MAKATI

GUADALUPE

MAKATI

SALCEDO
VILLAGE

URDANETA
VILLAGE

LEGASPI
VILLAGE

FORBES
PARK
NORTH

Manila
Golf Club

Fort
Bonafac

SAN
LORENZO
VILLAGE

PASAY
CITY

FORBES
PARK
SOUTH

Manila
Polo Club

American
War
Memorial
Cemetary

SAN
RAFAEL

DASMARIÑAS
VILLAGE

MAGALLANES
VILLAGE

Dilain Creek

Manila
Bay

BACLARAN

TAGUIG

N

PARAÑAQUE

Camp
Aguinaldo

M Metrorail statio

0   1 km

0   1/2

Government
- 9 Bangko Sentral
- 14 Center for International Trade and Exhibitions
- 11 Cultural Center of the Philippines
- 3 Department of Finance
- 5 Department of Tourism
- 1 Immigration Office
- 2 Malacañang Palace
- 12 Philippine International Convention Center

Offices and Landmarks
- 31 Asian Development Bank
- 23 British Embassy
- 32 Greenhills Commercial Center
- 22 King's Court Building
- 19 Makati Commercial Center
- 26 Makati Medical Center
- 16 Manila Domestic Airport
- 17 Ninoy Aquino International Airport
- 28 Philippine National Bank
- 25 Philippine Stock Exchange–Ayala
- 30 Philippine Stock Exchange–Tektite
- 27 Solidbank Building
- 6 US Embassy

Hotels
- 7 Admiral Hotel
- 8 Century Park Sherato
- 21 Hotel Inter-Continenta
- 15 Hyatt Regency Hotel
- 4 Manila Hotel
- 20 Nikko Manila Garden
- 24 Peninsula Manila Hote
- 18 Philippine Village Hote
- 29 Shangri-La EDSA Hote
- 10 Traders Hotel
- 13 Westin Philippine Plaz

Makati Business District

N

Malugay
Sen. Gil J. Puyat Avenue
H.V. De la Costa
Lakandula
Alfaro
Bautista
Sanchez
Tordesillas
SALCEDO VILLAGE
Valero
San Agustin
Herrera
Ayala Avenue
Salcedo
Adelantado
Salcedo
Sotto
Legaspi
Bolanos
Esteban
Ormasa
De la Rosa
Rodriguez
Hada
Castro
Alvarado
Gil
Villar
Seceno
ROXAS TRIANGLE
ROXAS TRIANGLE
Paseo de Roxas
San Ignacio
Sto. Domingo
Sto. Tomas
URDANETA VILLAGE
Cruzadas
Cabildo
Cerrada
Recoletos
Ninoy Aquino Monument
LEGASPI VILLAGE
Gamboa
Soria
Aguirre
Jimenez
Nieva
Perea
Gallardo
Legaspi
GREENBELT SQUARE
GREENBELT PARK
Greenbelt
Esperanza
Makati Avenue
Rizal Drive
North Drive
Urdaneta Avenue
East Drive
Hotel Drive
Pasay Road
Juan Luna
West Drive
South Ridge
MAKATI COMMERCIAL CENTER
Epifanio de los Santos Avenue (EDSA)
McKinley
SAN LORENZO VILLAGE

Office Buildings
- 13 ALPAP Bldg.
- 15 BA-Lepanto Bldg.
- 4 Chemphil Bldg.
- 16 China Bank Bldg.
- 12 Country Space I Bldg.
- 6 Doña Salustiana Dee Ty Bldg.
- 2 Don Jacinto Bldg.
- 11 Gammon Center
- 5 InterBank Bldg.
- 1 King's Court Bldg.
- 25 Locsin Bldg.
- 9 Pacific Bank Bldg.
- 18 Pacific Star Bldg.
- 7 PAL Bldg.
- 17 PCI Bank Tower
- 14 Philinvest Financial Center Bldg.
- 10 Solidbank Bldg.
- 3 Zeta Bldg.

Financial Institutions
- 15 Bank of America
- 10 Bank of Nova Scotia
- 17 Banque Nacional de Paris
- 16 China Bank
- 14 Deutsche Bank Asia
- 20 Equitable Bank
- 8 HongkongBank
- 5 InterBank
- 17 PCI Bank
- 21 Phil. National Bank
- 22 Phil. Stock Exchange
- 10 Solidbank Corp.

Airlines
- 4 Aerolift Philippines
- 11 Air India
- 11 Canadian Pacific
- 11 Cathay Pacific
- 9 Finnair
- 7 Philippine Airlines
- 16 Qantas
- 12 Swissair
- 12 Thai Airways
- 18 United

Embassies
- 6 Australian Embassy
- 2 Belgian Embassy
- 25 British Embassy
- 1 Dutch Embassy
- 6 Chilean Embassy
- 6 Danish Embassy
- 18 French Embassy
- 10 German Embassy
- 3 Italian Embassy
- 19 Japanese Embassy
- 11 New Zealand Emb.
- 13 S. Korean Embassy
- 17 Swedish Embassy
- 10 Swiss Embassy

Hotels
- 26 Intercontinental
- 27 Nikko Manila Garden
- 23 Manila Peninsula
- 24 Shangri-La Manila

✉ Makati Central Post Office

✚ Makati Medical Ctr.

Province of Bulacan
Caloocan City
Valenzuela
Quezon City
Malabon
Markina
San Juan
Manila
Mandaluyong
Pasig
Province of Rizal
Makati
Pateros
Pasay City
Taguig
Parañaque
Laguna de Bay
Las Piñas
Muntinlupa
Province of Cavite

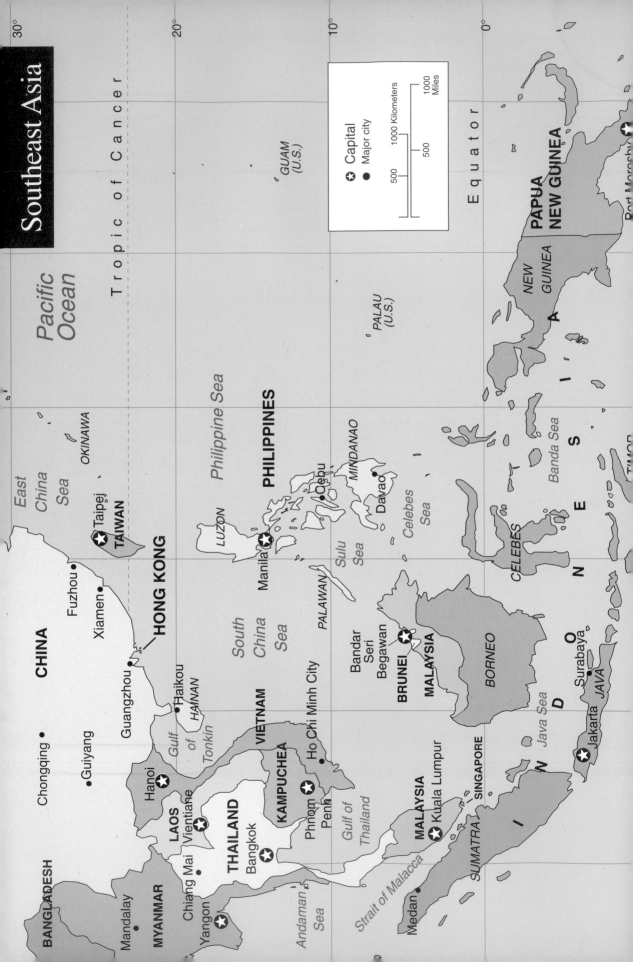

Southeast Asia

Tropic of Cancer

Pacific Ocean

Equator

Capital ✪
Major city ●

1000 Kilometers
1000 Miles
500
500

PAPUA NEW GUINEA

NEW GUINEA

Port Moresby ✪

PALAU (U.S.)

GUAM (U.S.)

Banda Sea

East China Sea

OKINAWA

Philippine Sea

PHILIPPINES

MINDANAO

Davao ●

Celebes Sea

CELEBES

TAIWAN

Taipei ●
✪

HONG KONG

Fuzhou ●

Xiamen ●

South China Sea

LUZON

Cebu ●

Manila ✪

Sulu Sea

PALAWAN

Bandar Seri Begawan ✪

BRUNEI

MALAYSIA

BORNEO

CHINA

Chongqing ●

● Guiyang

Guangzhou ●

Haikou ●
HAINAN

Gulf of Tonkin

Hanoi ✪

VIETNAM

Ho Chi Minh City ●

KAMPUCHEA

Phnom Penh ✪

Gulf of Thailand

MALAYSIA

Kuala Lumpur ✪

SINGAPORE

LAOS

Vientiane ✪

THAILAND

Bangkok ✪

Chiang Mai ●

Java Sea

SUMATRA

Strait of Malacca

Medan ●

Jakarta ✪

Surabaya ●
JAVA

BANGLADESH

Mandalay ●

MYANMAR

Yangon ✪

Andaman Sea

TIMOR

Business Culture

INTRODUCTION

In the Philippines, a country with a long and varied cultural history, knowledge of the local business culture is a must for international businesspeople. The Filipinos, who have been dealing with foreign traders for at least a millennium, are as diverse as their history. Chinese, Indian, Arab, and Indonesian visitors had already left legacies of their cultures and remnants of their wares long before the Spanish settled in the islands for more than 300 years, followed by people from the US, who held sway for another half-century.

With more than 90 spoken languages and dialects and a comparable number of indigenous tribal groups, the nation's population is remarkably diverse, even without considering the varied influence of foreign cultures. Nevertheless, it is possible to speak of a Philippine culture that is in some ways remarkably unified. However, in doing so, it is always necessary to remember the enormous diversity of peoples and cultures in this nation.

The aim of this chapter is to provide the international businessperson with an understanding of the essential character of business culture in the Philippines, while at the same time highlighting significant exceptions to the norms.

CONTENTS

ASIA WITH A WESTERN VENEER

For the Western businessperson, the Philippines has a very familiar feel, at least initially. With the third largest English-speaking population in the world, a Catholic majority, English-language media, the latest Western fashions, supermarkets, and fast-food chains, there is much to remind one of North America and Europe. But just below this rather thin Western outer layer lies an entirely different world, one that has much more in common with the rest of Asia.

It is in the delicate balance of these diverse cultural traditions that the Filipinos live their lives. Like the mostly submerged mountain chains that make up the more than 7,000 islands of the Philippines, much of the culture is hidden, not easily seen or understood by the casual foreign observer. Asians sometimes find the culture too Western, while those from the US and Europe are shocked to discover fine distinctions that remind them that they are in fact not at home, even though at first it may have seemed so. And for the nearly 70 million Filipinos, there is nothing more natural than to be, as some have said, Malay in family, Spanish in love, Chinese in business, and US in ambition.

THE EVOLUTION OF PHILIPPINE CULTURE

By the time Ferdinand Magellan discovered the islands in 1521, they had already been inhabited for more than 20,000 years. The earliest residents are thought to have been part of the Austronesian peoples, the prehistoric ancestors of the Chinese and all other Asian races. Even today, many of the upland tribal groups follow the patterns of this earlier age.

Contact with the outside world was minimal before roughly AD 900, when Chinese traders arrived with textiles, pottery, tools, and iron weapons to trade for pearls, coral, gold, and local handicrafts. Although the Chinese currently make up less than 1 percent of the population, Chinese culture, traditions, and beliefs are still much in evidence, especially in family structure, commerce, and the building crafts. The Chinese were followed by other traders, including Indians, Arabs, and other Muslim Southeast Asians.

Early in the 14th century, Islam spread from the Southeast Asian mainland into the southern Philippine islands, and it is still today the faith of roughly 5 percent of Filipinos. Although it is the largest minority in the country, the Muslim community—centered in Mindanao, Palawan, and the Sulu archipelago—remains for the most part outside the mainstream of national life. They are known locally as Moros, although some consider this term to be somewhat derogatory.

When the Spanish formally claimed the islands in 1565, they named the new territory in honor of King Philip II. The Philippines remained a Spanish colony until it was ceded to the US as part of the Spanish-American War settlement in 1898.

It would be difficult to overestimate the influence of the Spanish on the evolving Philippine culture, but certainly their most visible legacy is Catholicism. Approximately 83 percent of the modern population are members of the Roman Catholic Church. Another 9 percent are affiliated with the Philippine Independent Church or various other Protestant sects.

The US colonization of the Philippines (1898–1946) has been characterized by some Filipinos as 48 years in Hollywood after 300 years in church. Again the impact on the local culture was complex and extensive, but certainly the most striking feature is the continued, widespread use of English. The language of instruction during the past 70 years, English is still a marker of higher social class and education, but it is also understood by many Filipinos with relatively little formal education. Despite government efforts during the 1960s and 1970s to replace it with Pilipino (or "Filipino"; based largely on Tagalog, the most widespread native language and that of Luzon, the island on which the capital is located), English continues to be the main language of business and government. An estimated 40 percent of the population speak it today.

PHILIPPINE SOCIETY: VALUES, BELIEFS, AND BEHAVIORS

General Attitudes

Despite its diversity of native population and long history of foreign influence, Philippine culture is surprisingly homogeneous, especially when it comes to basic values. The great majority of Filipinos are bound together by common values and religion. In practice, whether Christian, Muslim, or animist, in both urban and rural settings, and in virtually all socioeconomic classes, Filipinos share a number of key beliefs and behaviors, including:

- demonstrating family and kinship loyalty
- honoring religious teachings and practices
- respecting the public image of self and others
- maintaining harmony in social situations
- avoiding direct confrontation and conflict

Family and Kinship

The basic social unit of Philippine life has always been the family, including distant relations and even nonrelatives such as godparents, sponsors, and longtime friends. The concept of kinship has historically been extended to include neighbors, friends to whom a debt is owed, and partners in commerce. Although kinship ties tend to be stronger in rural areas, they nevertheless play a significant role in urban life and often help to determine the dynamics of interaction at the highest levels in politics, business, and society.

The international businessperson will get farther, faster by recognizing the need to establish connections with prospective business partners or clients. Favors easily granted within the context of personal alliance may be unavailable to those attempting to operate from outside this system.

Family members and other kin are morally obligated to support each other, not only emotionally and socially, but often financially. The personal needs of the individual are less important than those of the kinship group, and willing self-sacrifice is expected from all family and kin.

Religion

Religion is at the center of most Filipinos' lives, not only guiding their thoughts and actions, but providing ritual and ceremony to mark virtually all major and minor life events from cradle to grave. The vast Catholic majority and the followers of Islam have each adopted and modified some of the ancient animist traditions that preceded them. The result in each case is a unique religious blend resulting in strong personal faith. In addition to the two major faiths, small communities of Buddhists, Taoists, and animists are also found, primarily in the rural and mountainous areas.

Visitors to the Philippines cannot help but notice the many religious festivals, ceremonies, and holidays that occur throughout the year. Among the majority of Catholics, the Lenten and Christmas seasons are especially important times, but city and community-based festivals on saints' days as well as baptisms and marriages, all reinforce the fabric and interconnectedness of family and community life. The sharing of these rituals and events provides opportunities for Filipinos to extend or receive favors and thus expand their personal alliances and kinship networks.

In the Muslim (Moro) community, the practices and rituals of Islam are very much a part of daily life. The faithful are called to prayer five times a day; holidays—such as Muhammad's birthday, the end of the month of Ramadan, and the start of the Muslim new year—are all scrupulously observed. And every year, many Filipino Muslims find a way to go on the ritual pilgrimage (hajj) to the holy city of Mecca that is required at least once during the lifetime of a devout Muslim.

Even today, in remote villages and communities throughout the islands, followers of the many animist traditions are heavily influenced by historical folk beliefs, traditions, and practices. Traditional rituals and ceremonies appealing to the spirits of the field, sky, home, or garden have been passed down through generations and influence the religious practices of many upland tribal groups.

Unfortunately, religion has also been a long-standing source of conflict in the Philippines, especially between the Christian majority and the Muslims, who have engaged for decades in secessionist guerrilla warfare in the south, particularly on the island of Mindanao. In addition, although recent government policies have moved in the direction of cultural pluralism, relations between the Catholic majority that dominates political and economic affairs and the largely alienated tribal minorities continue to be problematic.

Given the central role of religion in almost every Filipino's life, the foreign visitor should always remember to treat religious practice and belief with the utmost respect.

Self-Esteem and Public Image

The relationship between self and group is complex in Philippine culture. While individuals are morally obligated to place the group's interest above their own, there is also a universal concern with individual self-esteem and public image. Philippine culture encompasses the decidedly Asian concept of face with the Spanish concept of *amor propio*—love of self, often expressed as an easily offended sense of dignity. This seeming contradiction between conformity and individuality is resolved to the extent that each individual consciously considers words, thoughts, and actions in terms of potential effect on the standing of self and others.

The Philippine concept of *hiya* (literally, shame) defines and labels social behavior. Self-esteem is a function of whether others approve or condemn one's behavior. To be openly criticized or ridiculed in public or to fail to do what was expected results in *hiya* and a loss of self-esteem. Similarly, a feeling that one has not acted properly, or continues to

behave in a manner that is disapproved of by family or community leaves one with *hiya* and liable to censure or exclusion.

A Filipino colleague may not question what you say because of *hiya*. An employee who has been let go from his job may react violently out of *hiya*. If you wonder why a Filipino hesitates to bring up a problem, overlooks a long-overdue financial debt, or fails to point out a contradiction in the strategic plan, the answer will probably be connected to *hiya*.

Hiya has been likened to a sense of social propriety according to which individual behavior is the principal measure in gaining self-esteem and approval from the group. In such a system, it is essential that foreign businesspeople understand as much as possible about the assumptions and expectations of their business and social colleagues. To behave badly will result in serious breaches of etiquette that could, without the social newcomer's knowledge, disrupt relationships, fail to fulfill expectations, and close the door to further business development.

Harmony and Social Responsibility

Closely related to the need for self-esteem and approval is the high value placed on harmony and smooth interpersonal relations. In Tagalog, the word *pakikisama* sums up the very important cultural concepts of togetherness, camaraderie, and group obligation.

Pakikisama requires the individual Filipino to defer to group consensus, do what is necessary for the advancement of the group, and sacrifice individual welfare for that of the family, the community, or some other group. For example, ensuring that relationships run smoothly is usually thought to be more important than expressing personal opinions. Telling inconvenient truths or being overly frank is seen as an indication of lack of culture if as a result people feel uncomfortable.

Words or actions that might hurt another's feelings or be interpreted as showing lack of respect are to be avoided at almost any cost. As a result, it is sometimes difficult for the foreign businessperson to get to the bottom of things. Worse yet, questions and concerns that are expressed naturally in many other cultures are likely to be interpreted as insensitive at best or insulting at worst, and they could seriously damage a relationship.

The Debt Cycle

The currency of *pakikisama* is personal favors granted to, and accepted from, others. These debts of inner self are called *utang na loob*, and they represent far more than is contained in the Western concept "I owe you one." In the system of *utang na loob*, one is expected to repay a favor with interest and upon request.

Because most favors take the form of a service rendered, quantification of the relative value is impossible. As a result, the recipient of the favor is obligated to return a service or material gift that is thought to be equal to or greater than the original favor.

In any Filipino group, each individual has *utang na loob* to one or more of the other members, while others have *utang na loob* to him. In effect, these social debts bind the group together. Because of *utang na loob* to their group, Filipinos avoid establishing a debt relationship with someone from a rival or opposing group. To do so would certainly be deemed disloyal and would create a serious conflict of conscience.

The foreign businessperson should be aware of this system and of the responsibilities of creating a debt relationship with a Filipino. It is also important to understand the ways in which *utang na loob* works in business. For example, an employee might have only mediocre job skills; however, such an employee who has established a reserve of *utang na loob* with important people in the government or business community is likely to be very effective in getting the job done.

Conflict and Confrontation

In the cultural context described earlier, it should not be surprising that Filipinos try very hard to avoid conflict and confrontation. The culture has evolved a number of strategies and mechanisms to provide alternatives to direct communication of bad or difficult news. For example, intermediaries are often employed in situations where there is a possibility of embarrassment or insult for either party.

Job applications are often presented by a third party, who can be refused or rejected more easily than the applicant can. Children will approach one parent to act on their behalf in a conflict or grievance with the other. Family members or community leaders are frequently asked to present proposals or intercede in disputes with others. In fact, this practice extends to the highest levels of business and politics, which explains the critical role that intermediaries and introductions can play in business development.

PHILIPPINE BUSINESS CULTURE: VALUES, BELIEFS, AND BEHAVIORS

The Business Climate

Businesspeople will find a business climate in the Philippines that is receptive to multinational business development. The business structure is essentially Western, and there are many incentives to make foreign business welcome. As an example, the BOT (build-operate-transfer) center in Manila, which develops and oversees large-scale infrastruc-ture projects funded with foreign investment capital, has provided a model for the rest of Asia.

The headquarters for the Asian Development Bank is based in the Philippines, and the Asian Institute of Management annually trains young professionals from the region in international business practices. English is the language of business; hotel, conference, and business facilities are modern and well equipped; and there is a large supply of skilled as well as unskilled labor.

There are also some challenges to doing business. Periodic power failures, massive traffic jams, and temporary breakdowns in telephone and postal systems are relatively common, certainly by industrialized world standards. As is the case in many developing countries with a colonial heritage and a well educated professional population, the bureaucracy is both massive and slow to move. But these minor, though relentless, annoyances can all be dealt with, usually by Filipino employees and associates who understand the way the system works and are well integrated into it.

Business Style

Although many Philippine business practices are patterned on international models, the style and tone of business is much different from that in New York, London, Geneva, or even Tokyo. Establishing trust and a personal relationship is not only important, it is virtually required. As a result, things take time, and the foreign businessperson should plan on spending a considerable amount of time getting acquainted with Philippine colleagues, culture, and country.

Filipinos are warm and friendly. They value relationships and especially friendships, seeing them as essential ingredients in business and life in general. Filipinos expect you to be interested in them as individuals. Unlike the case in many other Asian cultures, the individual in the Philippines is not so much submerged in the group but is a representative of it, deserving of individual as well as collective respect and attention. For this reason, Filipinos are pleased if you show an interest in them and in their families, and they will want to take the time to learn about you before entering into a business relationship.

If you fail to recognize and treat a Filipino as an individual, you are unlikely to be successful in what you wish to accomplish. While Filipinos will do everything they can to uphold their reputation as being hospitable, concerned, and friendly, they expect foreign visitors to be respectful, interested, and polite in return. Without this reciprocal behavior, there can be little understanding.

Business and the Family

In the Philippines, family and family life are valued above work and business. Because of the cultural desire to prosper, reflect a good image of self and family, and avoid awkward situations, business and family matters are not often allowed to come into conflict, but when they do, the choice is clear. Expect employees who are called upon to deal with family matters to do so immediately and with less apparent regard for business priorities than might be seen in some other cultures.

Time spent with the family is not seen as an obligation, but as a privilege. Although the sense of duty is there, so is the sense of pleasure in being with one's family and fulfilling that which is expected. Weekends, holidays, and festivals are a chance to renew and strengthen family ties. And because the family is the primary source of strength in the society, company employees will resist and resent any business requirements that keep them away from family during these times.

In addition, Filipinos feel a strong obligation to do whatever they can for relatives and are sensitive to opportunities for helping family members. In business, this situation can clearly have an effect on hiring and promotion, awarding of contracts, establishment of business partnerships, choice of vendors, and even selection of participants in training and development programs. The international businessperson should be aware of this loyalty and attempt to deal with it indirectly and tactfully. In some instances, the creation of such an obligation may result in employees who are highly loyal and quite effective in actuality, even when they do not appear so on paper.

A Belief in Fate

Philippine culture places a strong emphasis on fate. Success and failure are attributed to fate more often and to a greater degree than to individual merit. Thus most people are content with their situation because they believe that fate has chosen it for them. A common expression in Tagalog is *bahala na,* which can be translated roughly as either "God wills it" or "accept what comes, bearing it with hope and patience." Natural as well as personal disasters are commonly greeted with expressions that translate as "it can't be helped" or "never mind, it was my fate."

This attitude has clear implications for such business-related activities as goal setting, performance reviews, promotion, and even competitive selling. As noted, Filipinos take great care to try to do what they think is right. But when they fail, their feeling of personal responsibility is buffered, at least to some extent, by their sense of fatalism. After an individual has done everything possible, it is up to fate to make the final determination.

Ethics and Legalities

Although the basic Philippine concepts of morality and ethics are similar to those of many foreign businesspeople, there are also important ways in which Philippine morality is unique. Much of the Filipino sense of right and wrong behavior has been influenced by the teachings of Catholicism, Islam, and native religions. As a result, Filipinos are concerned about their behavior in the eyes of their deity. However, Filipinos are also likely to give considerable weight to tradition, family duty, and responsibility to those with whom they have ongoing relationships. As noted, any failure to live up to these expectations is likely to produce a deep sense of shame that is likely to be more immediate and thus more powerful than the dictates of law or religion.

This outlook also has bearing on the long-standing—and, some argue, imported—tradition of bribery. The large bureaucracy in the Philippines almost ensures that few things will get done quickly or easily. In addition, one of the traditional perquisites of power has been the ability to demand and receive payment for services that in many cultures are seen as part of one's basic job responsibility. In modern times, this practice has created frustration, ethical dilemmas, and, in some cases, serious legal difficulties for foreign companies, businesspeople, and others operating in the Philippines.

Two traditional ways exist for dealing with the day-to-day results of this fact of life. One is to employ a Filipino who is skilled in obtaining the permits and signatures necessary for business activities. The other is to provide *lagay*, a small bribe viewed as a means of improving communication with the person whose help is required.

From time to time—and more so recently—there have been government proclamations and campaigns against corruption, graft, and bribery. There is also a growing sense of the ultimate cost of such corruption to the nation and the society; recent estimates of such costs during the 1970s and 1980s have been in the billions of US dollars. All of this is making it easier for foreign businesspersons to work together with their Filipino partners to develop a relationship that is in compliance with the laws and ethics of both countries.

DOING BUSINESS IN THE PHILIPPINES

What Filipino Businesspeople Expect

Because business is conducted on a personal basis, the international businessperson should be prepared to establish credibility and trust. If your company is well-known and has a good reputation in the Philippines, this should not be a problem, although you will still need to establish personal, individual relationships with your Filipino counterparts. However, if your firm is small, unknown, or new to the Philippines, you must devote greater effort to cultivating relationships. The groundwork for these contacts and references should be established before you attempt to introduce yourself.

The general pace is leisurely, and business is best done face-to-face in a convivial atmosphere. Small talk is prolonged, and time is taken to establish friendship and rapport. The international businessperson would be well advised to take the time to learn a little about Philippine history, culture, and values. Such knowledge reduces frustration with the relationship-building process and reflects the visitor's interest and sincerity.

In planning a trip or project, allow ample time to build trust and develop a working relationship. Do not try to rush the process: it will only slow things down. Long lunches and tea breaks are the norm, and the talk consists mainly of pleasantries. No matter what the topic under discussion or the final result of a meeting, it should always be allowed to wind down and end on a friendly note that will form the basis for a continuing future relationship.

Above all, Filipinos are sensitive to—and value in others—sincerity, friendliness, concern, respect for self and others, trustworthiness, and a desire to maintain harmony in relationship. Of course, they are also concerned with competence and ability to deliver, but only in the context of the character traits listed above. In the US and Europe, many cultures do business first and become friends as a result—a development that many view as optional and uneccessary. However, in the Philippines, it is the other way around, and business cannot be done with those who one is not willing to count as friends.

The Nationalist Factor

Filipinos are proud of their nation and its independence from foreign control. A sense of nationalism developed in the 19th century, and the best-known national hero is José Rizal, a martyr in the struggle for independence from Spain. More recently, nationalism has taken the form of a sensitivity to foreign domination of particular business sectors or levels of business activity. Filipinos report that only in recent times have they been able to secure top management positions in the foreign-owned businesses operating in their country. Until the late 1960s, most heads of religious and academic institutions were from outside the country, and entire industries—including the news media—were largely owned by foreigners.

In an effort to change this situation, the Philippine government has from time to time passed legislation and created restrictions on particular foreign groups or foreign-dominated businesses. For example, the nationalization of the retail trade in 1954 was widely seen as a strategy for eliminating Chinese control in that sector. Similar pressures on foreign-owned public utilities resulted in their sale to Filipino owners. It is clearly important for foreign businesspersons to be sensitive to Filipino nationalism and to be aware of recent or pending legislation that might have an effect on their business.

Government and Business

A popular saying among Filipino business people is, "For my friends everything; for my enemies the law." This sentiment accurately reflects the vulnerability of business to the enforcement of government laws, restrictions, and regulations. In almost all countries, business law by definition establishes the terms and conditions under which business can operate and prosper. In the Philippines, the issue has traditionally been primarily one of seemingly arbitrary legislation or the selective enforcement of existing laws and regulations.

Philippine law is especially strong in spelling out offenses, punishments, and adjudication procedures in almost all areas of business. This system is thought by some to reflect the need for smooth interpersonal relations and the avoidance of direct conflict. Government agencies and ministries have taken the lead role in disciplinary action in order to avoid direct face-to-face conflict in the workplace. For example, the termination of an employee involves *hiya* and therefore requires the employer to establish just cause with the Department of Labor. The Department in turn must authorize the termination, thus turning the drama of a potentially dangerous personal confrontation into a carefully choreographed, impersonal bureaucratic dance.

In the Philippines, the familiar role of the lobbyist in promoting and protecting business interests in the political realm is made even more important by the networks of relationships outlined earlier. The expansion of the kinship system to include favored associates is very much in evidence in national politics and the economy. Although recent governments have worked to stabilize the system and make it more arm's-length in nature, foreign businesspersons must still be alert to the potential dangers of arbitrary or selectively enforced government regulations that work against them but ignore better connected competitors.

Motivations of Filipino Businesspeople

For most Filipino businesspeople, financial rewards are generally less important than family interests and job satisfaction. This has resulted in a proliferation of titles in lieu of increases in salary: these boost satisfaction while costing little. While Philippine companies typically have a broad distribution of titles and job classifications, there is a wide gap between the highest paid employees and the rest. And of course, because the majority of businesses are family- owned, upper management is generally restricted to family members.

The Role of Women in Business

Traditionally women have always enjoyed greater equality in Philippine society than in most other Asian countries. Since before the Spanish colonial period, Filipinos have traced kinship bilaterally, and a woman's rights to legal equality and to inherit family property have been unquestioned. As mothers, daughters, and wives, they are responsible for holding the family together and for ensuring that an appropriate image of the family is conveyed to the outside world. The idealized Filipina is a woman who is shy, demure, modest, self-effacing, and loyal. Filipinas do not admire women who are aggressive or who mix freely and openly with men. Despite this, there is no implication of female social inferiority, and Filipinas have a good deal more visibility and participation in business than is typical among Asian cultures. Filipino women have for years served as senators, cabinet officers, Supreme Court justices, administrators, and heads of large businesses, and the national administration has been led by a woman president.

Filipinas are typically friendly, attentive, and conscientious as regards their responsibilities. However, this attentiveness, accompanied as it is likely to be with a carefully cultivated femininity, should not be mistaken as an invitation to anything more than a business relationship. Foreign businessmen should remember the general social prohibitions against open intimacy between the sexes.

BUSINESS ETIQUETTE

Greetings and Forms of Address

Filipinos greet each other by raising their eyebrows and then letting them fall as eye contact is made. This nonverbal form of hello is usually accompanied by a friendly smile and, between men, an informal handshake. A man should not initiate a handshake with a woman, although he may follow through if she extends her hand. The handshake should be light, not firm, and relatively short in duration. Women usually greet each other with a kiss on each cheek. When greeting children, let them initiate the process to show that they know how to convey respect. A Filipino child may grasp a visitor's hand and touch it against his or her own forehead as a gesture of respect.

Filipinos should be addressed as Mr., Ms., or Dr., as appropriate. Filipinos are respectful of all, regardless of station, so there is no distinction in address based on superior or subordinate relation-

ship, although Filipinos address superiors with the English "sir" or "ma'am" in both business and social contexts and are generally uncomfortable with a more informal approach. Visitors may also hear *po* or *ho*—roughly meaning "sir"—added when a superior or elder of either gender is addressed. Even beggars on the street are refused with the expression *patawarin po*, meaning "forgive me, sir." After a closer relationship has developed, it is common for people to use first names, however, in formal settings such as business meetings, professionals and senior managers should be addressed with titles or professional designations—for example, President Ramos, Engineer Fabella, Professor Camacho. In general, the foreign businessperson cannot be too respectful, regardless of status.

Dress

By all accounts, Filipinos dress well and judge others by their dress. Accordingly, the foreign businessperson should dress carefully and neatly, with attention to quality and taste. Despite the warm weather, a man should wear a jacket and tie to a business meeting and follow the lead of the hosts in removing it after arrival.

A woman should wear a business suit or matching outfit, preferably with a skirt and—despite the heat—stockings. Filipinas tend to be more fashion conscious than other Asian women, and foreign women who enjoy fashion can have a lot of fun. For evening social events, dressy pants and a top, a skirt with blouse, or a dress are all appropriate. Foreign women are not advised to try to wear the local butterfly-sleeved dress.

A Filipino man will often go to work in a light, intricately embroidered shirt; called a *barong tagalog*, this is worn outside the trousers. A short-sleeved *barong* made of cotton or polyester is appropriate in the daytime. For social events in the evening, a long-sleeved version, traditionally made of pineapple fiber and decorated with elaborate embroidery, is a traditional choice. Foreign businessmen who plan on spending a long time in the Philippines or returning often should consider purchasing one or more barongs. Not only are they lightweight and comfortable, but wearing them indicates an interest in Philippine culture and customs.

Jeans are acceptable for casual wear, but given the climate, lighter pants are recommended. Neither men nor women wear shorts on the street, and sandals will get you labeled as a "hippie."

Gestures, Body Language, and Style

The Philippines is a high context culture, that is, one in which the circumstances, tone, and manner of speech are liable to be as important as the words spoken. Filipinos do not speak in a belligerent, harsh, or loud manner. To do so could disrupt harmony, create conflict, damage interpersonal relations, or create shame.

Everyday conversation is almost always soft and gentle in tone, with low-key expressions of good humor and laughter representing the only common exception. A businessperson should never bark orders or scold someone in public. A firm and forthright—but not loud—tone can be appropriate, although even such a relatively restrained approach can cause problems. Never criticize someone in public; criticism should as tactful and indirect as possible and should be made in private.

When beginning a conversation, especially with a new acquaintance or a stranger, it is a good idea to start slowly. For example, when asking directions, the proper way to start is to say, "Excuse me, may I ask a question?" Even in the office, time should be taken to reestablish the personal connection before launching into the business of the moment. Inquiries about the health and well-being of the person whom you are addressing and their family are always welcomed as proper by Filipinos.

In the Philippines, the word "yes" is indeterminate: it can mean "yes," "maybe," "if that's what you want to hear," or "OK, if you say so." It can also mean "no, but I don't want to disappoint you or create a problem right now." For this reason, a "yes"—whether to a business agreement or dinner invitation—should be confirmed and, in the case of a business deal, eventually put into writing. Otherwise, a culturally based desire not to offend may end up as a major misunderstanding.

Much Filipino body language will be familiar to the foreign businessperson, but note the following:
- Laughter is a sign of enjoyment or pleasure, but is also used to mask embarrassment or unease.
- Beckon someone by holding your hand out palm down and moving your fingers in a scratching motion; do not curl your finger toward you.
- Standing with your hands on your hips indicates anger or confrontation.

Business Interactions

Business appointments in the Philippines should be arranged well in advance, especially if you are traveling from overseas. Ideally, arrangements should be made by someone who knows both you and the other parties who will attend. A Philippine government office or international consultant can help you in making appointments, but it is far preferable to be introduced by a mutual business colleague. All appointments should be confirmed, usually through the private secretary of the person with whom you will be meeting.

Cards Business cards are exchanged in the Philippines, but not as an integral a part of the greeting ritual as is the case in other Asian countries. Cards may be offered at the beginning of a meeting, but also may be exchanged at the end of a meeting. You may even find that your Filipino counterpart has not brought a business card to the meeting.

Seniority The Philippine deference to rank and status bears repeating in the context of business interaction. Age and seniority are very much respected throughout the Philippine business world. It is a good idea to be formal when first introduced to those of high rank or status, including senior members of your business associates' families and kinship groups. Senior government officials are especially sensitive to what they perceive as the lack of respect that lies behind informality.

Filipino Time When fixing a time for a meeting or other appointment in the Philippines, one of the parties is liable to ask, "Is that Filipino time or American time?" Sometimes "German time" or "Western time" replaces the American reference, but the idea is the same: Filipino time generally means the actual starting time will be a half-hour to an hour later. Good-natured clarification of which time is meant is likely to lessen the foreign businessperson's frustration.

Even when people try to be on time, traffic and weather often prevent it. In fact, sudden tropical rainstorms can flood even main roads within minutes. And even when it is dry, the traffic is horrendous by any standard, with delays of an hour or more being not uncommon. You should leave plenty of travel time, especially to other parts of the city, and you should not be surprised if people coming to meet with you are late.

Gifts A business gift is appropriate in the Philippines if an important, established relationship is involved. Otherwise, a gift is neither necessary nor expected. A foreign businessperson who decides to give a gift might consider one that is associated with his or her company or home country. Other appropriate gifts include foreign liquor (provided the recipient is not a Muslim) or subscriptions to English-language business magazines.

Negotiating

Although Filipinos have the reputation of being tough, capable negotiators, negotiation will most likely occur within the cultural context described previously in this chapter. Parties to the negotiation are unfailingly polite and are concerned with the welfare of the members of the other team. This does not mean that you will necessarily get what you want, but that the Filipinos are concerned with a mutually agreeable outcome and at the very least will observe the courtesies.

The Filipino negotiating team will act in concert, typically with one person of high rank doing most, if not all, of the talking. As always, direct confrontation is to be avoided, and especially troublesome points will sometimes be deferred or dropped until a better way can be found to resolve them.

Foreign negotiating teams should present a unified front and restrict any doubts, criticisms, or disagreements among themselves to private occasions away from their Filipino opposites. An exploratory "what if" or "devil's advocate" approach—characteristic of some negotiations in the US and Europe—can simply confuse a Filipino team. Foreign team members who pursue this role may be seen as disloyal or rude, and the Filipino team may not take the foreign team's position seriously.

A foreign team must keep in mind that the person who makes the decisions for the Filipino side is most likely not in the room. Thus, pressing for a resolution before the parties leave the table is liable to accomplish little except to make everyone uncomfortable. Negotiations are frequently accompanied by a parallel process of discussion and influence management with senior stakeholders who are not a party to the actual negotiating sessions.

A foreign businessperson who has a skilled and experienced member of the Philippine business community on the negotiating team will have an advantage in dealing with a Philippine business. It is extremely important that the terms of the agreement or proposed agreement be written down (although in practice, greater emphasis is placed on personal assurances). Also try to include an arbitration clause or other method for settling disputes.

Business Meals and Entertainment

You will almost certainly to be invited to dinner by your host or other Filipino business associates. If you are dealing with a Western businessperson, you will probably be invited home for a meal. Filipinos are more likely to entertain you in a restaurant. Manila in particular has countless restaurants serving a wide variety of cuisines, and your host will have a recommendation. If asked for a preference, the adventurous may request traditional Filipino *kamayan* food—that is, eaten with the hands.

Seafood restaurants serving Filipino dishes— grilled, broiled, or in soups—are among the best you will find anywhere. For the adventurous, there are restaurants connected with fish markets, where you first buy what you want and then give it to the chef to be cooked by the method of your choice.

Although business may be discussed over dinner, it may also be neglected in favor of other, more personal topics. Filipinos love to discuss a variety of subjects, but they especially enjoy talking about family. They typically ask many questions about your family and about family life in your country. The foreign businessperson should avoid introducing political or religious topics, and if asked about them, should be as indirect and nonjudgmental as possible while trying to change the subject. Criticism or complaints on any subject are best avoided.

In the Philippines, the host pays, and any attempt to avoid this custom is useless and ultimately rude. However, a foreign businesswoman should understand that it would be especially unacceptable for her publicly to pay for any meal, no matter who is the host. It is considered an insult for the visiting traveler to attempt to pay with a credit card beforehand.

The foreign businessman who has been entertained should reciprocate before returning home; women should do so in a way that does not force the payment issue. This is especially so if the business at hand has been successful, but is considered appropriate even if agreement has not been possible. Such courtesy not only reciprocates for courtesies extended by the Philippine host, but also keeps the lines of communication open for the future. Include Filipino spouses in an invitation to dinner, but not to lunch, where the conversation is more likely to be strictly business. It is a good idea to use the hotel restaurant or to ask your guests for a recommendation. Filipinos might try to pay even though they are guests, but under no circumstances should they be allowed to do so when you are reciprocating their hospitality.

In the Home

If you are invited to a dinner or party in a private home, plan to arrive about 30 minutes late; arriving on time might be taken as a sign of anxiety or greed. Phone ahead of time to confirm the invitation, which might have represented an impromptu, casual, and general expression of friendship rather than a specific invitation.

Cakes or fruit are appropriate gifts, as is imported high-quality brandy or whisky (provided the host is not Muslim). Always make a special point of greeting and saying good-bye to older people, and in conversation, direct questions to the father or husband. You will probably be entertained in the living room and should not expect to go into other areas of the house unless specifically invited. Children may make a brief appearance to be introduced, but are unlikely to remain when guests are being entertained. Large numbers of unfamiliar people may attend Filipino gatherings, even those that are explicitly for business purposes. When dinner is announced, wait until the Filipino guests rise before you move to the table; it is polite to appear reluctant to go to the table, and the host will often invite guests several times. Your host will seat you; sometimes the male guest is seated next to the host, with a female guest next to the hostess.

Customarily, Filipinos eat with a spoon in the

right hand and a fork in the left. Food is pushed onto the spoon with the fork. In the countryside, people at home often eat with their right hand, not using any utensils. Do not use your left hand, which—especially in the Muslim culture—is traditionally reserved for hygienic functions. Filipinos will often refuse food, drinks, or cigarettes when they are first offered, but then accept them the second time. Since most upper-middle class families have cooks, it is not customary to praise the food; instead, compliment your hostess on the flower arrangements or the house.

Always leave a little food on your plate, or it might appear that your host has not provided a sufficient amount. To indicate that you are finished, place your utensils horizontally on your plate. Dinner is usually followed by dancing and drinks, although Filipinas traditionally do not drink alcohol, especially in public. Plan to leave a party about 10 pm during the week or around midnight on the weekend.

ADAPTING TO VARIED PHILIPPINE BUSINESS ENVIRONMENTS

As detailed in this chapter, Philippine culture is surprisingly homogeneous, but there are some differences from region to region and among populations with different religions. The most significant variances from the norm are seen in rural areas and in regions with large Muslim populations. Although most foreign businesspeople will find themselves operating in the more cosmopolitan Manila area, more than half of the Philippine population still lives a rural, agrarian life.

Outside the Cities

In 1990 nearly 6 out of every 10 Filipinos lived in *barangays* (villages) consisting of 150 to 200 households. Many of the neighborhoods in these villages are essentially extended family units going back many generations. As a result, kinship relations, family obligations, and concern with public appearances and face are stronger than in the cities, where they nevertheless remain the determining factors in much of Philippine life. In the rural Philippines, traditional values continue to rule all aspects of life.

The foreign businessperson doing business in the countryside should be even more careful to follow the cultural information outlined in this chapter. Everything that is true of Philippine culture in Manila is even more true in the rural areas. It is especially important to establish personal references and identify intermediaries who have ties to the local business community. Outsiders are unlikely to make much progress until they are known and accepted by important members of the village.

Respect and deference should be given to elders in the community, and time should be set aside to establish personal relationships with key decision-makers and any others who can be expected to exercise particular influence. The foreign businessperson should be especially careful to avoid inadvertently transgressing local customs and beliefs. If you plan to work in the rural areas of the Philippines, you should certainly find a local partner to advise you.

Mindanao and the South

The largest minority in the Philippines, the Muslims (Moros) live principally in southern and western Mindanao, southern Palawan, and the Sulu Archipelago. Although undifferentiated racially and, to a large extent, culturally from other Filipinos, the Moros continue to remain outside the mainstream of national life. Since the early 1970s, they have called for the establishment of a separate Muslim state and have increasingly identified with the worldwide Islamic community, particularly the one in nearby Malaysia and Indonesia.

The foreign businessperson should not travel and do business in predominantly Muslim areas of the Philippines without first learning about the basics of Islamic culture and customs in general and those of the specific locale in particular. While there is a considerable overlap between Muslim mores and those in the rest of the country, certain expectations and prohibitions (alcohol and pork, among others) are unique to the Muslim community. The role of women is also very different. Religious teachings determine the basic fabric of society, politics, economics, and even criminal law. In 1990 the Philippine government established an Autonomous Region in Muslim Mindanao, giving Muslims regional control over some aspects of government.

FURTHER READING

Culture Shock! Philippines, 3rd ed., by Alfredo and Grace Roces. Portland, OR: Graphic Arts Center Publishing Company, 1985, 1992. ISBN 1-55868-089-6 248 pages.

Going International, by Lennie Copeland and Lewis Griggs. New York: Random House, 1985. ISBN 0-452-25864-2. 280 pages.

The Executive Guide to Asia-Pacific Communications: Doing Business Across the Pacific, by David L. James. New York: Kodansha, 1995. 240 pages, US$15.00.

Managing Cultural Differences, 3rd ed., by Philip R. Harris and Robert T. Moran. Houston, TX: Gulf Publishing Company, 1991. ISBN 0-88415-078-X. 638 pages. US$24.95.

Demographics

STATISTICAL SOURCES

The statistics gathered in this section represent a variety of sources and timelines. The data may vary somewhat from source to source, but should provide the reader with a solid background on trends in the Philippines. Most of the sources listed below are updated annually, and the most recent available were consulted for this chapter. A number of these statistical resources are now available online. Refer to the "Important Addresses" chapter, beginning on page 297, for listings of other statistical publications and sources.

Demographic Yearbook, New York: United Nations, Statistical Office

Europa World Year Book, London, England: Europa Publications Ltd.

Philippine Economic and Trade Statistics, Manila, Philippines: Board of Investments

Statistical Abstract of the United States, Washington, DC: US Department of Commerce

Statistical Abstract of the World, New York: Gale Research Inc.

Statistical Yearbook/Annuaire Statistique, Paris: UNESCO

World Development Report, New York: Oxford University Press (published for the World Bank)

World Economic and Social Survey, New York: United Nations

World Factbook, Washington, DC: US Central Intelligence Agency

World Population Projections 1994–95 Edition, Published for the World Bank, Baltimore and London: The Johns Hopkins University Press

World Resources, Washington, DC: World Resources Institute

World Resources: A Report by the World Resources Institute and the International Institute for Environment and Development, New York: Basic Books

Population

AVERAGE ANNUAL POPULATION CHANGE

1980–1985	1990–1995	2000–2005 (estimated)
2.58%	2.07%	1.7%

Source: World Resources

AGE DISTRIBUTION

	1994	2000
Under 5 years	12.9%	11.6%
5–14 years	24.4	22.5
15–64 years	59.0	61.8
65 years and over	3.7	4.0

Source: US Bureau of the Census, International Data Base

POPULATION PROJECTIONS

(in millions)

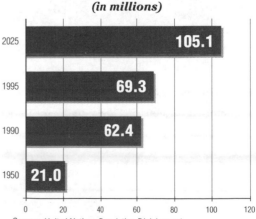

Source: United Nations Population Division and International Labour Office

POPULATION TRENDS

Population:	69,808,930
Population growth rate:	1.9%
Birth rate:	27.34 births/1,000 population
Death rate:	6.94 deaths/1,000 population
Net migration rate:	-1.18 migrants/1,000 population
Infant mortality rate:	50.8 deaths/1,000 live births
Life expectancy at birth	
Total population:	65.4 years
Male:	62.9 years
Female:	68.0 years
Total fertility rate:	3.35 children born/woman
Density (population per sq km):	233

Source: CIA World Factbook   All figures are 1994 estimates.

TOTAL POPULATION BY GENDER—1993

(by age group for country as a whole)

Age	Total (1,000)	Male (1,000)	Female (1,000)	% of Total
All ages	66,362	33,345	33,017	100
Under 1 yr.	1,776	908	868	2.68
0–4	6,879	3,524	3,355	10.37
5–9	8,305	4,252	4,053	12.51
10–14	7,861	4,020	3,841	11.85
15–19	7,085	3,632	3,453	10.68
20–24	6,239	3,194	3,045	9.40
25–29	5,560	2,775	2,785	8.38
30–34	4,873	2,348	2,525	7.34
35–39	4,162	2,012	2,150	6.27
40–44	3,358	1,672	1,686	5.06
45–49	2,602	1,312	1,290	3.92
50–54	2,103	1,051	1,052	3.17
55–59	1,710	840	870	2.58
60–64	3,849	1,805	2,044	5.80

Source: Philippine National Statistics Office

HEALTH CARE STATISTICS

Doctors per 1,000 (1988–1992)	Nurse-to-Doctor Ratio (1988–1992)	Hospital Beds per 1,000 (1985–1990)	Health Expenditures (as a % of GDP)
0.12	3.1	1.3	2.0

Population per Doctor	
(1970)	**(1990)**
9,270	8,120

Labor

EMPLOYED PERSONS BY MAJOR INDUSTRY—1993

Industry	Thousands	% of Total Workforce
Agriculture, forestry, fishing	11,219	45.8
Mining	132	0.5
Manufacturing	2,413	9.8
Electricity, gas, and water	102	0.4
Construction	1,124	4.6
Wholesale and retail trade, restaurants, and hotels	3,439	14.0
Transport, storage, and communication	1,315	5.4
Finance, insurance, real estate, and business services	497	2.0
Community, social, and personal services	4,250	17.3
Other (including government)	13	0.1
Total	24,504	

Source: Philippine National Statistics Office

EMPLOYED PERSONS BY OCCUPATION—1993

Occupation	Thousands	% of Total Workforce
1. Agricultural, forestry, and fisheries workers	11,127	45.3
2. Production and related workers	5,147	21.0
3. Sales workers	3,324	13.5
4. Service workers	2,079	8.5
5. Professional/technical	1,424	5.8
6. Clerical and related workers	1,030	4.2
7. Administrative, executive, and managerial	373	1.5
8. Other	31	0.1
Total	24,535	

Source: Philippine National Statistics Office

WORK STOPPAGES

	1991	1992	1993
Number of new strikes	151	115	119

Source: Philippine Department of Labor and Employment

EMPLOYMENT/UNEMPLOYMENT

	1991	1992	1993
Labor Force *(millions)*	25,630	26,290	26,805
Employed	22,939	23,766	24,504
Unemployed	2,691	2,524	2,301
Employment rate (%)	89.5	90.4	91.4
Unemployment rate (%)	10.5	9.6	8.6

Source: Philippine Department of Labor and Employment

LITERACY RATE

(in percentages)

Literacy Rate	1985	1991	2000
Total Population	87.7	89.7	92.8
Males	88.2	90.0	92.7
Females	87.3	89.5	92.9

Source: Statistical Abstract of the World

Cities and Territorial Divisions

POPULATION OF MAJOR CITIES

(1990 census)

Quezon City*	1,669,776
Manila*	1,601,234
Davao City	849,947
Caloocan City*	763,415
Cebu City	610,417
Zamboanga City	442,345
Pasay City*	368,366
Bacolod City	364,180
Cagayan de Oro City	339,598
Iloilo City	309,505
Angeles CIty	236,686
Butuan City	227,829
Iligan City	226,568
Olongapo City	193,327
Batangas City	184,970
Cabanatuan City	173,065
San Pablo City	161,630
Cadiz City	119,772

*Part of Metropolitan Manila

Source: Europa World Year Book

POPULATION BY REGION

(in thousands)

Region		1990	1995*
NCR	National Capital Region: Metro Manila	8,117	9,125
I	Ilocos	3,648	3,932
II	Cagayan Valley	2,395	2,627
III	Central Luzon	6,346	7,112
IV	Southern Tagalog	8,452	8,881
V	Bicol	3,995	4,331
VI	Western Visayas	5,518	5,988
VII	Central Visayas	4,699	5,175
VIII	Eastern Visayas	3,122	3,362
IX	Western Mindanao	2,510	2,816
X	Northern Mindanao	3,582	4,051
XI	Southern Mindanao	4,548	5,182
XII	Central Mindanao	2,074	2,350
CAR	Cordillera Admin. Region	1,169	1,291
ARMM	Autonomous Region on Muslim Mindanao	1,875	2,078
Total		62,050	68,301

Source: Philippines National Statistics Office   *Estimated

Ortigas business district, Manila

AREA OF THE LARGEST PHILIPPINE ISLANDS

Island Name	Area (sq km)
Luzon	104,688
Mindanao	94,630
Samar	13,080
Negros	12,710
Palawan	11,785
Panay	11,515
Mindoro	9,735
Leyte	7,214
Cebu	4,422
Bohol	3,865
Masbate	3,269
Others	23,087
Total	300,000

Source: Europa World Year Book

Inflation

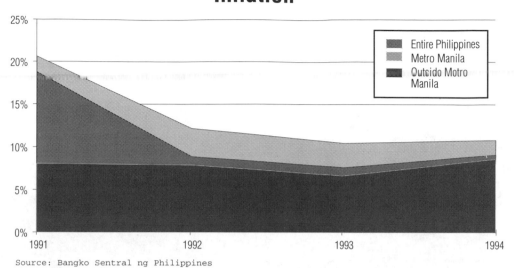

Source: Bangko Sentral ng Philippines

Media, Communications and Advertising

	1980	1985	1990	1991
Telephones in use (in thousands)	702	820	1,047	1,097
Televisions in use (in thousands)	1,000	1,500	3,000	2,800
Radios in use (in thousands)	2,100	3,550	8,600	8,810

OWNERSHIP OF MEDIA EQUIPMENT—1992

% of homes equipped with

Color television	23.0%
Videocassette recorder	14.0
Cable television	0.7

Source: International Marketing Data and Statistics 1995

ADVERTISING BY MEDIUM & OVERALL EXPENDITURES

(millions of pesos)

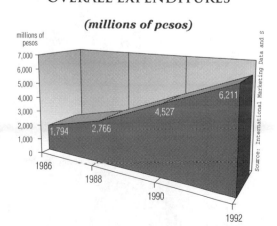

ADVERTISING BY MEDIUM 1992–1993

(as a proportion of total billing)

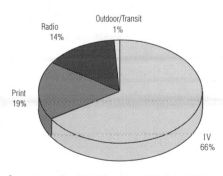

Source: International Marketing Data and Statistics 1995

Public Roads

PUBLIC ROADS BY SURFACE TYPE—1992

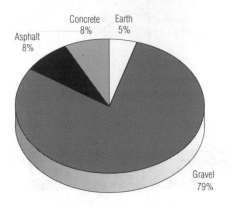

Asphalt 8%
Concrete 8%
Earth 5%
Gravel 79%

Source: Philippine Department of Public Works and Highways

PUBLIC ROAD GROWTH

(all types, in kilometers)

1986	158,498.90
1987	157,809.77
1988	157,447.53
1989	159,059.49
1990	160,380.11
1991	160,632.76
1992	161,694.95

Source: Philippine Department of Public Works and Highways

Energy

CONSUMPTION PER CAPITA

(kg of coal equivalent)

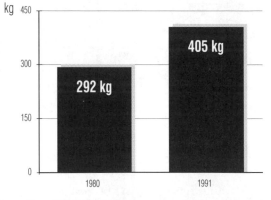

kg

292 kg (1980)
405 kg (1991)

Source: Energy Statistics Yearbook

TOTAL CONSUMPTION

(million metric tons of coal equivalent)

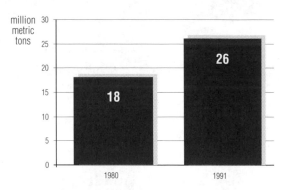

million metric tons

18 (1980)
26 (1991)

ELECTRIC, PETROLEUM & COAL PRODUCTION

	1980	1991
Electric energy production (bil. kWh)	18	26
Crude petroleum production (metric tons)	1,000,000	<500,000
Coal production (metric tons)	<500,000	1,000,000

Source: Energy Statistics Yearbook

Marketing

KEYS TO MARKETING IN THE PHILIPPINES

In the Philippines, selling a product can be as simple as signing a contract with a local sales agent or as complex as establishing a whole chain of companies in the country. The Philippine government is promoting a new linkage with world markets, and the government's "Philippines 2000" initiative—designed to better integrate the local with the international economy—is well underway. Markets have opened to foreign imports in many sectors as the government continues to lower tariffs, abandon import substitution policies of past years, and reduce trade barriers. Optimism is in the air, and the nation is taking determined steps toward achieving status as an "Asian Tiger."

Marketing in the Philippines is subject to conditions common among up-and-coming countries, plus a number of special issues inherent to a nation composed of far-flung islands. For example, Philippine infrastructure—transportation, utilities, and communications—is still developing. The national economy is shifting from a heavy agricultural orientation to a more balanced agro-industrial base.

CONTENTS

Many Filipinos are highly educated and skilled, and among major policy goals are the lowering of unemployment, the reduction of underemployment, and the raising of wages and the standard of living in general. Faced with a difficult environment, natural disasters, diverse and powerful minority interests, and the withdrawal of a substantial and economically important US military presence, the task seems daunting, but the Filipino people are finding ways to meet the challenges.

Doing business in the Philippines requires adaptation and innovation. The people have long been exposed to European and Western traditions, but their Asian heritage and culture is strong and must be recognized. With market and financial controls in a state of flux, a routine check on the current status of the law is essential before transacting business. Distribution channels have to account for the archipelagic geography of the country. Proper advance planning, assistance from Philippine professionals, and an understanding of legal and social conventions can ease a foreign businessperson's entry into this market.

It is not necessary to spend a fortune on research to learn whether there is a market for your products or services in the Philippines. This information is available from a variety of sources; this book is one. Your own government's commercial services and the Philippine trade associations and Chamber of Commerce are others. If you are persistent in asking for advice and referrals, you are likely to discover knowledgeable, experienced people whose job it is to help you wend your way through the mazes constructed by knowledgeable, experienced people whose job it is to get you lost.

One key is to keep initial costs as low as possible—perhaps through direct sales—until you have established a toehold. Another key is to seek out and establish firm, friendly relationships with Philippine nationals. It is important to answer inquiries personally, fill orders promptly, and offer

UTILIZING CUSTOMER INFORMATION

Once you have accumulated consumer information, the trick is in knowing what to do with it. The first step is to analyze the data in terms of the needs and preferences of potential customers, and the next is to formulate an effective sales strategy that will reach and appeal to the most likely buyers. The basic theory behind amassing information about consumer attributes is that consumer purchasing trends can be predicted from an analysis of these general characteristics.

Some businesses hire an information service company to generate, process, and distribute customer information about a particular market. These companies commonly assist in developing information systems tailored to the needs of the particular business. By subscribing to such a system, a businessperson can review financial management, research, marketing, purchasing, and administrative data. Market research firms can carry this analysis a step further, performing a professional review of the data and advising on the markets that appear to be most lucrative. For a full package of services—market research, analysis, and advertising development and placement—you might retain an advertising firm.

Regardless of whether you obtain the assistance of a local professional in marketing, you should at least gain a general familiarity with, if not in-depth knowledge about, the types of customer information available and how to use it. Most of this information falls into four areas: Demographics (customers' physical and environmental attributes), psychographics (what the customer thinks and values), buying patterns (what, where, and how often the customer buys and how much is spent), and media attraction (where they most often find out about what they buy). From a review of all this data, you can begin to target the market for a particular product, but if any part of the picture is missing, your analysis becomes less accurate and your marketing is likely to be less successful. Thus, to predict who will buy a product or service, you should

proceed to analyze customer information as follows:

1. *Determine the demographics*—the physical and environmental characteristics of potential customers: who they are in terms of such factors as age, education, geographical environment, earned income, and family status and structure.

2. *Add the psychographic data*—as manifested by the customers' preferred lifestyles—to find out why they act the way they do, why they want a product or service, why they prefer one item over another, what they are likely to spend their money buying, and what will be most likely to influence their decisions.

3. *Mix in buying patterns* to figure out how much purchasing power the potential customers have—how often they purchase a product, how much they spend, and where they go to buy it.

4. *Identify the media channels* that appeal most to the potential customers in order to penetrate the market most efficiently—that is, to "get the biggest bang for the buck."

Your research ideally will lead to an evaluation of the product itself to determine whether it is likely to fit the intended market, that is, whether the product will satisfy the current needs of the primary buyers. Research should suggest whether customers might consider the product a necessity or a luxury item (which in turn would indicate whether the product will sell regardless of its packaging and whether customers will make single or repeated purchases). Another factor that should become apparent is the frequency of purchase; this will help to determine how fast the customer base will have to grow to ensure the success of the business. You should also look at the product in terms of trends seen in the market data in an effort to anticipate whether the product will have to be altered, or the product line modified, to meet the changing needs and desires of the targeted customers.

responsive after-sales service. Above all, your company must make a genuine and explicit commitment to doing business overseas; otherwise the worst problems will come from within, not from the competition or the market. Export sales generate a momentum of their own. They pull in repeat business, new accounts, and offers from persons eager to do business with you—but not before you have laid the groundwork.

Marketing in the Philippines requires that you:
- Learn the demographic and geographic markets.
- Learn the ways of structuring or doing business in the Philippines.
- Determine the best marketing channels for your product.
- Determine the most effective means of advertising your product.
- Commit to exporting your product.

A review of the "Opportunities" chapter, beginning on page 29, will be helpful in highlighting opportunities for trading with Philippine businesses. Helpful contacts—in particular, trade associations, the chamber of commerce, and government agencies—are listed in the "Important Addresses" chapter, beginning on page 297.

WHO WILL BUY?

The Philippines is an archipelago of several thousand islands, together slightly larger than the state of Arizona, with a population of more than 70 million. Its population and markets are very diverse, with demands that range from the most basic to the most sophisticated products. Agriculture, mining, forestry, manufacturing, food processing, chemicals, pharmaceuticals, textiles, and apparel all are important sectors of the Philippine economy. Indeed, the question to ask is not "Is there a market?" but "What is the best market for the product or service in the Philippines?"

The answer must be derived from an evaluation of the intended and potential uses of the product or service, which in turn leads to identification of the most likely users. To sell a product or service successfully in today's increasingly open Philippine markets, one must recognize the customers most likely to use the product, determine the product attributes most likely to appeal to those customers, and tailor the merchandise—including quality, packaging, presentation, and pricing—accordingly.

Finding Customer Information

Detailed and reliable information on Philippine markets is fairly accessible to foreign entrepreneurs; almost all such market and demographic information is printed in English. For general demographic information such as population statistics, age distribution, consumer prices, housing, educational levels, inflation, unemployment figures, import/export trade information, and television, newspaper, and radio usage, the following sources provide fairly current and accurate information: Philippine Board of Investment, Philippine Department of Education, Philippine National Statistics Office, Philippine Department of Labor and Employment, Department of Trade and Industry, National Telecommunications Commission, and Philippine Survey and Research Center. A large number of international and region-specific magazines and other periodicals offer information on marketing and business in the Philippines, including *Manila Inc.*, *Business Asia*, *Asian Business*, *World Trade* magazine, and *Far Eastern Economic Review*.

Electronic (online) databases—accessed by computer modem via telephone lines—carry current news from abstracts of publications, periodicals, and articles. The National Trade Data Bank CD-ROM contains general information on the Philippines country and people, market research reports, and trade advisories compiled by the US Department of Commerce's International Trade Administration.

Trends in the Philippine Market

An international trader must keep up on developing trends when evaluating current customer information: the anticipation of shifts in markets can be as important as knowing current customer needs. Large-scale trends that affect Philippine markets include the following.

The population is roughly split—half is rural and half is urban, with much of the urban population concentrated in the Manila area. Of the roughly 70 million Filipinos living in the vast archipelago, 45 percent reside in urban areas—primarily metropolitan Manila. About 55 percent reside in rural areas, but the rural population is unevenly distributed, being densest on the main island of Luzon and in the Visayas islands.

The rapid growth in the Philippine population has led to internal migration. The lure of business opportunities and urban amenities has resulted in a significant population shift to metropolitan Manila. At the same time, settlements on the outskirts of Manila have been pushing toward the more remote foothills and coastal areas as the metropolitan area expands. Many Filipinos who want to buy property, especially at more reasonable cost, or who seek urban but less crowded surroundings have relocated to less densely populated Mindanao, resulting in significant growth in that region. Household mobility in general is of increasing importance.

The educational level of the Filipino population is quite high. The Philippines has one of the most highly educated populations in Southeast

Asia. Education is treasured within the culture. Filipinos expect high-quality products and are adept at comparison shopping.

The archipelagic geography of the Philippines influences the marketing structure. Because the Republic of the Philippines is made up of thousands of islands, marketing there requires the establishment of regional centers: this often results in increased distribution costs. Franchising and the use of local representatives with already established distribution chains are popular methods for marketing products throughout the islands. There is also a proliferation of small, isolated outlets that can be targeted through direct mail marketing or local sales agents.

The trend toward supermarkets, shopping malls, and discount superstores is on the rise. Retail trade is a dynamic economic sector, with average annual growth rates in sales ranging from 12 to 15 percent. The concept of one-stop shopping has resulted in several megamalls and shopping complexes in Metro Manila and other urban areas. This trend is expected to continue as industrial estates and outlying cities develop greater buying power. Wholesale and warehouse clubs are also developing market recognition and acceptance. Although direct investment in retail trade is limited to Filipino nationals, a significant and growing number of imports are distributed through domestically owned stores.

Customers and businesses are becoming increasingly aware of environmental concerns. In the last few years the Philippine Government has started turning serious attention to the environment. For example, in an attempt to improve compliance with regulations, new businesses must obtain certificate of compliance from the Department of Environment and Natural Resources (DENR) before they can register their operations. Concerned nongovernmental organizations have been even more active in publicizing and lobbying on these issues. As a result, a considerable amount of pressure has been put on manufacturing plants to comply with environmental regulations, and products that eliminate or decrease environmentally harmful residues and by-products are in greater demand.

The industrial sector represents a strong market for exporters to the Philippines. To take advantage of business incentives, many firms are seeking to increase their production of high-value-added exports. The government is promoting improvements in social and health services, the construction of homes, and the improvement of the country's infrastructure. A high demand exists for plastics, industrial chemicals, and other raw materials; upgraded technology; industrial machinery; and construction and telecommunications equipment.

WHERE IS THE MARKET LOCATED?

After determining the primary applications of a product and its most likely customers, you will need to review the Philippine regions and identify the ones where potential users of the product are concentrated. Although the government divides the country into 73 provinces and 15 different regions (Regions I–XII plus the Cordillera Administrative Region, National Capital Region, and the ARMM, or Autonomous Region in Muslim Mindanao), the Philippines is generally thought of in terms of three major geographic regions: Luzon, the Visayas, and Mindanao.

Geographic variation; differences in ethnic background, language, and dialect; and disparities in developmental levels are found throughout the country. Luzon Island, the site of Metro Manila, boasts the largest population, both urban and rural, and the greatest development; it is also the home of the most numerous indigenous group of Tagalog speakers, whose language forms the basis for the national tongue, Pilipino.

The rise in Philippine population has resulted in growing settlements in formerly undeveloped areas of the island of Luzon, the Palawan Islands (particularly Mindoro), the Western Visayas, and Mindanao Island. Outside of these specific zones of development, the economy depends largely on agriculture, much of which is subsistence based and highly localized.

Metro Manila

The fastest growing area in the country, Metro Manila (also referred to as the National Capital Region, or NCR) is home to approximately 11 million inhabitants. This region encompasses four central cities—Manila proper (1.8 million population), Quezon City (1.7 million), Caloocan City (765,000), and Pasay City (370,000)—and 13 surrounding municipalities.

Some 50 percent of Philippine industry is concentrated in the Manila area. The leading manufactured goods are foods, tobacco products, chemicals, pharmaceuticals, beverages, wood products, and apparel. Philippine business, finance, science, education, culture, and government are all centered in Metro Manila. Manila serves as the primary air gateway and shipping center for the country.

The Luzon Region

Although still dominated by Manila, the islands in the Luzon region are nevertheless more heavily developed than other areas of the country, and 20 percent of industry is located in the Luzon area, mostly in the Laguna area to the southeast of Metro Manila. The Luzon super-region includes the Cordillera Administrative Region in the north, Region I (Ilocos, located around Lingayen Gulf in the northwest), II (Cagayan Valley, on the northeast coast), III (Central Luzon, marked by the large central plain), IV (Southern Tagalog, including Mindoro and the Palawan Island group), and V (Bicol, consisting of the elongated peninsula extending to the southeast toward the Visayas).

Luzon Island, which includes two of the four major plains areas found in the country—the vast Central Plain and the Cagayan Valley—is home to much of the Philippines' developed plantation agriculture. The Luzon Central Plain is the country's rice producing area, and sugar cane, corn (maize), coconuts, pineapples, and bananas are also grown. Luzon also has forest, hydroelectric, and mineral resources, including the country's main copper and gold deposits. The main potential for gas and oil development lies in the area north of Palawan, although national ownership of this area is in dispute. This same area is one of the most productive for commercial fishing.

Northern Luzon is the location of the Baguio City Export Processing Zone (EPZ), which specializes in electronic equipment and precision components; the Bataan EPZ—the oldest and largest, located on the peninsula west of Manila Bay—which produces textiles and apparel, processed foods, wood and metal products, and chemicals; and the Cavite EPZ, Cavite Special Export Processing Zone (SEPZ), and Gateway SEPZ, all of which are located south of Manila. The Luisita Industrial Park and the First Bulacan Industrial City SEPZs are located north of Manila. The Clark Economic and Subic Bay Economic Freeport Zones are also located on Luzon west of Manila.

Laguna Province, southeast of Manila, is also becoming more heavily developed with the opening of Camelray Industrial Park, Laguna Technopark, Laguna International Industrial Park, and Light Industry and Science Park SEPZs. The Tabangao SEPZ has been established in Batangas Province. The Calabarzon Special Development Program is designed to further industrialize the area southeast of Manila, including the Provinces of Laguna, Batangas, Rizal, and Quezon.

The Visayas Region

The Visayas super region includes Regions VI (Western Visayas), VII (Central Visayas), and VIII (Eastern Visayas), centered on Cebu City—the oldest city in the Philippines—on Cebu Island and including the islands of Samar, Leyte, Bohol, Negros, Panay, and Masbate. Although Cebu City is generally acknowledged to be the second city in the Philippines and a major shipping center—handling much international and the majority of inter-Philippine distribution—it and its surrounding areas have yet to reach the level of development found in

Manila and Luzon. The development of the Mactan EPZ outside Cebu City, the Leyte Industrial Development Estate SEPZ, the Samar Island Special Development Project, and the Panay-Negros Agro-Industrial Development Projects are designed to rectify this situation by bringing more industrial and other opportunities to the Visayas. The Visayas also produce copper, gold, and manganese, and the waters to the north and west of the Visayas are prime fishing grounds.

The Mindanao Region

Although the Mindanao super-region has generally received little attention, it is one of the fastest growing areas in the country. The early Spanish avoided the area, which was heavily settled and defended by preexisting Muslim groups known as the Moros. The concentration of Muslims and the difficulty of incorporating them into the national culture and economy has historically resulted in conflict, and the Autonomous Region in Muslim Mindanao (ARMM)—consisting of the provinces of Tawi-Tawi, Sulu, Lanao del Sur, and Maguindanao—is the contemporary acknowledgment of this separateness.

Besides the ARMM (which includes parts of Regions IX and XII), Mindanao includes Regions IX (Western Mindanao, including the city of Zamboanga and the Sulu Islands stretching southwest toward Borneo), X (Northern Mindanao—northeastern Mindanao), XI (Southern Mindanao—actually southeastern Mindanao Island, including the regional center of Davao), and XII (Southwestern Mindanao). Mindanao has considerable forest, hydropower, and mineral resources—including copper and gold—but little industry or commercial agriculture, although multinational food processing firms are making increasingly large investments in facilities in the region. Plans call for the embellishment of the Iligan-Cagayan de Oro Industrial Corridor in the north and the South Cotabato-General Santos City Area Development Project in the southwest to encourage industrial development on Mindanao. The latter project in particular is to become the Philippine core portion of the designated East ASEAN Growth Area, a cooperative regional project designed to promote development among adjacent member states, particularly the Philippines, Indonesia, and Malaysia.

FROM A TOEHOLD TO AN ESTABLISHED PRESENCE

Entry into the Philippine market can be accomplished through a variety of channels: from established distribution channels, such as agents and importers, to joint venture/licensing arrangements, to direct marketing, and finally to the substantial investment of opening an office or subsidiary in the Philippines. Depending on such factors as intent,

TIPS FOR CHOOSING AN AGENT

- **Seek out an agent through:**

  Government services Contact services available from your own government agencies for export trade promotion.

  Trade associations Request information from national and local trade associations in the US about commission wholesalers in a particular industry and region.

  Trade fair contacts Exhibit or visit regional and national industry-specific trade fairs, which are typically attended by hundreds of wholesalers.

  Trade and telephone directories Search the listings for commission wholesale services within the directories that cover the regions that seem most appropriate for marketing your products.

  Newspaper, magazine, and trade journal listings Research the services offered by reviewing the advertisements of those that promote themselves.

  End users, retailers, wholesalers, industry experts, and exporters Consult with your contacts in the industry. Ask customers and potential clients for recommendations and references to their preferred commission wholesalers.

- **Investigate your prospective agent's:**

  Experience Find a wholesaler in the business of distributing, selling, or servicing foreign goods in general. Test the wholesaler's knowledge about your type of product and about the region you want to target in particular. If you want to sell wool rugs, find a wholesaler who promotes floor coverings and textiles, not one who deals with toys. No matter how good their reputation, if it is in the wrong field, it will not help your reputation.

  Financial status Ask for and review financial data on the agent's business. Request information from a credit bureau or bank.

  Reputation Check with the agent's references, including other clients and bankers, about dependability, ease of working relationship, and service problems.

  Strength Find out whether the agent is well established and has sufficient market penetration in the regions where you believe your product will sell.

  Goals Query the agent's intentions with respect to international trade generally and your relationship in particular. If you want a long-term commitment, make sure the agent wants one too.

  Conflicts of interest Be certain your agent is going to devote sufficient promotion time to your products and that your product will compliment, rather than be in direct competition with, others sold by the agent.

financial and physical size, product line, and potential Philippine markets, a company that wants to do business in the Philippines might start with any one of these channels or might decide to use a combined approach.

While there are advantages to being close to the markets, a significant presence in Philippine markets can actually be attained at a relatively low cost without establishing any direct business presence there. The goal is to determine how to reach the primary users of the product or service through the most effective, cost-efficient means, and then learn how to gain their repeat business.

Overall, a trader must weigh the advantages of using existing channels against the advantages of starting from scratch. Presumably, a local representative knows the markets—where they are, what the people need, and what the people will buy. By doing business through a local Filipino agent or distributor, an exporter can gain an overall knowledge of the markets, but leave the details to the on-site

representative. Test marketing through a few Philippine specialists can show the nature, location, and size of a market before heavier investment is made.

On the other hand, marketing through someone else will mean a loss, not only of some revenue, but also of at least some control over the process. The exporter will have to rely on the Philippine representative's investigation and marketing decisions. Moreover, the exporter's product will probably be only one of many handled by the distributor. Therefore, the selection of a distributor must be made carefully.

Listed below are several ways to enter the market. In considering each market penetration strategy, you should keep in mind the product involved and the most successful and cost-effective way of reaching your intended target market.

1. Exhibit at trade fairs and industry exhibitions

Trade shows and industry exhibitions are excellent means of getting market exposure and making contacts with local country representatives. Both private and public potential customers can be reached at these exhibits. The exhibitor can meet—in a single location and within a short time—suppliers, distributors, and retail outlet owners. You can also test the market response to your products and review the products and services offered by competitors and other exhibitors.

Advantages As an exhibitor, you will be approached on the spot by distributors who are interested in your product. Many have exhibits at the show, so you can meet a large number of salespeople and product specialists all at one time. Contacts can be made on many levels, from the smallest businesses to the largest corporations, from local distributors and agents to foreign business representatives. Never underestimate the importance of the personal touch that can be conveyed through such direct interactions. (For more ideas on how to get the most out of exhibiting at Philippine trade shows, refer to the "Trade Fairs" chapter, beginning on page 121.)

Disadvantages Exposure is limited to those companies and individuals attending the fair, and competition with other products targeted for the same industry may be intense. Immediate sales may not cover the costs of attending. The benefit to the business is realized over time and depends on whether the contacts at the event lead to the conclusion of a business arrangement later.

2. Hire a local agent/distributor

Agent or distributor arrangements, by which a foreign manufacturer or exporter appoints a Philippine company or individual to promote and sell its products, are common methods used by newcomers entering the country's markets. In particular, consumer goods—from food to household items—typically reach Filipino buyers through local distribution companies.

Agent and distributor firms can range in size from small (with fewer than 25 employees handling only a few specialized products for a limited number of manufacturers) to large trading companies (which handle a wide range of products and suppliers). Some firms focus only on the Metro Manila area, while others also serve provincial commercial centers such as Cebu, Davao, Iloilo, and Baguio. Regardless of which firm is ultimately chosen, the exporter should verify that the firm is registered to do business with the Philippine Securities and Exchange Commission (SEC).

Most Filipino agents and distributors offer a full range of services. Marketing is their usual responsibility: they suggest market strategies, arrange exhibits, and undertake to promote the product through the most effective means. They may agree

AGENT/DISTRIBUTOR SERVICE (ADS)

This customized service of the US Department of Commerce is designed to help US businesses locate overseas representatives. A US government employee at an overseas location (often operating through the US embassy or consulate; usually a national of the host country) contacts prospects and reports their level of interest in your product.

This service works well for many companies. However, it has limitations: it can be used only by firms entering a new territory or after they have served notice of their intent to discontinue the relationship with an existing distributor.

The lead time necessary for processing and receiving a response to an ADS request is generally between 60 and 90 days. For this reason advance planning is necessary. One way to shorten the time required is to inform ADS that you will be visiting the target country shortly and need priority service. They will set the process in motion and send information overseas; you should be able to collect the results abroad personally about 30 days after submitting your application.

You can expect anywhere from zero to six leads, with three being the norm. The quality of the leads varies with the preparer, the specific market, and the specificity of the product. By all means request the names of those distributors who were contacted but did not show interest (as well as those who did). This will eliminate duplications as you contact firms on your own.

Contact the US Department of Commerce, Washington, DC for more information.

to negotiate sales transactions, assist in getting quotations and financing, and advise on compliance with import regulations and permit requirements. Often they will direct the physical movement and storage of the product. The scope of the agent's or distributor's responsibilities should be spelled out precisely in the contract. It is imperative to tailor the contract for your specific product or service, for your company, and for the particular markets.

Advantages Using an established distribution

channel for imports will mean that the Philippine importer has already complied with import permit requirements and is familiar with customs requirements. Furthermore, the Filipino representative knows the market, culture, and language of the local target market. Finally, no laws impede the termination of an agent or distributor contract should either party decide to end the relationship. However, contracts typically specify that 30 days' notice must be given to cancel the agreement.

Disadvantages The representative will usually take a fee, a commission on sales, or both. Problems can arise unless a well-planned, comprehensive contract is signed at the start of the relationship. For example, will you expect your representative to participate in trade shows? To which markets is your representative allowed to sell? How much marketing or sales support—such as training and materials—will you supply? Which costs are to be borne by the representative and which by you? What will constitute unsatisfactory performance? For the agent or distributor relationship to succeed, not only must the duties and liabilities of both parties be clearly defined in the beginning, but the parties must understand each others' changing situations and, possibly, adjust the terms of their agreement accordingly.

3. Engage in direct marketing

Direct marketing is a popular method of doing business in the Philippines. The legalities of direct marketing are covered by the Consumer Code of the Philippines, and this type of business practice is restricted to 100 percent Filipino-owned corporations. However, foreign firms can engage in wholesale activities and then sell to Philippine distributors. This method of market entry is often chosen by firms that supply consumer products or specialized items for a relatively specialized niche market. For more information on direct marketing in the Philippines, contact the Direct Sellers Association of the Philippines.

Advantages This form of marketing allows direct access to large consumer and other end user markets. Specific markets can be targeted to the extent that mailing lists, directories, or other listings of particular end users are available. An exporter can avoid the cost of intermediaries by contacting likely customers directly.

Disadvantages Direct marketing is usually not the best means of selling a complex product, such as one that requires the explanation of various options and instruction on the product's use. This type of marketing is also only as effective as the accuracy of the method used to select potential customers. Direct sales often require a great deal of customer service support, and a high level of returns may be expected because the customer cannot actually judge the product prior to delivery.

4. Establish a franchise

In the Philippines, franchising has grown noticeably in recent years. The number of franchise agreements has more than doubled. This growth is expected to continue. Foreign-based franchises have found profitable niches in the developing Philippine market. International fast-food chains have been among the most successful franchises to date. Other industries that offer franchise opportunities include business services, printing, automotive parts and services, cosmetics and toiletries, health aids, children's stores, and laundry and dry cleaning services. The typical franchise operates under a master license agreement, by which a single entrepreneur controls a geographic territory and, in turn, licenses other business owners to operate individual franchise locations. Some franchises retain a majority of their own outlets and use employees as managers. However, the trend among foreign franchises operating in the Philippines is away from the direct operation of outlets and toward reliance on local entrepreneurs as owner-operators.

Advantages Franchising works well in the Philippines for the same reason that it works well in any country. That is, the franchisor benefits because the business can be expanded rapidly with minimal capital outlay in comparison with the cost of opening new branch offices. At the same time, control over the product, marketing, and delivery is not lost, as would occur under a license arrangement. The franchisee has the benefit of ownership, but also gains use of the name and business support of the franchisor, and so does not need to build a company from scratch.

Disadvantages A franchise operates as a separate business entity, and therefore must comply with the full range of Philippine labor, tax, registration, investment, and other commercial regulations. Franchisees must be chosen with care because the operation of the franchise will reflect on the reputation of the chain generally. The cost of supporting and monitoring an overseas franchisor can be significant.

5. Negotiate a licensing arrangement

In the Philippines, a licensing or technology transfer agreement refers to a contract entered into by and between a Philippine company that seeks management and manufacturing know-how and a foreign firm that offers to furnish the required knowledge in exchange for royalties on the items produced. The agreements typically include a license to use the foreign firm's trademark, trade names, and service marks. To allow for the remittance of royalties in full these contracts must be registered with the central bank (Bangko Sentral ng Pilipinas, or BSP).

Advantages Licensing has a special advantage for small Philippine companies that lack the resources—primarily capital and management resources—to expand internationally. Licensing is a fairly economic way of testing and developing a market that can later be exploited by direct investment. A licensor can transfer the technology for auxiliary processes without licensing the primary technology, thereby gaining a market for the primary products, farming out the final production aspects, and obtaining royalties on sales.

Disadvantages The license agreement is highly regulated by law. Agreement provisions and royalty amounts are dictated by statute, and the duration of such agreements is limited to 10 years, although agreements may be renewed indefinitely. The licensor usually begins to lose control over the production and marketing systems as the licensee gains the knowledge and skills being transferred. The relationship between the parties tends to evolve, and therefore honesty and fair dealing are essential qualities to look for from the start of the arrangement.

6. Establish a joint venture

An increasingly popular method for enterprises interested in starting business operations in the Philippines is through joint ventures with local businesses. This market entry strategy is attractive because a joint venture arrangement reduces the amount of capital the investor must put up because a local partner shares in the capital requirements of the venture. A Philippine partner can also provide the business with local marketing know-how and management skills.

Advantages The advantages of this strategy are the sharing of risk and the ability to combine strengths through a joint venture. Thus, a company with in-depth knowledge of a local market might combine with a foreign manufacturer.

Disadvantages A joint venture requires the sharing of rewards as well as risks. The parties must be able to work out difficulties that are likely to arise: trust and honesty are essential to the relationship. The joint venture agreement must be carefully drafted to protect each party against potential damages from the disruption of business or dissolution of the arrangement. Most parties agree to a short trial period for the venture, with options to continue the contract if all is still well when the initial period ends. Foreign investment in joint ventures is limited by Philippine law. (Refer to the "Foreign Investment" chapter, beginning on page 43, for more details.)

7. Open a branch office

Branch offices in the Philippines, which are considered extensions of the foreign parent company, are allowed to conduct all types of business operations that are approved by the Board of Investments (BOI), including marketing, rendering of services, processing or assembling of semifinished products, manufacturing, and licensing. Once BOI approval is obtained, the branch must secure a license from the SEC before it can engage in business in the Philippines.

Advantages The parent company oversees management and therefore maintains significant control over operations. A local office can offer prompt service with a personal touch, thus showing commitment to the customer. In some industries, especially in the high-tech area, a local representative can provide on-site installation and consulting services. Unlike a sales agent or distributor, branch office employees work exclusively for you.

Disadvantages Expenditures of funds and labor for finding, leasing, staffing, and outfitting a branch office can be substantial. Establishment of a branch office may be limited by law, and the business will be subject to government regulations on licensing, labor, registration, services, and taxation. Branch profits are subject to an additional tax at a rate of 15 percent. All of the company's assets worldwide, wherever located, may be subject to potential liability.

8. Establish a separately incorporated subsidiary

A subsidiary is a separate entity, distinct from the parent company. If the parent company has majority stock control of the subsidiary, the subsidiary must register with the BOI. Registration with the SEC as a domestic corporation is also necessary. Philippine law allows a parent company to maintain effective direction of a subsidiary through the establishment of control devices such as proxies and voting trust agreements. (Refer to the "Business Entities & Formation" chapter, beginning on page 185, for more specific information).

Advantages Since the subsidiary is separate and distinct from the parent company, the parent company is effectively insulated from subsidiary liabilities. If the foreign operations in the Philippines are expected to be profitable and there are plans to reinvest such profits in the business, it is usually better to establish a subsidiary, because dividends are taxable only as and when declared to a parent company.

Disadvantages Establishing a subsidiary is considerably more costly than entering the market through a local representative. For the most part, this path is taken by larger companies that already have some product acceptance within the market and that can afford to take a risk and carry the fledging operation until it becomes profitable. The subsidiary will be subject to all local laws, including restrictions on foreign investment. (Refer to the "Foreign Investment" chapter, beginning on page 43, for more information.)

9. Bid on public projects or procurement contracts

The Philippine government procures a great number of items, usually through competitive bidding. These include road building and maintenance equipment, cement, machinery and equipment for government projects, and military and defense equipment. The major government purchasers are the National Electrification Administration, National Power Corporation, National Irrigation Administration, and National Housing Authority, to name a few. The Philippine government procurement regulations permit a foreign company to bid on government projects only if the firm maintains a registered resident agent in the Philippines.

Advantages A successful bid can advance the reputation of a product and its supplier in Philippine markets. It can also result in new contacts in the private sector if the goods and services are open to public view.

Disadvantages Price concessions may be required in order to be chosen over other bidders. Some preferences for Philippine bidders may be allowed, and foreign companies may be further hampered by having to show that they can meet registration and import requirements, offer strict product guarantees, post bonds, and provide costly on-site follow-up services. (Refer to "Public Procurement" beginning on page 40 in the "Opportunities" chapter, for a discussion of the bidding process and additional information.)

10. Build a local manufacturing operation

Foreign companies that decide to open manufacturing operations in the Philippines have many options for locating their facilities. A variety of incentives are available from the Philippine government to enterprises that register in any of the trade zones, such as one of the export processing zones, the Philippine Veterans Investment Development Corporation industrial estates, or any of the several areas located throughout the country that are classified as less developed.

Advantages Incentives offered by the Philippine government to entice foreign investors, particularly in the export processing zones and less developed regions of the country, can make the difference in establishing a competitive local facility. Labor costs tend to be lower, which helps to keep the prices of foreign-invested goods competitive with products made by local manufacturers.

Disadvantages Foreign investment restrictions may bar local operations or limit them to the production of goods primarily for export. Management and technology will generally have to be imported to the Philippines, and training programs for local workers are likely to be necessary; all this represents additional expense to the company. (Refer to the "Business Entities & Formation" chapter, beginning on page 185, and to the "Foreign Investment" chapter, beginning on page 43, for additional information and considerations involved in setting up a business in the Philippines.)

ADVERTISING CHANNELS

Although price is usually the primary decision factor in purchases, quality and service are secondary concerns that can become of overriding importance depending on the nature of the product and the circumstances. In general, Filipino buyers look favorably on imported goods, which many consider to be superior to most domestic products, and will often purchase them, even at a premium, if budgetary considerations allow. And despite the general emphasis on price, people in the Philippines tend to be extremely brand conscious. Therefore, advertising can play a significant role in the sale of most goods, particularly nondurable consumer goods.

There exist several different advertising channels for marketing products and services in the Philippines. Television, radio, and other creative means are commonly employed by advertisers to attract the general public's attention. Television accounts for the bulk of advertising dollars spent (60 percent), although because it is disproportionately expensive, it represents a much lower percentage of actual ads run. Radio—which represents only 17 percent of total media expenditures—is the most common—and arguably most effective—medium because radios are more affordable and there are a large number of radio stations. About 85 percent of such broadcast media are commercial in nature, while the remaining 15 percent—about 50 stations—are nonprofits run by religious, educational, and government groups.

Philippine print media also provide channels for reaching consumers, and despite a generally high literacy rate—listed at about 85 percent—many rural consumers are beyond the effective reach of regular print media. Costing considerably less than broadcast media advertising, print advertising accounts for about 22 percent of ad expenditures but a much larger proportion of actual advertising run. The remaining 1 percent of advertising budgets are spent primarily on advertising using outdoor signage and cinema trailers. The use of public relations firms is also on the rise, particularly for special events and press releases. Because of the historically poor quality of telephone service—in the early 1990s, fewer than 5 percent of households had a telephone—and a lack of experience with mail advertising, direct marketing has yet to take hold in the Philippines.

The difficulties of transportation, communication, and general interaction posed by the Philippines' island geography are reinforced by the diversity of ethnic and linguistic groups present in the country. Although there is a readily recognizable Philippine culture, a multiplicity of languages and backgrounds complicates the task of designing an advertising message, no matter how effective the channel used to communicate it. Thus, all but the most experienced marketers will want to consult local specialists before committing to a major campaign.

Print Media

Newspapers More than 20 daily newspapers are published in Manila; other areas of the country are served either by the Manila papers or by local papers, most of which are smaller weeklys. The most widely circulated paper is the *Manila Bulletin*, with a weekday circulation of 260,000 and a Sunday circulation of 320,000. Other major newspapers are the *Manila Times*, *Manila Chronicle*, *Philippine Daily Inquirer*, *Philippine Star*, and *Manila Standard*. The major popular (tabloid) papers are *People's Journal*, *People's Tonight*, *Daily Globe*, *Tempo*, and *Balita*. All of these newspapers represent an expanding medium for advertising. For major dailies, advertising can cost as little as P28,000 (about US$1,125) per full page, with most ads running from P45,000 to P67,000 (about US$1,800 to US$2,700). Business papers charge as little as P22,400 (about US$900) per full page ad, with most ads running from around P48,600 to P68,000 (about US$2,000 to US$2,725).

Magazines Circulation of Philippine magazines has now outpaced that of daily newspapers. About 20 leading magazines—most in English—are regularly used by local advertisers. Most popular, broad-circulation magazines are published weekly, either as independent publications or as weekend supplements to the daily newspapers. There are also trade and professional journals with growing monthly circulations; most of these are also published in English. There is a journal for practically every trade or profession, including commerce, industry, engineering, marketing, insurance, architecture, agriculture, and medicine. (Refer to the "Important Addresses" chapter, beginning on page 297, for contact information.)

Television

While television has grown rapidly in the last decade, it is concentrated mostly in Manila and a few other urban centers. There are 37 television stations owned and operated by broadcasting networks. Five television networks broadcast mainly from Manila. Like the networks themselves, most of the television viewers reside in urban areas. Although nearly half of Metro Manila families own a television set, the corresponding nationwide figure is only 5 percent. The high cost of television sets, the absence of television stations in many parts of the country, and limited broadcasting ranges and reception difficulties have kept television from becoming a larger factor, especially in rural areas. A 30-second spot on broadcast television can cost between roughly P5,000 to P40,000 (about US$200 to US$1,600), depending on the time slot and other variables.

The Philippine cable television industry has also seen significant growth; in Metro Manila there are more than 50 channels available on cable. Today, more than 250,000 Philippine homes are connected to cable; however, thus represents less than one percent of the current four million Filipino households. Given these figures, the Philippine cable industry has considerable potential for expansion, and cable TV gives advertisers the power to reach a target market with far less expense and effort than does broadcast television. Because of this, cable TV is becoming more popular among local advertisers, although it remains relatively limited in its total reach.

Radio

The availability of inexpensive mass-produced transistor radio receivers and the growth of radio stations throughout the country have made radio the primary mode of communications in the Philippines. About two-thirds of all households own a standard FM or a portable transistor radio—or both. Radio is the least expensive medium for reaching the population, especially in rural areas. There are 230 AM radio stations and 78 FM stations in the Philippines.

However, there is little concentration in the radio industry. Of the 82 commercial radio networks operating in the Philippines, 55 are quite small, owning only one or two stations. Only four own more than 10 stations, with the largest operating a total of 24 radio stations located in various parts of the country. While this situation prevents operators from exercising a great deal of pricing power for their advertising, it also makes it difficult for advertisers to construct and implement large-scale campaigns. Rates for 30-second spots on FM radio usually cost between P350 and P800 (about US$15 to US$35), and

ELEVEN TIPS TO BOOST YOUR SALES

Even after having some success in Philippine markets, a trader needs to reevaluate regularly not only whether a product is selling, but whether it is being exposed to the most ideal market, or even reaching the intended market. These tips suggest ways to test the success of your market strategies and to explore new pathways.

1. Keep in contact with your most important customers and contacts.

Personal contact—by telephone, or fax, or in-country visits—can be critical to building a commercial relationship. For some businesses, indirect contact may be sufficient, but a trip needs to be undertaken to establish and grow the relationship.

2. Offer to demonstrate or send samples of your products.

If you supply Filipino merchants, the value of a presentation—with or without your physical presence—can be a key to acceptance. This is a highly effective—and usually inexpensive—sales booster.

3. Distribute promotional catalogs, brochures, flyers, and technical data to potential buyers, libraries, educational institutions, and industry associations.

These potential customers will be able to evaluate the material on their own and will understand who you are when you approach them. Follow up the materials with calls and additional promotional materials that focus on new releases and product improvements.

4. Respect language and cultural differences, and adapt your product and marketing as needed.

The profit motive generally operates across cultures, and the nationals of different countries often have many things in common. However, you must also recognize the substantial differences. A generic marketing program can fall flat and even build ill will in the process. What works in your country won't necessarily work in the Philippines. Your products and marketing techniques need to be suited to your target market. They must also be in line with government regulations. Learn the differ-

ences, respect them, adapt to them, and avoid multi-million-dollar mistakes. It's not only a courtesy to your customers, it's a necessity to your success in making your exports competitive within the Philippines.

Products may need to be modified for sale in different regions or to customers with diverse characteristics. National brands have been losing ground to goods tailored to regional markets—particularly from locally owned franchises and small local suppliers that know their customers well through personal experience. You can learn from this trend. Sometimes a slight variation in a product to reflect regional customer tastes and trends can mean all the difference to sales.

5. Focus your product promotion.

Concentrate your time, money, and efforts on a specific market or region, work to build lasting relationships and repeat business there, and then expand as your products gain their own reputation. Avoid wasting resources by targeting the most likely customers—for big spenders, look to retail and chain outlets; for low-income consumers, consider discount and large outlet stores; for high-tech and specialty items, contact industrial manufacturers and firms offering financial and commercial services. After successfully penetrating the most likely market and establishing a base, consider expanding your distribution into new markets.

6. Follow up on initial sales inquiries.

Pursue a lead. Establish a liaison for major accounts—a single person who will be responsible for working with a client from the start of a transaction, through delivery, to after-sales support.

7. Price your product to fit the market.

Do not be greedy and try to generate maximum profits. At the same time, don't underprice your merchandise. While there are many bargain hunters, there are also many who question the quality of products that come with an excessively low price tag. Price your product to match the market.

8. Establish a direct feedback system.

From the start, you should have a plan in place to measure the effectiveness of your marketing efforts. This may be as simple as the collection of sales receipt data, brief surveys of new customers, or postcard customer registration forms. For tracking purchases of consumer goods, a number of electronic systems—usually using product codes and scanners—are available.

9. Promote repeat business.

Some companies are now sending personalized thank you notes, reminder cards, and holiday greetings to their more treasured or large-ticket item purchasers. Some electronic tracking systems offer the option of processing a customer's preferences and automatically issuing discounts, advertising, or special offers to the customer on the spot or through the mail.

10. Deliver on time.

If you don't, someone else will. Failure to deliver on time can destroy a carefully built reputation. If you are delivering to an intermediary, a delay in your delivery will also undermine that party's reputation and most likely will cost you future sales. There's not much you can do to make ships go faster or airlines schedule more flights, but you can try your best to have your products ready to package on time. If necessary, you can stockpile your products at a Philippine facility. Do your best to avoid nasty interruptions at customs by finding the best possible freight forwarders and brokers. When you must (and can), forget the expense and deliver by a dependable courier service. This is especially true for important documents. The extra effort will go a long way toward establishing, fortifying, and expanding your reputation in the market.

11. Emphasize customer service.

Marketing becomes more effective if customers reached once return to buy again. Customer service is essential in developing repeat business; the treatment of your customers is as important as the quality of the product. Your representatives and personnel must be able to explain your product: what it is, what it will do, and how it operates. They must know not only the product, but also be able to relate to the customer. Your company's image is at stake.

---

between P300 to P1,600 (about US$12 to US$65) for AM radio, depending on time slot and other factors.

Advertising Agencies and Market Research Firms

Today more than 100 Philippine advertising agencies exist to assist in preparing and placing advertisements in various media. Most of these agencies have organized themselves like the US advertising agencies that have served as the model. Several market research companies located in Metro Manila offer a range of services, such as product and consumer research, trade surveys, advertising and media research, panel services, motivational research, and public opinion studies. (Refer to the "Important Addresses" chapter, beginning on page 297, for a list of major advertising agencies and market research firms.)

Public Relations Firms

Public relations (PR) is now an integral part of the Philippine advertising mix. Almost all top corporations—as well as government offices—now have PR divisions. In fact, many Filipino companies are cutting down on their advertising budgets, instead looking to PR firms to produce the same results at a fraction of the cost. The pleasant reality is that PR campaigns generally can get results similar to those of more conventional advertising, albeit less rapidly than with advertising.

The scope of public relations varies, depending on an agency's specialty. Some may specialize only in producing special events, while others include more general publicity within their scope of offerings. Special events are expensive, although generally not as expensive as comparable advertising. Nor does PR provide a gauge with which to evaluate the effectiveness of the expenditure, especially on a short-term basis, and there is no way of finding out the return on your investment in the short-term. The use of PR is best viewed as a long-term investment.

FITTING THE PRODUCT INTO THE PHILIPPINE MARKET

Under the Ramos administration, trade policy changes have begun to open the relatively closed Philippine economy, reversing 40 years of policy based largely on protectionism and import-substitution. During the past 10 years, the list of items subject to quantitative restrictions and preclearance has shrunk considerably. The major exception to this liberalization is in the agricultural sector, where products which account for 70 percent of sectoral production by value are still protected from import competition.

Although trade with the Philippines is now more

open than it was, foreign businesses will still encounter some tariffs, taxes, restrictions, and cultural differences. As such, it is important to familiarize yourself with a few surmountable hurdles that all companies interested in participating in the global marketplace must face.

Import Duties Customs duties on most imports are being compressed into a range from zero to 30 percent ad valorem, although rates of up to 50 percent are still applied to certain protected items such as rice, coconut oil, sugar, fruits, and luxury consumer goods. Reductions have been phased in over a five-year period ending in 1995.

Value-Added Tax (VAT) With certain exceptions, a VAT of 10 percent is imposed on goods imported into the Philippines. This tax is based on the total value used by the Bureau of Customs in determining tariff and customs duties.

Taxes on Operating Businesses Once the business is operational, it will be subject to one or more of the following taxes: manufacturer's or producer's sales tax, specific tax, income tax, and other business taxes.

Home Consumption Value (HCV) The Tariff and Customs Code requires use of HCV, or the domestic wholesale price at the first line of distribution in the home country (plus export packing and other export costs), rather than the export or invoice value of the goods shipped, as is the case in most modern economies. The use of HCV has greatly increased the landed cost of many imported products, significantly raising dutiable values in many cases. This means of calculation of tariffs raises significant revenues, but also serves to protect domestic operations by making foreign products less price-competitive. The government is giving serious consideration to abolishing the HCV system in the near future.

Nontariff Barriers

Under the Philippine Retail Trade Nationalization Law, only Filipino citizens and firms which are 100 percent Filipino-owned may engage directly or indirectly in retail business. However, manufacturers or processors selling to industrial or commercial consumers are exempted from the law.

Quantitative Restrictions/Quotas Recent trade reforms have eliminated most quotas on imports, although roughly 135 items remain subject to quotas. About 60 commodities will remain protected by quotas indefinitely for reasons of health, safety, or national security. These include chemicals for manufacturing explosives, dangerous drugs, and vehicle parts for the light commercial vehicle development program.

Service Barriers Foreign participation in domestic banks is currently limited to 30 percent. However, the Philippine government is seeking to liberalize foreign participation by allowing the entry of additional foreign bank branches, the expansion of existing foreign banks, and an increase in the maximum level of foreign participation in domestic banks. Foreign banks may not obtain a universal banking license, which would allow investment banking activities.

Documentation All importations covered by a formal entry with an invoice value of 5,000 pesos (about US$195) or more shall be subject to a fixed import processing fee of 250 pesos (about US$9.75). This fee shall be paid by the importer/consignee to the authorized agent bank.

Foreign Ownership Restrictions Foreign nationals are allowed to own up to 100 percent of domestic market enterprises except in those industries that are either completely restricted or limited to a certain percentage of foreign ownership. Currently, the following industries do not allow any foreign ownership: mass media, services involving the practice of a licensed profession (for example, engineering, law, and architecture), retail trade, cooperatives, private security agencies, and small-scale mining. (Refer to the "Foreign Investment" chapter, beginning on page 43, for more information on foreign ownership.)

Product Marking and Labeling

With certain exceptions, every imported or locally manufactured product must be labeled to indicate brand, trademark, or trade name, country of manufacture, physical composition, net weight and measure (in the metric system), and address of manufacturer.

Samples and Advertising Matter

Samples that are unsalable or of no commercial value and samples of medicine properly marked "Physician's Samples, Not for Sale" are permitted entry without payment of duty. Samples of commercial value also may be imported without payment of duty, provided the value of any single importation does not exceed US$1500.

Weights and Measures

From 1985 to the present, only 48 products have been fully converted to metric weights and measurements. There are in effect central bank circulars stating that no importation of nonmetric measuring devices, instrumentation, and apparatus will be allowed without prior clearance from the Bureau of Product Standards.

Cultural Differences

Although English is the dominant business language in the Philippines, numerous other languages are spoken, and Pilipino is the official national language. The Philippines have been ruled for centuries by Western cultures—first Spain and more recently the US—and Filipinos are thus familiar with Western culture and business operations. Despite these at least superficial similarities, it is important to remember that the Philippines is a sovereign country with its own culture and way of conducting business.

LEARNING TO LOVE EXPORTING: EIGHT IN-HOUSE RULES

1. Adopt a global strategy

Most companies become international by an incremental process rather than by strategic choice. While some companies are first attracted to foreign markets by unsolicited export orders, others respond to specific opportunities for developing supplies of resources, acquiring foreign technology, or achieving greater production efficiency through foreign operations.

The two basic reasons for having a global strategy are that most product and factor markets extend beyond the boundaries of a single country and that the competition that ultimately determines performance is not constrained to individual locations and national markets. To remain—or become—competitive, the strategy horizon for most companies must, therefore, encompass threats and opportunities of both domestic and foreign origin.

2. Eliminate as much guesswork as possible

You cannot become successful at exporting if you arbitrarily pick an overseas market and limit your business possibilities to your company's existing products or services. Instead, a company must seek to identify demand areas (within the Philippines or any other foreign markets) where its capability for performance against competitors is greatest, even though the specific customer needs that are to be met may differ from those the company has been meeting in the past.

Some important questions you must answer before taking the plunge into international marketing are:
- Do you need to make changes to your product?
- Who are the potential buyers, and how do you find such buyers?
- How will your buyer find you?
- Do you need to advertise or exhibit at a trade fair?
- How many different products can you sell?
- How much can you expect to sell?

3. Get management support and stick with the program

It is imperative for your company to have a long-term commitment to export marketing; successful export marketing is not realized as quickly as successful domestic sales. Additionally, there are many hurdles to overcome—personal, political, cultural, and legal, among others. In general, it will be about six to nine months before you and your overseas associates can even begin to expect to see a glimmer of success. In some cases, it may be even longer. Remember to be patient and keep a close, but not suffocating, watch on your international marketing efforts. Above all else, give the venture a chance to develop. More than a few companies have cut their international marketing and advertising budgets because of premature, misunderstood international marketing results. Again, commit to the medium (if not the long) haul.

4. Avoid an internal tug-of-war

Consultants report that one of the biggest obstacles to successful export marketing in larger companies is internal conflict among divisions within a company. Domestic marketing battles international marketing, while each is also warring with engineering—and everybody fights with the bean counters. All the complex strategies, relationship building, and legal and cultural accommodations that export marketing requires means that internal support and teamwork are crucial to the success of the venture.

5. Stick with export marketing even when business booms at home

Exporting is not something to fall back on when your domestic market falters; nor is it something to put on the back burner when business is booming at home. It is difficult to ease into exporting. All the groundwork, financial and management investment, and blood, sweat, and tears that export marketing will require means that a clear commitment is necessary from the beginning. Any other attitude as good as dooms the venture from the start—you may as well forget it. We cannot overstress this aspect: take the long-range view or don't play at all. Decide that you are going to export and that you are in it for the long haul as a viable, moneymaking, full-fledged division within your company.

6. Become personally familiar with your customers and distributors

To be successful in the long run, the person responsible for export sales within the company must become personally familiar with the overseas customers and distributors. Anything that acts as a filter between you and your customers and/or distributors must be seen as a negative.

7. Get expert assistance and advice

Getting expert assistance is very important, but it need not come from expensive consultants. An exporter can gather knowledge about competitors and other producers, often from their own clients.

The real challenge lies in knowing how to ask the right questions.

8. Respect your overseas market

No matter what product or service you are exporting, you must respect your overseas customers and their culture. Once this is accomplished you may realize that your product needs to be fine tuned or tailored for the local market. This may involve altering the product itself or simply repackaging or repositioning it. Whatever changes need to be made, the benefits usually outweigh the costs.

Business Entities & Formation

TYPES OF BUSINESS ENTERPRISES

Philippine law recognizes a variety of business forms, including the corporation, the branch office, the general and limited partnership, the representative office, the regional headquarters, and the sole proprietorship. All of these forms are available to a foreign investor, especially if working with a Filipino citizen. A formal arrangement with a Filipino citizen may be necessary before a foreigner will be permitted to establish an entity or engage in a particular line of business in the country because the nation's law still places limits on foreign equity holdings in some sectors of the economy. Apart from legal restrictions on ownership, an investor's choice of entity will hinge on numerous factors and circumstances, such as the desired degree of control over the business, acceptable amount of government supervision, anticipated duration of an investment, acceptable degree of exposure to liability, and preferred tax treatment. (Refer to the "Taxation" chapter, beginning on page 269, for a discussion of tax considerations.)

Restrictions on the foreign ownership of businesses in the Philippines are largely the remnant of years of insularity during prior regimes. They are disappearing slowly as the current government moves the country toward greater openness in the economy. The law currently allows foreign investors to own up to 100 percent of an entity's capital, as long as the entity's activity is not included among those designated on the Negative List adopted as part of the Foreign Investments Act of 1991.

The Negative List is both highly detailed and broad in coverage. It limits foreign equity in businesses ranging from cockfighting to any operations that could potentially compete with existing businesses funded with Filipino capital. Other specific business areas on the Negative List include mass media, retail trade, some agricultural industries, and professional activities such as medicine, law, accounting, and engineering. A specific percentage of minority foreign investment is allowed in a few areas—for example, up to 30 percent in advertising businesses and up to 40 percent in businesses engaged in exploiting Philippine natural resources, owning Philippine land, operating or managing public utilities, or those endowed with paid-up equity capital of less than US$500,000. Any foreign investor considering a particular operation in the Philippines would be wise to review the Negative List with care. (Refer to the "Foreign Investment" chapter, beginning on page 43, for additional discussion of the limits on investment.)

In general, the government of the Philippines prefers that foreigners own no more than 60 percent of a Philippine business entity; however, it relaxes this limit if the business is expected to bring substantial amounts of capital or employment into the country, materially stimulate exports from the Philippines, or further the growth of government-designated pioneer industries. For businesses falling into any of these three categories, the government will sometimes offer extra incentives, provided that the business qualifies under rules established by the country's Board of Investments (BOI) or the Philippine Economic Zone Authority (PEZA).

A foreign investor who is interested in ownership in a Filipino entity should bear in mind that ownership limits established by the Negative List do not necessarily preclude actual foreign control over

KEY REGULATORS AND REGISTRIES

The **Securities and Exchange Commission** (SEC), the chief agency overseeing business entities, is responsible for registering different forms of business and accepting annual filings.

The **Board of Investments (BOI)** determines whether corporations qualify for government incentives to do business under the Omnibus Investments Act of 1987 or the Foreign Investments Act of 1991. This Board releases annual lists of desirable business operations that will be entitled to receive incentives.

The **Philippine Economic Zone Authority (PEZA)** is generally charged with promoting foreign trade. It registers export-oriented enterprises located inside the boundaries of designated EPZs and determines whether these enterprises qualify for government incentives.

The **Central Bank (Bangko Sentral ng Pilipinas)** manages monetary policy and exchange controls and registers all foreign investments in the Philippines. Unless an investment is registered with the Central Bank, a foreign

investor can neither repatriate investment capital nor remit earnings to the investor's home country.

The **Department of Trade and Industry (DTI)** oversees many aspects of economic and industrial policy. Its bureaus handle the registration of several business forms, including sole proprietorships.

The **Technology Transfer Board (TTB)**, a division within the DTI, is a policy board responsible for regulating technology transfers and approving royalty rates for licensing agreements.

The **National Economic and Development Authority (NEDA)** is a central planning body responsible for devising and implementing general social and economic development policy in the Philippines. NEDA also supervises commissions related to the oil industry and price and wage controls.

The **Environmental Management Bureau (EMB)** polices industries to ensure compliance with environmental standards.

such an entity. Even if foreign ownership of a business venture is limited by law to a minority stake, the foreign investor can structure participation in the venture to ensure effective management control. Techniques commonly used to retain such control include the creation of an entity in which the majority Philippine ownership is spread among so many unconnected domestic investors that the foreign investor is in de facto control of the organization through plurality ownership. Other common arrangements include an express management contract between an entity and a foreign investor; a licensing agreement by which a foreign investor licenses intellectual property rights to the enterprise (an arrangement often coupled with a management contract to oversee the use of the licensed property); a voting trust agreement that confers shareholders' voting rights on a foreign investor acting as the trustee; pledges of shares and voting rights to foreign lenders that loan funds to the domestic enterprise; and simple voting agreements between shareholders that delegate voting control to the foreign investors.

The most common business form used by foreign investors in the Philippines is the corporation, typically the 60/40 corporation in which Filipino investors own 60 percent of the corporation and foreign investors own 40 percent. While many

foreign companies open branch offices in the Philippines, the operation of a branch leaves the foreign firm open to greater potential liability than does the incorporation of a separate Philippine subsidiary. Franchise agreements have become more popular in the Philippines in recent years, and many foreign companies choose to conduct their Philippine operations through simple agent or distributor contracts with resident Filipino agents. Other business forms, including partnerships and sole proprietorships, are usually undesirable for foreign investors because they offer neither favorable tax treatment nor limits on potential liability. Nor would these forms generally be considered appropriate vehicles for serious foreign operations in the Philippines.

Corporations

The most salient feature of a Philippine corporation, governed by the New Corporation Code, is limitation of liability. Once a corporation is properly organized, it is deemed by law to have an existence separate from its investors, and those investors are not liable for the obligations of the business beyond the amounts they have invested.

The limited liability factor is a major consideration behind the preference of foreign companies for the incorporation of a subsidiary rather than the establishment of a branch office. Use of the corporate form can limit the company's liability to assets located in the Philippines. In contrast, a branch office is regarded as an extension of the parent corporation, and therefore the parent's assets potentially become exposed to general liability, regardless of where they are located. In choosing between a Philippine corporation and a branch office, investors should also review the tax treatment accorded to these two types of entities in the Philippines. (Refer to the "Taxation" chapter, beginning on page 269, for a discussion of tax treatment.)

Articles of incorporation—the corporation's basic charter—must specify the corporate name, place of business, purpose, and term of existence; identify incorporators and directors; describe amounts and kinds of capital stock; enumerate shareholders' rights and obligations; and set forth rules of corporate governance. During the incorporation process, the articles are filed with the Philippine Securities and Exchange Commission (SEC), the chief agency supervising corporations. (See "Formation and Registration of Business Operations" on page 191.)

Capital The corporate ownership interests of investors are represented by certificates designating shares of stock. At least five shareholders are needed to form a corporation, and a maximum of 15 founding shareholders are permitted. The majority of a corporation's founding shareholders must be Philippine residents. Once formation is complete, a corporation can have any number of shareholders, unless it is a "close corporation," which by law may have no more than 20 shareholders.

No minimum amount of authorized capital is required to start a corporation, but at least 25 percent of a corporation's authorized capital must be subscribed, and at least 25 percent of that amount must be paid into the corporation at the time of incorporation. During its existence, a corporation can increase or decrease its authorized capital with the approval of the corporation's board of directors and two-thirds of the corporation's shares or shareholders.

In addition to the capital contributions of shareholders, Philippine corporations can obtain funds through the capitalization of retained earnings or the sale of bonds, commercial paper, and other forms of debt obligations.

Share Characteristics Philippine law allows a corporation to provide for different classes of stock, the characteristics of which are defined in the corporation's articles. Shares may have par value or no par value. Regardless of par value, investors must pay a fair value for shares, either in cash or in kind, and shares cannot be issued for a value of less than five pesos (about US$0.20).

In most corporations, owners of common stock are entitled to equal distributions of profits without any preference over other stockholders, while owners of preferred stock typically have first rights to fixed dividends and distribution of the principal upon liquidation. While owners of common stock are typically entitled to cast votes in shareholder meetings, with the weight of their votes depending on the extent of their stock ownership, owners of preferred shares usually have no voting rights, except in some unique situations detailed in the New Corporation Code. In corporations capitalized in part through foreign equity, common stock is often divided into "A" and "B" shares, with A shares being held solely by Filipinos and B shares by foreigners. Philippine law also authorizes the issuance of convertible stock, which owners can transform from one class to another at designated times and prices.

Shares of stock are generally transferable, although Philippine law restricts any transfers that would unfairly affect the rights of a corporation's creditors. For businesses in which foreign investment is restricted, the ownership of shares is limited to a certain percentage, and the transfer of shares is also restricted if the result would raise foreign equity holdings above the permissible level. In a "close" corporation, articles of incorporation can provide additional restrictions on share transfers, as long as these restrictions are written into the articles of incorporation and are stated on the certificates.

Directors Corporate directors generally have broad powers to manage Philippine corporations, at least to the extent authorized by the corporate articles and bylaws. However, before taking actions that would fundamentally alter the corporation—such as dissolving or merging it, changing its line of business, or disposing of most of its assets—directors must first secure the approval of shareholders. Each director must own at least one share of the corporation's stock, and the majority of the directors must be Philippines residents.

The shareholders elect the directors for the term of office specified in the corporate articles or bylaws. Once elected, the directors must hold their own election to select a president from among themselves. They must also choose a treasurer, who need not be a director; a secretary, who must be a Philippine citizen and resident; and any other officers required by the corporate articles or bylaws. A single director can hold any two of these positions at the same time. Under SEC rules, foreigners cannot serve as corporate officers.

The legal relationship between a director and a corporation is that of trustee. Thus a director has fiduciary duties to the corporation and its shareholders and cannot engage in any business outside the corporation than would create a conflict of interest.

Shareholders In addition to electing directors and evaluating corporate performance during ordinary annual meetings, shareholders are entitled to vote on any proposed increase in authorized capital, changes to the articles of incorporation, and proposals to dissolve the corporation voluntarily. Most of these acts require the vote of two-thirds of either the corporation's shares or shareholders. In close corporations, articles of incorporation can provide for alternative majority voting requirements. Philippine law recognizes voting trusts, by which shareholders can delegate to a trustee the right to cast their votes. Shareholders may also vote by proxy if absent from meetings.

If a merger is proposed, the shareholders are entitled to consider the merger plan and express any disagreement with it. If the merger is then approved by two-thirds of the shares and goes forward, any dissenting shareholders are entitled to leave the corporation and demand payment for the fair value of their shares.

Minority shareholders are also entitled to dissent and to demand payment for the fair value of their shares if a change is approved that will alter the articles of incorporation with respect to their relative rights and obligations, modify the term of incorporation, or result in the disposition of substantially all corporate property and assets. The Corporation Code establishes an appraisal procedure to determine rights to payment in these circumstances.

Dividends Directors are charged with determining and declaring dividends. Dividends may not be declared unless retained corporate earnings exceed the total paid-in capital of the corporation. Directors are required to declare dividends, unless the earnings are restricted under the terms of the corporation's obligations to its creditors, or to specific uses authorized by shareholders. Dividends are usually distributed to shareholders in proportion to their holdings.

Statutory Audits Corporations with authorized or paid-up capital of P50,000 (about US$1,925) or more must file annual financial statements that have been attested by an independent certified public accountant. This requirement also applies to any corporation with more than 20 shareholders and any corporations that sell shares to the public.

If a corporation's quarterly gross sales or earnings exceed P25,000 (about US$965), the corporation must file audited financial statements along with its tax returns. Managers of publicly held corporations must submit statements of their responsibility for the accuracy of information in the financial statements. Corporations involved in highly regulated industries, such as banking,

insurance, or public utilities, may be required to submit additional audited papers to regulatory government agencies.

Books and Records Under the Corporation Code, a corporation must maintain a journal and a ledger recording all business transactions, as well as a record of the minutes of directors' and shareholders' meetings and books identifying shareholders and detailing stock transfers. Other records may be required for some specific lines of business. Books of accounts must be kept in a native Philippine language, English, or Spanish, must be registered with the Bureau of Internal Revenue, and must be retained for at least three years. Businesses with gross quarterly sales of less than P5,000 (about US$195) can keep simplified books.

Shareholders and Internal Revenue officers are entitled to examine a corporation's official books and records.

Government Supervision All corporations face some degree of government supervision. Every corporation must submit financial statements, bank certificates verifying deposits of capital, and articles of incorporation and bylaws—plus any amendments of these—to the SEC. Corporations that wish to qualify for various incentive schemes offered by the government must file documents with other government agencies that monitor corporations, such as the BOI and PEZA. (See "Formation and Registration of Business Operations" on page 191.)

Dissolution and Liquidation The Corporation Code prescribes the circumstances requiring dissolution of a corporation. These include expiration of the term for which the corporation was formed as stated in its articles, judicial decrees ordering liquidation, Filipino legislation requiring dissolution, or a corporation's failure to begin conducting business within two years its incorporation. Shareholders can voluntarily dissolve their corporation by vote of two-thirds of the shares. The SEC can also force dissolution of a corporation after receiving a verified complaint that alleges serious and irrevocable dissent in corporate management.

After dissolution, the liquidation process is managed either by the board of directors, in which case liquidation should be completed within three years, or by a receiver or trustee over a longer period. Philippine law protects corporate creditors, so shareholders cannot appropriate corporate assets until creditors have been paid, after which shareholders are entitled to assets in proportion to their shareholdings. Procedures for distribution of assets on liquidation are usually written in the articles of incorporation. Holders of preferred stock are typically entitled to distributions before common stockholders.

Branch Offices

After the stock corporation, the branch office is probably the second most popular form used by foreigners doing substantial business in the Philippines. Although formation and registration of a branch office requires a number of formalities (see "Formation and Registration of Business Operations" on page page 191), a foreign investor who chooses the branch form does not face as many administrative challenges in establishing the formalities of management and control. A branch office is regarded as an extension of its parent company, and thus looks mainly to the home country's laws for rules governing operations and management.

However, operation through a branch office does have some disadvantages. Foreign investors often prefer to use a subsidiary because incorporation limits the investors' liability to the assets of the Philippine subsidiary. However, if a branch office is used, the assets of both the branch and the parent company could be at risk. The branch form—which entails 100 percent ownership by the parent company—may also present a challenge to a foreign business when trying to participate in a Philippine industry in which foreign equity participation is limited by law.

A branch office must meet specific capitalization requirements before the SEC will grant a license to operate. The parent company must demonstrate its solvency and good standing in its home country and must deposit in the Philippines cash or securities amounting to P100,000 (about US$3,850). The company must then deposit 2 percent of the branch's gross income in excess of P5 million (about US$192,000) during each fiscal year following the establishment of the branch.

Rules governing books and records, audit requirements, government supervision, and dissolution of a branch office in the Philippines are essentially the same as the rules for corporations.

Representative Offices and Regional Headquarters

The representative office offers a very limited vehicle to the foreign investor who merely wants to establish a largely symbolic presence in the Philippines. The representative office can offer company information, can promote products, and can take orders on behalf of a head office, but it cannot itself derive income from the Philippines or directly distribute products. Because it does not derive any Philippine income, the representative office is not subject to Philippine income tax. However, a representative office must annually remit into the Philippines from abroad enough cash to cover its operating expenses, or a minimum of US$50,000, and must register with the SEC.

The same restrictions on income derivation and annual remittance of at least US$50,000 apply to the regional headquarters. This type of entity can act on behalf of a multinational firm with affiliates, subsidiaries, or branches in the vicinity of the Philippines, but solely as a supervisory center involved in coordination and communication. Such a headquarters cannot directly manage any of a multinational firm's Philippine subsidiary or branch offices. The Philippine government encourages the establishment of regional headquarters by furnishing resident visa privileges to headquarters' employees; limiting income tax rates for these employees to 15 percent; allowing construction of a regional warehouse under certain conditions; and exempting the headquarters from some municipal registration requirements.

Partnerships

A Philippine partnership is formed whenever two or more investors contribute to a common fund and intend to share any resulting profits. The partnership is considered a legal entity separate from the partners, and it is taxed like a corporation. However, even though it is a separate entity, the partnership must be dissolved on the death of a general partner.

The Philippines recognizes both general and limited partnerships. In a general partnership, all partners are personally liable for the partnership's obligations. The limited partnership offers the advantage that only the general partners—of which there must be at least one—are subject to personal liability for the partnership's obligations. Limited partners are liable only up to the amount of their capital contribution to the limited partnership. There are no minimum or maximum limits on capital contributions to a partnership, but if the partnership's capital exceeds P3,000 (about US$115), the agreement creating the partnership must be recorded and filed with the SEC. A contract that establishes a limited partnership must clearly state the limited nature of the entity and must specify which partners are general and which are limited.

The partnership agreement governs most of the company's operations. It establishes the respective liabilities of the partners and the extent of each partner's responsibility for management of the partnership. In the absence of contrary provisions in the contract, any general partner can act on behalf of the partnership without limitation. In a limited partnership, the law prohibits any limited partner from taking part in the active management or control of the business. Under most partnership contracts, partners cannot transfer their interests or alter the terms of the contract without the consent of all the other partners. Partnerships are subject to the same audit requirements as corporations.

A partnership must be dissolved on the death of a partner or the occurrence of any conditions requiring dissolution as set forth in the partnership agreement. A dissolving partnership continues to exist until it has completed a winding up process, which is designed to protect creditors.

While partnerships are easily established and involve fewer administrative formalities than corporations or branch offices, they usually are not favored by foreign investors because they offer fewer protections from liability and, to function effectively, require a high degree of cooperation and unity among the partners. However, partnerships are sometimes used by foreign investors who wish to derive income from a foreign partnership to take advantage of tax laws in their own home countries.

Joint Ventures

Philippine law does not recognize a joint venture as a separate legal entity. A de facto Philippine joint venture may be created by organizing a domestic corporation or partnership to operate for a specific project of limited duration. Shareholders or partners then take the roles of joint venturers. Investors usually turn to the corporation rather than the partnership as their joint venture vehicle because corporations offer a greater degree of flexibility in management and control, while a partnership requires a high degree of trust and coordination between the partners.

Licensing and Franchise Agreements

Many foreign investors do business in the Philippines through licensing, technology transfer, and franchise agreements. These arrangements allow foreign companies to transfer intellectual property rights, technology, and training in operational procedures and services to Philippine businesses in return for royalties. Philippine law recognizes and enforces these agreements, but limits their duration: the arrangement cannot exceed 10 years (although they may be renewed). At one time, renewal of the agreement required the approval of the Philippine Technology Transfer Board (TTB), a requirement that has been eliminated in favor of less formal renewal options (although agreements may not be automatically renewed).

The law also imposes several requirements on licensing, technology transfer, and franchise operations. Such agreements must be registered with the Bureau of Patents, Trademarks, and Technology Transfer (BPTTT). In addition, the parties must register their agreement with the Philippine Central Bank before the foreign licensor can remit royalties to a home country. The agreement must allow the licensee to export any licensed products, and

mandates that royalty rates cannot exceed those set by the TTB. Approval is usually granted provided the royalty rate is not in excess of 5 percent of net sales; approvals of higher rates are possible, but must be justified. The TTB will often allow foreign licensors who assist Philippine licensees in the export of licensed products to charge higher royalty rates. Foreign licensors must also agree to have Philippine law apply to any disputes over a licensing agreement.

Foreign franchises usually involve master license agreements given by a foreign investor to a Philippine business operator, who in turn controls a broad geographic area and licenses other business operators to run individual franchise locations. In recent years numerous fast food and convenience store franchises have begun thriving in the Philippines, and markets appear ripe for other types of franchising arrangements.

Agency/Distributor Agreements

Many foreign companies use agency or distributor arrangements by which a Philippine representative does nearly everything required to sell and promote the company's products in the nation's markets. Agents can negotiate deals; move, store, and deliver products; and provide product services to Philippine customers. Foreign investors who retain agents in the Philippines must register agency agreements with the SEC.

A major focus of agency contracts is the delineation of property rights between the overseas principal and the Philippine agent. Carefully drafted provisions should describe the extent to which ownership interests are being transferred or retained by each party. Other essential provisions should apportion the extent of each party's liability in the event of any claims related to improper advertising in the Philippines, damage to products incurred in the movement or storage of goods, and warranties made to Philippine customers.

Disputes over agency agreements are usually governed by Philippine law, and a foreign company that employs an agent in the Philippines must observe Philippine labor law. Laws that govern termination of agents are relatively liberal, allowing termination at either party's behest, typically on 30 days' advance notice.

Sole Proprietorships

Foreign investors can establish sole proprietorships in the Philippines, but they seldom use this form of business. The sole proprietor has sole, unlimited liability for all of the business' obligations and is required to supply all necessary capital, making this form more suitable for very small ventures.

The establishment of a sole proprietorship entails

TECHNOLOGY TRANSFER AGREEMENTS

A technology transfer agreement (TTA) is essentially a licensing arrangement by which a foreign company transfers technological know how related to a manufacturing or other production process to a local company in exchange for royalties on the local company's sales. A TTA may also be a management and training contract, computer software license agreement, or transfer or license agreement for industrial property rights (such as copyrights, trademarks, tradenames, and patents).

Such agreements must be carefully drafted to define clearly the rights and obligations of the parties and to comply with Philippine law. Important provisions to be considered include the following:

1. General Intent A statement of the parties' general intent in forming the TTA, which should be for the benefit of the Philippines.

2. Specific Intent A statement of exactly why the arrangement will benefit Philippine labor, export, and industrial interests.

3. Identification of Technology A precise description of the technology transferred, including related documentation and any accompanying trademarks or other intellectual property rights. The parties should specify the particular industry, legal, consumer, or other standards that the technology must meet.

4. Transfer Terms Provisions specifying the time within which the transfer will be made, any related items to be furnished by the transferor (such as advertising, promotional, and marketing materials), and the training to be provided (including the number and position of the personnel, the training location, and the party responsible for paying training expenses).

5. Confidentiality Of utmost importance, a clause stating that all information, knowledge, technology, and materials furnished are proprietary in nature, plus the transferee's covenant of confidentiality. This covenant should obligate the transferee to take certain steps to protect the technology rights from unauthorized use and should specify that failure to do so will constitute a material breach and a ground for termination of the TTA.

6. Unlimited Development, Production, and Sales A clause that entitles the local company receiving the technology to export, set prices, conduct research, and produce products or provide services without restriction.

7. Ownership of Modifications A specification of which party will own, or of joint ownership in, any improvements or other modifications in the technology that either party makes or discovers during the TTA term.

8. Duration A clause that fixes the term of the agreement, which can be no more than 10 years. The parties may provide for renewal options, which can effectively extend the agreement indefinitely.

9. Termination An explanation of when either or both parties are entitled to terminate the TTA, listing exactly what must be returned to the transferor at the time of termination, and specifying the procedures for returning all materials. This clause should also cover the rights of the transferee after the TTA expires to continue to use the technology and any modifications.

11. Governing Law A statement that the TTA is to be interpreted in accordance with Philippine law.

12. Controlling Language If contract negotiations are held in, or the contract is translated into, more than one language, a provision identifying which language will used for purposes of interpreting the contract terms and the parties' intent.

13. Dispute Resolution A clause selecting the system—courts, arbitration, or other—on which the parties will rely to resolve a dispute that they cannot otherwise settle through negotiation.

little formality, although a foreign proprietor must register the business with the Department of Trade and Industry (DTI) and must register the amount of any investment with the Central Bank. A nonresident foreigner who runs a sole proprietorship in the Philippines should additionally appoint a resident agent and register the agency agreement with the SEC.

FORMATION AND REGISTRATION

Formation and Registration of Business Operations

This section outlines the procedures and documentation required to form and register most forms of business in the Philippines. Laws covering formation and registration are contained in the Philippines Corporation Code, Commercial Code, Civil Code, Foreign Investments Act of 1991, and Omnibus Investments Act of 1987. In addition, businesses are subject to the rules contained in lists and regulations promulgated by the SEC, BOI, PEZA, TTB, DTI, Central Bank, and other agencies. For example, in an attempt to achieve better compliance with environmental regulations, firms must furnish a certificate of compliance obtained from the Department of Environment and Natural Resources (DENR) with their applications in order to obtain BOI certification when needed.

The Philippine government has instituted a program of economic reform and has been steadily opening the Philippine economy to foreign investment and reducing barriers to trade. For the most part, Philippine citizens welcome foreign investment. Thus, a foreign investor who is considering whether to establish a Philippine business entity may face a maze of regulation, but the investor is also relatively unlikely to encounter either substantial administrative resistance to the business plan or biased treatment when commencing operations in the country. However, Philippine law still contains remnants of a restrictive system designed to favor local industry, and Philippine red tape alone is enough to warrant some. Setting up a business in the Philippines may require an investor to go beyond simple compliance with stated procedures and to seek interpretation of Philippine laws and regulations that are currently in flux as foreign trade and investment expands. It will also require patience and understanding.

An assortment of government agencies monitors business entities in the Philippines, and the complex bureaucracy can present a daunting prospect to the foreign investor who contemplates the establishment of a business there. All businesses in the Philippines must register with the appropriate authorities before commencing operations. Moreover, the formation of most business entities often requires prior government approval of the plan. For the foreign investor, this procedure will require a careful examination of the laws and rules that limit foreign equity participation in various business entities and industries, as well as the observation of operating requirements—such as minimum capital deposits to be made in the Philippines, residence requirements for corporate directors and agents, and maximum royalty rates on license or franchise contracts. Even if mandatory registration and approval requirements are minimal, foreign investors may want to register their entity with regulating agencies—such as the BOI and PEZA—for the purpose of receiving certification that the business is eligible for government business incentives, including tax breaks, simplified registration and audit procedures, and unrestricted use of consigned equipment.

Procedures

It is essential to obtain legal and accounting advice from professionals in the Philippines who know the national and local government structure and who are familiar with regulatory requirements, procedures, and conditions. Fostering personal relationships with such individuals, either directly or through a partner in the Philippines, will help to smooth the setup and operation process. These professionals can handle registration and obtain necessary approvals as efficiently as possible. They can also advise and recommend business structures that maximize compliance with laws and regulations while minimizing exposure to regulatory agencies. (Refer to the "Important Addresses" chapter, beginning on page 297, for listings of government agencies and legal and accounting firms.)

A brief summary of procedures involved in organizing various enterprises in the Philippines is given here. Armed with this knowledge, an investor should be able to monitor the progress and status of the required agency approvals and filings. An understanding of the general procedures should also allow the investor to identify the steps that will require advance planning and preparation so as to be ready to comply with the requirements when the time arrives for the next stage of the process.

All Foreign-Owned Business Operations and Investments Any foreign person or company desiring to establish a business presence in the Philippines must first obtain a license from the SEC, or, if organizing a sole proprietorship, from the DTI. To get a license, the person must complete all of the following:

- Appoint a Philippine citizen as a resident agent who can represent the foreign investor for any legal purposes in the country, and file this appointment with the SEC.
- Establish an office and file its address with the SEC.
- Register any investment with the Philippine Central Bank, and remit to the Philippine banking system the foreign exchange equivalent of the amount of the investment being registered (without this registration an investor will not be permitted to repatriate investment capital or remit profits to the home country).
- Transfer enough capital to the office to cover any potential liabilities in the Philippines,
- Provide proof that Philippine citizens can also do business in the investor's home country, and
- If the investor is a foreign corporation that wants to do business in the Philippines, file

charters and bylaws, statements of authorized and paid-up capital, names and addresses of directors and officers, and other standard corporate documents with the SEC.

Corporations To found a Philippine corporation, one or more incorporators—each of whom must own at least one share of capital stock—must subscribe to proposed articles of incorporation and file these, along with documents establishing the corporation's name, purpose, capitalization, location of its main Philippines office, and other matters, with the SEC. The following are the basic documents that must be filed with the SEC:

- Articles of incorporation and by-laws;
- The incorporator's Philippine taxpayer identification number;
- A promise to change the corporate name if it is similar to the name of an already existing corporation;
- A treasurer's affidavit verifying the deposit of paid-up capital;
- A bank certificate showing the deposit of paid subscriptions to capital;
- A statement of the corporation's assets and liabilities;
- A statement that the entity will observe SEC reporting requirements;
- An authorization allowing the SEC to check the corporation's bank account; and
- Documents detailing personal information on directors, officers, and shareholders.

If a corporation is funded wholly or partially with foreign equity, additional documents must be filed with the SEC to show that the incorporators have obtained certain prior approvals. These documents include:

- A certificate from the Central Bank verifying that the foreign equity funds have been transferred into the country and any foreign exchange has been converted into Philippine pesos;
- If the contributor of foreign equity is a corporation, a certified copy of the resolution of that corporation's board authorizing the establishment of a subsidiary corporation and office in the Philippines; and
- If the corporation's paid-in capital will be less than US$500,000 (about US$19,250), a certificate from the Philippine Department of Science and Technology certifying that the business involves high technology (without this certificate, a corporation in the technology field would run afoul of Philippine law limiting foreign equity in small Philippine corporations).

Once all the paperwork has been submitted to the SEC and is approved, the SEC will issue a certificate of registration. A corporation is considered a legal person as soon as this certificate is issued. To make the incorporation of companies involved in common lines of business as painless as possible, the SEC has instituted an "express lane" for processing papers, allowing it to accept all the required documentation and to issue a certificate of registration in a single working day. If a corporation does not fall within a category entitled to express lane treatment, its papers typically can take as long as a month to be processed.

After the SEC issues a certificate of registration, shareholders can organize the corporation at an initial meeting where the directors are elected. If an organizational meeting is not held, and the corporation does not commence business, within two years of the issuance of the certificate, the corporation is deemed to have been dissolved.

Filing fees are 0.1 percent of the corporation's authorized capital stock, but cannot be less than P200 nor more than P100,000 (about US$3,850).

Registering for Incentives The Philippine government offers incentives to some corporations provided they are majority-owned by Filipino citizens or engage in preferred areas of economic activity, such as export. Activities that qualify for incentives are set forth in the Omnibus Investments Code of 1987, the Foreign Investments Act of 1991, and in the annual Investment Priorities Plan promulgated by the BOI. Incentives typically include exemptions from various taxes and customs duties, simplified business filings and customs procedures, and unrestricted use of consigned equipment. To take advantage of these incentives, a qualified corporation must register with the BOI. This involves submission of the following:

- Articles of incorporation and by-laws;
- Proof of citizenship if registration is based in part on Philippine ownership;
- Audited financial statements and income tax returns for the previous three years;
- Various resolutions and a letter from the board of directors authorizing an applicant or agent to sign the required forms;
- Proof, usually by means of audited financial statements, that the enterprise has the financial ability to complete any proposed projects that make the corporation eligible for incentives;
- A project report or feasibility study prepared in a format given by the BOI;
- Various numbered BOI application forms; and
- A filing fee.

Corporations that are established in Export Processing Zones (EPZs) and that export all of their products may qualify for additional government incentives, including substantial tax breaks, even if the corporations are wholly owned by foreign investors. Corporations that locate in Subic Bay, a former US military station now being transformed into a freeport zone, may be eligible for these incentives, as well. To take advantage of EPZ incentives, a corporation must register with the PEZA by filing the following documents:

- An application form;
- A project feasibility study;
- A certificate against graft and corruption;
- Personal information sheets on corporation officers;
- A resolution from the board of directors appointing a corporate representative authorized to sign necessary papers;
- Audited financial statements for the previous three years;
- SEC and BOI certificates of registration; and
- Articles of incorporation.

Refer to the "Trade Zones" chapter, beginning on page 71, for discussion of these zones.

Branches A foreign company establishing a branch in the Philippines must file the following documents with the SEC:

- A certified copy of a resolution from the foreign company's home office authorizing the establishment of the branch;
- A reciprocity certificate showing that the foreign company's home country allows Philippine businesses to establish branches in that country;
- A power of attorney appointing a resident of the Philippines to represent the foreign company in matters concerning the branch;
- A statement subjecting the foreign company to various forms of legal process in the Philippines;
- A sworn statement of the foreign company's good financial standing;
- The foreign company's audited financial statements;
- Proof of inward remittance of the capital assigned to the branch;
- The foreign company's articles of incorporation and bylaws;
- A "Foreign Company Information Sheet"; and
- Any relevant certificates from other government agencies, such as the BOI or PEZA, if the branch has registered for incentives.

Registration for incentives requires the filing of all the documents with the BOI and PEZA that are required of a corporation.

After a branch secures a license from the SEC, the branch must also deposit with the SEC securities that are worth at least P100,000 (about US$3,850) to cover the branch's liabilities to current and future creditors. The branch must deposit these securities within 60 days of the SEC's grant of a branch license. If the branch's annual income exceeds a certain amount, it must file with the SEC additional securities amounting to 2 percent of any increases in its annual income.

Partnerships Any partnership with capital exceeding P3,000 (about US$115) must register with the SEC. The registration procedure echoes the process required for the formation and registration of a corporation, but with the partnership contract replacing the articles of incorporation in all required filings. A partnership that wants to register for incentives must submit to the BOI or PEZA the same documents as are required of corporations.

Sole Proprietorships An investor who wants to establish a sole proprietorship must complete all of the following steps:

- Register the total capital investment with the Central Bank.
- Remit the amount of capital investment to the Philippine banking system.
- Register the business with the Bureau of Trade Regulation and Consumer Protection, a division of the DTI.
- If the proprietorship qualifies for incentives, apply to the BOI, PEZA, or other relevant agency.
- If a foreign investor is not going to reside in the Philippines, appoint a resident agent to represent the proprietorship and to accept legal service.
- Register the agency agreement with the SEC.

Additional Reporting Requirements

Corporations with authorized or paid-up capital exceeding P50,000 (about US$1,925), branches of foreign corporations, and partnerships or individuals with gross quarterly sales, earnings, receipts, or production exceeding P25,000 (about US$965) all must file annual audited financial statements with the SEC. Corporations must file annual reports containing general information sheets in addition to the financial statements.

Businesses must determine if they are required to obtain any additional registrations or file any additional reports with municipalities in which they are located. The Philippine Local Government Code requires adherence to municipal or city requirements.

USEFUL ADDRESSES

In addition to the government agencies listed here, individuals or firms should contact chambers of commerce, embassies, banks and other financial service firms, local consultants, legal and accounting firms, and resident foreign businesses for assistance and information. (Refer to the "Important Addresses" chapter, beginning on page 297, for more complete listings.)

TEN REMINDERS, RECOMMENDATIONS, AND RULES

1. The corporation and the branch office are the business forms most popular with foreign investors in the Philippines. A subsidiary corporation in the Philippines limits a foreign owner's exposure to liability to the subsidiary's assets in the Philippines. A branch office could expose a foreign owner's assets outside the Philippines to business liabilities.

2. Foreign investors must sometimes work with Philippine partners to start some kinds of business entities because Philippine law restricts foreign equity in various types of business organizations and certain industries. Restrictions on foreign ownership of Philippine businesses are enumerated in a "Negative List" established by the Foreign Investments Act of 1991. The Philippine government encourages at least 60 percent ownership of most types of businesses by Philippine nationals, thus the most popular business form used by foreign investors is the 60/40 corporation, in which foreign investors own only 40 percent of the shares.

3. Although foreign equity in a venture is sometimes restricted to a minority stake, foreign investors can use numerous techniques, such as management contracts or voting trust arrangements to enhance their voting power and to give them greater effective management control over the business.

4. The joint venture is not a recognized business form in the Philippines. Investors run de facto joint ventures by forming small corporations, or sometimes partnerships, that have limited purposes and terms of duration with Philippine counterparts.

5. Many foreign businesses conduct operations under the aegis of simple licensing contracts or agency agreements. Licensing contracts involving technology transfers are monitored by the Philippine Technology Transfer Board (TTB), which limits the duration of contracts and approves royalty rates. Disputes over licensing contracts and agency agreements usually must be governed by Philippine law.

6. Although the Philippine government and most citizens welcome foreign investment, making administrative resistance or unofficial bias toward foreign business ventures per se uncommon, the complexity of the Philippine bureaucracy alone makes the establishment and fostering of personal relationships with members of Philippine government agencies advisable. Because registration, formation, and operation of a business entity requires contact with numerous government agencies and interpretation of numerous laws and regulations, it is also imperative that foreign investors seek professional assistance from consulting, legal, and accounting firms experienced in the establishment and operation of Philippine businesses.

7. Whenever a foreign investor or business owner contributes capital to a Philippine business, the amount of the investment must be registered with the Securities and Exchange Commission (SEC), and the investor must convert any foreign exchange into Philippine pesos and remit the amount of the investment into an account held through the Philippine banking system. Investments should also be registered with the Philippine Central Bank. If an investment is not registered with the Central Bank, an investor will not be entitled to repatriate the investment capital or remit any earnings to a home country.

8. The SEC is the chief regulatory agency monitoring corporations, branches, representative offices, regional headquarters, and partnerships. The SEC approves formation of these entities after receiving required documentation and fees, issues certificates establishing the legal personalty of these entities, and requires periodic submission of financial reports and other documents.

9. The BOI and PEZA are the main regulatory agencies that determine whether business entities are entitled to receive incentives—such as tax breaks or simplified registration or reporting requirements—offered by the Philippine government. Businesses that believe they are qualified for incentives must apply to these agencies.

10. In addition to observing requirements established by national laws (such as the New Corporation Code and Foreign Investments Act) and regulations promulgated by national agencies (such as the SEC and BOI), owners of Philippine businesses must check for any local permit or reporting requirements established by the Philippine municipalities in which the businesses are located.

Bangko Sentral ng Pilipinas (BSP)
(Central Bank of the Philippines)
A. Mabini St., cor. Vito Cruz St.
Malate, Manila, Philippines
Tel: [63] (2) 507-051, 593-380/1, 595-263, 582-372
Fax: [63] (2) 522-3987, 597-363

Bases Conversion Development Authority
2nd Fl., Rufino Center
Ayala Ave., cor. Herrera St.
1226 Makati, Metro Manila, Philippines
Tel: [63] (2) 813-5383, 864-006/9
Fax: (2) 813-5424/7
Prepares development plans and oversees the conversion of US military reservations.

Board of Investments One-Stop Action Center (BOI-OSAC)
Industry and Investments Bldg.
385 Sen. Gil J. Puyat Avenue
1200 Makati, Metro Manila, Philippines
Tel:[63] (2) 868-403, 816-127, 875-602
Fax: [63] (2) 819-1793, 819-1816, 819-1887, 851-166

Bureau of Export Trade Promotion
Department of Trade and Industry
5th Fl., New Solid Bldg.
357 Sen. Gil J. Puyat Avenue
Makati, Metro Manila, Philippines
Tel: [63] (2) 817-5298, 817-5203, 818-5701
Fax: [63] (2) 817-4923, 819-1816

Bureau of International Trade Relations
Department of Trade and Industry
361 Sen. Gil J. Puyat Avenue
Makati, Metro Manila, Philippines
Tel: [63] (2) 817-8087
Fax: [63] (2) 818-7846

Bureau of Patents, Trademarks and Technology Transfer
Department of Trade and Industry
361 Sen. Gil J. Puyat Ave.
Makati, Metro Manila, Philippines
Tel: [63] (2) 815-4919, 818-3109, 818-3944, 818-4128
Fax: [63] (2) 818-4145

Bureau of Trade Regulation and Consumer Protection
Department of Trade and Industry
2nd Fl., Trade and Industry Bldg.
361 Sen. Gil J. Puyat Ave.
Makati, Metro Manila, Philippines
Tel: [63] (2) 817-5280, 817-5340, 863-431, 818-5701
Fax: [63] (2) 810-9363

Environmental Management Bureau
6th Floor, Philippine Heart Center
East Avenue
Quezon City
Tel: [63] (2) 98-0421 x3627, 97-56-09
Fax: [63] (2) 97-32-54

National Economic and Development Authority (NEDA)
NEDA Bldg.
Amber Avenue
1600 Pasig, Metro Manila, Philippines
Tel: [63] (2) 631-5031, 631-3716, 631-0945 to 64
Fax: [63] (2) 631-3747

Philippine Economic Zone Authority (PEZA)
4th Fl., Legaspi Towers 300
Roxas Boulevard
Metro Manila, Philippines
Tel: [63] (2) 521-9725, 521-0585, 521-0546/7
Fax: [63] (2) 521-8659

Securities and Exchange Commission (SEC)
SEC Building
Epifanio de los Santos Ave.
Greenhills
Mandaluyong, Metro Manila, Philippines
Tel: [63] (2) 810-1145, 780-931/9
Fax: [63] (2) 722-0990
Registers and supervises business entities.

FURTHER READING

The preceding discussion is provided as a basic guide for those interested in doing business in the Philippines. The resources described in this section provide additional information on business law, investment, taxation, accounting, and procedural requirements.

Doing Business in the Philippines, Ernst & Young International, Ltd., 1995. Available from: Ernst & Young, 787 Seventh Ave., New York, NY, USA; Tel: [1] (212) 773-3000. Available in the Philippines from Punongbayan & Araullo, PO Box 7573, Domestic Airport (mailing address); 1300 Domestic Road, Pasay City, Metro Manila (post office lock box); or 6th Fl., Vernida IV Building, Alfaro St., Salcedo Village, 1200 Makati, Metro Manila, Rep. of the Philippines; Tel: [63] (2) 810-9741, 812-6091; Fax: [63] (2) 810-9748. Provides an overview of the investment environment in the Philippines together with information about taxation, business organizational structures, business practices, and accounting requirements.

Doing Business in the Philippines, Price Waterhouse World Firm Limited, 1993. Available from: Price Waterhouse, 400 South Hope St., Los Angeles, CA 90071-2889, USA; Tel: [1] (213) 236-3000. Available in the Philippines from Joaquin Cunanan & Co.-Price Waterhouse, PO Box 2288, Manila (mailing address); or BA-Lepanto Building, 8th Fl., 8747 Paseo de Roxas, Makati, Metro Manila, Rep. of the Philippines; Tel: [63] (2) 818-7622; Fax: [63] (2) 815-3514. Covers the investment and business environment in the Philippines and the audit, accounting, and taxation requirements.

Setting up in Business in Philippines, DTI Export Publications, 1994. Available from: DTI Export Publications, PO Box 55, Stratford-Upon-Avon, Warwickshire CV37 9GE, UK; Tel: [44] (89) 296212; Fax: [44] (89) 299096. Summary profile of the country's geography, people, trade, investment, and business environment.

Labor

THE LABOR ECONOMY

The Philippines is becoming increasingly attractive to many international operations seeking production centers in Asia. Skyrocketing wage costs in such previously low-cost locations as Taiwan, Hong Kong, and South Korea, coupled with growing shortages in production labor availability in these countries, are causing many companies with operations in Asia to seek more cost-effective sites for labor intensive production. The Philippines is proving to be a good source of generally well educated, skilled, and easy-to-train workers who are available at reasonable cost.

Companies considering the use of Philippine labor are likely to find many opportunities. At present, a relatively high proportion of the labor force is underemployed in low productivity, service sector jobs. Although the unemployment rate has been falling by about a percentage point each year, at 8.6 percent it remains high. This is due to such factors as the high rate of population growth, a lack of access to land, insufficient industrial job creation, and past political policies designed to protect domestic producers that often hindered economic growth and competitive upgrades.

The Philippine government has been campaigning to raise domestic wages. However, it has been somewhat constrained in this effort because it needs to do so without increasing the unemployment and derailing the still fragile economic recovery that could result from a higher cost structure. However, despite official efforts, real wages remain low, and a relatively powerless labor union system has been unable to do much to slow the deterioration in earning power. The Philippines is a culture in which education is highly prized, and a relatively large percentage of people in the workforce hold college degrees. Nevertheless, many highly trained workers have been able to obtain relatively low-skill clerical or production jobs, while others are out of work altogether despite their credentials. In short, the Philippines has a surplus of educated, cost-competitive, skilled labor at all levels in virtually all sectors of its diversifying economy.

Population

The Philippine population continues to grow at the rapid rate of 2.3 percent annually, although this rate has slowed somewhat from even higher average rates posted in recent decades. The 1990 census lists the population at 60.7 million, and in the mid-1990s it is estimated at around 70 million. Even if growth continues at today's somewhat slower rate, the Philippines will have more than 75 million inhabitants by the year 2000. At this rate, the Philippines needs to double its available stock of housing, schools, and health facilities every 29 years just to maintain the current level of services for its residents, much less improve them. Successes to date have been mixed.

In demographic terms, the population at all ages is about evenly split between male and female, but agewise the Philippine population is young: about 40 percent of the residents are less than 14 years of age, while 57 percent are younger than 20, and only 5 percent are older than 60. The number of people considered to be of working age (15 years and older) is expected to increase to more than 45 million (60 percent of the population) by the year 2000. Simply to provide employment for anticipated new entrants into the labor force—not to mention more and better paying employment for existing cohorts—the economy will have to generate more than one million

GOVERNMENT REGULATORS

Department of Labor and Employment (DOLE) DOLE is responsible overall for the regulation of employment in the Philippines. Its authority extends to three broadly defined areas: promotion of employment and apprenticeship; workers' protection and welfare; and promotion and maintenance of industrial peace based on social justice.

National Labor Relations Commission (NLRC) The NLRC coordinates programs and policies with DOLE, but is otherwise a separate agency. The NLRC oversees unfair labor practice allegations, job termination disputes, and other labor matters not strictly related to wages. It consists of one chairman and 14 commissioners. In combination with the National Conciliation and Mediation Board (NCMB), the NLRC serves as a quasi-judicial mechanism for hearing and adjudicating workers' claims, and it has exclusive appellate jurisdiction over all cases decided by labor arbiters.

Regional Tripartite Wages and Productivity Boards (RTWPBs) There are 15 regional boards, each representing a section of the country. The Boards assist the NWPC. Specifically, they are charged with developing plans, programs, and projects related to wages, income, and productivity improvements for their respective regions, as well as determining and fixing minimum wage rates. They also act on applications for exemption from prescribed wage rates.

National Wages and Productivity Commission (NWPC) The NWPC consults and advises the national government on wages and worker productivity. It formulates policies and guidelines on these issues; prescribes rules and guidelines for determining minimum wage and productivity standards; and reviews wage levels set by the RTWPBs for compliance with prescribed guidelines and national development plans. It also studies and disseminates information on wages and productivity and other related information on employment, cost of living, and labor costs.

jobs each year throughout the rest of the decade.

About 44 percent of the Philippine population lives in urban areas; Metropolitan Manila alone is home to seven million, one-tenth of the total population of the country. Other large urban centers include Cebu City, Davao, Iloilo, Zamboanga, and Baguio. Filipinos are of Malay stock with touches of Islamic, Hindu, Chinese, Spanish, and US influences. Ethnic Malays constitute a majority of the population, but there are significant Chinese, US, and Spanish minority communities throughout the archipelago.

Labor Force In 1993 the Philippine National Statistics Office numbered the total labor force (consisting of all Filipinos 15 years and older) at 26.8 million. Expanding at an average rate of 2.7 percent annually, the working age population is growing more rapidly than the total population (which increases 2.3 percent annually). The National Statistics Office attributes this phenomenon to the extended period of time that individuals remain in the eligible category once they enter the workforce, and to the increasing number of women who are entering the workforce. New entrants to the total labor force have averaged approximately 650,000 each year, including about 230,000 annual entrants to the pool for managerial and technical positions.

Labor Availability and Distribution by Sector

The relatively high level of unemployment among educated, potentially highly productive Filipinos in many areas of the country translates into the availability of a skilled and trainable workforce in a variety of labor market segments in a wide range of different locations nationwide. Nevertheless, labor can most readily be secured in urban areas. Because nearly 90 percent of all Philippine industry is located in the greater Manila area, aspiring workers tend to migrate to that locale.

In past decades, the agricultural sector (including fishing and forestry) provided the most employment, and it continues to account for a substantial share of jobs. The sector employed 45 percent of the total employed labor force in 1993. However, its share has been dropping slowly in recent decades; in 1960 this sector had employed 60 percent of the workforce.

The industrial and service sectors have not yet fully made up for the falling rate of agricultural sector employment. Employment in the industrial sector (including the manufacturing, mining, and construction industries) accounted for only 15 percent of the total employed workforce in 1993. Employment in various service industries (including commerce; financial, real estate, and business services; transportation, communications, and utilities; and personal and government services) accounts for about 40 percent of the workforce—versus only 25 percent in 1960.

Much of the growth in the services sector has been in the nature of small-scale enterprises or self-employment activities, such as street-hawking or vending, repair work, transportation, and personal services. Such endeavors are often referred to as "the informal sector," primarily because of the general lack of recordkeeping and a relative freedom from government regulation. This informal service sector is generally characterized by long hours and low wages, yet it constitutes an ever growing share of the employed labor force and contributes to the expand category of the underemployed.

Unable to find jobs at home, large numbers of Filipinos work overseas. The actual numbers of these guest workers is unclear, but their contribution to the economy is highly significant and important. Official remittances from overseas workers have equaled about 14 percent of merchandise exports, and the Bangko Sentral ng Pilipinas (BSP) estimates that actual remittances passing through "informal channels" might be as much as twice the documented amount. Even by the more modest official measure, export of labor is among the largest sources of foreign exchange in the economy, and it accounts for the fact that the Philippines—contrary to most developing countries—generally posts a surplus in trade in services.

The Philippine Overseas Employment Administration listed nearly 685,000 Filipinos as deployed overseas in 1993, up from 615,000 in 1991. Of these, nearly one-fifth represent seagoing Filipino workers involved in the merchant marine and serving on ships registered elsewhere. According to composite figures on land-based overseas Filipino employees, there were about 539,000 such guest workers abroad in 1993, up from 385,000 in 1988 (but down from the peak level of 550,000 in 1992). However, some observers estimate the total Filipino overseas workforce at around one million workers. (The government sometimes includes emigrants living abroad in its tally of overseas Filipinos, and through their remittances such overseas Filipinos are important to the economy whether or not they intend to return at some point in the future.)

Inasmuch as wages paid for overseas work have been a multiple of what Filipinos could expect to earn at home, such employment opportunities have been in great demand, and overseas migration is likely to absorb increasingly more Filipinos as long as the domestic economy continues to expand more slowly than the labor force. Workers from all sectors—including technical, construction, domestic, managerial, and services—participate in overseas employment.

Unemployment and Underemployment Trends

In July 1993 official figures listed employment at 91.4 percent, with 22.1 percent underemployed. Unemployment was thought to be 8.6 percent. These figures are not broken down by gender. As of mid-1995, unemployment was estimated at 8.8 percent.

Although the Philippines continues to suffer from high unemployment, unemployment as a percentage of the workforce has been slowly falling from a high of around 11 percent in 1991. However, it will be difficult to achieve further reduction unless job creation—which has not kept pace with workforce expansion—increases substantially. The US exit from vast former Navy base at Subic Bay in 1992 put additional pressure on the Philippine economy, resulting in the loss of an estimated 400,000 direct and indirect local jobs. The eruption of the Mount Pinatubo volcano in June 1991 immediately displaced about 600,000 workers; the effects of this natural disaster have yet to be overcome. Further contributing to the unemployment problem, at least in the short run, are the increases in the minimum wage mandated by the Wage Board in April 1994. These raised the basic nonagricultural daily minimum wage from P135 to P145 (about US$4.90 to US$5.26).

A longer-term problem remains: inadequate investment in the industrial economy and the decline in the number of new jobs created in this higher-value-added sector. This in turn has caused rapid growth in the service sector and in the resulting underemployment. Unemployment has tended primarily to effect young, inexperienced entrants into the labor force; these individuals are predominately relatively well educated and are not heads of households. By contrast, underemployment remains primarily a problem for the poor and less well educated and for older people. Up to 20 percent of male heads of households and 35 percent of female heads of households, although technically classified as employed, were unable to find more than 40 days of work per quarter during recent years.

In general, the turnover rate in the Philippines is relatively high, as high as 7.2 percent in Metro Manila and 6.5 percent in outlying urban areas. Contributing heavily to this high rate of turnover is the fact that companies hire non-regular employees (known as "casuals") when business improves, then terminate them as soon as business slackens. Observers further note that unemployment in the Philippines follows a seasonal pattern, in which unemployment rises substantially—two to three percentage points—during the first quarter and then ends the year at a much lower rate. Experts believe that the swing in the unemployment rate has to do with the production schedules found in the small firms that employ the overwhelming majority of salaried workers. Typically, these firms have a fairly high rate of turnover that occurs early in the year, as the low paid workers—especially young and female workers—either go out to look for better paying jobs or decide to temporarily leave the workforce. However, at the end of the year everyone wants to be employed in order to earn money for Christmas shopping. Neither employee nor employer loyalty is highly developed in the Philippines.

Nevertheless, the recent trend toward liberalization in the economy bodes well for the future employment picture. Several Japanese and South Korean industrial firms, faced with rising wages at home, are considering large investments in the Philippines, which could create more than a hundred thousand new jobs. Tourism, both domestic and international, is one of the largest growing contributors to the Philippine economy, and it is hoped that employment in this sector will double within the next few years.

Foreign Workers

Given the abundance of skilled or trainable labor and the scarcity of jobs, the Philippine government has traditionally discouraged the employment of foreign labor, except in particular specialized jobs for which no Filipinos are available. Entry visas and work permits are required for foreign personnel hired on either a permanent or temporary basis, and all foreigners seeking employment, whether as residents or nonresidents, must first secure an employment permit from the Philippine Embassy or consulate in their home country. Work permits may be issued to a nonresident foreigner or to the applicant employer after a determination of the nonavailability of a person in the Philippines who is competent, able, and willing at the time of application to perform the services for which the alien is desired.

In accordance with its recent efforts to liberalize the economy, and in order to encourage foreign participation in the economic development of the country, the government has liberalized the visa requirements for certain categories of foreigners. Foreign stockholders, investors, representatives of investment houses, and land developers are among the categories eligible for this special incentive. In addition, registered producer enterprises and firms in the Export Processing Zones are allowed to employ, within five years from registration (extendable for limited periods), foreign nationals to occupy supervisory, technical, or advisory positions; however, such foreign personnel should not exceed 5 percent of total employment in each category. The positions of president, treasurer, and general manager, or their equivalents, may be retained by foreign nationals if the majority of the capital stock of the firm is owned by foreign nationals. Foreign personnel for approved regional or area headquarters in the Philippines, as well as their respective spouses and unmarried children younger than 21 years of age, may be issued multiple entry special visas. Foreigners who invest at least US$75,000 in the Philippines (US$50,000 in tourism-related projects) may be issued a Special Investor's Resident Visa (SIRV), which allows the investor to reside in the Philippines for as long as the investment is maintained.

Under individual bilateral treaty provisions covering the US, Japan, and Germany, foreigners may be granted a treaty trader visa solely to carry on substantial trade, principally between the foreigner's country and the Philippines, or to direct and develop an enterprise in which the trader has substantial capital investment.

Foreign technicians may be admitted into the Philippines with a prearranged employment visa if

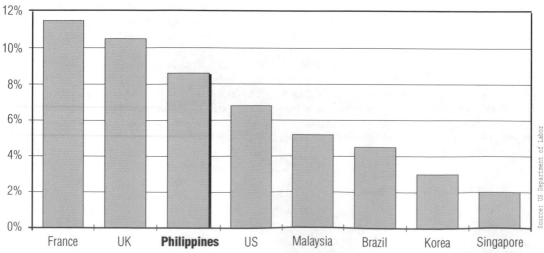

Comparative Unemployment—1993

Note: In virtually all cases actual unemployment is greater than official figures, which tend to understate this measure. This is particularly true of emerging nations, although developed, industrial nations are not immune. The figures given are derived from official sources and should be viewed primarily as a relative guide.

the skills they possess are not available in the country. However, to ensure the actual transfer of technology, the employer and the foreign technician must train at least two Filipino apprentices in the department for which the foreigner is being hired.

Individuals may come to the Philippines for business or pleasure using a temporary visitor's visa, allowing them to stay for a period of 59 days and extendable to up to one year. Every alien whose stay will exceed 59 days is required to register with the Commission on Immigration and Deportation or in areas outside Metro Manila with the office of the municipal or city treasure. Foreigners are generally permitted to stay in the Philippines without a visa for a period not exceeding 21 days. An alien who is admitted as a nonimmigrant can apply for resident status without departing from the Philippines.

HUMAN RESOURCES

The Philippine government is committed to increasing the general living standards of its population as it increases its competitiveness in the international marketplace. Its stated objectives for the period through 1998 are to have a healthier, better fed, better educated, and better sheltered citizenry; related goals include mechanisms that reduce the rate of population growth and provide better access to government social services and training programs for the poorest Filipinos. The Philippines is blessed with an abundance of young, educated, industrious, and willing workers. Already, the well developed educational system has produced an explosion of knowledge and entrepreneurial skills, along with a changing of the corporate guard to a younger generation imbued with a sense of capitalist professionalism and sophisticated managerial skills. As the effects of recent government policies become more widespread and assimilated into the economy at large, this trend should continue and expand.

Education

Filipinos have a deep regard for education, which they view as one of the main avenues for social and economic advancement. The government has invested heavily in education, and has expanded its availability tremendously, while at the same time increasing the quality of both elementary and secondary schools. Additional educational and manpower training programs are planned, with a focus on improving basic learning while also developing a critical mass of technical and professional personnel. The development of stronger links between education and industry figures prominently in this strategy. Many institutions of higher learning have developed work-study or apprenticeship programs with businesses. Although many of the Philippine elite continue to send their children to US colleges and business schools, the Philippines has developed sophisticated domestic college and post-graduate curricula in business subjects. MBA courses are available at about a half-dozen Philippine colleges, and the Asian Institute of Management, opened in the 1970s, has gained such prestige that it attracts top students from throughout the ASEAN region.

Since 1991 the education system has been able to serve a relatively large part of the population effectively, at least at the elementary level. The government education system offers six years of elementary instruction followed by four years of high school. Children enter elementary school—which is free—at the age of seven. Instruction is bilingual in Pilipino and English, although Pilipino—the national language—is being emphasized to an increasingly greater degree. The government, which counts as literate anyone who has completed four years of elementary school, lists the literacy rate at above 90 percent and is targeting 96.5 percent literacy by 1998. Literacy rates are virtually the same for men and women.

Some 97 percent of the relevant age group is enrolled in elementary education. High school enrollment rates are approximately 58 percent nationwide, but are somewhat lower on Mindanao and in the Eastern Visayas region. Enrollment in institutions of higher learning is approximately two million, and there are currently 55 universities throughout the country, turning out nearly one million graduates annually. The preferred fields of study are: business administration (36 percent), teacher training and education (16 percent), medical and health-related programs (16 percent), and engineering and technology (15 percent). The Philippines also trains an average of 500,000 technical-vocational graduates each year. These numbers are rising, with a 16 percent increase in student enrollment between 1987 and 1992. Like other countries, Philippine educational institutions vary in quality. Some universities are excellent—rivaling any in the world—while others are considered "diploma mills" that maintain relatively low standards.

It is generally recognized that the Philippines maintains an exceptionally good education system. The government and various universities offer numerous scholarship programs that provide students from low-income families with access to higher education. The Catholic and Protestant churches sponsor schools, and there are also privately owned, nonsectarian schools at all levels. Only about 6 percent of elementary students attend private schools, but this proportion rises sharply to about 63 percent at the secondary level and approximately 85 percent at the tertiary level. About a third of the private tertiary level school enrollment is in religiously affiliated schools.

Substantially more than 10,000 foreign students

study in the Philippines, mostly in the regular system, although there are at least three major schools for international students. Ethnic Chinese Filipinos have established their own system of elementary and secondary schools; classes in the morning cover the usual Filipino curriculum and are taught by Filipino teachers, while the afternoon is devoted to Chinese studies.

Unfortunately, this excellent education system has resulted in relatively little noticeable improvement in the economy. One of the most serious problems facing the Philippine economy is the large number of students who complete college but then cannot find a job commensurate with their educational skills. At best, they join the ranks of underemployed; more often than not, they are left idle, bored, and discontented.

Training

Traditionally, Filipinos have tended to view the attainment of educational credentials as a means of escape from manual labor and poverty. Thus it has not been easy to win broad-based popular support for vocational and other training programs. Nevertheless, the government has made a valiant effort to increase such nontraditional, nonacademic training programs in all sectors. Informal education and skills training is sponsored by several government agencies and other bodies, and private companies enjoy financial and tax advantages for promoting labor training and development programs. The National Manpower and Youth Council (NMYC) provided skills training for 1.2 million people between 1987 and 1992 in such subjects as electronics, automotive mechanics, garment manufacturing, and computers. In 1993 alone the NMYC provided basic, upgrade, and livelihood skills training to 165,000 trainees, providing placement assistance and on-the-job training to 22,819 trainees and 19,153 certified skilled workers.

Other government agencies contributed as well. Between 1987 and 1992 the Department of Labor and Employment (DOLE) trained more than 10,000 people each year under its Employments Apprenticeship Program, while the Department of Education, Culture, and Sports (DECS) trained more than two million people in livelihood skills development. The DECS Strategy Plan for the period 1993 to 1998 includes equipment upgrading for both public and private technical and vocational institutions, as well as increases in basic and functional literacy through community-based literacy and continuing education programs.

Training programs extend to private enterprise. Approximately 47 percent of production firms in the Philippines provide initial training to newly recruited production workers, ranging from 72 percent of all electronics firms to 32 percent of construction companies and 35 percent of basic metals firms. However, there is room for improvement. Fewer than one-third of firms provide established workers with training to improve their job skills and performance or to facilitate moves between similar jobs; firms actually offer this type of additional training range from about half (51 percent) in electronics to 18 percent in construction and 22 percent in wood products. Only one-quarter of Philippine enterprises provide training to enable workers to upgrade their skills and status; in fact only 12 percent of employers in construction and non-metallic mineral products offer such opportunities.

Women in the Workforce

Women enjoy most but not all of the legal rights and protections accorded to men. Philippine labor law specifically prohibits discrimination on the basis of sex and, although the Philippines is a traditionally patriarchal society, women seem genuinely to have benefited from this law. Women hold more and more positions of authority in business and are generally treated the same as their male counterparts. The government seems to go out of its way to avoid any hint of discrimination in the labor force; it rarely breaks statistics up by gender, so it is difficult to determine whether women actually enjoy all employment opportunities and equal pay for equal work. However, Filipinos are clearly accustomed to Western businesswomen, and most are not at all reluctant to deal with women in any capacity.

However, in keeping with its patriarchal traditions, Philippine law mandates special considerations for female employees, including restrictions on the hours (mostly daytime) that women may be employed, special health and sanitary requirements, and mandated childcare facilities in certain circumstances. The law also provides for paid maternity leave.

Women and girls in the lower economic strata remain particularly vulnerable to exploitation by unethical operators who promise employment overseas or arranged marriages with foreign men. Some of these women end up working as prostitutes or suffering abuse at the hands of their foreign employers. The Philippine government has publicly warned Filipino women to beware of such recruiters, but it has had no notable success in curbing such activities and has not made prosecution of such offenders a priority.

CONDITIONS OF EMPLOYMENT

Labor policies relating to terms and conditions of employment are contained in the Labor Code of the Philippines. All rights and benefits granted under this Code apply alike to workers, whether agricultural or nonagricultural, except as may otherwise be provided in the Code. In general, laws governing minimum wage and employee benefits vary widely, depending on the size, type, and location of a particular business. The enforcement of hours worked and overtime pay is managed through periodic inspections by the DOLE.

Working Hours, Overtime, Holidays, and Vacations

Workweek and Hours An employee may be required to work eight hours per day or 48 hours per week at the regular rate of pay. All establishments and enterprises may operate or open for business on Sundays and holidays provided that the employees are given the required weekly rest day of not less than 24 hours following every six consecutive normal work days. The normal working week in the manufacturing sector is 44 to 48 hours; a 40-hour week is generally observed in other sectors and is mandatory in the public sector.

The overtime rate must equal 125 percent of the regular pay rate. Night shift employees (working between 10 pm and 6 am) must be paid a premium of at least 10 percent above the regular wage. An employee is paid the regular daily wage on unworked regular holidays. Employees required to work on a scheduled rest day which is also a regular holiday receive additional compensation of 130 percent of the daily work rate. On regular holidays the overtime rate is 130 percent of the regular rate of pay, except in retail and service establishments that regularly employ less than 10 workers.

The general overtime regulations do not apply to government employees, management employees, field personnel, domestic help, those providing personal services, workers paid by the piece, or workers who are members of the family of the employer and dependent on that employer for support. Health personnel are also exceptions; their regular working hours are eight hours a day, five days a week, and they must be paid for work performed on the sixth day at a rate of 130 percent of their regular wage.

Generally, government offices are open Monday through Friday from 9 am to 5 pm; banks from 9 am to 3 pm; commercial offices from 9 am to 7 or 8 pm on weekdays and 9 am to noon on Saturdays. Retail shops are open from 9 am to 7:30 pm Monday through Friday.

Vacations Employees with at least one year of service are legally entitled to five days' leave with pay each year. However, the standard practice is to give two weeks of paid vacation and allow two weeks of paid sick leave annually, with the vacation leave increasing with years of service. Most employees take their yearly vacations during the months of June through September.

HOLIDAYS

The Philippines recognizes the following regular holidays:

New Year's Day	January 1
Araw ng Kagitingan	April 9
Maundy Thursday	March or April
Good Friday	March or April
Labor Day	May 1
Independence Day	June 12
Bonifacio Day	November 30
Christmas Day	December 25
Rizal Day	December 30

The president may proclaim any other day as a special public holiday.

When a legal holiday falls on a Sunday, the following Monday is generally not considered a holiday unless the president proclaims it as such. However, this is usually done, and most collective labor agreements contain this provision as well. In addition, there are many local holidays and festivals that occur throughout the year, including a different patron saint's festival in each city and town.

Special Leave

Women who have worked at least six months within the last twelve months may obtain maternity leave with full pay for at least two weeks prior to and four weeks after their date of delivery. Maternity leave is paid only for the first four deliveries. Employers are prohibited from discriminating against women due to pregnancy or related leave.

Employment of Minors

Many Philippine children face serious problems stemming from widespread poverty and government inability to intervene effectively. Child labor and truancy are all too common. Although there are still no truancy laws in the Philippines, the government has strengthened laws to stem the practice of child labor. Current legislation does allow employment under the age of 15—but basically only in an enterprise in which only members of the employer's family are employed and provided the employment does not interfere with the minor's schooling; moreover, the minor's employment must be under the direct and sole responsibility of a parent or guardian.Other exemptions are also allowed for employment in public entertainment, such as radio, theater, or television. In any event, the parent or guardian and employer are in every case required to ensure the minors health, safety, and morals, and are to provide for the child's education or training; they must also procure a work permit from DOLE prior to allowing employment of the minor.

Children between the ages of 15 and 18 may only be employed for certain hours and periods as determined from time to time by the Secretary of Labor and Employment. They may not be employed in undertakings which are deemed to be hazardous or deleterious.

It is recognized that a significant number of children are actually employed in the informal sector of the urban economy or as field laborers in more rural areas. Although the government is largely powerless to prevent such practices, it has taken steps to educate the population regarding health hazards to children working with pesticides in agricultural areas. The most serious violations of child labor laws occur in piecework or the contracting out of embroidery or other garment-related production, much of which is exported. The government has recently shown an increased willingness to become involved in such situations and has been actively investigating allegations of child labor abuses.

Hiring Policies

Philippine enterprises enjoy wide latitude in recruitment and hiring policies, as long as they comply with laws regarding sex discrimination, and foreign and child labor. However, many collective bargaining agreements to which employers are bound require the employer to hire union members if available and require promotion based on seniority, if possible.

The hiring of workers in the Philippines is charac-terized by an emphasis on both formal and informal screening. Potential employees must obtain and submit items such as police clearances and certificates or diplomas. Informal advantages include personal acquaintances inside the company who will vouch for the applicant; those with personal links inside the company have greater chances of being hired.

Termination of Employment

Philippine law provides employees with broad protections against termination at will and without cause. Employers are prohibited from terminating a regular employee except for just cause. The ill health of an employee constitutes just cause, but in such cases the employee is entitled to a minimum separation payment of one month's salary or one month's salary for every year of service, whichever is higher.

The employer may terminate the employment of a regular employee due to: the installation of labor-saving devices; redundancy; or retrenchment to prevent losses or closing the business; or cessation of operations. The company should first notify DOLE and the employee a minimum of one month before the intended date of termination. The payment of an amount equivalent to the employee's regular salary during the month long notice period will suffice in lieu of official notice to employees. In cases of termination due to the installation of labor saving devices or redundancy, the affected workers are entitled to separation pay equivalent to at least one month's salary or one month's salary for every year of service, whichever is more. In cases of retrenchment to prevent losses or closure, or in the cases of the cessation of operations not caused by serious business losses or financial reverses, the worker must receive separation

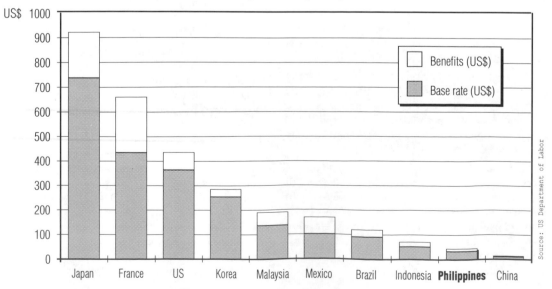

Comparative Average Weekly Wages—1992

Source: US Department of Labor

pay equal to one half of a month's pay for every year of service or one month's pay, whichever is higher.

Many employers are subject to the terms of collective bargaining agreements which provide for more stringent termination policies and larger separation payments.

Workplace Safety

Every employer must have first aid medicines and equipment in its premises, and it must take steps to train a sufficient number of employees in first aid treatment. Employers must also furnish free medical and dental care and facilities. If the work is hazardous, a part-time physician or dentist must be on the employer's premises at least two hours each workday. If the number of employees requires that a full-time physician be in attendance, the physician must remain on the employer's premises for eight hours each workday. If the work is considered nonhazardous, a physician or dentist may be kept on retainer, but need not be present on the premises.

In order to eliminate or reduce hazards in the workplace, the law provides comprehensive and mandatory occupational safety and health standards. DOLE is generally responsible for investigation and enforcement of safety laws, although some areas have special regional industrial safety inspections of establishments within their own jurisdictions. Little information is available on actual industrial and occupational health conditions, although it is recognized that workplace injuries and death are declining yearly. Multinational firms are generally considered to provide safer workplaces because they apply US, European, or Japanese standards of worker safety and health in order to meet the requirements of their insurance carriers.

WAGES AND BENEFITS

Labor Costs

Labor costs in the Philippines are relatively low. The minimum wage is low, and it represents the actual wage level in many industries; while benefits normally add up to only 30 percent of an employer's monthly salary and wage expenses. While there have been recent increases in minimum wage levels, these have often been accompanied—and more than offset—by devaluations in the peso. Even the highest minimum wage rates fall well below the estimated subsistence level for a family of six.

The average annual labor costs to the employer (including social charges and fringe benefits) is around P45,000 (US$1,800) for a low-skill production worker and P95,000 (US$3,850) for a college graduate with four years of experience. Independent surveys continue to demonstrate the competitive advantage of the Philippines, as far as both quality and cost of labor are concerned. Given its high level of education, relatively high productivity per worker, and widespread use of the English language, the Philippines offers very competitive labor costs for Western companies interested in setting up operations overseas.

Adding to the sometimes apparently arbitrary nature of wages in the Philippines is the fact that real wages have been depressed for some time, and significant wage differentials have developed across labor market segments that would appear to have similar characteristics.

Minimum Wages

Minimum wages are an important political and social institution in the Philippines, and the basic wage is effectively the minimum wage for much of the workforce. The system of minimum wages has in the past been periodically fixed by the government authorities through decrees or wage orders. Legislation enacted in 1989 transferred wage-setting authority to 15 tripartite regional wage boards, composed of representatives from employers, workers, and the governmental Wage Commission. The boards conduct ongoing studies of wage rates and other economic conditions in all industries within their regions. However, the wage-setting authority of the boards is ill-defined and has been subject to court challenge.

The current daily minimum wage rates in the Metro Manila area, implemented in April 1994, are as follows:

nonagriculture	P145.00 (US$5.60)
agriculture (plantation)	P135.00 (US$5.20)
agriculture (nonplantation)	P124.50 (US$4.80)
cottage/handicraft (more than 35 employees)	P133.00 US$5.10)
cottage/handicraft (fewer than 35 employees)	P131.00 (US$5.00)
private hospitals (more than 100 beds)	P145.00 (US$5.50)
private hospitals (less than 100 beds)	P141.00 (US$5.40)
retail/service (more than 15 workers)	P145.00 (US$5.50)
retail/service (11 to 15 workers)	P141.00 (US$5.40)
retail/service (10 or fewer workers)	P124.00 (US$4.80)

Despite labor's calls for an overhaul of the system and an across-the-board increase in the minimum wage, the government has preferred leaving responsibility for adjustments to the minimum wage with the regional boards. The boards' most recent round of wage scale reviews took place late in 1993. Acting on the basis of multiple—and often conflicting—criteria, inadequate economic data, and procedural confusions, the wage boards have produced a confusing welter of orders and exceptions. The highest minimum wage rates are in the Metro Manila area, with lower rates set for rural areas.

The wage increases were smaller and the minimum daily wage rates were lower for the other regions of the country; daily wages ranged from a low between P71.30 (US$2.74) and P114.35 (US$4.40) to a high between P93.50 (US$3.60) and P129.00 (US$4.96).

Not covered by minimum wage rates noted earlier are: household or domestic helpers, including family drivers and personal service workers; workers in some specially exempted retail-service establishments; employees of exporting firms; and the workers of distressed establishments when such establishments are specifically exempted from compliance by the Board. Special, sometimes arbitrary, and frequently changing, wage rates are set for these workers, as well as for various other classes of workers from time to time.

Some surveys indicate that 16 percent of 17,500 establishments nationwide were in violation of minimum wage standards, while in the national capital region—where enforcement is generally somewhat stricter—only about 7 percent of employers were in violation. However, observers note that compliance with minimum wage standards has been improving recently.

Social Security Benefits

It is mandatory for all private industry employees, including resident foreign employees, to be covered as of the date of employment by the Social Security System (SSS), which is funded through monthly premium contributions by the employer and employee, based on the latter's salary. Self-employed persons with a gross annual income of at least P1,800 (about US$69.26) must also be covered by the system. This system was created to provide employees and their families with protection against the economic hardships associated with disability, sickness, old age, and death. To ensure that employees obtain these benefits, employers are required to become members of the SSS from their first day of business operations. Government employees are covered by a separate but similar program, known as the Government Service Insurance System (GSIS).

Contributions are based on schedules issued by the SSS. Employee contributions are made through payroll deductions, which the employer remits monthly to the system along with its own contribu-

tion. The maximum combined monthly contribution is currently P588 (about US$22.63). The employer pays 40 percent, and the employee pays the remaining 60 percent. Employers' SSS contributions are tax deductible.

Standard SSS benefits include disability and/or retirement payments, a funeral benefit of P6,000 (US$230.88), sickness allowances, maternity leave of 45 days and maternity pay of as much as P6,000 (US$230.88), and miscellaneous loans of up to P8,000 (US$307.85).

Medical Benefits Both the SSS and the GSIS include compulsory medical coverage for all employees. Employers and employees are required to make equal monthly contributions to Medicare, a health care plan administered by the Philippine Medical Care Commission. The premium is based on each employee's salary, and it is remitted by the employer to the SSS (or GSIS); the employer contribution is a deductible expense. Medical benefits include hospitalization, medicine, surgery, and other fees. Benefits are payable directly to the hospital, physician, or pharmacy providing treatment.

Workers' Compensation Benefits The workers' compensation system provides immediate and automatic medical benefits, disability payments, burial expenses, and death benefits to workers and their dependents in the case of a work-connected injury or death. Coverage is compulsory for all employers and their employees covered by the SSS or GSIS and extends to Filipino citizens employed abroad by Philippine employers.

Yearly Bonus Philippine law requires employers to pay a thirteenth month's salary each year to all employees who have been employed at least one month. The payment is to be made by December 24th of each year. This is given in lieu of the Christmas bonus, mid-year bonus, profit sharing payments, or other cash bonuses that had been common. The law does provide that financially distressed companies may obtain an exemption from such payment in a given year.

Additional Benefits The Philippine Labor Code provides that an employer shall compensate for work-connected death or disability in addition to the benefits available from SSS or GSIS. Many employers also offer housing and educational loans, private pension plans, rice allowances, subsidized meals, transportation allowances, and life insurance benefits. Stock purchase plans have recently become a more popular benefit and means of providing additional compensation for employees. It is generally recognized that foreign personnel enjoy more generous fringe benefits than do local employees.

LABOR RELATIONS

General labor-management relations in the Philippines reflect the maturing understanding of both labor and management that economic success hinges on cooperation and the development of mutual interests. The turmoil of the immediate post-Marcos years has been replaced by a greater emphasis on dialogue involving unions, employers, and the government. Current labor relations are benefiting from clear-cut government policies, effective enforcement of labor laws, and improved management-labor relations as the parties become more accustomed to the use of collective bargaining. Fewer strikes have occurred in recent years. The number of labor stoppages has fallen by 30 percent during the past few years, while the number of productive man-days lost has been cut almost in half.

While the law is fairly clear, some labor organizations maintain that its provisions generally favor employers by giving them many avenues to declare a strike illegal and punish the strikers. The International Labor Organization (ILO) has criticized some specific provisions and claims that Philippine labor law is not in conformity with ILO Convention 87 of Freedom of Association. The labor law also bans strikes over unfair practices during the effective term of a collective bargaining agreement; this has been the subject of international criticisms as well.

The task of settling disputes and other labor issues falls to the Bureau of Labor Relations. It has the power to mediate and arbitrate intra-union disputes and to certify collective bargaining agreements. It has been quite effective in establishing compulsory arbitration mechanisms for settling unresolved issues in collective bargaining, unfair labor practice cases, money claims, and other cases arising from employer-employee disputes. The present system relies on collective bargaining as the basis of labor relations policy, but also permits government intervention in the form of conciliation, mediation, and arbitration efforts by DOLE and the Bureau of Labor Relations. The recent decline in work stoppages and man-days lost is thought to be a direct result of increased government intervention in these matters.

While DOLE has improved its labor-management settlement capabilities and made effective use of them in reducing strikes, It is placing increased emphasis on nongovernmental mechanisms for dispute resolution. Voluntary arbitration has come into greater use, and plant-level labor-management safety committees have been given the principal role in enforcing occupational safety and health rules. DOLE is also continuing to promote the establishment of labor-management cooperation programs and is setting up councils at the regional, industry, and plant levels to implement this program. More than 50,000 workers participate in these councils, all of which aim to improve labor-management communications and solve problems arising in the workplace other than those directly covered by collective bargaining agreements.

Unions and the Labor Movement

All workers, including employees of government corporations and most foreign employees but excluding managerial employees, have the right to organize, form, join, or assist labor organizations for purposes of collective bargaining. Employers are prohibited from terminating or otherwise discriminating against employees who exercise this right. Nonetheless, organized labor in the Philippines was slow to get going and remains relatively weak. Most union activity is in the manufacturing sector, with the degree of unionization varying by industry, from about 9 percent in the construction industry to more than 58 percent in basic metals. Total trade union membership in the Philippines as of October 1993 was just over three million workers organized in 5,757 active unions and three major federations. Approximately 656,000 workers were covered by 4,785 existing collective bargaining agreements.

The Trade Union Congress of the Philippines (TUCP) is the largest federation and represents workers from all sectors. Formed in 1974, it was designated the official labor center of the Philippines by the Marcos government. It still works closely with the government to resolve issues without resorting to work stoppages or other economic disruptions. The Kilusang Mayo Uno (KMU, or May 1st Movement), on the other hand, has a history of violent militancy in pressing for its members' demands. In 1980 the KMU brought together nine broadly based, more ideologically oriented unions. It calls for the formation of worker solidarity movements and advocates a nationalist oriented alternative to the prevailing economic and social policies of the government. During the late 1980s and early 1990s the Philippines was plagued by violent union activity involving injuries and deaths on both the government and labor sides. The level of labor unrest and violence has subsided noticeably as the economy and the political sector have stabilized. Today, the unions seem to understand that only by working with management and the government will the Philippines rid itself of its chronic low wages, high unemployment, and oversupply of labor.

Nevertheless, many foreign investors remain wary of the Philippine labor situation, despite the trend toward better understanding between labor and management. However, the hard-line leftist militant KMU has been losing its influence and credibility. This federation remains vocal and continues to be a major player in worker relations. Increasingly it finds itself at odds with other federations—the moderate TUCP or the Federation of Free Farmers, which represents agricultural workers—on important labor issues. Nevertheless, when the federations are able to unite on an issue, they are usually successful in forcing the government to treat labor's demands seriously.

In the international sphere, the Asian-American Free Labor Institute (AAFLI) of the American Federation of Labor–Congress of International Organizations (AFL-CIO) maintains a local office with a resident US representative and carries out an extensive program of technical assistance for TUCP. In addition to its activities in support of the service departments of TUCP, AAFLI has recently completed successful projects to establish Workers Legal Counseling Centers, which assist unions and workers in pursuing work-related financial claims and in the training of labor arbitrators, labor advocates, and grievance officers.

Workers' Rights

Right of Association The right of workers, including public employees, to form and join trade unions is assured by the Philippine constitution and subsidiary legislation and is freely practiced without formal government interference. Trade unions and trade union federations are largely independent of the government and of political parties. Unions have—and freely exercise—the right to form or join federations and to affiliate with international trade union organizations. Strikes in the private sector are legal, subject to certain procedural restrictions found in the Labor Code and imposed under emergency executive powers.

Restrictions include the obligation to provide notice, respect for mandatory cooling-off periods, and the need to obtain majority approval before calling a strike. The law also stipulates that all means of reconciliation must have been exhausted prior to declaration of a strike and that the strike issue has to be relevant to the labor contract or the law.

Right to Organize and Bargain Collectively Except for government employees, who are subject to certain restrictions, workers have the right to organize and bargain collectively guaranteed by law. The number of collective bargaining agreements in force has increased in recent years, as have the number of registered unions. Dismissal of a union official or worker attempting to organize a union is considered an unfair labor practice under Philippine law. Nevertheless, employers sometimes attempt to intimidate workers by threats of firings or closure. Allegations of intimidation and discrimination in connection with union activities are grounds for review by the National Labor Relations Commission (NLRC) as possible unfair labor practices. The NLRC and the National Conciliation and Mediation Board (NCMB) provide DOLE with quasi-judicial mechanisms for hearing and adjudicating workers' claims. The process has been slow, but no slower than other parts of the courts and the bureaucracy.

Labor law and practices are uniform throughout the country, including the Export Processing Zones (EPZs). The rate of unionization and the number of collective bargaining agreements concluded in most EPZs are similar to those in the rest of the country, although the proportions to date are much lower in the newer EPZs. However, some labor sources have complained that antiunion discrimination does exist in the EPZs, and the KMU has charged that one plant was closed after union activity took place there, but was later reopened under a different name to hire nonunion employees.

Prohibition of Compulsory or Forced Labor The Philippines has ratified the International Labor Organization (ILO) Convention 105, which prohibits forced labor and has the force of law in the country. However, the ILO has criticized provisions in the law that punish workers convicted for participation in illegal strikes with an obligation to perform labor while in prison. There have been no other reports of forced labor being practiced in the country.

Business Law

CONTENTS

THE PHILIPPINE LEGAL SYSTEM

INTRODUCTION

During the late 1970s and early 1980s Philippine business law incorporated numerous protective measures designed to insulate Philippine business from foreign competition. By the end of this period, Philippine regulatory agencies had evolved into substantial bureaucracies, sometimes requiring a foreign trader or investor to move through various agencies and comply with several layers of rules and regulations to complete a transaction. In the past decade the Philippine government has begun to unravel the country's often complex protective laws and regulations. The laws are changing rapidly, both in favor of foreign participation within the country and in promotion of more active Philippine participation in global markets.

In the May 1995 congressional elections, Filipinos endorsed the administration's pro-business, economic development platform designed to ease the entry of foreign capital into Philippine markets. The government has instituted—and continues to pursue—numerous legal reforms to remove or reduce bureaucratic obstacles that can delay business transactions and that encourage foreign investment in the Philippines. The atmosphere of reform is indeed promising, although foreign businesspeople should keep in mind that the opening Philippine economy is still a work in progress. All foreign businesses or investors must carefully investigate the most current legal and procedural requirements that apply to their particular business activities before commencing a transaction.

The information in this chapter is intended to familiarize the reader with important issues in Philippine commercial law, but it should not be used to

This introduction is based in part on interviews with Hector M. de Leon, Jr., of the Makati law office of SyCip Salazar Hernandez & Gatmaitan; Jose V.E. Jimenez of the Makati law office of Bengzon Narciso Cudala Pecson Bengson & Jimenez; and Cynthia D. Nuval-Ambrosio at the Makati law office of Villaraza & Cruz.

LEGAL GLOSSARY

acceptance An unconditional assent to an offer or one conditioned on minor changes that do not affect material terms of the offer. *See* counteroffer, offer.

agency The relationship between an agent and a principal. The agent represents and acts on behalf of the principal, who instructs and authorizes the agent to act.

attachment A legal process for seizing property before a judgment in order to secure the payment of damages if awarded; may be sought before or during the court action. Also referred to as sequestration. Example: a party who claims damages for breach of contract may request that a court issue an order freezing all transfers of specific property owned by the breaching party pending resolution of the dispute.

authentication The act of conferring legal authenticity on a written document, typically made by a notary public, who attests and certifies that the document is in proper legal form and that it is executed by a person identified as having authority to do so.

bailment A delivery of personal property by one person (the bailor) to another (the bailee) pursuant to a contract that requires the bailee to do something with the property—such as repair or transport it—and afterwards redeliver it to the bailor or otherwise dispose of it in accordance with the bailor's instructions. Example: a bailment arises when a seller delivers goods to a shipping company with instructions to transport them to a buyer at a certain destination.

capacity to contract Legal competency to make a contract. A party has capacity to contract if that party has attained the age required by law and has the mental ability to understand the nature of contract obligations.

chattel An item of personal property.

counteroffer A reply to an offer that materially alters the terms of the offer. Example: a seller who accepts a buyer's offer on condition that the goods will be made of a different material has made a counteroffer.

domicile The place where a party is living or located with no definite, present intention of moving away.

good faith A legal standard implying honesty in the conduct or transaction at issue, honesty of intention, or freedom from an intention to defraud, depending on the circumstances.

injunction A court order that either requires a party to do a specific act or prohibits that party from doing an act. Injunctions can be granted on a permanent or temporary basis, pending resolution of a dispute.

joint and several liability The liability of two or more persons who are responsible together and individually, allowing the harmed person to sue any or all of the wrongdoers.

juridical act An action intended to have, and capable of having, a legal effect, such as the creation, termination, or modification of a legal right. Example: The signing of a power of attorney is a juridical act because it gives legal authority to an agent.

juridical person An individual or entity recognized under law as having legal rights and obligations. Example: limited liability companies, corporations, and partnerships are entities recognized as juridical persons.

negligence A failure to act with reasonable care, possibly resulting in legal liability for harm to others.

offer A proposal that is made to a specific individual or entity to enter into a contract. The proposal must contain definite terms and must indicate the offeror's intent to be bound by an acceptance. Example: a buyer's order to purchase designated goods on certain delivery and payment terms is an offer. *See* acceptance, counteroffer.

pledge A bailment or delivery of property to a creditor to secure a debt. Also, a recorded security interest in a chattel.

power of attorney A written document by which one individual or entity (the principal) authorizes another individual or entity (the agent) to perform stated acts on the principal's behalf. Example: a principal may execute a special power of attorney (authorizing an agent to sign a specific contract) or a general power of attorney (authorizing an agent to sign all contracts for the principal).

reasonable care The level of care that an ordinary, prudent person would be expected to exercise under the same circumstances.

warranty An affirmation of fact regarding the characteristics, safety, or suitability of a product.

replace legal advice from a licensed attorney. Foreign investors should always review their business activities with attorneys who are familiar with international transactions, Philippine laws and regulations, and the laws of their own countries. (Refer to the "Important Addresses" chapter, beginning on page 297, for a list of law offices in the Philippines.)

BASIS OF THE LEGAL SYSTEM

From the late 1500s until its initial independence as a republic following the Spanish-American War in 1898, the Philippines was governed by Spain. From 1898 until the early 1940s, the country was a colony of the US. Consistent with these antecedents, Philippine law is a combination: a common law system modeled primarily on US law and a civil law system based largely on Spanish law. Judicial decisions may be based either on precedent set by past decisions (as under the US system) or on provisions codified in civil codes (as under the Spanish system). The Code of Commerce of Spain is technically still in effect in the Philippines, but many of its provisions have been superseded or altered by specific legislation and by the Philippine Civil Code, which became effective in 1950. Other statutes—for example, all legislation that pertains to the insurance industry—resemble US federal and state laws. In the course of litigation, Philippine lawyers often cite US case law, to which Philippine courts accord persuasive effect.

The US influence on Philippine law is most apparent in the Philippine constitution, which was ratified in 1987. It contains a bill of rights patterned after the one adopted in the US and establishes a tripartite government with powers delegated between executive, legislative, and judicial branches.

STRUCTURE OF GOVERNMENT AND LAWS

The Philippines is a republic consisting of 72 provinces and 61 chartered cities, including Manila, the country's capital. A president is elected by the direct vote of Philippine citizens and holds executive power. A bicameral legislature, comprised of a Senate with 24 members and a House of Representatives with as many as 200 elected members plus 50 members appointed by the president, exercises legislative powers. The country's highest court is the Supreme Court, comprised of a Chief Justice and 14 associate justices, all of whom are appointed by the president. The Supreme Court exercises powers of judicial review, meaning it may rule on the constitutionality of congressional legislation or acts of the executive. Lower courts include a Court of Appeals, regional trial courts, various municipal and tax courts, and the Sandiganbayan, which

handles some serious criminal cases and tries government employees charged with violations of anticorruption legislation. There are also specialized courts, such as the Shari'a District Courts which generally have original jurisdiction over cases relating to Muslims in the Philippines.

Historically, the executive branch of the government has been the strongest of the three branches of government and still tends to be the dominant branch. Through the president's cabinet, the executive oversees an extensive administration employing almost 3 million Philippine citizens. Nevertheless, the recent trend has been toward greater empowerment of congress and the judiciary. The 1987 Philippine constitution contains many clauses intended to prevent autocratic abuses of power by the Philippine executive.

The provinces have their own governors and the cities have their own mayors, but much significant government action still takes place at the national level.

In the international arena, the Philippines is a party to numerous bilateral and multilateral treaties and conventions. Many of these agreements accord special privileges and may protect the business and personal rights of foreign traders and investors doing business in the Philippines. They also serve as models and incentives for the revision of Philippine laws, and thus tend to indicate the type and direction of future changes that may be expected in domestic laws. (*See* the "Treaties" entry in the law digest, on page 230.)

LAWS GOVERNING BUSINESS

Foreign Investment and Companies The Philippine constitution, the 1991 Foreign Investments Act, the 1987 Omnibus Investments Code, various Investment Incentive Acts, and related regulations and lists promulgated by several government agencies—such as the Board of Investments (BOI), the Securities and Exchange Commission (SEC), the Philippine Economic Zone Authority (PEZA), the Department of Trade and Industry (DTI), and the Bangko Sentral ng Pilipinas (BSP, the central bank)—establish the legal framework for foreign investment. As noted later in this discussion, foreign investors who wish to own Philippine entities or property must take careful note of lists that prohibit their involvement in many lines of business or that encourage their involvement in other designated "pioneer" industries favored by the government.

Time limits and currency requirements for remittance of profits and repatriation of investments are detailed in laws and rules related to the BSP, codified in Philippine Republic Acts (key provisions include Republic Acts 265, 529, and 7653), the

THE INTERNATIONAL TRANSACTION: BASICS OF A ONE-TIME SALE

When dealing internationally, you must consider the business practices and legal requirements of the country where the other party to your contract is located. Parties generally have the freedom to agree to any contract terms that they desire, but the laws of your country or the other country may require a written contract. In some transactions, the laws may even specify all or some of the contract terms. Whether a contract term is valid in a particular country is mainly of concern in case you have to seek enforcement. Otherwise, you have fairly broad flexibility in negotiating contract provisions. However, you should always be certain to come to a definite understanding with the other party on four basic issues: the goods (quantity, type, and quality); the time of delivery; the price; and the time and means of payment.

For a small, one-time sale, an invoice or a simple contract may be acceptable. For a more involved business transaction or an ongoing relationship, a formal written contract is preferable in order to define clearly the rights, responsibilities, and remedies of all parties. Contracts that involve capital goods, high credit risks, or industrial or intellectual property rights will require special protective clauses. In preparing such contracts, it is essential to obtain legal advice from a professional who is familiar with the laws and practices of both countries involved.

For a simple, one-time deal, you need to consider at least the following clauses:

Contract Date

Specify the date when the contract is signed. This date is particularly important if payment or delivery times are fixed in reference to it—for example, "shipment within 30 days of the contract date."

Identification of Parties

Name the parties, describe their relation to each other, and designate any persons who are authorized to act for each party. The persons designated should also be the ones who sign the contract. If a person is signing on behalf of a company, you should be certain of that person's authority—request a written statement or corporate resolution if you are uncertain.

Goods

Description Describe the type and quality of the goods. You may simply indicate a model number, or you may have to attach detailed lists, plans, drawings, or other specifications. This clause should be clear enough that both parties fully understand the specifications and have no discretion in interpreting them.

Quantity Specify the number of units, or other measure of quantity, of the goods. If the goods are measured by weight, you should specify net weight, dry weight, or drained weight. If the goods are prepackaged and are subject to weight restrictions in the end market, you may want to ensure that the seller will provide goods packaged to comply with those restrictions.

Price Indicate the price per unit or other measure, such as per pound or ton, and the extended price.

Packaging Arrangements

Set forth packaging specifications, especially for goods that could be damaged in transit. At a minimum, this provision should require the seller to package the goods in such a way as to withstand transportation. If special packaging requirements are necessary to meet consumer and product liability standards in the end market, you should specify them also.

Transportation Arrangements

Carrier Name a preferred carrier for transporting the goods. You should designate a particular carrier if, for example, a carrier offers you special pricing or is better able than others to transport the product.

Storage Specify any particular requirements for storing the goods before or during shipment, such as security arrangements, special climate demands, and weather protection needs.

Notice Provisions Require the seller to notify the buyer when the goods are ready for delivery or pickup, particularly if the goods are perishable or fluctuate in value. If your transaction is time-sensitive, you could even provide for several notices to allow the buyer to track the goods and take steps to minimize damages if delivery is delayed.

Shipping Time State the exact date for shipping or provide for shipment within a reasonable time from the contract date. If this clause is included and the seller fails to ship on time, the buyer may claim a right to cancel the contract, even if the goods have been shipped, provided that the buyer has not yet accepted delivery.

Costs and Charges

Specify which party is to pay any additional costs and charges related to the sale.

Duties and Taxes Designate the party that will be

responsible for import, export, and other fees and taxes and for obtaining all required licenses. For example, a party may be made responsible for paying the duties, taxes, and charges imposed by that party's own country, since that party is best situated to know the legal requirements of that country.

Insurance Costs Identify the party that will pay the costs of insuring the goods in transit. This is a critical provision because the party responsible bears the risk if the goods are lost during transit. A seller is typically responsible for insurance until title to the goods passes to the buyer, at which time the buyer becomes responsible for insurance or becomes the named beneficiary under the seller's insurance policy.

Handling and Transport Specify which party will pay shipping, handling, packaging, security, and any other costs related to transportation, and enumerate those costs.

Terms Defined Contracts for the sale of goods most commonly use Incoterms—as defined by the International Chamber of Commerce in Paris—to assign responsibility for the risks and cost of transport. (Refer to the "International Payments" chapter, beginning on page 253, for explanations of the Incoterms.)

Insurance or Risk of Loss Protection

Specify the insurance required, the beneficiary of the policy, the party who will obtain the insurance, and the date by which it will have been obtained.

Payment Provisions

In a one-time transaction, the seller will typically seek the most secure form of payment before committing to shipment, while a buyer will want the goods cleared through customs and delivered in satisfactory condition before remitting full payment. If payments cannot be made in advance, parties most often agree to use documentary credits. (Refer to the "International Payments" chapter for an explanation of such payments.)

Method of Payment State the means by which payment will be tendered—for example, delivery of a documentary letter of credit or documents against payment; prepayment in cash or traveler's checks; or credit for a specified number of days.

Medium of Exchange Designate the currency to be used—for example, Philippine pesos, the currency of the other party's country, or the currency of a third country.

Exchange Rate Specify a fixed exchange rate for the price stated in the contract. You may use this clause to lock in a specific price and ensure against fluctuating currency values.

Import Documentation

Designate the documents for exporting and importing that each party will be responsible for obtaining, completing, and presenting to customs. Shipment of the goods, and even the contract itself, may be made contingent upon a party's having obtained in advance the proper licenses, inspection certificates, and other authorizations. (Refer to the chapters "Import Policies & Procedures" and "Export Policies & Procedures" for further discussion of these requirements.)

Inspection Rights

If the buyer will be given a right to inspect the goods before taking delivery, specify the party who will make the inspection—for example, the buyer, a third party, or a licensed inspector; the location where the inspection will occur—for example, at the seller's plant, the buyer's warehouse, or a receiving dock; the time at which the inspection will occur; the presentation of a certified document of inspection, if needed; and any requirements related to the return of nonconforming goods, such as payment of return freight charges by the seller.

Warranty Provisions

Limit or extend any implied warranties, and define any express warranties on property fitness and quality. The contract may, for example, state that the seller warrants that the goods are of merchantable quality, are fit for any purpose for which they would ordinarily be used, or are fit for a particular purpose requested by the buyer. The seller may also warrant that the goods will be of the same quality as any sample or model that the seller has furnished as representative of the goods. Finally, the seller may warrant that the goods will be packaged in a specific way or in a way that will adequately preserve and protect the goods.

Indemnity

Agree that one party will hold the other harmless from damages that arise from specific causes, such as the design or manufacture of a product.

Enforcement and Remedies

Timely Performance Stipulate that timely performance of the contract is essential. In the US, inclusion of this clause allows a party to claim breach merely because the other party fails to perform within the time prescribed in the contract. Although common in US

THE INTERNATIONAL TRANSACTION: BASICS OF A ONE-TIME SALE (cont'd)

contracts, a clause of this type is considered less important in other countries.

Modification Require the parties to make all changes to the contract in advance and in a signed written modification.

Cancellation State the reasons for which either party may cancel the contract and the notice required for cancellation.

Contingencies Specify any events that must occur before a party is obligated to perform the contract. For example, you may agree that the seller has no duty to ship goods until the buyer forwards documents that secure the payment for the goods.

Governing Law Choose the law of a specific jurisdiction to control any interpretation of the contract terms. The law that you choose will usually affect where you can sue or enforce a judgment and what rules and procedures will be applied.

Choice of Forum Identify the place where a dispute may be settled—for example, the country of origin of the goods, the country of destination, or a third country that is convenient to both parties.

Arbitration Provisions Although not yet a common remedy in the Philippines, arbitration can be used as an alternative to litigation for the resolution of disputes that arise. You should agree to arbitrate only if you seriously intend to settle disputes in this way. If you agree to arbitrate

but instead file suit, the court is likely to uphold the arbitration clause and force you to settle your dispute as initially agreed in the contract. This means you will have to arbitrate before you can have your day in court.

An arbitration clause should specify whether arbitration is binding or nonbinding on the parties; the country where arbitration will be conducted (which should be a country that has adopted the UN Convention on Recognition and Enforcement of Foreign Awards or a similar convention); the procedure for enforcement of an award; the rules governing the arbitration, such as the UN Commission on International Trade Law Model Rules; the institute that will administer the arbitration, such as the International Chamber of Commerce (Paris); the law that will govern procedural issues or the merits of the dispute; any limitations on the selection of arbitrators (for example, a national of a disputing party may be excluded from being an arbitrator); the qualifications or expertise of the arbitrators; the language in which the arbitration will be conducted; and the availability of translations and translators if needed.

Severability Provide that individual clauses can be removed from the contract without affecting the validity of the contract as a whole. This clause is important because it provides that, if one clause is declared invalid and unenforceable for any reason, the rest of the contract remains in force.

General Banking Act (Republic Act 337), and BSP regulations. (Refer to the "Currency & Foreign Exchange" chapter, beginning on page 243, for further information.)

If foreign companies wish to establish branches, subsidiaries, representative offices, or regional headquarters in the Philippines, they must adhere to the strictures of the Corporation Code of the Philippines, the Foreign Investments Act, and all applicable SEC rules and regulations. (Refer to the "Business Entities & Formation" chapter, beginning on page 185, for more information.)

Foreign persons who travel to the Philippines on business must comply with immigration laws codified in various Philippine Immigration Acts, Investment Incentive Acts, and the Alien Registration Act. Provisions of these laws are found in Philippine Commonwealth Acts 613 and 673 and Republic Act 562. (Refer to the "Business Travel" chapter, beginning on page 135, for more information.)

Local Companies The Corporation Code of the Philippines and attendant SEC regulations generally govern the formation and operation of Philippine corporations. These laws and rules establish the requirements and formalities with respect to applying for government approval and registration of a corporation. They also govern such matters as investor liability, company management, issuance of securities, and reporting and audit requirements. The regulatory and implementing authority of concerned government agencies—including the SEC, BOI, DTI, and PEZA—is described in the Corporation Code and related legislation.

Some types of companies are governed by industry-specific legislation, such as the Insurance Code of 1978 (modeled largely on California insurance law). Mining and banking are also covered by specific laws.

Companies that employ Philippine workers must comply with Philippine labor law, the provisions of which are dispersed throughout various Republic Acts, including Republic Act 6715 and 7610, and various Presidential decrees (including Presidential Decree 850, 442, 1519, and 1368). Foreign investors should be aware that Philippine labor law provides a comprehensive system of protections and benefits for Philippine workers and should carefully consult the relevant laws before hiring Filipino workers. (Refer to the "Labor" chapter, beginning on page 197, for more information.)

Commercial Activities The legal requirements of most ordinary business transactions are detailed in contract, agency, and remedy laws found in the Civil Code and Code of Commerce (also referred to as the Commercial Code). In many instances the rules of the Code of Commerce, which was inherited from Spain in 1898, have been superseded by more modern laws in the Civil Code. Many aspects of contract and sales law are further governed by case law that has interpreted the codified provisions. Particular types of transactions, such as contracts to which the Philippine government is a party or contracts involving technology transfer, may be covered by special Philippine legislation.

Most paper aspects of common financial transactions are governed by the Negotiable Instruments Law adopted by the Philippines.

The Philippine Statute of Frauds requires that documents representing specific types of contracts comply with certain formalities. Additional documentary requirements for transactions are listed in Civil and Commercial Code rules that govern acknowledgments, notarization, public records, and the like. The statutes sometimes contain forms to illustrate the legal format for documents.

Legal requirements for sales and mortgages of real property in the Philippines are covered in miscellaneous legislation, including Republic Act 4882, 2747, 2938, and 3135. Under a Land Registration Act, owners of property must register their titles and mortgages with the Registry of Deeds assigned to the relevant Philippine province. The Philippine constitution prohibits foreign entities from buying Philippine land, although a business entity with up to 40 percent foreign ownership is allowed to buy land. If land is leased, the lessor and lessee must observe landlord-tenant law, and the lease may be recorded in the Registry of Property.

Sales of personal property must comply with legal requirements in the Civil and Commercial Code, which apportions risks of loss between buyer and seller and details remedies available to either party on default of the other. Philippine law recognizes conditional sales and allows vendors to take security interests in goods sold. Philippine law also recognizes a pledge mechanism that allows a creditor to take a possessory interest in almost any type of movable property owned by a debtor.

Remedies Legal remedies for aggrieved creditors and unpaid sellers of property are contained in the Civil and Commercial Code, and related acts establish procedures for foreclosures on real property and chattel mortgages. The Philippine Rules of Court describe the procedure for executing a judgment. Debtors who are declared insolvent, whether voluntarily or involuntarily, must wind up their affairs in accord with the Insolvency Law of the Philippines, which is modeled after both the Spanish Commercial Code and California bankruptcy law.

Prescription laws in the Civil Code establish time periods within which actions must be brought to avoid loss of legal rights.

Restraint of Trade Article 186 of the Philippine Revised Penal Code deals with antitrust issues. It prohibits monopolies and other combinations or conspiracies in restraint of trade. Penalties for violation of the law include forfeiture of property by any entity involved in an unlawful combination and personal criminal liability for principals of any entity found to be in willful violation of the law.

Environmental Controls Environmental regulation is formulated and implemented by the Philippine Department of Environment and Natural Resources (DENR). The DENR requires that environmentally critical businesses periodically obtain Environmental Compliance Certificates and file environmental impact statements before conducting any business with the potential to degrade the environment. According to some observers, compliance with environmental regulations by some Philippine industries has been less than exemplary. Several organizations in the country are spearheading drives to publicize and investigate environmental issues and abuses, and the country is under international pressure in this area as well. Tougher government enforcement can be expected, and a business that establishes a facility in the Philippines is likely to be affected by stricter compliance measures.

Intellectual and Industrial Property Philippine intellectual property statutes—including copyright, patent, and trademark acts—are largely compatible with international norms as written. The Philippines is also a party to many international conventions on intellectual property (*see* "Practical Applications" on page 216 for an extended discussion). Under Presidential Decree 49, copyrights may be registered for most literary and artistic works, as well as computer programs and scientific models and designs. Depending of the material, registration affords protection extending fro more than 50 years. The Philippine Bureau of Patents, Trademarks, and Technology Transfer (BPTTT) oversees the registration of marks and inventions. The trademark statutes provide protection based on first use in the Philippines of a mark, while the patent laws protect the creation and use of a "new and useful" product, design, or invention, or the improvement of any of these.

The Rules of Procedure of the Philippine Technology Transfer Registry, a division within the BPTT, set legal requirements for technology transfer contracts between foreign businesses and Philippine entities.

Although no codified laws cover trade secrets, general provisions of the Civil Code and Philippine criminal statutes protect these secrets and other similar confidential information.

GEOGRAPHICAL SCOPE OF COUNTRY LAWS

The digest of laws in this chapter describes the national laws of the Philippines, which apply in the Philippine provinces and chartered cities. However, there may be differences in procedure between the Regional Trial Courts and Municipal or Metropolitan Courts, which have different and limited jurisdiction. Also, provinces, cities and municipalities may enact their own ordinances which supplement national laws. Thus foreign investors or businesses should always check the laws of the particular provinces where they plan to do business.

PRACTICAL APPLICATIONS

Significant Legal Considerations Probably the most significant legal issues facing a foreign investor or business arise from Philippine laws restricting the extent of foreign ownership in Philippine business entities and prohibiting or limiting the involvement of foreign investors in various types of industries. Many of these restrictions are slowly disappearing as the Philippines opens its doors to the international business community. Nevertheless, quite a few still appear in the Philippine constitution and in key legislation—such as the 1991 Foreign Investments Act and the 1987 Omnibus Investments Code. Moreover, application of the law may be relaxed somewhat with regard to foreign companies that offer to bring substantial capital into the Philippines, stimulate Philippine exports, or further the expansion of designated "pioneer" industries. A foreign investor must carefully consult these laws and related regulations, a task that requires the expertise of a Philippine lawyer. For a detailed discussion of these requirements, refer to the "Foreign Investment" chapter, beginning on page 43.

Foreign investors should be ready to deal with an extensive Philippine administration, which handles registration of business transactions, accepts and registers required deposits of foreign capital, licenses business entities, and performs many quasi-legislative and quasi-judicial functions in promulgating and applying rules and regulations that supplement and implement Philippine business law. These might include the BSP (which administers foreign exchange and currency law), the Bureau of Internal Revenue (which administers tax laws and regulations), the Bureau of Customs (which oversees tariffs and customs laws and regulations), and the SEC (which supervises nearly all business entities licensed to operate in the Philippines). Some foreign businesses have reported that the often unclear government registration, approval, and reporting regulations are made even more confusing by inconsistent agency practices. Rules are not always applied systematically and exemptions are sometimes granted arbitrarily. The idiosyncrasies of the system further recommend the services of a Philippine attorney familiar with the agencies involved.

A foreign business that intends to transfer technology to a person or entity in the Philippines must comply with detailed laws and regulations limiting the terms of technology transfer contracts. These laws were recently amended to bring Philippine technology transfer standards in closer accord with international norms. Nevertheless, such agreements are still subject to evaluation and approval by the BPTT. The standards for this evaluation are relatively vague: the BPTTT is authorized to consider the extent to which the agreement will benefit the Philippine parties and the nation's economy and the "reasonableness" of the royalties payable to the foreign business. The BPTTT also prohibits foreign parties from contracting for certain legal protections against liability in the Philippines. As a result of intrusive laws and regulations, the volume of technology transfer into the Philippines remains relatively low. (Refer to the "Business Entities & Formation" for discussion of technology transfer arrangements.)

Role of Legal Counsel Foreign investors transacting business in the Philippines can turn to nearly 38,000 Philippine lawyers for a wide variety of services, including assistance and advice in the negotiation of the terms of transactions, organization and management of business entities, negotiation and review of contracts, preparation and execution of legal instruments, procurance of government licenses and permits, negotiation of settlements, and litigation, should a business dispute move beyond amicable resolution. Given the legal system's derivation from both civil and common law systems, Philippine lawyers tend to work easily with foreign businesses from countries that apply either type of law.

THE US FOREIGN CORRUPT PRACTICES ACT

US business owners are subject to the Foreign Corrupt Practices Act (FCPA). The stiff penalties imposed under this act may make a US business owner reluctant to deal with a foreign company if there is even a hint of corrupt practice related to the transaction. The FCPA makes it unlawful for any US citizen or firm (or any person who acts on behalf of a US citizen or firm) to use a means of US interstate commerce (examples: mail, telephone, telegram, or electronic mail) to offer, pay, transfer, promise to pay or transfer, or authorize a payment, transfer, or promise of money or anything of value to any foreign appointed or elected official, foreign political party, or candidate for a foreign political office for a corrupt purpose (that is, to influence a discretionary act or decision of the official) for the purpose of obtaining or retaining business.

It is also unlawful for a US business owner to make such an offer, promise, payment, or transfer to any person if the US business owner knows, or has reason to know, that the person will give, offer, or promise directly or indirectly all or part of the payment to a foreign government official, political party, or candidate. For purposes of the FCPA, the term "knowledge" means both "actual knowledge" (the business owner in fact knew that the offer, payment, or transfer was included in the trans-action) and "implied knowledge" (the business owner should have known from the facts and circumstances of a transaction that the agent paid a bribe, but failed to carry out a reasonable investigation into the transaction). A business owner should make a reasonable investigation into the transaction, for example, if the sales represen-tative requests a higher commission on a particular deal for no apparent reason, if the buyer is a foreign government, if the product has a military use, or if the buyer's country is one in which bribes are considered customary in business relationships.

Legal Payments

The provisions of the FCPA do not prohibit payments made to facilitate routine government action. A facilitating payment is one made in connection with an action that a foreign official must perform as part of the job. In comparison, a corrupt payment is made to influence an official's discretionary decision. For example, payments would not generally be considered corrupt if made to cover an official's overtime if such overtime is necessary to expedite the processing of export documentation for a legal shipment of merchandise or to cover the expense of additional crew to handle a shipment.

A person charged with violating FCPA provisions may assert as a defense that the payment was lawful under the written laws and regulations of the foreign country and therefore was not for a corrupt purpose. Alternatively, a person may contend that the payment was associated with demonstrating a product or performing a preexisting contractual obligation and therefore was not for obtaining or retaining business.

Enforcing Agencies and Penalties

Criminal Proceedings The US Department of Justice (DOJ) prosecutes criminal proceedings for FCPA violations. Firms are subject to fines of up to US$2 million. Officers, directors, employees, agents, and stockholders are subject to fines of up to US$100,000, imprisonment for up to five years, or both.

A US business owner may also be charged under other federal criminal laws. On conviction, the owner may be liable for one of the following: (1) a fine of up to US$250,000; or (2) if the owner derived pecuniary gain from the offense or caused a pecuniary loss to another person, a fine of up to twice the amount of the gross gain or loss.

Civil Proceedings Two agencies are responsible for enforcing the civil provisions of the FCPA: the DOJ handles actions against domestic concerns, and the Securities and Exchange Commission (SEC) files actions against issuers. Civil fines of up to US$100,000 may be imposed on a firm, or on any officer, director, employee, agent, or stockholder acting for a firm. In addition, the appropriate government agency may seek an injunction against a person or firm that has violated or is about to violate FCPA provisions.

Conduct that constitutes a violation of FCPA provi-sions may also give rise to a cause of action under the federal Racketeer-Influenced and Corrupt Organizations Act (RICO), as well as under similar state statutes if such exist in a state with jurisdiction over the US business.

Administrative Penalties A person or firm that is held to have violated any FCPA provisions may be barred from doing business with the US government. Indictment alone may result in suspension of the right to do business with the government.

Philippine businesses routinely consult attorneys whenever they enter contracts or transactions involving significant funds or obligations, and Philippine citizens generally trust and esteem business lawyers. Only Philippine lawyers—who must be Philippine citizens, must complete a bachelor's degree in law, and must pass a bar examination—can practice before Philippine courts. Foreign attorneys can appear before the BPTT, not as legal counsel, but in their individual capacity, or as a member of a firm, or as an officer or authorized representative of a corporation or association. Non-Philippine lawyers cannot form partnerships with Philippine lawyers. Thus foreign businesses must retain Philippine lawyers to deal with most matters related to Philippine law. A non-Philippine attorney may render advice on the international aspects of commercial transactions and investments, and foreign attorneys can usually refer their clients to Philippine lawyers as needed.

The majority of Philippine lawyers familiar with international transactions are located in Manila. Firms can be contacted through referrals from foreign law firms and the Philippine listings in Martindale-Hubbell's *International Lawyers,* as well as through embassies and chambers of commerce.

Contracts With footholds in both civil and common law heritages, Philippine businesses and lawyers are familiar with both the traditional civil law contract (typically short, containing few detailed clauses, and instead referring to code provisions for specifics), and the common law contract (often elaborate, having detailed clauses expressly apportioning all of the parties' rights and obligations, and providing for all contingencies however remote). Because of the extensive US presence and involvement in Philippine affairs during the past century, Philippine businesses are perhaps most familiar with the latter type of document. However, the Philippine Civil Code, which accords the force of law to contracts and establishes standard remedies for their breach, is assumed as a backdrop to any continuing contractual relationship.

Each party to a business contract should retain separate legal counsel. Philippine lawyers may refuse to advise both parties to a contract so as to avoid the appearance of a conflict of interest.

Role of Notaries The notarial profession is quite important in the Philippines, where the commercial community emphasizes the formalities of documentation. All documents that constitute "public instruments"—such as a deed of sale of real property—are notarized. Also, notarization of a private document converts it into a public document and renders it admissible in court without further proof of authenticity. Notarization means that the notary attests to the personal appearance of the parties, to the identification of the parties present as the same persons who executed the document being notarized, and to the acknowledgment by each party present that the document was executed freely and voluntarily.

Notaries typically have law degrees and are appointed to two-year terms by Regional Trial Judges. A notary's authority usually only extends throughout a single Philippine province. While notaries ensure that documents are appropriately formalized, registered, and archived, they generally do not advise parties on the substantive aspects of business transactions.

Dispute Resolution Litigation in Philippine courts is not an optimal method of dispute resolution because delays and docket congestions have reached massive proportions. Delays of up to three years have been reported even in high-profile criminal cases, and civil cases can take six to eight years to settle. Courts rarely, if ever, comply with a law prescribing a 90-day limit for hearing a case, and one study of the Philippine tax court concluded that if the judges worked twice as fast, they could catch up with their backlog of cases in roughly 476 years.

Factors that affect the length of delay in court cases include the highly technical nature of Philippine legal procedure particularly in the areas of discovery and evidence, judicial lenience in granting postponements to parties in a case, and liberal filing of many motions to request interim rulings during the progress of a case. Lawyers commonly seek appellate review of a trial court's interim orders by filing petitions for certiorari, prohibition, or mandamus with the Philippine Court of Appeals or Supreme Court, a procedure that stays the proceedings in the main case.

Unlike in some of the neighboring Pacific Rim countries, litigation and the courts are considered a socially acceptable means of redress in the Philippines. Filipinos may seek court resolution of family disputes as well as business disagreements. This willingness to litigate has unfortunately contributed to congestion and delay in the overburdened legal system.

As in most common law jurisdictions, litigation costs vary according to the nature of a case's subject, the novelty or difficulty of the legal issues involved, the amount in controversy, the time spent by the lawyers, and the lawyers' relative professional standings. Filipino attorneys are highly educated and are paid accordingly, but the fees charged are in fact lower than those demanded by some attorneys in more developed countries. All Filipino attorneys are subject to the mandate in the Philippine Code of Professional Responsibility that the fee charged must be fair and reasonable.

Although complaints of corruption are not common, there is some perception in the Philippines that justice can be bought. As recently as 1988 public allegations of corruption were brought against Philippine Supreme Court judges. While some bias against foreigners may remain in the courts, the Philippine constitution guarantees both Filipino nationals and foreigners equal treatment under the laws.

Given the delay, cost, and risks involved in going to court in the Philippines, common sense must be applied: foreign businesses that contract with Philippine entities should structure their agreements to be clear and precise concerning:

- Various parties' rights and obligations in the event that a contract becomes impossible to perform;
- The procedure to be followed if one or both parties breach the agreement; and
- The events that can terminate the agreement and the procedure to be followed on termination.

Problems with the clogged judicial system in the Philippines may be alleviated, at least to some extent, in the near future because the government has embarked on a program of legal reform. In 1994 a sweeping judicial reorganization modified original and appellate jurisdiction in the Philippine courts in the hopes of achieving a more efficient legal system. A Rule on Summary Procedure was also enacted, allowing courts to dispose of some cases without regard to the technical procedural rules that have previously hampered expeditious determinations. The New Civil Code of the Philippines and an Arbitration Law set forth rules for voluntary arbitration of civil controversies. Other legislation establishes specific arbitration mechanisms for the construction industry and for labor-management disputes, and mediation of disputes between people residing in some cities or municipalities is actually compulsory under the Local Government Code.

The judiciary is also addressing congestion in the courts by encouraging compromise and settlement at all stages of a dispute, including while it is being litigated in court. Some judges have begun to suggest the use of alternative dispute resolution processes such as mediation, arbitration, and a party that has stipulated to arbitration in a contract instead files a complaint in a court, the court can dismiss the complaint. Although recourse to international arbitration is not the norm in the Philippines, it is becoming more common as the country opens its doors to foreign investment and multinational corporations accustomed to contracts with arbitration clauses. The Philippines accepts the principle of binding international arbitration and subscribes to the United Nations Commission on International Trade Law (UNCITRAL), which promulgates international arbitration rules. The Philippines is a member of the International Center for the Settlement of Investment Disputes (ICSID).

Aside from the courts and arbitral bodies, foreign investors and businesses should be aware that many of the regulatory agencies that constitute the Philippine administration are accustomed to overseeing and mediating trade disputes, although usually on an informal basis. For example, the DTI is often involved in disputes between Philippine vendors and foreign buyers. In practice, Philippine courts are apt to defer to an agency's view on legal matters related to the agency's purview.

Property Expropriation Concerns The current government of the Philippines—highly sensitive to foreign investors' need for clear property protection rights—has guaranteed investors' freedom from government expropriation except for a compelling public purpose and on payment of just compensation. In the event of any government taking for a public use, Philippine law allows a foreign investor to remit such compensation in the currency used for the original investment and at the exchange rate prevailing at the time of the original investment. The Philippine government is actively soliciting foreign involvement in massive projects designed to erect a modern industrial infrastructure. For this reason, the risk of cavalier disregard for foreigners' industrial property rights appears slim, despite the rather unhappy history of insecure private ownership in the Philippines. The Philippines is a member of the Multilateral Investment Guarantee Agreement (MIGA) and adheres to an Overseas Private Investment Corporation (OPIC) agreement through which foreign investors can insure any investments in the Philippines.

Intellectual and Industrial Property An extensive set of Philippine laws protects intellectual and industrial property rights, including patents, copyrights, and trademarks. The Philippines has signed a number of international treaties and agreements—including the Paris Convention for the Protection of Industrial Property, the Berne Convention for the Protection of Literary and Artistic Works, and an intellectual property chapter from the GATT Uruguay Round—that further secure these rights for foreign owners with property in the Philippines. The Philippines is also a member of the World Intellectual Property Organization (WIPO).

The BPTTT accepts applications for trademarks, trade names, service marks, and patents, and it registers these marks and patents where legal requirements are met. Foreign applicants must show that their home countries grant similar registration rights to Philippine citizens, and must appoint agents in the Philippines who can deal with matters related to applications.

Trademarks Trademark protection is accorded to the first user of a mark after the mark has been used in the Philippines for at least two months, and extends for a renewable 20-year period. A mark's owner must file an affidavit of use—or of justified non-use—every five years, or a mark's registration is canceled. Philippine law extends trademark protection only insofar as a mark is used with a specific class of goods and products closely related to those goods. Under current Philippine practice and pending Philippine legislation, an internationally recognized mark should definitely be registered for protection in the Philippines.

While the text of Philippine trademark law is generally consistent with international norms, the law has not been zealously enforced, and trademark counterfeiting is perhaps the most widespread violation of intellectual property rights in the country. Well-known international trademarks are frequently copied without permission. Even when the laws are enforced, punishments are too minimal to serve as an effective deterrent. Because many Philippine entities try to register foreign marks as their own, some foreign companies adopt strategies of defensive or preventive registration, continually registering their marks in the Philippines, regardless of whether they plan substantial commercial involvement in the country.

Patents Patent protection for utility models and industrial designs extends for five years; these patents may be extended for additional five-year terms. For most other inventions, the term is 17 years. Naturally occurring substances, including plants and animals, cannot be patented. If a patented product is not used commercially in the Philippines within two years of registration, or if Philippine demand for a patented product is not met, the owner of the patent must license the product. To the extent that the license involves technology transfer and the licensor wishes to charge a royalty exceeding 5 percent, the licensing agreement must be approved by the Technology Transfer Board. This compulsory licensing law, together with intrusive government review of technology transfer agreements, has made some international businesses reluctant to enter agreements involving use of their patents or technology in the Philippines.

Enforcement Despite the thrust of these laws and agreements, the Philippines has come under fire as a violator of international standards for protection of intellectual property rights. For example, Philippine copyright law has been criticized as overly broad because it allows reproduction and other use of published works in some cases without the authorization of copyright owners, and it allows sales of books in the Philippines without adequate payment of royalties to copyright owners. The Philippines has also been accused of lax enforcement, particularly in the areas of video works and computer software.

In response to its reputation as an indifferent enforcer of intellectual property rights, the Philippine government has authorized a host of public, private, and cooperative agencies to recommend, coordinate, and implement stricter measures. The Philippine government has also consistently expressed its commitment to international property protection standards as it signs additional international trade agreements. Whether such initiatives will prove effective remains to be seen. Enforcement efforts have been hampered by the congested condition of the Philippine court system. Nevertheless, there has been some effect, which some countries—including the US—have correspondingly acknowledged by upgrading the status of the Philippines on the "watch" lists that designate notorious violators of intellectual property norms.

To try to prevent infringement problems, foreign businesses should always insist on protective contractual provisions that clearly establish ownership of these rights during the contract term and after the business relationship terminates.

RELATED SECTIONS

Refer to the "Taxation" chapter for a discussion of tax issues in the Philippines; "Business Entities & Formation" for a description of the business forms recognized in the Philippines and organizational procedures; "Foreign Investment" for a discussion of relevant provisions and regulations; "Labor" for employment rules and standards; and "Import Policy & Procedures" and "Export Policy & Procedures" for discussion of rules involved in trade.

LAW DIGEST

Abbreviations used are: R.A.C., Revised Administrative Code of 1917; C.A., Commonwealth Act; R.A., Republic Act; C. of C., Code of Commerce of Spain of 1886, promulgated in the Philippines on Aug. 6, 1888; C.C. [n], Civil Code of the Philippines (R.A. 386), which took effect on Aug. 30, 1950; O.G., Official Gazette; R.P.C., Revised Penal Code, which took effect on Jan. 1, 1932; R.C., Rules of Court, which took effect on Jan. 1, 1964; P.D., Presidential Decree; L.O.I., Letter of Instruction; G.O., General Order; B.P. Batas Pambansa; and E.O., Executive Order.

ACKNOWLEDGMENTS

In the Philippines an acknowledgment may be taken before a notary public or any officer acting as notary public ex officio, such as clerks of Supreme Court, Judges of Regional, Metropolitan or Municipal Circuit or Trial Courts, Chief of Division of Archives, Patents, Copyrights and Trademarks, etc.

A person acknowledging an instrument who is liable to pay taxes on residence must exhibit a residence certificate showing payment thereof; an alien must exhibit an alien certificate of registration.

In a foreign country an acknowledgment may be taken before an ambassador, minister, secretary of legation, chargé d'affairs, consul, vice-consul, or consular agent of the Philippines acting within the country or place to which that official is accredited; or a notary public or officer duly authorized by law of that country to take acknowledgments of instruments in place where act is done.

When a party to the contract is an alien, in addition to a residence certificate, an alien certificate of registration number, the date and place of issuance thereof, and the date of the party's last annual report must be stated in the acknowledgment.

Authentication An acknowledgment of a document or official record made outside the Philippines by a notary public, commissioner of deeds, or other official authorized to take acknowledgments will not be admitted in evidence or recorded in the Philippines unless authenticated by an ambassador, minister, secretary of legation, chargé d'affairs, consul, vice-consul or consular agent of the Republic of the Philippines resident in the jurisdiction where made.

ALIENS

Aliens in the Philippines are entitled to protection of life, liberty, and property. Due process of law,

however, does not apply to political rights of aliens, although it does govern in respect to their civil rights. Undesirable aliens can be deported after an investigation and an opportunity to prepare a defense. Knowingly and fraudulently evading payment of internal revenue taxes is grounds for deportation, (R.A. 1093). The Philippine Immigration Act of 1940 (C.A. 673) created a Commission on Immigration & Deportation under supervision and control of Department of Justice.

Aliens are classified into immigrants and nonimmigrants. (C.A. 673, §§ 9, 13) Immigrants are further subdivided into "quota" and "nonquota" immigrants. "Quota" immigrants must not exceed 50 of any one nationality or without nationality for any one calendar year.

To be admitted, immigrants must present unexpired passports issued by governments of countries to which they respectively and originally reside or other document showing their origins and identities as prescribed by consular offices. (C.A. 613, §10).

A tax of P260 is collected for every alien over 14 years of age admitted in Philippines for stay exceeding 59 days. This tax is paid to Immigration Officer at port of entry.

Philippine Alien Registration Act of 1941 (C.A. 653) provides for compulsory registration and fingerprinting of resident aliens as well as aliens entering Philippines. The Alien Registration Act of 1950 (R.A. 562, as amended by R.A. 578 and 751) further provides for annual registration and payment of fees.

Right to Engage in Various Occupations or Commercial Activities Aliens cannot engage in retail business (R.A. 1180) or in businesses involving sale of rice or corn and by-products thereof (R.A. 3018). In bidding for government contracts like construction or repair of public works (C.A. 541) and purchase of articles for government (C.A. 138), preference is given to citizens of Philippines or to corporations organized under laws of Philippines and 75 percent owned by citizens. Aliens can engage in an overseas shipping business provided 60 percent of capital of shipping corporation organized under laws of Philippines is owned by citizens of Philippines (R.A. 1407). Authorization shall not be given for operation of public utilities except to citizens of Philippines or Philippine corporations at least 60 percent owned by Philippine citizens (§11, Art. XII, Constitution). Use, exploitation, and development of natural resources and establishment of educational institutions (except by religious groups) is limited to citizens of Philippines or to corporations 60 percent of capital of which is owned by such citizens. Aliens are excluded from ownership and management of mass media. Only citizens of Philippines or corporations or associations at least 70 percent of capital of which is owned by such citizens are allowed to engage in advertising industry. Participation of foreign investors in governing body of entities in such industry is limited to their proportionate share in capital and all executive and managing officers of such entities must be citizens of Philippines. (§11, Art. XVI, ibid.). In financing corporations three-quarters of all members of board of directors must be citizens of Philippines, and in financing partnerships, all managing partners must be citizens of Philippines. (R.A. 5980). At least 70 percent of the voting stock of any banking institution must be owned by citizens of Philippines except in the case of branches of foreign banks (P.D. 71). Under Investment Incentives Act, any registered enterprise engaged in a preferred area of investment and duly registered with the Board of Investments must be 60 percent owned by citizens of Philippines, and 60 percent of members of board of directors must be citizens of Philippines.

Property Aliens cannot acquire private land except through hereditary succession (§7, Art. XII, Constitution). Mortgages of real property to aliens are allowed, but alien mortgagees cannot take possession of mortgaged property except after default and only for purpose of foreclosure, receivership, enforcement, or other proceedings, and in no case for more than five years, and shall not bid or take part in sale of such real property in case of foreclosure (R.A. 4887). There are no restrictions on ownership of personal property.

The Anti-Dummy Law prohibits circumvention of the rules limiting foreign ownership, management, or control over enterprises, property, or business operations in the Philippines.

Corporations Owned or Controlled by Aliens No foreign corporation is permitted to transact business in Philippines or maintain any suit for recovery of any debt, claim, or demand whatever, unless it has a license required by law.

ARBITRATION

The Arbitration Law (R.A. 876) permits parties to submit to arbitration any controversy which may be the subject of an action, or parties to any contract may in such contract agree to arbitrate any controversy thereafter arising between them. Such submission or contract is valid, enforceable, and irrevocable, save upon such grounds for revocation of any contract. The arbitration must be in writing and subscribed by parties thereto.

The law is not applicable to controversies or cases subject to jurisdiction of National Labor Relations Commission.

Power of Arbitrators Arbitrators can administer oaths, subpoena witnesses, issue subpoena duces tecum, decide relevancy and materiality of evidence offered, and grant a rehearing.

Award and Judgment An award must be in writing, signed, and acknowledged by majority of arbitrators. At any time within one month after award is made, any party may apply to court having jurisdiction for an order confirming award.

ASSIGNMENTS

An assignment of credits is perfected in the same way as the contract of sale; but an assignment of a credit, right, or action produces no effect against third persons, unless it appears in a public instrument, or the instrument is recorded in the Registry of Property if the assignment involves real property. The assignment of a credit includes all accessory rights, such as a guaranty, mortgage, pledge, or preference.

The assignor in good faith warrants existence and legality of credit at time of sale but not of solvency of debtor.

A debtor may assign property to creditors in payment of debts. This assignment releases the debtor from liability only to the net amount of the property assigned. The assignment must be accepted by the creditors in order to become effective; an assignment cannot be imposed upon a creditor (37 O.G. 1444).

The assignment does not have the effect of making the creditors the owners of the property of the debtor, but gives to the creditors the right to proceed to the sale of the property.

ATTACHMENT

A writ of attachment may be had in any action brought for recovery of money or damages on a cause of action arising upon a contract or for fulfillment of an obligation; when defendant is about to depart from Philippines with intent to defraud creditors; in an action for money or property embezzled, fraudulently misapplied, or converted by defendant in a fiduciary capacity; in an action to recover possession of personal property unjustly detained, where it has been concealed, removed, or disposed of to prevent its being found or taken; when defendant has been found guilty of fraud in incurring obligation upon which action is brought; when defendant has disposed of, or is about to dispose of, property with intent to defraud creditors; and in an action against nonresident defendant on whom summons may be served by publication. An attachment may be had at time of commencing action or any time thereafter.

A claimant must post a bond to secure defendant against damage.

Levy All orders of attachment must be served by an officer of the court.

Real property is attached by filing with the registrar of titles of land a copy of the order of attachment and by leaving a similar copy of the order with the occupant of the property.

Stocks or shares of any corporation or company are attached by leaving with the head or managing agent of the corporation a copy of the order of attachment and a notice stating that the stock or interest of the defendant is attached.

Other types of property are attached through similar delivery of the order of attachment and notice to relevant parties.

Attachment may be discharged (1) when defendant gives a bond executed in favor of plaintiff equal to value of property attached; and (2) when defendant moves for an order of discharge on grounds that attachment was improperly and irregularly issued.

Some property is exempt from attachment and execution, including a debtor's home and land up to a certain value, some life insurance proceeds, and copyrights, among other property.

BANKRUPTCY AND INSOLVENCY

A solvent debtor who foresees the impossibility of meeting the debts may petition the court for a suspension of payment of the debts. If granted, a meeting of creditors is then held, and if they agree to the proposal for the settlement of debts made by the debtor, such settlement is declared binding upon all creditors. If the creditors fail to agree, they are then at liberty to enforce their legal rights.

An insolvent debtor owing debts exceeding US$500 may petition to be discharged from the debts. Three or more creditors who are residents of the Philippines may petition that a debtor be adjudicated insolvent upon a proper showing of one or more acts of insolvency.

At any time after three months after the adjudication of insolvency, but not later than one year after such adjudication, the debtor may obtain an order discharging all unpaid obligations provided the debtor has not committed any fraudulent acts.

COMMERCIAL REGISTER

Every owner of an establishment shall register in Bureau of Domestic Trade any name used in connection with business other than the owner's true name.

Registration fee is P110 for each name registered, renewable every five years.

It is unlawful for any person to use or sign with any name or style, without first registering such business name, or style, in the Bureau of Domestic Trade together with the person's true name.

CONTRACTS

A contract is a meeting of minds between two persons whereby one binds himself, with respect to the other, to give something or to render some service. Contracts without cause, or with unlawful cause, produce no effect whatever.

Excuses for nonperformance include: (1) contract refers to an obligation to deliver a determinate thing and the thing is lost or destroyed without fault of promisor; (2) contract refers to a debt which is later excused or renounced; (3) contract refers to obligation which later is merged in the characters of creditor and debtor in one and the same person; (4) contract is novated; and (5) contract refers to service which becomes so difficult as to be manifestly beyond contemplation of parties.

Applicable Law Law of place of making governs formalities of contract. Civil Code does not contain any conflicts rule respecting essential validity of contracts in general.

Distributorships, Dealerships, and Franchises Generally, contracts of distributorships, dealerships, and franchises involving domestic company are governed by laws on obligations and contracts instituted in Civil Code. Contracts of distributorship are governed by Civil Code provision on sales. Generally, contracting parties may establish whatever clauses, stipulations, terms, and conditions they may deem convenient, provided that they are not contrary to law, morals, good custom, public order, or public policy. Foreign companies can engage in wholesale activities, but not retail, because the Retail Trade Nationalization Law (R.A. 1180) restricts retail activities to Filipinos or Philippine corporations or partnerships wholly owned and controlled by Filipinos.

Technology transfer agreements include contracts between domestic companies and foreign companies and are governed by general contract law and by rules and regulations on technology transfer agreements issued by Bureau of Patents, Trademarks, and Technology Transfer.

All technology transfer agreements must be submitted for registration at Bureau of Patents, Trademarks, and Technology Transfer office. Some restrictive clauses are prohibited, including those which: (1) restrict directly or indirectly export of licensed products; (2) restrict use of technology supplied after expiration of technology transfer arrangement; (3) restrict manufacture of similar or competing products after expiration of technology transfer arrangement; (4) require payments for patents and other industrial property rights after their expiration, termination, or invalidation; (5) provide free of charge that major improvements made by technology recipient shall be communicated to technology supplier; (6) require that technology recipient shall not contest validity of any of patents of technology supplier; (7) restrict technology recipient from obtaining patented or unpatented technology from other technology suppliers; (8) restrict research and development activities of technology recipient; (9) prevent technology recipient from adapting imported technology to local conditions, or introducing innovations to it; (10) require technology recipient to keep part or all of information received under technology transfer arrangement confidential beyond reasonable period; and (11) exempt technology supplier from liability for nonfulfillment of responsibilities under technology transfer arrangement and/or liability arising from third-party suits brought about by use of licensed product or licensed technology.

Technology transfer agreements have a fixed term of 10 years with no automatic renewal, and royalties in excess of 5 percent may be allowed only upon prior approval of Bureau of Patents, Trademarks, and Technology Transfer.

COPYRIGHT

Copyrights may be registered for books, periodicals, music, visual works, computer programs, and a variety of other types of media.

The exclusive rights of a copyright owner include rights to: (a) print, reprint, publish, copy, distribute, multiply, sell, and make photographs and illustrations of the copyrighted work; (b) make any translation or other version or extracts of a work, or complete or execute it if it is to be a model or design; (c) exhibit, perform, represent, produce, or reproduce the copyrighted work in any manner for profit or otherwise; and (d) make any other use or disposition of the copyrighted work consistent with the laws of the land.

Application for registration should be filed with National Library.

Copyright lasts during lifetime of creator and for 50 years after death. In case of works of joint creation, period of 50 years shall be counted from death of last surviving co-creator.

Copyrights are not subject to levy and attachment.

EXECUTIONS

Execution may issue any time within five years after judgment becomes final. A sheriff must first attempt to satisfy a judgment out of the personal property of the debtor and then out of real property.

In enforcing execution against personal property, an officer must take possession of the property. In levying on real property, the officer must file with the registry of deeds of the province in which the property is situated a copy of the writ of execution, together with a description of the property and notice of the levy. Copies of such documents must be left with the occupant of the property.

Property sold under execution may be redeemed within one year thereafter.

Supplementary proceedings after execution was returned unsatisfied are available, allowing an execution creditor to examine the judgment debtor under oath as to property, business, or financial interests. Attendance of the party or witnesses may be compelled by an order or subpoena.

FOREIGN EXCHANGE

The Bangko Sentral ng Pilipinas (central bank) is authorized to suspend or temporarily restrict sales of foreign exchange and can subject all foreign exchange transactions to licensing requirements under §§ 70 and 74 of R.A. 265. Bangko Sentral has issued regulations relating to operation of foreign exchange and trade control in the Philippines.

FOREIGN JUDGMENTS

Foreign judgments have the following effects: (1) a judgment against a specific thing is conclusive upon title to the thing; and (2) a judgment against a person is presumptive evidence of a right as between parties and their successors in interest by subsequent title, but the judgment may be repelled by evidence of a lack of jurisdiction, lack of notice to a party, collusion, fraud, or clear mistake of law or fact.

FRAUDS, STATUTE OF

The following agreements must be in writing to be proved: (a) an agreement that by its terms is not to be performed within a year from its making; (b) a promise to answer for the debts, default, or miscarriage of another; (c) an agreement for the sale of goods at a price over P500, unless the buyer accepts and receives part of such goods; (d) an agreement for a lease for a longer period than one year or for the sale of real property; and (e) a representation as to the credit of a third person.

FRAUDULENT SALES AND CONVEYANCES

All contracts in which a debtor alienates property by gratuitous title are presumed to have been entered into in fraud of creditors if the donor did not reserve sufficient property to pay all debts contracted before the donation. Alienations by onerous title are also presumed fraudulent when made by persons against whom some judgment or writ of attachment has been issued. In addition to these presumptions, the design to defraud creditors may be proved in any other manner recognized by the law of evidence. Whoever acquires in bad faith property alienated in fraud of creditors must indemnify the creditors for damages suffered by them on account of the alienation.

Contracts made in fraud of creditors are rescindable.

Bulk Sales The sale, transfer, mortgage, or assignment of a stock of goods or materials otherwise than in the ordinary course of trade and the regular prosecution of the business, or of all or substantially all of the business or trade, or of all or substantially all of the fixtures and equipment used in and about the business, is fraudulent and void as against existing creditors of the vendor, mortgagor, etc., unless creditors are notified, including a detailed list of the property to be disposed of, and a statement regarding the sale is recorded with the Bureau of Domestic Trade. Violation of bulk sales law is punishable by fine and imprisonment. Action to attack sale must be commenced within four years after discovery of fraud (R.A. 3952).

IMMIGRATION

An alien coming to prearranged employment for whom issuance of a visa has been authorized in accordance with law may be admitted in Philippines as a nonimmigrant. Foreign nationals under employment contracts within purview of P.D. 66, and their spouses and unmarried children under 21 years of age, shall be permitted to enter and reside in Philippines during period of employment. They shall be subject to payment of usual visa and immigration fees. (L.O.I. 63)

An alien is entitled to enter Philippines under and in pursuance of provisions of a treaty of commerce and navigation (1) solely to carry on substantial trade principally between Philippines and foreign state of which the alien is a national, or (2) solely to develop and direct operations of an enterprise in which, in accordance with constitution and laws of Philippines, the alien has invested a substantial amount of capital; subject to the condition that citizens of Philippines are accorded similar privileges in foreign state of which such alien is a national. (R.A. 5171).

It is unlawful for any individual to bring into Philippines or employ any alien not duly admitted by any immigration officer. (C.A. 613, amended by R.A. 5701).

INTEREST

In 1983 the central bank suspended the ceiling of interest rates that may be charged or collected on loans or forbearance of money, goods, or credit. In the absence of any contract regarding interest rates, the rate shall be set at 12 percent per annum.

Compound interest cannot be allowed except by agreement. A lender cannot require that interest be paid in advance for more than one year.

Receipt of principal by a creditor gives rise to presumption that interest has been paid.

Usury Although the interest rate ceiling has been suspended, the usury law remains in effect and states that covenants and stipulations for higher rates of interest than are allowed by law are void, and usurers are subject to criminal prosecution.

LANDLORD AND TENANT

Unless a lease of real property is recorded in the Registry of Property, it is not binding upon third persons; every lease of real estate may be recorded. Leases for one year or longer must be in writing, but the testimony of a lessee or tenant shall be accepted as prima facie evidence of the terms of a covenant or contract which was not reduced to writing.

A lessee cannot assign a lease without the consent of the lessor. A lessee may sublet the thing leased, in whole or in part, without prejudice to the lessee's responsibility for the performance of the contract toward the lessor. A lessee may suspend the payment of the rent in case the lessor fails to make necessary repairs or to maintain the lessee in peaceful and adequate enjoyment of the property leased.

If the lease was made for a determinate time, it ceases upon the day fixed, without the need of a demand. If the period for the lease has not been fixed, it is understood to be from year to year, if the rent agreed upon is annual; from month to month, if the rent is monthly; from week to week, if the rent is weekly; and from day to day, if the rent is to be paid daily.

The maximum period allowable for duration of leases of private lands to aliens or alien-owned entities not qualified to acquire private lands in Philippines shall be 25 years, renewable for another 25 years upon mutual agreement of both lessor and lessee (P.D. 471). However, foreign investors investing in Philippines shall be allowed to lease private lands for a period not exceeding 50 years and renewable once for a period not exceeding 25 years (R.A. 7652).

If a lessee makes useful improvements which are suitable to the use for which the lease is intended, and provided the form or substance of the property is not altered thereby, the lessor upon the termination of the lease must pay the lessee one-half of the value of the improvements at that time; if the lessor refuses to pay, the lessee may remove the improvements. The lessor may judicially eject the lessee when: (1) the period agreed upon has expired; (2) the lessee does not pay the price stipulated; (3) either party violates any of the conditions agreed upon in the contract; or (4) the lessee devotes the thing leased to any use or service not stipulated.

LIENS

Those who furnish labor or materials for work undertaken by a contractor for a lump sum have no action against the owner except for the amount in which the latter is indebted to the contractor. Any person who has done work on personal property is entitled to retain the same as a pledge until paid.

LIMITATIONS OF ACTIONS

Actions to recover movables must be commenced prior to eight years from the time possession of the movables is lost.

Real actions over immovables must be commenced before 30 years from the time of loss.

A mortgage action must be commenced within 10 years.

Actions (1) upon a written contract; (2) upon an obligation created by law; or (3) upon a judgment must be brought within 10 years from the time the right of action accrues.

Actions (1) upon an oral contract; or (2) upon a quasi-contract must be commenced within six years.

Actions (1) upon an injury to the rights of the plaintiff; or (2) upon a quasi-delict must be commenced within four years.

All money claims arising from employer-employee relations must be commenced within three years.

These limitations are without prejudice to those specified in the Civil Code, in the Code of Commerce, and in special laws.

All other actions without periods otherwise fixed in other laws must be brought within five years from the time the right of action accrues.

The time for commencing all kinds of actions must be counted from the day on which they may be brought. The time for commencing actions which have as their object the enforcement of obligations to pay principal with interest or an annuity runs from the last payment of the interest or of the annuity.

The period for prescription of actions to demand the fulfillment of obligations declared by a judgment commences from the time the judgment becomes final. The period for prescription of actions to demand an accounting runs from the day the persons who should render the accounting cease in their functions. The period for the action arising from the result of the accounting runs from the date the result was recognized by agreement of the interested parties.

The limitation on commencement of actions is interrupted when they are filed before the court, when there is written extrajudicial demand by creditors, or when there is any written acknowledgment of debt by debtors.

MONOPOLIES AND RESTRAINT OF TRADE

Revised Penal Code, Art. 186 (amended R.A. 1956), makes it unlawful for any person (a) to enter into any contract or agreement or take part in any conspiracy or combination in restraint of trade or commerce, or to prevent by artificial means free competition in the market; (b) to monopolize any merchandise or object of trade or commerce, or combine with any other persons to monopolize merchandise in order to alter prices by unlawful or artificial means; (c) if the person or entity is an importer or manufacturer of foreign merchandise, then to combine in any manner with other persons for the purpose of making transactions which are prejudicial to lawful commerce, or of increasing the market price of any imported merchandise in any part of the Philippines. Penalties are higher if violations affect any food substance, motor fuel or lubricants, or other articles of prime necessity.

Any property possessed under any unlawful combination is forfeited to the Philippine government. If an offender is a corporation or association, the president and each one of the directors or managers of the corporation or association or its agent or representative in the Philippines who knowingly permitted or failed to prevent the commission of such offenses shall be held liable.

MORTGAGES

The instrument by which a mortgage is created should be recorded in the Registry of Deeds. A creditor cannot appropriate for himself mortgaged property or dispose of the property. A mortgagor can lease, sell, or mortgage property again without affecting the original mortgage contract.

Foreclosure is by action filed in a Regional Trial Court of the province where land is situated. A debtor has three months after judgment of foreclosure in which to satisfy judgment; otherwise court may issue execution and cause property to be sold by sheriff at public auction to satisfy judgment. When so stipulated in a contract, a mortgage may be foreclosed extrajudicially under R.A.3135, as amended.

A mortgagee who is disqualified to acquire or own lands of public domain in the Philippines shall not take possession of mortgaged property during the existence of a mortgage except after default, and then only for the purpose of foreclosing, receivership, enforcement, or other proceedings, and in no case for a period of more than five years from actual possession. A mortgagee shall not bid to take part in any sale of property in case of foreclosure (R.A. 4882).

Redemption There is no right of redemption after foreclosure sale except in cases falling under provisions of R.A. 2747, 2938, and 3135. In no case is redemption allowed after the sale of the mortgaged property has been confirmed by the court.

Deeds of trust are not extensively used, but a few deeds of trust have been executed in the Islands to secure bond issues.

A Pacto de Retro is a form of conveyance giving a seller the right of repurchase on or before a fixed date. If the seller fails to repurchase within the time fixed, the title is said to become "consolidated" in the buyer.

NOTARIES PUBLIC

Only qualified attorneys and certain public officials or persons qualified for the office of notary public may be appointed as notaries public. There is at least one notary in each municipality. Notaries are appointed by judges, usually for a term of two years. Every notary keeps a seal and a notarial register. Notaries are under the supervision of Regional Trial Courts, and their fees are fixed by law.

Notarial certificate must show date of expiration of commission.

PARTNERSHIP

A partnership in any form may be constituted by two or more persons. Every contract of partnership having a capital of 3,000 pesos or more, in money or property, as well as every partnership contract involving real property, must appear in a public instrument, which must be recorded with Securities and Exchange Commission. Failure to record this instrument does not affect liability of a partnership and its members to third persons.

The partnership has a juridical personality separate and distinct from that of the partners, even though the contract of partnership may not have been recorded.

A contract of partnership is void whenever immovable property is contributed thereto unless an inventory of said property is made, signed by the parties, and attached to the contract of partnership.

Limited Partnership This has as members one or more general partners and one or more limited partners. The limited partners are not bound by the obligations of the partnership. Persons desiring to form a limited partnership are required to sign and swear to a certificate, which must state, among other things, the name of the partnership, adding thereto the word "Limited"; the character of the business; the location of the principal place of business; the name and place of residence of each member, general and limited partners being respectively designated; the term for which the partnership is to exist; the amount of cash and description of property contributed by each limited partner; and the extent of each partner's participation in the profits. The certificate must be filed with the Securities and Exchange Commission.

Dissolution and Winding Up On dissolution the partnership is not terminated, but continues until the winding up of partnership business is completed. Grounds for dissolution of a partnership are enumerated in the law. Dissolution terminates all authority of any partner to act for the partnership, except so far as may be necessary to wind up partnership affairs.

PATENTS

Any invention of a new and useful machine, manufactured product or substance, process, or improvement is patentable, unless it is contrary to public order or morals or to public health or welfare. A mere idea, a scientific principle or abstract theorem not embodied in an invention, or any process not directed to making or improving a commercial product is not patentable. An application for a patent may be filed by an inventor or legal representative. An applicant who is not a resident of the Philippines must appoint an agent or representative in Philippines upon whom notice or process relating to application may be served. The term of a patent is 17 years from date it is issued, unless sooner revoked or canceled on grounds specified in law.

Where treaty, convention, or law affords similar privileges to citizens of the Philippines, an application which was also filed in a foreign country will be considered as filed on date it was filed in the foreign country as long as filing in Philippines is done within 12 months from the date on which any such foreign application is filed. No patent is granted for an invention patented or described in a printed publication in any foreign country more than one year before the date of filing of an application in the Philippines, or for an invention which has been in public use or sale for more than one year prior to such filing.

After two years from issuance of patent the patent office may grant a license under that patent if it should appear that, without satisfactory reasons, a patented invention is not being worked within Philippines; or that demand for patented article in Philippines is not being met on reasonable terms; or that refusal of patentee to grant license would prevent establishment of any new trade or industry or trade or industry already established would be unduly restrained; or that working of invention within Philippines is being prevented by importation of patented article; or if patented invention is necessary for public health or public safety (P.D. 1263).

A patentee whose rights have been infringed may recover damages and may secure an injunction for the protection of patentee's rights. Where damages cannot be readily ascertained, a patentee may be awarded a sum amounting to a reasonable royalty. Damages awarded may not be more than three times actual damages.

Industrial designs may be protected by their authors in the same manner and subject to the same provisions and requirements as relate to patents. The term of a design registration is five years from the date of registration, and may, on application, be extended another five years.

Fees The Bureau of Patents, Trademarks, and Technology Transfer publishes a schedule of fees for filing applications for patents. Fees vary depending on the type of patent and the status of the applicant as a "small" or a "big" entity.

The Technology Transfer Registry functions to (a) formulate policies that promote the inflow of technology into preferred sectors of activity; (b) establish standards on which to base relationships between parties to technology transfer arrangements; (c) encourage technology transfer arrangements by which bargaining positions of parties are balanced to avoid abuses of stronger position; and (d) measure extent of technology absorption and adaptation under technology transfer arrangements.

Technology transfer arrangements are contracts or agreements by and between domestic companies and foreign companies and/or foreign-owned companies that involve transfer of systematic knowledge for either manufacturing of products or rendering of services (E.O. 133).

PRESCRIPTION

By prescription one acquires ownership and other real rights through lapse of time and compliance with certain conditions (C.C. [n], §1106). Prescription runs against all persons and entities having full civil capacity. (C.C. [n], §1108.) In general, all things which are within commerce are susceptible to prescription.

PRINCIPAL AND AGENT

Under the new Civil Code, an agency is presumed to be employed for a compensation, and is either general or special. An agency couched in general terms comprises only acts of administration.

In certain cases, a special power of attorney is necessary. A special power to sell excludes the power to mortgage, and vice versa; a special power to compromise does not authorize submission to arbitration.

Third Persons So far as third persons are concerned, an act is deemed to have been performed within the scope of the agent's authority if such act is within the terms of the power of attorney, as written, even if the agent has in fact exceeded the limits of authority according to an understanding between the principal and the agent. Private or secret orders and instructions of the principal do not prejudice third persons who have relied upon a power of attorney or instructions shown them. The agent is responsible not only for fraud, but also for negligence.

If the agent had general powers, revocation of the agency does not prejudice third persons who acted in good faith and without knowledge of the revocation. Notice of the revocation in a newspaper of general circulation is a sufficient warning to third persons. The agency is revoked if the principal directly manages the business entrusted to the agent, dealing directly with third persons.

The agency shall remain in full force and effect even after the death of the principal, if it has been constituted in the common interest of the principal and of the agent, or in the interest of a third person. Anything done by the agent without knowledge of the death of the principal or of any other cause which extinguishes the agency, is valid and fully effective with respect to third persons who may have contracted with him in good faith.

RETAIL TRADE LAW

Retail business in Philippines is limited to Filipino citizens, and to associations, partnerships, and corporations, the capital of which is wholly owned by Filipinos. (R.A. 1180, amended by P.D. 714).

SALES

The goods which form the subject of a contract of sale may be either existing goods or "future goods," namely, goods to be manufactured, raised, or acquired by the seller after the perfection of the contract. If goods are to be manufactured specially for the customer and upon special order, and not for the general market, it is a contract for a piece of work rather than a contract of sale.

Price Gross inadequacy of price does not affect a contract of sale, unless it indicates a defect in the consent, or that the parties really intended some other act or contract. The fixing of the price can never be left to the discretion of one of the contracting parties. However, if the price fixed by one of the parties is accepted by the other, the sale is perfected.

Transfer of Ownership The contract of sale is perfected at the moment there is a meeting of minds upon the thing to be sold and upon the price. From that moment, the parties may reciprocally demand performance under the tenets of contract law. The ownership of the thing sold is transferred to the vendee upon actual or constructive delivery. The parties may stipulate that ownership in the thing shall not pass to the purchaser until full payment of the price.

Goods may be delivered to the buyer "on sale or return" to give the buyer an option to return the goods instead of paying the price, or delivered to the buyer on approval or on trial or on satisfaction, or other similar terms, in which case ownership passes to the buyer upon the stipulated conditions.

Warranties Unless contrary intention appears, there is an implied warranty that (1) the seller has the right to sell the thing at the time when ownership is to pass; and (2) the thing shall be free from any hidden faults or defects, or any charge or encumbrance not declared or known to buyer (C.C. Art. 1547).

Risk of Loss Subject to certain exemptions, and unless otherwise agreed, the goods remain at the seller's risk until the ownership is transferred to the buyer, but when the ownership is transferred to the buyer the goods are at the buyer's risk, whether actual delivery has been made or not. Certain exceptions apply to this general rule.

Reservation of Security Where there is a contract of sale of specific goods, the seller may reserve the right of possession or ownership in the goods until certain conditions have been fulfilled. The right of possession or ownership may be reserved notwithstanding the delivery of the goods to the buyer or to a carrier or other bailee. Where goods are shipped, seller and buyer may reserve rights of possession and ownership for security purposes through the form and transmission of bills of lading.

Lien Even if ownership of the goods has passed to the buyer, an unpaid seller of the goods has (1) a lien on the goods or right to retain them for the price while in possession of them; (2) if the buyer is insolvent, a right of stopping the goods in transit; (3) a right of resale, with certain limitations; and (4) a right to rescind, also with certain limitations. Where the ownership in the goods has not passed to the buyer, the unpaid seller also has the right to withhold delivery.

Installment Sales In an installment sale of personal property an unpaid seller may (1) require exact fulfillment of the obligation; (2) cancel the sale if the buyer fails to meet two or more installments; or (3) foreclose any chattel mortgage on the thing sold if the buyer fails to meet two or more installments. A seller has no further action against the purchaser to recover any unpaid balance of the price. The same rule applies to contracts purporting to be leases of personal property with option to buy.

Plural Sales If the same thing is sold to different buyers, the ownership is transferred to the person who first takes possession in good faith, if it is movable property. If immovable property, ownership belongs to the buyer who in good faith first records it in the Registry of Property.

Notices Required A person with a document of title has title to the goods subject to the terms of any agreement with the transferor of the title.

An unpaid seller may exercise right of stoppage in transit either by obtaining actual possession of the goods or by giving notice of claim to any carrier or other bailee with possession of the goods. Notice must be given at such time and under such circumstances that the carrier or bailee may prevent a delivery to buyer. An unpaid seller having a right of lien or having stopped the goods in transit may resell the goods. However, any failure to give notice of intention to resell the goods is relevant in determining whether a buyer was in default for an unreasonable time before the resale was made.

Applicable Law *See* topic "Contracts," subhead "Applicable Law" on page 223.

SECURITIES

Securities and Exchange Commission Laws under the Revised Securities Act (B.P. 178) are administered by the Securities and Exchange Commission, which has jurisdiction, supervision, and control over all corporations, partnerships, or associations with primary franchises and/or licenses or permits issued by the government to operate in Philippines.

No securities unless specifically exempt under provisions of the act may be sold in Philippines unless registered and permitted to be sold as provided in the act.

Registration of Brokers, Dealers, and Salespersons No broker, dealer, or salesperson may engage in business in Philippines as such unless registered as broker, dealer, or salesperson in the office of the Securities and Exchange Commission.

TRADEMARKS AND TRADE NAMES

Trademarks, trade names, or service marks used to distinguish goods, business, and services may be registered with the patent office, provided they are actually in use in commerce in the Philippines for not less than two months before an application is filed. If the applicant is not a Philippine citizen, the country of which applicant is a citizen must grant similar privileges to citizens of the Philippines. The certificate of registration remains in force for 20 years, provided affidavits are filed on the 5th, 10th, and 15th anniversaries of the issuance of the certificate attesting that the mark or name is still in use.

Infringement Any person who, without consent of a registrant, uses, sells, or advertises any reproduction or imitation of a registered mark or trade name is guilty of infringement. An injunction may be obtained to prevent infringement.

No imported merchandise which simulates or copies trademarks or trade names registered in the Philippines, or otherwise induces the public to believe that any article is manufactured in Philippines or in a country other than the place where it is in fact made, can be admitted into the Philippines.

A registered trademark or tradename may be assigned, but the assignment must be in writing, acknowledged before a notary public, and certified under the hand and official seal of the notary. An assignment is void as against any subsequent purchaser for value without notice, unless the assignment is recorded in the patent office. When the assignment is executed in a foreign country, the authority of the notary must be proved by the certificate of a diplomatic or consular officer of the Philippines.

An applicant for the registration of a mark or tradename, who is not a resident of the Philippines, must appoint an agent or representative in the Philippines upon whom notice or process relating to the application or registration may be served.

Firm Name, etc. A firm name, business name, or style must be registered in the Bureau of Domestic Trade, together with the true name of the owner and of any other persons having a joint or common interest in the firm or business.

TREATIES

The Philippines is a signatory to numerous international agreements and conventions, including trade and investment agreements with Korea, Switzerland, Australia, the US, and Germany.

The Philippines has signed tax agreements with Denmark, Sweden, Singapore, the UK, Canada, the US, France, Pakistan, Australia, Japan, Belgium, New Zealand, Finland, Indonesia, Austria, Thailand, Germany, Korea, Malaysia, The Netherlands, Italy, and Brazil. (Rev. Memo. Cir. No. 4-92).

The Philippines is not a party to: (1) Convention on Service Abroad of Judicial and Extrajudicial Documents in Civil or Commercial Matters; (2) Convention on Taking of Evidence Abroad in Civil or Commercial Matters; or (3) Convention Abolishing the Requirement of Legalization for Foreign Public Documents.

Financial Institutions

INTRODUCTION

The Philippine economy largely missed out on the wave of capital investment that poured into Southeast Asia during the 1980s. As a result, the Philippine financial sector has not yet evolved to the same degree as that found in some of its neighbors. In fact, some observers argue that the Philippine financial system has more in common with those found in some Latin American countries. Bank operating inefficiencies; foreign exchange reserve limitations; restrictions on foreign operations and ownership; a shortage of medium- and long-term capital for lending; and small, narrow, and shallow securities markets have limited financial and business development. However, despite these shortcomings, reforms initiated in the mid-1990s are having a positive effect on the development of the Philippine financial system.

The reconstituted central bank, Bangko Sentral ng Pilipinas (BSP), organized in 1993 to replace its insolvent, politically controlled predecessor, and a new, independent Monetary Board are paving the way for systemic stability. The enactment of the Foreign Investment Act of 1991 and the recent easing of restrictions on foreign bank entry into the Philippines is bringing fresh capital and world class financial operations and standards to the Philippines. In addition, the liberalization of foreign exchange controls is adding much-needed liquidity

and fostering investor confidence in the system.

The existing commercial banking system is growing more effective, but it remains highly concentrated, charges high nominal rates for its services, and typically lends only on a collateralized basis, usually only to the most creditworthy of business entities. For this reason, loans for small and medium-sized businesses are hard to come by. Funding from sources other than the banks remains undeveloped and limited. An informal credit market exists to serve these otherwise unfundable businesses, although it operates at extremely high rates and on an irregular, intermittent basis. However, financing may be available for projects in certain targeted growth sectors—such as export trade and government-promoted industrial and infrastructure project—from Philippine development banks or through multilateral institutions, such as the Asian Development Bank (ADB) and the International Bank for Reconstruction and Development (IBRD, or the World Bank).

Basic consumer banking and financial services such as checking or savings accounts, drafts, foreign currency exchange, credit cards, and mortgage loans are available at the largest commercial banks and to a lesser extent at some of the numerous local rural, savings, and mortgage banks. In addition, the influence of US institutions that have operated in the Philippines throughout the 20th century has created a business culture that is more inclined to cater to the retail financial services market than the business cultures of many other developing countries; such services are readily available for expatriates and foreign businesspersons. English is spoken in nearly all business and financial circles, and the years of Spanish and US influence have made the Philippines business culture more familiar to international—particularly European and Western—businesspeople than the business cultures of some of its Southeast Asia neighbors.

Philippine capital markets are relatively small, specialized, and undeveloped. No meaningful

CONTENTS

FINANCIAL GLOSSARY

cap In floating rate lending, an upper interest rate limit that will not be exceeded even if the market rate rises above the stated amount. In investing, a trading limit above which trading will be restricted. See floor.

capital adequacy A financial measurement of a financial institution's equity capital in comparison with the level of its liabilities. This ratio is used extensively by regulators and financial managers to measure the level of solidity of a particular entity. In general, the higher the capital adequacy measure, the lower the level of risk to the company's stock and bondholders.

capital formation Any process that directly or indirectly adds new capital to a business or economy. Capital can be formed through issuance of new securities, loan origination, or use of business earnings for capital investment or reinvestment. Capital formation is vital to the continued growth and stability of an economy, sector, or individual business.

commercial paper A negotiable, short-term instrument used in commerce. Types of commercial paper are: bills of exchange, promissory notes, and bank checks. Commercial paper is typically sold by a business, through a broker or dealer, to a lender or investor at a discount and is paid off at par at its maturity date (usually 30 to no more than 360 days later).

convertibility The ability to readily exchange one currency for that of another nation.

custodial services Management and safekeeping of securities or other negotiable instruments owned by an individual or company by a third-party financial institution.

derivatives Secondary financial instruments that are based on underlying assets or third-party contracts. Examples include index options, interest rate swaps, and asset-backed securities. These instruments are used primarily for investment hedging and speculation.

exchange-traded A description for a financial instrument bought and sold on a formal stock, futures, or options exchange.

factoring Discounting of an account receivable so as to obtain immediate payment. Factoring is used by businesses to gain short-term funding and to lower the level of accounts receivable on their balance sheet.

floor When the interest rate on borrowed funds is tied to the market rate, the parties can designate a minimum rate limit, known as the floor. Even if market rates drop below this level, the interest rate on the loan will not fall below the floor. In investing, a trading limit below which trading will be restricted. See cap.

foreign exchange reserves The amount of foreign currency (typically US dollars, deutsche marks, Japanese yen, or another "hard" or "reserve" currency) held by a nation's financial system as a reserve base, or financial backstop, for its international transactions and payments. The level of foreign exchange reserves is critical to the level of financial solvency for a nation's financial system.

letter of credit A document issued by a bank stating its commitment to pay a party (supplier/exporter/seller) a stated amount on behalf of a buyer (importer), as long as the seller meets specified terms and conditions.

liquidity (1) A company's access to cash to meet its financial obligations. (2) The availability of liquid funds in an economy. (3) The measure that compares a company's short-term assets with its short-term liabilities.

monetary policy A state-controlled, economic and financial tool used to manage price levels, activity, and solvency in the economy. Monetary policy is typically developed and managed by the Bangko Sentral ng Pilipinas (BSP), which can manipulate interbank interest rates, print new money (by issuing new government securities), change bank rules and regulations, and alter the level of the nation's reserve base.

offshore banking Banking operations officially transacted outside the country in question. In a host country, this would refer to a foreign entity's ability to bank at a host country's financial institution without regard to the foreign nation's rules and regulations. Entities typically utilize offshore banking facilities to escape more restrictive domestic banking operations, rules, and regulations in force.

over-the-counter market A marketplace for financial securities transactions conducted away from operating exchanges. Most such transactions take place electronically as distinct from within the open-outcry system on a stock exchange.

reciprocity The "mutuality of benefits," "quid pro quo," and "equivalence of advantages." In international transactions, the practice by which governments extend similar concessions to each other, as when one government allows certain financial practices or activities by foreign institutions within its borders in exchange for equivalent concessions for its own institutions to operate in the foreign institution's home country.

reinsurance A practice in the insurance industry of selling part of one insurance company's risk to another insurer specializing in such transactions to reduce the first firm's total risk. Reinsurance is essentially a secondary market for insured risks, allowing a company to transfer a portion of its risk exposure to another insurance company for a fee in order to diversify and mitigate excess risk.

retail banking Banking functions provided to the public at large (retail consumer market). Examples include deposit taking, checking accounts, consumer loans, and residential mortgages.

transparency The extent to which laws, regulations, agreements, and practices affecting transactions are open, clear, measurable, verifiable, and proceed according to established rules.

wholesale banking Banking functions provided to the business or industrial economy (wholesale market). These services include commercial lending, factoring, securities underwriting, and export financing.

spot price A price quotation for the immediate sale and delivery of a commodity or currency.

market exists to provide medium- and long-term credit, although a market for corporate bonds is beginning to emerge through the Philippine Stock Exchange. A healthy, growing money market is present, based primarily on an internationally recognized commercial paper market. In the absence of longer-term funding vehicles, this market is an important source of funding for Philippine business. The Philippine Stock Exchange, newly formed through the merger of the nation's two largest preexisting exchanges, has generally performed well, encouraged by increased political stability, improved reliability of continuous electrical power, and stabilized macroeconomic variables. Foreign capital inflows have risen greatly due to the recent liberalization of policies governing foreign ownership of assets in the Philippines, implementation of economic reforms, promotion of industrial programs, and increasing stability.

THE BANKING SYSTEM

Although the Philippines has never been thought of as a banking power, it does have a solid, effective, and profitable domestic banking sector. Due to historical government restrictions on bank licensing, and, hence, on competition, Philippine bank profit margins have been among the highest in the world. Despite reforms, critics contend that the system remains restrictive and inefficient. Nevertheless, with the restructuring of the BSP, liberalization of bank ownership rules and practices, and easing of restrictions on banking licenses for overseas operators, this sector is becoming more competitive and technologically proficient. As the size and scope of the sector increase, the availability and affordability of commercial loans are likely to improve, bolstering capital formation.

Today's Philippine banking system is highly concentrated: just five commercial banks control nearly half of the nation's banking assets. This effect is further compounded by the "unibank" system employed in the Philippines. Under this system, approved banks may handle investments and underwrite securities (investment banking functions) in addition to conducting traditional commercial bank deposit and lending activities. Because of past licensing restrictions and a limited banking market, foreign operators are few; together they account for less than 10 percent of all banking assets. For discussion purposes, the banking system can be divided into six main areas: the Philippine central bank, which manages the financial system; commercial banks; rural banks; thrift institutions; special government or development banks; and foreign banks.

Central Bank—Bangko Sentral ng Pilipinas (BSP)

The central bank, now known as the Bangko Sentral ng Pilipinas (BSP), was first established as the nation's central bank in 1949, three years after the Philippines gained independence from the US. Following the declaration of bankruptcy by the first Central Bank under a US$11 billion foreign debt load, the BSP was constituted according to the terms of the New Central Bank Act. Today's BSP is the sole issuer of the nation's currency (bank notes) and functions as the system's lender of last resort. The bank is responsible for the administration of monetary and credit policy and exercises regulatory authority over the banking system. It is also charged with maintaining internal and external monetary stability and preserving the international value and convertibility of the Philippine peso.

The BSP is governed by an independent Monetary Board. This board was recently restructured to further insulate the BSP from the political influence of the central government. The new seven-member board is comprised of its governor, a government cabinet member, and five independent members from the private sector (three of whom serve six-year terms and two of whom serve seven-year terms). Among the duties of the board are: determining exchange rate policy, setting peso spot price levels at which the BSP will buy and sell the national currency, establishing exchange rate trading bands (caps and floors), and determining money supply levels. Although some critics charge that the new BSP has yet to result in a central bank that is as truly independent of the government as many had hoped, most observers concede that BSP-led reforms have had a strongly positive impact on the Philippine banking system in general.

The BSP's effectiveness in improving the Philippine financial system is evidenced through several regulatory measures designed to reform the nation's banking system. In the past, most monetary policy has been oriented largely towards promoting economic development and has been specifically directed at officially approved activities such as agriculture and export production. Lately, the BSP has strengthened and improved the system by increasing minimum bank capitalization requirements (capital adequacy standards), creating a universal banking concept, liberalizing bank branching policies, relaxing foreign exchange regulations, and deregulating interest rates. These moves toward a more open, market-driven banking system follow a period during which heavy government control of the banking system and political and economic instability throughout the 1980s had rendered the Philippine financial system subservient to policy requirements and left it protected from market forces.

Commercial Banks

The national commercial banks dominate the Philippine financial system by providing the primary source of a wide range of services such as deposits, loans, currency exchange, and investment banking activities—for example, equity financing and securities underwriting. There are 34 institutions officially classified as commercial banks: 26 private domestic banks, 4 government and quasi-government-owned banks, and the Philippine branches of 4 foreign banks. The head offices of all commercial banks in the Philippines are located in metropolitan Manila. The domestic commercial banks have the most extensive nationwide branch network of all the bank types noted. Following Manila, Cebu City is the most active and competitive banking center; approximately 150 branches of 31 banks are present there, with most of the foreign banks having representative offices there as well. Davao, the third largest city in the Philippines, has a relatively large number of banking operations, although no foreign banks currently operate there.

The five largest domestic commercial banks, ranked in order of asset size, are: the Philippine National Bank, the Bank of the Philippine Islands, the Metropolitan Bank and Trust Co., the Far East Bank and Trust Company, and Citibank. Some of the other major commercial banks in the Philippines are: the Far East Bank, United Coconut Planters Bank, Philippine Commercial International Bank, Solidbank Corporation, and China Banking Corporation. The Philippine National Bank—still majority-owned by the government—is by far the largest bank in the country, accounting for more than 15 percent of the total assets in the commercial banking system. Large commercial banks are funded locally in the interbank debt market, as well as in the global debt and money markets. Deposits also continue to constitute a significant portion of the source of funding.

Until the early 1990s, the government was reluctant to license any new banking entities or even new branches of existing banks. Restrictions on new licenses were lifted in 1991, after nearly two decades of license denials by the Central Bank. Since the BSP began to liberalize its approach toward licensing, more than two dozen new entrants—almost half of them foreign—have begun competing with the existing operators for new operating licenses. This new competition should benefit both domestic and foreign borrowers and customers through lower loan rates, improved services, and wider access to funds and currencies.

Services Philippine commercial banks offer a wide variety of retail and wholesale banking services that are similar to those found in most developed nations. Short-term lending—primarily funds for working capital and trade finance—predominate, with medium- and long-term lending still in its infancy. Banks conduct a full array of trust operations, and most large Philippine commercial banks are involved in international operations, mainly through their correspondent relationships with foreign banks.

Recent reform measures allow commercial banks to operate Foreign Currency Deposit Units (FCDUs).

This service enables banks to accept foreign currency deposits, extend foreign currency loans to residents and nonresidents alike, and trade foreign exchange. The FCDUs are particularly important for overseas business entities and investors needing foreign currency exchange and loan services (both peso- and nonpeso-denominated) in order to operate in the Philippines.

Several of the larger commercial domestic banks operate as universal banks, or "unibanks." Approved out of a need to satisfy the growing demands of business for longer-term financing, unibanks engage in expanded investment banking services. These include the underwriting and investment services needed to create, place, and trade the longer-term securities that enable their clients to access the nascent debt market. The universal banking concept has also encouraged mergers to increase capital, promoting stability and profitability. Of the 32 licensed Philippine commercial banks, 14 have been licensed to operate as unibanks.

Philippine commercial banks are closely held, usually by prominent family-based business groups that date back to the Spanish and US colonial periods. Most private banks have their historic roots in the many family-owned banks established during the years between 1950 and 1965, when there were few entry barriers to the banking industry. During that period, there was no minimum capital requirement for establishing a bank, and 27 new banks were formed.

Government intervention in the private banking sector has historically been extensive. Restrictions on the issuance of new bank licenses and periodic interest rate controls imposed during the early 1970s, plus a string of rescue operations in the 1980s, served to keep the Central Bank directly involved in the banking system. A number of critics have voiced the opinions that the Philippine commercial banking system is still so restrictive that the BSP essentially manages a cartel. They argue that this situation serves to ensure healthy profitability for favored current operators by restricting new entrants and keeping interest rates artificially high to maintain a healthy spread favorable to the banks at the expense of consumers and the national financial system as a whole. Contrary to this view are the arguments that most government equity participation in the sector has been undertaken with the idea that it would be temporary in nature and was made in the context of assisting elements of the banking system during specific financial crises. The banks receiving such assistance have always continued to operate as private institutions. In addition, as part of more recent reforms, many foreign exchange controls, interest rate regulations, and licensing restrictions have been modified or entirely eliminated.

PHILIPPINE INTEREST RATES 1980–1994

	Discount rate	Treasury bill rate	Lending rate
1980	4.54	12.14	14.00
1981	6.69	12.55	15.33
1982	6.30	13.78	18.12
1983	8.05	14.23	19.24
1984	12.11	28.53	28.19
1985	11.50	26.72	28.61
1986	9.63	16.08	17.53
1987	9.08	11.51	13.34
1988	8.94	14.67	15.92
1989	9.64	18.65	19.27
1990	10.60	23.67	24.12
1991	10.75	21.48	23.07
1992	7.63	16.02	19.48
1993	6.51	12.45	14.68
1994*	7.45	14.70	16.44

*Note: partial year data. The lending rate was 18 percent in May 1995.

Source: International Monetary Fund, International Financial Statistics

Interest rates on loan funds have generally been higher than those available from overseas banks and in global capital markets because of relatively high domestic inflation and reserve requirements, a gross receipts tax, government interest rate controls, high credit and political risks, and restrictions on foreign exchange operations.

To provide incentive to the industry as well as to make markets more open, the government has decontrolled virtually all foreign exchange transactions; exceptions include (1) foreign currency loans and guarantees, and (2) foreign investments that require exchange purchases from the banking system to fund repatriation of capital and remittance of dividends and profits. The majority of these transactions must still be submitted to the BSP for approval. In short, the BSP continues to control foreign currency purchased or borrowed from Philippine banks for overseas investments and debt payments, but not through FCDUs or currency transactions conducted outside the banking system. Foreign borrowing will most likely be fully deregulated only after the nation's foreign currency reserves have risen substantially to a level that officials consider to be adequate to support such obligations. These restrictions represent remnants from the period of extensive US dollar flight during the foreign exchange crisis of 1983–1984.

Given their relatively protected franchise, profitability has not been a problem for Philippine commercial banks. Except during the currency crisis of the mid-1980s, Philippine bank profitability has been among the highest in the world. However, this profitability has been maintained in a somewhat artificial environment. Excluding the government-owned Philippines National Bank, nominal annual rates of return for banks have averaged approximately 20 percent during the past five years.

Foreign Banks

Only four foreign commercial banks—operating a total of 12 branches—do business in the Philippines. In addition, 13 other foreign banks maintain representative offices in the Philippines; although these are not permitted to carry on normal banking business, they serve important liaison functions with local businesses and correspondents.

Until recently, the last grants of full banking licenses to foreign banks were made in the 1940s. The four current operators—Citibank, Bank of America, Standard Chartered, and Hongkong and Shanghai Banking Corporation—are authorized to offer full retail and wholesale commercial banking services, although they are limited to operating only three branches apiece. In 1994 the Philippine government passed legislation to liberalize the entry of foreign banks, allowing them to establish branches, create majority- or wholly-owned subsidiaries or acquire up to 60 percent of an existing domestic bank's voting stock. The law allows up to 10 new foreign banks to establish branches over the next five years. Foreign banks are now allowed to trade foreign currency, open letters of credit, accept peso deposits, lend based on their peso deposits and reserves, and engage in trust operations. These reforms should improve the overall level of financial services by increasing competition and efficiency and encouraging the introduction of new services, products, and international standards.

The foreign banks' share of the Philippine market—based on their asset size—has actually declined from double digit levels in the late 1980's to approximately 9 percent in 1994. Observers attribute the reduction to the lifting of restrictions on that has allowed new entrants into the market rather than to any pullback from the Philippine market by foreign banks.

Offshore Banking

Approximately 18 offshore banking units (OBUs) operate out of the Philippines. These OBU operations are limited to foreign currency transactions such as the opening of trade letter of credits,

accepting remittances from overseas workers and converting them to pesos, and making and accepting foreign exchange placements on behalf of other financial institutions. The OBUs may not establish branches, handle outgoing foreign currency transactions by Philippine resident nationals, engage in any peso transactions, or perform any other banking activity. Thus, while they may perform certain specialized services well, they are not allowed to offer many of the generalized services needed by foreign businesspeople operating in the Philippines.

Development and Other Specialized Banks

The Philippines operates three specialized quasi-official development banks: the Development Bank of the Philippines, the Land Bank of the Philippines, and the Philippine Amanah Bank. These were originally organized at different times under different charters to serve specific divergent needs.

The largest and most comprehensive agency, the Development Bank of the Philippines (DBP) was organized in 1958 to take over the duties of its early post–World War II era reconstruction predecessor. The DBP is involved in numerous sectors and activities, including: the financing of agricultural production, energy generation and conservation projects; export promotion; and rural and commercial development programs. The bank offers industrial loans for the development of the large infrastructure projects needed to sustain economic growth and to promote industrial linkages within the economy. It is also especially active in supporting the production of inputs for small and medium-sized entities. Agricultural loans support food production to promote farmer self-sufficiency and raw materials production for the industrial sector. The DBP also provides construction financing for home development and commercial real estate projects; makes equity investments to complement various private initiatives; provides guarantees on domestic and foreign loans; and extends financing and consulting services to other private development banks. Trust operations and unibanking services are also available from the DBP. Loans are made both in local and foreign currency. The bank's funding sources include the BSP, foreign currency loans (primarily from the World Bank and the ADB), and issues of various debt instruments placed in domestic and international capital markets. Approved foreign investors and operators are eligible to apply for funding from the DBP.

The Land Bank of the Philippines (LBP) primarily finances government purchases of private lands for redistribution under various land reform programs. Created in 1963, the LBP's original mission was to complement the three prongs of the agrarian reform project: to provide land transfer financing; to provide farmer income and production assistance; and to implement capital redeployment by compensated former landowners. The LBP has full commercial banking powers, is involved in trust and unibank operations, and also functions as an FCDU.

Established in 1973, the Philippine Amanah Bank (PAB) was designed to provide savings and credit facilities for the large Muslim population in Mindanao in the southern Philippines. The bank functions as a commercial, savings, and development bank. It makes loans, invests for its own account, and provides various trust services. The PAB is funded through demand and time deposits and various debt securities, but mainly relies on government deposits and its own capital to finance its lending operations. The PAB is quite small compared with the other two development banks, and consequently, it plays a minor, somewhat more localized role with respect to foreign business-people wishing to operate in the Philippines.

Other Commercial Banks or Similar Institutions

Thrift and rural banks exist as the local counter-part of the larger, generally urban commercial and development banks to serve farmers and small businesspeople. There are more than 1,000 thrift and rural banks; however, cumulatively they control less than 5 percent of the nation's financial assets.

The thrift banking system was created in 1972 and is comprised of savings and mortgage banks, stock savings and loan associations, and private development banks. Some eight stock savings and mortgage banks operate under the provisions of the General Banking Act of 1948. These institutions collect funds from small savers and provide long-term credits, housing loans, and consumer financial services to their depositors. They also invest in domestic bonds and other securities. Most of these banks are based in the Manila area and have branches in various provinces. The savings and loan associations provide additional savings and credit to consumers, industry, commerce, and agri-culture. The Savings and Loan Association Act of 1963 governs the more than 60 savings and loan associations, which are found throughout the nation. Private development banks promote agri-culture and industry by providing medium and long-term credit facilities at advantageous interest rates and terms. The 42 banks are primarily supported by the larger DBP through stock owner-ship and short-term credit facilities.

Thrift banks now exercise a broad range of domestic banking powers and may even operate like commercial banks, provided they can demon-strate that they have sufficient capital. Many thrifts conduct trust operations, perform unibank func-tions, operate FCDUs, and deal in foreign exchange. Many now originate home mortgages for the nation's National Home Mortgage Finance Corpora-tion. Significant consolidation has recently occurred in the thrift industry as the institutions' powers have been broadened through an easing of license restrictions.

Philippine rural banks—established through the Rural Bank Act of 1952 and numbering more than 800—are the most numerous type of entity in the banking sector. Rural banks are relatively small, existing primarily to provide credit to small farmers and businesses. These entities generally operate as single units, but they are allowed to establish branches within their regional areas. They accept savings, time, and demand deposits and are funded by the larger government development banks, in much the same way as are the thrift banks. Many rural banks maintain direct links with larger commercial banks in order to offer various other banking services and the convenience of branches to their customers. Although large in number, the limited depth and scope of thrift and rural bank operations are such that they are unlikely to offer efficient or advantageous sources of services for foreign operations in the Philippines.

NONBANK FINANCIAL INSTITUTIONS

Specialized Commercial Financial Institutions

Although the commercial banking sector domi-nates the financial system, nonbank entities—such as finance companies, lending investors, mutual building and loan associations, venture capital companies, and nonstock savings and loan associa-tions—do play a vital role in Philippine credit and capital formation. Finance companies and lending investors constitute the largest elements in the Phil-ippine specialized commercial finance sector.

Finance companies operate as corporations or partnerships licensed by the Philippines Securities and Exchange Commission (SEC), although certain aspects of finance company operations are governed by the BSP. Finance companies first emerged in the 1950s to finance the mass distribu-tion of consumer durable goods from booming Phil-ippine factories. Now the largest segment of the private nonbank finance sector, finance companies are usually divided into quasi-bank and pure finance company entities.

When organized as a quasi-bank, a finance company may deal in commercial paper and borrow from the public. Because of their expanded powers, the quasi-bank finance companies are significantly larger than their pure finance company competitors, which are more restricted in their sources of funding. Both types of finance companies are active in buying and selling contracts, leases, chattel mortgages, and other forms of debt. Because there are only a handful of independent leasing companies, the finance companies also dominate the leasing sector and are active in leasing transportation equipment, machinery, and other equipment.

Many pure finance companies are "captive" finance subsidiaries of manufacturing companies. These captives act as financing arms of manufacturers who utilize their finance company subsidiaries as vehicles to support sales of their products to consumers. The largest and best-known of these are connected to manufacturers of automobiles, consumer durable household appliances, and small and large business equipment. These companies typically offer lending and leasing options to buyers of their parent company's manufactured products. The remaining entities in this subsector concentrate on the factoring of receivables and lending to market vendors.

A third subsector includes finance companies that are primarily money market operators. These groups act as dealers in commercial paper through nonrecourse sales and as brokers of direct transactions between borrowers and lenders or investors.

Lending investors are active competitors of finance companies. These firms typically use their own capital to offer a wide range of credit activities. However, they are generally most active in the short-term, noncollateralized loan market.

Specialized Consumer Financial Institutions

The bulk of consumer finance services are available from any of the large commercial banking groups. In addition, mortgages, secured and unsecured personal loans, credit cards, and other products are widely available from numerous mutual building and loan associations, nonstock savings and loan associations, and even from pawn shops. Foreign operators may use the services of these entities for personal needs; however, they are likely to find more comprehensive and more easily used services available from Manila-based commercial banks.

Insurance Companies

In 1992 the Philippine government opened the life and nonlife insurance sectors to new entrants. As was the case in the banking sector, the granting of new licenses had been suspended for decades. But unlike the banking sector, the insurance sector remains closed to foreign majority ownership. Currently, insurers must be domestically incorporated and can have no more than 40 percent foreign ownership. It remains to be seen how far reforms will go to further liberalize this sector of Philippine financial services.

All insurance companies are regulated by the Philippine Insurance Commission. This agency controls insurance operations through provisions governing such areas as policy pricing, capital adequacy, investment regulation, and benefit requirements. Fewer than 10 percent of Filipinos have any life insurance coverage. Many observers argue that this is largely the result of the high cost of insurance brought about by the below-market cost of policy loans to existing policyholders.

Philippine insurers offer a range of products including life, fire, marine, and health and accident insurance. The asset base of the industry—which represents less than one-third of that of private nonbanks—consists of policy loans, real estate loans, stocks, bonds, and time deposits. Nevertheless, despite these limitations, the industry is an important source of long-term capital for the economy. Nationwide there are approximately 150 licensed insurance companies, with the overwhelming majority writing only property and casualty insurance. If licensing restrictions were to be eased, it is expected that new competition would bring about lower life insurance premium costs and make the sector a larger and even more significant participant in the nation's financial arrangements.

Pension Funds

The Government Service Insurance System (GSIS) and the Social Security System (SSS) provide pension benefits to workers in the public and private sectors, respectively. Both are government-run and funded by compulsory contributions from employers and employees. The public pension system invests in government securities; housing, salary, commercial, and industrial loans; securities; and money market instruments. Private pension funds also exist and are funded from a combination of employer and employee contributions. Most of these funds are managed by third parties, such as life insurance companies or bank trust departments. Both the public and private pension systems are regulated by the Philippine government. Foreign operators are allowed to borrow from pension funds, but to date, activity has been very limited.

Underground Financial Operations

With legal market interest rates reaching as high as 40 percent and averaging around 15 percent in recent years, it would seem that the legitimate lending market has effectively usurped the role of the loan shark and the underground credit market. However, even at such high rates the demand for credit remains greater than the supply in the above-ground sector and unofficial financing is common. To varying degrees, personal patron-client, relationship-based credit arrangements exist in the Philippines, as is the case in much of the developing world. Less than creditworthy entities and individuals often apply to locally known individuals, including shop owners or employers, for credit.

Corruption has been pervasive in certain sectors of the Philippine economy for decades, and although much of it represents petty extractions at lower levels, it continues to play a role at higher levels as well. The current administration is attempting to crack down on some of the more blatant examples of corruption, but businesspeople must be aware of how deeply engrained it may be in certain methods of doing business. It is best to retain independent local talent to help navigate the system as efficiently as possible. Bribery is against the law, but occasionally foreign business executives will be approached. Be advised to stay clear of these situations.

The Philippines does have a high level of crime, including violent crime. Criminal elements in the police and military have periodically joined forces with criminal and other ideologically based groups to commit kidnapping, extortion, and other crimes. But contrary to some overseas perceptions, areas of lawlessness and military-rebel conflicts are generally known and well-defined. As is true in most other nations, the foreign operator-investor is best advised to first investigate and ask around before doing business in certain geographic or market sectors.

FINANCIAL MARKETS

The Securities Industry and Equities Markets

Despite the fact that the Philippines is generally not known as a major international financial center, recent global investor interest in emerging markets has resulted in considerable investor interest in the nation and an explosive expansion of the relatively small Philippine stock and bond markets. Increased foreign investor interest—coupled with the liberalization of local investment regulations allowing overseas investors free to buy as much as 100 percent of the equity of national companies operating in a number of sectors—has helped to promote substantial, more investor-friendly market reforms and improvements in exchange operations. The Philippine Stock Exchange (PSE), the new market for the nation's securities, is evidence of this evolution.

In early 1994, the larger and more senior Manila Stock Exchange and the smaller Makati Stock Exchange merged, forming the PSE, which operates as a dual-site market. The market conducts business through an electronic interlink, sharing a single price quote and a common issue listings system. Plans are underway for the PSE to trade under one roof in the near future. In early 1995, the total market capitalization of all listed stocks on the PSE amounted to approximately US$41 billion. This figure is up almost sevenfold from slightly less than US$6 billion in 1990. Trading is conducted from both the Manila and Makati locations on Monday through Friday from 9:30 am to 12:15 pm local time. An over-the-counter market (OTC) also exists to a limited extent. Unlisted stocks traded on the OTC consist primarily of bank shares.

Although stock market capitalization and accompanying liquidity has surged during the past five years, the PSE is still considered rather small and narrow relative to other exchanges operated by some of its Southeast Asian neighbors. Although the PSE lists approximately 180 firms, the market is highly concentrated, with the top five companies accounting for more than 50 percent of total market capitalization. In addition, active trading is limited to the 30 or 40 largest issues. The single largest firm, brewing giant San Miguel, alone represents nearly 13 percent of the entire market. Other top firms and their relative percentage share of the market share include the Philippine Long Distance Telephone Company (12 percent), Ayala Corporation (11 percent), Manila Electric Company (10 percent), Philippine National Bank (6 percent), Benpres Holdings (5 percent), and Ayala Land (3 percent). Most of these top firms are also quoted on other international exchanges.

Some structural impediments to stock market growth persist. Foreign broker-dealers are still prohibited from underwriting equity securities, thus limiting additional modernization because of a lack of competitive pressure. Further barriers to growth are found in the relatively outmoded back office operations, which have changed little since the Manila exchange first opened in 1927. However, improvements are being made. Book entry stock ownership, a basic operating procedure in more developed markets, has recently become available. Previously, stock certificates were entered into official books by hand and physically delivered to their new owners via courier. Many times the stock was traded away even before the certificate made it into the hands of the first new owner, creating additional backlogs.

Older stock issues exist in one of two forms: one restricted to Philippine national ownership and another available to both domestic and foreign investors. Historically, most trading consisted of restricted national shares, with the stock available to foreign investors being thinly traded, usually at a premium. Trading is changing rapidly as the large volume of new issues and recapitalization of older issues changes the makeup and activity patterns of the PSE.

In 1993 falling inflation and interest rates, greater political stability, and a lack of movement in developed markets combined to focus the attention of yield-hungry investors on opportunities in smaller emerging markets worldwide. In that year, the Philippine Stock Market Index (PSMI) shot up by more than 150 percent from the previous year, representing the best stock market performance in all of Asia and the second best in the entire world (the PSMI is composed of the 31 most heavily capitalized stocks listed on the exchange). Nearly US$2 billion flowed into the Philippine market in 1993.

Some 10 new companies went public on the exchange during 1993. The largest of these—the holding company Benpres—raised P3 billion (about US$111 million) in an initial public offering in November 1993; earlier in the year, the conglomerate JG Summit Holdings raised P2.8 billion (about US$103 million).

However, 1994 proved how vulnerable Philippine stocks can be—as shown by the periodic market corrections made primarily because of global interest rates and movements in other stock markets—regardless of how strong Philippine economic fundamentals may be independent of these factors. The market index fell by 16 percent during all of 1994, although because of currency appreciation, the PSMI still turned in the best market performance in the region. However, despite this drop, several new issues and large privatization deals took place, including the sale of shares in the state oil company, Petron, and the National Steel Company, adding P70 billion (US$2.7 billion) to total market capitalization. These moves provide evidence of growing confidence in the Philippine equity market through a broad shift in Philippine capital formation away from borrowing and toward equity financing. In addition, the outlook for the near future is quite good. With continued economic and political stability, foreign investment liberalization, and market operations improvement, the Philippine stock market should be a decent performer in the years to come.

Underwriting of equity issues in the Philippine market can only be done through Philippine majority-owned investment houses. These are typically subsidiaries of the unibanks, although some independent investment houses do exist. The unibanks have access to less expensive capital than the investment houses and generally dominate stock underwriting. Foreign commercial banks, unable to operate as unibanks, are currently precluded from participating in investment house activities. However, foreigners are allowed to own 100 percent of a domestically incorporated brokerage house, and several major foreign firms hold seats on the PSE, including Morgan Grenfell, Jardine Fleming, and units of Citibank and Bankers Trust.

Regulation and supervision of the securities industry is the responsibility of the SEC. In the past, surveillance of the markets by the SEC has been limited, with only a handful of staffers monitoring trading, leading some to characterize the Philippine markets as effectively unregulated. Complaints of kickbacks being required to obtain SEC approvals in some instances on matters ranging from securities registration to favorable decisions in enforcement cases have supported this cynical view. However, with billions of pesos now being raised through the stock market, the SEC's operations and abilities are becoming more critical than ever, prompting senior government officials to call for a restructuring of SEC management and reform its existing powers and operations.

Membership in the PSE is open to any incorporated company regardless of national affiliation. Foreigners wishing to acquire stock in an existing domestic corporation are free to do so in accordance with the rules, regulations, and limits of the Foreign Investment Act. Foreign ownership restrictions are still present in various sectors—including mass media, advertising, retail trade, and natural resource development. Foreign investors wishing to invest in securities listed on the PSE (including initial public offerings or offerings of additional shares in existing firms, stock rights, dividends, and stock splits) are required to register with the BSP or with a custodial bank. This filing may be accomplished through any authorized securities broker-dealer or underwriter.

Mutual funds in the Philippines are limited in size and scope, although new mutual fund products are being created and offered. Foreign investors wishing to invest indirectly in the Philippine market may do so through one of several Philippine market funds offered overseas.

Debt and Money Markets

The Philippine money market is the nation's most active source of short-term funds, outpacing the use of commercial bank funds several times over in both volume and turnover. Dating back to the early 1960s, three major submarkets continue to provide financing for the banking and industrial sectors. The interbank call loan market provides funds to banks through overnight borrowings and lending between individual banks and between individual banks and the BSP. The commercial paper market, initially developed in 1965, is one of the most popular and successful funding vehicles for larger creditworthy Philippine businesses. This market developed to fill the needs created by the shortage of funds available from commercial banks. Although available commercial bank funds were actually cheaper, banks found it difficult to compete with less cumbersome and operationally restrictive commercial paper. The third submarket—that in government treasury bills—constitutes a popular means of government funding and investor lending.

A bond market is emerging on the PSE, albeit slowly. Creditworthy Philippine companies wishing to obtain medium- and long-term funds have traditionally gone to willing commercial lending groups or to the Eurobond market. Other companies have satisfied their funding requirements by rolling over short-term credits as an alternative to paying for higher-cost, more restrictive longer-term loans. With the growth of a deep and liquid domestic bond market, Philippine companies may eventually begin to opt for this funding vehicle; however, participation to date has been limited. Creditworthy foreign operators looking for longer-term financing have the option of issuing debt on their own on international markets and converting funds into Philippine pesos for use by their local operations, or they may borrow within the local commercial bank lending market, albeit at higher rates.

Underwriting procedures for both foreign and domestic entities are rather straightforward and can be carried out by a number of domestic securities broker-dealers. However, foreign entities must register with either the SEC or the BSP prior to the issuance of any debt. There are no restrictions on foreigners regarding the amount and type of debt they may buy, sell, or trade. The relative illiquidity and periodic financial shocks afflicting local debt markets are important variables for foreign entities to consider in deciding on their funding profile.

The Philippine external foreign debt position has changed little during recent years. As of the beginning of 1995, Philippine foreign public debt amounted to approximately US$28 billion, with annual debt service payments amounting to approximately US$4 billion. This debt service is fairly high, in view of the fact that Philippine gold and foreign exchange reserves have hovered between US$4 billion and US$6 billion. Slower than anticipated economic growth in the early 1990s has limited the government's ability to stimulate the economy or introduce many of the large public infrastructure projects that it would like to undertake. As a result, the Philippines' debt rating remains below investment-grade, making debt financing in international markets relatively expensive. In light of this, the national government borrows heavily in domestic

markets, which traditionally has resulted in the crowding out of other potential local borrowers. Most government domestic debt is in the form of short-term maturities, and in recent years this debt service, combined with the service of foreign debt, has represented a significant drain on government resources and capabilities. However, with the resumption of real growth in 1993 and continued economic and political stability, the Philippines debt position should be improving in the near future.

Specialized Financial Markets

The Manila International Futures Exchange (MIFE) functions as the Philippines' main commodities and derivatives market. Established in 1986, the MIFE initially offered sugar and soybean futures contracts, expanding later into coffee and copra, all of which are domestically produced (in fact, the MIFE is the only exchange in the world offering a copra futures contract). The MIFE's first financial future— Philippine treasury bills—began trading in late 1990. This event signaled the beginning of real growth of the exchange's operations. Since then, futures trading volume has soared from fewer than 100,000 contracts annually to more than 1 million contracts. Five foreign currencies are now traded including contracts on US dollars, yen, Deutsche marks, sterling, and Swiss francs. However, it is important to note that the development of currency futures trading has been hampered in the past because of periodic currency crises and controls imposed by the Philippine government.

Exchange membership is open to Philippine nationals and foreigners. Five classes of members currently exist: founding, full, trade affiliate, associated, and individual market. Both founding and full members are seatholders with rights to trade on the floor. Trade affiliates, associated, and individual market members do not have direct trading privileges, but may take advantage of certain other trading and operating rights. The MIFE is regulated and controlled through the SEC.

FURTHER READING

This discussion has provided a basic guide to money, finances, financial institutions, and financial markets in the Philippines. Because the economic situation is changing so rapidly in the Philippines, authoritative, up-to-date sources on the structure and function of the financial sector are limited. Those interested in current developments may wish to consult the *Asian Wall Street Journal*. The *Asian WSJ* and the other periodicals listed below cover economic and financial developments in the Philippines.

Asia Money
(10 issues per year)
Euromoney Publications PLC
20th Fl., Trust Tower
68 Johnston Road
Wanchai, Hong Kong
Tel: [852] 2529-5009
Fax: [852] 2866-9046

Asian Wall Street Journal
(Daily, weekdays)
Dow Jones Publishing Co. Asia
GPO Box 9825
Hong Kong
Tel: [852] 2573-7121
Fax: [852] 2834-5291

Bangko Sentral Review
(Monthly)
A. Mabini St., cor. Vito Cruz St.
Malate, Metro Manila, Philippines
Tel: [63] (2) 507-051, 593-380/1, 595-263, 582-372
Fax: [63] (2) 522-3987, 597-363, 521-5224
Monthly review from the BSP

Far Eastern Economic Review
(Weekly)
GPO Box 160
Hong Kong
Tel: [852] 2508-4300
Fax: [852] 2503-1537

Manila Inc.
(Monthly)
Metro Manila Real Estate Magazine, Inc.
Ground Fl., Strata 2000
Emerald Avenue
Ortigas Center
Pasig, Metro Manila, Philippines
Tel: [63] (2) 632-0748 to 51
Fax: [63] (2) 631-2521

USEFUL ADDRESSES

Refer to the "Important Addresses" chapter, beginning on page 297, for a list of Philippine banks, securities brokers, insurance companies, government agencies, and other organizations. Some of the addresses listed below may be of particular interest.

Government and Trade Organizations

Board of Investments (BOI)
Industry and Investments Bldg.
385 Sen. Gil J. Puyat Ave.
1200 Makati, Metro Manila, Philippines
Tel: [63] (2) 818-1831, 868-403, 867-895, 875-602
Fax: [63] (2) 819-1887, 851-166

Insurance Commission
1071 United Nations Ave.
Manila, Philippines
Tel: [63] (2) 583-534, 57-48-86, 599-221/5
Fax: [63] (2) 522-1434

Philippine Chamber of Commerce and Industry
Ground Fl., Secretariat Bldg., East Wing
CCP Complex
Roxas Boulevard
Pasay City, Metro Manila, Philippines
Tel: [63] (2) 833-8591/3
Fax: [63] (2) 833-8895

Securities and Exchange Commission (SEC)
SEC Building
Epifanio de los Santos Ave.
Greenhills
Mandaluyong, Metro Manila, Philippines
Tel: [63] (2) 810-1145
Fax: [63] (2) 722-0990

Government Banks

Bangko Sentral ng Pilipinas
(Central Bank of the Philippines)
A. Mabini St., cor. Vito Cruz St.
1004 Malate, Metro Manila, Philippines
Tel: [63] (2) 507-051, 593-380/1, 595-263, 582-372
Fax: [63] (2) 522-3987, 597-363, 521-5224

Development Bank of the Philippines
PO Box 1996
Makati Central Post Office
1200 Makati, Metro Manila, Philippines
Tel: [63] (2) 818-9511
Fax: [63] (2) 817-2097

Philippine National Bank (PHILNABANK)
PNB Building
257 Escolta St.
1099 Escolta, Metro Manila, Philippines
Tel: (2) 402-051
Fax: (02) 496-091

Land Bank of the Philippines
LBP Bldg.
319 Sen. Gil J. Puyat Ave.
Makati, Metro Manila, Philippines
Tel: [63] (2) 818-9411
Fax: [63] (2) 843-3155

Financial Markets

Manila International Futures Exchange (MIFE)
7th Fl., Producers' Bank Building
Paseo de Roxas
Makati, Metro Manila, Philippines
Tel: [63] (2) 812-7776
Fax: [63] (2) 818-5529

Philippine Stock Exchange, Ayala Center
Ground Fl., Stock Exchange Bldg.
Ayala Ave.
Makati, Metro Manila, Philippines
Tel: [63] (2) 810-1145/6
Fax: [63] (2) 810-5710

Philippine Stock Exchange, Tektite
12th Fl., Tektite Tower 1
Tektite Road, Ortigas Center
Pasig, Metro Manila, Philippines
Tel: [63] (2) 634-5089, 634-5920
Fax: [63] (2) 634-7115

Currency & Foreign Exchange

EXCHANGE ARRANGEMENT

The currency of the Philippines is the Philippine peso. The authorities of the Philippines do not maintain margins with respect to exchange transactions, and exchange rates are determined on the basis of demand and supply in the exchange market. However, the authorities intervene when necessary to maintain orderly conditions in the exchange market and in light of their other policy objectives over the medium term. On December 31, 1993, the exchange rates for buying and selling were P27.5 and P27.9, respectively, per US$1. [As of June 30, 1995, the exchange rate was P25.575 per US$1.] The Central Bank of the Philippines [reorganized and renamed as the Bangko Sentral ng Pilipinas, or BSP, in September 1993] is not governed by the trading rules of the Bankers' Association of the Philippines in making its own purchases and sales of foreign exchange, except for transactions conducted at the trading center. Commercial banks trade in foreign exchange through the Philippine Dealing System (PDS) or by telephone.

ADMINISTRATION OF CONTROL

Exchange regulations are administered by the central bank on the basis of policy decisions adopted by the Monetary Board. Without prior approval, non-Philippine nationals not otherwise disqualified by law may engage in business in the Philippines or invest in a domestic enterprise up to 100 percent of their capital. Nonresidents may purchase foreign exchange from authorized agent banks only up to the amount they have converted into pesos.

Pursuant to Circular No. 1353, dated September 1, 1992 (superseded by Circular No. 1389) foreign exchange may be freely sold and purchased outside the banking system. Foreign exchange received in the Philippines or acquired abroad may also be deposited in foreign currency accounts. However, in order that foreign loans and foreign investments can be serviced with foreign exchange purchased from the banking system, the proceeds of such foreign loans and foreign investments must continue to be sold to authorized agent banks for pesos. All categories of banks (except offshore banking units) duly licensed by the central bank are considered authorized agent banks.

Commercial banks are allowed to maintain open foreign exchange positions, subject to the limitation that long and short positions do not exceed 25 percent and 15 percent, respectively, of unimpaired capital.

PRESCRIPTION OF CURRENCY

There are no prescription of currency requirements for outgoing payments, but all exchange proceeds from exports and invisibles must be obtained in prescribed currencies. These curren-

CONTENTS

DEALING WITH MONEY IN THE PHILIPPINES

Recognized Currencies

The monetary unit of the Philippines is the peso (P), which is divided into 100 centavos (c). The formal Pilipino spelling is "piso," but "peso" is the recognized standard usage. Currency and coin is issued only by the Central Bank of the Philippines—now called the Bangko Sentral ng Pilipinas (BSP). Coins are available in denominations of 1c, 5c, 10c, 25c, 50c, P1, and P2. Bank notes are issued in denominations of P5, P10, P20, P50, P100, P500, and P1,000. In the spring of 1995, P10 was worth about US$0.36, while P500 was worth US$18.14. Visitors will need smaller bills because small shops, vendors, and taxi drivers are often unable to change larger bills. In the provinces and rural areas, it can be extremely difficult to get change for larger bills—P100 and larger.

The Philippines recognizes a range of currencies; those of its trade and treaty partners are listed as eligible for inclusion in its foreign reserves and are therefore considered negotiable. Foreign currencies most widely used include the US dollar, British pound sterling, Swiss franc, deutsche mark, Canadian dollar, Italian lira, Australian dollar, and Japanese yen, all of which are familiar and readily convertible. Other currencies usually cannot be used, and travelers may have difficulty in exchanging them, even in Manila. The US dollar is the most common, and bills may be accepted in many areas of the country. Traveler's checks—especially (and sometimes only) US$-denominated traveler's checks—and major credit cards are generally accepted at many outlets and in many areas of the country.

Conversion of Currency

Foreign currency can be exchanged at the airport or at commercial banks, authorized foreign exchange dealers, and various outlets—especially in the downtown tourist district—such as tourist hotels and larger retail stores. You will need your passport to exchange funds (a photocopy will be taken with your first transaction). The best denominations to carry are the US$50 and US$100 bills; smaller bills may not be accepted. Only clean, crisp, straight bills will be accepted; bills that are less than pristine will be refused and are essentially nonnegotiable.

Contrary to the situation found in most places, cash (at least US currency) often receives a better rate than traveler's checks, which are usually exchanged for an amount discounted by approximately 5 percent.

Traveler's checks—denominated in US dollars from American Express, Bank of America, and Thomas Cook—are readily accepted; Eurocheques are not. Most commercial banks in Metro Manila and in provincial cities will change traveler's checks, and branches of the Philippine National Bank will always cash them, as will many licensed money changers. To cash and exchange traveler's checks, you will need the original receipt showing the serial numbers—as security against the negotiation of counterfeit or stolen checks.

Licensed foreign exchange dealers are efficient, but travelers should shop around for best rates and service charge schedule (some money changers may charge a service fee for quotes and comparisons). Foreign exchange rates are generally best in Metro Manila; transactions can cost as much as 20 percent in provinces when service charges and unfavorable rates are added.

In Manila, licensed money changers tend to cluster on Mabini Street—between Padre Faura and Santa Monica, and the corner of M H de Pilar and Padre Faura. Although rural areas may have no financial institutions that can negotiate foreign exchange, such exchanges can usually be made through hotels, albeit at relatively unfavorable rates. Some rural banks limit foreign exchange transactions to US$100 unless special arrangements are made.

An illegal foreign exchange black market exists, but even at best, the net gain would be measured in a few centavos per US$100 above standard retail market rates. Most black market money changers operate scams that prey on tourists. These involve miscounting, sleight-of-hand tricks (such as adding to the top of the pile during a count while simultaneously removing more bills from the bottom of the stack), the exchange or substitution of counterfeit currency, and a raft of similar maneuvers. Such transactions are not recommended.

Reconversion

A receipt is given for funds exchanged in legal transactions. To reconvert pesos to foreign exchange at the airport when leaving, you must present exchange receipts. You can reconvert an amount of pesos only up to the amount listed on the receipt. In general, foreign currency can be obtained for pesos only at the airport, although residents and nonresidents are legally allowed to buy foreign exchange for other than controlled purposes.

Credit Cards

MasterCard, Visa, American Express, Diners Club, and JCB are the most commonly accepted credit cards. Travelers should note that many establishments displaying the Visa logo actually accept only the Visa card issued locally by Equitable Bank. Holders of Visa or MasterCard can get a cash advance in pesos from branches of the Equitable Bank. American Express cardholders can get currency or traveler's checks from the American Express office. Amounts of up to US$500 can be obtained as a cash advance on the cards (up to US$1,000 on a Platinum Card) every 21 days; with the card plus a personal check, cardholders can obtain up to US$1,000 every 21 days. Other than this specialized use, foreign checks are not accepted in the Philippines.

Banking Services

Bank transfers are inefficient and complicated and can require up to 10 days to complete before funds are available. The Philippine National Bank and American Express are among those most accustomed to international transactions. Service is substantially improved if a local account is opened. For those who will be in the country for more than a few days or on a regular basis, a local bank account can greatly facilitate financial matters. Some Philippine banks can issue a local credit card, and many issue local automated teller machine (ATM) cards that make obtaining cash much easier. The use and number of ATMs is growing rapidly; the two main networks, BankNet and MegaLink, merged in August 1994, allowing customers virtual nationwide access. Philippine bank accounts are insured only up to the first P40,000 (about US$1,450). This is the maximum amount payable for all accounts maintained in the same name at all banks.

cies are as follows: Australian dollars, Austrian schillings, Bahrain dinars, Belgian francs, Brunei dollars, Canadian dollars, Deutsche marks, French francs, Hong Kong dollars, Indonesian rupiahs, Italian lire, Japanese yen, Kuwaiti dinars, Malaysian ringgit, Netherlands guilders, British pounds sterling, Saudi Arabian riyals, Singapore dollars, Swiss francs, Thai baht, UAE dirhams, US dollars, and other such currencies that may be declared acceptable by the central bank.

Payments may be made in pesos for exports to ASEAN countries, provided that the central bank is not asked to intervene in the clearing of any balances from this payment scheme. Authorized agent banks may accept notes denominated in the prescribed currencies for conversion into pesos.

NONRESIDENT ACCOUNTS

Bank accounts denominated in pesos may be opened in the names of individual or corporate nonresidents without the prior approval of the central bank. Nonresident accounts may be credited only with the proceeds from inward remittances of foreign exchange or convertible foreign currencies and with peso income from or proceeds of conversion of properties (real or personal) located in the Philippines and belonging to nonresidents. Nonresident accounts may be freely debited for peso withdrawals.

Both residents and nonresidents may maintain foreign currency deposit accounts with authorized agent banks in the Philippines (*see* "Proceeds from Invisibles," on page 249). Residents are allowed to maintain deposits abroad without restriction.

IMPORTS AND IMPORT PAYMENTS

Generally, all merchandise imports are allowed without a license. However, the importation of certain products is regulated or restricted for reasons of public health and safety, national security, international commitments, and development and protection of local industries.

Imports are classified into three categories: freely importable, regulated, and prohibited. Freely importable products may be processed by authorized agent banks without prior approval or clearance from any government agency. To import regulated products, a clearance permit is required from the appropriate government agency (including the central bank). Prohibited products are those that may not be imported under existing laws. Import arrangements not involving payments using foreign exchange purchased from the banking system, such as self-funded/no-dollar imports and importations on consignment basis, are allowed without prior approval from the central bank. Under the Comprehensive Imports Supervision Scheme (CISS), percip-

FOREIGN EXCHANGE ISSUES

Accounts and Procedures

The Bangko Sentral ng Pilipinas (BSP), formerly the Central Bank of the Philippines, is responsible for managing all Philippine financial affairs, including the foreign exchange system. Foreign exchange regulations are contained in BSP Circulars No. 1318, 1338, 1348, 1353, and 1389 (this last essentially consolidates most of the previous specific circulars). Exchange controls were in place prior to September 1, 1992, when the foreign exchange system was liberalized under Circular No. 1353. Since that time, foreign exchange can generally be bought and sold freely at market rates, which are set according to supply and demand. (This floating rate structure has been in place since the early 1970s, but free access to foreign exchange was restricted until this latest revision.)

Foreign and most domestic businesses may now hold foreign currencies (previously they had to convert foreign exchange into pesos). No effective limits exist on how much foreign exchange is brought in or out of the country. However, prior BSP approval is still required for removal from or entry into the country of any sum of Philippine national currency greater than P5,000 (about US$180). This restriction was designed to prevent currency speculation in other Asian markets, and approval is usually pro forma for most transactions. Dealers no longer need to have a license to operate in foreign exchange markets, and exporters are now free to obtain foreign exchange from any source—rather than just from local commercial banks. In short, the only restrictions that remain are on purchases of foreign exchange from the banking system for investment or debt service outside the country. The peso is effectively convertible and uncontrolled in sources and uses located outside the domestic banking system itself.

Foreign investors must register an investment to obtain foreign exchange to repatriate investment capital and remit earnings. Full and immediate outflows of these funds are allowed on presentation of evidence of registration (previously such funds were allowed out only on a delayed installment that varied by sector, industry, and terms of investment). Funds that originate from unregistered invest-ments—except those existing prior to March 15, 1973, and registered as such ex post facto—cannot be converted for export from the country. Holders of foreign exchange have the right to invest in domestic securities.

Resident and foreign firms and individuals can maintain foreign currency accounts in any acceptable settlement currency. In part, the shift to allow foreign currency accounts came from a desire to provide ways to attract back into the country some of the estimated US$20 billion-plus in flight capital that left the country during the 1980s. Accounts for proceeds of royalties, rentals, dividends, profits, and invisible payments are blocked unless the agreement or foreign investment from which the funds result has been registered. However, registration with the BSP can be via decla-ration to an authorized, designated custodian bank. External borrowings require advance prior BSP approval, which is obtained on a case-by-case basis. The proceeds of foreign borrowings must be sold to a local bank. Firms must report outstanding foreign indebtedness, and foreign exchange to service such obligations cannot be obtained unless the loans are registered and approved. Local borrowing is uncon-trolled; however, foreign firms must file semiannual status reports on all such local borrowing.

International Payments

International obligations can be settled in any accepted currency. The currencies of most trading partners are accepted, and special application can be made to the BSP for authorization to settle in another currency based on the circumstances. Acceptable payment arrangements include cash, letter of credit (L/C), documents against payment (D/P), documents against acceptance (D/A) and open account (O/A).

Accepted international procedures are followed. L/Cs must be opened by the date of shipment, with a separate L/C for each transaction. Amendments do not need to be approved. Only approved, eligible firms—those operating in manufacturing, the oil industry, public utilities, and raw materials import—can use D/A and O/A terms. However, intercompany O/As are allowed without approval (as long as transfer pricing guidelines—consisting of the requirement that such arrangements are uniform worldwide—are observed). Such D/A and O/A imports require a Bangko Sentral ng Pilipinas Release Certificate (BSPRC) indicating that the documents have been reviewed and registered. Commercial banks are not allowed to pay on unregistered transactions. Terms longer than 360 days require prior BSP approval. Banks are also being allowed to compete more freely on pricing for L/Cs, resulting in a sharp drop in such costs and greater competition among issuers. Self-funded and consignment imports require no approvals.

Foreign Reserves

Philippine international reserves (minus gold) have grown from only US$155 million in 1965 to US$6.1 billion at the beginning of 1995. This represents an all-time high and a substantial 30 percent rise from US$4.7 billion at the same time a year earlier. The BSP has attempted to manage the foreign reserve position to provide a growing cushion for the economy to enable it to become more stable and withstand fluctuations.

However, in late 1994, the BSP was allowing prepayment of foreign obligations and greater investment by Filipinos outside the country in order to reduce somewhat its "excess" foreign reserves and bring down an "overvalued" peso, aiding national exporters. This policy was short-lived, as in early 1995 the BSP began to tighten up in order to raise the value of the peso as a show of strength to counteract the chain reaction threat following the collapse of the Mexican peso.

Foreign Exchange and Financial Policy

In the past, when the peso tended to devalue, the BSP often sold US dollars at above-market rates to slow the fall of its currency. However, since the peso has recently been appreciating, making Philippine exports less competitive, the BSP has been buying foreign currency at below-market rates. The Department of Finance, a separate agency, has also been preparing a tax to be levied on "hot money" inflows, designed to discourage short-term volatile portfolio investments and allow better management of such foreign funds. The BSP has also lowered reserve requirements in the banking system to 17 percent from 20 percent to reduce interest rates and accelerate demand, which should promote spending that soaks up some of the excess supply of foreign funds. In 1995 the peso appreciated more than 12 percent against the weakening US dollar.

Meanwhile, some observers are arguing that the Philippines should shift its floating rate exchange system to a variation of the fixed rate system used recently by Argentina, pegging the peso to the US dollar to encourage greater stability in the country's foreign exchange markets.

---

ient inspection is required for imports valued at more than US$500 from all countries if they are declared in the shipping documents as off-quality, used, second-hand, scraps, off-grade, or a similar term indicating that the article is not brand new.

Commercial banks may sell foreign exchange to service payments for imports under letters of credit (L/C), documents against acceptance (D/A), documents against payment (D/P), open account (O/A) arrangement, and direct remittance. Letters of credit must be opened on or before the date of shipment and are valid for one year. Only one letter of credit may be opened for each import transaction; amendments to such an arrangement need not be referred to the central bank for prior approval. The D/A and O/A procedures are restricted to oil firms; producers and manufacturers, whether for the domestic or export market; franchised public utility concerns; and importers-traders importing raw materials required by domestic manufacturers.

Separate regulations apply to imports into specific regions by barter traders but these arrangements can be made without prior approval from the central bank.

PAYMENTS FOR INVISIBLES

Authorized banks may sell foreign exchange to residents for payments of any nontrade transactions against appropriate written applications without limit and without prior approval from the central bank, except for payments related to foreign loans or investments that require documentation showing central bank approval and/or registration.

Full and immediate repatriation of profits and dividends (net of taxes) accruing to nonresidents from all types of investment may be effected directly through commercial banks without prior approval from the central bank. However, service payments relating to foreign loans or foreign direct investments effected by purchases of foreign exchange through

PHILIPPINE FOREIGN EXCHANGE RATES

Philippine pesos per US dollar

	Year-End	Year-Average
1960	2.02	2.02
1965	3.91	3.909
1970	6.435	5.904
1975	7.498	7.248
1980	7.6	7.511
1981	8.2	7.9
1982	9.171	8.54
1983	14.002	11.113
1984	19.76	16.699
1985	19.032	18.607
1986	20.53	20.386
1987	20.8	20.568
1988	21.335	21.095
1989	22.44	21.737
1990	28	24.311
1991	26.65	27.479
1992	25.096	25.512
1993	27.699	27.12
1994	26.219	24.4
1995 (2nd qtr.)	25.575	—

Note: These data are graphed below.

Source: IMF, International Financial Statistics Yearbook, 1994

authorized agent banks are limited to those transactions whose original capital transfer is sold for pesos at authorized banks and has previously been registered with the central bank.

Dividends of current income arising from equity investments in nonpriority sectors made in connection with the program for the conversion of external debt into equity investments may not be transferred for the first four years after the investment is made; thereafter, such dividends and current income may be transferred.

Resident and nonresident travelers must have prior authorization from the central bank to take out more than P5,000 in domestic bank notes and coins or checks, money orders, and other bills of exchange drawn in pesos. When traveling abroad, citizens of the Philippines must pay a travel tax of P2,700 for first-class passage and P1,620 for economy-class passage. Reduced rates of P1,350 for first-class passengers and P810 for economy-class passengers are provided for groups of people traveling for recognized special purposes. Reduced rates of P400 for first-class passengers and P300 for economy-class passengers are provided for dependents of contract workers duly registered with the Philippine Overseas Employment Administration. Departing nonresidents are allowed to reconvert at airports or other ports of exit unspent pesos of up to a maximum of US$200 or an equivalent amount in other foreign exchange (calculated at prevailing exchange rates) without proof of sales of foreign exchange to authorized agent banks.

EXPORTS AND EXPORT PROCEEDS

Exports are allowed without restriction, except

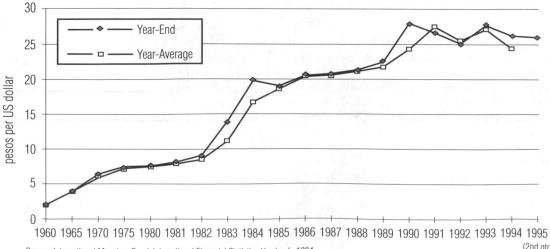

Philippine Foreign Exchange Rates
Philippine pesos per US dollar

Source: International Monetary Fund, International Financial Statistics Yearbook, 1994

(2nd qtr.)

for those that are regulated or prohibited for reasons of national interest. Exports of selected seeds and shoots of native plants, endangered fish and wildlife (including selected marine species), and stalactites and stalagmites are prohibited.

All exports must be covered by export declarations or permits. Authorized agent banks may issue and amend an export declaration without prior approval from the central bank. Payments for exports may be made in prescribed currencies, under the following forms without prior central bank approval: L/C, D/P, D/A O/A, cash against documents arrangements, consignment, export advance, and prepayment.

Foreign exchange receipts or earnings of residents from exports may be sold for pesos to authorized banks or outside the banking system, retained, or deposited in foreign currency accounts, whether in the Philippines or abroad, and they may be used freely for any purpose. There are no export taxes.

Trade with Bulgaria, Cambodia, Cuba, Romania, and the states of the former USSR no longer requires clearance.

PROCEEDS FROM INVISIBLES

There are no mandatory surrender requirements on proceeds from invisibles, and they may be used without restriction. Travelers may freely bring in any amount of foreign currency and up to P5,000 in domestic bank notes, coins, checks, money orders, and other bills of exchange drawn in pesos.

CAPITAL

All inward investments need to be registered with the central bank. The registration of a foreign investment with the central bank is required only if the foreign exchange is needed to service the repatriation of capital and remittances of dividends and profits originates in the banking system. Foreign exchange proceeds from registered investments and foreign loans must be sold to authorized agent banks for pesos in order to purchase foreign exchange for related servicing from authorized agent banks. When applications for new inward foreign investments (in kind or in cash) are reviewed, no priority or preference is given to the category of industry in which the investment is made, as long as (1) it does not violate the nationalization law and its requirements; (2) there is inward remittance for cash investments; and (3) investment in kind covers only machinery and equipment, raw materials, supplies and spare parts, and other items necessary for the operation of the invested firm. The law guarantees full repatriation of cash investment in export-oriented industries

that have been registered with the central bank, in enterprises registered with the Board of Investments (BOI), and in securities certified by the central bank and traded on the Manila and Makati Stock Exchanges.

Foreign companies are eligible to obtain loans in domestic currency from domestic sources, provided that they have a maximum debt-equity ratio of at most 60:40 in high-priority sectors, of 55:45 in medium-priority sectors, and of 50:50 in low-priority sectors. Investments in domestic commercial banks registered with the central bank may be repatriated without restriction.

Foreign direct investments need not be registered with the central bank, except when foreign exchange to service repatriation of capital and dividend net profit remittances are to be funded from the banking system. Foreign direct investments may be (1) foreign equity in Philippine firms or enterprises; (2) investment in government securities or securities listed on the stock exchange; or (3) investment in money instruments or bank deposits. Foreign direct investments may be in cash or in kind. Investments are permitted in connection with the Program for the Conversion of Philippine External Debt into Equity Investments. Under this program, most categories of external debt, including rescheduled debt, may be converted into equity investment. Investments duly registered with the central bank or an accepted custodian bank are entitled to full and immediate repatriation of dividends, profits, and savings without prior authorization from the central bank.

Outward investments by resident natural and juridical persons may be made freely, except those purchased from authorized agent banks that exceed US$1 million per investor per year; such investments require prior central bank approval.

All public and certain private sector loans from foreign creditors, offshore banking units, and Foreign Currency Deposit Units (FCDUs) must be referred to the central bank for prior approval.

These loans include (1) publicly guaranteed loans; (2) those covered by foreign exchange guarantees by local commercial banks; (3) those guaranteed by FCDUs and funded or collateralized by offshore loans or deposits; and (4) medium- and long-term loans obtained by private commercial banks and financial institutions for relending to public or private enterprises. Approval for public sector loans must be obtained before actual negotiations commence. Other private sector loans from the above-mentioned creditors require prior approval from and/or registration at the central bank only if they are to be serviced using foreign exchange purchased from the banking system. However, subject to certain conditions and requirements, the following short-term loans (not exceeding 360 days) do not require prior central bank approval and may be serviced out of foreign exchange purchased from the banking system: (1) loans of financial institutions for normal interbank transactions; (2) private sector export advances from buyers abroad; and (3) loans from FCDUs of commodity service exporters, producers, and manufacturers, including oil companies and public utility concerns.

Loans requiring prior central bank approval are normally expected to finance export-oriented and BOI-registered projects, projects listed in the Investment Priorities Plan and the Medium-Term Public Investment Program, and projects that may be declared priority under the country's socioeconomic development plan by the National Economic and Development Authority or Congress. Medium- and long-term loans may finance foreign exchange and local costs exclusive of working capital. Short-term loans may finance only foreign exchange requirements of projects, except preexport financing requirements, which may also be used to cover peso costs.

Terms of loans to be obtained by the national government and government corporations must be in accordance with the provisions of pertinent laws, although other loans may be made on terms similar to those prevailing in the international capital markets.

Seventeen foreign banks are operating offshore banking units in the Philippines. These units may engage in a wide range of foreign currency transactions with nonresidents and with other offshore banking units. They are permitted to lend to resident importers and exporters, provided that such loans do not have public guarantees, that the funds have been remitted from abroad and sold to the banking system, and that loans are authorized by the central bank. Offshore banking units may open and maintain deposit accounts in pesos exclusively with domestic agent banks to meet administrative and other operating expenses, and to pay designated local beneficiaries of nonresident Philippine or multinational companies the equivalent of foreign exchange remittances channeled through the offshore banking units' correspondent banks abroad. Offshore banking units may also sell inward remittances of foreign exchange to the central bank.

Under the Foreign Investments Act of 1991, non-Philippine nationals not otherwise disqualified by law may, upon registration with the Securities and Exchange Commission (SEC), conduct business in the country or invest in domestic enterprises up to 100 percent of capital unless participation is prohibited by existing law. However, enterprises seeking to apply for incentives, as well as foreign investors in export enterprises, must also register with the BOI.

All industrial enterprises, whether owned by nationals or nonnationals, shall comply with the environmental standards set by the government.

GOLD

Small-scale miners are required to sell all of their production to the central bank. All other forms or types of gold may, at the option of the owner or producer and with the consent of the central bank, be sold and delivered to the central bank. Producers are paid in Philippine pesos on the basis of the latest London fixing price and the prevailing Philippine peso-US dollar exchange rate. The gold so acquired is deemed to be part of official international reserves. The central bank may sell gold grains, pellets, bars, and sheets to local jewelry manufacturers and other industrial users upon application, or to banks only for resale to jewelry manufacturers and industrial users, at the central bank's gold-selling price plus a service fee to cover costs, including cost of conversion and packaging.

The exportation of gold in any form, except that produced by small-scale miners, is permitted. There are no restrictions on the importation of any form of gold except coin blanks essentially of gold and gold coins, and those without any indication of actual fineness of gold content.

Various denominations of gold coins have been issued by the Central Bank of the Philippines [BSP], as follows: a 1 Peso Paul VI coin (1970); a 1,000 Piso Ang Bagong Lipunan coin (1975); a 1,500 Piso IMF-IBRD coin (1976); the 1,500 Piso Ang-Bagong Lipunan coins (1977 and 1978); a 5,000 Piso Ang Bagong Lipunan coin (1977); a 2,500 Piso Douglas MacArthur centenary coin (1980); the 1,500 Piso Pope John Paul II coins (1980 and 1981); a 1,500 Piso Bataan-Corregidor coin (1982); a 2,500 Piso AquinoReagan coin (1986); and a 10,000 Democracy Restored coin (1992). Transactions in legal tender gold coins are governed by the provisions of Central Bank Circular No. 960 (Sections 175 and 176), dated October 21, 1983.

CHANGES DURING 1993

Administration of Control

April 13 Central Bank Circular No. 1389 setting forth the status of the central bank's rules and regulations on current accounts, capital accounts, foreign currency deposit units, offshore banking units, and representative offices of foreign banks was issued. The circular repealed provisions of other rules and regulations that are incompatible with the circular. Included among the changes were modifications to the list of prohibited exports and the liberalization of limitations in repatriating capital, profits, and dividends pursuant to foreign direct investments.

June 23 (1) Offshore banks were authorized to lend under trade facilities; (2) short-term loans from offshore banking units to private importers/exporters would be permitted, provided that there are no public guarantees of such loans and that foreign exchange has been remitted from abroad and sold to the banking system; assignment of loans by creditors would, however, require prior approval from the central bank (Central Bank Circular No. 1393).

September 15 (1) All references to the Central Bank of the Philippines in Circular No. 1389 were amended to read the Bangko Sentral ng Pilipinas; (2) offshore banking units were authorized to issue and register export declarations and open letters of credit for importations of resident-borrowers, provided that such importations would be funded by foreign currency loans from offshore banking units authorized by the central bank (Central Bank Circular No. 5 of Series 1993); (3) private sector loans not guaranteed by foreign governments or official credit agencies and used to finance imports of freely importable products under deferred letters of credit and private sector loans granted by foreign companies to their local branches were included on the list of loans that do not require prior approval from the central bank; and (4) applications to purchase foreign exchange for outward investments, whether or not prior central bank approval is required, were required to be accompanied by (a) a project feasibility study, investment proposal/ subscription agreement, bond/stock offering circular, and other documents showing the nature and place of the investment; and (b) a written undertaking to transfer to the Philippines and sell for pesos through authorized banks the dividends/ earnings or divestment proceeds from outward investments that were funded by foreign exchange purchased from authorized dealers.

International Payments

International transactions add an additional layer of risk for buyers and sellers that are familiar only with doing business domestically. Currency regulations, foreign exchange risk, political, economic, or social upheaval in the buyer's or seller's country, and different business customs may all contribute to uncertainty. Ultimately, however, the seller wants to make sure he gets paid and the buyer wants to get what he pays for. Choosing the right payment method can be the key to the transaction's feasibility and profitability.

There are four common methods of international payment, each providing the buyer and the seller with varying degrees of protection for getting paid and for guaranteeing shipment. Ranked in order of most security for the seller to most security for the buyer, they are: cash in advance, documentary letters of credit (L/C), documentary collections (D/P and D/A Terms), and open account (O/A).

Cash in Advance

In cash in advance terms the buyer simply prepays the seller prior to shipment of goods. Cash in advance terms are generally used in new relationships where transactions are small and the buyer has no choice but to prepay. These terms give maximum security to the seller but leave the buyer at great risk. Because the buyer has no guarantee that the goods will be shipped, he must have a high degree of trust in the seller's ability and willingness to follow through. The buyer must also consider the economic, political and social stability of the seller's country, as these conditions may make it impossible for the seller to ship as promised.

Documentary Letters of Credit

A letter of credit is a bank's promise to pay a seller on behalf of the buyer so long as the seller meets the terms and conditions stated in the credit. Documents are the key issue in letter of credit transactions. Banks act as intermediaries, and have nothing to do with the goods themselves.

Letters of credit are the most common form of international payment because they provide a high degree of protection for both the seller and the buyer. The buyer specifies the documentation that he requires from the seller before the bank is to make payment, and the seller is given assurance that he will receive payment after shipping his goods so long as the documentation is in order.

Documentary Collections

A documentary collection is like an international cash on delivery (COD), but with a few twists. The exporter ships goods to the importer, but forwards shipping documents (including title document) to his bank for transmission to the buyer's bank. The buyer's bank is instructed not to transfer the documents to the buyer until payment is made (Documents against Payment, D/P) or upon guarantee that payment will be made within a specified period of time (Documents against Acceptance, D/A). Once the buyer has the documentation for the shipment he is able to take possession of the goods.

D/P and D/A terms are commonly used in ongoing business relationships and provide a measure of protection for both parties. The buyer and seller, however, both assume risk in the transaction, ranging from refusal on the part of the buyer to pay for the documents, to the seller's shipping of unacceptable goods.

Open Account

This is an agreement by the buyer to pay for goods within a designated time after their shipment, usually in 30, 60, or 90 days. Open account terms give maximum security to the buyer and greatest risk to the seller. This form of payment is used only when the seller has significant trust and faith in the buyer's ability and willingness to pay once the goods have been shipped. The seller must also consider the economic, political, and social stability of the buyer's country as these conditions may make it impossible for the buyer to pay as promised.

DOCUMENTARY COLLECTIONS (D/P, D/A)

Documentary collections focus on the transfer of documents such as bills of lading for the transfer of ownership of goods rather than on the goods themselves. They are easier to use than letters of credit and bank service charges are generally lower.

This form of payment is excellent for buyers who wish to purchase goods without risking prepayment and without having to go through the more cumbersome letter of credit process.

Documentary collection procedures, however, entail risk for the seller, because payment is not made until after goods are shipped. In addition, the seller assumes the risk while the goods are in transit and storage until payment/acceptance take place. Banks involved in the transaction do not guarantee payments. A seller should therefore only agree to a documentary collection procedure if the transaction includes the following characteristics:

- The seller does not doubt the buyer's ability and willingness to pay for the goods;
- The buyer's country is politically, economically, and legally stable;
- There are no foreign exchange restrictions in the buyer's home country, or unless all necessary licenses for foreign exchange have already been obtained; and
- The goods to be shipped are easily marketable.

TYPES OF COLLECTIONS

The three types of documentary collections are:
- Documents against Payment (D/P)
- Documents against Acceptance (D/A)
- Collection with Acceptance (Acceptance D/P)

All of these collection procedures follow the same general step-by-step process of exchanging documents proving title to goods for either cash or a contracted promise to pay at a later time. The documents are transferred from the seller (called the remitter) to the buyer (called the drawee) via intermediary banks. When the seller ships goods, he presents documents such as the bill of lading, invoices, and certificate of origin to his representative bank (the remitting bank), which then forwards them to the buyer's bank (the collecting bank). According to the type of documentary collection, the buyer may then do one of the following:

- With Documents against Payment (D/P), the buyer may only receive the title and other documents after paying for the goods;
- With Documents against Acceptance (D/A), the buyer may receive the title and other documents after signing a time draft promising to pay at a later date; or
- With Acceptance Documents against Payment (Acceptance D/P), the buyer signs a time draft for payment at a later date. However, he may only obtain the documents after the time draft reaches maturity. In essence, the goods remain in escrow until payment has been made.

In all cases the buyer may take possession of the goods only by presenting the bill of lading to customs and shipping authorities.

In the event that the prospective buyer cannot or will not pay for the goods shipped, they remain in the legal possession of the seller; however he may be stuck with them in an unfavorable situation. Also, the seller has no legal basis to file claim against the prospective buyer. At this point the seller may:

- Have the goods returned and sell them on his domestic market; or
- Sell the goods to another buyer near where the goods are currently held.

If the seller takes no action the goods will be auctioned or otherwise disposed of by customs.

PROCEDURE

The documentary collection process has been standardized by a set of rules published by the International Chamber of Commerce (ICC). These rules are called the Uniform Rules for Collections (URC) and are contained in ICC Publication No. 322. (*See* "Further Reading" on page 267 for ICC addresses and a list of available publications.)

The following is the basic set of steps used in a documentary collection. Refer to the illustration on the following page for a graphic representation of the procedure.

① The seller (remitter, exporter) ships the goods.

② and ③ The seller forwards the agreed upon documents to his bank, the remitting bank, which in turn forwards them to the collecting bank (buyer's bank).

④ The collecting bank notifies the buyer (drawee, importer) and informs him of the conditions under which he can take possession of the documents.

⑤ To take possession of the documents, the buyer makes payment or signs a time deposit.

⑥ and ⑦ If the buyer draws the documents against payment, the collecting bank transfers payment to the remitting bank for credit to the seller's account. If the buyer draws the documents against acceptance, the collecting bank sends the acceptance to the remitting bank or retains it up to maturity. On maturity, the collecting bank collects the bill and transfers it to the remitting bank for payment to the seller.

DOCUMENTARY COLLECTION PROCEDURE

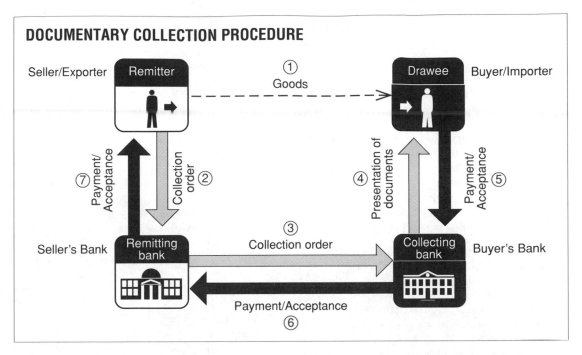

TIPS FOR BUYERS

1. The buyer is generally in a secure position because he does not assume ownership or responsibility for goods until he has paid for the documents or signed a time draft.

2. The buyer may not sample or inspect the goods before accepting and paying for the documents without authorization from the seller. However, the buyer may in advance specify a certificate of inspection as part of the required documentation package.

3. As a special favor, the collecting bank can allow the buyer to inspect the documents before payment. The collecting bank assumes responsibility for the documents until their redemption.

4. In the above case, the buyer should immediately return the entire set of documents to the collecting bank if he cannot meet the agreed payment procedure.

5. The buyer assumes no liability for goods if he refuses to take possession of the documents.

6. Partial payment in exchange for the documents is not allowed unless authorized in the collection order.

7. With documents against acceptance, the buyer may receive the goods and resell them for profit before the time draft matures, thereby using the proceeds of the sale to pay for the goods. The buyer remains responsible for payment, however, even if he cannot sell the goods.

TIPS FOR SELLERS

1. The seller assumes risk because he ships goods before receiving payment. The buyer is under no legal obligation to pay for or to accept the goods.

2. Before agreeing to a documentary collection, the seller should check on the buyer's creditworthiness and business reputation.

3. The seller should make sure the buyer's country is politically and financially stable.

4. The seller should find out what documents are required for customs clearance in the buyer's country. Customs brokers may be of help.

5. The seller should assemble the documents carefully and make sure they are in the required form and endorsed as necessary.

6. As a rule, the remitting bank will not review the documents before forwarding them to the collecting bank. This is the responsibility of the seller.

7. The goods travel and are stored at the risk of the seller until payment or acceptance.

8. If the buyer refuses acceptance or payment for the documents, the seller retains ownership. The seller may have the goods shipped back or try to sell them to another buyer in the region.

9. If the buyer takes no action, customs authorities may seize the goods and auction them off or otherwise dispose of them.

10. Because goods may be refused, the seller should only ship goods which are readily marketable to other sources.

Letters of Credit (L/C)

A letter of credit is a document issued by a bank stating its commitment to pay someone (seller/exporter/supplier) a stated amount of money on behalf of a buyer (importer) so long as the seller meets very specific terms and conditions. Letters of credit are often called documentary letters of credit because the banks handling the transaction deal in documents as opposed to goods. Letters of credit are the most common method of making international payments, because the risks of the transaction are shared by both the buyer and the seller.

STEPS IN USING AN L/C

The letter of credit process has been standardized by a set of rules published by the International Chamber of Commerce (ICC). These rules are called the Uniform Customs and Practice for Documentary Credits (UCP) and are contained in ICC Publication No. 500. (*See* "Further Reading" on page 267 for ICC addresses and list of available publications.) The following is the basic set of steps used in a letter of credit transaction. Specific letter of credit transactions follow somewhat different procedures.

- After the buyer and seller agree on the terms of a sale, the buyer arranges for his bank to open a letter of credit in favor of the seller.
- The buyer's bank (the issuing bank), prepares the letter of credit, including all of the buyer's instructions to the seller concerning shipment and required documentation.
- The buyer's bank sends the letter of credit to a correspondent bank (the advising bank), in the seller's country. The seller may request that a particular bank be the advising bank, or the domestic bank may select one of its correspondent banks in the seller's country.
- The advising bank forwards the letter of credit to the seller.

- The seller carefully reviews all conditions the buyer has stipulated in the letter of credit. If the seller cannot comply with one or more of the provisions he immediately notifies the buyer and asks that an amendment be made to the letter of credit.
- After final terms are agreed upon, the seller prepares the goods and arranges for their shipment to the appropriate port.
- The seller ships the goods, and obtains a bill of lading and other documents as required by the buyer in the letter of credit. Some of these documents may need to be obtained prior to shipment.
- The seller presents the required documents to the advising bank, indicating full compliance with the terms of the letter of credit. Required documents usually include a bill of lading, commercial invoice, certificate of origin, and possibly an inspection certificate if required by the buyer.
- The advising bank reviews the documents. If they are in order, they are forwarded to the issuing bank. If it is an irrevocable, confirmed letter of credit, the seller is guaranteed payment and may be paid immediately by the advising bank.
- Once the issuing bank receives the documents it notifies the buyer who then reviews the documents. If the documents are in order the buyer signs off, taking possession of the documents, including the bill of lading, which he then uses to take possession of the shipment.
- The issuing bank initiates payment to the advising bank, which pays the seller.

The transfer of funds from the buyer to his bank, from the buyer's bank to the seller's bank, and from the seller's bank to the seller may be handled at the same time as the exchange of documents, or under terms agreed upon in advance.

PARTIES TO A LETTER OF CREDIT TRANSACTION

Buyer/Importer	Buyer	Seller	Seller/Exporter/Supplier
Buyer's bank	Issuing bank	Advising bank	Seller's bank

ISSUANCE

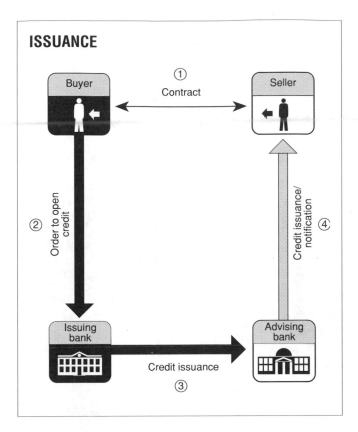

ISSUANCE OF A LETTER OF CREDIT

① Buyer and seller agree on purchase contract.
② Buyer applies for and opens a letter of credit with issuing ("buyer's") bank.
③ Issuing bank issues the letter of credit, forwarding it to advising ("seller's") bank.
④ Advising bank notifies seller of letter of credit.

AMENDMENT

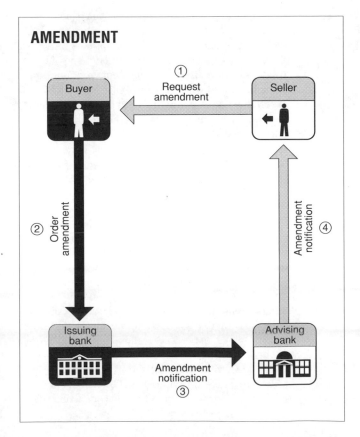

AMENDMENT OF A LETTER OF CREDIT

① Seller requests (of the buyer) a modification (amendment) of the terms of the letter of credit. Once the terms are agreed upon:
② Buyer issues order to issuing ("buyer's") bank to make an amendment to the terms of the letter of credit.
③ Issuing bank notifies advising ("seller's") bank of amendment.
④ Advising bank notifies seller of amendment.

UTILIZATION

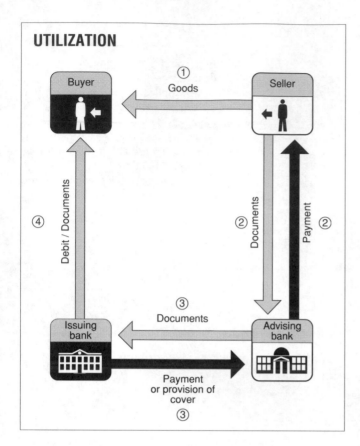

UTILIZATION OF A LETTER OF CREDIT

(Irrevocable, confirmed credit)

① Seller ships goods to buyer.

② Seller forwards all documents (as stipulated in the letter of credit) to advising bank. Once documents are reviewed and accepted, advising bank pays seller for the goods.

③ Advising bank forwards documents to issuing bank. Once documents are reviewed and accepted, issuing bank pays advising bank.

④ Issuing bank forwards documents to buyer. Seller's letter of credit, or account, is debited.

COMMON PROBLEMS IN LETTER OF CREDIT TRANSACTIONS

Most problems with letter of credit transactions have to do with the ability of the seller to fulfill obligations the buyer establishes in the original letter of credit. The seller may find the terms of the credit difficult or impossible to fulfill and either tries to do so and fails, or asks the buyer for an amendment to the letter of credit. Observers note that as many as half of all letters of credit are amended or renegotiated entirely. Since most letters of credit are irrevocable, amendments to the original letter of credit can only be made after further negotiations and agreements between the buyer and the seller. Sellers may have one or more of the following problems:

- Shipment schedule stipulated in the letter of credit cannot be met.
- Stipulations concerning freight cost are deemed unacceptable.
- Price is insufficient due to changes in exchange rates.
- Quantity of product ordered is not the expected amount.
- Description of product to be shipped is either insufficient or too detailed.
- Documents stipulated in the letter of credit are difficult or impossible to obtain.

Even when sellers accept the terms of a letter of credit, problems often arise at the stage in which banks review, or negotiate, the documents provided by the seller against the requirements specified in the letter of credit. If the documents are found not to be in accord with those specified in the letter of credit, the bank's commitment to pay is invalidated. In some cases the seller can correct the documents and present them within the time specified in the letter of credit. Or the advising bank may ask the issuing bank for authorization to accept the documents despite the discrepancies found.

Limits on Legal Obligations of Banks

It is important to note once again that banks deal in documents and not in goods. Only the wording of the credit is binding on the bank. Banks are not responsible for verifying the authenticity of the documents, nor for the quality or quantity of the goods being shipped. As long as the documents comply with the specified terms of the letter of credit, banks may accept them and initiate the payment process as stipulated in the letter of credit. Banks are free from liability for delays in sending messages caused by another party, consequences of Acts of God, or the acts of third parties whom they have instructed to carry out transactions.

TYPES OF LETTERS OF CREDIT

Basic Letters of Credit

There are two basic forms of letters of credit: the Revocable credit and the Irrevocable credit. There are also two types of Irrevocable credit: the Irrevocable credit not confirmed, and the Irrevocable confirmed credit. Each type of credit has advantages and disadvantages for the buyer and for the seller. Also note that the more the banks assume risk by guaranteeing payment, the more they will charge for providing the service.

Revocable Credit This credit can be changed or canceled by the buyer without prior notice to the seller. Because they offer little security to the seller, revocable credits are generally unacceptable to the seller and are rarely used.

Irrevocable Credit The irrevocable credit is one the issuing bank commits itself irrevocably to honor, provided the seller complies with all stipulated conditions. This credit cannot be changed or canceled without the consent of both the buyer and the seller. As a result, this type of credit is the most widely used in international trade. Irrevocable credits are more expensive because of the issuing bank's added liability in guaranteeing the credit. There are two types of irrevocable credits:

- **The irrevocable credit not confirmed by the advising bank (unconfirmed credit)** This means that the buyer's bank which issues the credit is the only party responsible for payment to the seller, and the seller's bank is obliged to pay the seller only after receiving payment from the buyer's bank. The seller's bank merely acts on behalf of the issuing bank and therefore incurs no risk.

- **The irrevocable, confirmed credit** In a confirmed credit, the advising bank adds its guarantee to pay the seller to that of the issuing bank. If the issuing bank fails to make payment the advising bank will pay. If a seller is unfamiliar with the buyer's bank which issues the letter of credit, he may insist on an irrevocable confirmed credit. These credits may be used when trade is conducted in a high risk area where there are fears of outbreak of war or social, political, or financial instability. Confirmed credits may also be used by the seller to enlist the aid of a local bank to extend financing to enable him to fill the order. A confirmed credit costs more because the bank has added liability.

Special Letters of Credit

There are numerous special letters of credit designed to meet specific needs of buyers, sellers, and intermediaries. Special letters of credit usually involve increased participation by banks, so financing and service charges are higher than those for basic letters of credit. The following is a brief description of some special letters of credit.

Standby Letter of Credit This credit is basically a payment or performance guarantee. It is used primarily in the United States because US banks are prevented by law from giving certain guarantees. Standby credits are often called non-performing letters of credit because they are only used as a backup payment method if the collection on a primary payment method is past due.

Standby letters of credit can be used, for example, to guarantee the following types of payment and performance:

- repayment of loans
- fulfillment by subcontractors
- securing the payment for goods delivered by third parties.

The beneficiary to a standby letter of credit can draw from it on demand, so the buyer assumes added risk.

Revolving Letter of Credit This credit is a commitment on the part of the issuing bank to restore the credit to the original amount after it has been used or drawn down. The number of times it can be utilized and the period of validity is stated in the credit. The credit can be cumulative or noncumulative. Cumulative means that unutilized sums can be added to the next installment whereas noncumulative means that partial amounts not utilized in time expire.

Deferred Payment Letter of Credit In this credit the buyer takes delivery of the shipped goods by accepting the documents and agreeing to pay his bank after a fixed period of time. This credit gives the buyer a grace period, and ensures that the seller gets payment on the due date.

Red Clause Letter of Credit This is used to provide the seller with some funds prior to shipment to finance production of the goods. The credit may be advanced in part or in full, and the buyer's bank finances the advance payment. The buyer, in essence, extends financing to the seller and incurs ultimate risk for all advanced credits.

Transferable Letter of Credit This allows the seller to transfer all or part of the proceeds of the letter of credit to a second beneficiary, usually the ultimate producer of the goods. This is a common financing tactic for middlemen and is used extensively in East Asia.

Back-to-Back Letter of Credit This is a new credit opened on the basis of an already existing, nontransferable credit. It is used by traders to make payment to the ultimate supplier. A trader receives a letter of credit from the buyer and then opens another letter of credit in favor of the supplier. The first letter of credit is used as collateral for the second credit. The second credit makes price adjustments from which come the trader's profit.

OPENING A LETTER OF CREDIT

The wording in a letter of credit should be simple but specific. The more detailed an L/C is, the more likely the seller will reject it as too difficult to fulfill. At the same time, the buyer will wish to define in detail what he is paying for.

Although the L/C process is designed to ensure the satisfaction of all parties to the transaction, it cannot be considered a substitute for face-to-face agreements to do business in good faith. It should therefore contain only those stipulations required from the banks involved in the documentary process.

L/Cs used in trade are usually either irrevocable unconfirmed credits or irrevocable confirmed credits. In choosing the type of L/C to open in favor of the seller, the buyer should take into consideration generally accepted payment processes in the seller's country, the value and demand for the goods to be shipped, and the reputation of the seller.

In specifying documents necessary from the seller, it is very important to demand documents that are required for customs clearance and those that reflect the agreement reached between the buyer and the seller. Required documents usually include the bill of lading, a commercial and/or consular invoice, the bill of exchange, the certificate of origin, and the insurance document. Other documents required may be copies of a cable sent to the buyer with shipping information, a confirmation from the shipping company of the state of its ship, and a confirmation from the forwarder that the goods are accompanied by a certificate of origin. Prices should be stated in the currency of the L/C, and documents should be supplied in the language of the L/C.

THE APPLICATION

The following information should be included on an application form for opening an L/C.

① **Beneficiary** The seller's company name and address should be written completely and correctly. Incomplete or incorrect information results in delays and unnecessary additional cost.

② **Amount** Is the figure a maximum amount or an approximate amount? If words like "circa," "ca.," "about," etc., are used in connection with the amount of the credit, it means that a difference as high as 10 percent upwards or downwards is permitted. In such a case, the same word should also be used in connection with the quantity.

③ **Validity Period** The validity and period for presentation of the documents following shipment of the goods should be sufficiently long to allow the exporter time to prepare the necessary documents and ship them to the bank. Under place of validity, state the domicile of either the advising bank or the issuing bank.

④ **Beneficiary's Bank** If no bank is named, the issuing bank is free to select the correspondent bank.

⑤ **Type of Payment** Availability Sight drafts, time drafts, or deferred payment may be used, as previously agreed to by the seller and buyer.

⑥ **Desired Documents** Here the buyer specifies precisely which documents he requires. To obtain effective protection against the supply of poor quality goods, for instance, he can demand the submission of analysis or quality certificates. These are generally issued by specialized inspection companies or laboratories.

⑦ **Notify Address** An address is given for notification of the imminent arrival of goods at the port or airport of destination. Damage of goods in shipment is also cause for notification. An agent representing the buyer may be used.

⑧ **Description of Goods** Here a short, precise description of the goods is given, along with quantity. If the credit amount carries the notation "ca.," the same notation should appear with the quantity.

⑨ **Confirmation Order** It may happen that the foreign beneficiary insists on having the credit confirmed by the bank in his country.

SAMPLE LETTER OF CREDIT APPLICATION

Sender American Import-Export Co., Inc. 123 Main Street San Francisco, California ———— Our reference AB/02	**Instructions** **to open a Documentary Credit** San Francisco, 30th September 19.. Place / Date

Please open the following [X] irrevocable [ ] revocable documentary credit	**Domestic Bank Corporation** Documentary Credits P.O. Box 1040 San Francisco, California
① Beneficiary Goodwill Trading Company 711-715 Rizal Avenue Manila Philippines	④ Beneficiary's bank (if known) Bank of the Philippine Islands BPI Building Ayala Avenue Makati, Metro Manila Philippines
② Amount US$70,200.--	Please advise this bank [ ] by letter [X] by letter, cabling main details in advance [ ] by telex / telegram with full text of credit
③ Date and place of expiry 25th November 19.. in San Francisco	
Partial shipments [X] allowed [ ] not allowed Transhipment [ ] allowed [X] not allowed	Terms of shipment (FOB, C & F, CIF) CIF San Francisco
Despatch from / Taking in charge at Hong Kong For transportation to San Francisco	Latest date of shipment 10th Nov. 19.. ③ 15 days after date of despatch Documents must be presented not later than

Beneficiary may dispose of the credit amount as follows ⑤

[X] at sight upon presentation of documents

[ ] after ....days, calculated from date of ....

[ ] by a draft due ....

drawn on [ ] you [ ] your correspondents

which you / your correspondents will please accept

against surrender of the following documents ⑥

[X] invoice   (....3......copies)

Shipping document
[X] sea: bill of lading, to order, endorsed in blank
[ ] rail: dublicate waybill
[ ] air: air consignment note
[ ]

[X] insurance policy, certificte   (.................. copies)
covering the following risks:
"all risks" including war up to
[ ] Additional documents final destination in
the USA
[X] Confirmation of the carrier that the
ship is not more than 15 years old

[X] packing list (3 copies)

⑦ Notify address in bill of lading / goods addressed to American Import-Export Co., Inc. 123 Main Street San Francisco, California	Goods insured by [ ] us [X] seller

Goods ⑧

1'000 "Record players ANC 83 as per pro forma invoice
no. 74/1853 dd 10th September 19.."

at US$70.20 per item

Your correspondents to advise beneficiary [ ] adding their confirmation [X] without adding their confirmation ⑨

Payments to be debited to our U.S. Dollars ....account no 10-32679150

NB. The applicable text is marked by [X]

E 6801 N 1/2 3.81 5000

American Import-Export Co., Inc.

Signature _____

For mailing please see overleaf

TIPS FOR PARTIES TO A LETTER OF CREDIT

Buyer

1. Before opening a letter of credit, the buyer should reach agreement with the seller on all particulars of payment procedures, schedules of shipment, type of goods to be sent, and documents to be supplied by the supplier.

2. When choosing the type of L/C to be used, the buyer should take into account standard payment methods in the country of the seller.

3. When opening a letter of credit, the buyer should keep the details of the purchase short and concise.

4. The buyer should be prepared to amend or renegotiate terms of the L/C with the seller. This is a common procedure in international trade. On irrevocable L/Cs, the most common type, amendments may be made only if all parties involved in the L/C agree.

5. The buyer can eliminate exchange risk involved with import credits in foreign currencies by purchasing foreign exchange on the forward markets.

6. The buyer should use a bank experienced in foreign trade as the L/C issuing bank.

7. The validation time stated on the L/C should give the seller ample time to produce the goods or to pull them out of stock.

8. The buyer should be aware that an L/C is not fail-safe. Banks are only responsible for the documents exchanged and not the goods shipped. Documents in conformity with L/C specifications cannot be rejected on grounds that the goods were not delivered as specified in the contract. The goods shipped may not in fact be the goods ordered and paid for.

9. Purchase contracts and other agreements pertaining to the sale between the buyer and seller are not the concern of the issuing bank. Only the terms of the L/C are binding on the bank.

10. Documents specified in the L/C should include those the buyer requires for customs clearance.

Seller

1. Before signing a contract, the seller should make inquiries about the buyer's creditworthiness and business practices. The seller's bank will generally assist in this investigation.

2. The seller should confirm the good standing of the buyer's bank if the credit is unconfirmed.

3. For confirmed credit, it should be determined that the seller's local bank is willing to confirm credits from the buyer and the buyer's bank.

4. The seller should carefully review the L/C to make sure these can be met: specified schedules of shipment, type of goods to be sent, packaging, and documentation. All aspects of the L/C must be in conformance with the terms agreed upon, including the seller's address, the amount to be paid, and the prescribed transport route.

5. The seller must comply with every detail of the L/C specifications; otherwise the security given by the credit is lost.

6. The seller should ensure that the L/C is irrevocable.

7. If conditions of the credit have to be modified, the seller should contact the buyer immediately so that the buyer can instruct the issuing bank to make the necessary amendments.

8. The seller should confirm with the insurance company that it can provide the coverage specified in the credit and that insurance charges in the L/C are correct. Insurance coverage is often for CIF (cost, insurance, freight) value of the goods plus 10 percent.

9. The seller must ensure that the details of goods being sent comply with the description in the L/C and that the description on the invoice matches that on the L/C.

10. The seller should be familiar with foreign exchange limitations in the buyer's country that could hinder payment procedures.

GLOSSARY

DOCUMENTS IN INTERNATIONAL TRADE

The following is a list and description of some of the more common documents importers and exporters encounter in the course of international trade. For the importer/buyer this serves as a checklist of documents he may require of the seller/exporter in a letter of credit or documents against payment method.

bill of lading A document issued by a transportation company (such as a shipping line) to the shipper that serves as a receipt for goods shipped, a contract for delivery, and may serve as a title document. The major types are:

- **straight (nonnegotiable) bill of lading** Indicates that the shipper will deliver the goods to the consignee. The document itself does not give title to the goods. The consignee need only identify himself to claim the goods. A straight bill of lading is often used when the goods have been paid for in advance.

- **order (negotiable or "shippers order") bill of lading** This is a title document which must be in the possession of the consignee (buyer/importer) in order for him to take possession of the shipped goods. Because this bill of lading is negotiable, it is usually made out "to the order of" the consignor (seller/exporter).

- **air waybill** A bill of lading issued for air shipment of goods, which is always made out in straight non-negotiable form. It serves as a receipt for the shipper and needs to be made out to someone who can take possession of the goods upon arrival—without waiting for other documents to arrive.

- **overland/inland bill of lading** Similar to an Air Waybill, except that it covers ground or water transport.

certificate of origin A document certifying the country of origin of the goods. Because a certificate of origin is often required by customs for entry, a buyer will often stipulate in his letter of credit that a certificate of origin is a required document.

certificate of manufacture A document in which the producer of goods certifies that production has been completed and that the goods are at the disposal of the buyer.

consular invoice An invoice prepared on a special form supplied by the consul of an importing country, in the language of the importing country, and certified by a consular official of the foreign country of origin.

dock receipt A document/receipt issued by an ocean carrier when the seller/exporter is not responsible for moving the goods to their final destination, but only to a dock in the exporting country. The document/receipt indicates that the goods were, in fact, delivered and received at the specified dock.

export license A document, issued by a government agency, giving authorization to export certain commodities to specified countries.

import license A document, issued by a government agency, giving authorization to import certain commodities.

inspection certificate An affidavit signed by the seller/exporter or an independent inspection firm (as required by the buyer/importer), confirming that merchandise meets certain specifications.

insurance document A document certifying that goods are insured for shipment.

invoice/commercial invoice A document identifying the seller and buyer of goods or services, identifying numbers such as invoice number, date, shipping date, mode of transport, delivery and payment terms, and a complete listing and description of the goods or services being sold including prices, discounts, and quantities. The commercial invoice is usually used by customs to determine the true cost of goods when assessing duty.

packing list A document listing the merchandise contained in a particular box, crate, or container, plus type, dimensions, and weight of the container.

phytosanitary (plant health) inspection certificate A document certifying that an export shipment has been inspected and is free from pests and plant diseases considered harmful by the importing country.

shipper's export declaration A form prepared by a shipper/exporter indicating the value, weight, destination, and other information about an export shipment.

INCOTERMS 1990

Incoterms are a codification of international rules for the uniform interpretation of common contract clauses in export/import transactions. Incoterms were developed by the International Chamber of Commerce (ICC) in Paris, France.

CIP—carriage and insurance paid to (... named place of destination)

"Carriage and insurance paid to..." means that the seller has the same obligations as under CPT, but with the addition that the seller has to procure cargo insurance against the buyer's risk of loss of or damage to the goods during the carriage. The seller contracts for insurance and pays the insurance premium. The buyer should note that under the CIP term the seller is only required to obtain insurance on minimum coverage. The CIP term requires the seller to clear the goods for export. This term may be used for any mode of transport including multimodal transport.

CPT—carriage paid to (... named place of destination)

"Carriage paid to..." means that the seller pays the freight for the carriage of the goods to the named destination. The risk of loss of or damage to the goods, as well as any additional costs due to events occurring after the time the goods have been delivered to the carrier, is transferred from the seller to the buyer when the goods have been delivered into the custody of the carrier.

"Carrier" means any person who, in contract of carriage, undertakes to perform or to procure the performance of carriage, by rail, road, sea, air, inland waterway or by a combination of such modes. If subsequent carriers are used for the carriage to the agreed destination, the risk passes when the goods have been delivered to the first carrier. The CPT term requires the seller to clear the goods for export. This term may be used for any mode of transport including multimodal transport.

CFR—cost and freight (... named port of destination)

"Cost and Freight" means that the seller must pay the costs and freight necessary to bring the goods to the named port of destination but the risk of loss of or damage to the goods, as well as any additional costs due to events occurring after the time the goods have been delivered on board the vessel, is transferred from the seller to the buyer when the goods pass the ship's rail in the port of shipment. The CFR term requires the seller to clear the goods for export. This term can only by used for sea and inland waterway transport. When the ship's rail serves no practical purpose, such as in the case of roll-on/roll-off or container traffic, the CPT term is more appropriate to use.

CIF—cost, insurance, freight (... named port of destination)

"Cost, Insurance, Freight" means that the seller has

the same obligations as under CFR but with the addition that he has to procure marine insurance against the buyer's risk of loss of or damage to the goods during the carriage. The seller contracts for insurance and pays the insurance premium.

The buyer should note that under the CIF term the seller is only required to obtain insurance on minimum coverage. The CIF term requires the seller to clear the goods for export.

This term can only be used for sea and inland waterway transport. When the ship's rail serves no practical purpose such as in the case of roll-on/roll-off or container traffic, the CIP term is more appropriate to use.

DAF—delivered at frontier (... named place)

"Delivered at Frontier" means that the seller fulfils his obligation to deliver when the goods have been made available, cleared for export, at the named point and place at the frontier, but before the customs border of the adjoining country. The term "frontier" may be used for any frontier including that of the country of export. Therefore, it is of vital importance that the frontier in question be defined precisely by always naming the point and place in the term. The term is primarily intended to be used when goods are to be carried by rail or road, but it may be used for any mode of transport.

DDP—delivered duty paid (... named place of destination)

"Delivered duty paid" means that the seller fulfils his obligation to deliver when the goods have been made available at the named place in the country of importation. The seller has to bear the risks and costs including duties, taxes and other charges of delivering the goods thereto, cleared for importation. While the EXW term represents the minimum obligation for the seller, DDP represents the maximum obligation.

This term should not be used if the seller is unable directly or indirectly to obtain the import licence. If the parties wish the buyer to clear the goods for importation and to pay the duty, the term DDU (delivered duty unpaid) should be used.

If the parties wish to exclude from the seller's obligations some of the costs payable upon importation of the goods (such as value added tax (VAT)), this should be made clear by adding words to this effect: "Delivered duty paid, VAT unpaid (... named place or destination)."

This term may be used irrespective of the mode of transport.

DDU—delivered duty unpaid (... named place of destination)

"Delivered duty unpaid" means that the seller fulfils his obligation to deliver when the goods have been made available at the named place in the country of importation. The seller has to bear the costs and risks involved in bringing the goods thereto (excluding duties, taxes and other official charges payable upon importation as well as the costs and risks of carrying out customs formalities). The buyer has to pay any additional costs and to bear any risks caused by his failure to clear the goods for import in time.

If the parties wish the seller to carry out customs formalities and bear the costs and risks resulting therefrom, this has to be made clear by adding words to this effect.

If the parties wish to include in the seller's obligations some of the costs payable upon importation of the goods (such as value added tax (VAT)), this should be made clear by adding words to this effect: "Delivered duty unpaid, VAT paid (... named place or destination)." This term may be used irrespective of the mode of transport.

DEQ—delivered ex quay (duty paid) (... named port of destination)

"Delivered Ex Quay (duty paid)" means that the seller fulfils his obligation to deliver when he has made the goods available to the buyer on the quay (wharf) at the named port of destination, cleared for importation. The seller has to bear all risks and costs including duties, taxes and other charges of delivering the goods thereto.

This term should not be used if the seller is unable directly or indirectly to obtain the import licence.

If the parties wish the buyer to clear the goods for importation and pay the duty the words "duty unpaid" should be used instead of "duty paid."

If the parties wish to exclude from the seller's obligations some of the costs payable upon importation of the goods (such as value added tax (VAT)), this should be made clear by adding words to this effect: "Delivered ex quay, VAT unpaid (... named port of destination)." This term can only be used for sea or inland waterway transport.

DES—delivered ex ship (... named port of destination)

"Delivered Ex Ship" means that the seller fulfils his obligation to deliver when the goods have been made available to the buyer on board the ship uncleared for import at the named port of destination. The seller has to bear all the costs and risks involved in bringing the goods to the named port of destination. This term can only be used for sea or inland waterway transport.

EXW—ex works (... named place)

"Ex works" means that the seller fulfils his obligation to deliver when he has made the goods available at his premises (i.e. works, factory, warehouse, etc.) to the buyer. In particular, he is not responsible for loading the goods on the vehicle provided by the buyer or for clearing the goods for export, unless otherwise agreed. The buyer bears all costs and risks involved in taking the goods from the seller's premises to the desired destination. This term thus represents the minimum obligation for the seller. This term should not be used when the buyer cannot carry out directly or indirectly the export formalities. In such circumstances, the FCA term should be used.

FAS—free alongside ship (... named port of shipment)

"Free Alongside Ship" means that the seller fulfills his obligation to deliver when the goods have been placed alongside the vessel on the quay or in lighters at the named port of shipment. This means that the buyer has to bear all costs and risks of loss of or damage to the goods from that moment. The FAS term requires the buyer to clear the goods for export. It should not be used when the buyer cannot carry out directly or indirectly the export formalities.

This term can only be used for sea or inland waterway transport.

FCA—free carrier (... named place)

"Free Carrier" means that the seller fulfills his obligation to deliver when he has handed over the goods, cleared for export, into the charge of the carrier named by the buyer at the named place or point. If no precise point is indicated by the buyer, the seller may choose within the place or range stipulated where the carrier shall take the goods into his charge. When, according to commercial practice, the seller's assistance is required in making the contract with the carrier (such as in rail or air transport) the seller may act at the buyer's risk and expense.

This term may be used for any mode of transport, including multimodal transport.

"Carrier" means any person who, in a contract of carriage, undertakes to perform or to procure the performance of carriage by rail, road, sea, air, inland waterway or by a combination of such modes. If the buyer instructs the seller to deliver the cargo to a person, e.g. a freight forwarder who is not a "carrier," the seller is deemed to have fulfilled his obligation to deliver the goods when they are in the custody of that person.

"Transport terminal" means a railway terminal, a freight station, a container terminal or yard, a multipurpose cargo terminal or any similar receiving point.

"Container" includes any equipment used to unitise cargo, e.g. all types of containers and/or flats, whether ISO accepted or not, trailers, swap bodies, ro-ro equipment, igloos, and applies to all modes of transport.

FOB—free on board (... named port of shipment)

"Free On Board" means that the seller fulfills his obligation to deliver when the goods have passed over the ship's rail at the named port of shipment. This means that the buyer has to bear all costs and risks of loss of or damage to the goods from that point. The FOB term requires the seller to clear the goods for export.

This term can only be used for sea or inland waterway transport. When the ship's rail serves no practical purpose, such as in the case of roll-on/roll-off or container traffic, the FCA term is more appropriate to use.

INTERNATIONAL PAYMENT TERMS

advice The forwarding of a letter of credit or an amendment to a letter of credit to the seller, or beneficiary of the letter of credit, by the advising bank (seller's bank).

advising bank The bank (usually the seller's bank) receiving a letter of credit from the issuing bank (the buyer's bank) and handling the transaction from the seller's side. This includes: validating the letter of credit, reviewing it for internal consistency, forwarding it to the seller, forwarding seller's documentation back to the issuing bank, and, in the case of a confirmed letter of credit, guaranteeing payment to the seller if his documents are in order and the terms of the credit are met.

amendment A change in the terms and conditions of a letter of credit, usually to meet the needs of the seller. The seller requests an amendment of the buyer who, if he agrees, instructs his bank (the issuing bank) to issue the amendment. The issuing bank informs the seller's bank (the advising bank) which then notifies the seller of the amendment. In the case of irrevocable letters of credit, amendments may only be made with the agreement of all parties to the transaction.

back-to-back letter of credit A new letter of credit opened in favor of another beneficiary on the basis of an already existing, nontransferable letter of credit.

beneficiary The entity to which credits and payments are made, usually the seller/supplier of goods.

bill of exchange A written order from one person to another to pay a specified sum of money to a designated person. The following two versions are the most common:

- **draft** A financial/legal document where one individual (the drawer) instructs another individual (the drawee) to pay a certain amount of money to a named person, usually in payment for the transfer of goods or services. Sight drafts are payable when presented. Time drafts (also called usance drafts) are payable at a future fixed (specific) date or determinable (30, 60, 90 days etc.) date. Time drafts are used as a financing tool (as with documents against acceptance D/P terms) to give the buyer time to pay for his purchase.
- **promissory note** A financial/legal document wherein one individual (the issuer) promises to pay another individual a certain amount.

collecting bank (also called the presenting bank) In a documentary collection, the bank (usually the buyer's bank) that collects payment or a time draft from the buyer to be forwarded to the remitting bank (usually the seller's bank) in exchange for shipping and other documents which enable the buyer to take possession of the goods.

confirmed letter of credit A letter of credit containing a guarantee on the part of both the issuing and advising bank of payment to the seller so long as the seller's documentation is in order and terms of the credit are met.

deferred payment letter of credit A letter of credit by which the buyer takes possession of the title documents and the goods by agreeing to pay the issuing bank at a fixed time in the future.

discrepancy The noncompliance with the terms and conditions of a letter of credit. A discrepancy may be as small as a misspelling, an inconsistency in dates or amounts, or a missing document. Some discrepancies can easily be fixed; others may lead to the eventual invalidation of the letter of credit.

D/A Abbreviation for "documents against acceptance."

D/P Abbreviation for "documents against payment."

documents against acceptance (D/A) *See* documentary collection.

documents against payment (D/P) *See* documentary collection.

documentary collection A method of effecting payment for goods whereby the seller/exporter instructs his bank to collect a certain sum from the buyer/importer in exchange for the transfer of shipping and other documentation enabling the buyer/importer to take possession of the goods. The two main types of Documentary Collection are:

- **documents against payment (D/P)** Where the bank releases the documents to the buyer/importer only against a cash payment in a prescribed currency; and
- **documents against acceptance (D/A)** Where the bank releases the documents to the buyer/importer against acceptance of a bill of exchange guaranteeing payment at a later date.

draft *See* bill of exchange.

drawee The buyer in a documentary collection.

forward foreign exchange An agreement to purchase foreign exchange (currency) at a future date at a predetermined rate of exchange. Forward foreign exchange contracts are often purchased by buyers of merchandise who wish to hedge against foreign exchange fluctuations between the time the contract is negotiated and the time payment is made.

irrevocable credit A letter of credit that cannot be revoked or amended without prior mutual consent of the seller, the buyer, and all intermediaries.

issuance The act of the issuing bank (buyer's bank) establishing a letter of credit based on the buyer's application.

issuing bank The buyer's bank which establishes a letter of credit in favor of the seller, or beneficiary.

letter of credit A document stating commitment on the part of a bank to place an agreed upon sum of money at the disposal of a seller on behalf of a buyer under precisely defined conditions.

negotiation In a letter of credit transaction, the examination of seller's documentation by the (negotiating) bank to determine if it complies with the terms and conditions of the letter of credit.

open account The shipping of goods by a seller to the buyer prior to payment for the goods. The seller will usually specify expected payment terms of 30, 60, or 90 days from the date of shipment.

red clause letter of credit A letter of credit which makes funds available to the seller prior to shipment in order to provide him with funds for production of the goods.

remitter In a documentary collection, an alternate name given to the seller who forwards documents to the buyer through banks.

remitting bank In a documentary collection, a bank acting as an intermediary, forwarding the remitter's documents to, and payments from the collecting bank.

revocable letter of credit A letter of credit which may be revoked or amended by the issuer (buyer) without prior notice to other parties in the letter of credit process. It is rarely used.

revolving letter of credit A letter of credit which is automatically restored to its full amount after the completion of each documentary exchange. It is used when there are several shipments to be made over a specified period of time.

sight draft *See* bill of exchange.

standby letter of credit A letter of credit used as a secondary payment method in the event that the primary payment method cannot be fulfilled.

time draft *See* bill of exchange.

validity The time period for which a letter of credit is valid. After receiving notice of a letter of credit opened on his behalf, the seller/exporter must meet all the requirements of the letter of credit within the period of validity.

FURTHER READING

For more detailed information on international trade payments, refer to the following publications of the International Chamber of Commerce (ICC).

How to Order ICC Publications

ICC Publications are available from ICC National Committees and Groups, which exist in 64 countries, or from:

ICC Publishing S.A.
38, Cours Albert 1er
75008 Paris, France
Tel: [33] (1) 49-53-29-23, 49-53-29-56
Fax: [33] (1) 49-53-29-02

ICC Publishing, Inc.
156 Fifth Avenue, Suite 308
New York, NY 10010, USA
Tel: [1] (212) 206-1150
Fax: [1] (212) 633-6025

Documentary Credit Rules Publications

Uniform Customs and Practice for Documentary Credits (1993 Revision) This sixth edition from the ICC came into force on January 1, 1994. The 49 articles of the new *UCP 500* are a comprehensive and practical working aid to bankers, lawyers, importers and exporters, transport executives, educators, and those involved in international trade transactions worldwide. Also available in bilingual English-Spanish and English-Russian editions. Order ICC No. 500, 1993 edition, 60 pages, US$9.95.

UCP 500 and 400 Compared An article-by-article comparison study between the 1993 revision and the 1983 revision to the *UCP*. This study also incorporates commentaries on the rationale for rewrite of the articles. Order ICC No. 511, 1993 edition, 135 pages, US$39.95.

ICC Guide to Documentary Credit Operations, by Charles del Busto. Offers a complete explanation of the documentary credit process including: international trade considerations; a list of political, legal and economic issues; documentary requirements; roles of the issuing and advising banks; types and uses of documentary credits. Contains graphs, charts and sample documents to illustrate and highlight important points as well as a suggested checklist for documentary preparation and examination. Also available in bilingual English-Spanish edition. Order ICC No. 515, 1994 Edition, 122 pages, US$34.95.

Standard Documentary Credit Forms Source-book of forms to use with *UCP 500*. Gives precise instructions about how the revised forms should be filled out. These standard forms have been developed on the basis of the UN's layout key and this alignment with other documents in international trade makes this publication an invaluable aid to all parties to a documentary credit. Order ICC No. 516, 1994 edition, 80 pages, US$29.95.

UCP 500 and Standby Letters of Credit: Special Report, by Brooke Wunnicke, Esq. and Diane B. Wunnicke. Focuses on sections of ICC's 1993 revision to *UCP 500* that relate to standby letters of credit. A John Wiley publication, distributed by ICC Publishing, Inc. Order ICC No. 938, 1994 edition, 100 pages, US$75.00.

Documentary Credits Insight A quarterly newsletter designed to keep you on top of worldwide letter of credit developments, which impact directly on your business. Published four times a year, DCI contains analytical commentary and up-to-the-minute information from the experts who drafted *UCP 500.* DCI also offers you a country-by-country update on documentary credit developments from correspondents in more than 25 countries. Must be ordered directly through ICC Publishing S.A. in Paris. Tel: [33] (1) 49-53-29-56 Fax: [33] (1) 49-53-29-02.

Incoterms Publications

Incoterms 1990 Defines the thirteen 1990 trading terms and specifies the respective rights and obligations of buyer and seller in an international transaction. Also available in bilingual Spanish-English and Russian-English editions. Order ICC No. 460, 1990 edition, 216 pages, US$27.95.

Guide to Incoterms 1990 Contains the full text of *Incoterms 1990* plus commentary illustrating how each Incoterm is interpreted in law and everyday practice. Order ICC No. 461/90, 1991 edition, 150 pages, US$49.95.

Taxation

CORPORATE TAXATION

TAXES ON CORPORATE INCOME AND GAINS

Corporate Income Tax Domestic corporations are taxed on their worldwide net taxable income. Resident foreign corporations are taxed on net taxable income, and nonresident foreign corporations are taxed on gross income derived from the Philippines. A resident foreign corporation (a branch) is one created under foreign laws and engaged in trade or business in the Philippines. Any other foreign corporation is considered a nonresident.

Rate of Corporate Tax Domestic and foreign

corporations are subject to tax at the rate of 35 percent.

Philippine-source income of foreign corporations taxed at preferential rates includes the following:

Sources of Income	Rate (%)
Interest income derived by offshore banking units (OBUs) from foreign currency loans granted to residents	10
Income derived by OBUs authorized by the Central Bank (CB) from foreign currency transactions with nonresidents, other OBUs, and local commercial banks, including branches of foreign banks authorized by the CB to transact business with OBUs	0
Gross Philippine billings of international carriers doing business in the Philippines	2.5
Rentals, lease, or charter fees derived by nonresident owners of vessels chartered by Philippine nationals	4.5
Rentals, lease, or charter fees derived by nonresident lessors of aircraft, machinery, and other equipment	8.5
Gross income of motion picture film owners, lessors, or distributors	25
Interest on foreign loans	20

Domestic and foreign enterprises registered with the Board of Investments (BOI) under the 1987 Omnibus Investment Code are granted an income tax holiday and exemption from certain other taxes and duties.

Capital Gains In general, capital gains are taxed in the same manner as ordinary income. However, capital gains on the sale of shares of stock in a domestic corporation are taxed at 10 percent on the

AT A GLANCE

CORPORATE TAXATION

Corporate Income Tax Rate (%)	35(a)
Capital Gains Tax Rate (%)	35
Branch Tax Rate (%)	35
Withholding Tax (%)	
Dividends (%)	0(b)(c)
Interest on Peso Deposits (%)	20(b)(d)
Royalties from Patents, Know-how, etc.	20(b)
Branch Remittance Tax (%)	15
Net Operating Losses (Years)	
Carryback	0
Carryforward	0

(a) Certain Philippine-source income of foreign corporations is taxed at preferential rates (see "Taxes on Corporate Income and Gains").

(b) If the recipient is a nonresident foreign corporation, the final withholding tax rate is generally 35 percent.

(c) Dividends paid to nonresident foreign corporations are subject to a 15 percent rate if certain conditions are met (see "Taxes on Corporate Income and Gains").

(d) Interest received by nonresidents on loans to Philippine residents is subject to a 20 percent final withholding tax.

PERSONAL TAXATION—MAXIMUM RATES

Income Tax Rate (%)	35
Capital Gains Tax Rate (%)	30*
Net Worth Tax Rate (%)	0
Estate Tax Rate (%)	35
Gift Tax Rate (%)	20

*See "Capital Gains and Losses."

first P100,000 and 20 percent on the excess over P100,000 if the shares are not traded through a local stock exchange. If the shares are traded on a local exchange, the tax is 0.375 percent of the gross selling price. Effective May 28, 1995, this rate was to be increased to 0.5 percent. A tax of 1 percent, 2 percent, or 4 percent is imposed on the gross sales price of shares sold in an initial public offering.

Administration Corporations must file quarterly returns within 60 days from the close of each of the first three quarters of the taxable year, whether calendar or fiscal, and a final or adjusted return on or before the 15th day of the fourth month following the close of the calendar or fiscal year. The corre-

sponding tax is paid at the time the return is filed.

Dividends Dividends received by a domestic or resident foreign corporation from a domestic corporation are not subject to tax. If the recipient is a nonresident foreign corporation, the 35 percent tax may be reduced to 15 percent if the country of domicile of the recipient does not impose any tax on income derived from outside such country or if it allows a credit for taxes deemed paid in the Philippines equivalent to 20 percent, which represents the difference between the 35 percent regular tax rate and the 15 percent preferential tax rate.

Foreign Tax Relief In the case of domestic corporations, tax credits are allowed for income, war profits, and excess profits taxes paid or accrued to any foreign country, subject to certain conditions. Alternatively, such income, war profits, and excess profits taxes may be claimed as a deduction from taxable income. Resident foreign corporations are not allowed to credit tax paid to foreign countries against Philippine income.

DETERMINATION OF TRADING INCOME

General The computation of income for income tax purposes must be in accordance with the accounting method regularly employed in keeping the taxpayer's books of account, provided that method clearly reflects income.

Other allowable deductions include the usual, ordinary, and necessary business expenses—interest, taxes, losses, bad debts, charitable and other contributions, and contributions to a pension trust—all of which are required to be in connection with the conduct of trade or business in the Philippines.

Inventories Inventory valuation must conform as nearly as possible to the best accounting practice in the trade or business and must clearly reflect income. The most commonly used methods of inventory valuation are cost and the lower of cost or market valuation.

Tax Depreciation Taxpayers are allowed to deduct a reasonable allowance for exhaustion and wear and tear (including obsolescence) of property used in a trade or business. The tax authorities have not specified permissible depreciation methods or rates. The only requirement is that the method used must be generally accepted in the particular industry. Depreciation methods that are generally acceptable include the straight-line method, declining-balance method, the sum-of-the-years' digits method, or any other method that may be prescribed by the Secretary of Finance. In general, motor vehicles may be depreciated over a period not exceeding five years. Resident foreign corporations may claim depreciation only on property located in the Philippines.

Head-Office Expenses A foreign corporation doing business in the Philippines through a branch is allowed to deduct from its Philippine-source income not only the expenses, losses, and other deductions actually incurred, but also a ratable part of expenses incurred by the head office that cannot be allocated directly to any particular branch or branches. This refers to the branch's share of head-office overhead or administrative expenses.

OTHER SIGNIFICANT TAXES

The table below summarizes other significant taxes:

Nature of Tax	Rate
A value-added tax (VAT), on the sale, barter, exchange, or importation of goods and properties and on sales of services; specific goods and transactions are exempt; in general, exports of goods and services are subject to a 0 percent rate (a new VAT law, which was to be effective on May 28, 1994, has been suspended because of a petition questioning the constitutionality of the new law; the new law would extend VAT to cover sales of intangible personal properties, real properties, and certain additional services and transactions)	10%
Documentary stamp tax	
Loan agreements, promissory notes, and government securities	P0.30 per P200 of the face value of the document
Stock certificates	
Original issue	P2 per P200
Transfer	P1 per P200
Other specified transactions and documents	Various

MISCELLANEOUS MATTERS

Foreign Exchange Controls The Philippines has liberal foreign exchange controls. To ensure repatriation of capital and remittance of profits, foreign investments must be registered with the central bank.

Transfer Pricing The method used by a corporation to fix prices should be consistent worldwide.

Related-Party Transactions The tax treatment of transactions between related parties is generally the same as the treatment of transactions between unrelated parties. However, a deduction may not be claimed for losses on sales or exchanges of properties or for interest incurred on transactions between related parties.

TREATY WITHHOLDING TAX RATES

The following are the maximum withholding rates for dividends, interest, and royalties provided under the treaties:

	Dividends (p)	Interest	Royalties
	%	%	%
Australia	15(a)	15(b)	15(c)
Austria	10(d)	15(b)	15(e)(f)
Belgium	15(g)	15(b)	15(c)
Brazil	15	15(b)	15(aa)
Canada	15(d)	15(b)(h)	25(e)(h)
Denmark	23.32(w)	13.3(w)	23.32(w)
Finland	15(j)	15(b)	15(s)
France	15(d)	15(b)	15(k)
Germany	10(l)	10(q)	10(r)
Indonesia	15(l)	15(b)	15(c)
Italy	15	15(b)	15(c)
Japan	10(t)	10(m)	10(n)
Korea	10(l)	15(b)	15(f)
Malaysia	15	15	15(c)
Netherlands	10(i)	15(u)	10(s)
New Zealand	15	15(b)	15(c)
Pakistan	15(o)	15(b)	15(c)
Singapore	15(o)	15(b)	15(c)
Spain	15(x)	15(y)	15(z)
Sweden	15(i)	15(b)	15(s)
Thailand	15(j)	15(b)	15(c)
United Kingdom	15(d)	15(b)	15(c)
United States	20(o)	15(b)	15(c)(e)
Nontreaty countries (v)	15/35	20/35	35

Note: Most treaties require that the recipient be the beneficial owner of the income for the preferential rates to apply.

(a) If rebate or credit is given to the recipient; otherwise, the rate is 25 percent.

(b) 10 percent if paid with respect to public issues of bonds, debentures, or similar obligations or, in the case of Austria and Korea, also if paid by a Board of Investments (BOI)-registered preferred pioneer enterprise.

(c) If paid by a BOI-registered preferred enterprise or, in the case of Belgium, Italy, Malaysia, Singapore, Thailand, and the UK, also if paid with respect to motion picture films or tapes for television or broadcasting: otherwise, the rate is 25 percent.

(d) If recipient holds 10 percent of the voting shares of the paying corporation (payer) or, in the case of Austria, also if the recipient holds 10 percent of the shares issued by the payer during the six months preceding the dividend payment date; otherwise the rate is 25 percent.

(e) Subject to the "most-favored-nation" provision of the treaty.

(f) 10 percent if paid by a BOI-registered preferred pioneer enterprise.

(g) If the dividend is tax-exempt in Belgium; otherwise, the rate is 20 percent.

(h) If the interest or royalty is taxable in Canada.

(i) If the recipient is a company (excluding a partnership in the case of Sweden) and if, during the part of the paying company's taxable year that precedes the date of payment of the dividend and during the whole of its prior taxable year, at least 10 percent of the voting stock of the paying company was owned by the recipient company: otherwise, the rate is 25 percent (Netherlands, 15 percent).

(j) If the recipient owns 10 percent (Thailand, 15 percent) of the voting shares of the payer.

(k) If the royalties are taxable in the country of residence of the recipient and, if they are paid by a BOI-registered enterprise engaged in preferred areas of activities or if they are paid with respect to motion picture films or works recorded for broadcasting or television; otherwise, the rate is 25 percent.

(l) If recipient holds 25 percent of the capital of the payer or, in the case of Korea, also if paid by a BOI-registered preferred pioneer enterprise; otherwise, the rate is 20 percent (Germany, 15 percent; Korea, 25 percent).

(m) If paid with respect to government securities, bonds, or debentures or if paid by a BOI-registered preferred pioneer enterprise; otherwise, the rate is 15 percent.

(n) If paid by a BOI-registered preferred pioneer enterprise; 15 percent if paid for the use of or the right to use motion picture films or films or tapes for radio or television broadcasting; otherwise, the rate is 25 percent.

(o) If the recipient holds at least 25 percent (Singapore, 15 percent; US, 10 percent) of the capital of the payer during the part of the payer's taxable year preceding the dividend payment date and during the prior year; otherwise, the rate is 25 percent.

(p) A preferential rate of 15 percent under the National Internal Revenue Code may be applied if the recipient's country of domicile allows a credit for taxes deemed paid in the Philippines equivalent to 20 percent, which represents the difference between the 35 percent regular tax rate and the 15 percent preferential rate.

(q) On compliance with certain requirements; otherwise, the rate is 15 percent.

(r) This rate applies if the royalties arise from the use of, or the right to use, any patent, trademark, design or model, plan, secret formula, or process; from the use of, or the right to use, industrial, commercial, or scientific equipment; or for information concerning industrial, commercial, or scientific experience. The rate is 15 percent if royalties arise from the use of, or the right to use, any copyright of literary, artistic, or scientific work, including motion picture films or tapes for television or broadcasting.

(s) If paid by a BOI-registered preferred enterprise or, in the case of Sweden and Finland, if paid for motion picture films or tapes for television or broadcasting or for the use of or the right to use any copyright of literary, artistic, or scientific work; otherwise, the rate is 25 percent (Netherlands, 15 percent).

(t) If the recipient holds 25 percent of the voting shares of the payer or 25 percent of the shares issued by the payer during the six months preceding the dividend payment date or if paid by a BOI-registered pioneer enterprise; otherwise, the rate is 25 percent.

(u) 10 percent if paid in connection with the sale on credit of any industrial, commercial, or scientific equipment or any loan of whatever kind granted by a bank or any other financial institution.

(v) See applicable footnotes to the "At a Glance" section.

(w) If the payer is a corporation engaging in certain preferred areas of investment that are listed in the treaty. For interest and royalties, the treaty rate applies only if the payer derives at least 80 percent of its gross income from the active conduct of business in such preferred areas of investment.

(x) The rate is 10 percent if the recipient is a corporation that holds directly at least 10 percent of the voting shares of the payer.

(y) The rate is 10 percent if the interest is paid in connection with the sale on credit of any industrial, commercial, or scientific equipment or if the interest is paid with respect to the issue of bonds, debentures, or similar obligations that are offered to the general public.

(z) The rate is 10 percent if the royalties are paid by a BOI-registered enterprise that is engaged in a preferred area of activities. The rate is 20 percent for royalties with respect to cinematographic films or tapes for television or broadcasting.

(aa) A 25 percent rate applies to royalties with respect to the use of or the right to use trademarks, cinematographic films, or films or tapes for television or radio broadcasting.

PERSONAL TAXATION

INCOME TAX—EMPLOYMENT

Who Is Liable

Citizens and resident aliens are liable for tax on worldwide income.

Residence is determined by the length and nature of the stay. A person who comes to the Philippines for a definite purpose that may be promptly accomplished is not deemed to be resident, but a person who comes for a definite purpose requiring an extended stay and who establishes a temporary home in the Philippines is considered resident. Aliens who reside in the Philippines with no definite intention concerning the amount of time of their stay are considered resident, even if they intend to return to another country to live. Aliens who have acquired residence in the Philippines remain residents until they depart with the intention of abandoning that residence.

Taxable Income

Taxable employment income consists of gross compensation reduced by allowable personal and additional exemptions. Gross compensation income includes all remuneration, whether paid in money or some other medium, for services performed for an employer, such as salaries, wages, emoluments and honoraria, bonuses, allowances such as transportation expenses and entertainment allowances, monetary and nonmonetary fringe benefits, taxable pensions and retirement pay, and other similar income.

For taxation of employment income of nonresidents, *see* "Nonresidents" on page 275.

Income Tax Rates

Tax on 1994 income is levied at the following rates.

Employment Income		Tax on Lower	Rate on
Exceeding	Not Exceeding	Amount	Excess
P	P	P	%
0	2,500	0	0
2,500	5,000	0	1
5,000	10,000	25	3
10,000	20,000	175	7
20,000	40,000	875	11
40,000	60,000	3,075	15
60,000	100,000	6,075	19
100,000	250,000	13,675	24
250,000	500,000	49,675	29
500,000	——	122,175	35

Spouses are taxed separately, not jointly, on all types of income.

Personal Deductions and Allowances

Taxpayers are allowed the following exemptions in 1994:

- Basic personal exemptions granted are P9,000 for single or legally separated married individuals without dependents; P12,000 for heads of families (unmarried or legally separated individuals with one or more parents, brothers, sisters, or legitimate, recognized natural or adopted children living with and dependent on them for their chief support, if the dependents are 21 years old or younger, unmarried and not gainfully employed or, regardless of age, if incapable of self-support because of mental or physical defect); and P18,000 for each married individual.
- For a married individual or head of family, an additional exemption of P5,000 is allowed for each dependent up to four (that is, a legitimate, recognized natural or adopted child, chiefly dependent upon and living with the taxpayer, if the dependent is 21 years old or younger, unmarried and not gainfully employed or if the dependent, regardless of age, is incapable of self-support because of mental or physical defect). Only one of two spouses may take such exemptions. The husband is deemed the proper claimant of additional exemptions unless he waives his right in favor of his wife. For legally separated spouses, additional exemptions may be claimed only by the spouse in custody of the child, and the total deductions claimed by both spouses must not exceed the maximum allowable exemption amounts.
- A special additional exemption of P4,000 is allowed to a single, married, or legally separated individual or head of family with gross income not exceeding P20,000. This exemption is available only to the spouse claiming the exemptions for dependent children.

INCOME TAX—SELF-EMPLOYMENT/ BUSINESS INCOME

Who Is Liable

Citizens and resident aliens who derive income from self-employment or the practice of a profession are subject to tax on such income under the Simplified Net Income Taxation System (SNITS).

Self-employed means persons engaged in business who derive their personal income from such business. This includes single proprietorships, manufacturers, traders, and proprietors of service shops.

Professionals means persons who derive their income from the practice of their profession, such as lawyers, doctors, dentists, and accountants. It also includes those who earn income from pursuit of an art or talent, such as artists and athletes.

Taxable Income

Gross income derived from whatever source (unless exempt) is reduced by allowable deductions to compute taxable income.

Income Tax Rates

Tax on 1994 income is levied at the following rates.

Business Income		Tax on Lower Amount	Rate on Excess
P	P	P	%
0	10,000	0	3
10,000	30,000	300	9
30,000	120,000	2,100	15
120,000	350,000	15,600	20
350,000	—	61,600	30

Partners of general professional partnerships are subject to a 15 percent tax on periodic distributions, including draws, advances, sharings, allowances, and stipends. This tax may be credited when a return is filed and income tax liability is calculated.

See "Nonresidents" on page 275 for taxation of self-employment or business income of nonresidents.

Deductible Expenses

Only the following direct costs are allowed as deductions from income derived from self-employment or professional income:

- Raw materials, supplies, and direct labor;
- Salaries of employees directly engaged in activities in the course or pursuant of the business or practice of their profession;
- Utilities expenses;
- Rent on business property;
- Depreciation;
- Contributions made to the government and accredited relief organizations for the rehabilitation of calamity-stricken areas declared by the President; and
- Interest paid or accrued in a taxable year on loans from accredited financial institutions, which must be proven to have been incurred in connection with the conduct of a taxpayer's profession, trade, or business.

For individuals whose cost of goods sold and direct costs are difficult to determine, a maximum of 40 percent of their gross receipts is allowed as a deduction.

A taxpayer may also claim the deductions listed here, but they may be claimed only once during the taxable year by any taxpayer.

DIRECTORS' FEES

Directors' fees are taxed as income from employment.

INVESTMENT INCOME

The following classes of income are subject to a final 20 percent withholding tax:
- Interest on peso deposits and yields, or any other monetary benefit from deposit substitutes, trust funds, and similar arrangements; and
- Royalties, prizes exceeding P3,000, and other winnings.

Dividends received from domestic corporations and a partner's share in the profits of a partnership that is taxed as a corporation are not taxable.

Rental income is considered business income and taxed at the rates described in the "Income Tax Rates" subsection of the "Income Tax—Self-Employment/Business Income" section.

RELIEF FOR LOSSES

Self-employed persons are not permitted to carry forward business losses to future years. Carrybacks are also not permitted.

CAPITAL GAINS AND LOSSES

In general, capital gains are taxed as business income. If an asset disposed of is held for no more than 12 months, tax is imposed on the entire capital gain; otherwise, only 50 percent of the gain is taxed.

Capital gains on the sale of shares of stock in a domestic corporation not traded on a local stock exchange are taxed at rates of 10 percent on the first P100,000 and 20 percent on the excess. The rate for shares traded on an exchange is 0.25 percent (final withholding tax) of the gross selling price.

Capital gains from the sale of real property located in the Philippines are taxed at a 5 percent rate. Computation of the gain is based on the higher of the gross selling price or fair-market value at the time of sale.

Capital losses are deductible only to the extent of capital gains.

ESTATE AND GIFT TAXES

An estate tax is imposed at graduated rates ranging between 5 percent and 35 percent on the transfer of a decedent's net estate valued in excess of P200,000. Citizens, regardless of whether resident at the time of death, and resident aliens are taxed on their worldwide estate. Special rules apply to nonresident aliens; *see* "Nonresidents" on page 275.

The net estate is computed by deducting the following amounts from the value of all the dece-

dent's property, real or personal, tangible or intangible, wherever situated:
- Allowable expenses, losses, indebtedness, and taxes;
- The value of property transferred for public use;
- The value of property subjected to estate or gift tax (subject to special rules) within five years prior to the decedent's death; and
- The value of the family home, not to exceed P1 million.

Estate tax rates for 1994 are set forth in the following table.

Value of Total Net Estate Exceeding P	Not Exceeding P	Tax on Lower Amount P	Rate on Excess %
0	200,000	0	0
200,000	500,000	0	5
500,000	2,000,000	15,000	8
2,000,000	5,000,000	135,000	12
5,000,000	10,000,000	495,000	21
10,000,000	——	1.545,000	35

To prevent double taxation of estates, the Philippines has concluded an estate tax treaty with Denmark.

Residents and nonresidents are subject to gift tax, which is payable by the donor on total net gifts made in a calendar year. Citizens, regardless of whether resident at the time of a gift, and resident aliens are subject to gift tax on worldwide assets. Nonresident aliens are subject to gift tax on their Philippine assets only. The following table provides gift tax rates for 1994.

Value of Total Net Gifts Exceeding P	Not Exceeding P	Tax on Lower Amount P	Rate on Excess %
0	50,000	0	0
50,000	100,000	0	1.5
100,000	200,000	750	3
200,000	500,000	3,750	5
500,000	1,000,000	18,750	8
1,000,000	3,000,000	58,750	10
3,000,000	5,000,000	258,750	15
5,000,000	——	558,750	20

SOCIAL SECURITY TAXES

Social security contributions are payable by all individuals working in the Philippines. The employee's contribution is approximately 3.4 percent and is withheld by the employer. The employer's contribution is approximately 5 percent. Self-employed persons may make voluntary contributions.

ADMINISTRATION

The tax year corresponds to the calendar year. An income tax return must be filed and the tax due paid on or before April 15 for income of the preceding year. If tax due is more than P2,000, it may be paid in two equal installments, the first at the time of filing the return and the second on or before July 15 following the close of the tax year.

Employers are required to withhold tax on the compensation of their employees. The tax withheld may be credited against tax due on the return. Individuals whose only income is salary income that does not exceed P60,000 and has been subject to withholding are not required to file tax returns.

Although spouses may compute their individual income tax liabilities separately based on their respective total taxable incomes, they file joint returns. Employment income earned by either spouse that does not exceed P60,000 is not reported, even if the employment income of both spouses together totals more than P60,000.

A separate return must be filed and any tax due paid within 30 days after each sale of shares not traded on a local stock exchange; a final consolidated return must be filed on or before April 15 for all stock transactions of the preceding year. For a sale of real property, a separate return should also be filed and any tax due paid within 30 days of each sale.

NONRESIDENTS

Nonresident Citizens Nonresident citizens deriving income from sources outside the Philippines are taxed at progressive rates of 1 percent to 3 percent of taxable income. To arrive at taxable income, the following deductions may be taken from gross income derived from foreign sources:

- A personal exemption of US$2,000 for a single or legally separated married individual or US$4,000 for a married individual or head of family; and
- National income tax paid to the government of the foreign country of residence.

If income is derived from Philippine sources, tax is also imposed on such income in the manner described for residents.

Nonresident Aliens Taxation of nonresident aliens depends on whether they are deemed to be engaged in trade or business in the Philippines. A nonresident who comes to the Philippines and stays for more than 180 days (total) during any calendar year is deemed to be doing business in the Philippines; any other nonresident is deemed not engaged in trade or business in the Philippines.

Nonresident aliens engaged in trade or business in the Philippines are generally taxed in the same manner as resident citizens and aliens on taxable income received from sources in the Philippines.

However, dividends, shares in profits of partnerships taxed as corporations, interest, royalties, and prizes in excess of P3,000 and other winnings are subject to final withholding tax of 30 percent of the gross amount. Capital gains on the sale of real property and shares in domestic corporations are taxed in the manner described in "Capital Gains and Losses." Tax deductions are allowed only if connected with Philippine-source income; no tax credits may be claimed for taxes paid to foreign countries. Losses may be deducted only if incurred in trade or business or if they arise from profit-oriented transactions in the Philippines. Depreciation or depletion deductions may be claimed only when the related asset is in the Philippines. Personal exemptions allowed to a nonresident are equal to those allowed under the income tax law of the nonresident's country of citizenship to Filipinos who are nonresident there, but they may not exceed the exemptions allowed to citizens or aliens residing in the Philippines.

Nonresident aliens not engaged in trade or business in the Philippines are subject to a final withholding tax of 30 percent on gross income from all sources in the Philippines. However, capital gains on sale of real property and of shares in domestic corporations are subject to the same tax as that imposed on citizens and resident aliens.

Aliens employed by regional or area headquarters of multinational corporations or offshore banking units established in the Philippines are subject to a 15 percent final tax on gross compensation income received. Aliens who are permanent residents of a foreign country but who are employed and assigned in the Philippines by service contractors or by subcontractors engaged in petroleum operations in the Philippines are also subject to a 15 percent final tax on gross compensation income received from the contractors or subcontractors. Gross compensation income includes salaries, wages, annuities, compensation, remuneration, and other compensation, such as honoraria and allowances, from such entities. Any other income earned by these alien employees in the Philippines is taxed under the rules described in the preceding two paragraphs.

For estate tax purposes, only that part of a nonresident alien decedent's estate situated in the Philippines is included in the taxable estate. Under specified conditions, deductions may be permitted for such items as expenses, losses, indebtedness, taxes, and the value of property previously subjected to estate or donor's tax or of property that has been transferred for public use.

DOUBLE TAX RELIEF/ DOUBLE TAX TREATIES

Foreign taxes (with certain exceptions) paid or incurred in connection with a taxpayer's profession, trade, or business may be deducted from gross income. Alternatively, citizens and, if reciprocity requirements are met, resident aliens may claim credit for income, war profits, and excess profits taxes due to any foreign country. The credit may not exceed the Philippine income tax multiplied by a fraction, the numerator of which is taxable income from foreign countries and the denominator of which is worldwide taxable income.

The Philippines has concluded double taxation treaties with the following countries.

Australia	Germany	New Zealand
Austria	Indonesia	Pakistan
Belgium	Italy	Singapore
Brazil	Japan	Sweden
Canada	Korea	Thailand
Denmark	Malaysia	United Kingdom
Finland	Netherlands	United States
France		

Transportation & Communications

INTRODUCTION

A poor transportation and communications infrastructure has severely inhibited overall economic growth in the Philippines, greatly hindering its ability to compete in the global business world. That said, it is possible—albeit with some difficulty—to travel and to send freight to any part of the country or abroad from most urban centers within the country. An extensive road network links some parts of the archipelago; the country has hundreds of ports, 25 of which may be considered major ones; it has two international airports, four alternate international airports, and about 180 smaller airports, plus plans to convert the former Clark Air Force Base into another international airport. Telephone service is available and is excellent between most pairs of urban centers as well as internationally. Still, overcrowded and poorly maintained roads, neglected ports, outdated airports, and generally inadequate telecommunications services all contribute to the difficulty of doing business in or with the Philippines.

To address these problems, the government in recent years has embarked on an ambitious campaign to update and expand the infrastructure. It is continually improving and adding to existing roadways and has aggressively sought to involve the private sector in such projects as upgrading and expanding its airport and seaport facilities; building

more overseas and interisland vessels; increasing the transmission capabilities of radio links among the islands; and installing additional telephone lines and teleprinter stations.

In particular, the Philippines has depended heavily on a build-operate-transfer (BOT) scheme designed to bring projects on line quickly by granting extended operating concessions to foreign investors who will install critical infrastructure. The initiative aims to encourage the private sector to invest in infrastructure projects using the following formula: build-own-operate, build-transfer, build-transfer-operate, build-lease-transfer, rehabilitate-operate-transfer, rehabilitate-own-transfer, develop-operate-transfer, and contract-add-operate. The government is relying on BOT arrangements for most of its major infrastructure initiatives, including highways, airports, and shipping services. An ambitious program of "Flagship Projects"—designed to upgrade the infrastructure vastly and quickly by focusing on key sectors— utilizing BOT schemes was launched in 1993.

Although early results of BOT projects are highly promising, many problems remain. Because of the level of need—many extensive projects must be built entirely from scratch, as there is often no existing base from which to build—the financial demands of many of the projects are daunting, even for large international consortia. And no matter how profitable a BOT project might look on paper, foreign companies must still weigh the potential political risk. Because of the scale of many of the projects envisioned, potential investors must evaluate whether the government can or will grant a rate of return that would make the project acceptably profitable; this could forestall full implementation of the government's ambitious plans.

With chronic budget deficit problems the Philippines has in any case been forced to scrimp on infrastructure spending. In some respects, this could be a blessing in disguise. If massive infrastructure construction were to occur too rapidly,

TRANSPORTATION GLOSSARY

bill of lading A document issued by a carrier to a shipper, signed by the captain, agent, or owner of a vessel, furnishing written evidence regarding receipt of the goods (cargo), the conditions on which transportation is made (contract of carriage), and the engagement to deliver goods at the prescribed port of destination to the lawful holder of the bill of lading. A bill of lading is, therefore, both a receipt for merchandise and a contract to deliver it as freight.

bulk cargo Cargo that consists entirely of one commodity and is usually shipped without packaging. Examples of bulk cargo are grain, ore, and oil.

charter A charter party or charter agreement is a lease or agreement to hire an airplane, vessel, or other means of conveyance to transport goods on a designated voyage to one or more locations.

consolidation The combining of less than a container load (LCL) of cargo from a number of shippers at a centrally located point of origin by a freight consolidator and the transporting of them as a single shipment to a destination point. Consolidation of cargo often results in reduced shipping rates.

containerization The practice or technique of using a boxlike device (container) in which a number of packages are stored, protected, and handled as a single unit in transit. Advantages of containerization include: less handling of cargo, more protection against pilferage, less exposure to the elements, and reduced cost of shipping.

customs broker An individual or firm licensed by a government to act for importers or exporters in handling the sequence of customs formalities and other details critical to the legal and speedy exporting and importing of goods.

freight forwarder A person engaged in the business of assembling, collecting, consolidating, shipping and distributing less than container load or less than truckload freight. Also, a person acting as agent in the transshipping of freight to or from foreign countries and the clearing of freight through customs, including full preparation of documents, arranging for shipping, warehousing, delivery and export clearance.

Incoterms 1990 A codification of international rules for the uniform interpretation of common contract clauses in export-import transactions. Developed and issued by the International Chamber of Commerce (ICC) Paris. (Refer to page 264 of the "International Payments" chapter for a complete list of Incoterms.)

intermodal transport The coordinated transport of freight, especially in connection with relatively long-haul movements using any combination of freight forwarders, piggyback, containerization, airfreight, ocean freight, assemblers, and/or motor carriers.

reefer container A controlled temperature shipping container, usually refrigerated.

roll-on, roll-off (Ro-Ro) A broad category of ships designed to load and discharge cargo which rolls on wheels. Broadly interpreted, this may include train ships, trailer ships, auto, truck and trailer ferries, and ships designed to carry military vehicles.

unitization The practice or technique of consolidating many small pieces of freight into a single unit for easier handling.

Warsaw Convention The informal name for The Convention for the Unification of Certain Rules Relating to International Carriage by Air, signed in Warsaw in 1929. An international multilateral treaty which regulates, in a uniform manner, the conditions of international transportation by air. Among other things, it establishes the international liability of air carriers and establishes the monetary limits for loss, damage, and delay.

waybill A document prepared by a transportation line at the point of a shipment, showing the point of origin, destination, route, consignor, consignee, description of shipment and amount charged for the transportation service; the waybill is forwarded with the shipment or by mail to the agent at the transfer point or waybill destination.

Definitions in this glossary are excerpted from the Dictionary of International Trade, copyright ©1994 World Trade Press.

the economy could not possibly handle the necessary payments. However, if the economy itself grows too fast, it will be slowed naturally by the limits of its infrastructure. Although the choice could cause the Philippines to endure several more years of slow economic growth, the government has held its expenditures on infrastructure during the last three years to less than 2 percent of GDP.

Compared with an average of 6.1 percent in developing countries and 5.8 percent for other high-growth areas, this seems unduly low. But it might be what the Philippines needs to allow itself the time and resources to put in place the infrastructure needed to service and sustain a growing economy.

WATER TRANSPORT

Most freight in the Philippines travels by water. Hundreds of shipping routes service both freight and passenger movements among the islands, and the Philippines is also heavily dependent on ocean shipping in its international trade. It has more than 400 operational ports classified as ports of entry, subports of entry, municipal ports, and private ports. Some 25 major ports—including those in Manila, Cebu, Batangas, Iloilo, and Zamboanga — annually clear more than 160,000 vessels engaged in international and domestic trade. Approximately 85 percent of all Philippine foreign trade passes through the Port of Manila, as does 90 percent of the imports to be subsequently distributed to other destinations via air, land or interisland water transport.

The interisland shipping industry is undergoing reforms to make it more market oriented. Current reforms include privatizing government-held maritime-related enterprises—such as shipbuilding and repair and vessel and harbor operations—and deregulation of routes, tariffs, and vessel acquisition. But, although the government has undertaken some measures to deregulate the shipping industry, it has delayed implementation of policies to privatize the country's ports, thus hindering its overall efforts. Shippers complain that the Philippine Ports Authority (PPA) still supervises over stevedoring operations too closely and that they still have to pay large sums for which they see little return. Nevertheless, beginning in 1993 the PPA has undertaken several port infrastructure projects designed to improve the efficiency of the water transport system. Many of these were conducted under the BOT program. The PPA predicts cargo traffic to exceed 150 metric tons by the year 2000, with annual ship calls projected to reach approximately 258,000. The PPA plans to establish a world class port system which will eventually be complemented by the development of an integrated intermodal transport chain.

Ports

The Philippines has more than 500 ports, 81 of which are national (the remainder are municipally owned and operated). Fewer than half of the national ports are open to international shipping. There are 202 government-operated ports that support the interisland shipping industry. The more important ports are in Manila, Batangas, Cebu, Iloilo and Zamboanga. The ports in Southern Tagalog and Western Mindanao do not handle cargo transportation, although they do handle substantial passenger traffic. In all, the Philippines has 38 ports of entry, 15 subports of entry, 225 municipal ports, 240 private ports, and 24 other national ports. Those equipped to serve international vessels are: Manila, Cebu, Iloilo, Cagayan de Oro, Davao, General Santos, Polloc, and Zamboanga.

Manila, the busiest national port, handles about 90 percent of the country's imports and more than 20 percent of its exports. A number of expansion and rehabilitation projects designed to reduce congestion in the Manila port area were shelved during the economic crisis in 1983, but have been revived; some have been completed. The Manila International Container Terminal Project, completed in 1990, has significantly eased congestion around the Manila port area. International cargo traffic is busiest at the South Harbor in Manila and the Manila International Container Terminal (MICT) located adjacent to it. South Harbor lies at the northeastern shoulder of Manila and has a shoreline of 2 km (1.25 mi). Protected by more than 3,000 m (10,000 ft) of rock barriers enclosing about 600 hectares (1,500 acres) of anchorage, it has five finger piers with a total berth length of 4,331 m (14,000 ft). These can accommodate 26 vessels at any given time. Twenty-seven berths are available at the anchorage. Containers can be loaded either at the South Harbor—which has a capacity of 6,485 20-foot equivalent units (TEUs)—or at the MICT.

A recent P560 million (about US$22.4 million) rehabilitation of South Harbor's five piers included the setting up of a fendering system for all piers, improvements in lighting and other facilities, and reinforcement for the piers. Manila's North Harbor, which handles domestic shipping, has also been rehabilitated recently. Aside from pier repairs, a new 500 m (1,640 ft) wharf with a reclaimed backup area was constructed from Pier 16 to the edge of the marine slipway. North Harbor now provides berthing facilities for deep-draft domestic vessels and ample working and storage spaces.

Cebu, the second largest port, has lined up a number of reclamation projects to expand its transshipment capacity. Its plans include the reclamation of 70 m (230 ft) of the Cebu International Port, with the addition of a container freight station and a bulk grain handling facility. Other projects include the South Mactan reclamation, the Consolación Port Reclamation, and the Cordova reclamation. The Cordova project will reclaim 1,600 hectares (4,000 acres) of shoreline area and set up a super container port and an economic and commercial area, including tourist facilities. The South Mactan project will reclaim 200 hectares (500 acres) for a containerized port while the Consolacion project will reclaim 100 hectares (250 acres) both for commercial and port facilities.

Cebu's 423,245 sq m (4.5 million sq ft) port has a quay length of 692 m (2,270 ft), a 3,831 m (12,565 ft) marginal wharf, three finger piers with total berthing length of 4 km (2.5 miles) and a backup area of 1.5 hectares (3.75 acres) for noncontainer-ized cargo. Its container terminal has a capacity of 10,000 twenty-equivalent-units (TEUs).

Manila International Container Terminal (MICT) Located beside South Harbor, the MICT is run by International Container Services, Inc. (ICTSI), a consortium which handles about one-half of all container traffic in the country. MICT handles about 75 to 80 percent of total container traffic at the Port of Manila. It has put in place, among other equipment: five post-panamax cranes including two 40-tonners, with four more to be acquired in the late 1990s; eight yard gantries; and straddle carriers. With the new equipment, its throughput capacity now ranges from 750,000 to 1 million TEUs, depending on dwell times.

ICTSI is also establishing an inland container terminal to help abate the country's traffic problems. The terminal, which will be linked to the Port of Manila, will be at Cabuyao, Laguna. The area, which already abounds with industrial companies, is expected to benefit greatly from the project. The terminal will serve as a loading point for export prod-ucts and is expected to boost the country's exports by approximately 18 percent. ICTSI is also looking to take over at least some of the wharves at Subic Bay. Although ICTSI is still small-fry compared with the container terminals at Singapore and Hong Kong, it has more than vindicated the government's decision to shift these services to private ownership.

Manila*

Transportation Service —Truck and barge.

Cargo Storage—Covered: 48,592 sq m (523,000 sq ft. Open: 36,963 sq m (398,000 sq ft).

Special Cranes—Heavy lift capacity is 75 tons. Container, 25 to 30 with 40 ton capacity.

Air Cargo—Ninoy Aquino International Airport (NAIA): Pasay City, 10 km (6.25 mi).

Cargo Handling—Containerized, bulk and general cargo can all be adequately handled by existing port equipment. Three (3) ore and bulk terminals, 1 tanker terminal and 1 Ro-Ro off-loading point provide specialized cargo handling capabilities.

General—Typhoons may occur between June and October. Annual rainfall is approximately 200 cm (79 in). Security measures have been increased at port, but goods should be packaged to deter theft and pilferage. The international container terminal is being upgraded (see preceding section).

Cebu*

Transportation Service —Truck.

Cargo Storage—Covered: 4,600 sq m (49,500 sq ft). Open: 10,000 sq m (108,000 sq ft) for break bulk and 50,000 sq m (538,000 sq ft) dedicated to container staging.

Special Cranes—Heavy lift capacity is 35 tons. Container, two with 25 and 35 ton capacity.

Air Cargo—Mactan International Airport: 15 km (9.5 mi), offers service to Manila.

Cargo Handling—Cebu's equipment can handle most general cargo. Motor vehicle spare parts and chemicals are among this port's primary commodi-ties. Covered storage is limited to export sheds owned and operated by private firms. Cargo may be stored in open area, covered by tarpaulins only.

General—Temperatures range from 17°C to 35°C (63° to 95° F) with annual rainfall of 180 cm (71 in). Typhoons can occur during the rainy season, which extends from June through September. A new inter-national port has been built. This includes a container freight station and bulk grain handling facility (see "Ports" on page 279).

Subic Bay The former US naval base at Subic Bay has begun attracting cargo traffic and is positioning itself as a major competitor of Singapore in the Asian transshipment market. The Subic Bay Metropolitan Authority has signed an agreement with Inchcape Pacific Ltd that allows the latter to use Subic Bay as a transshipment point for cargo traffic between Asia and the US. There are also marine cargo handling agreements with other Asian exporters in the works. In all, some 1,350 vessels called at Subic Bay in 1994, up from 225 in 1993. Of these, ships from four inter-national lines have been calling regularly: American President Lines, Maersk Line, Regional Container Lines PLC, and Madrigal–Wan Hai Lines.

Socsargen A huge redevelopment program is underway to expand and improve both the airport and port facilities in the area made up of South Cotabato, Sarangani, and General Santos City (Socsargen). Air traffic volumes are expected to increase to 210,000 passengers and 25,000 tons of agricultural and aquatic cargos by the year 2005. Socsargen will also benefit from the expansion of Makar Wharf, a strategic base port in the South. Makar Wharf is expected to handle an additional 594 million tons of cargoes and is scheduled for completion by 1998.

Shipping

Sea freight is the most common transport method used by exporters in the Philippines, and shippers have a wide choice of vessels, companies, and services. There are more than 850 registered operating vessels in the Philippines, with gross regis-

---

*Port facility information for Manila and Cebu in this section is excerpted from Ports of the World (15th ed.), copyright © 1994 CIGNA Property and Casualty Co., reprinted with permission from CIGNA Property and Casualty Companies.

tered tonnage totaling 2.8 million. Cargo ships represent about 95 percent of the total. There are about 480 Philippine-registered vessels, although fewer than 40 of these are actually Philippine-owned. The government has implemented regulations requiring certain exporters to utilize only Philippine-owned vessels for a stated percentage of their shipments, but there are many waivers and exceptions, and the requirements have already been revised more than once. For the most part, exporters have a free hand in choosing which vessel to use.

The most common choices are conference, nonconference, charter, and tramp. Conference vessels boast regular service, comprehensive and dependable routes, and stable rates. However, their services do not come cheap; their rates are generally about 15 to 20 percent higher than those of nonconference vessels. (Nonconference vessels commonly raise their rates proportionately whenever conference rates increase.) To take advantage of better rates, regular shippers can sign a shipper's contract with a conference vessel, which ensures them lower rates in exchange for regular shipping volumes. Carriers can waive standard rates and give a discount to a regular shipper on a case-by-case basis, although this must be done in accordance with conference approval procedures, which can take time. Thus flexibility as well as price are the advantages offered by nonconference over conferences ships. Exporters can hire charter ships to transport their goods anytime and anywhere, but the use of these is normally justifiable only for volume traders. Tramp ships, like taxis, go wherever cargos are available.

Three conference lines are operating in the Philippines: Philippine/Europe Conference (PEC), serving Europe and the Mediterranean; Australia/New Zealand Shipping Conference (ANZESC), serving Sydney, Melbourne, Brisbane, and Adelaide; and Asia North American Eastbound Route Agreement (ANERA), serving Asia and North America. Some nonconference vessels, including Taiwan's Evergreen Marine, provide scheduled service but quote freight rates independently.

AIR TRANSPORTATION

Airfreight and air express shipments, although more costly, may in many cases actually be the most cost-effective way to transport goods to and through the Philippines. With notoriously bad roads and almost nonexistent rail service, the only remaining choices are water shipments or airfreight. Because of its high cost, airfreight is still used mainly for products with a high value relative to weight, for perishable products, and for products that must reach the buyer very quickly. However, airfreight and air express shipments are becoming more popular for some imported merchandise as costs come down and service is expanded. In some circumstances, the greater costs incurred in shipping by air may be offset by savings in packing, handling, inventory documentation, and delivery. Semiconductor exports are always sent by air due to special transit requirements.

The biggest problem for Philippine shippers seems to be the lack of cargo space. Flying Tigers is the only international cargo freighter that serves Manila, although smaller shipments can be sent via FedEx, DHL, or United Parcel Service. Almost all of the passenger airlines that call at the NAIA have some available cargo space as well, but freight is liable to get "bumped" along the way, delaying delivery. And because rates from the Philippines are relatively low compared with rates from Japan or Hong Kong, carriers stopping someplace in their own countries tend to give priority to their own cargo (for which they can command the higher rates). Therefore, Philippine shippers often have to either wait in line to book cargo space or suffer through the possibility that their cargo will be off-loaded for a few days or weeks at some port along the way, or both. This problem affects shipments into the Philippines as well—especially those of raw materials—because most of the airlines pass through the busy trading posts such as Tokyo, Hong Kong, or Thailand. Savvy shippers therefore recommend the use of a reliable and established agent who does regular business with the shipping airline. Such agents are usually given good space allocation by the carriers with which they regularly do business.

A very rough guide to how much more costly it is to ship by air is illustrated by a 40 ft. container, weighing about 20 tons, from the Philippines to the US West Coast—roughly a 16-hour flight offered by several commercial carriers. This shipment would cost about US$3,000 (or 15 cents per kilogram) if shipped by sea. If it is sent by air, the cost rises as high as US$46,000 (or US $2.30 per kilogram).

There are 86 public airports in the Philippines, including two international airports (Manila's Ninoy Aquino International Airport and Mactan International Airport near Cebu City), and four alternate international airports (Laoag in Northern Luzon, Cubi Point in Central Luzon, Davao in Southern Mindanao, and Zamboanga in Western Mindanao), 12 trunk line airports, 37 secondary airports, and 31 feeder airports. There are also 143 private airports. Forty-two national airports offer scheduled air transport service and account for 99 percent of traffic. Most airfreighted exports are shipped from Manila. Increased passenger and freight traffic has made it necessary either to expand Manila's existing airport or to build a new international

PHILIPPINE TRANSPORTATION

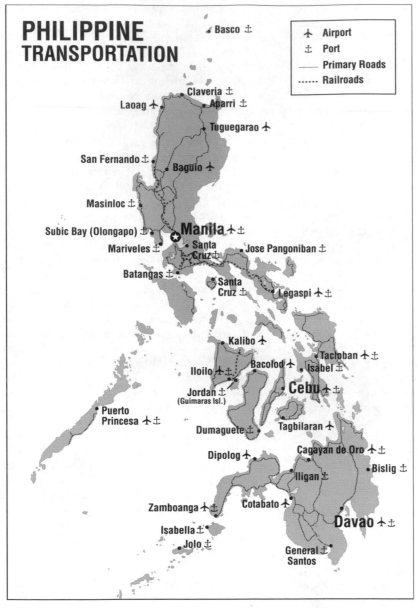

Legend	
✈	Airport
⊥	Port
───	Primary Roads
·····	Railroads

Basco ⊥

Claveria ⊥
Laoag ✈   Aparri ⊥
Tuguegarao ✈
San Fernando ⊥
Baguio ✈
Masinloc ⊥
Subic Bay (Olongapo) ⊥   **Manila** ✈⊥
Mariveles ⊥   Santa Cruz⊥   Jose Pangoniban ⊥
Batangas ⊥   Santa Cruz ⊥   Legaspi ✈⊥
Kalibo ✈   Tacloban ✈⊥
Iloilo ✈⊥   Bacolod ✈   Isabel ⊥
Jordan ⊥   **Cebu** ✈⊥
(Guimaras Isl.)
Puerto Princesa ✈⊥   Dumaguete ⊥   Tagbilaran ✈
Dipolog ✈   Cagayan de Oro ✈⊥
Iligan ⊥   Bislig ⊥
Zamboanga ✈⊥   Cotabato ✈
Isabella ⊥   **Davao** ✈⊥
Jolo ⊥   General Santos ⊥

handling equipment. Plans are underway, under the BOT program, to add both an international air cargo terminal and a domestic air cargo terminal thus expanding its passenger capacity by more than 20 percent to 11 million per year and doubling its cargo capacity to 500,000 tons. Additional access road networks in the area are also part of this plan.

NAIA is served by several international air carriers, including FedEx, United Air Lines, United Parcel Service, Continental, Japan Air Lines and others.

There is, as noted earlier, a competing, equally viable plan to build an entirely new international airport at Clark Air Force Base. The government maintains that both projects can be undertaken simultaneously and that Manila can then be served by two airports, much as in the case in Tokyo, New York, or Rome. However, it is unrealistic to presume that Manila can support two international airports—even the most optimistic growth forecasts project a limited number of passengers and cargo entering and leaving the country in the foreseeable future—and neither of the rival consortia is willing to proceed without assurance that the other will be stopped or at least significantly downgraded. Thus, although neither project had moved much beyond the planning stage by mid-1995, it is likely that at least some NAIA improvements will be made in the near future.

Cebu Mactan International Airport Located on Mactan Island just offshore of Cebu, this facility is the Philippines' only other airport offering international flights. Although direct flights from Cebu to the US West Coast are not yet available, discussions are underway, and direct service should soon be available. Most carriers serving Cebu will ship

terminal at Clark Air Force Base. Both are viable alternatives, and as of mid-1995 no final decision had been made.

Airports

Ninoy Aquino International Airport (NAIA) Manila's NAIA is the Philippines' premier airport for both cargo and passenger traffic. However, its facilities are largely inadequate even at its current volume of traffic, let alone at the increased volumes expected in the future. NAIA's current cargo capacity is 250,000 tons, and it can handle up to 9 million passengers per year, but it is already being asked to serve both cargo and passengers in excess of these amounts. NAIA currently has two runways and cargo freight, although it often must pass through Manila on its way in or out of the country.

Mindanao Although technically deemed an international airport, Davao Airport, the main airport on the island of Mindanao, is hardly an international gateway. Most airlines will carry freight, but it will be consolidated and transferred at Manila. There are also plans underway to develop an international airport at Zamboanga.

Davao The Asian Development Bank (ADB) recently approved the US$105 million development project for Davao's international airport to support the Philippines' efforts to prepare Davao City to become the country's gateway to the newly established Association of Southeast Asian Nations (ASEAN) growth polygon. This project includes the upgrade and expansion of the existing airport runway; improvement of air navigation and safety facilities; and expansion of current cargo capacity. Davao City is the center of business, finance, and international trade in Mindanao.

AIR CARRIERS

Philippine Airlines (PAL), the national carrier, provides domestic and international flights into and out of Manila as well as domestic service from the other public airports. Considered in the past to be notoriously inefficient, it has made some improvement following privatization in 1992. Domestic passenger service is also provided by the smaller private carriers Aerolift and Pacific Airways. Other domestic freight carriers include Circle Freight International, Sharp Travel Service, and Hecny Forwarders, Inc.

The top ten international airlines operating in the Philippines, all of which carry freight, are: United Airlines, Cathay Pacific Airways, Lufthansa German Airlines, Northwest Airlines, Singapore Airlines, China Airlines, Japan Airlines, Continental Air Micronesia, Qantas Airways, and Korean Airlines. International freight can also be transported to and from Manila and Cebu by PLA, LBC Express, Inc., Pakistan International Airlines, Air Canada, American Airlines, FedEx, Garuda Indonesia, Thai Airways International, and United Parcel Service. CAAC also accepts cargo, but has a limited number of flights to Manila.

Air courier service is recommended for transmittal of important documents to the Philippines. Companies offering courier services are DHL, TNT Skypak International, Eagle Courier, FedEx, United Parcel Service, World Courier Philippines, Airborne Express, and Republic Courier Service.

FedEx and DHL are the two international companies that have shown the most interest in operating in the Philippines. FedEx has contracted to create a facility similar to its Memphis, Tennessee hub at the former US naval base at Subic Bay, expected to reduce delivery times and increase freight capacity for its entire Asian operation. DHL has expressed its intention to buy 13 percent of PAL in order to give it better access to the smaller, regional airports in the Philippines. TNT Express is also building an Asian air network hub in Manila.

OVERLAND TRANSPORT: TRUCKING AND RAILROADS

Trucking

An extensive road network links much of the archipelago. The highway network is 160,000 km (100,000 mi) long, includes 11,000 bridges, and provides access to virtually the entire county. However, this is not to say that road transport is easy. Most roadways are overcrowded and under-maintained. Outdated design standards, substandard construction, inadequate and deferred maintenance, and damage from overloaded vehicles have all contributed over the years to the deterioration of many roads. Although an extensive rehabilitation and improvement program is being implemented under the BOT scheme, fewer than two-thirds of the roads in the Philippines are considered all-weather. Only about 16 percent of roadways are paved, while most of the rest are surfaced with gravel; about 5 percent are barely improved dirt roads. The government intends to make 100 percent of its national arterial roads suitable for all-weather use and to pave 94 percent of them by 1998; 95 percent of secondary roads are also to be upgraded to all-weather status, with 80 percent of these being paved. This is an ambitious undertaking, and given the present state of many of the roads, the country will probably continue to rely primarily on marine transport for the foreseeable future.

Although government statistics list trucking as the means of transport used to move more than 50 percent of Philippine freight, trucking is not really a significant factor in international trade in the Philippines. The road system is underdeveloped, the geography fragmented, and the trucking system often unreliable.

Railroads

Rail transport is poorly developed outside the Metro Manila area. Due to the fragmentation of land areas and the large amount of investment needed to build them, railroads have not been a significant mode of transportation. Nevertheless, railroads carry both freight and passengers on the islands of Luzon and Panay. The South Main Line—carrying both freight and passengers—runs 437 km (273 mi) from Manila to Albay (in the Bicol Region to the south). The government also plans to rehabilitate the currently unused North Main Line, which consists of 63 km (37 mi) of track connecting Manila and San Fernando (in Pampanga Province). There also is a light rail line, carrying passengers only, in Metro Manila, from Caloocan City (in the north) to Baclaran Terminal (in the south).

COMMUNICATIONS

Telecommunications

Telecommunications represents one of the primary deficiencies that have curtailed economic growth in the Philippines. In the past, the local exchange service was a regulated monopoly, dominated by the Philippine Long Distance Telephone Company (PLDT), which accounted for more than 94 percent of local lines (the government and several small carriers contributed the rest). The PLDT also dominated as the sole international gateway operator, while its wholly owned subsidiary cornered the fledgling cellular phone market. More concerned with maintaining its protected status and profits than with improving service, the closely held PLDT for many years simply neglected to provide adequate telecommunications services. By 1992 the backlog of applications for telephones had reached 800,000, nearly 500,000 of them in Metro Manila alone. It could take from two months to as long as two years to get telephone service, depending on specific circumstances.

To improve the efficiency, quality of service, and reliability of the Philippines' telecommunications industry, the government pushed to deregulate and demonopolize telecommunications, opening up the market to new private telecommunications firms. This opening sparked aggressive expansion and competition, and now there are more than 50 firms providing telecom service in the country. Many of these are backed by significant foreign providers eager to join this highly profitable industry. But the entry thresholds are high. Winning an international license requires that the operator establish 400,000 domestic lines within three years, while a cellular license requires the concessionaire to set up 300,000 lines within five years. Most ventures remain in the planning stage, although more are beginning to come on line.

In an attempt to hold onto its premier position, PLDT has reacted quickly with initiatives of its own. Looking to retain its current 90 percent of the market, it has launched its "Zero Backlog Program," which aims to increase telephone density to at least 17 per 100 in its franchise areas by adding almost one million new lines by 1996. It plans to install a further 1.5 million lines between 1997 and 2001. In addition, it has plans to increase the number of its local exchanges from 125 to 192; to improve the quality of its service by investing in a fiber-optic loop in the Makati business district of Metro Manila; and to upgrade connections linking the various segments of the national system. Still, many of its exchanges are using obsolete switching gear or are even operated manually. Only about 44 percent of its lines are digital; copper wire is still widely used and fiber optics have been introduced only since 1992. PLDT has quite a head start on its competitors in local exchange service, but the newcomers, with access to state-of-the-art technology through their foreign backers, may garner the edge in the international and cellular markets.

There are already eight new international gateway carriers operating facilities interconnected with those of PLDT. These companies have been assigned local service areas that they must develop along with their international and cellular operations. They plan to invest between US$600 million and US$2 billion each over the next few years to install new lines and build additional operations facilities; however, most of this investment is expected to go toward developing and operating the more lucrative international and cellular services rather than the less profitable local service. Although most services and pricing structures are relatively standard at the moment, the markets are expected to continue to develop, with new entrants setting up additional operations, following the idea that competition and specialization will provide more specific services at lower prices. For now, however, businesspeople in the Philippines must generally take what they can get and when they can get it, with regards to telecommunications systems and services.

In all, the telephone companies operate 216 telephone exchange stations, most of which are concentrated in Metro Manila or other major cities. The government-owned Telecommunications Office also provides (very limited) telephone and telegraph services in the rural areas. There are seven domestic record (telegraphic) carriers and three data communications carriers. The private record carriers serve 22 percent of municipalities with rudimentary, open-wireless, high-frequency facilities. There are 2,131 telegraph main stations and substations, and 122 telex main stations and substations. There are also four international record carriers and two domestic and international satellite systems.

Still, telephone density remains quite low, with an average density of about 3 lines per 100 inhabitants. Even Metro Manila, with the highest telephone density in the country, has only 7.3 lines per 100 inhabitants, and some outlying rural areas must make do with 1 line per 1,000 inhabitants. In short, the Philippines does not yet have adequate telecommunications service. The country's telephone density is among the lowest in the region, and the Philippines lags behind all other members of the Association of Southeast Asian Nations (ASEAN) in terms of telecommunications investment.

Local Telephone Services Local service is currently provided by the PLDT in most areas, or by smaller or government operators in a few rural areas. However, under the government's program to demonopolize the telecommunications industry, most regions will eventually be served by at least two carriers, giving customers a choice between the PLDT and one of its competitors. The government has divided the country into 11 separate telephone districts, for which it will issue licenses to operators who agree to provide local service in exchange for access to the more lucrative long distance and cellular markets. Such licensees must satisfy the government's requirements for equipment investment and line installation.

Local service area licenses have already been awarded to several firms, and line installation has actually begun in some places. In addition, the PLDT has installed nearly one million new lines, most of them in Metro Manila. The backlog of telephone applications has already lessened, and the waiting period has been shortened significantly—at least in some cases. Metro Manila is fairly well covered; the wait for telephone service there has generally dropped to about one month.

Long Distance and International Services Although still far behind the developed world and even its Asian neighbors, the Philippines is on the verge of offering a variety of innovative, competitive international telecommunications services to its businesspeople. The PLDT still retains a majority of the long distance market, but some of its competitors are giving it a run for its money. Eastern Telecommunications Philippines, Inc. has recently won the right to set up a global connection to the domestic phone network of PLDT. Other similar arrangements are expected to follow. Global Telecom, International Communications Corporation (ICC Telecom), and Bell Telecommunications Philippines (Belltel), all provide international telecommunications service.

Choices and services are still limited, and there are as yet few pricing options specifically tailored to the business client's needs and usage. However, the industry is moving rapidly, and many of the new competitors have access to the latest equipment and innovative marketing strategies through their foreign partners. Already, the number of international calls made in the Philippines has been growing at an annual rate of 27 percent. However, except in major urban areas, the quality of transmission remains problematic, and many telephone exchanges remain unconnected to the long distance network.

Mobile Telecommunications Services The use of cellular phones has expanded rapidly over the past four years, and there are now several companies operating in this field, led by PLDT and its affiliate, Pilipino Telephone Corporation (Piltel), as well as Express Telecommunications Corp. (Extelcom), Isla Communications, and Smart Information Technologies. The PLDT group controls about 83 percent of market share throughout the country, and provides the only cellular services in the Visayas islands or on Mindanao.

The networks still suffer from too few cell sites, too many connections, misuse of equipment, and the use of weak batteries by customers. All of these elements combine with the Philippines' hilly terrain to cause noise, crosstalk, dead spots, dropped calls, and congestion. The country also has one of the lowest cellular phone densities in the region— about 1.5 per 1,000 people, versus South Korea's 4, Taiwan's 9 and Australia's 22. However, the government hopes to have cellular phones in all major urban centers by 2010.

The limited number of telephone lines and the growing popularity of two-way radio and cellular phones have all helped the paging industry to prosper during the past few years. Pagers have become very popular among professionals, such as medical practitioners, sales engineers, insurance agents, real estate brokers, and senior management personnel. The paging system is the fastest-growing sector of the telecommunications industry, with recent growth reaching 43.5 percent a year. Professionals save substantial amounts of money by getting pagers in addition to their cellular phones. With a pager, cellular phone bills can be cut by 20 to 30 percent, and pagers can also receive and screen calls 24 hours a day. Subscribers can either call back immediately from the cellular phone at P4.50 (about US$0.17) for the first minute and P3.00 (about US$0.12) for each additional minute or wait until they get to the office or nearest pay phone and return the call for far less money.

Four types of pagers are available in the Philippines: tone only; tone and voice; numeric; and alphanumeric. A tone only pager produces a tone or beep when it receives a radio signal. A tone and voice pager produces a tone and thereafter transmits a voice message when it receives a radio signal. It usually has the capacity to receive a voice message lasting of up to 20 seconds, but it is incapable of storing messages. The more advanced (and more expensive) types of pagers are the numeric and alphanumeric pagers. Both types of pagers eliminate the need for subscribers to contact the paging service operator in order to retrieve incoming messages and can store messages for later retrieval. A numeric pager relays messages by displaying numeric codes on its liquid crystal display; alphanumeric pagers can also display headline news, stock quotes, and other similar brief messages.

Record Carrier Services There are about 2,824 operational telegraph stations nationwide. TELOF, the largest, has about 54 percent of the market. However, the Philippine Telegraph and Telephone Co. has both a digital and microwave backbone. It is the sole licensed provider of domestic packet switching and electronic mail service in the country.

There are four international record carriers, all of which offer such services as international telegraph, telex, fax, and leased circuits. Most carriers are also embarking aggressively into voice services to widen their scope of operations.

Public Telephones Red pay phones in sidewalk cubicles may be used only for local calls. Silver pay phones, usually found in department stores and commercial centers, may be used for either local or long distance calls. Private pay phones in small stores or in marketplaces and shopping arcades can be used for local calls.

Directory Assistance Throughout the country, dial 114 for directory assistance. For international direct dialing assistance, dial 112. Dial 108 for operator-assisted international calls, and call 109 for operator-assisted domestic calls.

The Future

The Philippines appears to be poised for phenomenal growth in the communications sector. Several companies are looking to install massive, fully integrated telephone networks using satellite and fiber optic technology. Most expect their operations to be 100 percent digital and state-of-the-art. The almost nonexistent baseline infrastructure and almost guaranteed huge demand are encouraging companies to bypass incremental development and, instead, avail themselves immediately of the latest technology to enact more ambitious plans.

This development should soon allow such services as call waiting (which alerts the subscriber to a second caller and enables the subscriber to put the ongoing call on hold and take the second one); caller ID (which allows the subscriber to determine a caller's phone number before answering); and the emergency network known as 911 in the US (a comprehensive set of local emergency services responding to a simple nationwide phone number). In addition, such features as credit card calls, conferencing, and voicemail will be available. Other electronic services such as audiotext, fax-on-demand, or online information services are also expected to become available eventually.

REGULATORY AGENCIES

Bureau of Air Transportation
Old MIA Road
Pasay City, Metro Manila, Philippines
Tel: [63] (2)832-3047, 831-8078, 832-3308
Fax: [63] (2) 833-1577

Bureau of Telecommunications
A. Roces Ave.
Quezon City, Metro Manila, Philippines
Tel: [63] (2) 964-391

Dept. of Public Works and Highways (DPWH)
DPWH Bldg.
Bonifacio Drive
Port Area, Metro Manila, Philippines
Tel: [63] (2) 475-865, 479-311, 482-011
Fax: [63] (2) 401-551, 401-683

Dept. of Transportation and Communications
3/F, Philcomcen Building
Ortigas Avenue
Pasig, Metro Manila, Philippines
Tel: [63] (2) 631-8761/3, 631-8666 to 85, 721-3781
Fax: [63] (2) 632-9985

Land Transportation Office
East Ave.
Quezon City, Metro Manila, Philippines
Tel: [63] (2) 922-9061/65
Fax: [63] (2) 921-9072

Manila International Airport Authority
Ninoy Aquino International Airport (NAIA)
Paranaque, Metro Manila, Philippines
Tel: [63] (2) 832-2938, 831-6205
Fax: [63] (2) 833-1180

National Telecommunications Commission
VIBAL Bldg.
Epifanio de los Santos Ave. cor. Times St.
Quezon City, Metro Manila, Philippines
Tel: [63] (2) 924-4042, 924-4008, 981-160
Fax: [63] (2) 921-7128.

Philippine National Railways
Management Center
Torres Bugallon St.
Kaloocan City, Metro Manila, Philippines
Tel: [63] (2) 362-0824
Fax: [63] (2) 362-0824

Philippine Ports Authority (PPA)
Marsman Building, Gate 1
22 Muelle de Francisco St.
South Harbor
1002 Port Area, Metro Manila, Philippines
Tel: [63] (2) 530-0875, 479-204
Fax: [63] (2) 530-1199, 486-237

Philippine Telegraph and Telephone Corp.
PT&T Spirit of Communication Center
106 Alvarado St.
Legaspi Village
Makati, Metro Manila, Philippines

Telecommunications Office (TELOF)
2nd Fl., Multipurpose Bldg.
A. Roces Ave.
Quezon City, Metro Manila, Philippines
Tel: [63] (2) 951-961, 974-747
Fax: [63] (2) 921-8977

Business Dictionary

PRONUNCIATION GUIDE

English and Tagalog (pronounced tah-gah-lawg) are the most common languages used in business in the Philippines today. The nation's official language is Pilipino, which is primarily based on Tagalog in combination with elements of other indigenous Philippine languages. Most Filipinos, especially in urban areas, speak at least some English, although the syntax and pronunciation may be unfamiliar to a visitor. Malay-based Tagalog incorporates words borrowed from other languages, including Chinese and Arabic. However, the strongest influences have been Spanish and English, reflecting long colonial exposure. Most borrowed words have a distinct Tagalog flavor; for example, adopted English words include halo (hello), gudnait (good night), and taksi (taxi).

Knowledge of a few common Tagalog words and phrases can help business travelers particularly in Metropolitan Manila, the country's primary business center and the heart of its Tagalog-speaking area. In other locales, a traveler may run into any of the dozens of distinct languages and dialects that are spoken throughout the country. Significant pockets of other Filipino languages—such as Cebuano in Cebu and Chavacano (a pidgin Spanish) in Zamboanga City on Mindanao—can be found. A businessperson may also run into Spanish speakers,

mainly in well educated, more traditional Filipino circles, and many of the languages throughout the Philippines have a strong Spanish flavor to them. Other distinct languages are present in the predominately Muslim communities on Mindanao (with its growing business center at Davao).

Notes on Pronunciation

Each of the five Tagalog vowels (a, e, i, o, u) is usually pronounced the same whenever it is used, regardless of adjoining consonants. The vowel *a* is pronounced somewhere between the way it sounds in *back* and in *father* in English, *e* as in *get*, *i* as in *police*, *o* as in *hotel*, *u* as in *rude*. Double vowels are pronounced separately (*oo* = ooh ooh), but the degree of stress given to specific vowel combinations varies.

The *p* and *f* are often interchanged; thus, a written *p* may be pronounced as *f* (Pilipino=Filipino). The consonant combination *ng* often sounds like *nang* when spoken, although the *na* may be softened or slurred into the rest of the word. Similarly, *mga* tends to be said as *manga* but may be softened by native tongues.

Pilipino words are formed from root words by adding prefixes (at the beginning), suffixes (at the end), or infixes (in the middle). The language is agglutinative, meaning that it combines strings of syllables to convey meaning. This can result in long, repetitive syllable chains that can be difficult for nonnative speakers.

Stress

In general, stress is placed on the next to the last syllable, but there are numerous exceptions. Many words stress the last syllable, and others have multiple stresses. English and Spanish influences, in particular, can be seen in the exceptions to the general rule. For pronunciation purposes, in this dictionary the letters underlined in a word carry the stress, as in hah-<u>loh</u> for halo (hello).

Pilipino uses the glottal stop, noted here with an apostrophe, in which the last vowel is pronounced abruptly by closing the epiglottis in the throat. This usually occurs in words that accent the next to the

Reviewed by Tagalog consultants Merdona C. Bautista and Carmelita R. Bernardo.

last syllable, but may also occur in combination with a final accent, resulting in a double stress at the end of a word.

Pilipino can be complicated because a word can have multiple meanings that depend on where the stress falls, and care must be taken because using the wrong stress can be humorous or misleading.

Forms of Address

Courtesy is expressed by adding the syllable *po* whenever addressing elders or other persons who are due respect. Thus, *po Ginoong Ramirez* is the formal address for *Mr. Ramirez*. As a general rule, the formal address should be used when speaking with someone you have not met before, with an older person, with someone of higher rank, or with any other person who should be shown deference, unless that person expresses a contrary preference. (Note that expressions in this short business dictionary are those suited for formal address.)

Persons who have earned a title are often addressed by it. Thus, a public official may be *Mr. Secretary* or *Mrs. Mayor*; a professional may be addressed as *Engineer Ramirez*. The spouse of a titled person may be also be addressed as *Mrs. Secretary* or *Mr. Mayor*, thus being included in their spouse's title.

BUSINESS WORDS AND PHRASES

GREETINGS AND POLITE EXPRESSION

English	Tagalog	Pronunciation
Hello	Halo	Hah-loh
Good morning	Magandang umaga	Mah-gahn-dang oo-mah-gah
Good afternoon	Magandang hapon	Mah-gahn-dang hah-pohn
Good night	Gudnait/Magandang gabi	Good-nah-yeeht/Mah-gahn-dang gah-bee
Goodbye	Paalam na po (by person departing)	Pah-ah-lahm nah poh
	Adyos po (by person left behind)	Ah-dee-ohs poh
Pleased to meet you	Nagagalak akong makilala kayo	Nah-gah-gah-lahk ah-kohng mah-keeh-lah-lah kah-yoh
How are you?	Kumusta kayo?	Koo-moost-ah kah-yoh?
Fine, thanks. And you?	Mabuti, salamat. At kayo?	Mah-boo-teeh sah-lah-maht. Aht kah-yoh?
Please	Paki lang	Pah-keeh lahng
Would you please . . . ?	Puede bang paki . . . ?	Pweh-deh bahng pah-keeh . . . ?
Excuse me	Ipagpaumanhin mo	Ee-pahg-pah-oo-mahn-heehn moh
I'm sorry	Ikinalulungkot ko	Ee-keehn-ah-loo-loong-koht koh
Congratulations	Maligayang bati	Mah-leeh-gah-yahng bah-teeh
Thank you	Salamat	Sah-lah-maht
Thank you very much	Maraming salamat	Mah-rah-meehng sah-lah-maht
You're welcome	Walang anuman	Wah-lahng ah-noo-mahn
I don't speak Tagalog	Hindi ako nakapag-sasalita ng Tagalog	Heehn-deeh ah-koh nah-kah-pahg sah-sah-leeh-tah' nahng Tah-gah-lawg
I don't understand	Hindi ko naiintindihan	Heehn-deeh koh nah-eeh-eehn-teehn-deeh-hahn

English	Tagalog	Pronunciation
I understand	Naiintndihan ko	Nah-eehn-teehn-deeh-hahn koh
Do you speak English?	Nagsasalita ka ba ng Ingles?	Nahg-sah-sah-leeh-tah' kah bah nang Eehng-lehs?
My name Is John Smith	Ang pangalan ko ay John Smith	Ahng pahng ah lahn koh ah yooh John Smith
Is Mr./Mrs./Miss Smith there?	Nandiyan po ba si Ginoong/Ginang/Gining Smith?	Nahn-deeh-yahn poh bah seeh Geeh-noh-ohng/Geeh-nahng/Geeh-neeng Smith?
yes	oo (informal)/opo (polite)	oh-oh/oh-poh
no	hindi/hindi po	Heehn-deeh'/heehn-deeh poh

CLOCK AND CALENDAR

English	Tagalog	Pronunciation
What time is it?	Anong oras na?	Ah-nohng oh-rahs nah?
At what time?	Sa anong oras?	Sah ah-nohng oh-rahs?
ten o'clock	ika sampu	ee-kah sahm-poo'
noon	tanghali	tahng-hah-leeh'
today	sa araw na ito	sah ah-rahw nah eeh-toh
yesterday	kahapon	kah-hah-pohn
tomorrow	bukas	boo-kahs
Monday	Lunes	Loo-nehs
Tuesday	Martes	Mahr-tehs
Wednesday	Miyerkules	Mee-yehr-koo-lehs
Thursday	Huwebes	Hoo-weh-behs
Friday	Biyernes	Beeh-yehr-nehs
Saturday	Sabado	Sah-bah-doh
Sunday	Linggo	Leeng-goh
official holiday	pista opisyal	peeh-hes-tah oh-peehs-yahl
festival day	pista	peeh-hes-tah
vacation	bakasyon	bah-kah-seeh-ohn
day off work	araw ng pahinga	ah-rahw nahng pah-eeng-ah

NUMBERS

English	Tagalog	Pronunciation
one	isa	eeh-sah
two	dalawa/dalwa	dah-lah-wah/dahl-wah
three	tatlo	taht-loh
four	apat	ah-paht

English	Tagalog	Pronunciation
five	lima	leeh-<u>mah</u>
six	anim	ah-<u>neehm</u>
seven	pito	peeh-<u>toh</u>
eight	walo	wah-<u>loh</u>
nine	siyam	seeh-<u>yahm</u>
ten	sampu	sahm-<u>poo</u>'
eleven	labing-isa	lah-<u>beeng</u> eeh-<u>sah</u>
twelve	labindalawa/labindalwa	lah-been- dah-lah-<u>wah</u>/lah-been-dahl-<u>wah</u>
thirteen	labintatlo	lah-been-taht-<u>loh</u>
fourteen	labing-apat	lah-<u>beeng</u> <u>ah</u>-paht
fifteen	labinglima	lah-<u>beehng</u> leeh-<u>mah</u>
sixteen	labing-anim	lah-<u>beeng</u> <u>ah</u>-neehm
seventeen	labimpito	lah-beem-peeh-<u>toh</u>
eighteen	labingwalo	lah-beeng-wah-<u>loh</u>
nineteen	labinsiyam	lah-been-seeh-<u>yahm</u>
twenty	dalawampu	dah-lah-wahm-<u>poo</u>
twenty one	dalawampu't isa	dah-lah-wahm-<u>poo</u>'t eeh-<u>sah</u>
thirty	tatlumpu	taht-loom-<u>poo</u>'
forty	apatnapu	<u>ah</u>-paht-nah-<u>poo</u>'
fifty	limampu	leeh-mahm-<u>poo</u>'
sixty	animnapu	ah-neem-nah-<u>poo</u>'
seventy	pitumpu	peeh-toom-<u>poo</u>'
eighty	walumpu	wah-loom-<u>poo</u>'
ninety	siyamnapu	seeh-yahm-nah-<u>poo</u>'
one hundred	isandaan	eeh-sahn-dah-<u>ahn</u>
one hundred fifty	isandaa't limampu	eeh-sahn-dah-<u>ah</u>'t leeh-mahm-<u>poo</u>'
two hundred	dalawandaan	dah-lah-wahn-dah-<u>ahn</u>
five hundred	limandaan	leeh-mahn-dah-<u>ahn</u>
one thousand	isanlibo	eeh-sahn-<u>leeh</u>-boh
one million	isang milyon/isang angaw	eeh-<u>sahng</u>-meehl-<u>yohn</u>/eeh-<u>sahng</u> <u>ahn</u>-gahw
first	una	<u>oo</u>-nah
second	pangalawa	pahng-ah-lah-<u>wah</u>
third	pangatlo	pahng-aht-<u>loh</u>

English	*Tagalog*	*Pronunciation*

DESTINATIONS

Where is the bus stop?	Saan ang hintayan ng bus?	Sah-<u>ahn</u> ahng heehn-<u>tah</u>-yahn nahng boos?
...airport?	...aerport?/paliparan?	...air-<u>pohr</u>?/ pah-lee-<u>pahr</u>-ahn?
...bank?	...bangko?	...<u>bahng</u>-koh?
...barber?	...barbero?	...bahr-<u>beh</u>-roh?
...business district?	...pook ng negosyo?	...poh-ohk nang neh-<u>goh</u>-seeh-oh?
...clothes store?	...tindahan ng damit?	...teehn-<u>dah</u>-hahn nang dah-<u>meet</u>?
...courthouse?	...hukuman?	...<u>hoo</u>-koo-mahn?
...copier/copy center?	...kopyahan?	...<u>kohp</u>-yah-hahn?
...drugstore/pharmacy?	...butika/parmasya?	...boo-<u>teeh</u>-kah/pahr-<u>mah</u>-seeh-yah?
...embassy?	...embassi?	...<u>ehm</u>-bahs-seeh?
...exhibition?	...eksibisyon?	...ehk-seeh-beeh-seeh-<u>yohn</u>?
...factory?	...paktorya?	...pahk-<u>tohr</u>-yah?
...grocery store?	...groserya?	...groh-<u>sehr</u>-yah?
...gym?	...himnasyum?	...heem-<u>nah</u>-seeh-yoom?
...hospital?	...ospital?	...ohs-peeh-<u>tahl</u>?
...hotel?	...otel?	...oh-<u>tehl</u>?
...market?	...palengke?	...pah-<u>lehng</u>-keh?
...police station?	...istasyon ng pulis?	...eeh-stah-see-<u>ohn</u> nahng <u>poo</u>-leehs?
...post office?	...pos opis?	...pohs <u>oh</u>-peehs?
...restaurant?	...restauran/karihan?	...rehs-tahwr <u>ahn</u>/<u>kah</u>-reeh-hahn?
...restroom/toilet?	...kubeta/kasilyas?	...koo-<u>beh</u>-tah/kah-<u>seehl</u>-yahs?
...women's?	...pambabae?	...pahm-bah-<u>bah</u>-eh?
...men's?	...panlalaki?	...pahn-lah-<u>lah</u>-keeh?
...seaport?	...daungang-dagat?	...<u>dah</u>-oong-ahng <u>dah</u>-gaht?
...train station?	...istasyon ng tren?	...eeh-stah-seeh-<u>yohn</u> nang trehn?
...wharf?	...daungan?	...<u>dah</u>-oong-ahn?

TRANSIT

Would you please call a taxi for me?	Puede bang paki tawag mo ako ng taksi?	<u>Pweh</u> deh bahng <u>pah</u>-keeh <u>tah</u>-wahg moh <u>ah</u>-koh nahng <u>tahk</u>-seeh?
Does this bus go to Makati?	Ang bus bang ito aypunta sa Makati?	Ahng boos bahng eeh-<u>toh</u> iyh-pah-poon-<u>tah</u> sah Mah-<u>kah</u>-teeh?
Please take me to Manila	Pakidala lang ako sa Maynila	Pah-<u>keeh</u>-dah-<u>lah</u> lahng ah-<u>koh</u> sah Mahy-<u>neeh</u>-lah'

English	Tagalog	Pronunciation
Where am I?	Saan ako naroroon?	Sah-ahn' ah-koh nah-roh-ohn?
This is the address	Ito ang direksiyon ito	Eeh-toh ahng deeh-rehk-seeh-yohn
How far is it?	Gaano kalayo?	Gah-ah-noh kah-lah-yoh?
turn right	pumakanan	poo-mah-kah-nahn
turn left	pumakaliwa	poo-mah-kah-leeh-wah'
stop	para	pah-rah
entrance	pasukan	pah-soo-kahn
exit	labasan	lah-bah-sahn
east	silangan	seeh-lahng-ahn
north/northward	hilaga/pahilaga	heeh-lah-gah/pah-heeh-lah-gah'
south/southward	timog/patimog	teeh-mohg/pah-teeh-mohg
west	kanluran	kahn-loo-rahn
hired driver/chauffeur	tsuper	tsoo-pehr
airplane	eroplano	eh-roh-plah-noh
bus (public)	bus (publiko)	boos (poo-bleeh-koh)
car	kotse	koht-seh
ferry	tawiran sa ilog	tah-weeh-ahn sah eeh-lohg
taxi	taksi	tahk-seeh
How much?	Magkano?	Mahg-kah-noh?
fare	pasahe	pah-sah-heh
ticket	tiket/bilyete	teeh-keht/beehl-yeh-teh
one-way (single) ticket	isang biyaheng (iisa) tiket	eeh-sahng beeh-yah-hehng (ih-ih-sah) teeh-keht
round trip (return) ticket	balikang biyahe (pabalik) na tiket	bah-leeh-kahng beeh-yah-eh (pah-bah-leehk) nah teeh-keht

TAKING CARE OF BUSINESS AT . . .

. . . The Bank

What is the exchange rate?	Ano ang kapalit na halaga?	Ah-noh ahng kah-pah-leeht nah hah-lah-gah?
I'd like to exchange some (dollars)	Gusto kong magpapalit ng mga (dolyar)	Goos-toh kohng mahg-pah-pah-leeht nahng mahng-ah (dohl-yahr)
Filipino currency	Kuwaltang Pilipino	Koo-wahl-tahng Peeh-leeh-peeh-noh
traveler's check	tsekeng pang-manlalakbay	tseh-kehng pahng-mahn-lah-lahk-bah-yeeh

English	*Tagalog*	*Pronunciation*
US dollar	dolyar ng US	<u>dohl</u>-yar nang Oo-Ehs
Can you cash a personal check?	Maaari mo bang palitan ang tsekeng personal?	Mah-<u>ah</u>-ahr-eeh' moh bahng <u>pah</u>-lee-tahn ahng <u>tseh</u>-kehng <u>pehr</u>-soh-nahl?

. . . The Hotel

I have a reservation	Mayroon akong reserbasyon	Mah-eehr-oh-<u>ohn</u> ah-<u>kohng</u> reh-sehr-bah-seeh-<u>yohn</u>
Would you give me a single/double room?	Maaari mo ba akong bigyan ng singel/doble na kuwarto?	Mah-<u>ah</u>-ah-reeh' moh bah ah-<u>kohng</u> beehg-<u>yahn</u> nang <u>seehn</u>-gehl/<u>doh</u>-bleh nah koo-wahr-toh?
Is there...	Mayroon bang...	Mah-<u>eehr</u>-oh-ohn bahng...
...air conditioning?	...eyr kondisyon?	...ehyr kohn-deeh-<u>seeh</u>-yohn?
...private bathroom?	...sariling paliguan?	...sah-<u>reeh</u>-leehng <u>pah</u>-leeh-goo-<u>ahn</u>?
...hot water?	...mainit na tubig?	...mah-<u>eeh</u>-neeht nah <u>too</u>-beehg?
May I see the room?	Puede bang tignan ko ang kuwarto?	<u>Pweh</u>-deh bahng <u>teehg</u>-nahn koh ahng koowahr-toh?
May I have my bill?	Pakibigay nga ang aking kuwenta/talautangan?	Pah-<u>keeh</u>-beeh-gay nahng-ah ahng <u>ah</u>-keehng cooh-<u>wehn</u>-tah/tah-<u>lah</u>-oo-tahn-gahn?
Do you accept credit cards?	Tumatanggap ba kayo ng mga kredit kard?	Too-<u>mah</u>-tahng-gahp bah kah-<u>yoh</u> nahng mahng-ah <u>kreh</u>-deeht kahrd?
I'd like the international (telephone) operator	Gusto ko ang opereytor ng telepono na pang-internasyonal	Goo-<u>stoh</u> koh ang oh-peh-<u>rehy</u>-tohr nahng teh-leh-<u>poh</u>-noh-nah pahng eehn-tehr-nah-<u>seeh</u>-<u>yohn</u>-al

. . . A Store

I'd like (three books)	Nais kong (tatlung mga aklat)	<u>Nah</u>-eehs kohng (taht-<u>loo</u>ng mahng-ah ahk-<u>laht</u>)
I'd like this one	Nais ko ito	<u>Nah</u>-eehs koh eeh-<u>toh</u>
I'd like these	Nais ko ang mga ito	<u>Nah</u>-eehs koh ahng mahng-ah eeh-<u>toh</u>
When does it open?	Kailan magbubukas?	Kah-eeh-<u>lahn</u> mahg-boo-boo-<u>kahs</u>
When does it close?	Kailan magsasara?	Kah-eeh-<u>lahn</u> mahg-<u>sah</u>-sah-<u>rah</u>?
How much?	Magkano?	Mahg-<u>kah</u>-noh?

FILIPINO TITLES

board of directors	lupon ng mga tagapamahala	loo-<u>pohn</u> nang mang-ah tah-gah-pah-mah-<u>hah</u>-lah'
chair	tagapangulo	tah-gah-pahng-<u>oo</u>-loh
manager	manedyer/tagapamahala	<u>mah</u>-neh-dyehr/tah-gah-pah-mah-<u>hah</u>-lah'

English	Tagalog	Pronunciation
assistant manager	katulong na tagapamahala	kah-<u>too</u>-lohng nah tah-gah-pah-mah-<u>hah</u>-lah'
president	pangulo/presidente	pahng-<u>oo</u>-loh/ preh-seeh-<u>dehn</u>-teh
vice president	pangalawang pangulo/bise presidente	pahng-<u>ah</u>-lah-<u>wahng</u> pahng-<u>oo</u>-loh/ beeh-seh preh-seeh-<u>dehn</u>-teh
supervisor	superbisor/tagapangasiwa	soo-pehr-<u>beeh</u>-sohr/ tah-gah-pahng-ah-<u>seeh</u>-wah'
marketing director	direktor sa pamimili	deeh-<u>rehk</u>-tohr sa <u>pah</u>-meeh-meeh-leeh
sales manager	manedyer sa pagtinda	<u>mah</u>-neh-dyehr sah pahg-<u>teehn</u>-dah
agent	ahente	ah-<u>hehn</u>-teh
partner	kabakas	kah-<u>bah</u>-kahs
accountant	akawntant/kontador	ah-<u>kahn</u>-tahnt /kohn-<u>tah</u>-dohr
attorney	atorni/abugado	ah-<u>tohr</u>-neeh / ah-boo-<u>gah</u>-doh
banker	bangkero	bahng-<u>kehr</u>-oh
engineer	inhinyero	eehn-heehn-<u>yehr</u>-oh
interpreter	interprete/tagasalin	eehn-tehr-preh-<u>teh</u>/tah-gah-<u>sah</u>-leehn
mayor	puno ng lunsod/meyor/alkalde	poo-<u>noh</u> nang loon-<u>sohd</u>/meh-yohr/ahl-<u>kahl</u>-deh
merchant	komersiyante	koh-mehr-seeh-<u>yahn</u>-teh
notary	notaryo	noh-<u>tahr</u>-eeh-yoh
physician	mediko/doktor	<u>meh</u>-deeh-<u>koh</u>/dohk-tohr
registrar	tagatala	tah-gah-tah-<u>lah</u>'

BUSINESS SLANG

A

ala suerte (ah-lah swehr-teh) Leave it to luck; not planned.

alembong (ah-lehm-bohng) Not businesslike; irresponsibly flirtatious.

amoy gatas ang hininga (ah-mohy-gah-tahs ang heeh-neehn-gah) Young in business; inexperienced; literally means "breath smells milk."

anghel de guardia (ang-hehl deh gwahr-deeh-yah) Guardian angel; a guide; an inspiration.

B

balasubas (bah-lah-soo-bahs) A debtor who avoids paying debts; a cheat.

basang sisiw (bah-sahng seeh-seehw) Born loser; ends up being humiliated; literally means "a wet chick."

bato sa buhangin (bah-toh sah boo-hah-ngeehn) The biggest in a crowd; literally "stone in the sand."

boliliaso (boh-leeh-leeh-yah-soh) A miscalculation; a mistake.

buwaya (boo-wah-yah) Greedy person; a person who doesn't play by the rules; literally means "crocodile."

busilak na puso (boo-seeh-lahk nah poo-soh) Goodhearted; literally "white-as-cotton heart."

D

dilang anghel (deeh-lahng ang-hehl) A person who makes good prognostications in business or life in general; "an angel's tongue."

dugong bughaw (doo-gohng boog-hahw) refers to royalty; in business, the cream of the crop; literally means "blue bloods."

G

gawang luko (gah-wahng loo-koh) A foolish act; a bad investment.

H

halik Satanas (hah-leehk Sah-tahn-ahs) A treacherous kiss; a bad recommendation; a bad endorsement; literally means "Satan's kiss."

hataw magmaneho (hah-tahw mahg-mahn-eh-oh) Careless manager; a person who drives carelessly.

hating kapatid (hah-teehng kah-pah-teehd) The fair sharing of profit or food; means "divided between brothers."

hugis puso (hoo-gees poo-soh) Beautiful; means "shaped like a heart."

K

kamay ng Diyos (kah-mah-eeh nang deeh-yohs) A blessed or divine effort; literally means "the hand of God."

kamay ni Satanas (kah-mah-eeh neeh Sah-tah-nahs) A businessperson to be avoided as a partner; "the hand of the devil."

kape at gatas (kah-peh aht gah-tahs) Opposites; in reference to colors, black and white; literally it means "coffee and milk."

kapit sa patalim (kah-peeht sah pah-tah-leehm) desperate attempt at survival; literally "hold onto a blade."

kapit-tuko (kah-peeht too-koh) Holding very tight; literally "holding on like a lizard."

karengkeng (kah-rehng-kehng) Not a serious venture; flirtation with futility; also a flirtatious person.

L

lakad pagong (lah-kahd pahg-ohng) In business, slow; hardly moving; literally means a "turtle's walk."

langoy aso (lah-ngohy ah-soh) Fast, swift; "swim like a dog."

ligaw tingin (leeh-gahw teeh-ngeehn) A silent attempt at a partnership; admiration in silence or from a distance.

lintik lang ang walang ganti (leehn-teehk lahng ahng wah-lahng gahn-teeh) Warning against double-crossing; literally means "Damned if I can't exact revenge."

M

mababa ang lipad (mah-bah-bah ahng leeh-pahd) Of low morals; no scruples; means "flies low."

mabigat ang paa (mah-beeh-gaht ahng pah-ah) Slow, hardly moves; literally "heavy foot."

mabigat dalhin (mah-beeh-gaht dahl-heehn) Heavy load; literally means "having a monkey on one's back."

mabilis pa sa alas kuatro (mah-beeh leehs pah sah ah-lahs kwah-troh) fast, agile; literally means "faster than four o'clock," an allusion to the hour of dismissal from class or work.

magaan ang dugo (mah-gah-ahn ahng doo-goh) An instant liking for somebody.

magaan ang kamay (mah-gah-ahn ahng kah-mah-eeh) A person who has good luck; a person who is lucky in business; literally "light-handed."

mahaba ang pisi (mah-hah-bah ahng peeh-seeh) One who can go far or succeed in business; literally means "long belt."

maikli ang pisi (mah-eehk-leeh ahng peeh-seeh) One who won't go far; one who does not have the means to succeed; literally means "short belt."

maitim ang budhi (mah-eeh-teehm ahng bood-heeh) A bad person; devilish; literally "black conscience."

makapal ang mukha (mah-kah-pahl ahng mook-hah) A shameless person; one without principles; literally means "thick face."

makati ang dila (mah-kah-teeh ahng deeh-lah) One who cannot keep a secret; a talkative person; "itchy tongue."

malaki ang ulo (mah-lah-keeh ahng oo-loh) In Tagalog, a person who has grown proud; an arrogant person; literally means "big head."

manggagantso (mahn-gah-gahn-tsoh) A person who betrays another; a back-stabber; in business, an untrustworthy person; literally means "he who acts like a goose."

mang-oonse (mahng-oh-ohn-seh) A double-crosser; a cheat.

maraming borloloy (mah-rah-meehng bor-loh-loy) Over-decorated; overly ornate or complex, as in a building or a business proposal.

matalas ang dila (mah-tah-lahs ahng deeh-lah) A merciless critic; one who condemns easily; literally means "sharp tongue."

matalas ang gunting (mah-tah-lahs ahng goon-teehng) A bureaucrat who demands a bribe; somebody who demands an undeserved payment; literally "sharp scissors."

matalas ang pangamoy (mah-tah-lahs ahng pahng-ah-mohy) One who spots an opportunity from a distance; one who has a nose for profits; means "sharp smell."

matang lawin (mah-tahng lah-weehn) Sharp-eyed; very observant; one who makes meticulous observations; literally "eagle's eye."

matiyagang manalangin (mah-teeh-yah-gahng mah-nah-lah-neehn) A conscientious worker; one who patiently pursues an objective; literally means "one who prays patiently."

mukhang anghel (mook-hahng ahng-hehl) A trustworthy person; "angel-faced."

N

nagsusunog ng kilay (nahg-soo-soo-nohg nahng keeh-lah-ee) One who works late into the night; a hard worker; literally means "burning his eyebrow."

namumulot ng mansanas (nah-moo-moo-loht nang

mahn-sah-nahs) Making an easy profit; a good business investment; literally means "apple picking."

ngiting aso (ngeeh-teehng ah-soh) Treacherous; insincere; "a dog's smile."

P

pabandying-bandying (pah-bahn-dyeehng-bahn-dyeehng) Irresponsible; going about life aimlessly with no plans.

panlalangis (pahn-lah-lahng-eehs) Overpraising someone to gain an advantage; literally means "using oil."

paradang pulis (pah-rah-dahng poo-leehs) Parking in an inappropriate, if not licentious, way; carelessly taking the wrong seat at a group gathering, such as at dinner or in a board meeting; "parking like a policeman."

parang kagat langgam (pah-rahng kah-gaht lahng-gahm) Light, not painful; means "like an ant's bite."

patutsada (pah-toot-sah-dah) Gimmicks; cheap tricks to promote a product.

perang Hapon (peh-rahng Hah-pohn) fake money; worthless currency; literally means "Japanese war money."

pindanggang magdamit (peehn-dahng-gahng mahg-dah-meeht) Not noted for sartorial elegance; a bad dresser; does not follow fashion trends.

Pulutin sa kangkongan (poo-loo-teehn sah kahng-koo-ngahn) A treasure found amidst a wasteland; inspiration that materializes out of thin air; means literally "pick up from among the kangkong plants."

punot-dulo (poo-noht-doo-loh) The cause of a bad result or unsuccessful ending; "the beginning and the end."

pusong anghel (poo-sohng ahng-hehl) A good-natured person; one who is kind or loving; "an angel's heart."

putok ng botse (poo-tok nang boht-seh) one who gets mad easily; one who often whines or complains; literally means "eruption of the mouth."

putok ng bulkan (poo-tohk nang bool-kahn) One who is very angry; means "volcanic eruption."

S

Sisid marino (seeh-seehd mah-reeh-noh) To leap without looking; to strike carelessly; to get into business without any planning; literally "a Marine's dive."

T

talak ng talak (tah-lahk nang tah-lahk) One who talks endlessly; "cackles like a chicken."

tapos na ang boksing (tah-pohs nah ahng bohk-seehng) Too late; the show is over; literally "the boxing is over."

tigas kamatis (teeh-gahs kah-mahteehs) Deceptively tough; something that is not as strong as it seems; literally means " tough as a tomato."

trabahong kalabaw (trah-bah-hohng kah-lah-bahw) Hard work; literally "the work of a carabao (water buffalo)."

tubig at langis (too-beehg aht lah-ngeehs) Cannot be mixed; socially incompatible; "water and oil."

tubong lugaw (too-bohng loo-gahw) Easy money; undeserved profit; literally "porridge profit."

tulis kampilan (too-leehs kahm-peeh-lahn) A rapier-like blade; a dangerous prospect or person.

tulog manok (too-lohg mahn-ohk) Light sleep; catnap; literally means "chicken sleep."

tulak ng bibig, kabig ng dibdib (too-lahk nang beeh-beehg, kah-beehg nang deehb-deehb) In Tagalog, insincere; stated without conviction; means "What the mouth says, the heart takes back."

tumatakbo ng matulin (too-mah-tahk-boh nahng mah-too-leehn) The act of being careless; acting without much thought; "running fast."

U

ugaling matsing (oo-gah-leehng mah-tseehng) Uncouth, without manners; bad behavior; literally "a monkey's behavior."

usapang lalake (oo-sah-pahng lah-lah-keh) Macho talk; tough talk; "talk between real men."

urong-sulong (oo-rohng-soo-lohng) A person who cannot make a decision and stick to it; one who is indecisive or frequently changes plans; literally means "advance and retreat."

W

walang gawang magaling (wah-lahng-gah-wahng-mah-gah-leehng) Incapable of doing good; not to be trusted.

walang modo (wah-lahng moh-doh) Uncouth; having no manners.

walang patawad (wah-lahng pah-tah-wahd) Forgives nobody or nothing; careless; not choosy.

Important Addresses

CONTENTS

INTRODUCTION

The following addresses have been gathered from a wide range of sources. We have attempted to verify each address at press time; however, it is likely that some of the information has already changed. Inclusion of an organization, product, or service does not imply a recommendation or endorsement.

Unless otherwise noted, all addresses are in the Philippines; the international country code for calling the Philippines is [63] and is not shown in the Philippine listings. City codes are given in parentheses (i.e., (2) for Manila), while non-Philippine country codes are in square brackets (i.e., [44] for the UK). Refer to page 149 of the "Business Travel" chapter for details on making telephone calls in the Philippines.

Local telephone numbers in Manila are either six or seven digits, but may be shorter in other cities. A list of dialing codes for major cities is on the following page.

Philippine addresses do not always follow a strict format. However, there are some common elements. Businesses often give a building name and floor number. The street address may or may not include a number, particularly if the organization is located in one of the bigger office buildings. You will frequently see addresses given as the intersection, or corner of two streets, indicated by "cor." or "cnr." There are four-digit postal codes in place, but they are still used relatively infrequently. The placement of the postal code is most often preceding the city name, but you may see it anywhere on the last line of the address. Manila addresses usually—but not always—indicate a section of town, followed by "Metro Manila." Some areas in the National Capitol Region of Metro Manila are: Caloocan City, Ermita, Intramuros, Las Piñas, Makati, Malate, Mandaluyong, Manila, Parañaque, Pasay City, Pasig, Quezon City, and San Juan.

TELEPHONE DIALING CODES IN THE PHILIPPINES

The largest islands of the Philippines are listed below, along with their main cities and the telephone dialing codes for those cities. The international dialing code for the Philippines is [63].

Island	Major City	Telephone Code
Bohol	Tagbilaran	(3823) or (38)
Cebu	Cebu	(32)
Leyte	Tacloban	(53)
Luzon	Angeles	(455)
	Baguio City	(74)
	Bataan	(47)
	Batangas	(43)
	Cavite	(96)
	Dagupan	(75)
	Lucena	(42)
	Manila (and Metro Manila)	(2)
	San Fernando (La Union Province)	(72)
	San Fernando (Pampanga Province)	(45)
	San Pablo	(93)
	Subic Bay (Olongapo)	(47)
	Tarlac City	(452)
Masbate	Masbate	(56)
Mindano	Butuan	(8522) or (8521)
	Cagayan de Oro	(8822)
	Davao	(82)
	Iligan	(63)
	Zamboanga	(62)
Mindoro	Calapan	(4661)
Negros	Bacolod	(34)
Palawan	Puerto Princesa	(48)
Panay	Iloilo City	(33)
Samar	Calbayog	(5741)

GOVERNMENT

PHILIPPINE GOVERNMENT AGENCIES AND ENTITIES

Government Offices

Asset Privatization Trust
10th Fl., BA-Lepanto Bldg.
8747 Paseo de Roxas
Makati, Metro Manila
Tel: (2) 861-619, 815-9201/5
Handles privatization of government assets

Bangko Sentral ng Pilipinas (BSP)
(Central Bank of the Philippines)
A. Mabini St., cor. Vito Cruz St.
Malate, Metro Manila
Tel: (2) 507-051, 593-380/1, 595-263, 582-372
Fax: (2) 522-3987, 597-363

Bases Conversion Development Authority
2nd Fl., Rufino Center
Ayala Ave., cor. Herrera St.
1226 Makati, Metro Manila
Tel: (2) 813-5383, 864-006/9
Fax: (2) 813-5424/7
Oversees conversion of military reservations, including former Clark Air and Subic Naval Bases

Board of Investments (BOI)
Industry and Investments Bldg.
385 Sen. Gil J. Puyat Ave.
1200 Makati, Metro Manila
Tel: (2) 818-1831, 868-403, 867-895, 875-602
Fax: (2) 819-1887, 851-166

Board of Investments (BOI)
Investment and Marketing Department
Industry and Investments Bldg.
385 Sen. Gil J. Puyat Ave.
Makati, Metro Manila
Tel: (2) 868-403, 816-127, 875-602
Fax: (2) 819-1793, 819-1816, 819-1887, 851-166

Board of Investments One-Stop Action Center
(BOI-OSAC)
Industry and Investments Bldg.
385 Sen. Gil J. Puyat Ave.
1200 Makati, Metro Manila
Tel: (2) 815-0702, 858-8322, 815-3731, 867-884
Fax: (2) 810-9728, 761-2165

Bonded Export Marketing Board
Ground Fl., Industry and Investments Bldg.
385 Sen. Gil J. Puyat Ave.
Makati, Metro Manila
Tel: (2) 856-127, 818-1831/9
Fax: (2) 810-9728

Bureau of the Animal Industry (BAI)
Visayas Ave.
Diliman
Quezon City, Metro Manila
Tel: (2) 966-883

Bureau of Air Transportation
Old MIA Rd.
Pasay City, Metro Manila
Tel: (2) 832-3047, 831-8078, 832-3308
Fax: (2) 833-1577
Provides, develops, constructs, maintains and operates airports, airways systems, and air navigation facilities

Bureau of Customs
Port Area
Manila
Tel: (2) 530-0966, 484-161/9
Fax: (2) 474-421/4, 530-0966, 818-2971

Bureau of Domestic Trade Promotion
2nd. Fl., Trade and Industry Bldg.
361 Sen. Gil J. Puyat Ave.
Makati, Metro Manila
Tel: (2) 817-5132, 817-5322
Fax: (2) 810-9363

Bureau of Export Trade Promotion
Department of Trade and Industry
5th Fl., New Solid Bldg.
357 Sen. Gil J. Puyat Ave.
Makati, Metro Manila
Tel: (2) 817-5298, 817-5203, 818-5701
Fax: (2) 817-4923, 819-1816

Bureau of Fisheries and Aquatic Resources
Arcadia Bldg.
Quezon Ave.
Quezon City, Metro Manila
Tel: (2) 965-498

Bureau of Food and Drugs
DOH Compound
Alabang
Muntinlupa, Metro Manila
Tel: (2) 842-4583, 807-0751
Fax: (2) 842-4603

Bureau of Forest Development
Visayas Ave.
Diliman
Quezon City, Metro Manila
Tel: (2) 964-826

Bureau of Internal Revenue
National Internal Revenue Bldg.
Diliman
Quezon City, Metro Manila
Tel: (2) 991-683, 965-644
Fax: (2) 922-4894

Bureau of International Trade Relations
Department of Trade and Industry
361 Sen. Gil J. Puyat Ave.
Makati, Metro Manila
Tel: (2) 817-8087   Fax: (2) 818-7846

Bureau of Patents, Trademarks and
Technology Transfer
Department of Trade and Industry
361 Sen. Gil J. Puyat Ave.
Makati, Metro Manila
Tel: (2) 815-4919, 818-3109, 818-3944, 882-350, 818-4128
Fax: (2) 818-4145

Bureau of Plant Industry
Department of Agriculture
692 San Andres
Malate, Manila
Tel: (2) 571-726, 571-776, 586-201
Fax: (2) 521-7650

Bureau of Product Standards
3rd Fl., Trade and Industry Bldg.
361 Sen. Gil J. Puyat Ave.
Makati, Metro Manila
Tel: (2) 817-5527, 817-5339, 817-9602
Fax: (2) 817-9870

Bureau of Telecommunications
A. Roces Ave.
Quezon City, Metro Manila
Tel: (2) 964-391

Bureau of Trade Regulation and Consumer Protection
Department of Trade and Industry
2nd Fl., Trade and Industry Bldg.
361 Sen. Gil J. Puyat Ave.
Makati, Metro Manila
Tel: (2) 817-5280, 817-5340, 863-431, 818-5701 to 35
Fax: (2) 810-9363
Registers and supervises sole proprietorships

Center for International Trade Expositions
and Missions
ITC Complex
Roxas Blvd., cor. Sen. Gil J. Puyat Ave.
Pasay City, Metro Manila
Tel: (2) 831-2201/9, 832-5001, 832-3982
Fax: (2) 832-3965

Center for Labor Relations Assistance
2nd Fl., Trade and Industry Bldg.
361 Sen. Gil J. Puyat Ave.
Makati, Metro Manila
Tel: (2) 817-5180, 866-878
Fax: (2) 817-5180

Civil Aeronautics Board
Old MIA Rd.
Pasay City, Metro Manila
Tel: (2) 833-6911, 833-7248
Fax: (2) 833-7266
*Regulates domestic and international airline operations
and issues licenses to domestic and international
airfreight forwarders*

Commission on Immigration and Deportation (CID)
Magallanes Drive
Intramuros, Metro Manila
Tel: (2) 407-651

Construction Industry Authority of the Philippines
6th Fl., Finman Bldg.
Tordesillas St.
Salcedo Village
Makati, Metro Manila
Tel: (2) 817-1230, 815-0710
Fax: (2) 818-1573
Licenses domestic and overseas contractors

Coordinating Council of the Philippine Assistance
Program (CCPAP)
14th Fl., Central Bank Bldg.
Ermita, Manila
Tel: (2) 521-4262, 521-4274, 507-051 x2917/8

Department of Agrarian Reform
Elliptical Rd.
Diliman
Quezon City, Metro Manila
Tel: (2) 997-031   Fax: (2) 973-968

Department of Agriculture
DOA Bldg.
Elliptical Rd.
Diliman
Quezon City, Metro Manila
Tel: (2) 998-741 to 65, 997-011
Fax: (2) 978-183, 995-140

Department of Budget and Management
Administration Bldg.
Malacañang Palace Compound
J.P. Laurel St.
San Miguel, Metro Manila
Tel: (2) 483-475, 521-2301
Fax: (2) 481-782, 530-1174, 483-475

Department of Education, Sports, and Culture
University of Life Bldg.
Meralco Ave.
1600 Pasig, Manila
Tel: (2) 632-1361/9, 633-6282
Fax: (2) 632-1371, 633-0805

Department of Energy
PNPC Complex
Merritt Rd.
Fort Bonifacio
Makati, Metro Manila
Tel: (2) 850-251, 852-850, 857-051/9, 851-021/9
Fax: (2) 817-8603, 851-021

Department of Energy
One-Stop Action Center
3rd Fl., DOE Bldg., PNPC Complex
Merritt Rd.
Fort Bonifacio
Makati, Metro Manila
Tel: (2) 851-021, x238, 815-2098
Fax: (2) 877-633
*Handles inquiries and provides information about
private power opportunities*

Department of Environment and Natural Resources
DENR Bldg.
Visayas Ave.
Diliman
Quezon City, Metro Manila
Tel: (2) 976-626/9, 976-671/5, 990-691
Fax: (2) 963-487, 922-6991

Department of Finance
DOF Bldg.
Agrifina Circle
Rizal Park, Manila
Tel: (2) 482-455, 507-051
Fax: (2) 530-0935, 461-015

Department of Foreign Affairs
DFA Bldg.
2330 Roxas Blvd.
Pasay City, Metro Manila
Tel: (2) 834-4000
Fax: (2) 832-3793, 832-0683

Department of Health
San Lazaro Hospital Compound
Rizal Ave.
Santa Cruz, Manila
Tel: (2) 711-6080, 711-9502/3
Fax: (2) 711-9509, 711-6055

Department of the Interior and Local Government
PNCC Complex
Epifanio de los Santos Ave., cor. Reliance St.
Mandaluyong, Metro Manila
Tel: (2) 622-8115, 631-8829, 631-8777
Fax: (2) 631-8830, 631-8814
*Responsible for roads, water supply and sanitation
facilities*

Department of Justice (DOJ)
DOJ Bldg.
Padre Faura St.
Ermita, Manila
Tel: (2) 599-271, 521-3721

Department of Labor and Employment (DOLE)
DOLE Executive Bldg.
Cor. Gen. Luna and San Jose Streets
1002 Intramuros, Manila
Tel: (2) 484-852, 530-0144, 470-264
Fax: (2) 530-1014, 472-857, 470 000

Department of National Defense
Camp Aguinaldo
Epifanio de los Santos Ave.
Quezon City, Metro Manila
Tel: (2) 721-9031, 721-9001
Fax: (2) 708-757

Department of Public Works and Highways (DPWH)
DPWH Bldg.
Bonifacio Drive
1002 Port Area, Metro Manila
Tel: (2) 475-865, 479-311, 482-011
Fax: (2) 401-683, 484-296
Responsible for roads, bridges, highways, flood control, drainage and shore protection, rural water supply, and urban infrastructure

Department of Science and Technology (DOST)
Gen. Santos Ave., Bicutan
Taguig, Metro Manila
Tel: (2) 837-2071, 837-3171, 822-0960/7, 823-8939
Fax: (2) 822-0564, 823-8937
WWW server: http://www.dost.gov.ph/index.html

Department of Social Welfare and Development
Batasan Pambansa Complex
Constitution Hills
Quezon City, Metro Manila
Tel: (2) 922-1811, 931-7916, 931-8101/7
Fax: (2) 741-6939

Department of Tourism
DOT Bldg.
T.M. Kalaw St.
Rizal Park, Manila
Tel: (2) 599-031 to 48, 585-528
Fax: (2) 521-7373/4, 522-2194

Department of Trade and Industry
Trade and Industry Bldg.
361 Sen. Gil J. Puyat Ave. Ext.
Makati, Metro Manila
Tel: (2) 818-5705 to 25, 818-1831, 818-5701
Fax: (2) 856-487

Department of Trade and Industry
Build-Operate-Transfer (BOT) Team
Industry and Investments Bldg.
385 Sen. Gil J. Puyat Ave.
Makati, Metro Manila
Tel: (2) 885-167, 818-1831 x230/7
Fax: (2) 816-4816

Department of Trade and Industry
Office of Special Concerns
357 Sen. Gil J. Puyat Ave.
Makati, Metro Manila
Tel: (2) 883-197, 817-3309, 817-5077

Department of Transportation and Communications
3rd Fl., Philcomcen Bldg.
Ortigas Ave.
Pasig, Metro Manila
Tel: (2) 631-8761/3, 631-8666, 721-3781
Fax: (2) 632-9985

Economic Intelligence and Investigation Bureau
Camp Aguinaldo
Epifanio de los Santos Ave.
Quezon City, Metro Manila
Tel: (2) 911-7821 Fax: (2) 911-7833

Environmental Management Bureau
6th Fl., Philippine Heart Center
East Ave.
Quezon City, Metro Manila
Tel: (2) 980-421 x3627, 975-609
Fax: (2) 973-254

Export Assistance Network
6th Fl., New Solid Bldg.
357 Sen. Gil J. Puyat Ave. Ext.
Makati, Metro Manila
Tel: (2) 818-8434, 819-1809
Fax: (2) 817-4923, 819-1816

Fertilizer and Pesticide Authority
6th Fl., Raha Sulayman Bldg.
Benavidez St.
Legaspi Village
Makati, Metro Manila
Tel: (2) 818-5115

Fiber Development Authority
Philfinance Bldg.
Benavidez St.
Legaspi Village
Makati, Metro Manila
Tel: (2) 818-7347

Freight Booking and Cargo Consolidation Center
(FBCCC)
Philippine Shippers Council
6th Fl., Filcapital Bldg.
Ayala Ave.
Makati, Metro Manila

Garment and Textiles Export Board
4th Fl., New Solid Bldg.
357 Sen. Gil J. Puyat Ave.
Makati, Metro Manila
Tel: (2) 817-4321, 817-4323
Fax: (2) 817-43-39

Insurance Commission
1071 United Nations Ave.
Manila
Tel: (2) 583-534, 574-886, 599-221/5
Fax: (2) 522-1434

Land Transportation Office
East Ave.
Quezon City, Metro Manila
Tel: (2) 922-9061/65
Fax: (2) 921-9072

Light Rail Transit Authority
Administrative Bldg., LRT Compound
Aurora Blvd.
Pasay, Metro Manila
Tel: (2) 832-0423 Fax: (2) 831-6449

Livestock Development Council
DA Compound
Elliptical Rd.
Diliman
Quezon City, Metro Manila
Tel: (2) 988-741

Local Water Utilities Administration
MWSS-LWUA Complex
Katipunan Rd.
Balara
Quezon City, Metro Manila
Tel: (2) 976-107, 976-203
Fax: (2) 922-3434

Maritime Industry Authority
PPL Bldg.
1000 United Nations Ave.
Ermita, Metro Manila
Tel: (2) 582-710

Metropolitan Waterworks and Sewerage System
Katipunan Rd.
Balara, Quezon City
Tel: (2) 922-3757, 922-2969
Fax: (2) 921-2887

Monetary Board
c/o Bangko Sentral ng Pilipinas
A. Mabini St.
Malate, Metro Manila
Tel: (2) 507-051, 593-380/1, 595-263, 582-372
Fax: (2) 522-3987, 597-363

National Agriculture and Fishery Council
Department of Agriculture
Elliptical Rd.
Diliman
Quezon City, Metro Manila
Tel: (2) 962-2706, 978-234, 988-608
Fax: (2) 922-8622

National Census and Statistics Office
c/o National Economic Development Authority (NEDA)
PO Box 779
Metro Manila
Tel: (2) 613-645   Fax: (2) 610-794

National Computer Center
Camp Gen. Emilio Aguinaldo
Cubao
Quezon City, Metro Manila
Tel: (2) 797-631   Fax: (2) 781-172

National Economic and Development Authority (NEDA)
NEDA Bldg.
Amber Ave.
1600 Pasig, Metro Manila
Tel: (2) 673-5031, 631-3716, 631-0945 to 64
Fax: (2) 631-3747

National Electrification Administration
3rd Fl., D&E Bldg.
1050 Quezon Ave.
Quezon City, Metro Manila
Tel: (2) 922-9009, 922-5688
Fax: (2) 922-9058

National Food Authority
Matimyas Bldg.
E. Rodriguez Blvd.
Quezon City, Metro Manila
Tel: (2) 712-1719

National Housing Authority
Quezon Memorial Elliptical Rd.
Diliman
Quezon City, Metro Manila
Tel: (2) 921-7828/97-8016
Fax: (2) 921-0444

National Irrigation Administration
2nd Fl., NIA Bldg.
Epifanio de los Santos Ave.
Quezon City, Metro Manila
Tel: (2) 922-2795   Fax: (2) 962-846

National Meat Inspection Commission (NMIC)
Bureau of Animal Industry
Visayas Ave.
Diliman
Quezon City, Metro Manila
Tel: (2) 924-3119   Fax: (2) 924-3118

National Statistics and Coordinating Board
2nd Fl., Midland Buendia Bldg.
Sen. Gil J. Puyat Ave. Ext.
Makati, Metro Manila
Tel: (2) 851-778, 896-1778
Fax: (2) 816-6941

National Telecommunications Commission
VIBAL Bldg.
Epifanio de los Santos Ave., cor. Times St.
Quezon City, Metro Manila
Tel: (2) 924-4042, 924-4008, 981-160
Fax: (2) 921-7128
Regulates telecommunications industry and formulates policies

Manila International Airport Authority
Ninoy Aquino International Airport (NAIA)
Parañaque, Metro Manila
Tel: (2) 832-2938, 831-6205
Fax: (2) 833-1180
Responsible for air traffic operations for domestic and international flights

Office of the Ombudsman (Tanodbayan)
c/o Department of Justice
Padre Faura St.
Ermita, Manila
Tel: (2) 599-271, 521-3721
Investigates complaints about public officials

Philippine Coconut Administration
Elliptical Rd.
Diliman
Quezon City, Metro Manila
Tel: (2) 994-501   Fax: (2) 921-6173

Philippine Economic Zone Authority (PEZA)
4th Fl., Legaspi Towers 300
Roxas Blvd.
Metro Manila
Tel: (2) 521-9725, 521-0546/7, 521-0585
Fax: (2) 521-8659

Philippine Information Agency
Visayas Ave.
Diliman
Quezon City, Metro Manila
Tel: (2) 922-7477   Fax: (2) 922-6543

Philippine National Railways
Management Center
Torres Bugallon St.
Caloocan City, Metro Manila
Tel/Fax: (2) 362-0824

Philippine Ports Authority (PPA)
Marsman Bldg., Gate 1
22 Muelle de Francisco St.
South Harbor
1002 Port Area, Metro Manila
Tel: (2) 530-0875, 479-204
Fax: (2) 530-1199, 486-237

Securities and Exchange Commission
SEC Bldg.
Epifanio de los Santos Ave.
Greenhills
Mandaluyong, Metro Manila
Tel: (2) 810-1145, 780-931/9
Fax: (2) 722-0990
Registers and supervises business entities

Tariff Commission
5th Fl., Philippine Heart Center
East Ave.
Quezon City, Metro Manila
Tel: (2) 998-106   Fax: (2) 921-7960

Telecommunications Office (TELOF)
2nd Fl., Multipurpose Bldg.
A. Roces Ave.
Quezon City, Metro Manila
Tel: (2) 951-961, 974-747
Fax: (2) 921-8977

State Corporations

Construction and Development Corporation
of the Philippines
TFC Bldg.
355 Sen. Gil J. Puyat Ave.
Makati, Metro Manila
Tel: (2) 876-061

Foreign Trade Service Corps
5th Fl., New Solid Bldg.
357 Sen. Gil J. Puyat Ave.
Makati, Metro Manila
Tel: (2) 819-1797, 812-7551
Fax: (2) 819-1816, 817-4923, 819-1793

National Development Co. (NDC)
Producers Bank Bldg.
371 Sen. Gil J. Puyat Ave.
Makati, Metro Manila
Tel: (2) 818-3284   Fax: (2) 815-4472

National Power Corporation
Cor. Quezon Ave. and Agham Roads
Diliman
Quezon City, Metro Manila
Tel: (2) 921-2998, 921-3541 to 80
Fax: (2) 922-4339

National Steel Corporation
377 Sen. Gil J. Puyat Ave. Ext.
Makati, Metro Manila
Tel: (2) 816-2036   Fax: (2) 815-2036
(Was this transferred to private sector in 1994?)

National Sugar Trading Corporation
Traders Royal Bank Bldg.
Aduana St.
Intramuros, Metro Manila
Tel: (2) 408-667

Philippine Cotton Corporation
4th Fl., JJACIS Bldg.
31 Shaw Blvd.
Pasig, Metro Manila
Tel: (2) 673-1476

Philippine Convention and Visitors Corporation
4th Fl., Legaspi Towers 300
Roxas Blvd.
Manila
Tel: (2) 575-031   Fax: (2) 521-6165

Philippine Dairy Corporation
Philsucom Bldg.
North Ave.
Quezon City, Metro Manila
Tel: (2) 998-741

Philippine Export and Foreign Loan Guarantee Corp.
(PHILGUARANTEE)
5th Fl., Executive Bldg. Center
Sen. Gil J. Puyat Ave., cor. Makati Ave.
Makati, Metro Manila
Tel: (2) 818-1316   Fax: (2) 817-2835

Philippine International Trading Corporation (PITC)
Philippines International Center
116 Tordesillas St.
Salcedo Village
1227 Makati, Metro Manila
Tel: (2) 818-9801, 818-6010, 818-6533
Fax: (2) 819-0562, 815-2302
Mailing address: PO Box 2253, 1056 Metro Manila

Philippine National Construction Corporation (PNCC)
PNCC Bldg.
Epifanio de los Santos Ave., cor. Reliance St.
Mandaluyong, Metro Manila
Tel: (2) 721-6584, 631-8431
Fax: (2) 631-5362

Philippine National Oil Company (PNOC)
PNOC Bldg.
7901 Makati Ave.
Makati, Metro Manila
Tel: (2) 817-5395, 859-961, 859-061
Fax: (2) 815-2721, 812-1070
Responsible for geothermal energy development, power plants, oil exploration

Philippine Postal Corp.
Liwasang Bonifacio
Metro Manila
Tel: (2) 471-411/3, 481-578
Fax: (2) 530-1169

Philippine Telegraph and Telephone Corp. (PT&T)
PT&T Spirit of Communication Center
106 Alvarado St.
Legaspi Village
Makati, Metro Manila

Private Development Corp. of the Philippines (PDCP)
Banker's Center
6764 Ayala Ave.
PO Box 757
Makati, Metro Manila
Tel: (2) 810-0231   Fax: (2) 819-5376

Wenagro Industrial Corporation
92 Mindano Ave.
Quezon City, Metro Manila
Produces and exports Philippine products

SPECIAL TRADE ZONES

Bases Conversion Development Authority (BCDA)
2nd Fl., Rufino Center
Ayala Ave., cor. Herrera St.
1226 Makati, Metro Manila
Tel: (2) 813-5383, 864-006/9
Fax: (2) 813-5424/7
Contact the BCDA for information on the conversions of the former Clark Air and Subic Naval Bases

Philippine Economic Zone Authority (PEZA)
4th Fl., Legaspi Towers 300
Roxas Blvd.
Metro Manila
Tel: (2) 521-9725, 521-04-19, 521-0546/7
Fax: (2) 521-8659, 521-0419

Subic Bay Metropolitan Authority (SBMA)
Bldg. 229, Waterfront Ave.
Subic Bay Freeport Zone
2200 Olongapo City
Tel: (47) 222-5454/6, 222-2731, 384-5849
Fax: (47) 222-5278
Manila telephone number: (2) 817-3994

Export Processing Zones

Baguio City Export Processing Zone (BCEPZ)
Loakan Rd.
Baguio City
Tel: (74) 442-6589

Bataan Export Processing Zone (BEPZ)
Mariveles
Bataan
Tel: (47) 935-4004   Fax: (47) 731372

Cavite Export Processing Zone (CEPZ)
Rosario
Cavite
Tel: (96) 437-6090   Fax: (96) 742-1022

Mactan Export Processing Zone (MEPZ)
Lapu-Lapu City
Cebu
Tel: (32) 400-590   Fax: (32) 400-591

Industrial Estates

Philippines Industrial Estates Association (PHILEA)
PHILEA Desk (OSAC)
Ground Fl., Industry and Investments Bldg.
385 Sen. Gil J. Puyat Ave.
Makati, Metro Manila
Tel: (2) 818-1831/9   Fax: (2) 810-9728

Carmelray Industrial Park
Carmelray Development Corporation
7th Fl., Rufino Plaza
Ayala Ave.
Makati, Metro Manila
Tel: (2) 810-6306   Fax: (2) 817-5051
Mailing address; industrial park located in Canlubang, Calamba, Laguna

First Cavite Industrial Estate
3rd Fl., First Bank Bldg.
Sen. Gil J. Puyat Ave.
Makati, Metro Manila
Tel: (2) 817-1308   Fax: (2) 817-0939
Mailing address; industrial park located in Langkaan, Dasmariñas, Cavite

Gateway Business Park
Gateway Business Holdings
Ground Fl., Jaycem Bldg.
104 Rada St.
Legaspi Village
Makati, Metro Manila
Tel: (2) 892-2916, 819-1146
Fax: (2) 817-9576
Mailing address; industrial park located in Amadeo Rd., Bgy. Jalavera, Gen. Trias, Cavite

Laguna International Industrial Park
Laguna International Industrial Park, Inc.
3rd Fl., Solid House Bldg.
P. Tamo Ext., cor. Lumbang St.
Makati, Metro Manila
Tel: (2) 859-041 to 52   Fax: (2) 819-5123
Mailing address; industrial park located in Ganado and Mamplasan, Biñan, Laguna

Laguna Technopark
Laguna Technopark, Inc.
Ground Fl., MSE Bldg.
Ayala Ave.
Makati, Metro Manila
Tel: (2) 814-7676   Fax: (2) 812-1386
Mailing address; industrial park located in Santa Rosa and Biñan, Laguna

Light Industry and Science Park of the Philippines
Science Park of the Philippines, Inc.
15th Fl., Solidbank Bldg.
Paseo de Roxas
Makati, Metro Manila
Tel: (2) 810-2931   Fax: (2) 819-0941
Mailing address; industrial park located in Diezmo, Cabuyao, Laguna

Luisita Industrial Park
Luisita Reality Corporation
119 De la Rosa St., cor. C. Palanca St.
Legaspi Village
Makati, Manila
Tel: (2) 818-3911, 818-1516
Fax: (2) 817-9309
Mailing address; industrial park located in Hacienda Luisita, San Miguel, Tarlac

EMBASSIES AND TRADE OFFICES OF THE PHILIPPINES

Argentina
Embassy of the Philippines
Juramento 1945
1428 Buenos Aires, Argentina
Tel: [54] (1) 781-4173

Australia
Embassy of the Philippines
PO Box 3297
Manuka, ACT 2603, Australia
Tel: [61] (6) 273-2535

Philippine Consulate General
Level 5, 122 Castlereach St.
Sydney, NSW 2010, Australia
Tel: [61] (2) 267-7500   Fax: [61] (2) 261-8412

Austria
Embassy of the Philippines
Brillrothstrasse 2/II/21
A-1190 Vienna, Austria
Tel: [43] (1) 318-7134   Fax: [43] (1) 318-7138

Bangladesh
Embassy of the Philippines
House NE (L) 5, Rd. 83
Gulshan Model Town
Dhaka 1212, Bangladesh
Tel: [880] (2) 605-945

Bahrain
Embassy of the Philippines
PO Box 26681
Bldg. 81, Rd. 3902, Block 339
Umm Al-Hassan, Bahrain
Tel: [070] 723-355

Belgium
Embassy of the Philippines
85 rue Washington
1050 Brussels, Belgium
Tel: [32] (2) 538-3807, 533-1807
Fax: [32] (2) 538-3234

Brazil
Embassy of the Philippines
SEN, Av. das Nações, Lote 1
70431, Brasília, DF, Brazil
Tel: [55] (61) 223-5143   Fax: [55] (61) 226-7411

Canada
Embassy of the Philippines
130 Albert St., Suite 606
Ottawa, ON K1P 5G4, Canada
Tel: [1] (613) 233-1121   Fax: [1] (613) 233-4165

Philippine Consulate General
60 Bloor St. West, Suite 409
Toronto, ON M4W 3B8, Canada
Tel: [1] (416) 967-1788   Fax: [1] (416) 967-6236

Philippine Trade Office
c/o Philippine Consulate
Suite 301–308, Rogers Bldg.
470 Granville St.
Vancouver, BC M4W 3B8, Canada
Tel: [1] (604) 685-7645

Chile
Embassy of the Philippines
La Gloria 17, esq. Apoquindo
Las Condes
Santiago, Chile
Tel: [56] (2) 208-1313

China (People's Republic of)
Embassy of the Philippines
23 Xiu Shui Bei Jie
Jian Guo Men Wai
Beijing, PRC
Tel: [86] (1) 532-1872, 532-3420

Egypt
Embassy of the Philippines
5 Sharia ibn el-Walid
Cairo (Dokki), Arab Republic of Egypt
Tel: [20] (2) 348-0396

France
Embassy of the Philippines
4 Hameau de Boullainvilliers
75016 Paris, France
Tel: [33] (1) 44-14-57-00   Fax: [33] (1) 44-47-56-00

Germany
Embassy of the Philippines
Argelanderstrasse 1
53115 Bonn, Germany
Tel: [49] (228) 267-990   Fax: [49] (228) 221-968

Philippine Trade and Investment Center
Asia Pacific Center
Kaise-Wilhelm Ring 20
5000 Köln 1, Germany
Tel: [49] (221) 144-483, 134-372, 136-477
Fax: [49] (221) 123-278

Hong Kong
Philippine Consulate General
21st Fl., Wah Kwong Regent Centre
88 Queen's Rd.
Central, Hong Kong
Tel: [852] 2810-0770, 2810-0963

Hungary
Embassy of the Philippines
Jozsefhegyi út 28–30
1025 Bucharest, Hungary
Tel: [36] (1) 155-4019   Fax: [36] (1) 155-2066

India
Embassy of the Philippines
50N Nyaya Marg
Chanakyapuri
New Delhi 100 021, India
Tel: [91] (11) 601-120   Fax: [91] (11) 315-1167

Indonesia
Jalan Imam Bonjol 6–8
Jakarta 10310, Indonesia
Tel: [62] (21) 310-0334   Fax: [62] (21) 315-1167

Iran
Embassy of the Philippines
PO Box 19395-4797
Tehran, Iran
Tel: [98] (21) 801-9619   Fax: [98] (21) 274-039

Iraq
Embassy of the Philippines
Hay Babel
Baghdad, Iraq
Tel: [964] (1) 719-3228

Israel
Embassy of the Philippines
PO Box 50085
Textile Center Bldg., 13th Fl.
2 Rebov Kaufman
Tel Aviv 60812, Israel
Tel: [972] (3) 510-2231   Fax: [972] (3) 510-2229

Italy
Embassy of the Philippines
Via San Valentino 12–14
00197 Rome, Italy
Tel: [39] (6) 808-3530   Fax: [39] (6) 808-4219

Japan
Embassy of the Philippines
11-24 Nampeidai-machi, Shibuya-ku
Tokyo 150, Japan
Tel: [81] (3) 3462-1216, 3464-4177, 3496-2731
Fax: [81] (3) 3462-2678

Phillipine Consulate General
4th Fl., Taiwa Bldg.
18-1 Akashi-machi, Chuo-ku
Kobe, Japan
Tel: [81] (78) 333-0461   Fax: [81] (78) 331-6869

Korea (South)
Embassy of the Philippines
559-510 Yeoksam-dong
Kangnam-ku
Seoul, Republic of Korea
Tel: [82] (2) 556-7133, 568-9131
Fax: [82] (2) 556-7418

Kuwait
Embassy of the Philippines
PO Box 26288
Safat 13123, State of Kuwait
Tel: [965] 532-9316   Fax: [965] 532-9319

Libya
Embassy of the Philippines
PO Box 12508
Sharia el-Dul
Tripoli, Libya
Tel: [218] (21) 35607

Malaysia
Embassy of the Philippines
1 Changkat Kia Peng
50450 Kuala Lumpur, Malaysia
Tel: [60] (3) 248-4233   Fax: [60] (3) 248-3576

Mexico
Embassy of the Philippines
Calderón de la Barca 240
Col. Reforma-Polanco
México, DF, México
Tel: [52] (5) 254-8055   Fax: [52] (5) 545-8631

Myanmar (Burma)
Embassy of the Philippines
56 Pyi Rd., 6-1/2 Mile
Yangon, Myanmar
Tel: [95] (1) 64010

Netherlands
Embassy of the Philippines
Laan Copes van Cattenburch 125
2585 EZ The Hague, Netherlands
Tel: [31] (70) 360-4820

Philippine Trade Promotion Center
c/o CBI
PO Box 30009
3001 DA Rotterdam, Netherlands
Tel: [31] (10) 433-0661   Fax: [31] (10) 404-5665

New Zealand
Embassy of the Philippines
PO Box 12042
Wellington, New Zealand
Tel: [64] (4) 472-9921   Fax: [64] (4) 472-5170

Nigeria
Embassy of the Philippines
Plot 152, No. 302, off Third Ave.
Victoria Island
Lagos, Nigeria
Tel: [234] (1) 614-684

Pakistan
Embassy of the Philippines
19, St. 1, Shalimar 6/3
PO Box 1052
Islamabad, Pakistan
Tel: [92] (51) 820-145

Papua New Guinea
Embassy of the Philippines
PO Box 5916
Boroko, Papua New Guinea
Tel: [675] 256-577

Peru
Embassy of the Philippines
José del Llano Zapata
Miraflores
Lima 18, Peru
Tel: [51] (14) 416-318   Fax: [51] (14) 420-432

Poland
Embassy of the Philippines
ul. Gornoslaska 22, m. 5
00-484 Warsaw, Poland
Tel: [48] (22) 219-523

Romania
Embassy of the Philippines
Stirbei Voda 87
Bucharest, Romania
Tel: [40] (1) 137-643

Russian Federation
Embassy of the Philippines
Karmanitsky per. 6
Moscow, Russia
Tel: [7] (095) 241-3870   Fax: [7] (095) 956-6087

Saudi Arabia
Embassy of the Philippines
PO Box 94366
Riyadh 11693, Kingdom of Saudi Arabia
Tel: [966] (1) 454-0777

Philippine Consulate General
PO Box 9113
Jeddah 21413, Kingdom of Saudi Arabia
Tel: [966] (2) 660-2101

Singapore
Embassy of the Philippines
20 Nassim Rd.
Singapore 1025
Tel: [65] 737-3977, 737-3332
Fax: [65] 733-9544

Spain
Embassy of the Philippines
Office of the Commercial Attaché
Calle Claudio Coello, 92
28006 Madrid, Spain
Tel: [34] (1) 576-5401/3   Fax: [34] (1) 575-8360

Sweden
Embassy of the Philippines
Skeppsbron 22
PO Box 2219
103-15 Stockholm, Sweden
Tel: [46] (8) 206-717, 204-718, 235-665
Fax: [46] (8) 247-105, 140-714

Switzerland
Embassy of the Philippines
Hallwylstrasse 34
3005 Berne, Switzerland
Tel: [41] (31) 351-4211   Fax: [41] (31) 352-3416

Taiwan
Philippine Trade and Investment Center
Manila Economic and Culture Office
PO Box 109-841
Taipei, Taiwan ROC
Tel: [886] (2) 723-2024, 723-2527/8
Fax: [886] (2) 723-2025

Thailand
Embassy of the Philippines
Office of the Commercial Attaché
760 Sukhumvit Rd.
Ampur Phra Kanong
10110 Bangkok, Thailand
Tel: [66] (2) 258-5382, 259-0139

Turkey
Embassy of the Philippines
Cayhane Sok. 24
Gaziosmanpaaa
Ankara, Turkey
Tel: [90] (312) 446-5831   Fax: [90] (312) 427-3987

United Arab Emirates
Embassy of the Philippines
PO Box 3215
Abu Dhabi, UAE
Tel: [971] (2) 345-664

Consulate General of the Philippines
PO Box 55058
Dubai, UAE
Tel: [971] (4) 236-526   Fax: [971] (4) 229-588

United Kingdom
Embassy of the Philippines
9A Palace Green
Kensington
London W8 4QF., UK
Tel: [44] (171) 937-1600/9   Fax: [44] (171) 937-2925

Office of the Philippine Commercial Counsellor
1A Cumberland House
Kengsington Court
London W8 5NX, UK
Tel: [44] (171) 937-1898, 937-7998
Fax: [44] (171) 937-2747

United States of America
Embassy of the Philippines
1600 Massachusetts Ave. NW
Washington, DC 20036, USA
Tel: [1] (202) 467-9300   Fax: [1] (202) 328-7614

Consulate General of the Philippines
3660 Wilshire Blvd., Suite 900
Los Angeles, CA 90010, USA
Tel: [1] (202) 387-5321

Consulate General of the Philippines
Philippine Center Bldg., 6th Fl.
447 Sutter St.
San Francisco, CA 94108, USA
Tel: [1] (415) 433-6666

Consulate General of the Philippines
2433 Pali Highway
Honolulu, HI 95817, USA
Tel: [1] (808) 585-6316

Consulate General of the Philippines
30 N. Michigan Ave., Suite 2100
Chicago, IL 60602, USA
Tel: [1] (312) 332-6458

Consulate General of the Philippines
Philippine Center
556 Fifth Ave.
New York, NY 10036, USA
Tel: [1] (212) 764-1330

Venezuela
Embassy of the Philippines
Quinta Taray
Avda. Tropical
La Floresta
Caracas, Venezuela
Tel: [58] (2) 284-2006

Vietnam
Embassy of the Philippines
E1 Trung Tu Diplomatic Quarter
Hanoi
Tel: [84] (4) 257-948   Fax: [84] (4) 257-873

FOREIGN EMBASSIES IN THE PHILIPPINES

Embassy of Argentina
6th Fl., ACT Tower
135 Sen. Gil J. Puyat Ave.
Salcedo Village
Makati, Metro Manila
Tel: (2) 875-655, 886-091   Fax: (2) 810-8301

Embassy of Australia
Doña Salustiana Dee Ty Bldg.
104 Paseo de Roxas
1200 Makati, Metro Manila
Tel: (2) 817-7911   Fax: (2) 817-3603

Embassy of Austria
4th Fl., Prince Bldg.
117 Rada St.
Legaspi Village
1200 Makati, Metro Manila
Tel: (2) 817-9191, 818-1581, 816-6116
Fax: (2) 813-4238

Embassy of Bangladesh
5th Fl., JEG Bldg.
150 Legaspi St.
Legaspi Village
Makati, Metro Manila
Tel: (2) 817-5010

Embassy of Belgium
6th Fl., Don Jacinto Bldg.
Cor. de la Rosa and Salcedo Streets
Legaspi Village
Makati, Metro Manila
Tel: (2) 876-571/4   Fax: (2) 817-2566

Embassy of Brazil
6th Fl., RCI Bldg.
105 Rada St.
Legaspi Village
Makati, Metro Manila
Tel: (2) 888-181, 810-9241
Fax: (2) 818-2622

Embassy of Brunei
Bank of the Philippine Islands Bldg.
11th Fl., Ayala Wing
Ayala Ave., cor. Paseo de Roxas
Makati, Metro Manila
Tel: (2) 816-2836, 816-2876

Embassy of Bulgaria
1732 Sampaguita St.
Dasmariñas Village
Makati, Metro Manila
Tel: (2) 818-1321

Embassy of Canada
9th Fl., Allied Bank Center
6754 Ayala Ave.
Makati, Metro Manila
Tel: (2) 815-9536, 815-9541, 810-8861
Fax: (2) 815-9595

Embassy of Chile
6th Fl., Doña Salustiana Dee Ty Bldg.
104 Paseo de Roxas
Legaspi Village
Makati, Metro Manila
Tel: (2) 810-3149, 815-0795
Fax: (2) 815-0795

Embassy of China (People's Republic of)
4896 Pasay Rd.
Dasmariñas Village
Makati, Metro Manila
Tel: (2) 853-148   Fax: (2) 818-4783

Embassy of Colombia
Araneta Center
18th Fl., Aurora Tower
Quezon City, Metro Manila
Tel: (2) 921-2701   Fax: (2) 921-2746

Embassy of Cuba
11th Fl., Heart Tower Condominium
108 Valero St.
Salcedo Village
Makati, Metro Manila
Tel: (2) 817-1192   Fax: (2) 816-4094

Embassy of Denmark
6th Fl., Doña Salustiana Dee Ty Bldg.
104 Paseo de Roxas
1200 Makati, Metro Manila
Tel: (2) 819-1906, 894-0086
Fax: (2) 817-5729

Embassy of Egypt
2229 Paraiso St.
Dasmariñas Village
Makati, Metro Manila
Tel: (2) 880-390/7   Fax: (2) 817-0885

Embassy of Finland
14th Fl., BPI Bldg.
Ayala Ave., cor. Paseo de Roxas
Makati, Metro Manila
Tel: (2) 816-2105/9   Fax: (2) 815-1401

Embassy of France
16th Fl., Pacific Star Bldg.
PO Box 3165
Makati Ave., cor. Sen. Gil J. Puyat Ave.
Makati, Metro Manila
Tel: (2) 810-1981/8   Fax: (2) 817-5047

Embassy of Germany
6th Fl., Solidbank Bldg.
777 Paseo de Roxas
1200 Makati, Metro Manila
Tel: (2) 892-4906, 864-900
Fax: (2) 810-4703

Embassy of India
2190 Paraiso St.
Dasmariñas Village
Makati, Metro Manila
Tel: (2) 872-445, 873-339
Fax: (2) 815-8151

Embassy of Indonesia
Indonesian Embassy Bldg.
185 Salcedo St.
Legaspi Village
Makati, Metro Manila
Tel: (2) 855-5061/8   Fax: (2) 818-4441

Embassy of Iran
4th Fl., Don Jacinto Bldg.
Salcedo and de la Rosa Streets
Legaspi Village
Makati, Metro Manila
Tel: (2) 871-561/3

Embassy of Iraq
1368 Caballero St.
Dasmariñas Village
Makati, Metro Manila
Tel: (2) 856-715

Embassy of Israel
Room 538, Philippine Savings Bank Bldg.
6813 Ayala Ave.
Makati, Metro Manila
Tel: (2) 885-320/9, 892-5329
Fax: (2) 819-0561

Embassy of Italy
6th Fl., Zeta Bldg.
191 Salcedo St.
Legaspi Village
Makati, Metro Manila
Tel: (2) 887-632, 892-4531, 874-531/4

Embassy of Japan
LC Bldg.
375 Sen. Gil J. Puyat Ave.
Makati, Metro Manila
Tel: (2) 818-9011, 816-1027
Fax: (2) 817-6562

Embassy of Korea (South)
3rd Fl., ALPAP 1 Bldg.
140 Alfaro St.
Salcedo Village
Makati, Metro Manila
Tel: (2) 817-5703/5, 817-5705
Fax: (2) 817-5845

Embassy of Libya
4928 Pasay Rd.
Dasmariñas Village
Makati, Metro Manila
Tel: (2) 817-3461

Embassy of Malaysia
107 Tordesillas St.
Salcedo Village
Makati, Metro Manila
Tel: (2) 817-4581/5   Fax: (2) 816-3158

Embassy of Mexico
814 Pasay Rd.
San Lorenzo Village
Makati, Metro Manila
Tel: (2) 857-323

Embassy of Myanmar (Burma)
4th Fl., Basic Petroleum Bldg.
104 Carlos Palanca Jr. St.
Legaspi Village
Makati, Metro Manila
Tel: (2) 817-2373   Fax: (2) 817-5895

Embassy of the Netherlands
9th Fl., King's Court Bldg.
2129 Pasong Tamo
1264 Makati, Metro Manila
Tel: (2) 812-5981/3, 887-753
Fax: (2) 815-4579

Embassy of New Zealand
3rd Fl., Gammon Center
126 Alfaro St.
Salcedo Village
Makati, Metro Manila
Tel: (2) 818-0916, 815-6301
Fax: (2) 815-4457

Embassy of Nigeria
2211 Paraiso St.
Dasmariñas Village
3117 Makati, Metro Manila
Tel: (2) 817-3836/7, 817-5152
Fax: (2) 815-2005

Embassy of Norway
6th Fl., Atlantica Bldg.
Cor. Salcedo and Herrera Streets
Legaspi Village
Makati, Metro Manila
Tel: (2) 881-111

Embassy of Pakistan
6th Fl., Alexander House
132 Amorsolo St.
Legaspi Village
Makati, Metro Manila
Tel: (2) 817-2772/6

Embassy of Panama
Room 501, Victoria Bldg.
129 United Nations Ave.
Ermita, Metro Manila
Tel: (2) 521-1233

Embassy of Papua New Guinea
2280 Magnolia St.
Dasmariñas Village
Makati, Metro Manila
Tel: (2) 810-8456/7, 816-1465
Fax: (2) 817-1080

Embassy of Peru
FM Lopez Bldg.
Cor. Legaspi and Herrera Streets
Legaspi Village
Makati, Metro Manila
Tel: (2) 818-8209, 818-7209

Embassy of Romania
1216 Acacia Rd.
Dasmariñas Village
Makati, Metro Manila
Tel: (2) 810-9491/3   Fax: (2) 810-9491

Embassy of the Russian Federation
1245 Acacia Rd.
Dasmariñas Village
Makati, Metro Manila
Tel: (2) 810-9614, 850-190, 810-9581

Embassy of Saudi Arabia
8th Fl., Insular Life Bldg.
6781 Ayala Ave.
Makati, Metro Manila
Tel: (2) 817-3371/3   Fax: (2) 816-1477

Embassy of Singapore
6th Fl., ODC International Plaza Bldg.
217-219 Salcedo St.
Legaspi Village
Makati, Metro Manila
Tel: (2) 894-596, 816-1764/5
Fax: (2) 818-4687

Embassy of Spain
5th Fl., ACT Tower
135 Sen. Gil J. Puyat Ave.
Metro Manila
Tel: (2) 818-3561, 818-5526

Embassy of Sri Lanka
5th Fl., Gammon Center Bldg.
126 Alfaro St.
Salcedo Village
Makati, Metro Manila
Tel: (2) 818-4142

Embassy of Sweden
16th Fl., PCI Bank Tower II
Makati Ave.
Makati, Metro Manila
Tel: (2) 819-1951, 817-5090
Fax: (2) 815-3002

Embassy of Switzerland
18th Fl., Solidbank Bldg.
777 Paseo de Roxas
Makati, Metro Manila
Tel: (2) 819-0202   Fax: (2) 815-0381

Embassy of Thailand
107 Rada St.
Legaspi Village
Makati, Metro Manila
Tel: (2) 815-4220, 815-4219, 816-0697
Fax: (2) 815-4221

Embassy of the United Kingdom
15th–17th Fl., Locsin Bldg.
6752 Ayala Ave., cor. Makati Ave.
Makati, Metro Manila
Tel: (2) 816-4849, 816-7116
Fax: (2) 819-7206

Embassy of the United States of America
1201 Roxas Blvd.
Ermita, Metro Manila
Tel: (2) 521-7116   Fax: (2) 522-4361

Embassy of Venezuela
6th Fl., MAJALCO Bldg.
Benavides St., cor. Trasierra St.
Legaspi Village
Makati, Metro Manila
Tel: (2) 817-9188, 817-9137
Fax: (2) 818-5103

Embassy of Vietnam
554 Vito Cruz
Malate, Metro Manila
Tel: (2) 500-364, 508-101
Fax: (2) 508-101

All addresses and telephone numbers are in the Philippines unless otherwise noted. The country code for the Philippines is [63].

TRADE ORGANIZATIONS

GENERAL BUSINESS AND TRADE ORGANIZATIONS

Cebu Chamber of Commerce and Industry
Room 104, WDC Bldg.
Osmena Blvd.
6000 Cebu City
Tel: (32) 99-312, 99-689

Chamber of International Trade
Ground Fl., Peralas Bldg.
646 Quezon Ave.
Quezon City, Metro Manila
Tel: (2) 712-0193

Confederation of Philippine Exporters
Room S-324, PICC-CCP Complex
Roxas Blvd., Metro Manila
Tel: (2) 832-0309, 831-9844

Employers Federation of the Philippines (ECOP)
4th Fl., ECC Bldg.
355 Sen. Gil J. Puyat Ave.
Makati, Metro Manila
Tel: (2) 816-3813   Fax: (2) 858-576

Makati Business Club
2nd Fl., Princess Bldg.
104 Esteban St.
Legaspi Village
Makati, Metro Manila
Tel: (2) 816-2658, 816-2660, 812-3812, 812-3753
Fax: (2) 816-2658, 812-3813

Manila Chamber of Commerce
410 Shurdut Bldg.
Intramuros, Metro Manila
Tel: (2) 498-321

Philippine Industrial Estates Association
PHILEA Desk
Ground Fl., Industry and Investments Bldg.
385 Sen. Gil J. Puyat Ave.
Makati, Metro Manila
Tel: (2) 818-1831/9   Fax: (2) 810-9728

Philippine Chamber of Commerce
7th Fl., ODC International Plaza
219 Salcedo St.
Legaspi Village
Makati, Metro Manila
Tel: (2) 817-6981

Philippine Chamber of Commerce and Industry
Ground Fl., Secretariat Bldg., East Wing
CCP Complex
Roxas Blvd.
Pasay City, Metro Manila
Tel: (2) 833-8591/3   Fax: (2) 833-8895

World Trade Center Metro Manila
15th Fl., Solidbank Bldg.
Paseo de Roxas
1200 Makati, Metro Manila
Tel (2) 819-7232, 819-7297
Fax: (2) 819-7205

FOREIGN BUSINESS ORGANIZATIONS

In the Philippines

American Chamber of Commerce of the Philippines
Corinthian Plaza, 2nd Fl.
Paseo de Roxas
1299 Makati, Metro Manila
Tel: (2) 818-7911   Fax: (2) 816-6359
Mailing address: PO Box 1578, MCC, Manila

American Chamber of Commerce of the Philippines
Cebu Chapter
Room 104, WDC Bldg.
Osmena Blvd.
6000 Cebu City
Tel: (32) 99-312, 70-469

American Chamber of Commerce of the Philippines
Davao Chapter
Room 507, Aldevinco Bldg.
C.M. Recto St.
8000 Davao City
Tel: (82) 79-369

Canadian Chamber of Commerce and Industry
Ground Fl., InterBank Bldg.
Paseo de Roxas
Makati, Metro Manila
Tel: (2) 812-8568

Euro Info-Office
3rd Fl., King's Court II Bldg.
2129 Don Chino Roces Ave.
Makati, Metro Manila
Tel: (2) 811-2234   Fax: (2) 818-8030

European Chamber of Commerce of the Philippines
5th Fl., Kings Court II Bldg.
Pasong Tamo
Makati, Metro Manila
Tel: (2) 854-747, 866-995/8, 854-4747
Fax: (2) 815-2688

Federation of Filipino-Chinese Chambers of Commerce
and Industry, Inc.
6th Fl., Federation Center Bldg.
Muelle de Binondo St.
Manila
Tel: (2) 474-921/5   Fax: (2) 530-1369

Philippine-US Business Council
5 E. Rodriguez Jr. Ave., cor. Pasig Blvd.
Pasig, Metro Manila
Tel: (2) 693-8576

US-ASEAN Council
Thomas Jefferson Bldg.
395 Sen. Gil J. Puyat Ave. Ext.
Makati, Metro Manila
Tel: (2) 818-4336

In the United States

Philippine-American Chamber of Commerce, Inc.
711 Third Ave., 17th Fl.
New York, NY 10017
Tel: [1] (212) 972-9326   Fax: [1] (212) 867-9882

INDUSTRY-SPECIFIC ASSOCIATIONS

Association of Broadcasters in the Philippines (KBP)
6th Fl., LTA Bldg.
118 Perea St.
Legaspi Village
Makati, Metro Manila
Tel: (2) 815-1990   Fax: (2) 815-1989

Association of Philippine Leathergoods Manufacturers
(APLEM)
51 Xavier St.
Greenhills, Metro Manila
Tel: (2) 706-894

Bankers Association of the Philippines
11th Fl., Sagittarius Bldg.
De la Costa St.
Salcedo Village
Makati, Metro Manila
Tel: (2) 851-711, 810-3858, 810-3859
Fax: (2) 812-2870, 810-3860

Cebu Gifts, Toys, and Housewares Manufacturers and
Exporters Association
Room 207, Jessever Bldg.
Fuente Osmeña, Cebu City
Tel: (32) 216-216   Fax: (32) 310-132

Ceramic Exporters and Manufacturers Association
c/o Cardinal Ceramics Mfg. Inc.
SAKAP Bldg.
121 Dao St.
San Antonio Village
Makati, Metro Manila
Tel: (2) 816-19-83, 816-1213
Fax: (2) 810-8707

Chamber of Agriculture and Natural Resources
of the Philippines
5th Fl., Rico House
Amorsolo St.
Legaspi Village
Makati, Metro Manila
Tel: (2) 856-296

Chamber of Furniture Industries of the Philippines
Unit H, 9th Fl., Strata 100 Bldg.
Emerald Ave.
Pasig, Metro Manila
Tel: (2) 673-7940, 673-8874

Chemical Industries Association of the Philippines
c/o Exxon Chemical Philippines
15th Fl., BA-Lepanto Bldg.
Paseo de Roxas
Makati, Metro Manila
Tel: (2) 816-2795   Fax: (2) 815-1686

Christmas Decoration Producers and Exporters
Association of the Philippines
Rm. 304, MCR Bldg.
495 Boni Ave.
Mandaluyong, Metro Manila
Tel: (2) 788-956, 788-957

Coffee Exporters Association of the Philippines
708 National Life Insurance Bldg.
Ayala Ave.
Makati, Metro Manila
Tel: (2) 816-2942, 810-0543, 819-0533

Computer Distributors and Dealers Association
of the Philippines (COMDDAP)
7th Fl., SEDCCO I Bldg.
Legaspi St., cor. Rada St.
Legaspi Village
Makati, Metro Manila
Tel: (2) 810-3814   Fax: (2) 815-6-31

Confederation of Filipino Consulting Organizations
c/o Development of Environmental Systems, Inc.
Room 307, Columbian Bldg.
160 West Ave.
Quezon City, Metro Manila
Tel: (2) 99-2382   Fax: (2) 99-2382

Confederation of Garment Exporters of the Philippines
Suite 103, Marlis Bldg.
121 Tordesillas St.
Makati, Metro Manila
Tel: (2) 818-0224, 861-059

Consumer Electronic Products Manufacturing
Association (CEPMA)
c/o Philippine Electrical and Allied Industries
Federation
3rd Fl., Ajinomoto Bldg.
Sen. Gil J. Puyat Ave.
Makati, Metro Manila
Tel: (2) 818-5487

Council of Engineering Consultants of the Philippines
c/o DCCD Engineering Corporation
SOL Bldg.
112 Amorsolo St.
Legaspi Village
Makati, Metro Manila
Tel: (2) 87-45-86/9, 818-2033
Fax: (2) 818-2142

Energy Management Association of the Philippines
Suite 6-H, 6th Fl., Don Tim Bldg.
5468 South Superhighway
Makati, Metro Manila
Tel: (2) 881-753   Fax: (2) 867-497

Fashion Jewelry and Accessories Association
51 Xavierville St.
Greenhills West
San Juan, Metro Manila
Tel: (2) 785-243, 706-842
Fax: (2) 721-6897

Federation of Fishing Associations of the Philippines
4th Fl., Domestic Insurance Bldg.
Bonifacio Drive
Port Area, Manila
Tel: (2) 403-724, 481-929

Filipino Shipowners' Association
Magsaysay Bldg., Room 512
520 T.M. Kalaw St.
Ermita, Metro Manila
Tel: (2) 598-662   Fax: (2) 503-164

Foreign Buyers Association of the Philippines
Suite 607, Philbanking Bldg.
Ayala Ave.
Makati, Metro Manila
Tel: (2) 818-9472   Fax: (2) 817-9160

Garment Business Association of the Philippines
Room 608, Doña Narcisa Bldg.
8751 Paseo de Roxas
Makati, Metro Manila
Tel: (2) 813-7418, 883-943, 883-946, 883-939

Guild of Philippine Jewelers
32 Greenhills St.
New Manila
Quezon City, Metro Manila
Tel: (2) 721-2451   Fax: (2) 721-5073

Hotel and Restaurant Association of the Philippines
Rm. 205, Regina Bldg.
Aguirre St.
Legaspi Village
Makati, Metro Manila
Tel: (2) 815-4659, 815-4661
Fax: (2) 815-4663, 810-3821

Metalworking Industries Association of the Philippines
55 Kanlaon
Mandaluyong, Metro Manila
Tel: (2) 792-173, 775-391

Packaging Institute of the Philippines
Rm. 216, Comfoods Bldg.
Sen. Gil J. Puyat Ave.
Makati, Metro Manila
Tel: (2) 817-2936, 827-8509
Fax: (2) 817-2936

Pharmaceutical and Healthcare Association
of the Philippines
Unit 502, One Corporate Plaza
845 Pasay Rd.
Makati, Metro Manila
Tel: (2) 816-7334, 816-0618
Fax: (2) 819-2702

Philippine Association of Finance Companies, Inc.
2nd Fl., PCCI Bldg.
118 Alfaro St.
Makati, Metro Manila
Tel: (2) 813-1541   Fax: (2) 819-3356

Philippine Association of Prawn Growers
c/o NPPMCI
Ground Fl., JTL Bldg.
North Drive
Bacolod City
Tel: (34) 24-426, 81-404

Philippine Banana Growers and Exporters Association
c/o Davao Fruits Corp.
State Condominium 1, Salcedo St.
Legaspi Village
Makati, Metro Manila
Tel (2) 817-0158

Philippine Chamber of Food Manufacturers, Inc.
8th Fl., Liberty Bldg.
Pasay Rd.
Makati, Metro Manila
Tel: (2) 865-011

Philippine Chamber of Handicraft Industries, Inc.
Rm. T-2, 3rd Fl., Sunvar Plaza
Pasay Rd., cor. Amorsolo St.
Makati, Metro Manila
Tel: (2) 887-734, 887-818

Philippine Coconut Producers' Federation, Inc.
2nd and 3rd Fls., Lorenzo Bldg.
Cor. Taft and Vito Cruz Streets
Metro Manila

Philippine Computer Society
6th Fl., Emmanuel House
115 Aguirre St., Legaspi Village
Makati, Metro Manila
Tel: (2) 818-4227, 817-1820
Fax: (2) 818-0381

Philippine Electrical, Electronics and Allied Industries
Federation
3rd Fl., Union-Ajinomoto Bldg.
331 Sen. Gil J. Puyat Ave.
Makati, Metro Manila
Tel [63](2) 876-081/9

Philippine Electronics and Telecommunications
Federation (PETEF)
6th Fl., Telecoms Plaza Bldg.
316 Sen. Gil J. Puyat Ave.
Salcedo Village
Makati, Metro Manila
Tel: (2) 813-6398, 815-8921
Fax: (2) 813-6397

Philippine Exporters Confederation, Inc.
(PHILEXPORT)
Philippine International Convention Center
Ground Fl., Money Museum
Roxas Blvd.
Manila
Tel: (2) 833-2407, 833-2531
Fax: (2) 831-3707

Philippine Fish Canners Association, Inc.
Room 106, Cabrera Bldg. I
130 Timog Ave.
Quezon City, Metro Manila

Philippine Food Exporters and Processors
Organization (PHILFOODEX)
Rm. 712, L 7 S Bldg.
1414 Roxas Blvd.
Manila
Tel: (2) 521-4466, 521-2299

Philippine Medical Association
PMA Bldg.
North Ave.
Quezon City
Tel: (2) 992-132, 973-514
Fax: (2) 974-974

Philippine Motor Association
683 Aurora Blvd.
Quezon City, Metro Manila
Tel: (2) 721-5761/4, 780-191
Fax: (2) 785-878

Philippine Plastics Industrial Association, Inc.
317 Rizal Ave. Ext., Grace Park, rear Block
Solidbank Bldg.
Caloocan City, Metro Manila
Tel: (2) 361-1160   Fax: (2) 361-1168

Philippine Software Association, Inc. (PSA)
Mezzanine, Republic Glass Bldg.
115 Aguirre St.
Legaspi Village
Makati, Metro Manila
Fax: (2) 818-5368

Philippine Sugar Millers' Association
14th Fl., Pacific Bank Bldg.
6776 Ayata Ave.
Makati, Metro Manila
Tel: (2) 815-1279, 810-1286
Fax: (2) 810-1291

Philippine Toy and Novelty Manufacturers Association
(Philtoy)
25 Quezon Ave.
Quezon Ave.
Quezon City, Metro Manila
Tel: (2) 711-7415, 732-5141
Fax: (2) 731-8477

Philippine Wood Processors and Exporters
Organization, Inc.
c/o Marigold Commodities, Inc.
131 F. Manalo St.
San Juan, Metro Manila
Tel: (2) 772-763

Pollution Control Association of the Philippines
Rm. 2115, 2nd Fl., V.V. Soliven Bldg.
Epifanio de los Santos Ave.
Greenhills
San Juan, Metro Manila
Tel: (2) 701-402, 703-409
Fax: (2) 701-487

Renewable Energy Association of the Philippines, Inc.
Department of Energy
PNPC Bldg.
Merritt Rd.
Fort Bonifacio
Makati, Metro Manila
Tel: (2) 851-021 to 31 local 245
Fax: (2) 852-298

Seaweed Industry Association of the Philippines
Room 307–308, Casa Mendoza
Ariston Cortes Ave.
Mandaue, Cebu City
Tel: (2) 84-012, 83-456

Semiconductor Electronics Industry Foundation, Inc.
(SEIFI)
5th Fl., Kings Court II
Pasong Tamo, cor. de la Rosa St.
Makati, Metro Manila
Tel: (2) 877-938, 866-995

Textile Mills Association of the Philippines (TMAP)
Alexander House
132 Amorsolo St.
Legaspi Village
Makati, Metro Manila
Tel: (2) 816-6605, 818-6601
Fax: (2) 818-3107

Textile Producers' Association of the Philippines
Rm 513, Downtown Center Bldg.
516 Quintin Paredes St.
Binondo, Metro Manila
Tel: (2) 499-069, 461-435, 530-1043

Tuna Canners Association of the Philippines
Room 106, Cabrera Bldg. I
130 Timog Ave.
Quezon City, Metro Manila

United Coconut Association of the Philippines (UCAP)
4th Fl., G and A Bldg.
2303 Pasong Tamo
Makati, Metro Manila
Tel: (2) 816-7495

Wooden Gifts and Accessories Manufacturers
Association, Inc.
6 South Bayview Drive
Sunset Village
Parañaque, Metro Manila
Tel: (2) 831-1316, 832-1633

FINANCIAL INSTITUTIONS

BANKS

Professional Association

Bankers Association of the Philippines
11th Fl., Sagittarius Bldg.
De la Costa St.
Salcedo Village
Makati, Metro Manila
Tel: (2) 851-711, 810-3858, 810-3859
Fax: (2) 812-2870, 810-3860

Government Banks

Bangko Sentral ng Pilipinas
(Central Bank of the Philippines)
A. Mabini St., cor. Vito Cruz St.
1004 Malate, Metro Manila
Tel: (2) 507-051, 593-380/1, 595-263, 582-372
Fax: (2) 522-3987, 597-363, 521-5224

Development Bank of the Philippines
PO Box 800
Makati Central Post Office
1200 Makati, Metro Manila
Tel: (2) 818-9511   Fax: (2) 817-2097

Philippine National Bank (PHILNABANK)
PNB Bldg.
257 Escolta St.
1099 Escolta, Metro Manila
Tel: (2) 402-051   Fax: (2) 496-091

Land Bank of the Philippines
LBP Bldg.
319 Sen. Gil J. Puyat Ave.
Makati, Metro Manila
Tel: (2) 818-9411   Fax: (2) 843-3155

International Development Banks

Asian Development Bank (ADB)
6 ADB Ave.
1501 Mandaluyong, Metro Manila
Tel: (2) 632-4444   Fax: (2) 741-7961
WWW server: http://www.aslandevbank.org

International Finance Corporation
World Bank Group
Bangko Sentral ng Pilipinas
A. Mabini St., cor. Vito Cruz St.
1004 Malate, Metro Manila
Tel: (2) 521-1664   Fax: (2) 522-0156

Commercial Banks

Allied Banking Corporation
Allied Bank Center
6754 Ayala Ave.
Makati, Metro Manila
Tel: (2) 818-7961   Fax: (2) 816-0921

Associated Bank
411 Quintin Paredes St.
Binondo, Metro Manila
Tel: (2) 476-061

Bank of Commerce
Boston Bank Center
6764 Ayala Ave.
Makati, Metro Manila
Tel: (2) 817-4906   Fax: (2) 817-2426

Bank of the Philippine Islands
BPI Bldg.
Ayala Ave.
Makati, Metro Manila
Tel: (2) 818-5541   Fax: (2) 715-8434

China Banking Corporation
China Bank Bldg.
Cor. Paseo de Roxas and Villar Streets
1200 Makati, Metro Manila
Tel: (2) 817-7981   Fax: (2) 815-3169

CityTrust Banking Corporation
379 Gil J. Puyat Ave.
Makati, Metro Manila
Tel: (2) 818-0411   Fax: (2) 815-2595

Equitable Banking Corporation
262 Juan Luna St.
1006 Binondo, Metro Manila
Tel: (2) 409-061, 407-011, 242-7101
Fax: (2) 496-613, 241-5984

Far East Bank and Trust Company
FEBTC Bldg.
Muralla St.
1002 Intramuros, Metro Manila
Tel: (2) 401-020/1

Metropolitan Bank and Trust Company (Metrobank)
Metrobank Plaza
Sen. Gil J. Puyat Ave.
Makati, Metro Manila
Tel: (2) 818-3311, 810-3311
Fax: (2) 817-6248, 810-1531

Philippine Banking Corporation (Philbank)
6797 Ayala Ave., cor. Herrera St.
Makati, Metro Manila
Tel: (2) 718-0901, 817-0901
Fax: (2) 817-0892

Philippine Commercial International Bank (PCI Bank)
One PCI Bank Towers
Makati Ave., cor. H.V. de la Costa St.
Makati, Metro Manila
Tel: (2) 817-1021   Fax: (2) 818-3946

Philippine Trust Company (Philtrust Bank)
Philtrust Bldg.
United Nations Ave., cor. San Marcelino St.
Metro Manila
Tel: (2) 573-961   Fax: (2) 815-3140

Pilipinas Bank
ACT Tower
135 Sen. Gil J. Puyat Ave.
Makati, Metro Manila
Tel: (2) 819-1931   Fax: (2) 815-3140

PNB Republic Bank
Legaspi Towers 300
Roxas Blvd. cor. Vito Cruz
Metro Manila
Tel: (2) 817-8981

Prudential Bank and Trust Company
Ayala Ave.
Makati, Metro Manila
Tel: (2) 817-8981   Fax: (2) 817-5146

Rizal Commercial Banking Corporation
RCBC Bldg.
333 Sen. Gil J. Puyat Ave.
Makati, Metro Manila
Tel: (2) 819-3061   Fax: (2) 818-1089

Security Bank and Trust Company
SBTC Bldg.
6778 Ayala Ave.
Makati, Metro Manila
Tel: (2) 818-7677   Fax: (2) 816-4213

Solidbank Corporation
Solidbank Bldg.
Cor. Juan Luna and Dasmariñas Streets
Binondo, Metro Manila
Tel: (2) 831-2821

Traders Royal Bank
TRB Tower
Roxas Blvd.
Pasay City, Metro Manila
Tel: (2) 831-2821/3   Fax: (2) 831-2494

Union Bank of the Philippines
SSS Makati Bldg.
Ayala Ave.
Makati, Metro Manila
Tel: (2) 892-0011   Fax: (2) 818-6058

United Coconut Planters Bank
Makati Ave.
Makati, Metro Manila
Tel: (2) 818-8361   Fax: (2) 818-6863

Foreign and Offshore Banks

American Express International Banking Corp. (USA)
3rd Fl., Corinthian Plaza
Paseo de Roxas
Makati, Metro Manila
Tel: (2) 818-6731   Fax: (2) 817-2589

Bank of America, NT&SA (USA)
BA-Lepanto Bldg.
8747 Paseo de Roxas
Makati, Metro Manila
Tel: (2) 815-5000, 815-8046
Fax: (2) 815-5895

Bank of Nova Scotia (Canada)
9th Fl., Solidbank Bldg.
Paseo de Roxas
Makati, Metro Manila
Tel: (2) 817-9751   Fax: (2) 817-8796

Bank of Tokyo (Japan)
5th Fl., Ayala Bldg.
Makati, Metro Manila
Tel: (2) 892-1976   Fax: (2) 816-0413

Banque Nacional de Paris (France)
Ground Fl., PCI Bank Tower II
Makati Ave.
Makati, Metro Manila
Tel: (2) 815-8821

Barclays Bank PLC (United Kingdom)
4th Fl., Dolmar Gold Tower Bldg.
107 Alvarado St.
Legaspi Village
Makati, Metro Manila
Tel: (2) 815-9291/3   Fax: (2) 816-2526

Citibank, NA (USA)
Citibank Center Bldg.
8741 Paseo de Roxas
Makati, Metro Manila
Tel: (2) 815-7000   Fax: (2) 815-7703

Deutsche Bank Asia (Germany)
17th Fl., Filinvest Financial Center Bldg.
8753 Paseo de Roxas
Makati, Metro Manila
Tel: (2) 817-3961, 817-2961   Fax: (2) 817-2861

Hongkong & Shanghai Banking Corporation
(Hong Kong)
Royal Match Bldg.
6780 Ayala Ave.
1226 Makati, Metro Manila
Tel: (2) 810-1661, 877-031, 814-5200
Fax: (2) 817-1953

International Bank of Singapore
7th Fl., Corinthian Plaza
Paseo de Roxas
Makati, Metro Manila
Tel: (2) 817-9951

International Corporate Bank
InterBank Bldg.
111 Paseo de Roxas, cor. Legaspi St.
Makati, Metro Manila
Tel: (2) 818-6511   Fax: (2) 815-4442
*Acquired by private investors, including the American
Express Corporation, in 1987*

Korea Exchange Bank (S. Korea)
19th Fl., Metrobank Plaza
Sen. Gil J. Puyat Ave. Ext.
Makati, Metro Manila
Tel: (2) 817-2178   Fax: (2) 818-0074

Standard Chartered Bank (Hong Kong)
7901 Makati Ave.
Makati, Metro Manila
Tel: (2) 850-961   Fax: (2) 815-3084

STOCKS AND COMMODITIES

Exchanges and Supervising
Government Agencies

Securities and Exchange Commission
SEC Bldg.
Epifanio de los Santos Ave.
Greenhills
Mandaluyong, Metro Manila
Tel: (2) 810-1145, 780-931/9
Fax: (2) 722-0990
Registers and supervises business entities

Manila International Futures Exchange
7th Fl., Producers' Bank Bldg.
Paseo de Roxas
Makati, Metro Manila
Tel: (2) 812-7776   Fax: (2) 818-5529

Metropolitan Stock Exchange
SEC Bldg.
Epifanio de los Santos Ave.
Greenhills
Mandaluyong, Metro Manila

Philippine Stock Exchange, Ayala Center
Ground Fl., Stock Exchange Bldg.
Ayala Ave.
Makati, Metro Manila
Tel: (2) 810-1145/6   Fax: (2) 810-5710

Philippine Stock Exchange, Tektite
12th Fl., Tektite Tower 1
Tektite Rd., Ortigas Center
Pasig, Metro Manila
Tel: (2) 634-5089, 634-5920
Fax: (2) 634-7115

Brokerage Houses

BT Brokerage Inc.
The Pacific Star Bldg.
Makati Ave., cor. Sen. Gil J. Puyat Ave.
Makati, Metro Manila
Tel: (2) 819-0231   Fax: (2) 818-7349

BZW (Asia) Ltd.
4th Fl., Dolmar Gold Tower
107 Carlos Palanca St.
Legaspi Village
Makati, Metro Manila
Tel: (2) 818-8930   Fax: (2) 8186-2526

Baring Securities Inc.
18th Fl., Pacific Star Bldg.
Makati Ave., cor. Sen. Gil J. Puyat Ave.
Makati, Metro Manila
Tel: (2) 810-7701   Fax: (2) 819-1256

Citicorp Vickers Phils. Inc.
5th Fl., Citibank Center
8741 Paseo de Roxas
Makati, Metro Manila
Tel: (2) 815-7685   Fax: (2) 815-7014

Cititrust Securities Corp.
3rd Fl., CityTrust Bank Bldg.
379 Gil J. Puyat Ave.
Makati, Metro Manila
Tel: (2) 818-0411   Fax: (2) 817-3813

Credit Lyonnais
14th Fl., Pacific Star Bldg.
Makati Ave., cor. Sen. Gil J. Puyat Ave.
Makati, Metro Manila
Tel: (2) 817-1616   Fax: (2) 817-7145

Crosby Securities Inc.
19A Rufino Pacific Tower
6784 Ayala Ave.
Makati, Metro Manila
Tel: (2) 811-0180   Fax: (2) 811-0207

DBS Securities Inc.
11th Fl., Sage House
110 Herrera St.
Legaspi Village
Makati, Metro Manila
Tel: (2) 812-8361   Fax: (2) 815-1113

Dharmala Securities Inc.
2nd Fl., OPPEN Bldg.
349 Sen. Gil J. Puyat Ave.
Makati, Metro Manila
Tel: (2) 819-3123   Fax: (2) 873-164

HG Asia Securities Inc.
5th Fl., Pacific Star Bldg.
Sen. Gil J. Puyat Ave., cor. Makati Ave.
Makati, Metro Manila
Tel: (2) 812-9123   Fax: (2) 812-7909

Jardine Fleming Exchange Capital Securities Inc.
2nd Fl., Corporate Business Center
151 Paseo de Roxas St.
Makati, Metro Manila
Tel: (2) 813-8519   Fax: (2) 813-5366

Kim Eng Securities
11th Fl., Pacific Bank Bldg.
6776 Ayala Ave.
Makati, Metro Manila
Tel: (2) 894-5305   Fax: (2) 894-5308

Morgan Grenfell Phils. Securities Inc.
3rd Fl., Makati Stock Exchange Bldg.
6767 Ayala Ave.
Makati, Metro Manila
Tel: (2) 813-0553   Fax: (2) 817-0863

Peregrine Securities Phils. Inc.
Ground Fl., Makati Stock Exchange Bldg.
6767 Ayala Ave., cor. Herrera St.
Makati, Metro Manila
Tel: (2) 816-3471   Fax: (2) 819-2654

Sun Hung Kai Securities Inc.
17th Fl., BA-Lepanto Bldg.
8747 Paseo de Roxas
Makati, Metro Manila
Tel: (2) 813-2041   Fax: (2) 817-5880

UBP Securities Inc.
3rd Fl., Makati Stock Exchange Bldg.
6767 Ayala Ave., cor. Herrera St.
Makati, Metro Manila
Tel: (2) 815-6519   Fax: (2) 815-6299

Urbancorp Investments Inc.
Urban Bank Square
Urban Ave.
Makati, Metro Manila
Tel: (2) 856-268   Fax: (2) 819-1278

INSURANCE

Regulatory Agency

Insurance Commission
1071 United Nations Ave.
Manila
Tel: (2) 583-534, 574-886, 599-221/5
Fax: (2) 522-1434

Insurance Companies

Central Surety and Insurance Co.
2nd Fl., UniversalRe Bldg.
106 Paseo de Roxas St.
Legaspi Village
1200 Makati, Metro Manila
Tel: (2) 817-4931   Fax: (2) 817-0006

Empire Insurance Co.
2nd–3rd Fl., Prudential Life Bldg.
843 Arnaiz Ave.
Legaspi Village
1229 Makati, Metro Manila
Tel: (2) 815-9561   Fax: (2) 815-2599

Equitable Insurance Corporation
4th Fl., Equitable Bank Bldg.
262 Juan Luna St.
Binondo, Metro Manila
Tel: (2) 498-991

FGU Insurance Corp.
BPI Bldg.
16th–18th Fl., Ayala Ave.
1226 Makati, Metro Manila
Tel: (2) 817-0971   Fax: (2) 817-9806

Makati Insurance Co. Inc.
4th Fl., Builders Center Bldg.
170 Salcedo St.
Legaspi Village
Makati, Metro Manila
Tel: (2) 815-9236   Fax: (2) 818-3320

Mercantile Insurance Co. Inc.
Mercantile Insurance Bldg.
Cor. Gen. Luna and Beaterio Streets
Intramuros, Metro Manila
Tel: (2) 493-791

Metropolitan Insurance Co.
Oledan Bldg.
131 Ayala Ave.
Makati, Metro Manila
Tel: (2) 810-8151

Paramount Insurance Corporation
15th Fl., Sage House
110 Herrera St.
Legaspi Village
Makati, Metro Manila
Tel: (2) 812-7956   Fax: (2) 813-3043

Philippine American General Insurance Co. Inc.
AIU-Philhome Bldg.
De la Rosa, cor. Alvarado St.
Legaspi Village
Makati, Metro Manila
Tel: (2) 817-8726

Rizal Surety and Insurance Co.
2nd-3rd Fl., Prudential Life Bldg.
843 Arnaiz Ave.
Legaspi Village
Makati, Metro Manila
Tel: (2) 815-9561   Fax: (2) 815-2599

World-Wide Insurance and Surety Co. Inc.
4th Fl., Cardinal Bldg.
999 Pedro Gil St., cor. F. Agoncillo St.
Metro Manila
Tel: (2) 593-290

SERVICES

ACCOUNTING AND CONSULTING FIRMS

Note: Many of these firms have offices in other Philippine cities and worldwide

Alas Group
PO Box 2839 MCC
Manila
Tel: (2) 810-1701   Fax: (2) 812-4632
A member of Horwath International

Coopers & Lybrand
c/o Carlos J. Valdes
MCPO Box 2431
Makati, Metro Manila
Tel: (2) 857-706   Fax: (2) 819-1740

Diaz Murillo Dalupan
PO Box 3119
Manila 1099
Tel: (2) 864-325   Fax: (2) 817-5766
Part of Deloitte Touche Tohmatsu International

Joaquin Cunanan and Company
8th Fl., BA-Lepanto Bldg.
8747 Paseo de Roxas
Makati, Metro Manila
Tel: (2) 818-7622/6, 818-9103/5
Fax: (2) 815-3514
A Price Waterhouse firm; mailing address: PO Box 2288, 1099 Manila

KMPG Fernandez Santos & Lopez
MCPO Box 1659
Makati, Metro Manila
Tel: (2) 812-8331

Laya, Manabat, Salgado & Co.
MCPO Box 3483
Makati, Metro Manila
Tel: (2) 818-9492   Fax: (2) 816-6595

Punongbayan & Araullo
6th Fl., Vernida IV Bldg.
Alfaro St.
Salcedo Village
Makati, Metro Manila 1200
Tel: (2) 810-9741, 812-6091
Fax: (2) 810-9748
A member of Ernst & Young International

SGV & Co.
PO Box 589
Manila 1099
Tel: (2) 819-3011   Fax: (2) 819-0872
A member of Nexia International

SyCip, Gorres, Velayo & Co.
6760 Ayala Ave.
Makati, Metro Manila
Tel: (2) 819-3011   Fax: (2) 819-0872
A member of Arthur Andersen & Co

ADVERTISING AGENCIES

AB Communications
20th Fl., Pacific Star Bldg.
Sen. Gil J. Puyat Ave., cor. Makati Ave.
Makati, Metro Manila
Tel: (2) 815-8466/8   Fax: (2) 815-8493

Ace/Saatchi & Saatchi Advertising
9th Fl., Feliza Bldg.
108 Herrera St.
Legaspi Village
Makati, Metro Manila
Tel: (2) 810-1901 to 20
Fax: (2) 812-5035

Campaigns & Grey
12th Fl., Velero Towers
Velero St.
Salcedo Village
Makati, Metro Manila
Tel: (2) 818-3861/3   Fax: (2) 810-3854

Core Alliance
7th Fl., SEDCCO Bldg.
Rada St., cor. Legazpi St.
Makati, Metro Manila
Tel: (2) 816-3766   Fax: (2) 815-9034

Dentsu, Young & Rubicam, Alcantara/Manila
704 Pablo Ocampo Sr. St.
Manila 1072
Tel: (2) 574-681/9   Fax: (2) 521-8129

J. Walter Thompson Co. (Philippines)
Ramon Magsaysay Center
Manila Central Post Office
PO Box 1399
Ermita, Metro Manila 1099
Tel: (2) 599-831/9   Fax: (2) 521-1024

Jimenez/DMB&B
23rd Fl., Pacific Star Bldg.
Sen. Gil J. Puyat Ave., cor. Makati Ave.
Makati, Metro Manila
Tel: (2) 815-8318   Fax: (2) 815-8333

Lintas Manila
PO Box MCC 1081
Makati, Metro Manila
Tel: (2) 811-1111   Fax: (2) 811-0130

Ogilvy & Mather (Philippines) Inc.
14th Fl., Solidbank Bldg.
777 Paseo de Roxas
Makati, Metro Manila
Tel: (2) 813-3001   Fax: (2) 819-2604

PAC/BBDO
Dominion Bldg.
833 Pasay Rd.
Makati, Metro Manila 1200
Tel: (2) 892-8331   Fax: (2) 817-8761

Taipan Bozell
2nd Fl., DPSI Business Center
210 N. Garcia St., Bel Air II
Makati, Metro Manila
Tel: (2) 894-5157   Fax: (2) 894-5159

LEGAL SERVICES

Bar Association

Philippine Lawyers' Association
PO Box 2082
Manila
Tel: (2) 741-2650

Law Firms

Angara Abello Concepcion Regala & Cruz Law Offices
ACCRA Bldg.
122 Gamboa St.
Legaspi Village
Makati, Metro Manila
Tel: (2) 817-0966
Fax: (2) 816-0109, 812-4897

Balgos & Perez Law Office
5th Fl., Corinthian Plaza
Paseo de Roxas
Makati, Metro Manila
Tel: (2) 818-6451   Fax: (2) 810-0792

Bengzon Zarranga Narciso Cudala Pecson Bengson & Jimenez Attorneys & Counsellors at Law
6th Fl., SOL Bldg.
112 Amorsolo St.
Legaspi Village
1229 Makati, Metro Manila
Tel: (2) 815-9071/8, 810-8235, 810-8581
Fax: (2) 817-3251, 813-0081

Bito Lozada Ortega & Castillo Law Offices
ALPAP Bldg.
140 Alfaro St.
Salcedo Village
Makati, Metro Manila
Tel: (2) 818-2321   Fax: (2) 810-3153

Carag Caballes Jamora & Somera
2nd Fl., The Plaza Royale
120 Alfaro St.
Salcedo Village
Makati, Metro Manila
Tel: (2) 812-5246/8
Fax: (2) 818-8971, 815-1436

Castillo Laman Tan & Pantaleon Law Offices
4th Fl., Valero Tower Condominium
Valero St.
Salcedo Village
Makati, Metro Manila
Tel: (2) 817-6791   Fax: (2) 819-2725

V.E. Del Rosario & Partners
Rasadel Bldg.
1011 Makati, Metro Manila
Tel: (2) 818-6011/3, 877-876/7
Fax: (2) 818-0194

Feria Feria Lugtu & La Ó
Ferlaw Bldg.
366 Cabildo St.
1002 Intramuros, Metro Manila
Tel: (2) 479-182, 478-040, 407-196
Fax: (2) 530-0582

Gozon Defensor & Parel Law Offices
15th Fl., Sagittarius Condominium
H.V. de la Costa St.
Salcedo Village
Makati, Metro Manila
Tel: (2) 816-3716/9   Fax: (2) 817-0696

Laurel Law Offices
15th Fl., JMT Corporate Condominium
Ortigas Center
Pasig, Metro Manila
Tel: (2) 634-2711   Fax: (2) 633-8680

Puno and Puno Law Offices
5th Fl., Hongkong Bank Center
San Miguel Ave.
Pasig, Metro Manila
Tel: (2) 631-1261   Fax: (2) 631-2517

Quisumbing Torres & Evangelista Law Office
Pacific Star Bldg.
Makati Ave., cor. Sen. Gil J. Puyat Ave.
Makati, Metro Manila
Tel: (2) 817-3016   Fax: (2) 817-4432
Associated with Baker & McKenzie

Romulo, Mabanta, Buenaventura, Sayoc
& de los Angeles
4th Fl., King's Court I Bldg.
2129 Pasong Tamo
Makati, Metro Manila
Tel: (2) 815-3011   Fax: (2) 810-3110

Siguion Reyna Montecillo & Ongsiako Law Offices
9th Fl., Philcom Bldg.
8755 Paseo de Roxas
Makati, Metro Manila
Tel: (2) 810-0281   Fax: (2) 819-1498

SyCip Salazar Hernandez & Gatmaitan Law Offices
105 Paseo de Roxas
Makati, Metro Manila
Tel: (2) 817-9611, 817-9811
Fax: (2) 817-3896

Tan Mazano & Velez
11th Fl., Pacific Bank Makati Bldg.
6776 Ayala Ave.
1200 Makati, Metro Manila
Tel: (2) 818-3249, 818-6701
Fax: (2) 817-7358

Villaraza & Cruz Law Offices
5th Fl., LTA Bldg.
118 Perca St.
Legaspi Village
Makati, Metro Manila
Tel: (2) 818-9836
Fax: (2) 816-7057, 817-1324

MARKET RESEARCH FIRMS

Andersen Consulting
SGV Development Center
105 de la Rosa St.
Legaspi Village
Makati, Metro Manila
Tel: (2) 817-0301   Fax: (2) 817-2397

Asia Pacific Center for Research
Suite 321, Secretariat Bldg.
PICC, Roxas Blvd.
Pasay City, Metro Manila
Tel/Fax: (2) 831-3524

Feedback, Inc.
Suite 114, Limketkai Bldg.
Ortigas Ave., Greenhills
San Juan, Metro Manila
Tel: (2) 721-4456   Fax: (2) 79-8727

FSA (Phils.), Inc.
3rd Fl., Philippine Social Science Center
Marcos Ave.
Diliman
Quezon City, Metro Manila
Tel: (2) 978-741   Fax: (2) 976-846

Leverage International (Consultants), Inc.
5th Fl., PS Bank Bldg.
Ayala Ave.
Makati, Metro Manila
Tel.: (2) 810-1389   Fax: (2) 810-1594

Philippine Survey and Research Center, Inc.
PSRC Bldg.
Cor. Calbayog and Kanlaon Streets
Mandaluyong, Metro Manila
Tel: (2) 77-4802
Fax: (2) 77-4805

Total Research Needs-MBL, Inc.
155 Panay Ave.
Quezon City, Metro Manila
Tel: (2) 96-1102   Fax: (2) 922-2860

TRANSLATORS AND INTERPRETERS

Executive Centerpoint
106 Legaspi St.
Legaspi Village
Makati, Metro Manila
Tel: (2) 815-9872, 818-8825

Westin Philippine Plaza
Cultural Center Complex
Roxas Blvd.
Manila
Tel: (2) 832-0701

EuroComm
81-I Masikap Extension
Teachers' Village, Metro Manila
Tel: (2) 922-3961   Fax: (2) 922-3861

Mandarin Oriental Business Center
Makati Ave., cor. Paseo de Roxas
Makati, Metro Manila
Tel: (2) 816-3601 x2327/9

TRANSPORTATION

Bureau of Air Transportation
Old MIA Rd.
Pasay City, Metro Manila
Tel: (2) 831-8078, 832-3308, 832-3047
Fax: (2) 833-1577
Provides, develops, constructs, maintains and operates airports, airways systems, and air navigation facilities

Civil Aeronautics Board
Old MIA Rd.
Pasay City, Metro Manila
Tel: (2) 833-6911, 833-7248
Fax: (2) 833-7266
Regulates domestic and international airline operations and issues licenses to domestic and international airfreight forwarders

Land Transportation Office
East Ave.
Quezon City, Metro Manila
Tel: (2) 922-9061/5   Fax: (2) 921-9072

Light Rail Transit Authority
Administrative Bldg., LRT Compound
Aurora Blvd.
Pasay, Metro Manila
Tel: (2) 832-0423   Fax: (2) 831-6449

Manila International Airport Authority
Ninoy Aquino International Airport (NAIA)
Parañaque, Metro Manila
Tel: (2) 832-2938, 831-6205
Fax: (2) 833-1180
Responsible for air traffic operations for domestic and international flights

Philippine National Railways
Management Center
Torres Bugallon St.
Caloocan City, Metro Manila
Tel: (2) 362-0824   Fax: (2) 362-0824

Philippine Ports Authority
Marsman Bldg.,
22 Muelle de Francisco St.
South Harbor, Metro Manila
Tel: (2) 530-0875, 479-204
Fax: (2) 530-1199, 486-237

AIRLINES AND AIR CARGO CARRIERS

Major Philippine Carriers

Philippine Airlines (PAL)
PAL Bldg.
Legaspi St.
Legaspi Village
1059 Makati, Metro Manila
Tel: (2) 816-6691, 819-1771, 818-0111
Fax: (2) 817-86890
The Philippines' national carrier

Abotiz Air Transport
General Aviation Area
Domestic Airport
Pasay City, Metro Manila
Tel: (2) 831-2294   Fax: (2) 831-3978

Aerolift Philippines
Ground Fl., Chemphil Bldg.
851 Pasay Rd.
Legaspi Village
Makati, Metro Manila
Tel: (2) 812-6711, 817-2361

Pacific Airways
3110 Domestic Airport Rd.
Pasay City, Metro Manila
Tel: (2) 832-2731/2

Foreign Carriers

Air Canada
Cityland Condominium II
Esteban St., cor. Herrera St.
Makati, Metro Manila
Tel: (2) 810-4461   Fax: (2) 810-5131

Air France
7th Fl., Century Towers Bldg.
100 Tordesillas St.
Salcedo Village
Makati, Metro Manila
Tel: (2) 815-6963   Fax: (2) 815-6969

Air India
Gammon Center Bldg.
Alfaro St.
Makati, Metro Manila
Tel: (2) 815-1280, 815-2441
Fax: (2) 817-8720

Alitalia
The Gallery Bldg.
Amorsolo St.
Makati, Metro Manila
Tel: (2) 850-265, 812-3351
Fax: (2) 818-7312

American Airlines
Olympia Condominium
Makati Ave., cor. Santo Tomas St.
Makati, Metro Manila
Tel: (2) 817-8645, 810-3228
Fax: (2) 810-3230

British Airways
Ground Fl., 135 Filipino Merchants' Bldg.
Corner Legaspi and Dela Rosa Streets
Makati, Metro Manila
Tel: (2) 817-0361   Fax: (2) 819-0410

Canadian Airlines International
Allied Bank Center
Ayala Ave.
Makati, Metro Manila
Tel: (2) 810-2656

Canadian Pacific Airways
Gammon Center Bldg.
Ayala Ave.
Makati, Metro Manila
Tel: (2) 815-9401

Cathay Pacific
Ground Fl., Gammon Center
126 Alfaro St.
Salcedo Village
Makati, Metro Manila
Tel: (2) 815-9417   Fax: (2) 815-2445
Hong Kong carrier

China Airlines
Ground Fl., Arcade
Manila Midtown Hotel
Manila
Tel: (2) 590-086, 599-460
Fax: (2) 821-3467
Taiwanese carrier

Continental Air Micronesia
Ground Fl., SGV Bldg.
6760 Ayala Ave.
Makati, Metro Manila
Tel: (2) 818-8701

Egypt Air
Windsor Tower Bldg.
163 Legaspi St.
Legaspi Village
Makati, Metro Manila
Tel: (2) 831-0661, 815-8476/9
Fax: (2) 818-3454

Finnair
Pacific Bank Bldg.
Ayala Ave.
Makati, Metro Manila
Tel: (2) 818-2601, 818-2621

Garuda Indonesian Airlines
Ground Fl., The Peninsula Manila
Ayala Ave., cor. Makati Ave.
Makati, Metro Manila
Tel: (2) 862-205, 818-1731
Fax: (2) 818-1662

Gulf Air
Ground Fl., Windsor Tower Bldg.
163 Legaspi St.
Legaspi Village
Makati, Metro Manila
Tel: (2) 817-6909, 815-8229
Fax: (2) 819-7436

Japan Airlines
Hotel Nikko Manila Garden
Epifanio de los Santos Ave., cor. Pasay Rd.
Makati, Metro Manila
Tel: (2) 812-1591, 810-9786
Fax: (2) 817-1718

KLM Royal Dutch Airlines
160 Alfaro St.
Salcedo Village
Makati, Metro Manila
Tel: (2) 815-4790, 815-9701
Fax: (2) 819-5680

Korean Air
Ground Fl., LPI Plaza
124 Alfaro St.
Salcedo Village
Makati, Metro Manila
Tel: (2) 815-8911, 815-9261
Fax: (2) 815-0737

Lufthansa German Airlines
Legaspi Park View Condominium
134 Legaspi St., cor. Palanca St.
Legaspi Village
Makati, Metro Manila
Tel: (2) 810-4596, 810-5089
Fax: (2) 812-9463

Malaysian Airline System
Ground Fl., Legaspi Towers 300
Roxas Blvd., cor. Vito Cruz
Manila
Tel: (2) 575-761, 586-893
Fax: (2) 571-780

Northwest Airlines
9th Fl., Athenaeum Bldg.
160 Alfaro St.
Salcedo Village
Makati, Metro Manila
Tel: (2) 819-7431, 819-7341
Fax: (2) 815-6455

Pakistan International Airlines
Ground Fl., Colonnade Bldg.
Carlos Palanca St., cor. Legaspi St.
Legaspi Village
Makati, Metro Manila
Tel: (2) 818-0441, 813-2618
Fax: (2) 813-2618

Qantas Airways
Ground Fl., China Bank Bldg.
Paseo de Roxas
Makati, Metro Manila
Tel: (2) 815-9491
Fax: (2) 810-5008

Royal Brunei
Ground Fl., Saville Bldg.
Sen. Gil J. Puyat Ave., cor. Paseo de Roxas
Makati, Metro Manila
Tel: (2) 817-1631/4
Fax: (2) 812-6389

Sabena Belgian Airlines
Ralph Anthony Suite
Arkansas St., cor. Maria Orosa St.
Ermita, Metro Manila
Tel: (2) 508-636   Fax: (2) 508-639

Saudia Arabian Airlines
114 Cougar Bldg.
Cor. Valero and Herrera Streets
Salcedo Village
Makati, Metro Manila
Tel: (2) 818-4722, 818-7866
Fax: (2) 810-8813

Scandinavian Airline System (SAS)
F&M Lopez Bldg.
Legaspi St.
Makati, Metro Manila
Tel: (2) 810-5050   Fax: (2) 810-0798

Singapore Airlines
138 H.V. De la Costa St.
Salcedo Village
Makati, Metro Manila
Tel: (2) 810-4966, 810-4951
Fax: (2) 815-2527

Swissair
2nd Fl., Country Space I Bldg.
Sen. Gil J. Puyat Ave.
Makati, Metro Manila
Tel: (2) 818-8351/4   Fax: (2) 815-3350

Thai Airways
2nd Fl., Country Space I Bldg.
Sen. Gil J. Puyat Ave.
Makati, Metro Manila
Tel: (2) 815-8421/7, 815-8431
Fax: (2) 817-4044

United Airlines
Pacific Star Bldg.
Makati Ave., cor. Sen. Gil J. Puyat Ave.
Makati, Metro Manila
Tel: (2) 818-7321, 818-5421/4
Fax: (2) 817-4682

Vietnam Airlines
Anson Arcade
Pasay Rd., cor. Paseo de Roxas
Makati, Metro Manila
Tel: (2) 874-878

INTERNATIONAL FREIGHT FORWARDERS AND COURIERS

Many of these organizations also provide customs broker services.

Airborne Express
c/o RAF International
152 Quirino Ave., cor. T. Alonzo St.
Tambo
Parañaque, Metro Manila
Tel: (2) 832-5527   Fax: (2) 832-5929

Airfreight International Manila Inc.
Salud Dizon Bldg.
Parañaque, Metro Manila
Tel: (2) 833-0708, 833-0696, 833-8529

Associated Freight Consolidators, Inc.
Cargo Center, Nayong Pilipino Complex
Mia Rd.
Pasay City, Metro Manila
Tel: (2) 832-2701   Fax: (2) 833-3779

Cargo Bridge Philippines Corp.
Rm. 7-D, Country Space I Bldg.
Sen. Gil J. Puyat Ave.
1200 Makati, Metro Manila
Tel: (2) 812-7118   Fax: (2) 818-9004

CBFM International Cargo Forwarders Corp.
4279 Emilia St.
Palanan
Makati, Metro Manila
Tel: (2) 831-3447

Circle Freight International (Philippines) Ltd. Inc.
CFIP Bldg.
Ninoy Aquino Ave.
Parañaque, Metro Manila
Tel: (2) 831-4631   Fax: (2) 831-5090

CPI Transport, Inc.
592 Quirino Ave.
Tambo
1701 Parañaque, Metro Manila
Tel: (2) 831-9366, 831-8042
Fax: (2) 833-1395

DHL
Philcox Bldg.
Domestic Rd.
Pasay City, Metro Manila
Tel: (2) 811-010, 834-0418
Fax: (2) 831-1986, 813-5260

Dimerco Express (Phils.) Inc.
170 Quirino Ave., Tambo
Parañaque, Metro Manila
Tel: (2) 831-0041/5   Fax: (2) 832-5693

Dimerco Express (Phils.) Inc.
9 Borromeo Arcade
F. Ramos St.
Cebu City
Tel: (32) 72795, 52-866
Fax: (32) 832-5693

All addresses and telephone numbers are in the Philippines unless otherwise noted. The country code for the Philippines is [63].

Emery Transnational Air Cargo Corp.
PO Box 7557, Naia
Ninoy Aquino Ave.
Parañaque, Metro Manila

FedEx
c/o Airfreight 2100
U-Freight Warehouse
3rd Fl., Unit 2
Bgy., Vitales
Parañaque, Metro Manila
Tel:(2) 833-7586/9   Fax: (2) 833-3288

FedEx
c/o Airfreight 2100
4th Fl., Robinson's Galleria
Epifanio de los Santos Ave.
Mandaluyong, Metro Manila
Tel: (2) 632-9849

Global Freight Forwarders Inc.
Don Tim Bldg.
5468 S. Superhighway
Makati, Metro Manila
Tel: (2) 817-5521, 816-1771
Fax: (2) 817-4461

GRM International, Inc.
707 Unit P, Q, & R
Columbia Airfreight Complex
Ninoy Aquino Ave.
Parañaque, Metro Manila
Tel: (2) 832-2761   Fax: (2) 833-0224

Hecny Forwarders, Inc.
30 San Luis St.
Pasay City, Metro Manila
Tel: (2) 833-2561/8   Fax: (2) 831-0084

Legaspi International Forwarders
Unit M, R & S, Commercial Bldg.
Sucat
Parañaque, Metro Manila
Tel: (2) 832-1831   Fax: (2) 832-2185

LEP International Philippines, Inc.
Skyfreight Bldg.
Ninoy Aquino Ave.
Parañaque, Metro Manila
Tel: (2) 831-7201   Fax: (2) 833-3790

MSAS Cargo International
Ground Fl., Ding Velayo Sports Center
Domestic Airport Rd.
Pasay City, Metro Manila
Tel: (2) 833-8967   Fax: (2) 833-8980

RAF International Forwarding (Phils.) Inc.
6th Fl., NBR Bdlg.
Cityland 10 Condominium
H.V. de la Costa St.
Makati, Metro Manila
Tel: (2) 485-391   Fax: (2) 812-9212

Rapid Air Freight, Inc.
6 Eleven Bldg.
Naia Rd.
Pasay City, Metro Manila
Tel: (2) 8312-7281   Fax: (2) 832-2876

Rass Forwarders, Inc.
Room 21, Cargo Center
Nayong Pilipino Complex
Mia Rd.
Pasay City, Metro Manila
Tel: (2) 831-3895   Fax: (2) 833-6157

Sea-Land Service, Inc.
2nd–3rd Fl., Dynavision Bldg.
108 Rada St.
Legaspi Village
Makati, Metro Manila
Tel: (2) 866-931/4

Shulman Air Freight International Phils. Inc.
2304 B1-B2 MacLane Center
64 Dasmariñas St.
Binondo, Metro Manila
Tel: (2) 495-876   Fax: (2) 488-148

Sky International
15th Fl., Federal Tower
57–59 Dasmariñas St.
Manila
Tel: (2) 470-830/9, 478-691/2
Fax: (2) 530-0568, 492-056

TNT Express Worldwide
Ground Fl., Morning Star Center
347 Sen. Gil J. Puyat Ave.
Makati, Metro Manila
Tel: (2) 817-2871
Fax: (2) 819-1373

UPS
c/o Delbros Cargo Center
Manila
Tel: (2) 832-1565/9
Fax: (2) 834-0431

Westward Airship International, Inc.
110 Carlos Palanca Jr. St.
Ground Fl., Doña Angelas Garden
Legaspi Village
Makati, Metro Manila
Tel: (2) 818-8233   Fax: (2) 818-7594

SHIPPING FIRMS

Aboitiz Jebsen Bulk Transport Corp.
3rd Fl., King's Court Bldg.
2129 Pasong Tamo
Makati, Metro Manila
Tel: (2) 887-451/4   Fax: (2) 815-2860

Aboitiz Shipping Corporation
110 Legaspi St.
Legaspi Village
Makati, Metro Manila
Tel: (2) 208-332   Fax: (2) 818-4814

American President Lines
ECJ Condominium
Cor. Arzobispo and Santa Lucia Streets
Intramuros, Metro Manila
Tel: (2) 498-831/4

Asian Shipping Corp.
50 N. Bay Blvd.
Navotas, Metro Manila
Tel: (2) 268-585, 205-464, 213-813, 210-104

Candano Shipping Lines, Inc.
6th Fl., Victoria Bldg.
429 United Nations Ave.
Ermita, Metro Manila
Tel: (2) 503-306/9

Carlos A. Gothong Lines, Inc.
Quezon Rd.
Reclamation Area, Cebu City
Tel: (32) 211-181   Fax: (32) 212-265

Eastern Shipping Lines, Inc.
ESL Bldg.
54 Anda Circle
2803 Port Area, Metro Manila
Tel: (2) 401-081   Fax: (2) 489-708

Loadstar Shipping Co., Inc.
Loadstar Bldg.
1294 Romualdez St.
1007 Paco, Metro Manila
Tel: (2) 598-071/4   Fax: (2) 521-8061

Luztevco (Luzon Stevedoring Corporation)
Tacoma and Second St.
Port Area, Metro Manila
Tel: (2) 742-0261

National Shipping Corporation of the Philippines
Knights of Rizal Bldg.
Bonifacio Drive
Port Area, Metro Manila
Tel: (2) 473-631   Fax: (2) 530-0169

Philippine Pacific Ocean Lines
Delgado Bldg.
Bonifacio Drive
Port Area, Metro Manila
Tel: (2) 478-541

Philippine President Lines, Inc.
PPL Bldg.
1000-1046 United Nations Ave.
Metro Manila
Tel: (2) 509-011

United Philippine Lines, Inc.
UPL Bldg.
Santa Clara St.
Intramuros, Metro Manila
Tel: (2) 498-961

MEDIA AND INFORMATION SOURCES

All publications are in English unless otherwise noted.

DIRECTORIES AND ANNUALS

American Chamber of Commerce of the Philippines Membership Directory
American Chamber of Commerce of the Philippines
2nd Fl., Corinthian Plaza
Paseo de Roxas
1299 Makati, Metro Manila
Tel: (2) 818-7911   Fax: (2) 816-6359
Mailing address: PO Box 1578, MCC, Manila

Annual Report, Central Bank of the Philippines
(Annual)
Bangko Sentral ng Pilipinas
A. Mabini St., cor. Vito Cruz St.
Malate, Metro Manila
Tel: (2) 507-051, 593-380/1, 595-263, 582-372
Fax: (2) 522-3987, 597-363

Asian Computer Directory
(Monthly)
Washington Plaza
1st Fl., 230 Wanchai Rd.
Wanchai, Hong Kong
Tel: [852] 2832-7123   Fax: [852] 2832-9208

Asian Printing Directory
(English/Chinese, Annual)
Travel & Trade Publishing (Asia)
16th Fl., Capitol Centre
5-19 Jardines Bazaar
Causeway Bay, Hong Kong
Tel: [852] 2890-3067   Fax: [852]2895-2378

Asia-Pacific Journal of Operational Research
(Annual)
Operational Research Society of Singapore
National University Singapore
Department of Math
Singapore 0511
Tel: [65] 772-2737   Fax: [65] 779-5452

Asia Pacific Leather Directory
(Annual)
Asia Pacific Leather Yearbook
(Annual)
Asia Pacific Directories, Ltd.
6th Fl., Wah Hen Commercial Centre
381 Hennessy Rd.
Hong Kong
Tel: [852] 2893-6377   Fax: [852] 2893-5752

Asia-Pacific Travel Index
(Annual)
Asian Business Press Pte. Ltd.
100 Beach Rd.
2600 Shaw Tower
Singapore 0718

ASTRAD: ASEAN Trade Directory
(Annual)
Peter Isaacson Publications Pty. Ltd.
46-50 Porter St.
PO Box 172
Prahran, Vic. 3181, Australia
Tel: [61] (3) 520-5555   Fax: [61] (3) 525-2983

Bankers Handbook for Asia
(Annual)
Dataline Asia Pacific Inc.
3rd Fl., Hollywood Center
233 Hollywood Rd.
Hong Kong
Tel: [852] 2815-5221   Fax: [852] 2854-2794

Buyers Guide to Philippine Manufacturers and Exporters
(Annual)
Trade Development Publishing House
Suite 2505-A, Tektite Towers
Ortigas Complex
Pasig, Metro Manila
Tel: (2) 631-8276   Fax: (2) 631-2521

Directory of Philippine Electronics Exporters
Directory of Philippine Gifts and Housewares
Directory of Philippine Leather Goods and Footwear
Directory of Philippine Processed Foods Exporters
Department of Trade and Industry
Trade and Industry Information Center
4th Fl., Industry and Investments Bldg.
385 Sen. Gil J. Puyat Ave.
3117 Makati, Metro Manila
Tel: (2) 818-5705   Fax: (2) 856-487

Fookien Times Yearbook
(Annual)
Fookien Times Publishing Co., Inc.
13th and Railroad Streets
Port Area, Metro Manila
Tel: (2) 401-871
Annual report of trends and events in the Philippines.

Key Directory for Construction Professionals
(Annual)
Heart Publications Inc.
Suite 204, Heart Bldg.
7461 Bagtikan St.
1200 Makati, Metro Manila
Tel: (2) 819-3566

Kompass Philippines
(Annual)
Kompass First East Asia Inc.
Ground Fl., Star Center Bldg.
Sen. Gil J. Puyat Ave.
1200 Makati, Metro Manila
Tel: (2) 884-781   Fax: (2) 812-2290

Philippines Business Directory
(Annual)
Massmark Philippines
PO Box 3333
1073 Manila
Tel: (2) 805-0955

Philippines Government Directory
(Annual)
The Diplomatic Post Publishing Corp.
981 Padilla St.
San Miguel, Metro Manila
Tel: (2) 833-2818   Fax: (2) 833-3858

Philippine Media Directory
(Annual)
Azur Publication Inc.
J.P. Rizal St.
Santa Maria, Bulacan
Tel: (97) 721-4332

Philippine Mining and Engineering Journal Annual & Directory
(Annual)
Business Masters International
55 U.E. Tech Ave.
University Hills
Malabon
Rizal, Luzon

Philippine Products Magazine
Trade Development Publishing House
Suite 2505-A, Tektite Towers
Ortigas Complex
Pasig, Metro Manila
Tel: (2) 631-8276   Fax: (2) 631-2521

Philippine Trade and Industry Directory
(Annual)
Philippine Chamber of Commerce and Industry
7th Fl., ODC International Plaza
219 Salcedo St.
Legaspi Village
Makati, Metro Manila
Tel: (2) 817-6981

Philippine Yearbook
(Annual)
National Census and Statistics Office
c/o National Economic Development Authority (NEDA)
PO Box 779
Metro Manila
Tel: (2) 613-645   Fax: (2) 610-794

Philippines 5000
(Annual)
Credit Information Bureau, Inc.
3rd Fl., Secretariat Bldg., PICC
CCP Complex
Roxas Blvd.
Pasay City, Metro Manila
Tel: (2) 833-3303   Fax: (2) 834-1317
Financial reference containing the official ranking of the country's top 5,000 corporations

Who Supplies What from Europe? A Guide to European Products Marketed in the Philippines
European Chamber of Commerce of the Philippines
5th Fl., King's Court II
Pasong Tamo
Makati, Metro Manila
Tel: (2) 811-2234

World Jewelogue
(Annual)
Headway International Publications Co.
907 Great Eagle Center
23 Harbour Rd.
Hong Kong
Tel: [852] 2827-5121   Fax: [852] 2827-7064

DAILY NEWSPAPERS

Philippine News Agency
Media Center
Maharlika Broadcasting System
Bohol Ave.
3005 Quezon City, Metro Manila
Tel: (2) 976-661

Philippine Information Agency
Visayas Ave.
Diliman
Quezon City, Metro Manila
Tel: (2) 921-7941

Asian Wall Street Journal
(Monday–Friday)
Dow Jones Publishing Co. (Asia)
GPO Box 9825
Hong Kong
Tel: [852] 2573-7121   Fax: [852] 2834-5291

Business World
(Monday Friday)
Business World Publishing Corp.
4th Fl., Diamond Motor Bldg.
Ortigas Ave.
Greenhills
San Juan, Metro Manila
Tel: (2) 799-291, 793-934

Malaya
(Daily)
People's Independent Media, Inc.
C.C. Castro Bldg.
38 Timog Ave.
Quezon City, Metro Manila
Tel: (2) 983-271/6

Manila Bulletin
(Daily)
Bulletin Publishing Corp.
Cor. Muralla and Recoletos Streets
Intramuros, Metro Manila
Tel: (2) 473-621
Largest English-language daily. Also publishes Panorama
magazine

Manila Chronicle
(Daily)
Manila Chronicle Publishing Corp.
371A Bonifacio Drive
Port Area, Metro Manila
Tel: (2) 810-6941/4   Fax: (2) 481-085

Manila Times
(Daily)
La Vanguardia Publishing Co.
Cor. Scout Santiago and Ojeda Streets
Quezon City, Metro Manila
Tel: (2) 964-448

Morning Times
(English, Visayan)
Zulueta St.
PO Box 51
Cebu City, Cebu
Tel: (32) 77-032

People's Journal
(Daily; English, Pilipino)
Philippines Journalists Inc.
Times Journal Bldg.
Railroad St., cor. 19th and 20th Streets
Port Area, Metro Manila
Tel: (2) 486-872

Philippine Daily Inquirer
(Daily)
PO Box 2050
1099 Manila
Tel: (2) 700-620/9

GENERAL BUSINESS PUBLICATIONS

ASEAN Business Quarterly
(Quarterly)
Asia Research Pte. Ltd.
PO Box 91
Alexandra Post Office
Singapore

Asian Business
(Monthly)
Far East Trade Press
2nd Fl., Kai Tak Commercial Bldg.
317 Des Voeux Rd.
Central, Hong Kong
Tel: [852] 2545-7200   Fax: [852] 2544-6979

Asiaweek
(Weekly)
Asiaweek Ltd.
199 Des Voeux Rd.
Central, Hong Kong
Tel: [852] 2815-5662   Fax: [852] 815-5903

Business Asia (Weekly)
Country Forecasts: Philippines (Quarterly)
Country Reports: Philippines (Quarterly)
Economist Intelligence Unit
111 West 57th St.
New York, NY 10019-2211, USA
Tel: [1] (212) 554-0600   Fax: [1] (212) 586-1181

Business Journal
(Monthly)
American Chamber of Commerce of the Philippines
Corinthian Plaza, 2nd Fl.
Paseo de Roxas
1299 Makati, Metro Manila
Tel: (2) 818-7911   Fax: (2)   816-6359
*Mailing address: PO Box 1578, MCC, Manila; US-
Philippine trade and news*

Far Eastern Economic Review
(Weekly)
GPO Box 160
Hong Kong
Tel: [852] 2508-4300   Fax: [852] 2503-1537

Manila, Inc.: The Magazine of Philippine Business and Style
(Monthly)
MMREM, Inc.
Ground Fl., Strata 200
Emerald Ave.
Ortigas Center
Pasig, Metro Manila
Tel: (2) 632-0748   Fax: (2) 631-2521

Philippine Business and Industry Index
(Annual)
Library Integrated Service Cooperative
PO Box 192
University of the Philippines Campus
1101 Quezon City, Metro Manila
Tel: (2) 921-9231
Indexes and abstracts Philippine business publications

Philippine Business Magazine
Philippine Chamber of Commerce and Industry
7th Fl., ODC International Plaza
219 Salcedo St.
Legaspi Village
Makati, Metro Manila
Tel: (2) 817-6981

Philippine Business On-Line
Eiger Consulting and Information Service
7 Mt. Fairweather St.
Filinvest I
1119 Quezon City, Metro Manila
Tel: (2) 931-6744
WWW server: http://www.eunet.ch/asarte/pbo/
index.html
*A World Wide Web server and bulletin board service
that debuted June-July, 1995*

Philippine Business Report
Department of Trade and Industry
Trade and Industry Information Center
4th Fl., Industry and Investments Bldg.
385 Sen. Gil J. Puyat Ave.
3117 Makati, Metro Manila
Tel: (2) 818-5705   Fax: (2) 856-487

Philippine Economic Journal
(Quarterly)
Philippine Economic Society
PSSC Bldg., PO Box 205
University of the Philippines
Diliman
Quezon City, Metro Manila

Philippine Letter
(Semimonthly)
Asia Letter Group
GPO Box 780
Hong Kong
Tel: [852] 2526-2950   Fax: [852] 2526-7131

Philippine National Bank Economic Brief
PNB International
Philippine National Bank Public Information Office
PNB Bldg.
257 Escolta St.
1099 Escolta, Manila
Tel: (2) 402-051   Fax: (2) 496-091

Philippine Quarterly of Culture and Society
(Quarterly)
San Carlos Publications
6000 Cebu City

Philippine Review of Economics and Business
(Semiannual)
University of the Philippines
College of Business Administration
School of Economics
Diliman
1101 Quezon City, Metro Manila

Philippines Inc.
(Monthly)
Business Media, Inc.
912 Pasay Rd.
Makati, Metro Manila
Tel: (2) 857-498, 855-303

World Executive's Digest
(Monthly)
World Executive's Digest, Inc.
3rd Fl., Greenbelt Drive
Legaspi Village
Makati, Metro Manila
Tel: (2) 818-3289   Fax: (2) 818-5177

BUSINESS AND TAXATION GUIDES

Country Commercial Guide: Philippines
National Technical Information Service (NTIS)
5285 Port Royal Rd.
Springfield, VA 22161, USA
Tel: [1] (703) 487-4650, 487-4099
*More than 100 Country Commercial Guides are published
by the International Trade Administration of the US
Department of Commerce and are available in paper or
diskette versions. Also on the National Trade Data Bank
CD-ROM from NTIS*

Doing Business in the Philippines
Ernst & Young International, Ltd.
787 Seventh Ave.
New York, NY, USA
Tel: [1] (212) 773-3000
*Available in the Philippines from Punongbayan &
Araullo, 6th Fl., Vernida IV Bldg., Alfaro St., Salcedo
Village, 1200 Makati, Metro Manila; Tel: (2) 810-9741,
812-6091; Fax: (2) 810-9748*

**Philippines: The HSBC Group Business Profile
Series**
The Hongkong and Shanghai Banking Corp. Ltd.
1 Queens Rd.
Central, Hong Kong
Tel: [852] 2822-1111   Fax: [852] 2810-1112

Doing Business in the Philippines
Price Waterhouse
400 South Hope St.
Los Angeles, CA 90071-2889, USA
Tel: [1] (213) 236-3000
*Available in the Philippines from Joaquin Cunanan &
Co.-Price Waterhouse, PO Box 2288, 1099 Manila; Tel: (2)
818-7622/6, 818-9103/5; Fax: (2) 815-3514*

Investors' Guide to the Philippines
M. Pilipinas, Inc.
PO Box EA-414
Ermita, Metro Manila
Tel: (2) 911-4665   Fax: (2) 911-4619
*A reference book for investors, entrepreneurs, and
businesspeople*

Philippines in the Heart of Asia
American Chamber of Commerce
2nd Fl., Corinthian Plaza
Paseo de Roxas
Makati, Metro Manila
Tel: (2) 818-7911/3   Fax: (2) 816-6359

Philippines: Where It's the Best to Invest
Philippines: The Right Investment Site
BOI Annual Report
Individual Summary of Weekly Approved Projects
Board of Investments (BOI)
Industry and Investments Bldg.
385 Sen. Gil J. Puyat Ave.
Makati, Metro Manila
Tel: (2) 868-403, 867-895, 875-602
Fax: (2) 819-1887
*Other publications on specific industry sectors, such as
cocoa products, computer software and services,
electronics, are also available from the BOI*

Setting up in Business in the Philippines
DTI Export Publications
PO Box 55
Stratford-upon-Avon
Warwickshire CV37 9GE, UK
Tel: [44] (1189) 296-212   Fax: [44] (1189) 299-096

STATISTICAL PUBLICATIONS AND SOURCES

Department of Environment and Natural Resources Annual Report
(Annual)
Department of Environment and Natural Resources
DENR Bldg.
Visayas Ave.
Diliman
Quezon City, Metro Manila
Tel: (2) 976-626/9, 976-671/5, 990-691
Fax: (2) 963-487, 922-6991

Department of Trade and Industry Annual Report
(Annual)
Department of Trade and Industry
Trade and Industry Information Center
4th Fl., Industry and Investments Bldg.
385 Sen. Gil J. Puyat Ave.
3117 Makati, Metro Manila
Tel: (2) 818-5705   Fax: (2) 856-487

Economic Indicators
(Monthly)
National Statistical Coordination Board
NEDA Bldg.
Amber Ave.
1600 Pasig, Metro Manila
Tel: (2) 673-5031, 631-3716, 631-0945 to 64
Fax: (2) 631-3747

Philippine Statistical Yearbook
(Annual)
National Economic Development Authority (NEDA)
NEDA Bldg.
Amber Ave.
1600 Pasig, Metro Manila
Tel: (2) 673-5031, 631-3716, 631-0945 to 64
Fax: (2) 631-3747

Selected Statistics in Agriculture
(Annual)
Department of Agriculture
Bureau of Agricultural Statistics
BEN-LOR Bldg.
1184 Quezon City, Metro Manila
Tel: (2) 992-641
Also publish Development Indicators in Philippine
Agriculture *(Annual)*, Livestock, Poultry, and Fishery
Statistics Bulletin *(Annual)*, Rice and Corn Situation
Outlook *(Quarterly)*, Retail Market Price Bulletin
(Weekly)

Statistics for Entrepreneurs
The Countryside in Figures
(Annual)
National Statistical Information Center
Ground Fl., Midland Buendia Bldg.
403 Sen. Gil J. Puyat Ave.
Makati, Metro Manila
Tel: (2) 862-469

Yearbook of Labor Statistics
(Annual)
Bureau of Labor and Employment Statistics
Department of Labor and Employment (DOLE)
DOLE Executive Bldg.
Cor. Gen. Luna and San Jose Streets
1002 Intramuros, Manila
Tel: (2) 484-852, 530-0144, 470-264
Fax: (2) 530-1014, 472-857, 470-986
Also publishes Current Labor Statistics *(Monthly)*,
Labor and Employment Statistical Report *(Quarterly)*,
Occupational Wages Survey *(Annual)*

INDUSTRY-SPECIFIC PUBLICATIONS

Asia Computer Weekly
(Bimonthly)
Asian Business Press Pte., Ltd.
100 Beach Rd. #26-00, Shaw Towers
Singapore 0718
Tel: [65] 294-3366   Fax: [65] 298-5534

Asiamac Journal: The Machine-Building and Metal Working Journal for the Asia Pacific Region
(Quarterly; English, Chinese)
ATA Journal: Journal for Asia on Textile & Apparel
(Bimonthly)
Adsale Publishing Company
21st Fl., Tung Wai Commercial Bldg.
109-111 Gloucester Rd.
Hong Kong
Tel: [852] 2892-0511
Fax: [852] 2838-4119, 2834-5014

Asia Mining
(Monthly)
Asiaworld Publishing House, Inc.
7514 Bagtikan, cor. Pasong Tamo
3117 Makati, Metro Manila
Tel: (2) 874-348

Asian Architect and Contractor
(Monthly)
Thompson Press Hong Kong Ltd.
Tai Sang Commercial Bldg., 19th Fl.
24-34 Hennessy Rd.
Hong Kong

Asian Aviation
(Monthly)
Asian Aviation Publications
2 Leng Kee Rd. #04-01, Thye Hong Centre
Singapore 0315
Tel: [65] 4747088   Fax: [65] 4796668

Asian Computer Monthly
(Monthly)
Computer Publications Ltd.
Washington Plaza, 1st Fl.
230 Wanchai Rd.
Wanchai, Hong Kong
Tel: [852] 2932-7123   Fax: [852] 2832-9208

Asian Defence Journal
(Monthly)
Syed Hussain Publications (Sdn)
61 A&B Jelan Dato, Haji Eusoff
Damai Complex
PO Box 10836
50726 Kuala Lumpur, Malaysia
Tel: [60] (3) 442-0852   Fax: [60] (3) 442-7840

Asian Electricity
(11 per year)
Reed Business Publishing Ltd.
5001 Beach Rd. #06-12, Golden Mile Complex
Singapore 0719
Tel: [65] 291-3188   Fax: [65] 291-3180

Asian Electronics Engineer
(Monthly)
Trade Media Ltd.
29 Wong Chuck Hang Rd.
Hong Kong
Tel: [852] 2555-4777   Fax: [852] 2870-0816

Asian Hospital
(Quarterly)
Techni-Press Asia Ltd.
PO Box 20494
Hennessy Rd.
Hong Kong
Tel: [852] 2527-8682   Fax: [852] 2527-8399

Asian Hotel & Catering Times
(Bimonthly)
Thomson Press (HK)
19th Fl., 23-34 Hennessy Rd.
Tai Sang Commercial Bldg.
Hong Kong
Tel: [852] 2528-3351   Fax: [852] 2865-0825

Asian Manufacturing
Cargonews Asia
(Bimonthly)
Far East Trade Press Ltd.
2nd Fl., Kai Tak Commercial Bldg.
317 Des Voeux Rd.
Central, Hong Kong
Tel: [852] 2545-3028   Fax: [852] 2544-6979

Asian Medical News
(Bimonthly)
MediMedia Pacific Ltd.
Unit 1216, Seaview Estate
2-8 Watson Rd.
North Point, Hong Kong
Tel: [852] 570-0708   Fax: [852] 570-5076

Asian Meetings & Incentives
(Monthly)
Travel & Trade Publishing (Asia)
16th Fl., Capitol Centre
5-19 Jardines Bazaar
Causeway Bay, Hong Kong
Tel: [852] 2890-3067   Fax: [852] 2895-2378

Asian Oil & Gas
(Monthly)
Intercontinental Marketing Corp.
PO Box 5056
Tokyo 100-31, Japan
Fax: [81] (3) 3667-9646

Asian Plastic News
(Quarterly)
Reed Asian Publishing Pte., Ltd.
5001 Beach Rd. #06-12, Golden Mile Complex
Singapore 0719
Tel: [65] 291-3188   Fax: [65] 291-3180

Asian Printing: The Magazine for the Graphic Arts Industry
(Monthly)
Travel & Trade Publishing (Asia)
16th Fl., Capitol Centre
5-19 Jardines Bazaar
Causeway Bay, Hong Kong
Tel: [852] 2890-3067   Fax: [852] 2895-2378

Asian Security & Safety Journal
(Bimonthly)
Elgin Consultants, Ltd.
Tungnam Bldg.
Suite 5D, 475 Hennessy Rd.
Causeway Bay, Hong Kong
Tel: [852] 2572-4427   Fax: [852] 2572-5731

Asian Shipping
(Monthly)
Asia Trade Journals Ltd.
7th Fl., Sincere Insurance Bldg.
4 Hennessy Rd.
Wanchai, Hong Kong
Tel: [852] 2527-8532   Fax: [852] 2527-8753

Asian Sources: Computer Products
Asian Sources: Electronic Components
Asian Sources: Fashion Accessories
Asian Sources: Gifts & Home Products
Asian Sources: Hardware
Asian Sources: Timepieces
(All publications are monthly)
Asian Sources Media Group
22nd Fl., Vita Tower
29 Wong Chuk Hang Rd.
Wong Chuk Hang, Hong Kong
Tel: [852] 2555-4777   Fax: [852] 2873-0488

Asian Water & Sewage
(Quarterly)
Techni-Press Asia, Ltd.
PO Box 20494, Hennessy Rd.
Hong Kong
Fax: [852] 2527-8399

Asia Pacific Broadcasting & Telecommunications
(Monthly)
Asian Business Press Pte., Ltd.
100 Beach Rd. #26-00, Shaw Towers
Singapore 0718
Tel: [65] 29423366   Fax: [65] 29825534

Asia Pacific Dental News
(Quarterly)
Adrienne Yo Publishing Ltd.
4th Fl., Vogue Bldg.
67 Wyndham St.
Central, Hong Kong
Tel: [852] 2525-3133   Fax: [852] 2810-6512

Asia Pacific Food Industry Business Report
(Monthly)
Asia Pacific Food Industry Publications
24 Peck Sea St. #03-00, Nehsons Bldg.
Singapore 0207
Tel: [65] 222-3422   Fax: [65] 222-5587

Asiatechnology
(Monthly)
Review Publishing Company Ltd.
6-7th Fl., 181-185 Gloucester Rd.
GPO Box 160
Hong Kong
Tel: [852] 2832-8381   Fax: [852] 2834-5571

Asia Travel Guide
(Monthly)
Interasia Publications, Ltd.
190 Middle Rd. #11-01, Fortune Center
Singapore 0718
Tel: [65] 339-7622   Fax: [65] 339-8521

Bldg. & Construction News
(Weekly)
Al Hilal Publishing (FE) Ltd.
50 Jalan Sultan #20-06, Jalan Sultan Centre
Singapore 0719
Tel: [65] 293-9233   Fax: [65] 297-0862

Business Traveller Asia-Pacific
(Monthly)
Interasia Publications
13th Fl., 200 Lockhart Rd.
Wanchai, Hong Kong
Tel: [852] 2574-9317   Fax: [852] 2572-6846

Cargo Clan
(Quarterly)
Emphais (HK), Ltd.
10th Fl. Wilson House
19-27 Wyndam St.
Central, Hong Kong
Tel: [852] 2521-5392   Fax: [852] 2810-6738

Catering & Hotel News, International
(Biweekly)
Al Hilal Publishing (FE) Ltd.
50 Jalan Sultan #20-26, Jalan Sultan Centre
Singapore 0719
Tel: [852] 2293-9233   Fax: [852] 2297-0862

Construction and Engineering
(Monthly)
Asiaworld Publishing House
7514 Bagtikan, cor. Pasang Tamo
3117 Makati, Metro Manila

Early Warnings
(Monthly)
Situation, Trends, and Outlook (STO)
(Quarterly)
The Marketing Unit
Philippine Statistical Association (PSA), Inc.
2nd Fl., PSS Center
Commonwealth Ave.
Diliman
Quezon City, Metro Manila
Tel: (2) 964-471   Fax: (2) 964-548
Reviews of the agribusiness sector

Electronic Business Asia
(Monthly)
Cahners Publishing Company
275 Washington St.
Newton, MA 02158, USA
Tel: [1] (617) 964-3030   Fax: [1] (617) 558-4506

Energy Asia
(Monthly)
Petroleum News Southeast Asia Ltd.
6th Fl., 146 Prince Edward Rd. W
Kowloon, Hong Kong
Tel: [852] 2380-5294   Fax: [852] 2397-0959

Far East Health
(10 per year)
Update-Siebert Publications
Reed Asian Publishing Pte.
5001 Beach Rd. #06-12, Golden Mile Complex
Singapore 0719
Tel: [65] 291-3188   Fax: [65] 291-3180

Farming Today
(Monthly)
Room 201, Catalina Bldg.
New York St.
Cubao
Quezon City, Metro Manila

Lloyd's Maritime Asia
(Monthly)
Lloyd's of London Press (FE)
Rm. 1101 Hollywood Centre
233 Hollywood Rd.
Hong Kong
Tel: [852] 2854-3222   Fax: [852] 2854-1538

Media Asia
(Quarterly)
Asian Mass Communication Research and
Information Center
39 Newton Rd.
Singapore
Tel: [65] 251-5105   Fax: [65] 253-4535

Media: Asia's Media and Marketing Newspaper
(Biweekly)
Media & Marketing Ltd.
1002 McDonald's Bldg., 46-54 Yee Wo St.
Causeway Bay, Hong Kong
Tel: [852] 2577-2628   Fax: [852] 2576-9171

Medical Progress
(Monthly)
Marsmann & Co.
Room 404, Kalaw-Ledesma Condominium
117 Gamboa St.
Legaspi Village
Makati, Metro Manila
Tel: (2) 816-4734

Medicine Digest Asia
(Monthly)
Rm. 1903, Tung Sun Commercial Centre
194-200 Lockhart Rd.
Wanchai, Hong Kong
Tel: [852] 8939303   Fax: [852] 8912591

**Philippine Architecture, Engineering, and
Construction Record**
(Monthly)
PAENCOR Inc.
154 Araneta Ave.
PO Box 1295
Quezon City, Metro Manila

Philippine Law Journal (Quarterly)
Philippine Law Report (Monthly)
University of the Philippines
Law Publishing House
Diliman
Quezon City, Metro Manila

Philippine Law Gazette
(Monthly)
D4 Don Felipe St.
Pilarville Subdivision
Tandang Sora
1107 Quezon City, Metro Manila
Tel: (2) 974-536

Philippine Lumberman
(6 issues per year)
PAENCOR Inc.
75 Mother Ignacia Ave.
Roxas District
Quezon City, Metro Manila

Philippine Mining and Engineering Journal
(Monthly)
Business Masters International
55 U.E. Tech Ave.
University Hills
Malabon
Rizal, Luzon

Philippines Transportation
(Monthly)
c/o Manuel Vijungco, Publisher
PO Box 998
Manila

Philippine Tax Journal
(Monthly)
Room 203, University Center Bldg.
1985 Recto Ave.
Manila

Polymers & Rubber Asia
(Bimonthly)
Upper West St.
Reigate Surrey RH2 9HX, UK
Tel: [44] (1737) 242-599   Fax: [44] (1737) 223-235

Sugarland Magazine
(Monthly)
Sugarland Publications
Room 207–209, Sugar Center Bldg.
San Juan St.
Bacolod City, Negros
Tel: (34) 22-643
About the sugar industry

Travel News Asia
(Bimonthly)
Far East Trade Press, Ltd.
2nd Fl., Kai Tak Commercial Bldg.
317 Des Voeux Rd.
Central, Hong Kong
Tel: [852] 2545-3028   Fax: [852] 2544-6979

Travel Trade Gazette Asia
(Weekly)
Asian Business Press Pte., Ltd.
100 Beach Rd. #26-00 Shaw Towers
Singapore 0718
Tel: [65] 2943366   Fax: [65] 2985534

RADIO AND TELEVISION

Government Agencies

Department of Transportation and Communications
3rd Fl., Philcomcen Bldg.
Ortigas Ave.
Pasig, Metro Manila
Tel: (2) 631-8761/3, 631-8666, 721-3781
Fax: (2) 632-9985

National Telecommunications Commission
VIBAL Bldg.
Epifanio de los Santos Ave. cor. Times St.
Quezon City, Metro Manila
Tel: (2) 924-4042, 924-4008, 981-160
Fax: (2) 921-7128
Regulates telecommunications industry and formulates policies

Professional Organization

Assocation of Broadcasters in the Philippines (KBP)
6th Fl., LTA Bldg.
118 Perea St.
Legaspi Village
Makati, Metro Manila
Tel: (2) 815-1990/2   Fax: (2) 815-1989

Radio and Television Networks

ABS-CBN Broadcasting Corporation
Mother Ignacia Ave.
Quezon City, Metro Manila
Fax: (2) 921-5888
Television and radio network

Banahaw Broadcasting Corporation
Capitol Hills, Diliman
3005 Quezon City, Metro Manila
Tel: (2) 961-109
Radio and television network

Far East Broadcasting Co.
PO Box 1
0560 Valenzuela, Metro Manila
Tel: (2) 292-1152
Fax: (2) 292-4724, 359-9490
Radio network

GMA Rainbow Satellite
Republic Broadcasting System (RBS)
RBS Bldg.
Epifanio de los Santos Ave.
Diliman
Quezon City, Metro Manila
Tel: (2) 997-021
Radio and television network

Inter-Island Broadcasting Corporation
Broadcast City
Capitol Hills, Diliman
Quezon City, Metro Manila
Tel: (2) 976-137   Fax: (2) 968-556
Television network

Maharlika Broadcasting System
Media Center
Sgt. Esuerra Ave.
3005 Quezon City, Metro Manila
Tel: (2) 922-0880
Television and radio network

Nation Broadcasting Corporation (NBC)
NBC Tcwer
Epifanio de los Santos Ave.
Guadalupe
1200 Makati, Metro Manila
Tel: (2) 819-5673   Fax: (2) 819-7234
Radio network

Philippines Broadcasting Service (PBS)
Bureau of Broadcast Services
Office of the Press Secretary
4th Fl., Philippine Information Agency Bldg.
Visayas Ave.
Quezon City, Metro Manila
Tel: (2) 924-2607   Fax: (2) 924-2745
Radio network; oversees Bureau of Broadcast Services and Office of Media Affairs

Radio Philippines Network
Broadcast City
Capitol Hills, Diliman
Quezon City, Metro Manila
Tel: (2) 977-661   Fax: (2) 984-322
Radio and television network

Index

GOODWILL

58 YEARS

Goodwill Trading Co., Inc. continues to serve the Filipino reader offering a wide array of reading and educational materials.

1938

Today, **GOODWILL BOOKSTORE** has grown to become one of the Philippines' most respected and leading names in the book publishing, retailing, importation and distribution.

1960

JMC Press, Inc.

one of the pioneers in local textbook development; it takes pride in being the only publisher of medical textbooks in the Philippines.

1969

EDCA Publishing and Distributing Corporation

an affiliate, specializes in servicing librarians' requirements; makes information accessible to a wide customer base by introducing and marketing CD Roms and other electronic information products and services.

1977

Katha Publishing Co., Inc.

develops and produces textbooks for the college level, including textbooks in video cassette form; is now publishing books on herbal medicine.

A Tradition of Goodwill and Excellence

1987

World Magazine & Book Distributors, Inc. - THE MAGAZINE SOURCE

distributing over 1000 titles from the US and UK. Its products and outlet network combine to make its magazine distribution in the Philippines formidable.

1994

Kiddie Camp Play and Learn Funworld

the only daycare center in the Philippines located within a bookstore, Kiddie Camp offers learning activities with the element of fun supported by a wide array of books for children.

1995

Goodwill Infolink Multimedia Circuit

one of the first to distribute and market information using both electronic and conventional formats in the Asia Pacific Region - knowledge at your fingertips. (This division is located at the 3rd Floor of the Goodwill Center at the Glorietta Complex.)